THE INFORMANT

GARY MAY

THE
Informant

THE FBI, THE KU KLUX KLAN, AND THE MURDER
OF VIOLA LIUZZO

YALE UNIVERSITY PRESS   NEW HAVEN & LONDON

Published with assistance from the Louis Stern Memorial Fund.

Set in Scala type by Duke & Company, Devon, Pennsylvania.
Printed in the United States of America.

Library of Congress Cataloging-in-Publication Data
May, Gary, 1944–
The informant : the FBI, the Ku Klux Klan, and the murder of Viola Liuzzo / Gary May.
   p. cm.
Includes bibliographical references and index.
ISBN 0-300-10635-1 (alk. paper)
1. Liuzzo, Viola, 1925–1965. 2. Rowe, Gary Thomas. 3. Murder—Alabama—Lowndes
County. 4. Civil rights workers—Alabama—Biography. 5. Informers—Alabama—
Biography. 6. Ku Klux Klan (1915–). 7. United States. Federal Bureau of Investigation.
8. Undercover operations—Alabama. 9. Selma–Montgomery Rights March, 1965. I. Title.
E185.98.L58M395 2005
323'.092'309073—dc22

2005002067

A catalogue record for this book is available from the British Library.

10 9 8 7 6 5 4 3 2 1

In loving memory of Stuart Jerome, my uncle, who taught me that writing is all about storytelling. And for Morley and Donna, who were always there when we needed them. And for Archie, Mitch, and Darcy, my best friends.

CONTENTS

Preface   ix

Acknowledgments   xiii

1 Undercover Man   1

2 One Hell of a Good Job   22

3 Serious Business   51

4 Bombing Matters   79

5 Cat and Mouse   105

6 Season of Suffering   125

7 Night Riders   150

8 This Horrible Brew   184

9 A Slight Case of Murder   211

10 Parable of the Two Goats 233

11 A Temple of Justice 251

12 Taking the Sun Away 273

13 Digging In 287

14 Pain and Anguish 316

15 A Search for the Truth 336

Epilogue: Dealing with the Devil 364

Notes 373

Index 417

IN MARCH 1965, a Detroit housewife and mother of five was murdered in Alabama; it became one of the most important but overlooked racial murders of the 1960s. Viola Liuzzo went to Selma to join thousands of her fellow citizens in the historic Voting Rights March. Late on the night of March 25, she was shot to death by a group of Alabama Klansmen, thereby becoming the only white woman to lose her life in the civil rights movement. Incredibly, the Klansmen were captured within twenty-four hours because one of them, Gary Thomas Rowe, Jr., was a secret FBI informant. Besides the personal consequences for her family and friends, Liuzzo's murder had far-reaching national consequences. It shocked America and galvanized the civil rights movement, contributing to the enactment of one of the most important pieces of legislation in American history, the Voting Rights Act of 1965.

Her killing prompted President Lyndon B. Johnson to become personally involved in the case. In an act without precedent in the history of the presidency, he announced the arrest of Liuzzo's killers over national television and warned Klansmen "to get out of the Klan now and return to a decent society—before it is too late."

But what perhaps gives the Liuzzo case its historical importance and even contemporary relevance is the light it sheds on the FBI's secret informant system, which continues to this day. Gary Thomas Rowe, Jr., was the FBI's most important informant in the Alabama Ku Klux Klan from 1960 to 1965, and besides being present in the car when the Klansmen shot Liuzzo, he was involved in a number of violent incidents in the history of the civil rights movement. To protect Rowe's true identity and collect the information it wanted, the FBI allowed Rowe to attack blacks, Freedom Riders, and other civil rights workers without fear of arrest and prosecution. In effect, the FBI protected the very terrorists it hoped to destroy.

Today, the United States is engaged in a war against domestic and international terrorism, and, it is argued, one important weapon is informants who will penetrate terrorist groups and help prevent future violence. The experience of Gary Thomas Rowe suggests that the opposite can be true: In order to protect their cover, informants commit the very acts they are supposed to forestall and therefore make U.S. intelligence agencies complicit in these crimes.

Based on declassified FBI records, trial transcripts, and interviews with FBI agents, members of the Liuzzo family, and others involved in the case, this book is also the story of two extraordinary people—Gary Thomas Rowe, Jr., and Viola Liuzzo. Rowe, called Tommy by his friends, was a brawler, a liar, a womanizer, and perhaps a murderer, personally recruited by the FBI in 1960 to infiltrate the Alabama Klan. His enemies would later call him a "maniac" and a "Judas goat" who "sold his soul for 30 pieces of silver." His admirers included J. Edgar Hoover, who, according to Rowe, once told him, "You're one of the greatest Americans this country has ever had." Later, however, Rowe came to believe that the FBI had betrayed him, and he publicly attacked the Bureau in interviews before congressional committees and on national television. "My whole life was the FBI," he once said. "I was a red, white, and blue flag. I gave my life for my country and got screwed."

Viola Liuzzo was equally controversial. To segregationists, she was an "outside agitator," a drug addict who went to Alabama to sleep with black men. To feminists, she was a hero, a woman liberated before her time, willing to leave her five children—the youngest just six years old—to fight for civil rights. Her colleagues in that struggle consider her a martyr who gave her life for justice; she is honored on plaques bearing her name at the site where she died and many other places where the civil rights movement is commemorated.

All too often, both Rowe and Liuzzo have been wrenched from the context of their lives to further political or legal agendas, and seeking the truth about them is one of this book's goals. They are traditionally seen as polar opposites, but in fact they shared a number of common experiences: Both grew up in the South in near poverty; both left school in the eighth grade; both were married multiple times; both searched for personal fulfillment in self-created crusades. Rowe saw himself not as an informer, "a snitch," but as an "undercover man" working inside the Klan for the FBI and his country. Liuzzo devoted her life to attacking injustice wherever she saw it—in the towns and cities of her youth and later in the hospitals where she briefly worked, in the Detroit school system where her children were educated, and finally in Alabama, where "her people" were denied the right to vote. The two never met, but their collision on a rainy night in rural Alabama changed their lives forever.

ACKNOWLEDGMENTS

IN MARCH 2002, I had the pleasure of meeting Diane McWhorter, author of *Carry Me Home: Birmingham, Alabama, the Climactic Battle of the Civil Rights Revolution*. Her book discussed, in part, the early career of FBI informant Gary Thomas Rowe, so we had a lot to talk about. When she had to leave, I asked her to inscribe my copy of her book. She wrote: "To Gary May—Fellow Stalker of the late, great Gary Thomas Rowe. Maybe we'll yet find him . . ."

After five years of stalking Rowe, I'm not sure that it's possible for anyone to capture him with total accuracy, but I tried. Many people helped me in that quest. My greatest debt is to Dean A. Robb, Esquire, the Liuzzo family attorney, who generously gave me access to his records and allowed me to quote from them. If all attorneys were as selfless as Mr. Robb, the profession would not be held in such low esteem. This book may have been written, but it would not have been published without the wise counsel of John W. Wright, my agent. He advised me on how to navigate the tricky shoals that are the modern publishing world and eventually steered me to a safe harbor at Yale University Press. There, I found Lara Heimert, every writer's dream editor. She was brilliant and supportive, and this book has profited immeasurably from the care she devoted to it. Thanks, too, to her colleagues Phillip King, Molly Egland, Keith Condon, Mary Pasti, Susan Laity, Christina Coffin, Liz Pelton, and especially the wonderful Jessie

Dolch, superb practitioner of an ancient art today rarely seen—copyediting. Her hard work is evident on every page of this book. I'm also very fortunate that Yale sent the manuscript to Professor Richard Gid Powers to review. The preeminent historian of the FBI, Professor Powers's suggestions forced me to examine more clearly the central questions raised by Rowe's relationship with the FBI. I also often turned to Diane McWhorter for information about Birmingham, and she was always kind enough to come to my aid.

Family and friends of Viola Liuzzo granted me interviews that gave me insight into her complex personality. I'm especially indebted to Mary Liuzzo Lilleboe, who spoke so candidly about her mother. Mrs. Liuzzo's sister, Rose Mary Sprout, and family friend Gordon Green helped too.

Those who knew Gary Thomas Rowe, Jr., were not as cooperative, with some important exceptions. I spent an afternoon with former FBI Special Agent Neil Shanahan, who regaled me with stories about his informant's life in Birmingham during the mid-1960s. Chuck Lewis, who covered Rowe for ABC News, gave me many hours of his time over many years, which allowed me to reconstruct an important chapter in the history of investigative journalism. Rick Journey of Birmingham's Fox News channel WBRC shared his impressions of the always elusive Tommy Rowe. Linda Seigler, of Savannah, Georgia, described Rowe's final years and tried to persuade his family to speak with me. I had a memorable conversation with Rowe's eldest daughter from his first marriage, but his sister Betty said only that it was "too painful" to talk about her brother, while a Rowe son turned me away more bluntly: "Don't you fuckin' call me no more," he said. I very much regret that they wouldn't help reconstruct Rowe's early life, which is one of this book's shortcomings. While historians should always document their sources, occasionally it becomes necessary to grant someone anonymity in exchange for important information. Two people made such a request, and I granted it, regrettably.

For a historian of recent America, the Freedom of Information/Privacy Act is an invaluable tool for opening important collections of classified documents, so I need to thank Maria Lasden of the FBI and Wilson J. Moorer of the Federal Bureau of Prisons for their work on my behalf. Analysts in the Justice Department's Office of Professional Responsibility helped me gain access to its records on Rowe. Acquiring photographs proved to be difficult, but many people helped to find the ones I wanted.

Bret Bell, an investigative reporter for the *Savannah Morning News*, checked the paper's files for me, and Luciana Spracher, a skillful researcher, became my link to its photo staff members Julia Mueller and Sarah Wright. A special thanks to Bob Mathews, who scanned the photo of Rowe used on the book's cover. Thanks also to Jeff Bridgers and Bonnie Cole at the Library of Congress; Tiffany Miller at Bettmann/Corbis, Kevin O'Sullivan at AP/ Wide World, and Michael Gorman at WireImage.

Those at home are always harder to thank. My daughter Joanna read drafts of chapters and made good suggestions on improving them, and my son Jeff, a terrific historian, took time away from his graduate work to solve my computer problems and format the manuscript. My wife, Gail, has been with me through three books and has somehow managed to remain optimistic and cheerful when I needed it the most. Any errors of fact or interpretation are, of course, my own.

CHAPTER ONE

Undercover Man

LOYAL MCWHORTER WORKED AT the Kelly Ingram VFW Club in down-town Birmingham, a favorite watering hole of off-duty cops, traveling salesmen, and members of the Alabama Ku Klux Klan. McWhorter was a Klansman himself and a member of the Klan Bureau of Investigation, or KBI, which found and screened people who wanted to join the "Hooded Order." In the winter of 1960, McWhorter had his eye on one particular man—Gary Thomas Rowe, Jr., or Tommy, as he was known around town. Rowe looked like a "good red-neck Klansman," McWhorter thought, red-headed with blue eyes, standing about six feet tall and weighing a stocky 220 pounds. Frequently Rowe boasted that he could "whip anybody's ass" and enjoyed proving it at the Starlight Club, the Blue Note, and other bars along the Strip, Birmingham's tenderloin district. Sometimes Rowe worked as a bouncer at the VFW Club, and McWhorter admired how easily he threw drunks out the door. He had tried previously to recruit Rowe but had failed. Rowe thought grown men wearing sheets was silly, and he seemed to lack the passionate hatred of blacks that most Klansmen felt. Neverthe-less, this time McWhorter was determined to get him.[1]

But there were things about Rowe that troubled McWhorter. Rowe had friends at the Bureau of Alcohol, Tobacco, and Firearms and spoke often of prowling through the Alabama backwoods with agents searching for illegal stills and, when they found them, helping to destroy them. In return for his help, the ATF would sell him surplus rifles at bargain prices; his favorite was a carbine that looked like a Thompson submachine gun. Rowe also barhopped with Birmingham police officers who let him ride around in their squad cars on night patrol. One rumor had it that he worked for the CIA or even the FBI. Rowe was a mystery—part self-proclaimed "hell raiser," part amateur cop. McWhorter worried that if Rowe joined the Klan, he'd sell them out to the Feds, or to the few Birmingham cops who were not themselves Klansmen.[2]

Still, landing Rowe would be a personal victory, one that McWhorter badly needed; he'd been stealing money from the cashbox of his local Klan group and feared that he was about to be discovered. He decided to make one final check before openly discussing membership with Rowe. Sometime in late March, McWhorter telephoned the Birmingham FBI field office and asked whether Gary Thomas Rowe worked there. Who was calling? an agent asked. McWhorter refused to give his name and repeated the question. No, said the agent, he'd never heard of the man. What made him think that Mr. Rowe had anything to do with the Bureau? Just something he'd heard at the VFW Club, probably a mistake, McWhorter replied, and then hung up. He was satisfied that Rowe wasn't an agent or an informant.[3]

The FBI did not dismiss the call as coming from a local crackpot; it was evidence that a man named Rowe might be impersonating an agent, a crime the FBI took most seriously. Every agent was familiar with J. Edgar Hoover's most sacred commandment: "Thou shall not embarrass the bureau." Therefore, Special Agent Barrett G. Kemp, twenty-eight years old and a recent graduate of the FBI Academy, was assigned to investigate. After discussing the case with veteran agents Charles B. Stanberry and Byron McFall, Kemp visited the VFW Club, where he talked with several bartenders, including Loyal McWhorter, whose nervousness persuaded Kemp that he had made the call. A check of the Bureau's files on Rowe revealed that he was born in Savannah, Georgia, in 1933; left school after completing the eighth grade; served in both the Georgia National Guard and the Marine Reserves; and was married briefly, divorced, and a father by the age of eighteen when he married again. He also had been arrested, twice, for carrying a concealed weapon, and again in 1951 for impersonating a police officer, but the charges had been dismissed. He was well known to ATF agents, Kemp discovered, and to the Birmingham police, who told many wild stories about Rowe's adventures. He had tried to become a county sheriff, but his application was rejected because he lied when claiming to be a high school graduate. He was considered a "cop buff," someone who desperately wanted a life in law enforcement but was unqualified for the job. The resulting disappointment might explain his habitual brawling and carousing, even though he had a wife and several children to support. Friends joked about how Rowe's wife, Dorothy, would dutifully lay out his clothes as he prepared for a night on the town with his buddies or a date with one of the many women who found him attractive. Klan members throughout the state knew and liked him, but he had never joined.[4]

Kemp concluded that McWhorter's call was part of an effort by the Klan to recruit Rowe. He had all the characteristics of an Alabama Klansman: He was young, twenty-six, and strong, with a hair-trigger temper and a habit of solving problems with his fists. He had an eighth-grade education and a police record, and he was familiar with firearms and explosives. His career history was checkered. He was currently working as a machinist at a Birmingham dairy, but he had also been a construction worker (laid off when the government contract expired), ambulance driver (fired for taking on unauthorized passengers), meat packer, bartender, and bouncer. He was not a rabid racist, but he had no affection for blacks or their "white nigger" allies who were causing trouble throughout the South.[5]

The qualities that made Rowe an ideal Klansman also made him an ideal Klan informant for the FBI. In the 1950s, the Bureau had successfully penetrated the American Communist Party by placing informers pretending to be Communists into local cells. That model was now to be duplicated in the 1960s with the Ku Klux Klan. Young agents like Barry Kemp were constantly encouraged to recruit and maintain informants inside the criminal world and were rated on their success. Now, given the emergence of the civil rights movement and southern resistance to it, that world included both the movement and organizations like the Klan. Rowe's friendships with members of the ATF and cops might prove advantageous, providing the FBI with information and valuable links to Klan sympathizers inside the police department and city government.[6]

If Rowe expressed an interest in working for the Bureau, he would receive an extensive background investigation. FBI files would be checked for derogatory information—a serious criminal record might disqualify him. His personal history (health, marital status, armed services and employment records) would be examined for evidence of stability, reliability, discretion, and integrity. If Kemp and his superiors concluded that Rowe could be used "without danger of embarrassment to the Bureau," he would become a Potential Confidential Informant—(Racial), forced to remain in limbo for another undetermined period until FBI Headquarters determined that he was ready to be a full Confidential Informant, controlled and directed by Agent Kemp.[7]

Bureau regulations did not require that the informant be "lily white," as one agent put it. Indeed, the FBI recognized that "the most productive informants are criminally inclined" or were already career criminals— "double crossers," Hoover called them. But there were specific transgressions that the FBI considered serious enough to disqualify a person: an unsatisfactory military record, drug or alcohol addiction, and "sexual perversion," which usually meant homosexuality. Would Rowe be attracted to the informer's secret life? Barry Kemp decided to ask him.[8]

Recruiting informers is an art. First, the agent circles the target casually, then slowly moves in, learning the subject's strengths, weaknesses, desires. Rowe was easy to read: This was a man with one real hunger, to be a cop, and only the absence of a high school diploma had stood in his way. Kemp could imagine Rowe's frustration, riding around with fat Birmingham cops, men weaker than he and certainly no smarter. Yet they had the badge and the right to carry a gun and use it. That would be the prize Kemp would offer Rowe: to work for the Bureau, not as an "informer," a dirty word that was never spoken, bringing to mind derelicts who sold rumor and gossip for money. Instead, Rowe would be an "undercover man," an "investigator for the FBI." Kemp's invitation would instantly fulfill a life's dream.[9]

Dorothy Rowe answered the door when Kemp first dropped by late on the afternoon of April 4, 1960. She saw a tall, thin man, handsome and impeccably dressed in a charcoal gray suit and matching hat—everyone's idea of the typical G-man. (Jimmy Stewart had just played one in the popular film *The FBI Story*.) The agent touched the brim of his hat in greeting and asked to see her husband. "My God, honey," Dorothy exclaimed, "there's an FBI man to see you!" Tommy hurried to the door, examined Kemp's credentials, and invited him in.

"Wha'd I do?" Rowe asked nervously.

Probably nothing, Kemp said, just a routine investigation. Then he told him about the call from the VFW Club, which suggested that Rowe had said or implied that he was a government agent. They had to check these things out, certainly Rowe could understand that. Didn't he have a long interest in law enforcement, even tried to join the county sheriff's office?

That part was true, Rowe said. He had always wanted to be a police officer but had never finished high school. He was close to many Birmingham cops: "A lot of them had stag parties together. We'd run around . . . and . . . drink and chase girls." But he strongly denied telling anybody that he was an FBI agent.

Did he know the bartenders at the club? Loyal McWhorter and Bob Coker? Kemp asked.

Yes, he often hung out there, sometimes worked the door, went "drinking and bullshitting" with both men.

Did he know if they belonged to any organizations like the Ku Klux Klan? Had they ever asked him to join the Klan? Was he a Klansman?

Rowe said he didn't know the men that well, they were just casual friends. But he did admit that he had been asked to join the Klan.

Kemp rose abruptly, ending the conversation. That clears things up, he said, although he might visit Rowe again, if he didn't mind.

Kemp returned four days later with some good news. The case of the mysterious phone call was definitely closed, he told Rowe. It was probably just McWhorter checking him out for possible Klan membership. Then, almost as an afterthought, he asked: "What do you think about the Klan?"

"A bunch of assholes," Rowe said.

Kemp laughed. Why did he say that?

"I don't think a man would have to hide behind a bed sheet to go out and bust somebody in the god-damn head."

What would it take to get him into the Klan?

"I don't want to get involved with those god-damned people," Rowe said. "They're crazy. . . . But you show me any reason and I'll see what I can do for you."

"I'm going to be very honest with you," Kemp said. "I've had some talks with people before I came here and I understand that you're a pretty good man. I'm talking . . . physical[ly]. . . . You could knock that wall down if you wanted to. . . . You've got balls." How would Rowe like working for the Bureau inside the Klan? It would be a great service to the country.

"You're on," Rowe replied, without a moment's hesitation.

"And that's how he got me," Rowe later explained, "the FBI was God." Being selected to work for the Bureau was "a very proud day" in his life.[10]

A few days later, the Klan made its move. While Rowe was playing pool at the VFW Club, McWhorter asked whether he could take him out for a cup of coffee—there was a man he wanted him to meet. Rowe agreed, and they drove to the Post Office Cafe in downtown Birmingham where Rowe was introduced to Clarence Grimes, a Klan organizer from Montgomery. Grimes and McWhorter wanted him to join the Alabama Knights of the Ku Klux Klan, they said. Rowe expressed interest, but he wanted to know more about the organization. Let's talk in the car, McWhorter said, and while Rowe drove around town, the two men briefed him about Klan life. Locally, the Klan was divided into six groups, or Klaverns—in Pratt City, Woodlawn, Bessemer, Center Point, Fairfield, and downtown Birmingham. Headquarters was in Montgomery, where Bobby Shelton, the Imperial Wizard, presided. The initiation fee was $12.50, and monthly dues were just $1 plus sixty-seven cents to pay for various costs. A member's robe cost from $12 to $15, depending on whether you wanted it made from bridal satin. Rowe could save money by having his wife make it instead of the seamstress they usually used. Each Klavern focused on the activities of "the colored population and no white persons were investigated unless a white woman was involved . . . with a Nigger."[11]

Rowe was also told that he would soon be approached by a member of the Klokan Committee, which screened new members. He would receive a membership blank to fill out and undergo a thorough investigation, which might take as long as six weeks, before he learned whether he was accepted. That was fine, Rowe told them. He would "kick it around . . . see what happens." Later, Rowe telephoned Kemp and reported on the meeting with McWhorter and Grimes. Kemp was pleased. "Let's see what's on their minds," he said. "Go back and follow it through." Kemp told Rowe he would meet with him again soon. He then spoke with Clarence M. Kelley, the special agent in charge of the Birmingham field office, who gave his permission to open a 137 File—the special designation for informants —on Gary Thomas Rowe, Jr.[12]

Several weeks passed before Rowe again heard from the Klan. On

May 21, he met with Bill Holt, whose membership in the Klan transformed this slim, ordinary looking forty-three-year-old pipe fitter into the Klokan Chief, one of the Klan's top officials, in charge of investigating new members. The delay, Rowe learned, was McWhorter's fault; he had been found misappropriating Klan funds and skipping meetings but had been "chastised." Holt would act as his formal sponsor and gave Rowe the official Klan application form. It read:

> I, the undersigned, a native born, true and loyal citizen of the
> United States of America, being a white male Gentile person
> of temperate habits, sound in mind and a believer in the tenets
> of the Christian religion, the maintenance of White Supremacy
> and the principles of a pure Americanism, do most respectfully
> apply for membership in the Knights of the Ku Klux Klan
> through Klan No. Eastview 13, Realm of Alabama.
>   . . . If I prove untrue as a Klansman I will willingly accept
> as my portion whatever penalty your authority may impose.[13]

Bill Holt watched as the applicant signed "Tommy Rowe," filled in his home address, and dated the form. Rowe was also asked to submit a "klecktokon," a form on which he listed the names and addresses of references, his occupation (Plant Utility—White Dairy), his age (he was twenty-six but added four years, as he had when he joined the National Guard at age fourteen), height (he added an inch to bring him to six feet), and weight (212 pounds). He also gave Holt $24.50, to cover his initiation fee and one year's dues paid in advance.[14]

Holt had misgivings about Rowe. According to Rowe's later recollection, Holt looked him "straight in the eye" and said: "God-damn, we got so many leaks in there . . . I don't know what to do. I personally have took on to investigate you because you got a lot of connections with police officers and . . . we don't want to get set up here." But Rowe lashed back at his critic, putting him on the defensive: "Hey, you think I'm setting you up, you take your organization and get screwed."

Holt backed off, apologizing for his outburst: "If you're straight, you'll make us one hell of a Klansman."

"Whatever," Rowe told him. "If you want me, call me. If you don't, no big deal."[15]

While Rowe waited for final word from the Klan, Kemp prepared him

Gary Thomas Rowe, Jr., a self-proclaimed "hell-raiser,"
was the FBI's choice to infiltrate the Alabama Ku Klux
Klan in 1960. (UPI-Bettmann/Corbis)

for his secret life. One evening in June, Kemp drove Rowe to a secluded spot where they parked and talked for an hour. First—and most important—Rowe must understand that his work for the Bureau was "voluntary and confidential and that in no way could he consider himself an FBI employee." He would be reimbursed for expenses (such as initiation fees and dues) and paid cash for information he provided, but this would not constitute a regular salary. At first, Rowe resisted being paid for his services but was persuaded that the additional income would provide a "nest egg" for his children's education. Second, he must avoid violence, and certainly not instigate it. "Don't start anything," Kemp told him. "Don't be the one to jump up and say 'let's go.'" If he committed violent crimes, the Bureau would disown him and treat him like a common criminal.

But despite this warning, Rowe would soon face a dilemma regarding violence that he and Kemp did not discuss. To obtain information as well as to protect his own cover and his life, he would have to join his fellow Klansmen in what they called "missionary work"—assaulting black and white troublemakers and other "outside agitators" who were undermining the "southern way of life." His primary goal was to collect information; "he was not to act as peacemaker" inside the Klan.[16]

If his job description sounded more like that of the traditional informer rather than the undercover man he yearned to be, it didn't occur to Rowe. Rowe had "a more romantic conception of his role," a Justice Department investigator noted later. Whatever Kemp might say, Rowe always considered himself an "undercover man for the FBI." In fact, Kemp's other instructions reinforced Rowe's view of himself as a daring spy for the Bureau. The secret world of intelligence had a certain amount of "tradecraft," and Rowe was given a code name—Karl Cross—to use when communicating with the FBI field office. He was to mail his reports to a "John Robertson" at a blind post office box in Birmingham. After leaving Klan meetings, Rowe must not immediately telephone Kemp; instead, he should drive around for twenty to thirty minutes to make sure he wasn't being followed. He should make calls from public telephones that couldn't be easily tapped. So it is not surprising that Rowe would see himself as an "undercover agent" rather than a mere "snitch."[17]

Rowe finally heard from Bill Holt late on the afternoon of June 23. "I'm going to take you for a ride tonight," Holt told him on the phone.

"Where we going?" Rowe asked.

"Can't tell you," Holt said but added that at last Thursday's meeting of Eastview Klavern No. 13, Rowe had been elected to join the Klan.

But Holt was still suspicious, as Rowe learned when he picked him up around 6:30. "We're having to be a little more careful with you," Holt said. "We've got a good background [check] on you . . . but . . . I'm just a little nervous. I want to satisfy myself." Then he asked Rowe to put on a blindfold.

"That's a bunch of bullshit," Rowe protested. "I'm not going any place blindfolded." It was required, Holt said; new members were not to know the location of the meeting hall. Rowe relented: "If that's going to make you happy, I'll do it."[18]

They drove around in circles for a while, or so it seemed to Rowe, and then they finally stopped. He was helped out of the car and taken by the arm to a fire escape attached to the side of a building. Holt helped him up the forty or so steps to a landing, where Rowe heard Holt knock three times on a door, scratch something on the wood, and knock again. A voice made "a weird-ass sound," Rowe thought; Holt mumbled something, and the door opened. (Later, Rowe learned that it was all part of Klan ritual: the precise number of knocks, scratching an "X" on the door, and the request for a password.)

Holt removed the blindfold and Rowe found himself face to face with a man in a black hood and robe—the kind worn only by officers of the Klan. It was the Klarogo, keeper of the password, guardian of the gate that separated the "alien world" from the realm of the Hooded Order. Then the Night Hawk appeared, the Klansman responsible for taking care of new members as well as the Klavern's safety during the meeting. He took Rowe down a narrow hall and put him in a room with another initiate. There they waited for what seemed like an eternity. Through the walls, Rowe could hear people arguing. (Later, he was told that a Klansman was on trial for adultery; photographs were distributed to prove the accusations. The guilty man was fined fifty dollars and ordered to "clean up" after meetings and social events for the next four months. If he refused, he would be expelled from the Klan, which would also alert his wife to the affair.)[19]

Another Klansman joined Rowe and the other man, introducing himself as Earl Thompson, whose friends called him Shorty because of his diminutive size. Thompson explained that before being allowed to take the sacred oath of membership, they must answer affirmatively "The Ten Questions." If they failed to answer even one, they could not join the Klan:

1. Is the motive prompting your ambition to be a Klansman serious and unselfish?
2. Are you a native born, white, Gentile American Citizen?
3. Are you absolutely opposed to and free of any allegiance of any nature to any cause, government, people, sect or ruler that is foreign to the United States of America?
4. Do you believe in the tenets of the Christian religion?
5. Do you esteem the United States of America and its institutions above any other government, civil, political, or ecclesiastical, in the whole world?
6. Will you, without mental reservation, take a solemn oath to defend, preserve and enforce same?
7. Do you believe in clannishness and will you faithfully practice same towards Klansmen?
8. Do you believe in and will you faithfully strive for the eternal maintenance of white supremacy?
9. Will you faithfully obey our constitution and laws and conform willingly to all our usages, requirements, and regulations?
10. Can you always be depended on?[20]

Rowe and the other man answered yes to each question and then were taken into a spacious auditorium with enough seats to accommodate hundreds of Klansmen. On a stage sat the most important officers: the Exalted Cyclops, or E.C., as they called him, head of the local Klavern; the Klaliff, his chief assistant and second in command; the Klabee and the Kilgrapp, treasurer and secretary, respectively; and the Kladd, the Klan version of a court bailiff. On the main floor—a few feet from the stage (territory known as "holy ground")—stood an altar on which rested an open Bible, a sword, a pitcher of water, and "a fiery cross of light bulbs."

The Exalted Cyclops came forward and, as the lights dimmed, Rowe was commanded to put his left hand over his heart, raise his right hand, and receive the oath of allegiance. He swore "in the presence of God and man" to "forever keep sacredly secret the signs, words and grip and any and all other matters" pertaining to the Hooded Order, and "most sacredly vow" to never "yield to bribe, flattery, threats, passion, punishment, persecution, persuasion, nor any other enticements whatever coming from . . . any person or persons, male or female for the purpose of obtaining from me . . . secret information. I will die," Rowe affirmed, "rather than divulge the same, so help me God."[21]

Only one more ritual remained: the Eye of Scrutiny. With the room in darkness, a line of hooded Klansmen, holding lighted flashlights under their chins, approached Rowe and the other initiate, staring intently at them. Rowe thought everything was all right until one Klansman looked him in the eye, moved on to the other new member, and then suddenly turned around as if to challenge Rowe's suitability for membership. But no challenge occurred, the lights came up, and he received a membership card or "passport" into his new world. "I was now a bona fide Klansman," he later wrote, "properly naturalized into Klavern Palace 13, Birmingham, Alabama. This was to be my base of operations as an undercover man for the next five years."[22]

Rowe was joining an organization that was almost one hundred years old. Born in Tennessee in 1866 as a reaction against the Northern-imposed Reconstruction state governments, the Ku Klux Klan's goals were clear—"punishing impudent Negroes and negro loving whites," especially the many Republicans who moved south at the end of the Civil War. Led by former Confederate general Nathan Bedford Forrest (the first Grand Wizard), the Klan succeeded in subverting those governments that tried to protect the newly freed slaves from racist terror, and restored white supremacy to the South. Blacks were shot, drowned, and lynched in such great numbers that one Texas official complained that "it is impossible to keep an accurate record" of those who perished. By 1877, Reconstruction ended, and with it the first chapter in the Klan's history.[23]

The Klan returned in the 1920s, larger and stronger than before—a truly national organization that elected governors and senators throughout America. This Klan (except in the South and Southwest) was less overtly racist than its predecessor. It hoped to restore America's former white Anglo-Saxon purity, which had been taken away, Klansmen believed, during the growth of an urban, industrial, multiethnic society early in the twentieth century. Roman Catholicism became its chief target, the Church representing an alien faith seeking domination, especially in 1928, when New York governor Al Smith, a Catholic, sought the presidency. Internal scandals, the Depression, and World War II ended the second era of the Klan, but not for long.[24]

The civil rights movement, originating in the South during the years after World War II, and the Supreme Court's decision in *Brown v. Board of Education of Topeka* in 1954 revived both the Klan and other "vehicles of racial hate," such as the White Citizens Council. The council, home to "respectable" business leaders and local merchants, was created in Mississippi in 1954 after the *Brown* decision, and in the decade that followed, chapters spread throughout the South. Civil rights workers considered its members "Klansmen without their hoods," an apt description considering the organization's goals, expressed by the lawyer who established Alabama's group: "We intend to make it impossible for any Negro who advocates desegregation to find and hold a job, get credit, or renew a mortgage." The Klan, at this point, was less well organized than its white-collar counterpart because it was splintered into so many state groups—in Texas, the Carolinas, Florida, Arkansas, Alabama, and Georgia—that it took time before it was structured into one organized body. In the early 1950s, Georgia's Eldon Edwards reigned supreme—creating his own organization, U.S. Klans, Knights of the Ku Klux Klan. Within five years, it had chapters in eight other states. In Alabama, a tire salesman named Bobby Shelton coveted Edwards's empire of fifteen thousand Klansmen.[25]

Whereas the Klan of the nineteenth century appealed to Americans of all classes, that of the 1950s and 1960s attracted men of lesser achievement. The members of Rowe's Eastview Klavern No. 13 were drawn almost exclusively from working-class ranks: They were truck drivers, mechanics, gas station operators, small farmers, bricklayers, and especially Alabama's steelworkers. They were average in every way (most of Rowe's colleagues were around five feet eight inches tall, with brown hair and brown eyes), easily lost in a crowd. They found a comfortable and comforting home in the Klan. The members cared for one another. If a Klansman abused his family, they investigated it and tried to put a stop to it. The Klan also gave the men a history, an elaborate system of rituals, companionship, and a status they might otherwise be unable to achieve. But most important, it gave powerless men a sense of personal power. In a state infected by racism and fearful of black aspirations, Klansmen were the guardians at the gate, allowed by the Big Mules—those who dominated Alabama's economic and political life—to exert their authority through violence, as long as their victims were black. History and the prevailing political, economic, and social order were on their side.[26]

At first, Tommy Rowe's Klan life was disappointing. In daylight, Eastview Klavern No. 13 was merely the second story of Morgan's Furniture Store in northeast Birmingham. The Exalted Cyclops, Robert Thomas, was a thirty-nine-year-old railroad worker of no particular distinction. The meetings, held every Thursday night, quickly became boring. Rowe was both surprised and disappointed: "I thought we was going to . . . [learn] how to throw bricks, . . . burn the buildings, flog the people," he later said. "But we didn't. It was like 'so and so' was sick this week, we're going to take up a little collection, and they're having a problem down at Loveland's or Woolworths."[27]

Most meetings consisted primarily of angry talk, which Rowe recorded in his earliest reports, about the Klan's traditional enemies. There was angry talk about Catholics: "Mr. Wheeler got up and said that something had to be done about the Catholic Sisters playing Momma to the nigger boys and girls at the schools where they go. Also, he said that the Sisters sleep in the same place with nigger men, and the Priest was personally seen with his arm around colored women at the school."[28]

The possibility that Senator John F. Kennedy, a Roman Catholic, might become president sent shock waves through the Klan. "The South has no hope, so the people must be prepared to fight," said the Exalted Cyclops. "It is a sure thing that he is out to ruin the South. The next President is supposed to take full charge of the Federal Housing Program, Civil Rights issues, Federal Aid for schools, and if he does try to change things here there will be blood flowing on the streets." One Klansman asserted, to loud applause, that there were two ways "to stop that damn Communist [Kennedy]; that was to get someone to fill his face full of acid, or to use one of the guns that they had dry rotting away to shoot him with."[29]

There was angry talk about Jews: "The E.C. spoke about the Care Program. . . . They were always after money; that only about 12 cents of every dollar ever reached over there; that the Jews and the Catholics were getting the rest of it to help fight the South. He said that Judaism and Communism are the same thing."[30]

There was angry talk about the NAACP: At a Klan rally in Moulton, Alabama, Imperial Wizard Bobby Shelton told the crowd that the NAACP had stated approvingly that "white women wanted to be held and loved by the Negro man; that 70% of the white women had met Negro men and made love to them one time or another. And if that's what white women wanted, why should they not be allowed to make legal love out of it." The Klan Bureau of Investigation also had "concrete proof" that Senator Kennedy "is a member of the NAACP and has been a card carrying member since sometime in 1953. He was given this membership by Mrs. Franklin Roosevelt's son."[31]

And most of all there was angry talk about interracial sex. A white woman named Ruby Sims was "supposed to be selling herself to colored men for $8.00 for 15 minutes a time," Rowe learned in July. Rowe, Shorty Thompson, Jack Crawford, and Leroy "Monk" Rutherford were sent to look for her at the Irondale Trailer Park where she "is supposed to stay a lot, but we could not find her. She also goes to the Mayflower café a lot. We are supposed to try and find her again," Rowe reported to Kemp. The Klan in Scottsboro, Alabama, was having similar problems and asked the Eastview Klavern for help: Two young girls (one was the sheriff's granddaughter) were caught repeatedly having sex with two older black men, who had been jailed but were released on bond. The members "voted to send a legal representative to help out."[32]

The sighting of a woman who seemed to be black lounging at the Guest House Motel swimming pool provoked a lively discussion on how Klansmen could identify authentic blacks and what they should do about it. Hubert Page, the Klan's Grand Titan in charge of northern Alabama, told the assembled that the previous Sunday his wife, Mary Lou, took their young son to the motel's open house and saw "a colored woman in a bathing suit, sitting on the side of the pool with two little white children." Two Birmingham cops were also there and passed by her "five or six times," without asking her to leave. Mary Lou Page "got mad," rushed home, and told Hubert, who asked her whether she might have been mistaken. Maybe she had seen an Indian woman. "No, it was a nigger woman," Mary Lou said, "so [Hubert] got mad" and phoned the local authorities, who promised to look into it. "Then Glenn Wheeler got up and told the men to be careful, that he met some people over where he works that look just like colored people but are not. So Hubert got up and told him that if they had wool on their heads, then they had to go. There was talk from Billy Jackson about going over to the Motel to tear it up a little but Hubert said not at this time."[33]

But there was more than just idle angry talk, too. Klan members felt that a more aggressive Klan was needed in response to a more aggressive civil rights movement. Earlier that year black students in Tennessee had created sit-ins that soon spread to restaurants and department stores throughout the South. Rowe, who had learned "Lethal Judo" in the Marine Reserves and liked to show it off at the VFW Club, was asked to teach it to his fellow Klansmen. One night he demonstrated "how to disarm a person with knife and pistol, . . . [and] also how to break a man's back." He did suggest, however, that the men "go slow in trying to learn this" because they could seriously injure themselves.[34]

Klansmen were also encouraged to arm themselves; a permit to buy a pistol could easily be acquired from Jefferson County deputy sheriff Raymond Belcher simply by showing him a Klan membership card. (Sheriff Robert Bragg later told Rowe that "his office and his regular men would be at our [the Klan's] service day or night. All we had to do was call them; that his home would be open to us if we wanted to hold any kind of meeting out that way." Bragg and Belcher often turned to the Klan to handle problems that the police couldn't solve.) Klansmen, like Rowe, who couldn't afford to buy a gun, were loaned the money by the Klavern treasurer. With the fifty dollars Shorty Thompson gave him, Rowe was able to pick up a fine .22-caliber revolver at the Pig Trail Inn in Homewood. He was also required to buy a small baseball bat, which he gave to Thompson, who returned it to Rowe after he had hollowed it out and filled it with about five ounces of lead. At the next meeting, Rowe noticed a box filled with dozens of bats, which were made available to all Klansmen.[35]

Protecting the Klan from internal enemies was equally important and demanded imaginative ideas. On one occasion, the Klan experimented with hypnosis. At a meeting on August 3, Klansman Fred Henson, a gas station attendant and amateur hypnotist, put Gene Reeves "to sleep." He then asked him a series of questions (which Rowe later recorded): How old was he? Where did he live? How many children did he have? Did he "really hate Niggers and would he let his children date [them]?" Reeves "mumbled something about killing them all." Henson told him that Mrs. Reeves was there and, when he was awakened, he would have a burning desire to make love to her. Shorty Thompson was asked to play the role of Mrs. Reeves, and when Reeves was brought out of the trance, he began to fondle Thompson and then burst into tears. The Klansmen were very impressed by this demonstration and planned to use hypnosis on those they suspected of being informers; they also thought it would provide "a little fun along with business."[36]

But they didn't use hypnosis on Rowe the night they accused him of being an informant, which happened a few months after he had joined the Klan. "Hey bro," Rowe recalled Albert Peek saying at the end of a regular meeting, "I want to talk to you a minute before you leave." Rowe said "sure" but watched uneasily as Peek locked the front door. Then from behind a nearby soda machine, Peek pulled out a sawed-off shotgun and turned toward Rowe.

"You got your gun with you, bro?" Peek asked.

"I got my pants on, haven't I," Rowe replied.

"Let me have your goddamn gun."

"What the hell is going on," Rowe said quietly, although he knew he was in trouble. ("I remember very vividly saying . . . to myself, 'oh, fuck, I'm dead,'" he later recalled.)

A few Klansmen grabbed him and took him up on the stage to face Imperial Wizard Shelton. Bill Holt said, "You might as well talk to us, we know you're a FBI agent."

Trying to brazen it out, Rowe replied: "Man, you are full of shit. You guys don't . . . know what you're talking about." For a second he thought he might run for the open window, but he knew he'd never make it down the fire escape alive. Then his street-fighter's instincts took over; he grabbed Shelton around the neck, put a choke hold on him, and said, "You cocksucker, I'll kill your fucking ass; I ain't done nothing. I'm working for this goddamn organization."

"Let me go, let me go," Shelton gasped. Rowe did, realizing that the whole thing might just be a stunt. "I don't give a shit," he told them. "I'm probably a hell of a lot better Klansman than you ass holes are." Then Shelton said: "Goddamn, man, I was just testing you. I don't have anything on you. I just wanted to see what you was going to do."

"Well," Rowe said, "I goddamn near killed you and died of a heart attack." The men burst into laughter and the incident was over. "From that day until the day I left the Klan," Rowe said later, "Bobby Shelton protected me." But many Klansmen continued to suspect Rowe of being an FBI informant.[37]

Most nights were nowhere near as exciting, however. Occasionally, somebody would suggest an aggressive action, but it was rarely carried out. There was, for example, Operation Wholesale Day, recommended by Hubert Page at a meeting in August. The targets were blacks who insisted on exercising their constitutional right (affirmed by the U.S. Supreme Court in 1956) to sit anywhere they wished on city buses, including the front, where whites believed that only they were entitled to sit. At the appointed time, Klansmen would board buses and beat blacks with their loaded baseball bats, bicycle chains, blackjacks, and other weapons. "We will be notified a day ahead," Rowe noted, "where to meet, who will go with whom, and who will go where. This is supposed to last all day—hitting colored people and running. If we pass a person we know is with us and the law has him, we are to help him get away at all costs." At the next meeting, Page introduced a visitor, a man dressed in a white suit—not the typical Klansman garb—a city official, perhaps, who told the group that Wholesale Day was soon approaching and "he knew it was going to be the sparkplug of action in Alabama against the niggers, and we could count on his support all the way." The Exalted Cyclops added that "all Klansmen were to be on the alert; that as soon as they finished making plans so they would be able to have the most men present, they would pass the word." But the word never came, and Wholesale Day never took place.[38]

Like Rowe, Special Agent Kemp was puzzled by the Klavern's apparent inaction because Eastview No. 13 had the reputation of being one of the most dangerous groups in Alabama. He wondered whether his "undercover man" might not be reporting everything he observed. His doubts led to an angry confrontation between the two men in early August. "We need to talk," Rowe later recalled the agent saying after he had described the latest Klan meeting. Kemp picked him up and they drove to a deserted location. "What else happened?" Kemp asked.

"Nothing," Rowe said.

"There were no other discussions about anybody being [beaten] or hurt?"

"No, sir."

"You didn't go in late?"

"No, sir."

"Well, then," Kemp said, his voice rising, "I think you're holding back on me."

Rowe was hurt and annoyed. "Why am I here?" he asked. "I'm here because I love the FBI and my country. You know, you didn't beat me with a stick to get me here. If you don't believe what I'm telling you, then you go get yourself some other son-of-a-bitch. . . . Every god-damned thing I told you went on in that meeting, no more no less. . . . There's just nothing happening, absolutely nothing. . . . If you don't believe me, send me home."

Kemp lied to him, saying that he had another informant in the Klavern who told him that Klansmen had gone "night riding"—burning crosses and breaking windows. "Damned if I can't figure it out," he said wearily. "I know it's going on."

Rowe noted that sometimes, after the meetings ended, Klan officers left together; perhaps they met secretly and plotted the actions Kemp described. There were also smaller teams, consisting of the most trusted Klansmen, who were selected to perform missionary work. Often, one team didn't know what the others were up to. Rowe reminded Kemp that he had been in the Klan only about six weeks; he was making friends, but these things took time.[39]

Next time, Rowe should "be among the last to leave," Kemp ordered; perhaps he could join the leaders for a beer, feel them out, see if something more was going on. And "try to get in" those missionary groups.[40]

Kemp was worried about more than a few burned crosses and busted windows; he feared that the Bureau might terminate Rowe. He had sent Washington a report on July 25, describing Rowe as cooperative, "emotionally stable," and likely to develop into an "excellent informant." He also asked for permission to continue developing their relationship, looking toward Rowe's eventual promotion to Confidential Informant. But on August 8, J. Edgar Hoover denied his request and ordered a full investigation of Rowe: Who was he? Where did he come from? Why did he wish to work for the FBI? Kemp could still receive information Rowe voluntarily submitted, but he could not attempt to direct or control his activities. Hoover was extremely sensitive about associations that might embarrass the Bureau: Six months earlier, every field office was reminded of the need for "a thorough, intensive background investigation and careful personal scrutiny" of those who entered into this odd compact with the FBI. Hoover was right to raise questions about Rowe's past. Kemp's report was poorly researched and marred by factual errors; it didn't explain Rowe's earlier arrests for carrying a concealed weapon and impersonating a police officer. Also ignored was Rowe's first marriage to Margaret Blair in 1951 and the child from that brief union, the daughter Rowe never mentioned or considered a part of his family. All this suggested that Rowe might not be as emotionally stable or reliable as Kemp believed.[41]

Ten days after Kemp received Hoover's orders, Rowe's chances of becoming a full-fledged informant suddenly increased. The meeting of Eastview Klavern No. 13 that changed Rowe's life began promptly at 7:30 on Thursday evening, August 18, 1960. After the usual opening ceremonies, an older Klansman named Pitts rose to complain about how the Klavern was being managed. The top positions, he said, were all going to the younger men who were new to the Klan. It just wasn't fair. Exalted Cyclops Robert Thomas took immediate offense; if people weren't happy with his leadership, he would resign. Grand Titan Hubert Page immediately defended Thomas—if the E.C. left, he would too. Pitts said again that "the older men should hold offices"; a vote was called, and Pitts was soundly defeated.[42]

Bill Holt rose to his feet and announced that because of back problems, he "could hardly get around" so could no longer serve as Klokan Chief. The men voted for his resignation and Shorty Thompson nominated Tommy Rowe. Rowe, aware of the developing rift between the Klavern's generations (at an earlier meeting he noted that younger members were treating the elders harshly), shrewdly declined. He certainly wanted the position, he told the group, but because he had just joined the Klan in June, he thought the job should go to a more experienced member. Pitts nominated Thompson, who at age forty-four was eighteen years older than Rowe, but he was ineligible because he was already serving as treasurer. Holt quickly asked that the nominations be closed, so only one name was put to a vote—Tommy Rowe was elected unanimously. Page remarked that "he thought Tommy would make a good man [and] . . . could pick anyone in the Klavern to help him and any member that did not answer his call had better have a good reason for not showing up."[43]

Rowe was thrilled. After barely eight weeks in the Klan, he had suddenly risen to a critical position. The Klokan Chief reviewed all new membership applications and was responsible for protecting the Klavern from outside interference during its weekly meetings. He knew that Kemp would also be pleased; no other "undercover man" could surpass him in providing the Bureau with such important, inside information. Writing his report later that night, he joked, "I would suggest that you watch this fellow Tommy, because he is in complete charge of security for the Klavern." FBI Headquarters would reward Rowe's achievement in November by informing Kemp that Gary Thomas Rowe had been appointed Confidential Informant—(Racial). Kemp was authorized to direct his activities but should "at all times" be careful to make sure that Rowe was "not a plant," that is, a double agent acting for the Klan.[44]

Now, as a Klavern officer, Rowe was admitted to the inner circle where important issues were discussed and the more violent actions were contemplated and sometimes carried out. One such event was the annual cross burning at Birmingham public schools. On September 1, 1960, after the conclusion of the Klavern's meeting, Hubert Page asked a group of younger Klansmen to remain in the hall. After the rest left, the door was closed and locked. Page told them that they had been chosen to burn this year's crosses. First, they were organized into twelve "Action Squads," each consisting of three men, and were given their assignments. Page gave them his telephone number, which they were to use if they were arrested. Tell the police nothing, he cautioned; just call him and "he would be right down with a bondsman" to free them. Then they left, with Rowe among them, and during the following two and a half hours, they burned wooden crosses at schools in Woodlawn, North Birmingham, Cahaba Heights, and seventeen other locations. It might not have been the most exciting evening, but, for Rowe, it was better than watching Henson the hypnotist put Klansmen to sleep.[45]

Cross burning was considered an activity that FBI informants were supposed to avoid, but there is no evidence in Rowe's informant file that he was criticized for his activities. Although Kemp knew that Rowe participated, the final report forwarded to Headquarters didn't mention his direct involvement—only that cross burning occurred on the night of September 1. No one in the Birmingham field office or in Washington asked about his role. Without anyone in authority authorizing it, the leash connecting the informant to the Bureau was becoming looser; Rowe was given more freedom to participate in the very acts the FBI said were forbidden. In April 1961, the leash broke completely.

CHAPTER TWO

One Hell of a Good Job

FRED HENSON, THE KLAVERN hypnotist, was the first member of Eastview Klavern to hear about the little black boy in Odenville. It was disgraceful how old man Forman and his wife, Pauline, brought the kid into town, taking him everywhere he didn't belong, into the grocery store and the ice cream parlor, and worst of all, the barbershop, where Orman Forman had the boy's hair cut. Forman claimed that the four-year-old was his maid's child, and they were just taking care of him while Cora Lee (whom they had raised since she was nine years old) went to Detroit in search of work. The Klan didn't believe him. Although Forman was sixty-nine, the townspeople thought the child was actually his own son, the result of an illicit affair with the maid. The barber considered "taking care of" Forman himself, but he didn't want to feel like a bully. Forman was an old man, a bald-headed little guy only a few inches taller than five feet. So the barber complained to the St. Clair County sheriff's office. Townspeople were "raising all mighty hell about it," he told the cops, threatening to set fire to the barbershop "if he didn't quit cutting the kid's hair." The deputies agreed that Forman's stunts were "causing a lot of trouble," but they did nothing. So the barber turned to the Klan for help.[1]

Henson told Eastview members John Jones and Gene Reeves, who thought the story was worse than disgusting, a little missionary work was obviously needed. They checked with Exalted Cyclops Robert Thomas, who approved a visit designed to frighten Forman into moving the child elsewhere. On Sunday morning, April 2, 1961, Henson and his friends drove to the Forman place in East Birmingham, a large ranch house set well back in the woods and less than three miles from Odenville. It was a nice secluded spot, perfect for what they had in mind. They didn't go up to the house that day; this was just a reconnaissance mission. They would confront Forman later, after the Klavern meeting on Thursday night.[2]

Tommy Rowe heard about the proposed trip just before the start of the meeting on April 6; "there was a little missionary work to do," Shorty Thompson told him. At nine o'clock he and other Klansmen would leave the hall to move some heavy equipment—that was their cover story, and the other members would be their witnesses. At the appointed time, Rowe met his buddies in the parking lot behind the department store. Henson filled them in on their mission. Some wanted to just warn the old couple; others urged that they "beat the hell out of the[m]," while a visitor from Odenville said, "Well, we don't want to see the kid anymore." Somebody else replied, "That [can] be handled too." They crowded into two cars and headed for the Forman home, arriving an hour later. They hid one car off the highway and drove the second silently down the long dark road to the circular driveway in front of the house. Klansmen Bobby Frank Cherry, Charles Cagle, and the others hid in the woods nearby. Rowe stood near the porch steps as Bill Holt and Fred Henson, wearing their Klan hoods, knocked on the front door.[3]

"Who's there?" Forman called out.

"Our car broke down out on the highway," Holt said; "we need a phone." "OK," Forman answered, "come around to the side entrance." There, he began to unlatch the door. Suddenly, there was a blinding flash of light. Inside the house, Pauline Forman had turned on the floodlights illuminating the front yard, where she could see a group of strangers caught in a frozen tableau. "Be careful, there's men out there!" she warned her husband. The side door was open enough for Holt, Henson, and Rowe to grab both Formans and pull them onto the porch. "This is the son-of-a-bitch we want," Mrs. Forman later recalled one of the men saying. Holt pulled a .22 pistol from his pocket and pointed it at Pauline, who was almost as old and as tiny as her husband. Henson cried: "Bill! Please don't shoot that woman!"[4]

Hearing himself identified, Holt turned and cursed Henson, giving

Pauline a chance to run back into the house. Klansman L. B. Earle followed her, looking for the telephone; when he found it, he ripped it off the wall and carried it away.[5]

Outside, three Klansmen grappled with Forman, whose strength surprised Rowe. Holt had a pillowcase and, with Rowe's help, tried to put it over Forman's head. "Kill the old mother-fucker," Rowe later recalled Holt saying. Then Pauline Forman appeared with a .30-caliber German Luger in her hand. Placing it on her husband's shoulder, she pointed it at Holt, telling him she'd shoot if Orman wasn't released.[6]

Pandemonium erupted. The Klansmen turned Forman loose and ran for the cars. Bobby Frank Cherry and Robert Conaway (a part-time deputy sheriff in Irondale) fired at least three shots at the Formans but missed. Orman Forman, now armed with a .22, returned fire, but his gun jammed after two shots. "It was a hell of a mess," Rowe said later. Klansmen were running every which way. Charles Cagle ran into a boulder and shattered his knee. Rowe heard Bill Holt "holler 'Aw shit!'" and saw him fall into a ravine; Rowe thought Holt had been shot by Mrs. Forman. When Rowe reached his car, he looked back to see Pauline Forman in hot pursuit. "God-damn," he thought, "here comes old Granny tracking down the steps popping pellets at everybody's ass." He threw his car into reverse, stopping momentarily to pick up stray Klansmen, then rushed down the long road and onto the highway. In the backseat, he could hear a Klansman sobbing "Oh my God, oh my God." A few minutes later, he pulled over to help the stricken man. The other Klan car followed him. "Where you hit? Where you hit?" Rowe asked him, while feeling around his chest for wounds. There were none, but the man continued to repeat "Oh my God." "Shit," said another Klansman, "there's nothing wrong with him. He's just scared to death. Put him in my car. We won't have no more God-damn problems with him." The car sped off with its prisoner, whom Rowe never saw again.[7]

At a predetermined rendezvous spot in Irondale, Rowe found a dispirited group, more Keystone Cops than Knights of the Ku Klux Klan. They nursed their cuts and bruises and bickered among themselves: Why did Bobby Frank fire that first shot? Shouldn't he be "chastised," or worse? Some wanted to return to the battlefield to rescue their missing comrades, Charlie and Bill. They did, but found no one. A good Samaritan later found Cagle limping along the highway and gave him a ride. Holt had dodged the bullet and, more embarrassed than injured, spent the night hiding in the woods. Eventually, he was picked up by a friendly deputy sheriff who successfully persuaded Alabama state troopers to let him go home. Klansman Jones, who had planned the escapade with Henson and Reeves, was so shaken by the evening's events that he resigned from the Klan a few days later.[8]

It was well after midnight when the FBI field office patched Tommy Rowe through to a sleeping Barry Kemp. Rowe's tale was a mix of fact and outlandish fiction. At first he said that Gene Reeves led the group, pulled Forman outside, and tussled with him until Mrs. Forman appeared, blasting away with her Luger; "15–20 shots were exchanged," and Forman fell against the front door, possibly shot. Klansmen were also hurt; one screamed repeatedly, "Oh my God." The Klan "only intended to warn Forman concerning the negro boy and no violence was intended," Rowe claimed. Three days later, Rowe revised his story—Bill Holt replaced Reeves as the man in charge. Rowe may have been genuinely confused or he wanted some revenge against the man who suspected him of being an informant. Mrs. Forman later "tentatively" identified Bill Holt and Rowe as the men she saw assaulting her husband. Kemp later telephoned the field office, which sent an "urgent" teletype to Headquarters describing the events, but it omitted Rowe's direct involvement.[9]

The informant and his contact agent met again on April 10. Kemp strongly warned Rowe to avoid violent situations. Rowe lied, claiming that he didn't know about the planned assault on Forman until they left the hall; he thought they were going to move furniture, but by that time it was too late to leave. And he was fed up with Kemp's lectures: "You can't go out with carloads of 15 men and say, 'hey I'm going to stand and look at you beat these damn people,'" he asserted. "You either got to get in there or leave it alone or you're gonna get killed." Rowe insisted that he had saved Forman's life—"they was going to kill him right there," he said —and persuaded Kemp that he was the hero that night. "Tommy actually broke up the fight and protected the people and got the Klan out of there," Kemp later testified, asserting that trying to diffuse violent incidents was "basic" to Rowe's nature.[10]

When the FBI interviewed the Formans, they said nothing about one brave Klansman who tried to save them. Kemp never tried to corroborate Rowe's story and expressed remorse for criticizing him. "We have to by law instruct you that you are not to participate in any violence," Rowe later remembered him saying. "However, I know you have to do this. . . . But you have to get the information. That's the important thing: get the information."[11]

The leash was broken. Rowe was now free to do pretty much what he wanted as long as he didn't kill anybody and, above all, got the information the Bureau wanted. The FBI would protect him. The memos about the Forman incident that Kemp sent to Washington said nothing specific about Rowe's actions that night; once again, he merely had been the passive observer reporting on events from afar. And, in a progress report on his informant sent to Headquarters in June, Kemp praised Rowe for quickly furnishing the identities of the assailants (Kemp omitted Rowe, of course) and the reason for the attack. In the end, it was a good night for Tommy Rowe. His actions persuaded his friends that he was fully committed to the Klan's missionary work; his FBI handler thought him a hero; and the Bureau got its precious information, which went into the files and gathered dust. For the Formans and the cause of law enforcement, it was a bad night. Both Pauline and Orman were badly shaken, and without Pauline's brave intervention they might have been beaten or killed. No one was ever charged in the crime, let alone convicted.[12]

Rowe's next violent encounter—the most serious of his career save for the killing of Viola Liuzzo—would be more difficult for the FBI to cover up. This time, a photograph captured Rowe and other Klansmen beating an innocent bystander during a Klan attack on Freedom Riders on Mother's Day 1961. Of that event, a secret Justice Department report would later conclude: "Of the hundreds [involved] . . . Rowe was one of the handful most responsible for the violence."[13]

Not long after the Forman incident, the Congress of Racial Equality (CORE) formally announced that an interracial group of thirteen, soon to be known as the Freedom Riders, would travel on buses into the Deep South to determine whether the U.S. Supreme Court's recent order desegregating waiting rooms, restaurants, and bathrooms in bus terminals was being followed. James Farmer, CORE's national director, informed the president, the attorney general, the chair of the Interstate Commerce Commission, the director of the FBI, and the heads of the Greyhound and Trailways bus companies of their planned trip from Washington, D.C., to New Orleans, where they hoped to arrive on May 17, the seventh anniversary of the Supreme Court's *Brown* decision. As Farmer expected, his letters received no reply. "Our intention," he asserted, "was to provoke the Southern authorities into enforcing the law of the land. . . . We were counting on the bigots of the South to do our work for us."[14]

Birmingham's bigots were preparing a reception they wanted the Freedom Riders to remember for the rest of their lives. The plan originated with Theophilus Eugene "Bull" Connor, Birmingham's short, gravelly voiced police commissioner, whose hostility toward blacks was unrivaled among city officials. His chief lieutenants, W. W. "Red" Self and Tom Cook, both Birmingham police officers, would handle the details, and the Klan would do the missionary work—insulating both Connor and the police from any charges that might result from the assault. Red Self turned to his drinking buddy and fellow VFW Club bouncer Tommy Rowe to act as liaison between the police and the Klan. On April 13, Self called Rowe and invited him to go for a ride in his squad car. Since this was one of Rowe's favorite pastimes, he enthusiastically agreed. As they drove around town, Self told him that the Birmingham police "needed to get ahold of some people in the Klan that can keep their god-damned mouth shut, something big is coming to Birmingham, some Freedom Riders in busses. We want some people to meet them . . . and beat the shit out of them." Could he put them in touch with Klan officials? Rowe agreed to help, passing Self's request along to Hubert Page, who set up a series of meetings with Connor, Imperial Wizard Bobby Shelton, and other Klan officials. And, a few days later, Rowe met with Tom Cook, the police sergeant in charge of "Racial Matters," which meant threatening civil rights leaders in Birmingham and gathering derogatory information on Martin Luther King, Jr.[15]

Over a cup of coffee at Ivan's Drive-In Restaurant, Cook told Rowe what was in store for the Freedom Riders. When they entered the Greyhound and Trailways bus terminals, Sergeant Cook said, the Klan would be given fifteen minutes to "Beat 'em, bomb 'em, kill 'em, I don't give a shit. There will be absolutely no arrests. You can assure every Klansman in the country that no one will be arrested. . . . We don't ever want another Freedom Rider coming through Alabama again. I want it to be something they remember as long as they live. . . . Now, when you get the signal from Red to get the hell out of there, leave then, we've only got about two, three minutes at the most [before] you'll be swarmed with officers." As a sign of good faith, Cook gave Rowe documents claiming to prove Martin Luther

King's link to the Communists, which he wanted passed on to Shelton. Rowe didn't receive the specific details of the plan to attack the Freedom Riders; although Bobby Shelton had reassured Cook that Rowe could be trusted "100%," he still wondered whether Rowe could be an FBI informant and even called the Bureau to ask whether Tommy was "one of [their] people." So Rowe wasn't included in the discussions at the highest level and wasn't given specific orders until May 11, three days before the Freedom Riders were scheduled to arrive in Birmingham.[16]

That night, at a meeting of Eastview Klavern No. 13, Grand Titan Hubert Page told the Klansmen about the impending events. Two busloads of Freedom Riders were expected in Birmingham sometime on Mother's Day, Sunday, May 14. The first would arrive at the Greyhound bus station in the morning, the second at the Trailways depot later that afternoon. The Imperial Wizard wanted every man to realize how serious this crisis was: "professional agitators" were traveling through the Deep South causing "troubles," threatening to use all-white bathrooms and restaurants in bus terminals, and to "sit-in" to protest segregation. And they were about to invade Alabama. They should be stopped at the state line, Bobby Shelton said in a public statement issued on May 4, but if Alabama troopers and city police couldn't handle the job, the Klan and "all other true white people . . . would stop them any way they can." Robert Creel, Exalted Cyclops of the Bessemer Klavern, suggested that they determine what routes the buses were taking so that he "and a few picked men," hidden in strategic places on the highway, "could put a few loads of buckshot" into them. Rowe quickly objected to such talk during the meeting because "the walls had big ears." Page agreed and told Creel "to be careful" when talking on the floor.[17]

All Klansmen were now "on alert," Page continued, and should stay close to their phones during the weekend, awaiting "a call to the cause." If the Klan failed to respond, the Hooded Order would be ruined. Accordingly, sixty Klansmen, organized into six Action Squads and led by the Klavern's most energetic fighters, would be specially picked to greet the Freedom Riders at the Greyhound bus station, if they got that far.[18]

After the meeting, Hubert Page took Tommy Rowe aside and gave him a fuller briefing. Bull Connor had told them, "By God, if you are going to do this thing, do it right!" When members of CORE tried to integrate the bus terminal restaurant, Connor wanted Klansmen to provoke a fight that would then be blamed on the blacks. Beat them until they looked "like a bulldog got a hold of them," he said. If any tried to use the bathrooms, they were to be stripped naked and pushed outside where they would be arrested, and he would see that they were sent to the penitentiary. Klansmen would have fifteen free minutes to do their missionary work, but if, by chance, some didn't escape in time and were arrested, he guaranteed that their sentences would be light. They should leave their Klan membership cards at home and carry only guns that were registered. Klansman Gene Reeves would make sure that there were enough bats, chains, and pipes for everyone. Rowe was told that he would have a special job to do Sunday morning: Not only would he be in charge of his own Action Squad, but he and the other leaders (Bill Holt, L. B. Earle, Lloyd Stone, Gene Reeves, and Shorty Thompson) should try to stay out of the fight and, instead, watch for CORE officials, follow them to their hotels, and give them a beating that would send them running for their lives. Rowe would also be the chief link between Tom Cook and the Klan; a special telephone in the terminal would provide an open line between the two men. The entire state organization was expected to show up on Sunday, but five Klaverns were on "special call": Gardendale, Warrior, Helena, Bessemer, and Eastview No. 13. Hundreds, perhaps thousands, of Klansmen, armed and ready, would be in Birmingham Sunday morning.[19]

Rowe visited the Bessemer Klavern the following night to make a personal plea for full participation. He reminded the crowd that they had all been sent a "Fiery Summons," the most urgent communication a Klansman could receive: They must "drop everything, leave work, get out of a hospital bed," to answer the Klan's call. They all knew that the Freedom Riders were coming, and, well, "they was going to have a little surprise party" for them; the Klansmen should be at the Greyhound bus station by ten o'clock Sunday morning. It was Mother's Day and they were going to teach those "mother-fuckers" a lesson they would never forget.[20]

The FBI knew everything about the coming attack—the time, the place, the assailants, even their choice of weapons—but it did nothing to prevent it. A Justice Department task force investigating Rowe's career as FBI informant later called it "unfortunate" that, given the information Rowe provided, Hoover didn't order agents to the scene or, just as important, inform the U.S. Marshals Service or Attorney General Robert Kennedy. The Bureau's passivity can be explained by several factors, besides Hoover's

well-known hostility toward Martin Luther King and the civil rights movement. First, it believed that the maintenance of domestic order was solely
the responsibility of state and municipal law enforcement agencies, or in
the case of outright insurrection, the U.S. Army, and Hoover wouldn't
intervene unless there was solid evidence that a federal law was being
violated. (The recent Civil Rights Act of 1960 gave the FBI the authority
to investigate bombings if there was evidence that the explosives had been
brought in from another state and the suspects were fleeing across state
lines.) Oddly, there is no sign that the Bureau ever considered that the
Klan would be interfering with interstate travel, a federal responsibility.
Furthermore, current Bureau regulations stated clearly that in the case of
"general racial matters [such] as race riots, civil demonstrations and similar
developments," the FBI had no jurisdiction except in cases "where some
subversive influence was at work" or a statute was being violated. Apparently, the FBI considered only Communists and not the Klan a "subversive
influence."[21]

Second, the FBI considered itself chiefly an investigative body without
a protective responsibility or function. "We most certainly will not act as
bodyguards for anyone," Hoover once stated, and every agent followed
this rule. Special Agent Barry Kemp, when later asked who would protect
Americans from violence if the local police force was absent, replied: "It
wouldn't [be] me. I was just a private citizen . . . with no police powers.
. . . I was not the guardian of anybody's freedom."[22]

If the FBI didn't feel strongly about protecting the victims of violence,
such was not the case when it came to protecting their informant, the
man one FBI official called "our ace in the hole." This was their chief objective. Sharing Rowe's reports with others risked revealing his identity
and, perhaps, his life. So when Headquarters authorized Special Agent
in Charge Thomas Jenkins to inform Birmingham chief of police Jamie
Moore on May 12 that there might be "some violence" ahead, Jenkins was
ordered to be as vague as possible—he was not to mention the Ku Klux
Klan or the Greyhound bus station. "Any time we furnish information to
the Birmingham Police Department," FBI Supervisor Clement McGowan
told the field office, "we should be most meticulous to protect the informant
and the source of information." McGowan believed that "we could give
an adequate alert without being completely specific." Jenkins telephoned
Moore and advised him "in accordance" with his instructions. When they

spoke a second time, late on May 13, Moore told Jenkins that he would be out of town on Mother's Day, fulfilling a family obligation he couldn't avoid. If Jenkins needed to give them any additional information, he should speak with Sergeant Thomas Cook, who would be in charge in his absence. And, sure enough, when the field office received the news on the morning of May 14 that the Freedom Riders had left Atlanta and were proceeding to Alabama, Jenkins passed the information on to the very man he knew was preparing the attack. Later asked why he didn't tell Chief Moore that he suspected Cook of collaborating with the Klan, Jenkins said: "I didn't want to compromise the informant. I couldn't afford to compromise the informant." And why did he give any information to Cook? "He was the one who was supposed to be in charge of the Birmingham Police Department at that time. Who else was I going to call?" Jenkins should have anticipated what happened next: Cook telephoned Rowe at the Greyhound bus station to report that the Freedom Riders were on their way.[23]

Mary Spicer probably wasn't thinking about Freedom Riders when she boarded the Trailways bus in Atlanta on Sunday, May 14. The twenty-five-year-old black woman was headed for Birmingham to be married. Her fiancé was a twenty-nine-year-old shoe salesman named George Webb, and the wedding was to occur as soon as they could arrange it. Only moments before leaving, she hurried to telephone George that her bus would arrive at the Trailways depot at 4:05 p.m. He and his aunt, Monti Morris, would be there to meet her; she would have no trouble finding him—he planned to wear his best blue suit and light gray fedora, and just in case that wasn't enough to make him stand out in the crowd, he would be wearing red socks.[24]

When Spicer took her seat in the rear of the bus, she paid little attention to the other passengers—mostly blacks traveling alone. But there were several white men wearing T-shirts, chinos, and sullen expressions, and a racially mixed group of seven (three whites and four blacks) and others who seemed to be associated with their party—reporters, Spicer would later learn. Curiously, the group split up. The whites—an elderly couple and a middle-aged man—sat in the rear, the spot traditionally reserved for blacks, while the four young black males sat in the front, among the white passengers. Some passengers whispered that these must be "those Freedom Riders" they had heard about. The driver came aboard and introduced himself as "Pat" Patterson, and the bus left the terminal.[25]

The trip was tense but uneventful, although one man who left the bus at the last stop before Alabama told Freedom Rider Charles Person: "When you niggers get to Alabama, you'll get what's coming to you." They reached Anniston, Alabama, around three o'clock and stopped for fifteen minutes. Those who disembarked—including Spicer, the elderly white man, and two Freedom Riders, Charles Person and Herman Harris, who were assigned to check whether the restaurants and bathrooms were accessible to blacks—were surprised to find that all the facilities were closed; the terminal was quiet as a tomb. Anybody wanting something to eat or drink would have to cross the highway, where a restaurant and a gas station could accommodate them. Spicer, perhaps afraid to enter an "all-white" restaurant, got a soda from a beverage machine, while the older white man got drinks and sandwiches at the restaurant. When they returned to the bus, they reported the odd circumstances to the driver, who was also baffled. Then a porter came aboard and told Pat Patterson that Marshall Long, the Trailways dispatcher, was calling him from Birmingham.

In the station, Patterson learned that earlier that day a Greyhound bus carrying Freedom Riders had been attacked by an angry mob at Bynum, a few miles from Anniston and along the route their bus was supposed to follow. The tires were slashed, windows were smashed, and a firebomb was tossed inside the bus, choking the passengers with its billowing black smoke. They had no choice but to run outside, where the mob (mostly local Klansmen) beat them with sticks and metal bars until a state trooper fired a warning shot, which stopped the attack. Dispatcher Long ordered Patterson "not to leave the station without plenty of police protection." A uniformed police officer who accompanied Patterson from the terminal urged him to move all black passengers to the rear of the bus because the mob was still in the area.[26]

"Folks, I'm not going to drive away from here," Patterson told the passengers over the loudspeaker, "because a Greyhound bus down the street a few miles was just burned to the ground and the passengers are being carried to the hospital by the carloads—because of this"—he stopped and pointed to the Freedom Riders in the front of the bus. "A mob is waiting for our bus and will do the same to us unless we get these niggers off the front seat." To Person and the other blacks he said, "If you'll go to the back, I think I can get you through." Silence. Again he asked them, but there was no response. The police officer, who was listening from the bus steps, joined Patterson, asking them to "reconsider things. I'm not for either side," he said, "but there is really a mess down the road." If they didn't follow the driver's orders, "the police would not risk their lives" protecting them. The four black students didn't move or speak. "OK driver, take them through," said the disgusted officer, leaving the problem to Patterson, who wouldn't budge. The silence was broken by a pregnant woman who began to scream hysterically; Patterson quickly escorted her off the bus, leaving the agitated passengers to themselves.[27]

Suddenly, about eight or nine white men got up, "all talking at once," cursing the blacks and demanding that they give up their seats. "We don't want to be burned," they said, "niggers get to the back of the bus." One Freedom Rider explained that they were "interstate passengers" and could sit where they wished. When the blacks remained seated, a white man grabbed Charles Person by his necktie, slapped him across the face, and tried to pull him toward the rear of the bus. The nineteen-year-old Morehouse student, true to his nonviolent creed, did not react, which only enraged the whites even more, and several rushed over to hit him. His white colleagues—James Peck, a forty-six-year-old veteran CORE activist, and Walter Bergman, a retired college professor, at sixty-one the oldest of the group—hurried to the front to talk with the men, but they, too, were attacked. Peck, Mary Spicer later told the FBI, "was beaten until the men couldn't beat him any longer and they left him alone." Bergman received blows to the face and head and was thrown to the floor, despite his wife Frances's pleas to leave him alone. Isaac Reynolds, Ivor Moore, and Herman Harris were also attacked and lay in the aisle next to their fallen comrades. The white men began to push them to the rear but found it tough going; several picked up Charles Person and threw the 160-pound man over the seats to the back of the bus. Walter Bergman, unable to crawl fast enough to satisfy the thugs, was repeatedly kicked in the back: "There is so much NAACP in this nigger lover that he can't even get up," said one of his attackers. When they tired of kicking Bergman, the men picked him up and dragged him to a seat in the "blacks only" section. Although there was no one left to beat, one white man, his face flushed an angry red, continued to scream at them and had to be restrained by his wife.[28]

By the time the driver and the police officer returned to the bus, the assault was over. Walter Bergman, his left cheek swollen and eye partially closed, was comforted by his wife, who also tried to wipe the blood from

James Peck's face. The others had various cuts and bruises, but amazingly, the injuries appeared to be superficial, although Bergman would later suffer a stroke during routine surgery, leaving him confined to a wheelchair for the rest of his life; his physicians attributed it to the blows he received that day. The "spokesman" for the whites, a tall, thin man, wearing a plaid jacket and bow tie, announced that "the bus is now segregated, we can go on now." The officer told the Freedom Riders that, since he had not observed the attack, there was nothing he could do: "If you damn niggers had moved to the back of the bus when they told you," he said, "there wouldn't have been anything said or done." He did, however, offer to record their complaints. No one accepted his invitation. The white men asked him to leave his gun and nightstick behind, to ensure that "they'd have no more trouble," but he kept his weapons and left. Patterson started the bus and they drove off, taking a new route that would bypass the mob and the burned-out Greyhound bus.[29]

The whites continued to carefully watch the Freedom Riders during the remainder of the trip: "They sat half turned and were looking at us from Anniston to Birmingham," James Peck later told the FBI. And when Peck rose to get something to eat from a box on the seat in front of him, one of his attackers asked: "Where do you think you're going? Stay right there." Peck ignored him and got the box. Black journalist Simeon Booker (who had secretly sent the Freedom Riders' schedule to the FBI on May 4) tried to calm the angry whites by giving them something to read—copies of *Jet Magazine*, featuring a story on the Freedom Rides.[30]

In Birmingham, Rowe spent these hours conferring with Cook on the telephone, prowling around the terminal, and watching the activities at City Hall located across the street from the Greyhound bus station, where Police Commissioner Bull Connor ruled and the city police made their home. Connor had kept his word: No cops were on the street, and Rowe could see a steady stream of police cars going down the ramp to the parking garage beneath the building, and remaining there. Connor was in the "Detective Room" most of the day and was asked by a reporter, who was "scared because there were so many men hanging around the bus station," whether he planned to send police. Connor replied: "No, there's no use in doing that. It's just another bus coming in."[31]

The turnout did not prove to be as large as Hubert Page expected, but several hundred "heavy-set men" did show up, dressed casually in sport shirts as if they were attending a sporting event. A few were Birmingham cops dressed in civilian clothes. Journalist Howard K. Smith, reporting for CBS News, watched them move "restlessly in and around the terminal, looking and waiting." Some gathered on street corners, others sat in cars parked nearby. They were, a local reporter told Smith, "Klansmen minus their robes."[32]

Imperial Wizard Bobby Shelton was there, driving his Cadillac around the building and directing journalists "to places where the action was taking place." Also present were two especially virulent racists whom even the Klan called "poison"—Jesse B. Stoner and Edward Fields, the former an ex-Klansman and legendary hate merchant, the latter a twenty-nine-year-old chiropractor and self-proclaimed "Anti-Black and Anti-Jewish crusader." Together they ran the National States Rights Party, which had its headquarters located nearby because Birmingham, Fields said, "is a perfect place for my kind of work." The Imperial Wizard considered them a threat to the Klan, siphoning off members who wanted more action. When Rowe and Page bumped into the two men that morning, they almost came to blows: Page threatened "to whip their ass when they got through with the niggers." Fields reminded Page that they were all working for the same cause—white supremacy—and should ignore their differences, at least for today.[33]

The hours dragged by without a sign of the enemy. Where were the buses? The first was long overdue. Then a rumor began to circulate through the crowd: Something had happened in Anniston; the bus had been burned, people killed. Rowe took another call from Cook (he later estimated that they spoke a dozen times that day): It was true, the Greyhound bus had been stopped, but the Trailways bus was now nearby, due to arrive soon at the depot four blocks away. "Get your people and go up there!" Cook ordered. Rowe rushed through the terminal, yelling: "Come on, come on, we're going to be late! They're going to be there before we get there!" "He was the commando," a Klansman later remarked. "That's how he got those other boys to follow him."[34]

It must have been an "astonishing sight," Rowe later thought—hundreds of men running and walking down the streets of Birmingham on a beautiful spring afternoon, "carrying chains, sticks and clubs. . . . we barged into the bus station and took it over like an army of occupation. There were Klansmen in the waiting rooms, in the rest rooms, in the parking area. A bus official said, 'Get the shoeshine boy out; the Klan is here.'"[35]

The Trailways bus finally arrived in Birmingham at 4:15. Marshall Long, the dispatcher, came aboard to distribute cards for the passengers to record the day's events, but the angry whites in the front of the bus pushed him aside and left. One hurled a final insult at Peck and the Bergmans: "You damned Communists," he said, "why don't you go back to Russia. You're a shame to the white race." To the blacks, he added, "You're a shame to the nigger race." Ignoring the taunts, the Freedom Riders stepped off the bus.[36]

Person and Peck, his face still caked with blood, walked down the long dark corridor leading to the "all-white" waiting room; despite their injuries, they were to be that day's "test team," checking the terminal's facilities, directly confronting the most insulting signs of segregation. Walter Bergman, the official observer, followed a little ways behind. The whites-only waiting room might have been a comfortable spot to spend some time until one's bus arrived—there were shooting galleries and pinball machines—but not today. Somewhere between twenty and thirty men lined the walls, Person and Peck discovered as they pushed open the swinging doors and entered the room. "You black son-of-a bitch," Klansman Gene Reeves barked at Charles Person. "Don't you know you're not supposed to go in [here]? The colored waiting room is right around the corner." He took Person by the arm and turned him around, while another man grabbed Peck and they started for the doorway. Rowe saw Edward Fields take off his sunglasses and yell, "Get that son-of-a bitch!" Then, "all hell broke loose," Rowe said later. The group surged around the two Freedom Riders, pushing them into a corner near the pinball machine. Then the whites began to play human pinball, shoving Person from man to man. When they tired of this game, they took the two Freedom Riders out to the corridor, crowded now with anywhere from fifty to one hundred people. There, Person and Peck were knocked to the floor and beaten with brass knuckles, key rings, chains, pipes, and leaded bats, and, in Rowe's case, by fists and feet.[37]

For a time it was bedlam. "Fists and arms were flying everywhere," one participant later noted, "you couldn't tell who was beating whom." "A bloody ass mess, terrible, a damn free-for-all," Rowe called it. "Whites was hitting whites, everybody was just swinging, and whatever . . . you could find was hit." L. B. Earle, the Klansman who had torn the phone off Orman Forman's wall a month earlier, chose a poor time to go to the bathroom. When he stepped back into the corridor, the riot was in full swing. The mob, unaware that he was one of them, attacked him, leaving seven deep gashes in his head. Howard K. Smith noticed that Peck was beaten "very badly" and that his face "was soon a mass of red." When Peck and Person lost consciousness, the crowd dispersed, looking for other victims.[38]

At some point, Person got up, his head bleeding slightly, and ran out into the street where he caught a bus, rode it a few blocks, and then got off. Then he suddenly remembered that he had forgotten his fallen comrade, James Peck, but was too weak to return to the station to look for him.[39]

Howard K. Smith found Peck lying in the now deserted hallway. He and Walter Bergman got Peck to his feet and out to the street, where they tried to flag down a cab to take him to the hospital. One cab pulled over to the curb, but when the driver saw Peck's "bloody condition he sped off again." Smith ran to get his own vehicle, but when he returned, Bergman and Peck were gone. Later, he learned that a cab had finally stopped and taken the men to the home of Reverend Fred L. Shuttlesworth, leader of the civil rights movement in Birmingham. Bergman found his wife already there; she and the other Freedom Riders, Ivor Moore and Herman Harris, and the journalist Simeon Booker had managed to slip away from the terminal unnoticed. Shuttlesworth immediately took Peck to the segregated Carraway Methodist Hospital, which refused to treat him, so they drove to the Jefferson Hillman Hospital, where doctors used fifty-three stitches to close his six head wounds.[40]

Mary Spicer was the last to leave the bus. Her fiancé, George Webb, unaware of the trouble inside the terminal, embraced and kissed her. His aunt also welcomed her to Birmingham. She took the young woman's hatbox and suggested that they get her bags and meet in the parking lot. Webb and Spicer hurried inside to the baggage room but didn't get far before a group of white men accosted them. "Let's get them," one said, "let's get all of them." Webb pushed Spicer out the way. "Get the hell out of here unless you want to get the same thing," Tommy Rowe told her, and she ran screaming from the terminal. Webb turned, hoping to escape too, but four men surrounded him. He bent over, trying to protect himself, when one man, who Rowe thought was possibly a disciple of Fields, hit Webb on the right side of the head with a baseball bat. The men from Eastview Klavern No. 13—Bill Holt, Gene Reeves, and Rowe—punched and kicked him in the back and side and tore at his clothes. Webb struggled and kicked back, hitting someone, but couldn't break their hold. Then Red Self appeared at Rowe's side: "Tommy, Tommy, Tommy," he said, "get the fuck out of here! Troops is coming! Your fifteen minutes is up." Fifteen minutes? It seemed to Rowe like "we was there for hours." He turned away from Webb and hollered at the crowd, "Get out of here! Get out of here! Cops is coming!" Men began yelling "Go! Go!" and the crowd took off in every direction. "They were . . . exhilarated," Howard K. Smith later observed, "really in good spirits. They were out of breath, panting, they had a good physical exercise, they had done what they came to do, and seemed to be quite pleased, . . . joking with one another as they ran out and jumped in their cars."[41]

Rowe and his friends stuck around, continuing to beat Webb, when suddenly there was a flash of light. Rowe looked behind him and saw a man with a camera taking their picture. "Get that camera!" he yelled, and the four rushed off, allowing Webb a chance to run toward the exit. Other white men pursued him. Someone yelled, "Run nigger, run!" They caught up with him outside near the buses. Gene Reeves hit him in the face with his fist, and Webb fell backward over a baggage cart. Lying there, his body "sagging in the middle," he made an even better target—Reeves "jumped" on Webb, "stomping him." Webb heard somebody say "they wanted to give him a lesson," which consisted of three blows to the face and kicks in the shoulder. Somehow, he managed to get up and run, "falling and stumbling in a dazed condition," startling passersby who saw him "bleeding profusely from the head," his handsome blue suit torn to shreds. Eventually, he found his aunt's car in the parking lot, and she and Spicer took him home. Unable to reach the family's physician, they took him to the Hillman Emergency Center for treatment.[42]

Tommy Langston, the staff photographer for the *Birmingham Post-Herald,* had arrived at the Trailways station almost a half hour before the bus did. Everything seemed normal. Other journalists and photographers were standing around the parking lot chatting, so he felt no sense of urgency. He walked down a nearby alleyway and did some window shopping at Acton's Camera Store, until he saw a black woman running from the terminal screaming that someone was being beaten. Realizing that this was his cue, he rushed to the terminal and found the corridor filled with men beating somebody—he was too far away to see what was happening. Jerry McLoy, a *Post-Herald* reporter trapped among the crowd, waved to Langston, hoping he would take a picture, but the photographer didn't see him.[43]

A few minutes later, Langston got another chance near the baggage counter. He saw a man with a club raised over his head and, "on the spur of the moment," clicked the shutter. When the flash went off, somebody yelled, "Let's get that son-of-a-bitch," and Rowe and his accomplices left George Webb and raced toward Langston. He turned and ran outside, but they caught up with him in the parking lot. He crouched, trying to protect his four-hundred-dollar camera, but the men laid into him, swiping his back with a chain and beating his head with a leaded baseball bat. A man in a "red plaid shirt" jerked the camera from Langston's arms and tried to tear it apart with his bare hands; when that failed, he threw it on the ground, smashing it. Langston scrambled away, but the group followed, "grabbing, punching, and kicking." Then they saw another photographer taking pictures and went after him. Forgetting that his car was parked nearby, a dazed Langston staggered down the street. He hoped to find a cab, but none appeared, so he walked to the *Post-Herald* office. A colleague later picked up his broken camera and discovered that the film was not exposed and could still be printed.[44]

Bud Gordon, a writer and photographer for the *Birmingham News*, was walking back to his car when he heard someone yell, "There's another one," and noticed that he was being followed by the men who had attacked Tommy Langston. "Let's get him," cried Grand Titan Hubert Page, but the other man said all they needed was the camera. That man, whom Gordon later called "the big fellow," was in fact Tommy Rowe; he asked Gordon whether he had taken any pictures, and when Gordon said he had, Rowe "ripped" the camera from his hand. He tried to break it open to get at the film but only damaged the camera. Hoping that cooperation might spare him a beating, Gordon offered to remove the film. Rowe handed the camera back, and Gordon clicked it open and pulled out the film pack, which Rowe tore up and threw on the ground. "Knock hell out of him!" an unknown Klansman encouraged Rowe, but this time Rowe turned away from a fight. He and the others started to leave but ran into another reporter-photographer, Tom Lankford. Rowe told Gordon to take Lankford's camera, but the reporter held it tight until Rowe grabbed it and, in the scuffle that followed, the film was exposed. Rowe took the photographic plates and ran off. Down the street, Klansmen Ray Graves and Bill Holt joined Rowe, and the three walked on. As they turned the corner onto Nineteenth Street, they nearly collided with Sergeant Red Self. Seeing Rowe, Self "shook his head and smiled as they went by."[45]

Clancy Lake was Rowe's last victim that afternoon. The news director for WPAI Radio had parked his mobile unit with the station's call letters on its door behind the Birmingham post office and run the half block to the rear of the Trailways terminal. He arrived in time to see Webb receive his beating from "a short, chunky man" and then dash away; he also heard "yelling and screaming" as others fought. He rushed back to his car, turned on his two-way radio, and prepared to broadcast the events he had just witnessed. As he began his report, he saw the "chunky man" walking across the street with two others who looked like they had just come from a fight; they were all talking and laughing, obviously enjoying the moment. Then they saw Lake and stopped. The microphone he held in his hand must have looked like a camera, Lake thought, because now they rushed toward him.[46]

Lake quickly rolled up his front window and locked the doors, his broadcast becoming a call for aid—"Help, help, police," Lake cried. Graves lifted up the car's hood, reached in, and tore out some wires. Holt pulled out a blackjack and hammered the window nearest to Lake. It shattered, dusting the reporter with glass chips, momentarily blinding him. As Rowe ran around to the passenger side, he saw a police car drive by, then stop at a red light; it was close enough, Rowe said later, that the uniformed police officers "could have easily reached out . . . and touched Bill Holt." (It would have been a friendly touch—the officer driving was Floyd Garrett, nephew of a veteran Klansman named Bob Chambliss.) But Lake, thinking the officer would rescue him, yelled, "Send the soldiers, the people have gone crazy." When the light changed, the police car drove away. Rowe then attacked the window with his feet, making a lot of noise but breaking nothing. "Use your blackjack!" Graves yelled. Rowe did, and after a few licks, the window shattered. He unlocked the door and grabbed Lake, dragging him from the car and pulling the microphone from the radio.[47]

Although there was no sign of a camera, the men demanded that Lake turn over his film. Lake said he had no camera, no film, but they didn't believe him. They tore off his coat and ripped his shirt but found nothing; Holt checked the car, ransacking the glove compartment. Where was the damn camera? they asked again. When Lake didn't answer, they threw him against the post office wall. A crowd gathered; Lake begged them to help, but nobody did. The Klansmen swung their blackjacks at him, but Lake ducked, avoiding contact. Then the sounds of sirens nearby distracted the Klansmen and Lake broke away, running for the terminal. Looking back, he saw the men walking confidently down the street toward City Hall. Later, Lake wrote that he considered himself "the luckiest person involved in the violence. Any one of the three swipes at me with the black-jacks might have split my skull open."[48]

When Rowe and the others were out of sight, they ran into Shelton, who gave them a ride back to the bus terminal parking lot. As they approached the rear of the station at the corner of Eighteenth Street and Seventh Avenue, Rowe noticed a group of blacks writing down the license plate numbers of their automobiles. Rowe, Graves, and Holt jumped them and a brief fight ensued. Then they got into Rowe's car and drove away.[49]

When Rowe arrived home at about five o'clock, he found his wife, Dorothy, angry and upset over the disheveled way he and the others looked, so he changed his blood-stained clothes. Preparing for an evening of war stories with his fellow Klansmen, Rowe was interrupted by a telephone call from Sergeant Cook, reporting that yet another Freedom Rider bus was soon arriving at the Greyhound station, so Rowe and the four other Klansmen left the house. Dorothy Rowe noticed that two men in a black sedan picked them up.[50]

They didn't find another bus, but they did find blacks who hadn't yet been attacked; so another fight began, with Rowe doing most of the punching until one of his opponents pulled a knife and slashed at Rowe's throat. The fight that ensued didn't last long, but Rowe remembered it the rest of his life. "I heard 'My God, baby brother, look out!'" Rowe later recalled. "When I looked up, I saw a black swing at me . . . I thought he was going to hit me in the face . . . instead he cut my throat. Starting on the left side just under my jawbone, he slashed down to my windpipe. For a few seconds I just stood there watching my blood splash over both of us."[51]

"Hubert Page said, 'oh, fuck, Tommy, he cut your throat . . . Are you all right?'

"I said, 'Yeah, I'm all right,' but I was getting to feel kind of weak.

"'Get in the car, get in the car,' Page said."[52]

He knew of a doctor in Pinson, thirty miles away, who treated Klansmen wounded doing missionary work, so they rushed Rowe there. Dr. E. James Moore charged fifteen dollars for treating him, which was easily covered by Rowe's health insurance and the seventy-five dollars the Bureau gave him for expenses incurred that day. In the future, when Rowe described these events in his memoir, he claimed that he almost died, but FBI records tell a different story. They indicate that Rowe's injury didn't prevent him from trying to contact Sergeant Cook and then arranging a meeting later that evening with his friend Red Self in south Birmingham. "Don't worry about the beating of the Negroes," Self told him, suggesting that he go home and get a good night's sleep because they had done a good job. Rowe may have gone home, but not to sleep. At 12:15 a.m., he telephoned Special Agent Kemp to give him a detailed report (which later filled five single-spaced pages) on the day's developments. This was not the behavior of a man who, just a short time before, had been near death.[53]

The violence at the bus terminal seemed to bother Kemp less than the news that Rowe was injured. "What did you say?" an astonished Kemp asked him.

"I got my throat cut," Rowe said again.

Kemp was furious: "You son-of-a bitch!" he yelled. "I told you never to get involved in any violent activities." Kemp gave Rowe "the riot act," he later testified: "I was very, very mad. . . . I just couldn't believe that [Rowe] would be involved in an altercation."[54]

The morning brought more trouble, spread across the front page of the *Birmingham Post-Herald*. It was Tommy Langston's picture of the beating of George Webb, which the Klansmen thought had been destroyed along with the camera. Not to be outdone, the *Birmingham News* ran Clancy Lake's personal account of the assault in the parking lot, accompanied by a picture of the newsman as he might have appeared that day—a prisoner in his own car, looking out through a shattered window at Rowe and the others. An angry Tom Cook called Rowe early to tell him that his picture was front-page news. What had gone wrong? Why didn't the Klan get all the film? he wanted to know. Rowe thought they had. No, Cook said, the film was inside Langston's smashed camera, lying on the ground for an hour and a half before anybody thought to look at it. By that time, "it was too late for him to do anything about it." Get the paper, Cook demanded.

The Klan led an assault on the Freedom Riders at Birmingham's Trailways bus station on Mother's Day, 1961. Rowe, who organized the attack with the FBI's knowledge, also participated enthusiastically: He's the man bending over the victim in the right foreground. (Tommy Langston, *Birmingham Post-Herald*)

Rowe did. Under a headline that read GANGS BEAT UP PHOTOGRAPHER AND TRAVELERS IN BUS CLASHES was the photograph, prominently featured across five columns in the center of the page above the newspaper's fold. It showed four men bending over a fallen figure. Other men were also seen encouraging the beaters, or just standing around calmly smoking cigarettes; one looked directly at the camera and smiled. In the right-hand corner a heavyset man either held or beat the victim—his broad back faced the camera, but to anyone who knew him well it was obviously Tommy Rowe.[55]

Could Rowe identify anybody else in the picture? Cook asked. Rowe named three Klansmen, including his friend Bill Holt, but said that he didn't know the man in the dark jacket holding a pipe up over his head getting ready to bring it down on the crouched victim. He guessed that he was one of Dr. Fields's people. "Well," Cook concluded, "if it hadn't been for the picture nothing would have been said or done" about the melee at the bus terminal.

"Aw shit," Rowe recalled saying. "What am I supposed to do now, come turn myself in?"

"Bullshit," Cook said. "Go on about your business. I'll take care of it." But if he or any of the others were picked up for questioning, they should "stick to the original story that the people of CORE were to blame for everything."[56]

Barry Kemp's reaction to the photograph is difficult to determine. Years later, when Rowe's career was the subject of public controversy, Kemp testified under oath that he didn't see the photograph that morning. Rowe, on the other hand, recalled Kemp saying: "Jesus Christ, Tommy, we're all in shit. The Director is going to have a heart attack, roll over and do flip-flops when he sees this." Copies of the photograph were already on their way to Headquarters. Kemp supposedly stared at the picture intently for a few minutes and then pointed at the photo: "Who's that right there?"[57]

"Me," Rowe replied.

"Shit, I'm going to ask you again, who's that, look at it very close, who's that?"

"Me," Rowe said again.

"Who else does that look like besides you?"

Rowe thought for a moment, then remarked that perhaps the man resembled Klansman Charles "Arnie" Cagle, another veteran of the Forman assault.

"Look at that very closely," Kemp said again. "Is that Arnie Cagle?"

Rowe wouldn't play the game: "No, sir, that's me."

"No," Kemp said angrily, "that's Arnie Cagle. . . . Goddamn, we [are] all in trouble. To the day you die, if you're 99 goddamn years old, I don't care who asks you—if the Director comes down and looks you in the eye and says, 'Who's that?'—you [say] that's Arnie Cagle."[58]

Perhaps this conversation never occurred, or if it did, Rowe distorted or exaggerated Kemp's orders, which Kemp said he never gave. But FBI records indicate that Kemp *did* see the photograph on the morning of May 15 and discussed it with Rowe at that time and several times that week. Furthermore, Agent Neil Shanahan, who later became Rowe's FBI handler, recalled Rowe telling him that the FBI had instructed him to never "reveal himself as being in the picture. . . . he should tell everybody that's a picture of [Arnie Cagle]."[59]

But worse than this was the deception that followed. Protecting the informant was the rule, even if it meant lying to one's superiors in the field office and Washington. On May 17, Kemp sent a report to Thomas Jenkins, the special agent in charge, containing a highly distorted view of the events that had occurred the previous Sunday. According to Rowe, the attack on James Peck and Charles Person was the sole responsibility of Edward Fields, the Birmingham extremist, and his band of "young punks." Fields had "planned everything," Rowe claimed, despite his earlier reports to the contrary. The Klan desired a "peaceful" demonstration when the bus arrived, but those hopes "went awry because of the incident created by Dr. Fields." During the riot Rowe and his colleagues were outside, behind the bus station, and therefore couldn't have participated in the beating of the Freedom Riders, George Webb, and Tommy Langston. The Klansmen did obtain film from photographers in the parking lot, but they cooperated, no cameras were destroyed, and no one was hurt.[60]

The fight with newsman Clancy Lake was a bit more difficult to explain, because Rowe had already admitted being involved. Difficult, but not impossible, given Rowe's creative imagination and Kemp's desire to protect his informant. It seems that Rowe and his friends Bill Holt and Ray Graves were just strolling along, minding their own business, when suddenly they were confronted by a wild man, later identified as Lake, who shouted, "Stop right there! I saw you bastards." Curious, the men crossed the street to learn why Lake was using such "vile language" and verbally abusing them. But Lake wouldn't talk with them; he ran to his car, locked himself in, and started to talk into a microphone. In order for them to get an explanation, Rowe and the others found it necessary to break into Lake's car. Once the windows were broken and the door opened, Lake "lunged" from the car, "backed himself against the Post Office wall and raised his fists . . . as if he wanted to fight." They asked him politely why he was still cursing them but received no reply. Defending themselves, they hit back, but Lake ran away. As for Rowe's near-death experience later that day, the less said the better. Once again, Rowe was the innocent victim of a gang of blacks who caused a fight in which Rowe was injured, and was later treated by a physician. No additional details were provided.[61]

Did Barry Kemp intentionally mislead his superiors, or did he honestly think that Rowe's account was true? The Justice Department task force that later investigated Rowe provided an answer: "The evidence available [to Kemp] within hours after the incident was such that it would have been difficult for [Kemp] not to have known the full extent of Rowe's involvement. However, there is nothing in FBI files which indicates [Kemp] brought this information to the attention of Birmingham's Special-Agent-in-Charge or Headquarters." It was the ultimate conclusion of the task force that Kemp was guilty of "cover[ing] up Rowe's violent activities [and] . . . acting improperly."[62]

Kemp was not the only one to misinform his superiors. Thomas Jenkins, the head of the field office, had often received information from Clancy Lake in the past, and the newsman gave him a personal report of what was done to him on May 14. But in his report to Washington, Jenkins ignored Lake's story, as well as many articles appearing in the press and his agents' own witness statements. "Rowe was not personally involved in the fighting at the Trailways Bus Depot," he assured Director Hoover, and during the Lake attack he was simply "present" and denied striking the newsman.[63]

Rowe now emerged as the only hero of the Mother's Day attack. In a fitness report written a few weeks later, Kemp described Rowe as "stable in character and trustworthy, . . . and it appears that he is very cautious in his . . . dealings with his fellow Klansmen." No reference was made to the role Rowe played in facilitating and executing the attack. Thomas Jenkins was even more fulsome in his praise of Tommy Rowe: The "informant is, without doubt, the most alert, intelligent, productive, and reliable informant on Klan and racial matters currently being operated by the Birmingham office. He has . . . been of material assistance . . . in such matters as the Trailways Bus incident, . . . when he was seriously injured in performing his duties for the FBI."[64]

Because of his excellent work, the FBI gave Rowe a special bonus of $125, plus an extra $50 "for medical expenses for an injury received." With his usual pay of $90, Rowe received a grand total of $265—not bad for a couple of hours of work, although Rowe, who loved few things more than a good brawl, probably considered it sport.[65]

The Bureau also thought Rowe helpful in the investigation that led to the arrest of five suspects, but in fact, it was their presence in Langston's photograph that led to their arrest. Jesse Oliver Faggard, a twenty-year-old unemployed baker who lived with his parents in Alton, Alabama, was charged with assault with intent to murder for his participation in the beating of Tommy Langston. At first, he denied involvement, claiming that he "meant to hold [the Freedom Riders] back without any licks or bloodshed" because he "didn't go in for any rough stuff." Later, however, he confessed to belonging to the group that attacked the photographer. When no witnesses appeared to testify against him, the charge was reduced to disorderly conduct. His father, Jesse Thomas Faggard, a forty-eight-year-old carpenter, was just part of the crowd, as was John Hampton Thompson, a forty-seven-year-old house painter. The Faggards and Thompson, all members of a Tarrant County chapter of the Klan that had disbanded in March, received thirty days in jail and a thirty-dollar fine. Melvin Dove, the Bessemer Klansman who smiled at Langston's camera, was also charged with disorderly conduct, despite the fact that eyewitnesses claimed that he beat up two elderly black men on May 14; eventually, all charges against Dove were dropped because of lack of evidence. Herschel Acker, the man with the pipe, was charged with assault with intent to murder George Webb, but each of his three trials ended in a mistrial, and he was killed in an accident before he could be tried again.[66]

None of these men had any connection to Rowe, which may well have been the reason why they were prosecuted rather than Bill Holt and Hubert Page. Although Rowe had given Holt's and Page's names to the Bureau and they were well known to the Birmingham police, they were never considered suspects. The protective veil that covered Rowe now extended to two of the Eastview Klavern's most violent members. They, too, could escape punishment for almost any crime simply because their arrest might lead to Rowe's exposure and the end of his career as an informant.

The Freedom Riders did not fare as well as their attackers. The entire group was determined to press on to Montgomery despite "their swollen faces, surgical stitches and lungs still burning with smoke." On Monday, May 15, Reverend Fred Shuttlesworth took them to the Greyhound bus station, but the fever that had gripped the city since the previous day still ran high. Mobs of angry whites were said to be ready to launch another attack, and police had to use dogs to keep them back from the terminal. After arriving safely, the Freedom Riders learned that no bus company would carry them. Hurt, exhausted, and dispirited, they decided to escape from Birmingham by plane, telling themselves that they had achieved their purpose: alerting the nation to the evils of segregation. But once this news reached the mobs, they raced to the municipal airport, again detaining the Freedom Riders, who waited for someone to help them.[67]

Help came in the form of John Seigenthaler, one of Robert Kennedy's closest aides. The attorney general, like his brother, President John F. Kennedy, was annoyed by this seemingly needless domestic crisis on the eve of JFK's first summit meeting with Nikita Khrushchev, but he stepped in to get the Freedom Riders out of town. He and the president had no prior warning of the planned Klan assault and learned about events only as they occurred. On Mother's Day night, the Justice Department, rather pathetically, asked the FBI for "details" about what had happened—President Kennedy wanted to know. Seigenthaler, a southerner, was sent to Birmingham to work with police and airline officials to arrange a flight to New Orleans. But takeoff was delayed for hours because of bomb threats, many phoned in by members of the Eastview Klavern. Hubert Page and several Klansmen drove to the airport, hoping to see the "agitators' faces," but Page turned away because the area was "too hot." At midnight, the Freedom Riders finally left Birmingham.[68]

On May 17, a new group of Freedom Riders came to Birmingham—Nashville activists who felt that the civil rights movement was doomed if the journey wasn't completed as planned. Rowe reported that Hubert Page wanted the Klan to intercept them on the highway, offering to escort blacks and whites to a nearby town; those who refused would be beaten. Shorty Thompson was told to ready the Klavern's most prized possession, a submachine gun, but the Freedom Riders reached the city earlier than Page expected and were arrested and jailed. For the next twenty hours, they went on a hunger strike and sang freedom songs, both to keep up their spirits and to annoy their jailers until they were released. Bull Connor had them put in a car and promised to drive them back to Nashville. He did, chatting amiably with his passengers until they reached the Alabama–Tennessee border, where he abruptly stopped and dropped them off. It was "in the middle of nowhere, in the middle of the night," Freedom Rider John Lewis later wrote, "seven of us standing all alone . . . [in] Klan country."[69]

They managed to find a phone and arranged transportation back to Birmingham, where they tried to get a bus to Montgomery. Eighteen hours later they were on their way, escorted by police cars and helicopters, but when they reached the state capital the authorities disappeared, and the

Freedom Riders were attacked by a mob that beat them to the ground. John Doar, first assistant to the head of the Justice Department's Civil Rights Division, observed the assault as it happened and reported it to Washington: "A bunch of men . . . are beating them. There are no cops. It's terrible. . . . People are yelling, 'Get 'em, get 'em.' It's awful." When John Seigenthaler tried to help one victim, he was knocked unconscious and lay on the ground for almost half an hour before police took him to the hospital.[70]

Now, the president acted. Nearly four hundred U.S. marshals were sent to Montgomery, and the attorney general sought an injunction prohibiting the Klan from interfering with interstate travel. The marshals' first task was to rescue Martin Luther King, Jr., who had come to the city to support the civil rights workers, and twelve hundred congregants besieged at the First Baptist Church by angry whites, who threw rocks and then firebombs through the windows and attacked anyone caught outside. Governor John Patterson of Alabama, although a friend of the Klan, agreed to call out the National Guard and state troopers to assist federal authorities.[71]

The Freedom Riders pressed on. Under the protection of police and the National Guard, they made it to Jackson, Mississippi, where they were promptly arrested after entering all-white facilities. Although they received fines and suspended sentences, they refused to leave jail until Jim Crow laws were abolished. The movement spread to other states and drew more than one thousand people—black and white, young and old, Jew and Gentile—into its ranks. In September, the attorney general asked the Interstate Commerce Commission to officially outlaw segregation in interstate and intrastate travel, from buses to bathrooms, but it wasn't until 1962 that CORE declared victory and ended the Freedom Rides.[72]

For Tommy Rowe, this should have been a happy time. He came through the Mother's Day assault almost unscathed. Red Self assured Rowe that he had no reason to worry about anything that occurred that day; in fact, Clancy Lake, after looking at mug shots of possible suspects, told the police that he couldn't identify any of the men who had attacked him. Rowe was home free, with a new scar on his throat, visible evidence to the Klan that he was both brave and loyal. Those who doubted him were now silenced, and there was even talk that he might become the Klavern's next Exalted Cyclops. His reputation inside the Bureau was also enhanced: Barry Kemp thought he had done "one hell of a good job" and considered him "the finest informant" ever to infiltrate the Klan.[73]

Then, early in June, came a blow he did not expect: Barry Kemp was leaving the FBI. Kemp had received an offer to join an Ohio law firm and, judging it a "golden opportunity," submitted his letter of resignation to the special agent in charge on May 20. Perhaps anticipating trouble, Tommy Rowe was the last person he told. "I picked up Tommy . . . and we drove out in the mountains south of Birmingham and we talked," Kemp later testified. "Why are you doing this?" Rowe asked, obviously shocked and hurt. "I don't want you to leave."

"I'm going into private practice," Kemp said.

"If you're leaving, I'm leaving," Rowe said.

"No, I don't want you to quit, Tommy. You've done a good job, you are very important. I want you to stay on."

Rowe started to cry, saying, "You realize I was doing this for you."

"No, you didn't do it for me," Kemp said. "You do it for your country, you do it for your government, that's the reason."

Rowe was adamant, insisting that if Kemp left, he would too. The next day, Kemp introduced Rowe to his boss, Tom Jenkins, and they drove to a deserted street where the agents spent forty-five minutes trying to persuade Rowe to stay on, which he finally decided to do, reluctantly.[74]

But Rowe was still very upset. Barry Kemp had rescued him from a dreary existence as a part-time bartender, bouncer, and machinist at the White Dairy; he was transformed into an undercover agent of the FBI, entering a world of midnight meetings, code names, mail drops, dangerous scrapes, bizarre adventures, and the chance to raise hell without having to worry about the consequences. "Tommy and I were pretty close," Kemp said later. "He felt a close bond toward me . . . and he felt . . . I was letting him down." What would the future hold now that Kemp was gone? Rowe wondered.

As the movers packed Kemp's belongings on his final day in Birmingham, Rowe appeared with a gift for Kemp, a shirt and tie he had personally selected. He gave the gift to Mrs. Kemp to pass along. "He didn't want to see me," Kemp noted, "because he was still very hurt that I was leaving. That was our relationship."[75]

CHAPTER THREE

Serious Business

THE MONTHS THAT FOLLOWED the Mother's Day assault were a time of transition for Tommy Rowe and the Klan. Rowe had to adjust to his new FBI handler while the Klan tried to transform itself from a regional racist cult into a larger organization that would appeal to all Americans. Both found the changes difficult to make.

When Rowe learned that his new contact might be Charles B. Stanberry —or C.B. as the veteran agent was called—he protested strongly. "Get a long stick," he told Special Agent in Charge Thomas Jenkins, "and shove it up your ass. I don't like the man, won't have nothing to do with the man." The choice of Stanberry seemed logical given Rowe's status as the FBI's most important informant. Stanberry was considered the field office's expert on "Racial Matters," having served in Birmingham since 1945. But his strengths—knowledge and experience—were, to Rowe, dangerous weaknesses. He preferred a much younger man, like Kemp; Stanberry had joined the FBI in 1941, when Rowe was eight years old. Rowe thought he had spent too many years behind a desk, had lost his edge, and was just "dumb," perhaps even "senile." C.B., who had sometimes worked with Rowe when Kemp was unavailable, would schedule a meeting in the most public of places and at the busiest times when the Klan might spot them. Rowe liked deserted parking lots, street corners, alleys, and woods, where he and Kemp would talk in the middle of the night. C.B., in his tailored gray suit and hat, stood out "like a sore thumb"; put him in a crowd of five thousand people and everybody would know he was an FBI agent.[1]

Stanberry also had a more conservative approach to handling informants. He believed that an undercover man could obtain valuable information without resorting to violence. "We didn't want to have trouble," he later testified. "You had to impress on them not to engage in violence and leave it to their good judgment, hope and pray that they would do like you say." Rowe thought this was unrealistic; prayer was of little use when you found yourself in the middle of a riot. "It was time for him to retire," Rowe said; "he didn't know what the hell he was doing, and was going to get us killed." There was just no way that he would work with C. B. Stanberry.[2]

Rowe's power to reject those agents he didn't like and choose those he did was a sign of his growing importance to the Bureau. Although Byron McFall, a courtly midwesterner, was also a veteran agent and more than a decade older than Rowe, Rowe found him acceptable and agreed to work with him. Unlike C.B., he had not spent most of his career deskbound in Birmingham but had served in a number of posts—in Detroit, Cleveland, Salt Lake City, Little Rock, and Oklahoma City—before coming to Birmingham in 1958.

McFall was happy to take on Rowe because of his value to the Bureau, which increased McFall's own status in the field office. He later admitted that he didn't know Rowe's history—not even his recent involvement in the attack on the Freedom Riders. But he understood the difficulties Rowe faced. For the record, McFall told him not to break the law, not to instigate or engage in violence, and to "act like a gentleman." But he understood that sometimes Rowe might be trapped in situations where a bit of chain-wielding would be necessary to protect his cover. That was paramount—exposure might be fatal. Rowe called him "Mac," although his friends called him Ron, and liked his "dinky hats." McFall would kid Rowe about his womanizing, and eventually the two established a "cordial," if not close, working relationship. So on June 12, 1961, with McFall as witness, Rowe again formally signed an agreement pledging his services to the FBI, while promising to be both discreet and nonviolent.[3]

At first, there was little for Rowe to report to his new handler. The city was filled with new FBI agents investigating the violent incidents in Montgomery, Anniston, and Birmingham. Their presence and the federal injunction prohibiting Klan interference in interstate travel had the Klan temporarily on the run. Exalted Cyclops Robert Thomas refused to attend Klan meetings and ordered the destruction of membership records. During a meeting held on June 1, Shorty Thompson suggested that the Klan "go underground and meet in small groups in private homes." Bill Holt, veteran of the Forman and Trailways beatings, denounced Thompson and persuaded the members to continue holding their regular Thursday meetings at the Klavern hall. Nothing else of importance was discussed that night, Rowe later noted, because the group believed "it would get back to the FBI. It appeared that the people present were quite afraid of the Federal Injunction and further Federal action."[4]

Although no member of the Eastview Klavern was arrested for beating the Freedom Riders in May, many were questioned by the FBI, and they resented how the agents approached them at work or at home. To protect his cover, the FBI also "interrogated" Rowe, although the time was spent creating an alibi and an explanation for the scar on his throat. Agents came up with a reasonable story: He cut himself while shaving with a straight razor. The Birmingham police, though aware that Rowe was one of the men in Tommy Langston's picture, never interviewed him, but the Bureau had acted wisely. Some Klansmen asked Rowe whether the FBI had pulled him in for a talk, and he could convincingly say that the Feds had harassed him, too.[5]

Gradually, life returned to normal. The visiting agents left, and the Klan, with Robert Thomas officiating, resumed meeting at the Klavern hall. But they took extra measures to warn new members of the fate that befell those who snitched. During a "naturalization" ceremony on June 15, Hubert Page pulled one initiate from the line, claiming that he recognized him as one of the photographers at the Trailways station on Mother's Day. Rowe "knocked him down," and with the help of Henson, the hypnotist, they dragged him to a back room. A few minutes later, they paraded him before the Klansmen, announcing that they were now going to take the informer to Lake Purdy and "dump him." The new members were never told that it had all been a stunt arranged to frighten them—the photographer was a trusted Klansman who spent the rest of the evening drinking with Henson and Rowe.[6]

The three drunken Klansmen might have found the charade amusing, but to Imperial Wizard Bobby Shelton it was a step designed to bring needed discipline to the Klan. The increased federal presence after Mother's

Day—the FBI agents, the U.S. marshals, the National Guard—led to an increased militarization of the Klan. At a special meeting on June 21, Shelton announced the creation of a new eighteen-man Security Guard. Its responsibilities included interrogating those who failed to regularly attend meetings and pay dues, and forcing them back into the ranks. Even officers were checked; if they missed more than two meetings in succession "without a real good reason," they would be replaced. Guardsmen would make sure that no Klan official employed "colored people" in their homes; working them outside in fields or gardens was "OK but not in your house." The new guard would also protect "high officials" who visited Alabama and would lead the effort to attract new members. Only men of a certain physical size—"big men"—would be selected to serve in this important group. They would wear specially designed uniforms consisting of white trousers and skin-tight long-sleeved shirts made of gabardine (or less expensive material if the Klan could find it); red ties and black paratrooper boots with white leather laces completed the outfit. A small black sword would hang on the left side of their webbed belts, a black nightstick on the right. The old-fashioned hood would be replaced by a white crash helmet bearing the initials "S.G." on the front and decals of the Confederate and Alabama state flags on the earpieces. The Security Guard, Rowe told Special Agent McFall, would "be the beginning of a new kind of Klansman," adding that two men had been chosen to lead the corps—Monk Rutherford and Tommy Rowe. Rowe later gave the Bureau a Polaroid snapshot of four guards wearing their new outfits.[7]

In keeping with this martial spirit, Klansmen would be taught how to march and would be accompanied by their own color guard. Hubert Page was confident that Governor John Patterson would provide them with eighteen state flags, "since the Klan is responsible for maintaining segregation in Alabama." They would also be taught how to use weapons and such martial arts as ju-jitsu and karate. "The time had come when the men had to stand up and be ready to fight the whole government if necessary," proclaimed one official at a state rally late in June, "to get the rights of the South back. That from this day on . . . the Klan means business."[8]

The new Klan not only meant business, it would now be run like a business. It would have a chief executive officer (Shelton), an "Imperial Headquarters" housed in a remodeled lawyer's office on the fourth floor of Tuscaloosa's Alston Building, and a secretarial and public relations staff.

The Klan would also buy Shelton a house trailer "so that his office would be with him all the time." Furthermore, through raised dues, Shelton would receive a regular salary, freeing him to work for the Klan full time. He would travel throughout the country to create new Klaverns and bring old independent ones under his banner and also work with local law enforcement agencies "to prevent integration of the races lawfully." At Indian Springs, Georgia, in July, Shelton successfully brought a number of splinter groups into a new organization named the United Klans of America; at age thirty-two, he was the youngest Imperial Wizard in the Klan's history.[9]

To broaden its base, the Klan planned to create a "Universal Klan" that would attract members from the northern states now just "waking up to the fact that the colored people and the Puerto Ricans are taking over the North." In charge of this effort was Wally Butterworth, who, according to Rowe's reports, was "supposed to be a nationally known radio and television personality" and had "plenty of proof about how the Communists have infiltrated the higher positions in the government." Butterworth would visit the North, speak to sympathetic audiences, and organize local Klaverns. After paying a one-time registration fee of ten dollars, dues would be one dollar per month, which entitled members to a free subscription of the weekly Klan newspaper, *The Fiery Cross*. In no time, it was hoped, the entire white race would belong to the United Klans of America.[10]

To demonstrate their confidence in a Klan-dominated future, the Klan scheduled a major rally for October 28, 1961, at the Dixie Speedway in Midfield, Alabama. It would be advertised as an anti-Communist rally, to attract as many people as possible (Shelton hoped that thirty thousand would attend), but once everyone was there, they would receive "a good Klan talk" that would produce baskets full of cash and hundreds of new members. "The Rally must be one of the biggest of them all," Hubert Page declared. Klansmen must get their families and friends to turn out; Wally Butterworth would set the audience afire with one of his electric speeches, and the honored guests included young Atlanta students, disguised to protect their identities, who would reveal the horrors of forced integration in their city schools. The Security Guard was responsible for their safety and "if necessary, they would not hesitate to beat or shoot anyone trying to harm or unmask the[m]." Page would see that every Guardsman carried a new .45-caliber pistol, and, said Exalted Cyclops Robert Creel of Bessemer, if they were arrested, each must "go to his death swearing he is not a Klansman. If they have a hundred pictures of him and if everybody in the courtroom from the judge on down knows he is lying, he will still say he is not a member."[11]

A special meeting of officers and Action Squad leaders was held on October 24 to make sure everything was ready for the rally. Fifty thousand handbills had been distributed (none bearing the mark of the Klan), so a huge crowd was expected. The Security Guard was not in uniform, but they were ordered to wear their best suits and red ties so they could be easily identified as they made their way through the audience, gathering donations and distributing membership applications. Reporters and photographers were invited to attend, and this time they were allowed to take pictures of everyone except the visitors from Atlanta. The Klansmen were excited but also apprehensive: If the rally failed to meet their expectations, Hubert Page warned, "the Klan would be dead."[12]

The Dixie Speedway, home of stock car racing, was accustomed to vehicular disaster—cars crashing, tires flying toward the crowd, an occasional explosion and death. But the anti-Communist rally that began at 7:30 on Friday evening, October 28, 1961, was a human disaster from beginning to end. The stars of the evening, the students from Atlanta, were yanked from the program at the last minute because it was thought that their presence might be too inflammatory. So the audience, which numbered only about 450 people, rather than the hoped-for 30,000, was treated to five speakers whose talks, Rowe later reported, "were all about the same things." Wally Butterworth described how Washington was demanding that "coloreds and whites socialize and integrate" but did not inform the nation that 80 percent of the black population carried venereal disease "and it would not be long before the white population would have it." If the government didn't abandon its support of the civil rights movement, Butterworth warned, "the people will openly revolt against them." Others attacked the "nigger-loving Kennedys" and their allies, the Jews. JFK "would never allow another election and would try to use the same tricks as Fidel Castro . . . to stay in office. The white people should be prepared to fight to the death to stop this from happening." As for the Cold War, it was nothing but a Zionist conspiracy: "The Jews have been the cause of wars for years and years."[13]

The Imperial Wizard, although bitterly disappointed by the low turnout, tried to persuade the audience that in the near future the "Klan would be the strongest organization in the country and the people will know that anyone in public office will be a Klan man." In the 1920s, the heyday of the Hooded Order, the Klan had "cleaned up the government and the same thing was taking place now."[14]

Shelton didn't excite the crowd and people drifted away, the noise of automobiles drowning out the pledge made by a Florida Klansman that "all Florida units were waiting for the word from the Imperial Wizard as to what he wanted done and they would follow him all the way." For now, Bobby Shelton wanted cash and directed Hubert Page to start passing the buckets before everybody left. Exalted Cyclops Robert Thomas reminded Page that the handbills stated that the rally was free; to seek donations would "hurt the Klan." Page "really got mad," Rowe noted; they had always "passed the hat" at these affairs, he insisted, so he ordered the Security Guards to rush to the gates, "stop people and ask for donations." But it was too late: The guards managed to collect only thirty dollars and received just one new-member application instead of the three hundred Shelton had hoped for. Nearly every Klan official was "really angry over the way things turned out," Rowe later reported, and instead of gathering together to celebrate the event over dinner, as was their custom, the men went home alone.[15]

The Dixie Speedway fiasco didn't kill the Klan as Hubert Page feared, but for the men of Eastview Klavern it was a jinx they couldn't shake. At the first Klavern meeting following the rally, only a few members showed up. Worse, they discovered that their sacred crosses and altars were mysteriously missing, preventing them from "rededicating" the men through the traditional rituals. After discussing this mystery, Page finally admitted that he had loaned the objects to friends, although he wouldn't identify them. Klansman Wheeler was next to apologize: The film he had selected to show that night was unavailable, so the Klavern was treated to a repeat performance of *Communism on the Map*, right-wing propaganda at its worst. Bored, the men ended the meeting early.[16]

Ten days later, at a statewide meeting, other problems were discussed. Monthly reports and dues weren't arriving at Imperial Headquarters on time—or at all. Bessemer's Robert Creel was openly contemptuous of everyone; if the men didn't do their jobs, he warned, they would be removed, "and that went from the Imperial Wizard on down." Page again apologized for the low turnout at the speedway. He sent registered letters to heads of all the state Klaverns, but they were returned marked "addressee unknown," so he asked officers to make sure that he had the right locations. Bill Holt apologized for the poor attendance at the last Eastview meeting, explaining that he had thought it was only for officers so he, and the many men he had told, had stayed home that night. Klansman Dunnagan angrily remarked that "everyone should work or quit."[17]

More bad news was reported on December 7. The *Fiery Cross*, the Klan newspaper, was selling so poorly that payments couldn't be made on the equipment purchased; a collection agent showed up at Imperial Headquarters demanding the money owed (two thousand dollars) or the return of the printing press, letter folder, and addressograph. Funds were also lacking to pay Klan spokesman Wally Butterworth more than fifty dollars a week, which was "not good enough for a man of his talents," Rowe noted. (Shelton asked Rowe and other Eastview officials to lend one hundred dollars to the struggling PR man; the FBI field office was willing to put up the money, but Headquarters didn't think it appropriate for the Bureau to finance Klan activities and employees.) Members refused to seek Klan offices. Some nominated Shorty Thompson for E.C., but he declined because he worked the night shift at Hughes Aircraft. Rowe, too, was unable to seek the post because his job at the White Dairy prevented him from reaching the hall in time to prepare for the meetings. Henson the hypnotist appreciated being nominated to serve as Klavern treasurer but admitted that "he did not know how to figure well."[18]

The members became restless, talking and joking among themselves until the Exalted Cyclops ordered them to pay attention or leave. And those who left should "stay gone because they were not real Klansmen." That led Hubert Page to jump up and proclaim loudly that he was a "real Klansman" and thought the rest were, too. The hall became quiet as "the men looked around and stayed seated."[19]

Rowe and others in the secret Action Squads, however, continued to lead more exciting lives. Here, in the smaller groups, plots were hatched to crush "race mixing" at Alabama restaurants and nightclubs. On a cold Saturday night early in December, a group of Eastview and Bessemer Klansmen, armed with leaded bats and sawed-off shotguns, visited a nightclub called The Barn to "take violent action" against black musicians reported to be dancing with white waitresses. "All were ready for action,"

Rowe later noted. Shorty Thompson wanted to "burn the Barn and get rid of it," but the attack was called off because the club was too crowded.[20]

Disappointed but still looking for action, the Eastview group found a better opportunity for mayhem at the Krystal Kitchen, a popular Klan café in North Birmingham. Rowe, accompanied by Gene Reeves and Andrew "Buddy" Galelyn, went inside to pick up hamburgers and coffee for themselves and the others waiting outside in their cars. Galelyn ("big . . . and pretty strong and pretty mean," Rowe thought) spotted five blacks seated at the counter: Emory Anthony, his wife, Delores, and three friends who were waiting to pick up an order of barbecue sandwiches. "You goddamn niggers," Galelyn screamed, "get out of here!"

Frightened, Delores Anthony asked her husband and friends to leave, but the group didn't move fast enough for Galelyn. "Ain't no fucking Niggers coming in the Krystal," he said. "Goddamn it, move or I'll kill you!"

As they started to leave, Galelyn went berserk. Slipping on a pair of brass knuckles, he grabbed Anthony and started to beat him. Rowe and Reeves joined him, knocking Anthony to the floor and kicking him. When Delores Anthony started screaming, a white man named Rodney Cooper told them to stop or they'd have to deal with him. "That won't be much of a problem," Reeves said, and he and Rowe attacked him. "Then," Rowe said later, "the shit broke loose."

Cooper was no match for the stronger, heavier Klansmen (both Rowe and Reeves weighed well over two hundred pounds). They dragged Cooper outside and threw him into the street where a passing car swerved onto the sidewalk to avoid hitting him. The attack on Cooper gave the Anthonys a chance to slip away. Rowe and Reeves returned to the Krystal Kitchen, where a fistfight had developed between the Anthonys' three friends and other Klansmen who joined the fray. In the distance, sirens could be heard, prompting Reeves to tell the cook and waitresses that if they talked, the Klan would kill them. By the time the police arrived, the fight had spilled out into the street and was almost over. Rowe chased the black men around to the rear of the building; two got away, finding sanctuary in a nearby church, but Rowe and Reeves were able to beat up the third.

Rowe and his party were arrested and charged with assault with intent to commit murder. Police searched their cars and found the baseball bats and shotguns. They were about to be taken off to the Southside City Jail when Shorty Thompson, in violation of Klan rules to keep their identities secret, informed the sergeant in charge that they were all Knights of the Ku Klux Klan, just having a little fun with a "bunch of niggers" who had invaded the Krystal Kitchen. That changed everything: "Take your weapons and go home," the sergeant said. "You've done enough good for one night." So, "we hauled ass out of there," Rowe later said.

Everyone got away except Klansman Gary Gregory. He mouthed off to one of the cops, who arrested him for carrying a concealed weapon (a knife with a ten-inch blade). On the way to the jail, they picked up "an intoxicated white woman" and, placing her in the backseat with Gregory, invited him to have sex with her; he had "done a good job that night," said one of the cops, "and thought he might like to have a little fun." He was held for a few hours and then released. Just for the record, the police questioned the cook, the waitresses, and the victims of Klan violence; none could identify the assailants. Emory Anthony may have been reluctant to speak because a Birmingham detective brought several suspects to Anthony's home for an impromptu lineup.[21]

Rowe reported the incident to his FBI handler, but McFall put nothing in the record about Rowe's own participation in the assault on the black men and their ally Rodney Cooper. (Indeed, Rowe's report simply described the events without noting his own role.) Rowe later admitted that he beat at least two people and also claimed that he told Byron McFall everything that occurred, but McFall, when questioned later, said that he couldn't remember the events. It's possible that Rowe lied about the extent of his involvement, or exaggerated it, although later FBI interviews with the victims indicate that Rowe was, for the most part, telling the truth. McFall probably didn't give the special agent in charge a full picture of the assault, perhaps because he considered Rowe's actions defensive; by participating in the fighting he was protecting himself from both exposure and being hurt. Such details, almost by definition, would not have been included in the report. Therefore, all that Headquarters received was a one-paragraph description without any reference to Rowe's involvement. And nobody—not his FBI contact or the special agent in charge or Washington Headquarters—asked him why he had failed to alert the Bureau about the impending attack on The Barn.[22]

The FBI continued to allow Rowe to raise hell without consequences during 1962. To usher in the new year, "Unknown Subjects," as the FBI called them, bombed three black churches in Birmingham in the hours before midnight on January 16; nobody was hurt. At 12:20 a.m. Rowe telephoned Agent McFall to report the news. He, of course, had nothing to do with the explosions but thought his Klavern was involved. He then abruptly ended the call because, he said, he was with a Klansman and had made up an excuse to get away to contact McFall. When they talked again the next morning, Rowe told McFall that while someone was dynamiting the churches last evening, he and fellow Klansman Harry Walker were paying a visit on a black man and a white woman who were said to be living together, perfect targets for "head knocking." But when they arrived at their apartment on Fifty-fifth Place, nobody was home. During their ride, they discussed the bombings and Walker noted that it seemed like the work of Bobby Frank Cherry, an Eastview member who had participated in the assault on the Formans in 1961.

Asked later whether Rowe's reports, coming so soon after the last bombing, might suggest advance knowledge or participation, McFall said, "No." On the contrary, he was "proud of [Rowe] for being on the ball," acting as any good citizen should who happened to hear an explosion and then reported it to the FBI. The Unknown Subjects were never identified, and the Bureau expressed no interest in the January bombings. The special agent in charge never mentioned them in his quarterly report to Hoover, and no investigation was ordered. Bobby Frank Cherry was just one more nutty Klansman, whose knowledge of explosives won him the nickname "Cherry Bomb." Had the Bureau acted more vigorously, it might have prevented one of the worst crimes of the civil rights era the following year.[23]

The Action Squad struck again in April at a carnival in Bessemer, part of that city's celebration of its Diamond Jubilee. Blacks were seen on the rides and visiting the booths, "mixing with and molesting white people," one Klan officer reported, so a "select group" of Klansmen from Eastview and four other Klaverns were ordered to stop it. The official FBI account of the event simply stated that "several Negroes were battered around and two Klansmen were arrested" but never prosecuted. And once again, Rowe was the invisible man quietly observing and then recording events for FBI archives. But his version differed from the official history. Momentarily feeling like a real FBI agent, Rowe later claimed that he tried to prevent violence. Klansmen arrived at the carnival armed with "chains, . . . [tiny] bats with lead heavy ends, night sticks, sawed off shotguns, pistols, blackjacks, GI garrison belts with bolts and nuts screwed into them, and broomsticks with lengths of chain nailed on," Rowe said. Seeing a Bessemer policeman nearby, Rowe walked toward him, one hand in his pocket opening up a hole through which his own chain could fall to the ground in a clatter, attracting the officer's attention. It did. "What the hell are you doing?" the officer asked Rowe.

"Nothing," Rowe said, looking down at the chain at his feet.

The officer picked up the chain and said, "You dumb shit, put this back in your pocket. Goddamn, you're going to get us all in trouble." Noticing a half dozen Klansmen with weapons stuffed in their pockets, the officer said, "I'll be back in a minute. Wait right here," then left. A few minutes passed and then another cop escorted Rowe to a nearby stall, where the other policeman held six boxes of popcorn. "Take them goddamn clubs, bats, guns, whatever the hell you got," he told Rowe, "and put it in the popcorn boxes. I don't want that shit falling on the ground no more. When the signal comes down, you can take it out of the popcorn box and do whatever you want to do." Rowe took a box, put the chain inside, and covered it with popcorn. He motioned to the other Klansmen, who came over and followed his lead.

Unlike Rowe, Bessemer Klansman Gene Thomas wanted to fight and began the assault by attacking blacks with a chain and a special blackjack, wrapped with fishing line "to do more damage." The others quickly joined in. "Everybody was fighting," Rowe said, "it was black against white . . . and some white against white." Asked later if he "beat anyone that day," he said, "Yes . . . I don't know how many people. A hell of a bunch of them." McFall received a full report, Rowe later insisted, and the agent expressed no concern about the violence that had occurred. When McFall was later asked whether he could recall the Bessemer carnival and other violent events Rowe might have participated in, he said no.[24]

For more than a year the FBI had permitted Rowe to attack whomever he pleased, in order to defend himself, protect his cover, and obtain information the Bureau wanted. His victims included an elderly couple, Freedom Riders, photographers, and blacks who crossed Alabama's color line. In the summer of 1962, a new and ultimately far more dangerous problem arose—would the FBI allow its informant to commit murder?

When Rowe arrived for a meeting of the Eastview Klavern on July 19, Shorty Thompson took him by the arm and the two entered a small room off the main meeting hall. Already awaiting him were two of the Klavern's most violent members—Bill Holt and John "Nigger" Hall, so called because of his dark complexion and similar character: He once proudly admitted to throwing acid at blacks. Hall told them that they had received a special assignment from Grand Titan Hubert Page. A recent federal court decision had desegregated the Dobbs House Restaurant located at Birmingham's airport, and according to Sergeant Tom Cook of the police department, Reverend Fred L. Shuttlesworth was expected to lead blacks there, demanding admission and service. Even worse, two white women from Detroit would "hold hands with some of the negroes," once they were seated. Both Mayor Arthur Hanes and Police Commissioner Bull Connor were "tired of the way things [were] going in the racial situation," Page had said, "but . . . their hands were tied." According to Cook, Reverend Shuttlesworth had two bodyguards who went with him everywhere. They would be disarmed. A Birmingham policeman on duty would add to the confusion by faking a heart attack, and while the other Klansmen were beating the blacks, some would "encircle" Shuttlesworth, and Nigger Hall would "kill him with a knife." If black demonstrators showed up without their leader, the Klansmen were supposed to beat them with chains and clubs, and those who were "consorting" with white women would be taken away to receive "rougher treatment."

Bull Connor and other officials had long wanted to eliminate Reverend Shuttlesworth. In 1956, he had signaled his intention to take on Bull Connor by organizing the Alabama Christian Movement for Human Rights (ACMHR). The following year, he joined Martin Luther King in establishing the nonviolent Southern Christian Leadership Conference (SCLC). Shuttlesworth's racist enemies bombed his home and church and beat him with whips and chains when he tried to enroll his daughters in an all-white high school. "If you can't take it, you can't make it," he once said. "We mean to kill segregation or be killed by it."[25]

Rowe later claimed that he tried to prevent the assassination. Killing Shuttlesworth, he told the group, would "only cause more trouble," and anyway, "someone [else] will step into his shoes." His colleagues disagreed and were "too worked up to listen to reason." Rowe and Ernie Faulkner would "handle" the bodyguards. Other assignments would be made after the meeting.

When all gathered together again, it was announced that Klansmen should be "on call" during the weekend of July 21 and 22, ready to "attack some Negroes"; their squad leaders would fill in the details later.[26]

Later that night, Rowe and the others met with Hubert Page, who gave them more of the plan. "This is serious business," Page said. Only the Klan could do what the police could not—stop "the Negroes . . . now." The Klan would receive fifty thousand dollars to help them achieve that objective. If the police arrested them at Dobbs House, they would be protected; and in the unlikely event that they were tried and convicted, Governor Patterson would pardon them, "even if they should receive the death sentence." Rowe and Faulkner would kill the bodyguards using untraceable handguns supplied by Sergeant Cook. Bill Holt volunteered "to shoot Shuttlesworth but Page insisted it be done quietly with a knife," wielded by Nigger Hall. And Page gave them one last warning: "If word leaked out the lives of the informer and members of his family would not be worth a plugged nickel even if it took twenty years to get them."[27]

Page's warning frightened Rowe. Of the half dozen men who knew of the plot, all were "dyed in the wool" Klansmen, Rowe told Byron McFall when they met the next day. Hall and Holt, in particular, were able and willing to murder the Reverend. He was sure to be identified as the informer if Shuttlesworth wasn't killed. Rowe's "own position was precarious." The Klansmen expected him to be at Dobbs House that weekend, and if he wasn't, it would raise suspicions so high that his life would be in jeopardy.[28]

McFall immediately informed the special agent in charge, H. A. Fitzgibbon, who sought advice from Headquarters before doing anything that might endanger Rowe. His view, and those of others in the Birmingham field office, was that releasing information, however important, threatened the informant, so the Bureau should proceed with the utmost care. The man who decided that Shuttlesworth's life was worth more than Rowe's was Clement L. McGowan, Jr., chief of the FBI's Civil Rights Division, a veteran agent who had handled such cases for two decades. Although McGowan certainly wanted to protect Rowe, it was his firm belief that when dangerous situations arose, the FBI should never "sit on" information; "you've got to disseminate it even if it blows your informant," McGowan once noted. He therefore instructed Fitzgibbon to tell Birmingham's mayor and police chief, the Alabama director of public safety, and Reverend Shuttlesworth about the plan.[29]

On July 20, fewer than twenty-four hours after Rowe first learned of the plot, FBI agents contacted Shuttlesworth in Cincinnati, where he recently had moved to become pastor at the Revelation Baptist Church, and told him of the Klan's intentions. His change of locale had not weakened his commitment to the ACMHR, he told the agents, and he *did* plan to visit Dobbs House—but on July 30, not this weekend. Nevertheless, he thanked the FBI for alerting him to the dangers he might face and promised to keep the Bureau informed of his future movements. When Rowe and his fellow conspirators showed up at Dobbs House that Saturday and Sunday, they found a heavy police presence that permitted a group of blacks to successfully integrate the restaurant.[30]

The aborted plot did increase Rowe's chances of exposure. When the plan fell through, the Klan's Hubert Page told Rowe that someone had been "talking too much," implying that it might be him. Not long after this encounter, Rowe attended a special meeting of Klavern officers where the Imperial Wizard announced that he had caught an FBI informant, a man named Vickery, who was sentenced to death. Rowe managed to remain cool although, as he later told McFall, he was "scared to death." In the years ahead, there would be several attempts to eject Rowe from the Klan.[31]

Rowe's position became even more precarious in August, but this time the danger came from the FBI. Rowe's "dedicated woman chasing" often amused and confounded agents, who could never understand how a man like Rowe could attract so many women. Dorothy Rowe was not amused and, finally fed up with Rowe's behavior, demanded a trial separation, the first step toward a possible divorce. Since Mrs. Rowe knew that her husband was an informant, the FBI was afraid their breakup might blow Rowe's cover or, worse still, embarrass the Bureau. McFall apparently thought Dorothy Rowe's patience was endless, because just a month before, when preparing the quarterly report on Rowe, he had noted that "there has been no indication of any marital difficulties." Had he known of Rowe's troubles, McFall would have described them in the report's section on "Stability and Reliability," because an informant's personal problems might affect his ability to perform his duties. When Rowe told him he was moving out, the two met for several hours, discussing every aspect of Rowe's marriage.[32]

On August 5, McFall prepared a four-page, single-spaced memorandum explaining Rowe's problems and recommending that he be retained. He began with a brief history of Rowe's career, highlighting the Trailways bus incident on Mother's Day 1961, during which, McFall wrote, Rowe "was seriously injured in performing his duties for the FBI." McFall also noted that "the files of the Bureau are replete with other incidents of violence which informant has reported to this office prior to the actual incident," another exaggeration omitting those episodes that Rowe did not report either before or after they occurred. McFall's conclusion: Rowe was, "without doubt, the most alert, intelligent, productive, and reliable informant on Klan and racial matters currently being operated by the Birmingham office."[33]

The cause of Rowe's marital problems, McFall argued, was not his womanizing, but rather Mrs. Rowe's failure to fulfill her conjugal responsibilities: "The wife is vitally interested in her church work and, according to the informant, since the birth of their last child, has demonstrated a 'frigid' attitude . . . making the normal marital relationship unworkable." Their "incompatibility," he reassured the Bureau, would not "cause them to commit violence against each other," nor would it become widely known in the neighborhood. Despite the friction that led to the separation, Dorothy Rowe had always been a good informant's wife—"cooperative . . . and especially appreciative" of the extra income Washington supplied. This alone would guarantee that she would never reveal her husband's secret life. There was no reason to worry that this problem would hinder Rowe's effectiveness; on the contrary, living alone, he would have more time to expeditiously complete his reports and do the Bureau's bidding. And since he was also a man of "strong principles," who had agreed to continue supporting his wife and children, there was a good chance that the marriage might survive.[34]

The special agent in charge approved McFall's memo and sent it to Headquarters. J. Edgar Hoover replied quickly, permitting Rowe to continue as an FBI informant, but his contact agent should "be extremely alert to any development" that might require a reconsideration of Rowe's status.[35]

Like Rowe, Eastview Klavern No. 13 was also experiencing problems. The Imperial Wizard's attempt to transform the Klan from a small clique of racists into a broad anti-Communist movement had failed. By 1963, the average attendance at weekly meetings had dropped to twenty-three and was often smaller. The initiation fee was reduced to try to help attract new members. Money was scarce so at each meeting Klansmen were asked to buy a lottery ticket—the lucky winner received a British Enfield rifle. Special rings, cuff links, and tiepins were sold only to bona fide

Klansmen. For a dollar, one could buy Klan-created license plate tags bearing an imprint of the Confederate flag and the words "Keep Alabama Southern." When Bobby Shelton couldn't afford a new suit, he asked the Klavern to chip in to buy him one until an affluent member volunteered to pay the entire bill. Yet, despite its financial problems, the Klavern spent two meetings discussing its plan to someday buy nineteen acres of land in North Birmingham, where they would build the Klan's version of a posh country club, featuring a meeting hall, a pistol and rifle range, a recreation center, and a lake—a place "where all Klansmen would be welcomed." It was never built.[36]

Klavern meetings were generally dull, which may explain why it was difficult to recruit new members. D. W. Griffith's *The Birth of a Nation*, the epic film celebrating the founding of the Klan, was often shown, but its length prevented Klansmen from conducting other business. One entire session was devoted to discussing a Florida fishing trip that was to be partly financed by local businessmen as a reward for the Klan's help in electing George C. Wallace as governor (they passed out campaign leaflets and tore down those of his opponent).

Eventually, Klansmen began to show interest in other organizations that were appearing in Alabama. The newest was the United Americans for Conservative Government (UACG), an umbrella organization that included the Klan, the White Citizens Council (consisting mostly of businessmen who believed in the Klan but didn't want to lose status by joining it), the National States Rights Party, and the John Birch Society. The group had an air of respectability that the Klan lacked—candidates for the Birmingham City Council had sought votes at one meeting, although none had ever visited the Eastview Klavern seeking its political endorsement. In February, Rowe saw nine Eastview Klansmen at a UACG meeting. Leaders of the group boasted that the organization had grown quickly from 21 members to 438.[37]

There was also talk about creating a state militia, which would be called Volunteers for Alabama. "All members present seemed to be in favor of affiliating" with it, Rowe reported on April 11, especially because it had "the blessing of Governor George C. Wallace." Future meetings to discuss the new group were scheduled, and among the expected speakers was General Edwin A. Walker, "a virulent anti-Communist and strict segregationist," who resigned from the U.S. Army in 1961 after President

Kennedy removed him from command because of his extremist political views. (Ironically, on the evening of April 10, someone fired a shot at General Walker in his Dallas home, but Walker was unharmed; the would-be assassin was later identified as Lee Harvey Oswald.)[38]

Some Klansmen rejected both organizations and soon began meeting secretly in a small shack tucked away in a remote area under the bridge where Highway 280 crossed the Cahaba River. The Cahaba Boys, as these most disaffected and violent Klansmen came to be known, not only would pose a threat to Tommy Rowe but would commit the most horrendous atrocity in Birmingham's history.[39]

As the men of Eastview were seeking new avenues through which to express their anger, Martin Luther King came to Birmingham. Like the Klavern, King's own movement was temporarily stalled. His effort in 1961 to desegregate Albany, Georgia, had failed primarily because its affable police chief, Laurie Pritchett, had studied King's tactics and decided to "overcome non-violent protest with non-violent law enforcement." He treated demonstrators with civility, placing those he arrested in jails throughout the county to avoid overcrowding. When King himself was jailed, Pritchett ordered the cell cleaned and supplied his prisoner with a radio and plenty of reading material. King returned the favor: On Pritchett's wedding anniversary, he canceled a demonstration so the chief could spend the day with his wife. Without a public confrontation with segregationist forces that would capture the public's attention and pressure President Kennedy to act, King was all but powerless. "We killed them with kindness," said an Albany official when King withdrew. King badly needed a new strategy and a victory.[40]

He found both in Birmingham in 1963, "the most segregated city" in America. Schools, restaurants, hotels, motels, public swimming pools, hospitals, and cemeteries were all closed to blacks, and only a few blacks were allowed to vote. So many bombings occurred in the black residential section of town that it became known as Dynamite Hill. Racism and segregation were the twin pillars supporting business, government, and society. Those blacks who dared to challenge the existing order, the *New York Times* once noted, faced "the whip, the razor, the gun, the bomb, the torch the club, the knife, the mob, the police and many branches of the state's apparatus."[41]

Room 30 of the black-owned Gaston Motel became King's headquarters where he and his aides developed a new approach to fighting segregation, called "Project C—for Confrontation." Instead of pressuring local government to change the city's ways, King chose its businesses, hoping that boycotts and sit-ins and marches would cripple Birmingham's economic life and force department and variety store owners to compel the politicians there and in Washington, D.C., to act. His chief public enemy could not be the pleasant Chief Pritchett, so he turned his attention to the fiery racist Bull Connor, the architect of the attack on the Freedom Riders on Mother's Day 1961.[42]

King hoped that Connor would give in to his worst instincts and commit a public atrocity that would capture the nation's attention. He did. Demonstrators were roughly arrested, and the jails were soon filled to capacity. King turned to the city's high school and even elementary school students for help. They responded with enthusiasm. On May 3, as more than a thousand young protesters poured out of the Sixteenth Street Baptist Church, which had become the civil rights movement's center in Birmingham, Bull Connor let loose his police. They beat young blacks with their nightsticks and allowed attack dogs to leap and bite, tearing clothes and flesh. Then came the city's fire hoses; people rolled and tumbled like rag dolls under their force and were swept away. By the end of the day, almost thirteen hundred teenagers and children were in jail. Television brought these images into American homes; watching the pictures, President John F. Kennedy said later, made him sick.[43]

Justice Department officials flew to Birmingham to meet with local business leaders, and on May 10, King and his aides called a press conference at the Gaston Motel to announce that a settlement had been reached. The stores King had targeted agreed that within the next ninety days they would desegregate drinking fountains, restrooms, lunch counters, and dressing rooms. They also promised to employ blacks in jobs that served the public; within sixty days, a black patron could be helped by a black clerk. A biracial committee would soon be created to deal with the racial issues that divided the city. Labor unions stepped forward to pay the bail to release the jailed demonstrators. It was not everything King had sought, but it was enough for the time being.[44]

The men of Eastview watched these events but were not involved. At a Klavern meeting in late April, Exalted Cyclops Thomas ordered Klansmen "not to go downtown" and to let the police handle the demonstrators. It had been almost two years since the attack on the Freedom Riders, but it seemed like those heroic days were over. Perhaps the public rally to be held on May 11 would restore some of the Klan's past glory. Everyone was encouraged to attend that, and Rowe and the other Security Guards should wear their uniforms and make certain that no harm came to the Imperial Wizard and the other dignitaries scheduled to appear.[45]

The rally took place at the Moose Lodge near Bessemer. Klansmen from Georgia, South Carolina, Texas, Florida, and Tennessee joined their Alabama brothers. Rowe, dressed in his Security Guard uniform, estimated that the crowd numbered perhaps three thousand, although only a third remained for the entire event. The Imperial Wizard called on them to boycott stores that had agreed to King's demands; reading a list of the stores and their owners, he noted that "most of them were Jews or foreigners." He praised Bull Connor's troops for the excellent way they handled the demonstrators and pledged the Klan's help if they needed it. "Klansmen would be willing to give their lives if necessary to preserve segregation in Alabama," he proclaimed.[46]

The rally ended around 10 p.m., but for the Eastview Klansmen, the evening was just beginning. There was especially important missionary work to do; if luck was with them, they would kill Martin Luther King and his brother A. D. King that night. At 10:45, Unknown Subjects bombed A. D. King's home and parsonage. King, who was in bed, rushed into the smoke-filled living room where he found his wife, Naomi, "dazed but unhurt," and together they hurried to take their five children to safety. Fortunately, they left through the back door, because another, more powerful bomb exploded near the front porch, shattering the door and blowing its parts through the living room where the Kings had recently stood. Within a few minutes about a thousand angry blacks appeared, and a clash with white police and firefighters seemed imminent. Reverend King, however, was able to settle the crowd down temporarily, until about an hour later, when they heard another loud explosion.[47]

This time, the bombers' target was Room 30 of the Gaston Motel, where they hoped to kill Martin Luther King. King wasn't there, but the bomb destroyed the room below and left a "five by five foot" crater in the motel's west wall. Two house trailers nearby were also demolished. The crowd at A. D. King's home joined others at the motel, swelling into an enraged mob of more than twenty-five hundred people. What followed was "the first race riot of the modern civil rights era." Homes, cars, and stores were looted and burned. Bricks and bottles were thrown at whites who were taunting the crowd. State troopers carrying double-barreled shotguns arrived, as did Sheriff Jim Clark, leading his own posse on horseback. They rushed into the crowd, beating them with their rifles, and attacked innocent bystanders on their porches. Nobody was killed, but more than fifty were injured. News reporters and civil rights leaders were held prisoner at gunpoint in the motel's lobby. A. D. King telephoned the FBI and told the dispatcher, "This whole town has gone berserk." Asked what the Bureau's reaction was, King replied, "They say they'll look into it."[48]

At least one FBI agent—Rowe's contact agent Byron McFall—was frantically looking into it. His informant had promised to call him after the rally but hadn't. Where was Tommy Rowe? McFall telephoned Rowe repeatedly at home but there was no answer. Finally, at 3:00 a.m., Rowe checked in. "All hell was breaking loose downtown," he told McFall. That wasn't news to McFall—he had visited the sites of the bombings. Where had Rowe been for the past five hours? McFall demanded to know. With Klansmen, Rowe replied, none of them responsible for the bombings, or so he claimed. But he did have a suspect. At 2:30 a.m., according to Rowe, he and three colleagues—Hubert Page, Bill Holt, and Holt's nephew, Don Luna—drove to a deserted parking lot at the A&P Market on Tuscaloosa Avenue for a secret meeting with a black man who was Page's spy inside the black community. The cause of the night's trouble, the man said, was a group of Black Muslims, as many as 160, who had recently arrived in Birmingham. They bombed King's home and the Gaston Motel, hoping the Klan would be blamed for the destruction. "Mr. Curly," the man told Page, "those guys are trying to send you men to the penitentiary."

Page pulled out his gun, cocked it, and aimed it at the man's face. "If you're lying to me, you son of a bitch, I'll kill you on the spot," Page said.

"Mr. Curly as long as I have worked with you, you know I wouldn't lie," the man replied. The group accepted his explanation and drove off. Rowe went to the VFW Club, and when it was safe, he called McFall.[49]

McFall apparently doubted Rowe's story and wanted an immediate meeting. He pressed Rowe for details about the rally and where the most likely suspects went when it ended. He didn't like Rowe's answers; witnesses had seen four white men in a fast-moving car throw the bomb at the motel—the exact number in Rowe's party, which included Bill Holt, an experienced bomber. Rowe and the others could easily have bombed the motel and still met their black contact two hours later.

More specific evidence suggests that Rowe *was* involved in the Gaston Motel bombing. Historian Diane McWhorter believes that the bombing was "the best planned Klan action since the Freedom Riders were ambushed on Mother's Day, 1961." Her research revealed that every Klansman who might be suspected had established ironclad alibis for their whereabouts that evening. "Dynamite Bob" Chambliss, who had been bombing black homes since the 1940s, was seen partying late into the night at a local nightclub with Troy Ingram, another Klan bomber. Bill Holt and Exalted Cyclops Robert Thomas were supposedly at the local jail at midnight, paying the bond of Klansman George Pickle, an alcoholic pill popper, whose arrest earlier that day had all the earmarks of a planned operation. Either Thomas signed his name and Holt's or local police wrote their names on the form, allowing Holt to appear as if he had been present when, in fact, he was bombing the Gaston Motel. Other evidence suggests that McWhorter may be correct. It's extremely unlikely that the Exalted Cyclops would drive to the Birmingham jail at midnight to assist Pickle, who on February 14 was "censured" by the Klavern and suspended for sixty days for publicly boasting that he was a Klansman and also threatening the owner of a beer tavern who didn't want to buy one of the new license tags.[50]

McWhorter also argues that, besides trying to kill King, Holt saw the action as a way to test Rowe's loyalty—no FBI informer would bomb a motel, he reasoned. Other FBI reports record the comments of Bob Chambliss and Nigger Hall that suggest a Klan connection to the bombing. "If anyone ratted on him," Dynamite Bob said, "he would expose the roles" of Robert Thomas and Bobby Shelton, who were said to have authorized the attack, as well as the identities of the men who carried it out. And Hall once told Rowe, "I guess me and . . . Bobby Shelton are the only ones that actually know what happened on the night of May 11." Rowe replied, "[You're] really talking drunk talk now." "Drunk talk Hell!" Hall said. "I'm really going to tell that Shelton off." While not definitive, such remarks strongly imply Klan involvement.[51]

Determining the truth is difficult. Rowe later claimed that he didn't bomb the motel, but he often lied or exaggerated his role to both Klansmen and the FBI. One of Rowe's contact agents later said that "he told me everything," but he often thought Rowe's reports were exaggerated "just to make himself look good, a macho . . . tough guy." For this reason, and the agent's reluctance to reveal everything Rowe was up to, FBI records frequently contain no mention of Rowe's violent activities, imagined or real.[52]

There are more questions than answers. Why would Rowe quickly inform McFall of the plan to assassinate Fred Shuttlesworth ten months earlier but remain silent about the plot against King? Many of the Klavern's prominent members seemed to know of the impending bombing, so it seems unlikely that Rowe did not know about it as well, and he had ample time to alert McFall. (Since he wore his Security Guard uniform at the rally—complete with white crash helmet and black paratrooper boots— it's likely that he went home to change into clothes more suitable for missionary work; he could have alerted the Bureau at that time.) Perhaps Rowe felt that he must participate to protect his cover, especially given his problems with Bill Holt, whose doubts about Rowe, McWhorter notes, intensified after the abortive attempt on Shuttlesworth's life. There is evidence that on the night of the bombing, Rowe and Holt quarreled and even pulled guns on each other. Holt's feelings toward Rowe were also complicated by Holt's belief that Rowe was having an affair with his wife.

More clear is the FBI's response. If Byron McFall suspected that Rowe was involved, he kept his doubts to himself. In a report written for the special agent in charge, McFall *did* note that Rowe was unreachable for several hours but described his excuse without comment. The later report that went to Washington never even mentioned the missing informant and, in fact, accepted Rowe's version of events: The Klan, J. Edgar Hoover was told, was not responsible for the bombings on May 11, 1963. And nine days later, McFall submitted an evaluation in which he rated the informant "EXCELLENT." Once again, the FBI decided to protect its informant rather than investigate whether he had broken the law.[53]

If the bombing of the Gaston Motel was meant as a test, Rowe didn't completely pass it. Although he still retained the confidence of Imperial Wizard Shelton, he couldn't entirely allay the suspicions of his comrades, as he learned again in June. That month brought a new crisis for the Klan. A federal court ordered the admission of two qualified black students, Vivian Malone and James Hood, to the University of Alabama at Tuscaloosa. For the men of Eastview Klavern No. 13, the end of segregation at the university was another serious blow to the southern way of life, and they yearned to act. Yet at a Klavern meeting on June 6, Klansmen were told not to interfere with the enrollment. The Klan was still under the federal injunction issued at the time of the Freedom Riders assault, and Shelton feared that open defiance might lead to his arrest. Furthermore, Governor George Wallace promised to "stand in the school house door" to stop the admission, and the Klan didn't want to interfere with the dramatic moment when he directly challenged Justice Department officials on June 11.

During a break, Robert Thomas gave Rowe more information about the Imperial Wizard's recent activities. Shelton and Grand Dragon Hubert Page had just met with Wallace and Governor Ross Barnett of Mississippi, whose own state university had been integrated in September 1962. The men made a "secret pact" that once tempers cooled and federal authorities let down their guard, the Klan would kidnap the black students on both campuses and publicly lynch them. In his report to McFall, Rowe characterized such talk as "somewhat fantastic" but was "reporting it as he heard it."[54]

Rowe was therefore surprised to receive a telephone call from Klansman Herman Cash on Saturday afternoon, June 8, announcing that he and other select Klansmen had been chosen to immediately go to Tuscaloosa to "tear up . . . and bomb" the university. Rowe knew that Cash was a well-known alcoholic whose brother Jack owned Cash's Barbeque, a popular Klan "restaurant and beer joint," where many a plot was hatched, but now he seemed sober and serious. Rowe was told to report there at 4:00 p.m. and to bring his rifle. Cash said the order came from "the man down in the country," an expression that usually meant Bobby Shelton, so Rowe was eager to go. He immediately telephoned McFall, who urged him to make sure that the Klansmen and their weapons traveled in Rowe's car and to call again before they left. The Highway Patrol would be alerted to watch for Rowe's green-and-white Chevrolet with its whip antenna, and if everything worked as it should, the men would be arrested and their arsenal seized.[55]

When he arrived at Cash's Barbeque, Rowe found the men already assembled. Among them were three Klansmen—Gene Reeves, Charlie Cagle, and Ross Keith—who had recently been very unfriendly to Rowe. Like Rowe, Reeves was a veteran of the assault on the Formans, the Freedom Riders, and the Krystal Kitchen patrons, but he had also come to doubt Rowe. So had Cagle, who carried scars from his night at the Formans.

He had messed up his knee after colliding with a boulder that night, which may in part explain why he hated Rowe and once told Bobby Shelton he thought Rowe was an FBI informer. Keith had been recently investigated by Rowe and other members of the Klokan Committee for allegedly mistreating his family, a charge that was later dropped, but Keith blamed Rowe for the unpleasantness he had experienced. Rowe feared that these three men might lead to trouble for him, although the last two should pose no problem. Herman Cash seemed very nervous, perhaps because he had lent his car to the Gaston Motel bombers or, as one police informant later said, "took part in the bombing." And Ellis Dunsmore was certainly no threat to Rowe—he was a retired butcher and one of the oldest members of the Klan.[56]

When Rowe said he had to call his girlfriend Helen Metcalf (who knew that Rowe worked for the FBI and agreed to pass his information along to McFall), Keith became suspicious. "Get off that god-damned phone, man," Rowe later recalled him saying, "you're going to get us all killed." Rowe explained that he was just saying good-bye to Helen. "Bullshit," Keith replied.

"Here, take the god-damned phone and say hello to her," Rowe said. Keith took the phone and, to his astonishment, found Metcalf on the line. "I'll be a son-of-a bitch," he said, returning the phone to Rowe. As he walked away, Keith told Gene Reeves, "It's Helen, all right." "God-damn," Reeves said, "I thought I had him."[57]

Rowe wasn't out of trouble yet. When he offered to drive the men, Reeves said no. He preferred using Cagle's car. Knowing that the Highway Patrol would be looking out for his car, Rowe pressed, saying, "Hell, let's go in mine. [Cagle's] is going to fall apart." Reeves still refused and Rowe didn't want to push him more. He walked to his car and started to remove the weapons he had brought, which included a Thompson submachine gun he called "baby." Reeves blocked him again: "We got all the stuff we need over here, let's just go."

"I'd sure like to carry my baby with me," Rowe insisted, reaching into the trunk for the Thompson.

"Screw your baby," Reeves said, "let's go." They would go in two cars, Reeves finally decided. Rowe would ride with Herman Cash in his '58 Chevy along with Keith and Dunsmore while Reeves and Cagle would travel alone with their stockpile in the trunk—pistols loaded and ready to fire, nightsticks, sabers, bayonets, and, courtesy of Cash, a bale hook. Rowe later claimed there were more weapons—several shotguns, two hand grenades, and a bazooka.[58]

The trip proceeded without incident until 7:20 p.m., when they reached the outskirts of Tuscaloosa. Looming ahead was a Highway Patrol roadblock. Officers had been told to expect a green-and-white Chevrolet, so the first ones to approach Cash's car were confused. "This is not the fucking car," Rowe recalled one saying to the other. "[But] it's got a whip antenna," his colleague answered, "so I thought I better flag him down." The Klansmen were ordered to get out of their cars, and it became immediately apparent that officers had found the men they were looking for: Rowe was wearing his Klan Security Guard uniform, and Ross Keith had a pistol pushed down the front of his pants. "Don't put your hand on the gun," the nervous officer told Keith, "put your hand on top of the car." As Keith leaned against the car, the officer cried, "Hey, hey, this is them, this is them," and to Rowe "it seemed like half the world came out of those ditches" that ran along Highway 11. Dozens more Highway Patrol officers suddenly appeared, and their leader, Major Bill Jones, checked the cars for weapons, found them, and charged the six men with violating Alabama's Firearms Act.[59]

The Klansmen were taken to a room on the University of Alabama campus, where they were interrogated. Rowe and the others claimed that they were headed to a Klan rally. Their job as security officers was to "police" it, which explained all the weapons they carried. Herman Cash began to come apart at the seams, fearful that somehow his connection to the Gaston Motel bombing might be revealed. Rowe watched his shaking hand try to light a cigarette and told him, "Hey Herman just don't pay these god-damned people no mind, man, just play it cool baby, you're all right."

"I don't know what's wrong with me, I just don't understand it," Cash said and began to visibly shake. Reeves tried to calm him, slapping his shoulder and saying, "Hey, it ain't no big thing, just don't say a word . . . don't even tell them your name." Cash promised to be silent.

State Investigator Ben Allen (a former Klansman, according to Rowe) invited Rowe outside for a drink of water. "Somewhere in your organization you got a big ass snitch," Rowe recalled Allen saying, because the FBI had informed the Highway Patrol that the Klansmen were headed for

Tuscaloosa. And as for Cash, Allen said, "you better get in there and tell that cat to keep his god-damned fucking mouth shut about that god-damned bombing. . . . I don't know how much that goddamned man knows but . . . I can blow your whole fuckin' organization up in ten minutes if you don't get his ass outta here."

When they returned to the room, Allen could see that Cash was still shaking. "What the hell is wrong with you?" Allen asked him. "You're not worried about that [bombing] are you?" At that, Cash became completely unraveled. "I don't know nothing," he cried, "I don't know nothing. Please, please, look I'll get down on my hands and knees. Just let me go, if you let me go, you'll never see me again." When Allen left, Rowe told Cash: "If you don't straighten up I'm gonna kill your goddamned ass when we leave here . . . you won't never see home." All Cash could say was "Oh, my God, oh my God."

Actually, given the sympathetic state investigators and Highway Patrol officers, Cash had nothing to worry about. A few hours later, all six were released and none went to trial. Charlie Cagle lost his job, but the worst the others experienced was the embarrassment of the front-page headline, "Jefferson men arrested with weapons near U of A," and the story that listed their names in the next morning's Birmingham News. An accompanying picture showed their pistols, nightsticks, bayonets, and sabers.

That same day, Rowe and Exalted Cyclops Robert Thomas returned to Tuscaloosa to pick up the weapons, which, thanks to Bobby Shelton, who had talked to a friendly judge, proved to be no problem at all. When Rowe and Thomas arrived at the courthouse, they found a party for a newly elected district attorney in progress, and the judge handed them glasses of champagne and invited them in. "I want to thank you men," the judge told Rowe and Thomas, "you're outstanding American citizens. I wish we had 10,000 more like you guys." The Justice Department task force that later investigated Rowe's career praised him for passing on the news that was "responsible for preventing what might have been serious bloodshed."[60]

George Wallace kept his promise to stand in the schoolhouse door at high noon on June 11, but he stepped aside when confronted with a federalized Alabama National Guard, so the integration of the University of Alabama was relatively peaceful. But it marked another defeat for the Klan. Rowe later said, with characteristic exaggeration, that fifty thousand

Klansmen were ready to join the governor in resisting the "Central Government," but Wallace never asked for their help. Also troubling was President Kennedy's announcement that night that he would soon send Congress a strong civil rights bill designed to give blacks access to public accommodations. In a televised address to the nation, Kennedy said: "If an American, because his skin is dark, cannot eat lunch in a restaurant open to the public; if he cannot send his children to the best public school available; if he cannot vote for the public officials who represent him; if, in short, he cannot enjoy the full and free life all of us want, then who among us would be content to have the color of his skin changed and stand in his place?" Calling the civil rights crisis a "moral issue . . . as old as the Scriptures . . . and as clear as the American Constitution," the president said that America "for all its hopes and all its boasts, will not be fully free until all its citizens are free."[61]

Watching the president's speech in his home in Atlanta, Martin Luther King was "overjoyed." Medgar Evers, the NAACP's brave field secretary, heard Kennedy's words as he drove to his home in Jackson, Mississippi. It was after midnight when he arrived there. He parked his car in the driveway and walked up the path toward his house where his wife and children were waiting for him. Across the street a rabid segregationist named Byron de la Beckwith, hiding in the bushes, shot Evers in the back; he died moments later. Just as the bombing of the Gaston Motel followed quickly after King's success in Birmingham, so the murder of Medgar Evers occurred after the successful integration of the University of Alabama and Kennedy's speech. The civil rights movement's accomplishments were producing a severe reaction from its foes, whose revenge turned triumph into tragedy.[62]

CHAPTER FOUR

Bombing Matters

IN JULY 1963, THE MEN of Eastview Klavern No. 13 faced a new crisis. The U.S. Court of Appeals for the Fifth Circuit announced that Birmingham schools must integrate when the school year began in September. The Klansmen were already on record expressing their opposition. At a meeting earlier that summer, Hubert Page declared that "it was open season" on anyone, even whites, who supported integration. He admitted to once believing "that to beat or hurt one white person would do more harm than beating a hundred Negroes," but the Klan was in "trouble" and "they might as well do the real job. . . . He did not want the men to waste a month to start. . . . If they had something to handle, start now." But before they could act, they had to deal with the most dangerous of the splinter groups that were forming—the Cahaba Boys, who believed that Eastview had become "soft" and ineffectual in the face of what they saw as a Negro Revolution.[1]

The prime organizers of the Cahaba Boys were the Blantons: eighty-year-old "Pop" and his twenty-five-year-old son Tommy. Although born a Catholic, Tommy Jr. hated Catholics even more than blacks and Jews, especially if they happened to live next door. When he learned that his neighbor was a Catholic, he threw paint on her new car and bottles and rocks at her home, and doused her daughter's car with acid. His FBI file contained notations that he had "a history of psychopathic behavior" and was "a degenerate of the worst sort." Since many FBI agents were Catholic, they too became chief targets of Blanton's harassment. An agent recalled that his wife received a visitor one afternoon. When she opened the front door, a uniformed man, whose nearby truck identified him as an undertaker from the local funeral parlor, told her he was there to pick up her husband, Agent Martin. Mrs. Martin fainted dead away. When her husband learned of this cruel prank, he exploded in anger; his fellow agents had to restrain him from rushing after Tommy Blanton.[2]

Dynamite Bob Chambliss was also attracted to the new group. Rowe later recalled him saying, "Goddamn white people are getting kicked around and the niggers are taking over." If the men of Eastview—"you assholes," Chambliss called them—"can't do something about it," he knew people who could. Chambliss first joined the Klan when he was twenty years old, reportedly after watching The Birth of a Nation, and during the next twenty-seven years, he rose to become Exalted Cyclops of the Robert E. Lee Klavern. He resigned in 1951 because of "unfavorable publicity," he later said, the result of his "one-man war" against blacks, Catholics, and Jews. In the mines and quarries of Alabama, he learned about dynamite and, in 1947, first used it to destroy the home of a black man who, with the help of black attorney Arthur Shores, legally won the right to move into a white neighborhood. He had found his life's work. In 1956, he bombed Fred Shuttlesworth's Bethel Baptist Church, and by the end of the decade Chambliss was responsible for Fountain Heights, where blacks were trying to move, becoming known as Dynamite Hill. His friendship with longtime police commissioner Bull Connor won him a job in the city garage and also protected him from prosecution for his numerous crimes. Now, in 1963, he was a balding fifty-nine-year-old with ulcers and "stomach spasms," whose crooked grin and cold blue eyes frightened even his own wife.[3]

Fearful that the Cahaba Boys would siphon Eastview members (Troy Ingram and George Pickle were also defecting), Klokan Chief Shorty Thompson, Rowe, and five other Eastview Klansmen were ordered to find the Cahaba Boys' hidden shack and talk with the turncoats. On the night of August 15, they fortified themselves with liquor and tramped around the Cahaba River area until 11 p.m. when, drunk and exhausted, Nigger Hall suggested that the easiest way to locate the shack was to ask Ingram or Chambliss where it was. All seven agreed that was a good idea and, squeezing themselves into Rowe's Chevrolet, they drove to Ingram's home.

Ingram wasn't happy to see them, and as the conversation proceeded, Rowe noticed Mrs. Ingram appear at the door with a gun in her hand. Ingram started to retreat, but Hall grabbed his head "and dragged him out of the house." Mrs. Ingram asked her husband if she should call the police and Thompson replied, "If you want your husband back in one piece, you'll calm down and go to bed." The conversation resumed in Rowe's car and continued for two hours. Thompson noted that they had been long-time friends and "brothers in a common cause" and wondered why Ingram was trying to change the Klan "contrary to Shelton's wishes." Ingram denied this and blamed Chambliss "for any wrongdoing" that might have occurred. They eventually released Ingram unharmed.[4]

How could the Klavern persuade Chambliss and the others that East-view was still strong and vibrant? One way would be to employ Chambliss's favorite technique for terrorizing the black community. At around 9:30 on the night of August 20, the sound of a dynamite explosion echoed again on Dynamite Hill when someone bombed the home of attorney Arthur Shores, Chambliss's old foe. The bomb shattered the front windows and demolished the garage, but Shores was in the rear of the house and wasn't injured. A crowd, growing quickly from three hundred to a thousand, pelted police and firefighters with bricks. More police arrived, nearly a hundred, some armed with submachine guns. They fired bursts into the air above the rioters. Reverend A. D. King climbed atop a police car and urged the people to disperse: "If you are going to kill someone," he said, "kill me. . . . We are going to win this town regardless of what they do. Stand if you must [but] stand in love not violence." His plea failed; the mob threw more rocks and police moved against them, firing over their heads. It took an hour for order to be restored.[5]

Tommy Rowe telephoned his FBI contact later that night. In this first report to the FBI, Rowe said that two Action Squads were "working on some problem" that night but he didn't know anything more. However, he was certain that Nigger Hall and his group had nothing to do with the Shores bombing. But over the next few days, he changed his mind. During a break at a Klavern meeting on August 22, he later told McFall, Exalted Cyclops Robert Thomas approached a group that included Ross Keith and Rowe and joked, "You fellows were almost on top of that one the other night, weren't you?" Keith laughed, noting that they were so close that "his ears rang for thirty minutes afterward." The next night, while drinking at the Log Cabin Tavern, Rowe told Keith that most people felt he and his friends had bombed the house. Keith just grinned "sheepishly" and said, "I know that some of you fellows . . . thought that." "But your ears were ringing that night," Rowe reminded him. Keith said nothing further about the bombing.

Nine months later, when the FBI again asked Rowe about the bombing, he suddenly recalled new details: Keith and the others, whom he now named—Nigger Hall, Charles Cagle, and H. A. White, the man everyone called "Sister" because, Rowe noted, "he was a little on the feminine side" —were on a mission near Shores's home and, given the comments Keith later made, Rowe now concluded that they had been responsible for the bombing.[6]

In 1977, during an interview with Birmingham police officials, Rowe gave the fullest, most detailed account of what happened that night, which, because it is supported by other evidence, points to Rowe's own participation in the Shores bombing. This is the story Rowe told: Keith and Sister White rode to Shores's home on their motorcycles and placed the bomb while Cagle and Hall, who had driven to Dynamite Hill, watched for trouble. But the bomb went off "prematurely," Rowe recalled Keith saying, blowing "me down the goddamned alley. I thought I was a dead son of a bitch. . . . The blast was so fucking loud it almost blew my eardrums out." Indeed, his ears rang so badly he sought medical attention later that night. The bomb was made by a man who had not yet taken his Klan oath—Ronnie Tidwell, a twenty-eight-year-old unemployed electrician whom Keith and White called, with good reason, "a piss poor bomber."[7]

Rowe reported none of this to McFall in 1963 or 1964, although he claimed that he did. If so, then McFall failed to record it for his superiors. Rowe's recollections, fourteen years after the event, seem like those of an observer rather than the recipient of another's tale. Furthermore, FBI records indicate that on August 8, twelve days before the bombing, Rowe left a Klavern meeting early with Hall and Keith "to check out a problem" he never identified. Similarly, on August 15, five days before the bombing, Rowe again went "to check out a problem," this time with Keith, Hall, White, and "an unidentified man." These forays, in the company of the men who later bombed Shores's home, may have been reconnaissance trips to determine whether Shores had bodyguards or any other special protection. If Rowe, by his own admission, joined these men on an unidentified mission two weeks in a row, it doesn't seem unreasonable to conclude that he was probably with them the third night when the bombing occurred.[8]

There is no documentary evidence to prove that Rowe was involved in the Shores bombing, but if he was, and Rowe mentioned it at all to the FBI, his active participation wouldn't have been recorded. During 1962 and 1963, Rowe had a history of being close to bombings in Birmingham. Furthermore, the guilty parties were among his closest friends within the Klan, the men he regularly spent his evenings with either carousing or carrying out Klan missions.

More problems developed in Birmingham as the school year began on September 4, 1963. Three schools—Graymont Elementary and West End and Ramsay High Schools—were preparing to admit only five black children, but opponents protested by carrying signs ("Communist Jews Behind Race Mixing") and throwing rocks, prompting a police response. This minor violence led Governor Wallace to issue an executive order banning integration "for the sole and expressed purpose of preserving the peace."[9]

That night, at around 9:35, bombers struck again at Arthur Shores's home. The force of the explosion blew the front door into the living room, narrowly missing the attorney. His wife, who was reading in their bedroom, was thrown to the floor, but both survived with only a few bruises. The riot that followed was the worst yet. One black man was killed and another injured and hospitalized, both the victims of buckshot fired by police shotguns, but one officer later said, "There was a lot of people shot that night . . . by the Birmingham police." (The dead man, John Coley, resembled Fred Shuttlesworth so strongly that some felt his killing was another failed attempt to assassinate the Reverend.)[10]

Where was Tommy Rowe that night? Rowe's informant file contains no record of an immediate or even a delayed report to McFall—which is unusual because Rowe contacted his handler after a significant event—or any evidence that the FBI tried to find him. The quarterly report McFall later prepared for Washington, a detailed description of Rowe's activities based on a total of twenty-eight reports McFall received between June 8 and September 20, doesn't even mention the September 4 bombing. After a month's investigation, the field office noted tersely, "no definite suspects developed." It wasn't until May 1964 that Rowe provided the Bureau with information about that night—and it wasn't much. He recalled that Nigger Hall and his Action Squad (Sister White, Ross Keith, Bill Holt, Gene Reeves, Charles Cagle, and Harry Walker, Chambliss's nephew) spent the evening at a nightclub in Irondale, making sure that it didn't cater to blacks. Therefore, they couldn't have bombed Shores's home, and Rowe didn't know of any other possible suspects. Rowe's report was slipped into the Bureau's files named "Bombing Matters."[11]

The absence of an immediate report, and Rowe's reticence, might be explained by his account of where he was and what he was doing that night—defending himself against a black rioter whom he says he shot and killed. According to Rowe, he was driving near where the bombing occurred and, coming around a curve, suddenly found himself in the midst of the riot. He saw blacks drag a white man from a taxi while others were beating a woman and child. Then, "a great big ass black man" came toward him with a brick in his hand. The crowd yelled, "Kill him, kill him." As the man with the brick "reared back," ready to throw, Rowe pulled out his .38 revolver and shot him in the chest. Then he "stomped the gas" and took off fast.[12]

When he came to a barrier manned by motorcycle cops, several police cars, and an officer holding a shotgun, he stopped. "Whew!" Rowe told the sergeant. "Better get some people back there, I think I just killed a man."

The officer strolled over, "just as nonchalant as shit," Rowe recalled. "You all right?" he asked.

"Yeah."

"What's going on?"

Rowe was badly shaken and said again, "You better get some people in there. There's a lot of people getting killed down there."

"Did anybody get your tag number?" the officer asked.

"How the hell do I know if anybody got my tag number?" said an exasperated Rowe. "There was . . . a thousand goddamned niggers back there."

"Now, you're sure you're not hurt?" he asked again. "Think carefully. It's very important. Did anybody have a chance to get your damn tag number?"

"Sir, I don't know," Rowe said.

"Get the hell out of here, okay? Good shooting."

Rowe "went straight as a goddamned board home" and immediately called Byron McFall. After Rowe explained what had happened, noting the officer's reaction—"the damnedest thing: This sergeant told me to go home"—McFall said, "Oh, shit. Did he get your driver's license?"

"Didn't even ask me for it," Rowe said. "Told me: 'Good shooting.'"

"Okay," McFall said. "I'll get back to you in a bit." According to Rowe, McFall investigated and told him he'd found a black man who was shot in the eye. Rowe insisted that he had "hit this nigger right in the chest." McFall said he would do more checking.

He didn't speak with McFall until the next day, Rowe claimed, when they met in a grocery store parking lot. Had he reported the incident to the Birmingham police? McFall asked. Yes, Rowe replied. Then McFall allegedly said, "You're right, you killed him. Did the Sergeant . . . recognize you?" "No," Rowe said, it was the first time he ever saw that officer. "Forget this," McFall supposedly said. "Just sit tight and don't say anything else about it."

Later, when this incident became the subject of controversy, Agent McFall called Rowe's story "absolutely untruthful," and a coroner's investigation revealed that the only fatality that night was caused by a shotgun, not the revolver Rowe carried. If Rowe didn't kill the man, he might have just wounded him. Rowe didn't think so, but Birmingham police documents suggest that he might have been generally truthful about what happened that night. In every version of this story Rowe told, details differed except one: He remembered seeing rioters attacking a cab. Records indicate that a cab driver named P. L. Jarvis *was* hit by a brick at 10:15 on the night of September 4, 1963, in the area where Rowe said the assault occurred. Jarvis wasn't seriously hurt and received quick treatment for "a small cut on the side of his head." This incident adds some corroboration to Rowe's account. And if the shooting occurred at 10:15 at Sixth Avenue and First Street North, it places Rowe near Shores's home not long after the bomb exploded. Was it merely another in a long line of coincidences that Rowe was nearby when the second Shores bombing occurred?[13]

There is apparently little doubt about Rowe's involvement in the next Birmingham bombing, on September 7, 1963. When investigators asked him about it, Rowe said, "I was in on that." The Klansmen's evening that night began with a lavish affair sponsored by the United Americans for Conservative Government in the Redmont Hotel's Emerald Room. The guest of honor was their hero—Governor George Corley Wallace. For the occasion, the Klan's internal squabbling was temporarily forgotten. The Cahaba Boys, Bob Chambliss, and Troy Ingram were there as well as the Klan's Imperial Wizard, Tommy Rowe, Robert Thomas, and others from throughout the state. Seated near Wallace, at his request, was Edward Fields, head of the National States Rights Party, whom the governor praised for helping fight the integrationists. Two days earlier during an interview with the *New York Times*, Wallace had said: "What this country needs is a few first class funerals, and some political funerals, too." Tonight he expressed surprise that the recent city bombings had not claimed any black lives, evidence, he thought, that the bomb throwers were "nigras" hoping to win sympathy for their cause. The audience cheered.[14]

Later, when a group of Eastview Klansmen visited with their brethren at the Bessemer Klavern, there was talk about making the governor's wish come true. "Baby brother, we got a goody," Rowe recalled Robert Creel saying. "You'll like this, [it's] right up your alley." "Well, what you got?" Rowe asked. A fabulous way to conclude the night's festivities, Bessemer's Exalted Cyclops said. Someone had suggested that since they missed getting King at the Gaston Motel, they should bomb the country home of the motel's black owner, A. G. Gaston, a millionaire businessman who owned most of Birmingham's black business district. There was talk that Gaston was giving rifles to the Black Muslims and was so well protected at his mansion, called The Castle, in the North Birmingham woods that nobody "in the world" could touch him. One Klansman said, "Why don't we . . . go out and bomb the son-of-a-bitch?"[15]

Rowe later claimed that he tried to block this plan. "No, that ain't going to work," he supposedly told them. "What I'd do, I'd just go out there and kick . . . [his] goddamn ass. You tell me the guard has got shotguns and carbines and crap, let's just go take the shit away from him." Some liked this idea, but Ernie Faulkner and Bill Holt preferred bombing. The discussion grew "heated." A Bessemer Klansman named William Orville Eaton—later involved in the murder of Viola Liuzzo—volunteered to do the job himself. A serious heart condition had caused him to retire early, and Eaton thought he had only a few months to live. "Eaton was quite a fanatic," Rowe noted, "every other word was let's kill the bastard . . . he wanted to go up to the president and blow him away." Now, Eaton said, "Just drive me up to the gate, give me the goddamn bomb and I'll just walk up to them and let it go off." While Eaton was offering himself as a human sacrifice, Bessemer Klansman Gene Thomas left the group briefly and then returned with a package; inside were a bottle and a glass jug filled with diesel fuel that, if they were lucky, would set Gaston's mansion afire. And so, despite Rowe's misgivings, the means of destruction was agreed upon.[16]

It was raining heavily when the Klansmen arrived at Gaston's Castle in the woods, according to Rowe, so making their way to the house proved difficult. They crawled the last few yards and then suddenly came upon not a horde of bodyguards but a single "heavy-set black man" who was setting down his shotgun so he could light a cigar. They backed away from him as quietly as they could; Rowe never understood why they weren't seen. Two Klansmen ran toward the house and lobbed the two homemade bombs toward the front windows; one hit the house and burned out, but the other crashed through the window, setting drapes, a lamp shade, and a rug on fire. Nobody was injured. Bob Creel slapped a sticker on the side of the house that read, "The KKK Is Watching You," and the men ran back to their cars. They returned to the Bessemer meeting hall in a "jubilant" mood, Rowe said, thinking the attack "funny as hell," laughing at the "dumb ass guard" and "slapping each other on the back for a job well done."[17]

Later, Rowe claimed that he gave the Bureau a full report on the Castle bombing, but his file contains nothing about the incident. McFall's October 1963 quarterly report on Rowe's activities never mentions it, nor does the field office's October status report on "Bombing Matters." And when Rowe was reinterviewed in May 1964, agents didn't ask him about it. Both the Justice Department and the FBI apparently considered the bombing unimportant because the department never authorized the Bureau to investigate it and Hoover never expressed an interest in doing so.[18]

But the FBI couldn't ignore the next bombing. Claiming more lives than any previous attack, and young ones at that, it made headlines around the world and is remembered today as one of the most tragic events of the 1960s. On Sunday, September 15, at 10:20 a.m., an explosion tore through the basement of the Sixteenth Street Baptist Church, where Martin Luther King had recruited demonstrators in May. Killed instantly were three fourteen-year-old girls, Carole Robertson, Cynthia Wesley, and Addie Mae Collins, along with Denise McNair, who at age eleven was the youngest. Addie Mae's sister, thirteen-year-old Sarah, blinded and "spewing blood" from the twenty-one pieces of glass in her face, eyes, chest, and legs, somehow managed to find her way out of the wreckage that once was the women's lounge where the girls were dressing for the Sunday service. Sarah would spend two months in the hospital; doctors saved her life but had to remove her right eye. Sixteen others—parishioners and people just walking past the church—were injured. "In church! My God, we're not even safe in church," cried one anguished woman. The church's pastor, John Cross, told reporters, "We've been expecting this all along, waiting for it, knowing it would come, wondering when." He had become accustomed to canceling meetings because of the many bomb threats he received during the past few months, but nothing had happened—until now. "We haven't underestimated the extremists," Cross noted. "We've known right along there were people in this town capable of anything. Even this."[19]

An angry crowd threw rocks and pieces of glass at the police and sheriff's deputies, who responded by firing shotguns over their heads, forcing them into nearby streets and alleys. Miraculously, no widespread rioting occurred, as after the Shores and Gaston Motel bombings, but senseless violence claimed two other lives that day. Birmingham police shot a black teenager in the back, saying that he ran away after throwing rocks at them. And in a Birmingham suburb, Larry Joe Sims and Michael Lee Farley, two sixteen-year-old Eagle Scouts, were riding a red motor scooter covered with Confederate stickers when they came upon two black boys on a bike. Sims shot at them, killing one, thirteen-year-old Virgil Ware. (Sims and Farley surrendered to police the next day, confessing their crime. Reporters asked the sheriff's office why they murdered Ware, a boy they didn't know and had never seen before; a deputy replied, "They didn't give any reason.") In all, the Sixteenth Street Baptist Church bombing and its aftermath caused six fatalities, none older than sixteen.[20]

The FBI responded immediately. The Civil Rights Act of 1960 authorized it to investigate a possible violation of federal law—in this case the transportation of dynamite across state lines for criminal purposes and the apprehension of those responsible if they fled to another state. Ten special agents (and staff) flew immediately to Birmingham, and lab technicians followed later. The Bureau named the case BAPBOMB.[21]

Although this was going to be a "no-holds-barred" investigation, Director Hoover controlled it completely; nothing would be shared with local authorities or the Justice Department, which he accused of leaking information to newspapers and magazines. This included Hoover's nominal boss, Attorney General Robert Kennedy. When Assistant FBI Director Al Rosen asked Hoover whether Kennedy should receive a detailed report of the Bureau's efforts even though he had been briefed earlier by another official, Hoover said: "No. What Evans told him is sufficient. We want results, not publicity." Over the next few months, more than two hundred agents went to Birmingham, part of the largest investigation, it was said, since the FBI tracked down John Dillinger.[22]

City, state, and federal governments acted, too. President Kennedy expressed his sorrow and outrage and federalized the Alabama National Guard, placing several units on alert. Deputy U.S. Attorney General Burke Marshall and two assistants were sent to Birmingham. By evening, at the governor's order, 150 officers from the Alabama Highway Patrol were policing the city—but blacks protected their own neighborhoods.[23]

Bombing cases were always difficult to solve, and BAPBOMB proved to be no exception. Agents scouring the site of the explosion found only debris—no parts of safety fuses or blasting caps, no fragments of timing devices. The bomb destroyed everything that could be used as evidence, except for a piece of wire and a chunk of red plastic, which looked like it might have once been a fishing bobber. The police officer who found it gave it to an FBI agent, who apparently lost it—something that often happened in complicated cases, or so the FBI claimed. The crime scene outside the church was also a mess. Congregants, police, emergency medical technicians, and journalists had walked all over it; nothing of value was found. Explosives were plentiful in Birmingham; one could buy a stick of dynamite in a local hardware store. "Everybody and his brother knows how to dynamite," a journalist noted. "Miners use it. Contractors use it to dig ditches through underlying limestone. Farmers blow stumps with it, farm kids learn to fish in the creek with dynamite when they are about 13." The Du Pont and Hercules corporations had plants outside Birmingham, and both produced dynamite. All this made nearly every citizen a potential suspect.[24]

Despite these obstacles, the FBI worked on. Field offices in the region were ordered to check on their own Klansmen or members of hate groups to determine whether any might have been involved in the Birmingham bombing. Within two days, Washington received similar responses from Atlanta, Savannah, New Orleans, Knoxville, Jacksonville, and Tampa: "All bombing suspects accounted for" or "No pertinent information developed." In Atlanta, agents recorded the remarks of a Klansman who said he would never help the FBI because they were "the Gestapo for the Kennedys and the Communist Jews." If he had his way, he added, "agents would be tried for treason and hanged."[25]

Birmingham was always the center of the investigation. The day after the bombing, Attorney General Kennedy asked the Bureau's Courtney Evans whether there were "any good leads." Evans told him that there was "nothing of a concrete nature to report," although agents were interviewing thousands of citizens—anyone who might have recently seen suspicious people in the city. In 1964 Assistant Director Rosen said that they "practically [tore] Birmingham apart."[26]

Many in the South believed that blacks or Black Muslims had bombed the church and urged Hoover to investigate them. Georgia's powerful senator Richard B. Russell told the FBI's C. D. DeLoach "that the Negroes might have perpetrated this incident in order to keep emotions at a fever pitch," and feared that the Kennedy administration might block the prosecution of the guilty parties to avoid embarrassing the president while Congress was considering his civil rights bill. Or, Russell added, the Communists might have done it. Russell hoped Hoover would look "into all angles" and never "suppress evidence" for political purposes. DeLoach assured him that the director wasn't excluding anyone from investigation, and if any administration tried to use the FBI to serve its political ambitions, "they would certainly regret it." At the same time, a private citizen wrote Hoover: "I have every reason to believe this crime was committed by a member of the Black Moslems, loaded on Hashish. . . . The Black Moslems are fanatics . . . weed heads and junkies . . . and would have no qualms to do this if it would make a liar out of Wallace, put the South in a worse light [and] foment hate among their race." Hoover made sure that agents interviewed the members of Birmingham's small Black Muslim group and looked into King's recent movements, too.[27]

So strong were the rumors that civil rights activists had blown up the church that U.S. Attorney Macon L. Weaver issued a public statement hoping to dispel them. The story was circulating through the city that the church basement had been stocked with explosives and that one of the four girls accidentally knocked a bottle of nitroglycerine into a box filled with dynamite, causing the explosion. Willie Green, the church janitor, knew what had happened, it was claimed, so the FBI hid him away to prevent the truth from coming out.

It was also widely believed, one newspaper article stated, that the Justice Department was "trying to cover up any clues to the crime that may damage the Negro cause." U.S. Attorney Weaver assured Birmingham's citizens that when the guilty party, "regardless of who he may be," was apprehended, he would be brought to justice. He also noted that the church janitor was questioned "extensively" by police and released. The FBI interviewed Willie Green twice, and his polygraph test indicated that he had been "truthful." But this news was not revealed, reflecting Hoover's desire to keep everything within the Bureau. Shown an article featuring Weaver's remarks, Hoover angrily scrawled on the page: "Why do we furnish a . . . publicity seeker with any information? I had indicated that I did not want U.S. Atty talking for the FBI."[28]

Although the physical evidence didn't point to a specific suspect, the most obvious candidates were Alabama's Klansmen or members of the right-wing National States Rights Party. And the best way to identify the actual bombers, Hoover always believed, was through the information supplied by informants, chief among them Gary Thomas Rowe. Later, Rowe claimed that he played a major role in solving the crime: "Within two weeks . . . the FBI came to me and said, 'well, you gonna get a hell of a raise out of this . . . probably get rich off this,' " he stated in 1975. He said there was "no doubt" in the minds of the FBI that he gave them the names of the bombers.[29]

Rowe's recollection was false. In fact, the evidence reveals that Rowe, whether consciously or inadvertently, steered the FBI away from the real culprits, had difficulty explaining his own whereabouts the night the bomb was placed, and was unable to correctly identify the men who were eventually convicted for bombing the church—Bob Chambliss, Tommy Blanton, and Bobby Frank Cherry—until December 1964. By this time, fifteen months after the event, just about everybody in the Bureau knew who was responsible. Rowe's failure to produce important information is so stark when compared with the other events he reported during his five-year career—the attack on the Freedom Riders and the plot against Reverend Shuttlesworth, for instance—it suggests that he may possibly have had prior knowledge that the church was going to be bombed or that he actually participated in the action.

On the morning of September 15, Rowe was awakened at nine o'clock by Special Agent Byron McFall calling to check in, as he did every morning. The only thing Rowe had to report was that at 4 a.m. he had been awakened suddenly by a noise that sounded like an explosion. Did McFall know anything about it? He didn't, but promised to look into it and call Rowe back. He did, at 9:30. Nothing for them to worry about, McFall said; a boiler at the Southern Electric Steel Company blew up—it was just an "industrial accident." Rowe promised to contact him if anything developed that day, and the conversation ended. Less than an hour later, the phone rang again, and this time McFall's news was terrible. Someone had bombed the Sixteenth Street Baptist Church, and according to radio reports "at least one person was dead, maybe more."[30]

Who could have done this? McFall asked. Rowe didn't know but doubted that the Klan was involved because the church was deep in "Mau Mau Country," Rowe's name for the black section of town. But McFall wanted names, so Rowe gave him six: Bill Holt, Ross Keith, Nigger Hall, Charles Cagle, and Sister White, the group that lately had been together doing missionary work; then, almost as an afterthought, he added Shorty Thompson, although Thompson wasn't part of Hall's Action Squad. He also stressed that he had no solid information to indicate that any of the men were responsible for the bombing. However, he would call them to see if he could learn anything.

Mrs. Keith answered the phone at her house and told Rowe that her husband was out, John Hall had picked him up earlier that morning. Nobody answered the phone at the homes of Nigger Hall, Sister White, or Shorty Thompson, and Rowe couldn't call Cagle, who didn't have a phone. This is what Rowe told McFall when he called a few minutes later. Rowe seemed confused. When these guys were out and about, they usually called him, but not this time. McFall instructed Rowe to stay home on the chance that they might contact him. Then McFall asked for details about each man—where they lived and worked, what they looked like—approximate height, weight, hair and eye color, if Rowe knew. McFall would check his information with the Bureau's files. If any of the men was involved, Rowe noted, it was likely to be Bill Holt, the Klansman who had volunteered to shoot Reverend Shuttlesworth. In fact, just a few weeks earlier, Holt had boasted to him that he had bombed Negro homes several times in the past, and Rowe learned through his police contacts that Holt had once been arrested for "attempted house bombing."[31]

While Rowe waited for a call that never came, McFall checked his files on the six men and arranged for two agents to be assigned to search for each man and follow them for the rest of the day. Later, McFall insisted that Rowe played an essential role at the outset of the case, giving the Bureau "a sense of direction." By pointing them toward the men who Rowe felt were the most dangerous members of the Eastview Klavern, the FBI could move immediately to investigate the ones most likely to have committed the crime.[32]

Basking in the glow of what he thought was Rowe's achievement, McFall failed to notice something peculiar about what he learned from Rowe that morning. Everybody knew that Birmingham's most experienced bomber was Robert Chambliss. Just the previous month Rowe told McFall that Bobby Shelton had said that Chambliss and a small group of four men were responsible for "all the bombings." Shelton seemed in awe of Chambliss, Rowe later reported to McFall. Dynamite Bob was "quite a Klansman," Shelton said, the "equal to three or four" of those who were currently in the Klavern. Given Chambliss's reputation, this wasn't exactly news, but it is surprising that Rowe failed to mention the Cahaba Boys— Chambliss, Tommy Blanton, Troy Ingram, and Bobby Frank Cherry, famous for his "Cherry bombs." Was Rowe's omission merely an accident, or was he intentionally pointing the FBI in the wrong direction because he was involved in the bombing?[33]

During the week that followed, Rowe learned little about who might have been behind the bombing. On Monday, he visited with Robert Thomas. "Goddamn the shit hit the fan, didn't it?" Rowe recalled Thomas saying.

"It sure did," Rowe replied, "was anybody hurt?"

Thomas looked confused: "I understand there was a bunch of kids hurt . . ."

Rowe interrupted him. "No, come on, now, you know what the hell I mean. Is the guys all right?"

The usually mild-mannered Thomas suddenly became abrupt. "I don't know nothing about that," he told Rowe and then took him outside, away from Thomas's wife, Mildred. "Hey man," he said, "just play it cool . . . Mildred is just . . . all upset."

"I didn't know," Rowe said. "I just came over to see if everybody was all right."

Thomas gave him an odd smile and said, "I don't know nothing about [it]."[34]

At Thursday night's Klavern meeting on September 19, there was a good bit of joshing about the bombing. Bill Holt asked Hubert Page what he was going to do with all that reward money, implying that Page knew who had planted the bomb and would turn them in. Page played along, saying that after he got the money, he would lend every Klansman twenty dollars. Shorty Thompson seemed to take this exchange seriously because he then asked Page whether he knew who did it. "You don't know him," Page replied.[35]

Unfortunately, whoever bombed the Sixteenth Street Baptist Church wasn't finished. At 1:30 a.m. on September 25, an explosion awoke the people on Center Street South. Tommy Rowe, who happened to be nearby, reported it to the FBI field office only four minutes later. According to Rowe, he had just dropped off his girlfriend Helen Metcalf at her new apartment when they heard "a heavy explosion which even shook them momentarily." Rowe hurried to find a phone booth to call it in (nobody asked him why he didn't use Metcalf's phone). After calling the field office, he contacted Agent McFall. While they were talking, a police car sped by but then stopped when Officers J. D. Allred and Jimmy Vines spotted Rowe, whom they both knew. "What's happening?" Allred asked him. They, too, had heard the blast and were on their way to the scene. Rowe put his hand over the receiver and said, "I don't know." The officers then took off fast, headed south toward Center Street. As Rowe began talking again, he heard another blast, also coming from Center Street. He told McFall he would investigate and report again later.[36]

Allred and Vines were close by when the second explosion went off, and they saw immediately that it was a deadly shrapnel bomb—something Birmingham's bombers had never used before. The first explosion was supposed to bring out a crowd, and indeed, black residents at 1601 Center Street South were milling around the area as police arrived. The second bomb was designed to maim or kill by spewing out jagged nails, bolts, and pieces of pipe. Police and FBI agents later found shrapnel embedded in the front doors or the sides of seven homes across the street from the blast. In some cases, nails and bolts went through the doors and into the homes, where they penetrated furniture. Fortunately, no one was injured that morning, but the force of the explosion also broke windows, shattered a wooden light pole, and blew a hole in the sidewalk.[37]

At 3:12 a.m., Rowe again telephoned the field office. The dispatcher told him that Officers Vines and Allred wanted to speak with him before he went home—it was "very important" that they see him. Rowe sometimes rode around Birmingham with Allred and Vines, so he knew where to look for them. They were eating breakfast at Alley's Drug Store when Rowe arrived, yelled hello, and started to approach them. But a sergeant suddenly appeared and joined the men, who pointedly ignored Rowe as if they had never seen him before, so Rowe quickly left. He caught up with them a few days later. The officers were upset; they wanted the Klan to know that they didn't care how many "niggers" were killed, but these shrapnel bombs might kill cops, too.[38]

When Justice Department investigators later asked Special Agent Mc-Fall if he thought it peculiar that Rowe had again reported another bombing within minutes of its occurrence, he said no. "[He's] doing a good job if he's there somewhere where he knows what's going on. There would be no percentage in him trying to commit violence. He wouldn't gain anything by it." McFall was wrong: Rowe's participation in the bombings could help him greatly with both the Klan and the Bureau. If he moved from beatings to bombings, it would reassure his fellow Klansmen that he was one of them, which in turn would put him in a position to provide the Bureau with important information. Ironically, as the violence increased, so did his value to the Bureau.[39]

Perhaps McFall might have considered Rowe a suspect if he had known that his alibi for the evening of September 25 didn't hold up. Rowe's girlfriend Helen Metcalf, later asked whether she had been with him that night, returning home about 1:30 a.m., when they heard an explosion, told investigators that "she was *not* with Rowe when the bomb went off . . . at Center Street." But McFall never interviewed Metcalf, and the bombers were never identified or caught.[40]

The FBI's major focus remained on BAPBOMB. Rowe's chief subjects —Hall, Keith, Holt, Cagle, Thompson, and White—were polygraphed, but only Nigger Hall emerged as one of the likely suspects. But those who never made Rowe's short list, the Cahaba Boys, acted like suspects too. Just a few hours after the church bombing, two FBI agents appeared at

Chambliss's home. He reluctantly let them in but was obviously uncomfortable in their presence. When he asked whether he could get his cigarettes from the next room, the agents jumped up as if, Chambliss later said, "he was going after his gun." One agent followed him anyway. Repeating the story for his fellow Klansmen, Chambliss said that he told the "nigger-loving SOBs if they didn't have a search warrant to get the hell out of the house, or I'd get my shotgun and move them out."[41]

On September 25, two agents returned to talk to Chambliss and found him about to climb into his truck. Asked where he had been last night when Center Street was bombed, he pointed at his truck and said, "Right here with this thing" and wouldn't answer other questions. When he pulled away, he was apparently so angry that he crashed his truck into a utility pole, damaging it and slightly injuring himself.[42]

When agents visited Chambliss a third time, at the auto parts company where he worked, he invited his bosses to watch him "tell the FBI where they can go." Since Chambliss hated Catholics almost as much as he did Jews and blacks, he informed the agents that "72% of [you] bastards are Roman Catholics under the control of that yellow traitor Bobby Kennedy, [you] had better leave me alone." Waving his hands and pointing a finger at the agents, he said, "Stay away from my house and don't talk to my wife and relatives any more. . . . I'm warning you. I'm going to sue you; you're trying to drive me crazy." The FBI men noted that if he truly had nothing to hide, there was "no reason for his . . . wild attitude, and that he was not acting like an innocent man." They urged him to cooperate. The sooner their investigation was complete, the sooner they would go away. After more "crude remarks" about harassment, Chambliss stopped talking.[43]

Tommy Blanton's FBI polygraph test seemed to confirm his involvement in various bombings. Did he know who had bombed the Sixteenth Street Baptist Church? No, he said, the answer producing a sharp rise in blood pressure. Was he parked near the church at two o'clock in the morning of September 15? No, Blanton said, and his breathing quickened. Was Robert Chambliss with him that night? No, and his blood pressure shot up again. The technician concluded "that Blanton has direct knowledge of and participated to some extent in the bombing of 16th Street Baptist Church, the Gaston Motel, and possibly the bombings on Center Street." When he showed Blanton the results of his test, Blanton turned dead white and looked like he was going to faint. Blanton's alibi for the weekend of the church bombing, provided by his girlfriend Jean Casey, also didn't prove to be true, according to the polygraph. Asked, "Did Tommy tell you he bombed the church," and "have you withheld information from the FBI in this case," Casey answered deceptively. When her test results were explained to her, she insisted she was telling the truth and then became "hysterical."[44]

During an interview with the FBI on October 4, Blanton tried to punch one agent and knife another. The agents arrested Blanton and dragged him down to the field office, where he was more cooperative. He agreed to permit the FBI to search his apartment and told agents that Chambliss recently said he had bought dynamite and planned to make a shrapnel bomb. While he remained in custody, agents entered Blanton's apartment and planted a listening device that would later record incriminating statements about the church bombing.[45]

Troy Ingram also flunked his polygraph. His answers to the pertinent questions—did he have prior knowledge that the church was going to be bombed, did he bomb the church, and were bombs ever made in his basement—caused "a classic textbook type pattern of deception across the board," the analyst concluded. Although Ingram complained that he had a painful cyst under his scalp that accounted for his reactions, he didn't convince the agents, who strongly believed that Ingram and Chambliss had blown up the church. Ingram's test also indicated involvement in the Gaston Motel bombing, one or both of the attacks on Arthur Shores's home, and the Center Street bombing. The FBI interviewed Ingram's wife, who described him as a good husband and father, "not the type of person to be involved in violence." Like other potential witnesses, she viewed photographs of nineteen individuals connected to the case. Omitted that day, as it was every time agents interviewed a subject, was a picture of Gary Thomas Rowe.[46]

When FBI agents interviewed Bobby Frank Cherry, he told them, "I would kill a nigger if he bothered me." He also confessed to recently firing his rifle at a group of blacks who had the nerve to come near his house. His polygraph revealed that he had earlier bombed a house, knew who bombed the church, and was withholding evidence.[47]

The FBI's interviews pointed toward Blanton, Ingram, Cherry, and Chambliss as the perpetrators of the church and other bombings, but polygraph results weren't admissible in court, so the FBI investigation seemed to have hit a wall. "Alibis furnished and checked to no avail" was the constant refrain of agents as they interviewed both major and minor subjects. Alabama authorities, hoping to be the first to break the case, misinterpreted the Bureau's activity and concluded that they were close to making arrests. So they decided to move first. After conferring with Bobby Shelton, who had criticized the bombing, at least publicly, because it hurt the Klan's image, Colonel Al Lingo, Alabama's top law enforcement officer, ordered the Alabama Highway Patrol on September 29 to arrest Robert Chambliss, John Hall, and Charles Cagle. Shelton and Gene Reeves even accompanied Highway Patrolmen on their way to pick up the suspects.[48]

Lingo chose these three because both the FBI and state investigations revealed that early on the morning of September 5, Hall and Cagle (with his wife in tow) picked up a case of dynamite at Robert Chambliss's house and, not wishing to be caught with it, buried it in a field not far from Hall's home in Gardendale. Then Cagle, still nervous, asked a friend to dig it up and bury it somewhere else. Presumably, some of that dynamite was used to bomb the church. The case against the three was so weak that no officer would sign the possession charge form so Colonel Lingo signed it himself. (The FBI later learned that "responsible police officers were infuriated by . . . Lingo.") "We certainly beat the Kennedy crowd to the punch," crowed Governor Wallace after the men were taken into custody.[49]

But Chambliss, Cagle, and Hall didn't stay in jail long. All they could be charged with was possession of dynamite, which in Birmingham was tantamount to jaywalking. Chambliss went to trial and was acquitted. The charges against Hall and Cagle were later dropped. J. Edgar Hoover complained loudly that his investigation had been damaged; from now on Klansmen would quickly hire lawyers and keep their mouths shut.[50]

For John Nigger Hall, his arrest for possession of dynamite meant one thing: The Klan was setting him up to take the fall for the church bombing. His suspicions pointed to Chambliss. An FBI interview on September 15 had convinced him that the Bureau knew of the dynamite transfer, so he confronted Chambliss at a Klavern meeting four days later. Chambliss denied that he had told the FBI about Hall and Cagle's late-night visit to his home, but Hall didn't believe him. Desperate and afraid, Hall now turned to the only people he believed could protect him—the FBI. At first, Hall was a prime suspect in the church bombing—second on Rowe's list of the men capable of such an act. On September 25, Hall took a polygraph test, and the results definitely indicated knowledge of and possible planning or participation in the church bombing. Hall rejected these findings, insisting that "Black Muslims or other Negro groups" were responsible.[51]

Then in October, after his arrest, Hall's relationship with the FBI began to change. He started showing up at the field office, volunteering news he had picked up secondhand: that Tommy Blanton had remarked to a group of people that he "could tell you something about that [church] bombing"; that Herman Cash often complained to Hall that Blanton used to stop by his home early in the morning, inviting him to join Blanton in beating up Negroes. Although none of this information was critical, the FBI saw it as a sign that Hall wanted to cooperate, so at his request, they gave him another polygraph on October 15 that produced entirely new results: Although Hall may have bombed the Gaston Motel and other places before May 1963, now there was no evidence that he had participated in the church bombing. Although the FBI knew that the thirty-six-year-old truck driver was a convicted felon, "threw acid on Negroes," was chosen to murder Reverend Fred Shuttlesworth, drank excessively, beat his wife, and continued to be a prime suspect in a number of unsolved bombings, the Birmingham field office recommended to Washington that Hall become an FBI informant.[52]

Although Headquarters knew Hall's history, it didn't deter them from appointing him a Potential Confidential Informant, with his own code name and monetary rewards for information. Indeed, under the rules that governed the FBI's informant system, Hall's extensive criminal history made him all the more attractive. Hall's contact agent later noted, "If you want to catch fish, you've got to get into the water." Hall remained on the FBI payroll for the next two years but never caught any fish.[53]

Neither did Rowe, but Special Agent McFall continued to praise Rowe in both his quarterly reports and the periodic informant evaluations—Rowe was rated "Excellent" in late November—that he sent to Washington. He also recommended an increase in Rowe's monthly payments—up to $250 "for services rendered" and $60 for expenses. Hoover approved the request. Rowe now earned three times as much money as he received in February 1962.[54]

Ironically, much of Rowe's reporting now concerned the FBI's new informant Nigger Hall. Rowe reported his frequent drunkenness (at one poker party, Rowe estimated that Hall drank nine bottles of beer), describing him often as "very drunk" and "feeling no pain." Rowe recalled a visit to a junkyard in 1962, where for twenty-five cents each, Hall bought twenty-five empty hand grenades, noting that they could be filled with explosives. There was a Klavern meeting early in 1963, Rowe remembered, when Hall spoke authoritatively about constructing a shrapnel bomb that could "hurt a lot of Niggers." Rowe also noted that at a more recent meeting Hall admitted to telling Chambliss, Ingram, and Holt how to make a shrapnel bomb and thought that Ingram probably made the one used at Center Street. Holt, hearing all this, expressed his displeasure. "Those kinds of thoughts might get you buried," Rowe recalled Holt saying, to which Hall replied that anybody who tried to bury him better come at him from behind.[55]

None of this helped the FBI as the church bombing case dragged into the new year. On May 7, 1964, Rowe met with agents J. Brooke Blake and John Downey to review BAPBOMB. Rowe had "no idea" who the bombers were, he told the agents. If this surprised Blake, he didn't record it in his report. By this time, almost everybody in the field office knew their identities; even Hall, in December 1963, named Chambliss, Blanton, and Cherry. Neither agent had reviewed Rowe's previous statements or they would have noticed that Rowe's story had changed. Asked where he was the night before the bombing, Rowe said he spent the evening at a bar, drinking with Ross Keith, Charlie Cagle, Nigger Hall, and Sister White, who were going to pick him up early the next morning to watch blacks try to integrate Birmingham's churches. Rowe forgot that he had told McFall nine months earlier that those four men were the most likely suspects.

Rowe also unveiled a new version of how he learned about the bombing. He had been awakened at eleven o'clock—not by Byron McFall, as actually happened that morning, but by a call from Mary Louise McCord, the dispatcher at the Birmingham Police Department and a girlfriend who knew he was an FBI informant. "Thank God, honey, you're at home," Rowe claimed she said.

"What the hell is the matter?" Rowe replied.

"You didn't bomb the church."

"What church?"

"Hey, I'm happy you're at home and I know you're not involved. You better call the office; some little black kids have been killed down at the church and we're fixing to dispatch ambulances and units but I had . . . to be sure you were at home."

"Jesus Christ, are you serious? Where did it happen?" Rowe asked.

"Sixteenth Street Baptist Church . . . we've got to get units rolling."

Rowe said he hung up and immediately called the Bureau. "I want to tell you about the bombing," he told the FBI's telephone operator.

"Hey, hey, slow down," the man laughed. "There's no bombing. This is the first time I've ever known you to give me [a] bad scoop. . . . Did you have a good night?" Then, the operator abruptly stopped talking and asked Rowe to hang on.

He did, for ten minutes, or so he said.

"Jesus fucking Christ," said the operator when he returned. "Our switchboard is lit up like a Christmas tree . . . it went down and there's kids killed"—and he ended the call.[56]

Later, Rowe would add new characters and other events to this story. He claimed that he spent the weekend with Helen Metcalf, beginning Friday night with drinks at the VFW Club. Then, as he was taking her home, he passed the Sixteenth Street Baptist Church and saw a familiar car nearby driven by Tommy Blanton, with Bob Chambliss in the passenger seat. He caught up with them, flashed his lights, and the men talked. Chambliss flirted with Metcalf while Rowe asked Blanton what they were doing. Heading to Robert Thomas's home, Blanton said, but Rowe knew that he wasn't going in the right direction if that was his destination. Rowe told McFall on Saturday about seeing the two Klansmen, but the agent didn't think it significant. Metcalf spent Saturday night with Rowe and was in bed beside him when Mary Louise McCord called. Rowe told all this to McFall, he claimed. But McFall never recorded this part of the story, probably because Rowe never said it at the time. What *was* recorded were Rowe's remarks on December 10, 1964. It was now his "firm belief," he told Blake, that the church had been bombed by that group of angry refugees from Eastview No. 13—Robert Chambliss, Tommy Blanton, Bobby Frank Cherry, and Herman Cash, with help from Hubert Page and Bill Holt. Time would prove him almost right; he forgot Troy Ingram, who, with Chambliss's help, probably built the bomb. When it failed to explode on time, he went to check it and arrived to see it explode; witnesses saw a man who looked like Ingram limping away from the church, helped by another who was probably Tommy Blanton.[57]

Why Rowe decided to change his alibi is a mystery, because it only planted the seeds for further trouble. Alabama authorities later discovered that Birmingham police dispatcher Mary Louise McCord wasn't working that Sunday in September when Rowe said she called him in the morning. Federal investigators later contacted Helen Metcalf, who had remarried and refused to confirm or deny her presence with Rowe that weekend. And there was no reason for Rowe to telephone the field office to tell them about the bombing; the sound of the explosion, which reminded one eyewitness of a fleet of jets breaking the sound barrier, easily reached the FBI building located just a few blocks from the church.[58]

Almost everybody in Eastview Klavern No. 13 seemed to know that something was going to happen at the church that Sunday, most thinking that it would occur in the middle of the night when the building was unoccupied. Chambliss, not a popular fellow with the Eastview men, nonetheless received an unusual number of phone calls Saturday night. Shorty Thompson called, as did Ross Keith, Gene Reeves, Hubert Page, and, not surprisingly, Chambliss's cohorts in crime, the Blantons—father and son —and Bobby Frank Cherry. After talking with Chambliss, they went out on the town, creating alibis for one another. Ross Keith, Sister White, and Nigger Hall drank at a Birmingham bar and later spent the hours after midnight at a viaduct near Bessemer. Bobby Shelton was working late in his Tuscaloosa office along with Gene Reeves, who was mimeographing pamphlets to pass out at a prosegregation rally scheduled for Sunday afternoon. At 11:00 p.m., Shelton later claimed, news reached him that a group of angry blacks armed with rifles was headed his way. He alerted Exalted Cyclops Robert Thomas, who was visiting Bill Holt and his wife. Holt and Reeves were dispatched to a truck stop in Bessemer to head off the blacks. Hubert Page and his wife joined friends at a late-night bowling alley. Only Rowe had difficulty explaining where he was that night. Perhaps he believed that he didn't need an alibi because the FBI would protect him no matter what.[59]

Rowe's multiple stories also raise the possibility that he might have joined those who placed the bomb. It's hard to believe that Rowe, who was involved in so many violent events, was the only one of his group of Klan companions to be unaware of what was planned for Sunday, September 15, at the Sixteenth Street Baptist Church. When Rowe was polygraphed in the late 1970s, the results were mixed: One test indicated that he had prior knowledge, and the other, direct involvement. Doubts about his role would continue for the rest of his life.

Rowe contributed little to the case that the Birmingham field office finally built against the bombers. Agents found several eyewitnesses (unknown to Rowe) who could place Chambliss and Blanton at the church at around 2 a.m., eight hours before the bomb exploded; and two members of Chambliss's own family—his niece and sister-in-law, who heard him make incriminating statements—were willing to testify at trial. Twice in 1965 the Birmingham field office asked FBI Director Hoover for permission to consult with the U.S. attorney and the local prosecutor, neither of whom knew the identities of alleged perpetrators or the nature of the evidence against them because Hoover refused to share information. Both times, Hoover turned them down. "From an evaluation of the evidence received thus far," Hoover wrote the special agent in charge on May 19, 1965, "the chance of successful prosecution in State or Federal Court is very remote." Although Hoover constantly reminded his agents "that the reputation of the FBI depends upon your ability to solve [the bombing]," he would not act unless the case was rock solid. Hoover didn't bother to seek the counsel of the attorney general or other Justice Department divisions (such as Civil Rights) before reaching these conclusions. Ignoring his field agents, who "believed the climate of opinion . . . is very favorable toward . . . prosecution," Hoover believed strongly that no Alabama jury would convict white men, even for the murder of black children.[60]

Other factors may also have influenced Hoover's decision to oppose prosecution at that time. Some evidence was tainted by illegal taps on Klansmen's telephones and the installation of microphones in their homes through unlawful entry. The twelve hundred pages of transcripts obtained through such surveillance were useless in court. (When the Justice Department asked to see them anyway, Hoover refused their request.) A public trial might also expose the FBI's informants, chief among them Gary Thomas Rowe, revealing his history of violence committed while employed by the Bureau. Finally, there was a potentially damaging secret hidden within BAPBOMB. That case of dynamite that Nigger Hall and Charlie Cagle picked up on September 5, 1963, didn't just connect them to Chambliss and the church bombing; it connected the FBI, too. When agents interviewed Hall on September 15, they made it clear that they were aware of the dynamite transfer, probably through surveillance. Indeed, Chambliss's niece later claimed that the Bureau had a photograph of Hall and Cagle moving the box. In short, the FBI knew ten days before the death of the four young girls that the most dangerous Klansmen—likely responsible for a summer filled with bombings—had a box of dynamite, and they didn't alert the Birmingham police, who could have seized the crate and arrested the men. It might have been enough to have prevented the bombing of the church.[61]

Hoover's failure to act, later called "a serious error" by the Justice Department task force investigating Gary Thomas Rowe, didn't end the Bureau's investigation; on the contrary, agents were ordered to work harder, cultivate more informants, and even harass Klansmen, hoping one would crack and incriminate the bombers. But it wasn't until 1977 that a young Alabama attorney general named Bill Baxley persuaded an Alabama jury to convict Robert Chambliss of murder. Another courageous prosecutor, U.S. Attorney Doug Jones, finally brought the last two living suspects—Tommy Blanton and Bobby Frank Cherry—to trial in 2001 and 2002. They were found guilty. "Justice delayed," said Jones, "is still justice."[62]

CHAPTER FIVE

Cat and Mouse

ROWE'S LAST FOURTEEN MONTHS in the Klan brought new challenges: changes in the Bureau, the Eastview Klavern, and his personal life; more accusations that he was an FBI informant; and increased racial tensions as the civil rights movement returned to Alabama. Rowe also seemed more willing to defuse or prevent Klan violence during this period, perhaps a response to the guilt he might have felt about either knowing of or failing to prevent the bombing of the Sixteenth Street Baptist Church. One of Rowe's FBI handlers later thought that Rowe felt awful about the death of the four girls and that he had let the Bureau down.

In January 1964, Rowe learned that Byron McFall was leaving the Bureau for a job in the private sector. He would not miss McFall and felt none of the emotional turmoil that accompanied Kemp's departure in 1961. Although McFall was his handler for two and a half years—longer than any other agent—they weren't close. McFall often called Rowe "boy," which annoyed Rowe. When Rowe later wrote his memoir, he never mentioned McFall. "McFall was an old-timer," said an agent who knew him well. "Rowe needed 'Action Jackson' on his case." McFall's successor would be Special Agent J. Brooke Blake, if Rowe agreed. Blake had joined the FBI in 1955 after earning a law degree at the University of Baltimore Law School, served in Baltimore and Pittsburgh, and then in 1962 came to Birmingham, where he worked for the major theft squad. After September

15, 1963, he was switched to the group of agents investigating BAPBOMB. Before that fall he had no contact with Rowe; he didn't even know his code name, but he knew his reputation. From briefings and office memos, he realized that the man McFall called BH-248 "was somebody of major importance to the government."[1]

Blake was McFall's personal choice to succeed him, and the two men frequently met with Rowe for coffee and conversation, an audition of sorts. "He was a . . . pretty big guy, about 220 . . . a tough character," Blake later recalled. "He always wanted to be a cop and a person who, like all informants, you had to control. He was the type that would run off and put his safety in jeopardy . . . if you didn't dominate him." Blake also knew that an agent's success depended on the quality of his informants, so he very much hoped that Rowe would accept him and was honored that he was being considered for the job. Blake was nervous—"the transition of an informant from one agent to another is a very difficult thing," he noted —but Rowe took to him immediately. "He likes you," McFall told him, "and we think it will work." Rowe considered Blake "a formidable fighter . . . not a man to take any guff from the Klan." But it was those very qualities that almost got Blake killed just a month after becoming Rowe's handler.[2]

The occasion was the annual Klan convention, or Klanvocation. Imperial Wizard Shelton was pleased that this year representatives from six states, and two "Klan sympathizers" from Nova Scotia, would gather at Birmingham's Tutweiler Hotel on February 9–10 to hear speeches, discuss problems, and dine together at an elaborate banquet. It was to be a public event; Birmingham's mayor and Governor Wallace were invited, and members of the press could cover it without the usual fear of being beaten by angry Klansmen. No robes and hoods this time. Klansmen were ordered to wear their best suits and ties, and anyone found drinking faced a ninety-day suspension. But they were allowed to bring their guns. "We'll bring in some kind of an arsenal," one Klansman told a Klavern meeting on January 23, pushing aside his coat to display a pistol.[3]

At the end of a meeting on the night of February 7, Bill Holt asked Rowe whether he had any electric blasting caps left over from the case he had received more than a year earlier from the Warrior Klavern's James Moore. Holt wanted four, and Rowe agreed to provide them the next morning when they checked in at the Tutweiler Hotel. Rowe later informed Blake, and he was told to go ahead. If the switch took place, Rowe said, he would walk to the right of Holt or whoever actually received them. Blake and other agents would be on the scene and would follow Holt to see what became of the blasting caps. Blake thought it a good chance "to prevent . . . a bombing," he said later. "God knows, we had enough of them."[4]

But when Rowe tried to give Holt the blasting caps, which he had wrapped individually in pink toilet paper and put in a tobacco pouch, Holt refused to take them, noting that there were FBI men all over the place and he was "hotter than a firecracker." So Rowe gave the pouch to a Bessemer Klansman named "Big John" Burnette, a friend of Gene Thomas's who accompanied the men as they walked through the lobby toward the hotel's exit—Rowe walking to Burnette's right, as planned. Outside, they ran into Brooke Blake and John Downey. Rowe recalled Blake saying to Thomas, "Hello, sweetie." "Do you know who those fuckers were?" Thomas asked his friends. No, they said. They were FBI, Thomas explained, and they had recently badgered him in an interview. Burnette became very nervous—he didn't want to be caught carrying blasting caps.[5]

Blake and Downey followed the three Klansmen down the street. "I'm going to kill the son-of-a-bitch, he's screwing me his last time," Rowe recalled Thomas saying. Hoping to lose the agents, the three Klansmen turned into a nearby alley. When Thomas saw that there was no way out of the alley and that they would have to turn around and face the agents, he said, "I'm going to kill the fucker if he comes down this alley" and pulled out his gun.

Rowe panicked. For the first time in his career, he faced a fatal choice: let Thomas shoot Blake and Downey or try to prevent it and blow his cover. "You're not really going to kill him," Rowe said to Thomas.

But Thomas replied, "I'm going to kill the fucker."

According to Rowe, Blake said to the three Klansmen, "Get out of the goddamn alley. . . . I'll come up and kick the shit out of all three of you."

Rowe decided to take a chance. Stepping forward, he said, "Hey, you want to fight, cocksucker, you fight me. . . . I'll whip your goddamn ass." That seemed to break the tension, and Blake turned and walked away.[6]

It's likely that Rowe added some invented details to this story, and his later description doesn't entirely conform to his contemporary reports. Nonetheless, Blake remained convinced that Rowe was prepared to break cover to save his life. "I think it goes to the merits of the rapport [between] an informant and the handler," he said later.[7]

The year 1964 also brought a new Exalted Cyclops, ending, at least temporarily, the reign of Robert Thomas. Thomas, now forty-four, had long been attacked for reacting mildly to the civil rights activists, causing some fellow Klansmen to suspect that he was an FBI informant. Many also thought him hypocritical and weak for ordering Klansmen to get rid of their Negro help while his wife, Mildred, insisted that she keep her own black maid. Thomas's successor was Ronnie Tidwell, an ex-con whose coming to power worried Rowe. He thought Tidwell, who usually carried two pistols, was a "hothead" and "a radical," he told Blake, and "harder to control than Robert Thomas." Rowe recalled that Tidwell's answer to Martin Luther King's demonstrators was to send in the Klansmen with their shotguns blazing.[8]

Tidwell wanted to create a more militant Klavern. A licensed brown belt, he taught judo and karate, bought new gymnastic equipment, and gave the Eastview men instructions on how to make bombs. In a private meeting held in late March, Tidwell urged the Action Squads to go after blacks seen in white areas. "I want the Negroes terrorized for being . . . where they don't belong," he said. "No holds barred, use blackjacks, buckshot, and chains." If Klansmen were arrested, he would provide them a lawyer—his father, Ira. Tidwell also decided to focus his energies on destroying the American National Bank of Birmingham—an integrated institution that hired blacks and encouraged them to open accounts. Rowe played a key role in defeating Tidwell's plans.[9]

In order to restrain Tidwell, Rowe first befriended him. At a Klavern meeting on April 2, he stood by Tidwell when two members tried to overthrow him. "Bad reports" about Tidwell were circulating, said Robert Chambliss, who still attended Eastview meetings while remaining a Cahaba Boy. Tidwell, an unemployed electrician, had recently left his wife and was living in a trailer on his father's property; that, and his criminal record, cast doubt on his fitness as Exalted Cyclops. Loel Rogers, a Chambliss ally, volunteered to take Tidwell's place. Rowe stepped in, arguing that Klan procedures weren't being followed; before an officer is removed, there must be a trial. Then he attacked Rogers personally. As a Klansman, "all he ever did was pass out literature downtown," while Rowe and others fought and went to jail. Let Tidwell alone, Rowe argued; at last, they had an E.C. "who was not scared to do something." Rowe received enthusiastic applause.

Tidwell stayed on and relied on Rowe for advice, especially on how to deal with the American National Bank.[10]

Tear gas might work well, Tidwell told Rowe on the morning of April 14. It could cause confusion and panic, giving the Klan a chance to beat "a few Negroes." Dynamite would be better, but fearing a tapped phone, Tidwell spoke in code: "Something ought to be deposited in the bank, but I don't have any money." Rowe knew what he was talking about and said that he didn't have any money either. Tidwell had one final idea, to "toss a couple of hand grenades into the window at the bank." Rowe thought the police presence would be too great, so he urged him to delay the attack. Tidwell said he would consult Robert Thomas, who was now Grand Titan of northern Alabama, and, if he approved, would go ahead.[11]

It turned out to be a long day. Rowe's phone didn't stop ringing. Among his callers were nine Birmingham cops, two department "complaint clerks," and Jefferson County's chief deputy sheriff. All had the same message: The bank was "hot"; Rowe should tell the boys to stay away. Don't even go downtown, said Deputy Sheriff Raymond Belcher. Rowe reached Thomas at 8:00 p.m. The Grand Titan was strongly opposed to an attack on the bank. The area was "saturated with police," Thomas said; there was no sense in losing good men in what would be a suicidal mission. He planned to meet with Tidwell later that evening and would order him to drop the plan. Anyway, Thomas laughed, having "all the niggers" at the American National Bank might be a good idea because it would "get them out of our banks."

At 10:30 p.m., Thomas checked in. Nothing would happen that night, he assured Rowe, but beyond that, he didn't know. Tidwell was angry and had told Thomas, "The people of Birmingham are tired of the Klan's in-action." Rowe called Blake later that night. For the present, everything was OK, he said, but the crisis wasn't over.[12]

FBI agents spent most of that night and the following morning watching Klansmen's homes, but nothing happened. Rowe was awakened by an early call from Blake. Tidwell had given them the slip; did Rowe know where he was? He might be with his girlfriend, Rowe said, or at the Talley Ho Club, one of his favorite hangouts. Blake also reported that Klansman Harry Walker, Robert Chambliss's nephew, had been seen with Tidwell and Thomas the day before. What did that mean? There were two possibilities,

Rowe said. Walker and Thomas might have been "baby sitting" Tidwell, making sure no violence would occur. Or, and this was more ominous, perhaps he and Tidwell were planning something, as Walker was an Action Squad leader.[13]

Deputy Sheriff Belcher gave Rowe more bad news that morning. Officers had seen Tidwell the previous day with Bob Chambliss and Gene Thomas (who had recently shot a black laborer picketing U.S. Pipe in Bessemer), and today Tidwell and Thomas had disappeared. Belcher was afraid that they might bomb Arthur Shores's home again and felt that only Rowe could find them. "The FBI, City, and State are out and they . . . should get their butts home," Belcher told Rowe. It turned out to be a false alarm: Tidwell surfaced later that day and had apparently decided to follow Robert Thomas's orders to leave the bank alone, for the time being. Thomas had given him a new job, he told Rowe, and ordered Rowe to get his Action Squad ready for missionary work on April 18. He invited Rowe to meet him for drinks at eleven that night, when he would explain their new assignment.[14]

Thomas had already briefed Rowe on what was coming, so Tidwell's news didn't surprise him. According to the Birmingham police, "Negro males were dating white teenage girls and carrying on immoral activities" at the Shannon Mines strip pit, Tidwell told Rowe and his men, Ross Keith and Cecil Hanson, over drinks at the New Yorker Restaurant. As a newly appointed squad leader, Rowe was responsible for choosing the punishment. He thought "flogging" was appropriate, but Tidwell wanted something stronger. As the group drove to the strip pit, Rowe noticed that everyone carried pistols except Hanson, who had two rifles. They spent the night overlooking the scene, waiting for the couples to appear. Tidwell seemed "very jumpy" and Rowe was convinced he wanted to use his gun; somebody was bound to get killed. Hoping to prevent a bloodbath, Rowe tried "to calm Tidwell down" and repeatedly told the men that they should flog only the youngsters. When nobody showed up by daybreak, they left.[15]

Five days later, at an April 24 Klavern meeting, Ronnie Tidwell resigned as Exalted Cyclops. He cited as reasons the "friction" caused by his holding the position, a new job, and the desire to seek election as constable in Irondale, where, he probably thought, he could do as he pleased without interference. Robert Thomas recommended that Rowe become Exalted

Cyclops, but Rowe immediately nominated Gene Reeves—an Eastview veteran less reckless than young Tidwell—and Reeves got the post. Perhaps Rowe thought his show of support for Reeves might woo him away from the group that continued to suspect he was an informer.[16]

What Brooke Blake called "the shadows of suspicion" intensified during the summer of 1964, probably because of Rowe's recent behavior. Every time Klansmen called for action, Rowe was opposed: He saved Blake's life at the Tutweiler Hotel; he blocked Tidwell's efforts to bomb the American National Bank; he chose flogging instead of murder for the interracial couples; and on April 19, he resigned as head of his Action Squad. (Hoover didn't want him to hold a position where he would be responsible for instigating violence, but he was allowed to remain with the group.) And whenever he was asked to serve as Exalted Cyclops, he declined. Not even Rowe's more violent activities could convince those who suspected Rowe that they were wrong. In May, at Birmingham's Legion Field ballpark, Rowe got into a fight with a black man who accidentally spilled hot dogs and beer on him. When he felt somebody grab him from behind, he "spun around and . . . knocked him on his ass." It was an angry police officer who then "jumped up" and pulled his gun, which Rowe took away from him. Rowe wasn't arrested—proof, his enemies probably thought, that he had friends in the Bureau. And, of course, he did, although when Bureau agents were told of Rowe's fistfight they dismissed it as "a piece of trivia," because the event wasn't Klan-related and Rowe was always allowed to do what he wanted on his own time.[17]

July 4, 1964, began with a celebration, but for Tommy Rowe the day ended dismally. He was in Lakewood Park in Atlanta, Georgia, at a "Patriot's Rally Against Tyranny." The featured speakers that night were two great sons of the South: Governor Ross Barnett of Mississippi and Alabama's George C. Wallace. Eleven thousand people listened as Barnett attacked the Civil Rights Act of 1964, signed into law two days earlier by President Lyndon B. Johnson, whom Barnett called a "counterfeit confederate . . . who [might] someday resign from the white race." Suddenly two black men and a white woman (later identified as members of the Student Nonviolent Coordinating Committee, or SNCC) booed and hissed the governor, causing the crowd to go wild. "Kill 'em!" "Hit 'em," and "We want Wallace," the people cried, while others attacked the three with their fists and metal folding chairs. As the civil rights workers were taken away, Governor Wallace rushed to the podium and tried to calm the crowd, and then delivered a rousing speech.[18]

Later that evening, Rowe joined a select group of Klansmen that included Imperial Wizard Bobby Shelton, Grand Titan Robert Thomas, and the Grand Dragons of North Carolina, Tennessee, and Georgia. Shelton told Rowe that Bill Holt had formally accused him of being an FBI informant. Not mentioned were the earlier accusations of Gene Thomas, the Klansman who had been with Rowe during the attacks at the Bessemer carnival and A. G. Gaston's mansion and had wanted to shoot Agent Blake at the Tutweiler convention. Thomas had never liked or trusted Rowe and was jealous of the younger man's prominence in the Klan. He told Shelton that he had twice seen Rowe leaving the federal building that housed the FBI's field office. Thomas asked Rowe what he had been doing there and later recalled that Rowe told him "some kind of bull story. . . . He wouldn't ever give you a straight answer." Thomas was convinced that Rowe was an FBI informant and urged the Imperial Wizard to eject Rowe from the Klan. But Shelton, still trusting Rowe, rejected the request. Thomas kept his concerns to himself, but Holt was quite public about his dislike of Rowe, which forced Shelton to act.

The Alabama Klan's chief lawyer, or Imperial Klonsel, Matthew Hobson Murphy, had hired private investigators to learn "just what [his] allegiance is." If the charges were untrue, Rowe was told, he would be cleared and Holt "banished" from the Klan. Standing up for Rowe, Robert Thomas maintained that what was really bothering Holt was his wife's infidelity —Rowe was "playing around" with her, as were other Klansmen. Murphy promised to have an answer within two weeks.[19]

In the days that followed, Rowe took extra precautions: watching for strangers walking close behind him, avoiding the spots where he usually met Blake, checking his small apartment for bugs or other signs that somebody had been there. He found nothing out of the ordinary. Robert Thomas called him on July 13 to say that the secret hearing was scheduled for July 15. But on the appointed day, Thomas told Rowe that the meeting had been postponed and gave no reason. Rowe felt better; perhaps he wouldn't be challenged after all. But Blake warned him that it might be a trick and urged him not to relax. Above all, Rowe must not "reveal his identity under any circumstances." Rowe seemed jaunty, confident that he could handle anything that came. "Anybody with a little guts can play cat and mouse with these people," Rowe supposedly said. If he was cleared, his position would be "greatly enhanced and his future use more valuable."[20]

Eastview's meeting on July 16 began normally and reassured Rowe that nothing was going to happen. It was an "open house," so Klan wives were present and everyone seemed to be in a festive mood. *The Birth of a Nation* was shown, and it was close to eleven o'clock when the film ended and Rowe got ready to leave the hall. Then, Robert Creel, by this time a Grand Dragon at the state level, called the meeting to order and asked lawyer Matt Murphy to come forward. Rowe had been tricked, and his confidence disappeared: "[I was] just about ready to crap in my jeans," he said later. Murphy then announced that although he had found no evidence that Gary Thomas Rowe was an FBI informer, he still had his doubts. To make absolutely certain, he wanted to meet with Rowe and "feel him out."

Nigger Hall rescued Rowe. "Let me ask you something," he said to Murphy. "Would you know Tommy Rowe if he was to walk in that god-damn door?"

"Absolutely. Absolutely," Murphy said.

"When was the last time you seen him?" Hall asked.

"Two weeks ago."

"If you got any questions to ask Rowe, . . . move over two inches and you'll be touching him."

Murphy, startled by this turn of events, was speechless. Rowe turned and faced him. "Murphy, you're a queer son of a bitch," he later recalled saying. To the others, Rowe proclaimed: "This man has accused me of being an FBI agent to Klansmen all over Birmingham and he's endangering my life. He says he's got photos and film; make him put them on the table."

"You're too willing," Murphy said.

"You're damn right I'm willing; I haven't done anything." Then Rowe reared back, ready to punch Murphy, but some Klansmen stepped between them. "You old bastard," Rowe said, "be damn sure you know what you're doing tonight, because if I don't kill you, I'm going to sue hell out of you."

Hall then asked Murphy, "Is he snitching on us?"—reminding the lawyer that he had personally told Hall that Rowe was an informant.

Murphy stuttered nervously, admitting only that he "might be able to prove Rowe is a snitch." Bill Holt spoke up, denying that he had ever accused Rowe of anything. Knowing that was a lie, Rowe ripped Holt's shirt and slapped his face. Grand Dragon Creel shouted at the men, telling them to stop fighting or "he would pull the Klavern's charter unless order was restored." Holt and Murphy were told that they would be investigated to determine whether they were trying to wreck the Klavern. If the charge was true, Holt would be dismissed and Murphy fired from his job as the Klan's attorney. That brought an end to the confrontation and the evening's events. Rowe felt that he had been completely exonerated, although Creel later told him that if he found out that Rowe really was an FBI informant, he would kill him. Although Rowe was never again officially accused of being an informant, there were Klansmen, like Gene Thomas, who continued to suspect him, and Rowe was careful to keep his eye on them. And Creel's threat indicated that he would never be able to relax completely. Agent Blake later agreed, saying, "They sure as heck didn't trust Tommy ever."[21]

With Birmingham momentarily quiet, Rowe's life during the next two months was fairly normal, and he spent his time on personal concerns. His marriage finally ended in divorce, so he was now responsible for alimony and child support. Meeting the payments was difficult because his job at the White Dairy was coming to an end. His boss hated the Klan and, knowing of Rowe's membership, constantly taunted him about it. So Rowe quit that summer and, with the Bureau's help, went to work for the Jefferson Distributing Company, selling and then delivering beer in a company truck. He accepted a cut in pay but told Blake he didn't mind because the regular schedule left him more time for Bureau work. Blake thought Rowe's decision worth praising and informed Headquarters that he was confident Rowe would discharge his new duties "without embarrassing the Bureau or revealing his identity." But when summer ended and the demand for beer declined, Rowe, lacking seniority, was the first to be laid off. The only work he could find was helping out part-time at a local bar. Concerned that Rowe might take a job that interfered with his FBI duties, the Bureau arranged for him to work at Pizitz's Department Store as a floorwalker, watching customers for signs of shoplifting. He hoped this job would last; the hours were all right and he earned more money than he had as a truck driver and bartender.[22]

Amid this uncertainty, J. Brooke Blake resigned from the FBI in late September, and Rowe again had to adjust to a new contact agent. This proved to be easy. Agent Neil Shanahan was in his early thirties and was warm, outgoing, and amusing. Blake thought him "very sharp . . . a type of person that would relate to Tommy right away." Shanahan knew how important Rowe was both to the Bureau and to his own career—Blake had called Rowe "the best informant we had in the Ku Klux Klan." Shanahan also enjoyed Rowe's company. "He was a man of simple pleasures. [He] likes girls, smokes a pipe, drinks beer, a [good] person to chat with . . . a man's man," he later said.[23]

Shanahan soon learned for himself how valuable Rowe could be. At a Klavern meeting on September 17, Ronnie Tidwell reported that "race mixing" was going on at the Flame Club, a black-owned establishment in Fairfield that also catered to whites—mostly college students, or as the Klan preferred, "thrill-seeking beatniks." Rumor had it that white girls had been seen there dancing with black men. Everyone agreed that this must be stopped as soon as possible, so a five-man Klan delegation went to the club to see for themselves.[24]

On Saturday night, September 26, Tommy Rowe, accompanied by Gene Thomas, Cecil Hanson, and Curtis Doles, entered the Flame Club and were shown to a table. The club was crowded with nearly three hundred people, mostly black. Over cocktails and beer, the Klansmen discovered that the rumors were true; "whites and coloreds were sitting together, dancing, kissing," Rowe later claimed. These "open displays of affection" angered the Klansmen and they left quickly without finishing their drinks. On their way to Bessemer, Gene Thomas told them he was going to stop at a nearby gas station to telephone a friend who he thought could help them. A few minutes later, a Bessemer police car arrived, and its occupant, a Lieutenant Barnes, spoke with Thomas and Rowe. After Thomas explained to the officer what they had seen at the Flame Club, Barnes said, "What do you need?" Thomas replied, "Dynamite, hand grenades, and a submachine gun." Barnes said he would see what he could do and drove off. A half hour later, he was back with everything Thomas had ordered: eight sticks of dynamite, a Thompson .45-caliber submachine gun, and about a half dozen hand grenades. The Klansmen then headed for the Klavern hall to devise a plan using Barnes's gifts.

Calls went out to other brethren, and soon about thirty-five men had gathered. Thomas explained what they were about to do: Two sticks of dynamite would be placed at the rear of the club, and when they exploded, the men would throw a few grenades inside, forcing the people into the street, where the Klansmen, situated at several strategic spots, would blast away with the machine gun and other automatic weapons. Everyone thought this was a splendid idea, and they got everything ready. Rowe apparently thought it impossible to get away briefly to phone Shanahan, so he climbed into Thomas's car, which led the others to Fairfield. But as they approached the Flame Club, they noticed several Fairfield police cars out front. Cops were everywhere, putting down an altercation and dragging blacks to their squad cars. Thomas stopped immediately to let Curtis Doles run back to alert the others that the attack was off, for now.[25]

The following night, Rowe, Thomas, and Hanson met with Grand Titan Robert Thomas, who listened to their plan and told them to try again next Saturday night. But three days later, Robert Thomas canceled the attack after Imperial Wizard Shelton informed him that the assault was "politically inappropriate." Thomas asked Rowe to meet with his old friend and Klan sympathizer, Deputy Sheriff Belcher of Jefferson County, to see whether there was a legal way to accomplish their goal. Rowe informed Shanahan of these events, and although the Bureau worried that it might endanger the informant, it notified local police and the owner of the Flame Club of possible trouble.

Belcher was happy to help out. Like Thomas, he emphasized legal remedies when he saw Rowe and Hanson on October 3, sounding like "Mr. Law Enforcement." Klansmen should "act like normal citizens," he told them, "and file their complaints through the proper channels if they wish to have the Flame Club closed." He suggested another visit to the club to look for violations of the law and gave them a checklist to follow. Was "bootleg whiskey" being sold? Did any of the customers have weapons? Were any patrons minors? Were prostitutes working the club, and did they offer interracial sex? Then Belcher relaxed and became his old self. If the men found no evidence of illegality, he assured them, he would give them what they needed—"wildcat whiskey" and drugs ("benny pills"). Once Rowe and Hanson planted them on the premises, the club would be raided and closed.[26]

By October 13, the latter plan had been adopted, and Belcher told Rowe that everything was set: The liquor and the pills could be picked up at any time. Once Belcher learned that the goods were in place at the club (under the sink in the men's bathroom was a good spot), officers working for Alcoholic Beverages Control (ABC) would be tipped off, sweep through the building, find the stash, and close the club. And that was how it was accomplished. On October 14, ABC officers raided the club, discovered the illegal substances, and shut it down.[27]

Everyone (except possibly Gene Thomas, who preferred destroying the club and its patrons) was happy with the outcome. At a Klavern meeting on October 22, Robert Thomas read a letter from Imperial Wizard Shelton praising Tommy Rowe and other Klansmen who "had discovered a dangerous situation of race mixing . . . at the Flame Club . . . and, at personal disregard for their own safety and well-being, entered this club on a Saturday night and associated with armed Negroes and gained sufficient evidence that enabled law enforcement officials to close the club." Rowe promised Shanahan that he would get a copy of Shelton's letter for the Bureau. Shanahan was very pleased with Rowe's achievement, preventing "a possible holocaust." In his quarterly report for the special agent in charge, Shanahan wrote: "It is the opinion of the contacting agent that had the informant not been able to provide information to the Bureau . . . , an attack on this club with dynamite, hand grenades and machine guns would have occurred which might have resulted in death or injury to as many as 100 persons." Nothing was said to Washington about Rowe's role in smuggling bootleg whiskey and pills into the club—in effect, framing the club's owner, who was guilty of nothing more than allowing blacks and whites to socialize together.[28]

Early in 1965, the civil rights movement again changed Rowe's life. The Civil Rights Act of 1964 gave blacks access to public accommodations—hotels, motels, theaters, restaurants, and the like—at least theoretically. Segregationists resisted these gains, and change was achieved slowly and over many years. But more important than blacks' opportunity to buy a hamburger was their ability to vote—which had long been denied them in the South. Gaining access to the ballot box was the next critical objective of civil rights workers, and in the struggle that ensued, Selma, Alabama, became the major battleground.

Selma typified the challenges facing the civil rights movement. Slaves and cotton had been the foundations of its economic success since the city was founded in 1820. An important slave market flourished there, and its proximity to the Alabama River allowed cotton owners to ship their crop to Mobile and beyond. In the twentieth century, a different kind of slavery existed for Selma's blacks: Jim Crow laws, sharecropping, and total segregation kept them poor and isolated. Less than 1 percent of the black population of Dallas County was registered to vote. Civil rights groups, such as Martin Luther King's SCLC and the more militant SNCC, began working there early in the 1960s but had made little progress by 1965. Selma was the home of the first White Citizens Council, and Sheriff Jim Clark ruled with an iron fist. For the movement, Selma would be Birmingham redux: Civil rights workers would demonstrate for the right to vote until Clark snapped and hauled them off to jail, arousing the nation's conscience and forcing President Johnson to send a voting rights bill to Congress. The strategy worked, but it cost four lives.[29]

Martin Luther King, Jr., and the television cameras that now accompanied him, arrived in Selma on January 2, 1965, a few days after he received the Nobel Peace Prize. More than seven hundred people crowded Brown Chapel African Methodist Episcopal Church and heard him say: "When we get the right to vote, we will send to the statehouse not men who will stand in the doorways of universities to keep Negroes out, but men who will uphold the cause of justice. Give us the ballot."

Sheriff Clark said "Never," the word emblazoned on a button he wore on his coat. When Amelia Boynton, a longtime movement activist, marched on the courthouse on January 18, Sheriff Clark, holding a club, yelled, "Where are you going?" Before she could answer, "Clark grabbed me by my coat, propelled me around and started shoving me down the street," she later recalled. "I was stunned. I saw cameramen and newspaper reporters around . . . and I said, 'I hope the newspapers see you acting this role.'" He said, "Damn it, I hope they do." And they did. The next day, the *New York Times* and the *Washington Post* featured a photograph of Clark manhandling Boynton on their front pages.[30]

Ten days later, the men of Eastview Klavern No. 13 went on alert. Because of the marches and demonstrations in Selma, Robert Thomas told them that they should be prepared to go there if needed to support the local authorities. Part of that preparation entailed the collection of new arms, which Rowe had observed and recorded for Neil Shanahan a few months earlier when he was in Jacksonville, Florida, at a Klan rally. Socializing with Grand Dragon Creel and other officials in Creel's motel room, Rowe saw a shoebox protruding from under the bed, which he later determined held two bundles of dynamite—fourteen sticks in all, with blasting caps attached. He assumed the package was headed for Alabama. Further- more, while riding in Gene Thomas's car one day, he had noticed, when Thomas opened the console separating the front bucket seats, six hand grenades. Thomas's car also carried a double-barreled shotgun.[31]

This was only a small part of the Klan's arsenal. Shanahan asked Rowe to compile a list of Eastview and Bessemer Klansmen and their weapons. Of the eighteen he was able to survey, he found a total of eighteen pistols and thirty-five rifles (including shotguns and three machine guns); four had hand grenades, and one, FBI informant Nigger Hall, had dynamite. Gene Thomas, now Bessemer's Exalted Cyclops, had the largest collection of weapons: two pistols (a .38 and a .45), an automatic shotgun, three 303 Enfield rifles, a 30-30 Winchester rifle, two M-1 rifles, a Browning automatic rifle, a German automatic machine pistol, and hand grenades and blasting caps. Not listed was Thomas's bullwhip, which was hidden in the family's washing machine. Thomas and his Klan brothers were ready for Selma.[32]

In Selma and the other small towns where civil rights organizers went, the violence escalated. On February 18, after an enthusiastic rally at the Zion Methodist Church in Marion, a crowd of about four hundred marched to the Perry County Courthouse. They never made it. Arrayed before them was a group of more than two hundred angry law enforcers —Marion police officers, Perry County deputy sheriffs, state troopers led by Colonel Al Lingo, and townspeople brandishing clubs. Nearby was Sher- iff Jim Clark chatting with reporters. Suddenly there was a scream from the church behind them. Elderly parishioners, unable to march, were flee- ing police, who were forcing them into the street. Someone turned off the streetlights, and in the darkness that now covered marchers and troopers alike, the cops and deputies rushed into the crowd. Some, like twenty-six- year-old Jimmy Lee Jackson and his mother, fled to a nearby café, seek- ing safety. Police came after them and beat Mrs. Jackson, and during the struggle that ensued, Jimmy Lee was shot. A few days later, he died.

Jackson's death galvanized the movement. Some called for a march on Montgomery, where they wanted to lay Jackson's body on the capitol steps. From this impractical scheme grew the idea of a march from Selma to Montgomery on Sunday, March 7. After church that morning, six hun- dred marchers began the fifty-four-mile trek but were stopped while trying to cross the Edmund Pettus Bridge leading to Montgomery. When Sheriff

Clark yelled, "Get those god-damned niggers," troopers on horseback and volunteer police attacked the group, beating them with bullwhips, bats, and electric cattle prods until they fell back, blinded by tear gas.

The day would be remembered as Bloody Sunday, and television brought the assault into American homes that evening—images of charging horses, billowing tear gas, and swinging clubs. ABC News interrupted its Sunday night movie, *Judgment at Nuremburg*, for a report that included stark footage of the violence on the Edmund Pettus Bridge. It was estimated that more than 48 million Americans watched these horrific scenes.

"*Unhuman*. No other word can describe [it]," journalist George B. Leonard later wrote. "I was not aware that at the same moment people [everywhere] were feeling what my wife and I felt; that at various times all over the country . . . people would drop whatever they were doing; that some of them would leave home without changing clothes, borrow money, overdraw their checking accounts; board planes, buses, trains, cars; . . . that these people, mostly unknown to one another, would move for a single purpose: to place themselves alongside the Negroes they had watched on television." One of those people was a thirty-nine-year-old housewife, mother, and college student in Detroit named Viola Liuzzo. The events of Bloody Sunday caused her to break down and cry. A few weeks later, she left her family and her classes at Wayne State University to go to Selma.[33]

So did James Reeb, a white Unitarian minister from Boston. After dinner on the night of March 9, Reeb and two fellow ministers, unfamiliar with Selma's streets, wound up outside the Silver Moon Cafe, a known Klan hangout, where four thugs attacked them. One clubbed Reeb, fatally fracturing his skull. "Here's how it feels to be a nigger down here," screamed his killer.[34]

In the days that followed Bloody Sunday, demonstrators calling for the swift passage of a voting rights act marched in more than eighty cities. President Lyndon B. Johnson was deluged with telegrams from citizens and members of Congress. Wanting to be remembered by history as the "civil rights president," Johnson called Congress into special session on March 15 and went before them to deliver the greatest speech of his presidency. He announced that he would soon send them the strongest voting rights bill in U.S. history. The cause of black Americans "must be our cause too," he told the somber chamber, "because it is not just Negroes, but really all of us who must overcome the crippling legacy of bigotry and injustice." Then, shocking segregationists and civil rights activists alike, who thought they would never hear these words spoken by a southerner, let alone a president, Johnson said: "And we shall overcome." Everyone leaped up as one. One presidential aide noted, "In the galleries, Negroes and whites . . . wept unabashedly."[35]

Although the civil rights movement had won an extraordinary victory, organizers still planned to march on Montgomery to present to Governor Wallace a list of grievances. Invitations to join them had been sent to members of the clergy, educators, and show-business personalities—anyone of good heart who was nonviolent. Their four-day Voting Rights March would start in Selma on Sunday, March 21, and end at the steps of the capitol in Montgomery, where Martin Luther King would address them. Their luck held again when, on March 17, federal judge Frank M. Johnson granted King's request and issued an injunction ordering that the march be allowed to take place without interference. Governor Wallace complained that the state lacked the resources to protect the marchers, so President Johnson, armed now with Judge Johnson's edict, federalized the Alabama National Guard and sent FBI agents, military police, two thousand army personnel, and U.S. marshals to Selma, bringing Washington's protective presence to the more than three thousand participants.[36]

For the men of Eastview Klavern No. 13, this was a nightmare come true. A second Reconstruction had brought federal troops again to the South, and they were stunned and angry. Grand Dragon Robert Creel quoted Imperial Wizard Shelton at a meeting on March 16: "People are getting up in arms all over the State and saying that if the Negroes can march, so can the white people." The normally phlegmatic Robert Thomas thought a new tactic appropriate: Instead of confronting demonstrators in groups, a single Klansman should go to Selma, find a tall building overlooking the civil rights workers, drop a grenade on them from the building's top, and then "calmly walk away." He quickly changed his mind, however, ordering Klansmen to stay away from the city unless ordered to go there. Perhaps he and Tommy Rowe would visit Selma in a week or so to evaluate the situation.[37]

The Klan's first concrete plan was to mimic King: "If the niggers can demonstrate," Creel said, "so can the white people." They would have a white people's march on that same Sunday, but from Montgomery to Selma so they would pass the others on their way to the capital. The Klan received a permit to march, but members then decided to drive rather than walk. They would assemble at Montgomery's Patterson Field and then set out a few minutes after King's people left, their final destination Selma's Cramton Bowl. It would be a splendid "Klancade," one thousand automobiles packed with Klansmen, dwarfing King's marchers, humiliating them. But they were supposed to be polite: No "catcalls," threats, or curses would be tolerated. And they must not carry weapons—no chains, no bats, and certainly no guns that might cause an arrest. If there was violence, Creel warned, "he would see to it that they were punished." Imperial Wizard Shelton told reporters that Klansmen were not gangsters or "riffraff" but "very modern and progressive people." (To be prepared should violence occur, however, their arsenal would be available, carried by wives and girlfriends who would accompany them on the trip.)[38]

Tommy Rowe kept Neil Shanahan informed of these developments; between March 16 and March 21, they met or spoke on the telephone at least seven times. Rowe couldn't believe that the Klan would settle for a peaceful demonstration. At both the Eastview and especially the Bessemer Klavern meetings, people seemed bitter and disappointed that there would be nothing more than a pleasant Sunday drive. Rowe later recorded their comments: "If we can have bloodshed in Saigon, we can have it here," and "If we are to have bloodshed, it's better to have it in Selma, where our families aren't involved." Grand Dragon Creel was especially upset, drinking heavily, Rowe observed, and "in a very nasty mood." He thought Creel had "some plan up his sleeve involving violence," he told Shanahan on the night of March 20.[39]

Perhaps the man with the violent plan was Robert Thomas, Rowe learned the next morning. Rowe was supposed to meet the others at the Bessemer Klavern hall, but Thomas told him to come to his house and drive with him instead; he had "his reasons," he explained. Rowe, Thomas, Jack Crawford, and Monk Rutherford, their driver, left for Montgomery at ten o'clock, stopping along the way at the Triple J Ranch House for breakfast. Afterward, Thomas met a man in a pickup truck in the parking lot. Rowe watched them move two Browning automatic rifles (with bipods), twelve magazines of ammunition, and a box said to hold twenty-five hand grenades and six landmines from the man's truck to the trunk of Rutherford's blue Pontiac. Then they joined their colleagues at Patterson Field for an uneventful but disappointing drive to Selma. No "head-on confrontation" occurred once they saw the presence of the troops guarding the marchers. Most Klan cars turned off the highway or found other ways to reach Selma. And instead of thousands of Klansmen riding in a thousand cars, the actual numbers, Rowe estimated, were closer to 250 men in a hundred cars. FBI agents, Neil Shanahan among them, met the Klancade at Cramton Bowl, taking down license plate numbers and looking for women with weapons, but none were there.[40]

By that time, Rowe and the others were ready for supper, and Thomas directed them to a nearby motel and restaurant. When they finished eating, they did not return to Rutherford's car. Thomas pointed to a middle-aged man in a dark business suit standing outside a motel room and remarked, "There he is now." When Thomas led the group toward him, the man waved excitedly, saying "No, no, no." Rowe had seen state troopers in the restaurant; perhaps that's what worried the man. Thomas ignored the warning, and the two men talked alone for a few minutes. Then Thomas borrowed Rutherford's keys, started the car, and swung it around so the trunk faced the man's motel room. Rowe couldn't see what they did next, but the trunk was raised, so he assumed that the weapons were moved into the room. Thomas came out and stood silent for a few minutes, perhaps checking to see whether he had been observed. Then he motioned to Rowe and the others to get in the car and they returned to Birmingham. Thomas never identified either man or told them why the weapons were picked up and delivered to someone they had never seen before, but Rowe feared they would be used against the marchers later that week.[41]

Rowe told all this to Neil Shanahan at nine o'clock that night, but the agent didn't attach much significance to the story. He was distracted by a new crisis that had filled his day: Bombers were back in Birmingham. At 8 a.m., he had rushed to a black Catholic church on Center Street after a church official had discovered a green box filled with fifty pounds of dynamite attached to a ticking clock. Shanahan called an ordnance team from Fort McClellan to defuse the bomb. While they were carefully cutting the timer's wires, a police officer found an identical box a hundred yards away, near Arthur Shores's home; it, too, was disarmed. Then more bombs were found in an alley behind the Gaston Funeral Home. Radio and television stations alerted the city to the danger, and at four o'clock some teenagers found a fifth green box in an incinerator at all-black Western High School in Ensley. Not long afterward, Shanahan and the demolition team disarmed the sixth bomb, found under an abandoned bread truck near a home once owned by A. D. King. The FBI called the case GREENBOMBS. It's therefore not surprising that Shanahan found nothing new or imminently dangerous in Rowe's report about the transfer of arms.[42]

More bombs were discovered during the following week, including one that exploded at four o'clock in the morning behind a garage in North Birmingham. Another was found at the home of a Birmingham councilwoman, and a third outside the mayor's bedroom window. (The mayor defused it himself.) Shanahan and more than forty agents investigated the case. "I was up to my waist . . . and maybe higher in Green Bombs," he later recalled, so he didn't speak to Rowe until early on the morning of Thursday, March 25. It was the climactic end of the march in Montgomery, and, Shanahan learned, Rowe, Gene Thomas, and two other Bessemer Klansmen were going there, just to look things over. Shanahan didn't think the trip significant, and after checking with his boss, he told Rowe "fine," which meant "stay straight, keep your eyes open, don't get involved in anything, but furnish us the information." At 9:23 a.m., Shanahan sent the following message to Headquarters and field offices in Mobile and Selma, which would disseminate it to local police and other authorities: "BH 248-R ADVISED TODAY SIX [*sic*] MEMBERS OF UNITED KLANS OF AMERICA, INC., KKK, DEPARTED NINE A.M., FROM BESSEMER, ALA., EN ROUTE MONTGOM-ERY, BEING DRIVEN BY EUGENE THOMAS IN SIXTYTHREE CHEVROLET, RED AND WHITE, SIXTYFIVE ALABAMA TAG ONE B DASH THREE SIX NINE FOUR. PURPOSE OF TRIP NOT KNOWN. THESE SIX ONLY KNOWN KLANSMEN OF BIR-MINGHAM AREA EN ROUTE TO MONTGOMERY. END." He did not add these words: CONSIDER ARMED AND DANGEROUS.

Asked later by a lawyer representing the family of Viola Liuzzo whether he added that warning, Shanahan said, "Probably. I'm not absolutely cer-tain, but I think I did."

"You should have, anyway; you'd agree with that?"

"Yeah," Shanahan said.[43]

CHAPTER SIX

Season of Suffering

ON THE MORNING OF the last day of her life, Viola Liuzzo had a feeling that somebody was going to be killed. Later, when she was on the front page of every prominent newspaper and the subject of national controversy, many dismissed her concerns as the product of an overwrought imagination, a symptom of a troubled mind.

But on that day, the fear of death was real. It was shared by the president of the United States, FBI agents, civil rights activists, and Dr. Martin Luther King, Jr., who thought he might be assassinated. It was March 25, 1965, a moment when thousands of Americans, like Liuzzo, were about to complete the last leg of a march from Selma to the state capitol in Montgomery, demanding that blacks be allowed to vote. National Guardsmen lined the route, helicopters hovered overhead looking for snipers' nests, and FBI agents checked for explosives that might be hidden under bridges. "It looked like a war scene," Deputy Attorney General Ramsay Clark, the highest ranking Justice Department official on the scene, later recalled. "I expected violent assaults at any time. We'd drive up and down the road endlessly, looking at places where . . . it might occur. . . . We had reports of violence-prone people . . . drawn to the scene like a moth to a candle." Clark called the march "Walking through the valley in the shadows of death."[1]

President Johnson thought the last leg of the journey on March 25, from St. Jude's Church, just inside the city limits, to the marble steps of the state capitol, "potentially very dangerous." "I worked until about 2 a.m. and then went to sleep," he told an aide, "and I've been up an hour or so watching television [NBC televised events as they occurred] and reading reports and seeing how things are going in Montgomery. . . . Today's the big day."[2]

Viola Liuzzo was determined to be part of that big day. Before setting out on her journey on March 16, she explained to one of her professors why she was going to Selma. She was deeply moved by the suffering of "my people," and identified with the victims in Selma, as if "I were one of the Selma victims, not just a spectator." Through that identification, she recalled a time when she was sixteen years old and felt intense physical pain from a severe attack of inflammatory rheumatism. For four days, she received no help or medication for the pain. She knew that for those suffering in Selma, "every moment drags ever so slowly."[3]

Liuzzo's identification with those who suffered from intense physical or emotional pain was characteristic, and her use of the words "my people" was no accident. Although she would later be called an "outside agitator," she thought of herself as southern, having spent her formative years in rural Georgia and Tennessee. She was born on April 11, 1925, in California, Pennsylvania, her first home a tiny cabin with a dirt floor and no indoor plumbing. The town, named by those who stopped there briefly before heading west to seek their fortunes, employed men like her father, Heber Gregg, who worked in its coal mines.[4]

Gregg, a handsome country boy from Mount Vernon, Tennessee, joined the American Expeditionary Force at age seventeen and fought in France during World War I. After the war, he joined a different army— that of the unemployed who could find work only in the Pennsylvania coal mines, where miners earned fifty cents a day. He was put in charge of the cars that went in and out of the mines on mechanical tracks, and one day he noticed that the switching mechanism was giving off sparks. Fearing that this might be dangerous, he warned his supervisor, who told him to ignore it and go back to work. Heber Gregg had only dim memories of what happened next—an explosion that put him in the hospital. When he awoke, he discovered that his left hand had been amputated by doctors trying to save his life. Gregg fought the company, seeking to revoke his dismissal and win compensation for his injury, but in those days

Viola Liuzzo pictured in 1951, when she was twenty-six years old. (UPI-Bettmann/Corbis)

there were no government or union protections to help him. With no money to hire a lawyer, he was forced to accept what the company offered him in settlement—eight dollars. With no job and only a few dollars in his pocket, Gregg was reminded of the bad luck that seemed to plague his family: His father, a circuit-riding preacher, had been murdered by a thief who stole his only possession, a twenty-dollar gold piece.[5]

While working in Pennsylvania, Heber Gregg met and married young

Eva Wilson, a teacher, who became the family's financial support. In 1931, the Gregg family moved to the South; Heber was "a wanderer," his daughter later observed. They lived in five different states during Viola's childhood, rarely remaining in one place long enough for her to make friends or finish a year of school with the same class. Such "constant moving from place to place," Liuzzo's biographer notes, left her "with a lifelong sense of restlessness. In her mind there always seemed to be something just beyond her present circumstances, something waiting for her."[6]

Her life grew harder when Heber developed neurological problems caused by untreated syphilis he had contracted in France. He spent many years seeking treatment in veterans' hospitals, resulting in a separation that weakened the bonds between father and daughter. Viola grew up in near poverty "in one-room shacks" in Georgia and then Tennessee, where, in 1936, the family finally put down roots after Eva Gregg gave birth to another daughter. Eva was unable to work for a time, so the Gregg family was forced to go on relief and Viola quit school at age fourteen to help her family through the crisis. Experience had taught her what it meant to be an underdog fighting the injustices of an indifferent world, although the family didn't embrace the racism that often characterized impoverished southern whites. Once, when she was a teenager, she stole money from a store's cash register—not to spend on herself but to give to a black child whose life was more barren than her own.

In 1941, when Viola was sixteen, she ran away from home to marry a man she had met in Knoxville who was more than twice her age. She realized immediately that she had made a terrible mistake and left him the next day; the marriage was quickly annulled. But she would always be attracted to older men, and they found her irresistible. She was a strikingly beautiful young woman—petite, with strawberry blonde hair and gray eyes, "very vivacious, [and] explosive," said journalist Gordon Green, who knew her then.[7]

After the Japanese attack on Pearl Harbor, the Greggs moved again, this time to Ypsilanti, Michigan, where Heber briefly ran a grocery store and Eva worked for Ford Motors, whose plant became part of the national defense effort. They lived in Willow Run Village, erected by Ford to house the many who were employed there. In February 1943, eighteen-year-old Viola married again. Her Greek-American husband, George Argyris, was thirty-six and the owner and operator of a cafeteria at the Champion Spark

Plug Company in Hamtramck, where she also worked. Home became a duplex apartment on Blaine Street not far from Highland Park.

During this time Viola met a black woman from Mississippi, Sarah Evans, who became her lifelong best friend. Evans worked in a grocery store on Linwood Avenue, and there on a Saturday morning she first saw Viola. As she later recalled, "This pretty little woman came into my store looking for pepper," a commodity Evans's boss hoarded because it was in short supply during wartime. He told Viola they had no pepper, although Evans knew there was plenty on hand for the owner's best customers. "There was just something about this lady," Evans said, "she was so open and friendly, so lively," that she revealed that they did have pepper for sale. Her boss was furious. "He could have killed me—probably should have fired me," she said, but he reluctantly sold Viola what she wanted. Sensing that Evans might be in serious trouble, Viola said, "You know, you're the kind of woman I like. You're not afraid to speak up, to stick your neck out. Maybe we could get together and talk sometime," and, with that, a bond was formed. They would meet frequently in the Argyris home for coffee and conversation, mostly about the South, which, Evans said, "for all its foolishness, . . . was a place we both missed."[8]

At that time and place, such a relationship was extraordinary and perhaps even dangerous. Detroit was a racial tinderbox, a longtime home of the Ku Klux Klan, now crowded with both blacks and southern whites drawn there by wartime jobs. Adequate housing for blacks was almost nonexistent. Most were forced to inhabit the city's east side, where almost two hundred thousand people were crowded into a substandard ghetto misnamed Paradise Valley. On a muggy Sunday night in June 1943, Detroit exploded into the worst race riot in its history. Its immediate origins were unclear: A fight between black teenagers and white sailors broke out at a popular amusement park, and rumors of atrocities committed by both sides led to pitched battles that spread throughout the city. Black mobs stopped streetcars and beat white riders. Whites formed their own packs and roamed the city looking for black victims. "Jesus, but it was a show!" said one young rioter. "We dragged niggers from cars, beat the hell out of them, and lit the sons of bitches' autos. I'm glad I was in it! And those black bastards damn well deserved it." President Franklin D. Roosevelt was forced to send in six thousand troops to crush the insurrection. When it was over, thirty-four were dead—almost two-thirds of them black and most shot by Detroit police; nearly seven hundred were injured; property damage was estimated at almost $2 million. It's not known where Viola Argyris and Sarah Evans were during Bloody Week, as Detroiters called it, but the racial violence didn't destroy their friendship.[9]

Evans became not only Viola's best friend but her confidante and advisor. When Viola gave birth to her daughters Penny in 1946 and Mary in 1947, Evans was there to help with the babies. Viola's children were always her greatest joy, but they weren't enough to save a failing marriage. By all accounts, George Argyris was "a good, gentle, hard-working man," a loving husband and a good provider for his family, but, Evans thought, he was "unsympathetic to Viola's ambitions and interests" and couldn't match her passion and energy.[10]

Briefly, she was attracted to Gordon Green, a young Canadian studying for a master's degree at the University of Michigan who lived near her parents at Willow Run. "She was a strikingly beautiful young girl with a southern accent," Green later recalled, "a woman of considerable appeal . . . and quite liberated." He was especially impressed by her racial tolerance, which other southerners he met in Detroit did not share.[11]

While Sarah Evans cared for her daughters, Viola returned to work, but not in George's cafeteria. The New Olympia Bar on Grand Avenue was more to her liking. Close to Olympia Stadium, a major sports complex, the bar attracted boxers, wrestlers, hockey players—patrons far more interesting than those who frequented the Argyris Cafeteria. Although only a waitress, she earned a good salary and felt for the first time a sense of financial independence. This troubled George, who wanted a more traditional wife and mother for his children. Unable to resolve their differences, they mutually agreed to a divorce in 1950. The children stayed with their mother, who returned to her parents' home in Willow Run, but George Argyris continued to see Penny and Mary. Viola retained some affection for George and felt guilty for what had happened to their marriage; before leaving for Alabama in 1965, she visited her former husband "to apologize . . . for her part in what happened between them."[12]

Viola was not alone for long. At the Olympia Bar, one group stood apart from the athletes who were usually there: union men, tall, husky, obviously tough. One was a Teamster named Anthony James Liuzzo, a thirty-seven-year-old Italian American whose immigrant father, like Viola's, worked the coal mines in Carbondale, Pennsylvania. Liuzzo was barrel-chested and darkly handsome, with a prominent nose, fleshy lips, and narrow hooded eyes that conveyed warmth or menace. There was an air of danger about him. He and Viola took to each other immediately. Their pasts seemed intertwined: poverty, coal mines, small dusty towns, the struggle of organized labor to protect workers like the Heber Greggs of America, the exploited, the maimed, those tossed aside when Big Business had no further use for them. After her divorce became official in 1951, they married.[13]

Viola's second daughter with Argyris, Mary, once described her mother's marriage to Jim Liuzzo as "a combination of 'I Love Lucy' and 'Who's Afraid of Virginia Woolf.'" During its first seven years, Viola was often pregnant. She gave birth to Thomas in 1951 and Anthony Jr. in 1955. After Tony's birth, she again became pregnant but was frequently ill; Mary remembered her mother experiencing diabetic comas, caused perhaps by gestational diabetes. She repeatedly experienced miscarriages. Viola was "devastated," but she became pregnant again in 1958. It was a difficult pregnancy, requiring several hospitalizations, and when Sally was born in August 1959, she was severely malnourished. The physicians didn't expect her to live, and she received the last rites of the Catholic Church. But Viola wouldn't accept the prognosis. "Vi was determined to bring that kid through," Jim later said. "And you know, she did."[14]

In spite of her history of miscarriages and difficulties after Sally's birth, Viola became pregnant again in 1959—her ninth pregnancy in nine years, and her last. It was also the cruelest, because the child, a son named Joseph, lived only a few hours and then died. Unable to overcome her feelings of intense sadness, Viola was hospitalized for two weeks and treated for "postpartum psychosis," an extreme form of depression.[15]

She returned to her family feeling better, but it wasn't the end of her problems. Jim Liuzzo was a first-generation Italian American who believed in "old virtues," especially as far as women were concerned. He had difficulty understanding or appreciating his wife's many enthusiasms and idiosyncrasies—for example, her habit of bringing home stray animals, "anything that was hurt and needed a hand." Her charity also included "down-and-out people," her son Tony later recalled. "She would . . . feed them and get them help. Then they'd rip us off and my dad would go crazy."[16]

Jim Liuzzo adopted Penny and Mary in 1956, but his relations with them were also troubled. "I loved him," Mary later said, "but he was a

Viola Liuzzo and husband Anthony "Jim" Liuzzo with their youngest daughter, Sally, in 1962. (UPI-Bettmann/Corbis)

really mean, dark man." The children weren't allowed to talk at the dinner table, and one night when the forced silence produced fits of laughter, their father, "his face contorted with hate . . . reached over with his fork like he was really going to stab [us] with it." He frightened and demeaned them. When Mary received some pink lipstick as an eighth-grade graduation present and proudly made herself up, her stepfather told her she looked like "a streetwalker." Penny received similar treatment. Mary never heard Jim "call my sister Penny by her first name; he always called her by some rude name. And he was mean to my brothers and they were *his* kids." Their mother "would try to soften [Liuzzo] up a lot," encourage him to act more kindly toward the children, but the tension created by his behavior remained constant. Only young Sally, her father's favorite, was immune to this treatment.[17]

Jim's profession as a "business agent" for the Teamsters added to the family's problems. Viola's biographer, Mary Stanton, insists that "Jim held a responsible management position with the Teamsters," but stepdaughter Mary admitted that her stepfather led "a very criminal life." In 1953, he and five other Teamsters were arrested and accused of "soliciting and accepting payments from truckers, contractors, excavators and road builders under threats of injury to person or property"—in short, extortion. The charges against Jim were later dropped because of lack of evidence, but the other Teamsters were held for trial. A few months later, he was investigated for alleged violations of labor laws but was never indicted.[18]

Jim's work also affected his children. If someone called to speak to their father, they were told to say that he wasn't home, even if he was. They noticed that every morning he carefully examined his car before starting the engine. For them, life at home was "scary."[19]

Viola viewed her husband's labor organizing activity as heroic, even romantic, given her background. "She never believed he did anything wrong," Mary said. When James R. Hoffa (for whom Jim Liuzzo worked sometimes as a bodyguard) was convicted of conspiracy and mail fraud in 1964, she wrote an angry letter to the editor of the *Detroit Free Press* expressing her support for the Teamsters' leader. But she couldn't entirely dismiss his lifestyle—the excessive drinking and gambling and his relationships with other women. All this caused fierce arguments between the two Liuzzos, which the children witnessed.[20]

The children never felt any lack of affection or support from their mother, however. They saw her as intense, energetic, emotionally sensitive, intellectually curious, nurturing, and maternal. Profoundly aware of the mistake she had made in leaving school early, she instilled in her sons and daughters the idea that "education was a necessity of life." Learning didn't stop when the school day ended. She took them to art museums, plays, and concerts. The family library was packed with books reflecting Viola's many interests—literature, theology, philosophy, and medicine.[21]

The early 1960s was a difficult time for Viola Liuzzo. As she approached her thirty-sixth birthday in March 1961, she decided to create a career for herself beyond homemaker and mother. Enrolling at Detroit's Carnegie Institute, a trade school for medical technicians, she focused her energies on demanding night courses. She was popular with her in-structors and fellow students. There were group study sessions at the Li-uzzo home, and afterward spirited debates about current issues such as civil rights and interracial marriage, which she had no problem accepting.[22]

Viola graduated with honors in March 1962, but she quit her first job at Parkview Medical Center in August after only two months because of a disagreement over the center's unfair treatment of female employees. Unlike their male counterparts, they were prohibited from receiving over-time pay. When a colleague was suddenly dismissed without any future financial support, Viola offered the woman her own paycheck and mounted a campaign to expose the hospital. She telephoned the police to report that she was planning to steal a microscope and even gave them a descrip-tion of her car. When they stopped her, she insisted on being taken into custody, but because she had broken no laws, the police let her go without filing charges.[23]

Another part-time job at Detroit's Sinai Hospital also ended quickly after a disagreement over the best way to run the hospital's tissue lab. Her superior later remembered Viola as "eager and vivacious" but also "very excit-able," "quite easily upset," and "not a very competent worker." Another physi-cian thought better of her and later recommended that she be reinstated.[24]

Instead, she returned to school—this time at Wayne State University, where she found it difficult taking a seventeen-hour course schedule while also running her home, although Sarah Evans was there to help. She man-aged to complete the fall semester in 1962 but felt "great tension and pres-sure" trying to excel and was exhausted and often depressed. In January 1963, she admitted herself to Wayne County General Hospital because of "depression and agitation." Her physical examination revealed no major problems, but there was concern about her weight, which had increased to 144 pounds on a five-foot one-and-a-half-inch frame. After talking with Viola, Dr. Norman T. Samet noted: "She felt that she was unable to take care of her household because of the nagging and pressure that she receives from her husband. She had the idea that if she didn't admit herself to the hospital she might kill herself and her family."[25]

During the next five days, she improved and actually seemed to "relish" her interviews with psychiatrists and looked forward to interacting with more-troubled patients, which the doctors thought were inappropriate re-actions, indicative perhaps of a more serious mental illness. When Dr.

Samet asked Viola about her college work, she said that she hoped one day to become a doctor. Dr. Samet's response was to write in her chart, "Statements like these . . . raise the question of a possible schizophrenic condition." Another of Samet's observations merits attention: Viola Liuzzo, he noted, "has been rather unhappy and dissatisfied with the role of home-maker and has sought a number of desperate ways, including going to school full-time to find some niche or some status for herself other than that of housewife." Later that same year, Betty Friedan's book *The Feminine Mystique* explored the same issues that were haunting Viola, issues that Dr. Samet considered signs of mental illness.[26]

Dr. Samet had recommended psychotherapy, so Viola began meeting with Dr. Abraham Elson on August 2, 1963. "I need to unravel and uncover family problems, and solve them," she said, admitting that she "nags her family . . . and her husband when upset." Dr. Elson proved to be a more sensitive and understanding therapist. After their first session, Elson found her "anxious [and] nervous," but he felt there was no evidence of psychosis or schizophrenia. He also noted that Viola was "coming to a cri-sis in her life, a passage between young adulthood and impending middle age, and she felt unfulfilled and alienated, as many women do, and she was looking for respect and to improve her self-esteem."[27]

Dr. Elson also learned that sixteen-year-old Penny had become a further source of concern for Viola. Penny's relationship with her stepfather had deteriorated because Jim thought her too young to date or even attend so-cial events with her friends. Penny's mother stood by her, and the ensuing arguments left Penny depressed and feeling guilty, believing that she was the cause of her parents' discord. Thinking that she would be happier liv-ing with her grandparents in Ypsilanti, she packed and moved in with them, but after returning home during the summer her depression intensi-fied and she was hospitalized for three weeks. When she was discharged, she again went to Ypsilanti, hurting her mother deeply and precipitating another emotional crisis.[28]

In September, after a tumultuous argument with her husband, Viola called the police and the "city physician," urging them to arrest him because, she said, he was "crazy." Jim, "in desperation," called Dr. Elson, who rushed to the house and spent two hours trying to calm her down. "My temper is angry and vicious," she told Elson. "I have a mongrel temper at times. My husband has a Dago [temper]." She did not go back to school that fall.[29]

The year 1964 brought additional family problems. In January, she telephoned Dr. Elson and again reported that life among the Liuzzos was "too much" for her. Fifteen-year-old Mary, once "very, very close" to her mother, now rebelled against her. In love for the first time, she wanted to marry her boyfriend, and Viola, remembering her own disastrous marriage at age sixteen, fought back. And there was Penny's continued refusal to come home, which was supported by Eva Gregg, who now questioned her daughter's sanity. For a time, Viola explored whether there was any legal action available to compel Penny to come home, but then she changed her mind, choosing instead to focus her energies on a public issue she thought would benefit all children.[30]

This time the target of her indignation was the Detroit Board of Education, which, because of a new law, allowed students to leave school at age sixteen. Viola felt that she had been seriously handicapped by dropping out of school at fourteen, so this cause meant a great deal to her. She met with school officials, but they claimed they could do nothing; it was the law, and only the state legislature could change it. So Viola decided on a more dramatic form of protest—removing her own children from their schools and teaching them at home.[31]

Tom and Tony enjoyed the time they spent with their mother, but Mary was furious. She was an honor student who looked forward to attending college, and the time she missed from school ruined her academic record. After forty days, Viola was cited for violating Michigan law, and although the school board sought a compromise, she insisted on being arrested. Judge Joseph Gillis postponed a hearing, hoping that the matter could be quietly resolved—the school board didn't want to prosecute— but when she later returned to court, she pleaded guilty. The judge (who later called her a "professional crusader") fined her fifty dollars and placed her on one year's probation.[32]

Viola Liuzzo's crusade brought about the reverse of what she desired. School policy remained unchanged, and Mary, deeply resentful of the harm done to her, ran away from home briefly and then went to live with Viola's parents in Port Oglethorpe, Georgia.[33]

Shortly after Mary's departure, Viola disappeared without telling her family where she was going. Her husband called the police two days later, on July 16, and reported her missing, but she began to send him letters —some written from churchyards and cemeteries where she sometimes spent the night. He finally learned that she had driven to Montreal, where she was visiting Gordon Green, her former neighbor in Willow Run. Green later recalled that she seemed to be "a bit erratic," "a little excitable," and "disturbed." But within a few days she seemed fine again. Jim Liuzzo flew to Montreal, and with Green and his wife, they drove Viola back to Detroit.[34]

Amid her emotional turmoil, Viola found time in early September for what became the last adventure she would share with her sons. Ostensibly, they were going to visit Mary and Viola's parents in Georgia, but her real purpose was to introduce her "citified" sons to the South—her homeland. They drove leisurely, exploring back roads, camping out every night in parks and fields, sometimes even in cemeteries.

On one especially beautiful night in the Tennessee woods, Viola pointed upward to a star-filled sky and said: "Look at the stars and the woods. This is your heritage. Not what you see in the cities. Not the money and the buildings. This is what people were born for. *This* is your heritage." Tom later remembered that she seemed to have "an inner sense . . . telling [me] . . . that she might not always be there. Maybe she knew . . . just how fragile this life is and how quick it can be taken from you . . . , but she seemed to want to instill in me something I could keep forever after she was gone."[35]

When they returned home, Viola found that Penny had run away (though she eventually turned up unharmed). Viola's emotional problems worsened, and she eventually reached a breaking point. When her probation officer saw her on September 21, she noted that "Viola rambles . . . so it is very difficult to follow any one train of thought. She is probably above average intellectually, however, she is quite disturbed." A week later, she attempted suicide by taking an overdose of a sedative. Penny, believing her mother had a serious "viral infection," rushed her to the hospital, where Viola's stomach was pumped. After almost a week of psychotherapy, she was moved to Detroit Memorial Hospital. She told physicians that "she felt depressed and lonely" since Mary had moved away; on October 5, she was discharged into Dr. Elson's care. When Elson saw her ten days later, he thought she seemed "more relaxed," but on November 5 Viola was again in crisis, and the doctor rushed to her home. She had just learned that Mary, still living in Georgia, had married a boy she barely knew. Mary was just sixteen, the same age Viola was when she first married. She was heartbroken, "despondent," Elson later said; she didn't even know her new son-in-law's name. Again, the doctor managed to calm her down.[36]

In 1965, Viola Liuzzo found a new passion: the civil rights movement. She had always sympathized with the struggle for black equality and had joined the NAACP at Sarah Evans's suggestion, but her direct involvement in the movement didn't occur until March 1965. During her therapy in 1964, she never once talked about civil rights with Dr. Elson, and he was surprised when he later learned that she had gone to Alabama. But as a student at Wayne State, Liuzzo observed the ferment developing on campus and joined students who met with Reverend Malcolm Boyd (nicknamed the "Espresso priest"), with whom they discussed Bloody Sunday and the recent murders of Jimmy Lee Jackson and James Reeb. Boyd mentioned that some Wayne State students were going to Alabama to participate in the forthcoming Voting Rights March from Selma to Montgomery, and Liuzzo immediately expressed interest in joining them. On March 16, she and her fellow students marched on the federal building in Detroit to protest Alabama's brutality and later that night decided it was time to go to Alabama.[37]

The first to learn of her intentions was Sarah Evans, who pleaded with Liuzzo to reconsider, but she refused. She asked Evans to take care of Tom, Tony, and Sally while she was gone, and if something happened to her, to remain by their side. Evans agreed, as always. Liuzzo threw some clothes and textbooks in a paper bag and telephoned her husband to tell him that she was leaving for Selma. Jim and Penny were both strongly opposed to the trip and told her so. Her daughter thought she would never see her mother again and offered to take her place. She laughed off Penny's concerns: She would "live to 'pee' on Penny's grave," she told her, and then became serious—"I need to be there." Going south would also give her an opportunity to see Mary, the new Mrs. Barry Johnson. Then Jim got on the phone. "Look, Vi," he said, "come on home and let's talk this over, then if you still want to go I'll give you the money to fly." "No," she replied, "It's everybody's fight. There are too many people who just stand around talking, I'm going," and she hung up. The other, younger Wayne State students decided to remain at home while Viola Liuzzo, alone, drove a thousand miles into the Deep South. On Friday, March 19, 1965, she arrived in Selma.[38]

Pulling up at the twin-towered Brown Chapel, the movement's headquarters in Selma, she met two black teenagers, Sam Edmonson and Lewis "Tadpole" Miller, who identified themselves as civil rights workers and then asked to borrow her car. People by the thousands—doctors, lawyers, members of the clergy, nuns, teachers, representatives from business and labor, celebrities, and ordinary folks—were arriving at bus and train stations and at Dannelly Field, Montgomery's airport, and the boys wanted to join the caravan heading to pick them up. Without a moment's hesitation, Liuzzo gave them the keys to her powder blue 1963 Oldsmobile, and off they went.[39]

Inside the chapel, she signed a visitor's registry and was assigned a family to room with and a job at the hospitality desk. A young man walked her to the nearby George Washington Carver Apartments, a two-story brick housing project built in 1951 for Selma's blacks, to the home of Mrs. Willie Lee Jackson and teenage daughter Frances, who, only five weeks before, had given birth to a baby boy. Mrs. Jackson worked at a Selma café and in her spare time prepared food for the demonstrators. She had also made her small apartment available for civil rights workers to use as sleeping quarters; by the time Viola Liuzzo arrived, it was crowded with six other demonstrators, plus Mrs. Jackson and her family. "She was . . . very sweet . . . , no stranger," Mrs. Jackson later recalled. "She came right in and picked up our ways right away. She said she came to Selma because she thought she could help . . . , after a while, you had the feeling you had known her for a long time."[40]

Later that afternoon, Liuzzo walked back to Brown Chapel, stopping first at the transportation office to see about her car. There she met Leroy Moton, a nineteen-year-old Selma native who had recently joined Martin Luther King's SCLC and was now in charge of moving people around the city in rented cars or vehicles that were volunteered for that purpose. Moton was hard to miss: At six feet three inches, he was more than a foot taller than Liuzzo. He was rail thin, with a long face and horn-rimmed glasses that always seemed to be slipping down his nose. He was gentle and sincere, but also rather comic—the SCLC transportation coordinator didn't even have a driver's license. Moton knew both Sam and Tadpole and reassured Liuzzo that her car was safe. She agreed to formally turn it over to him for the duration of the march and filled out the necessary papers. Moton promised that he would personally care for her car.[41]

She spent her first evening in Selma talking with Mrs. Jackson and playing with her grandson. She cradled the baby and helped Frances feed him and put him to bed. When the baby awoke in the middle of the night,

Leroy Jerome Moton, a nineteen-year-old civil rights activist, was Viola Liuzzo's passenger in her car the night she was murdered. (UPI-Bettmann/Corbis)

Liuzzo was there to give Frances the benefit of her experience as a mother. "Viola was devoted to that grandbaby of mine . . . ," Willie Lee Jackson later noted.[42]

On Saturday, she began working at the hospitality desk, greeting weary and nervous travelers who came to Selma from all across America. One clergyman later described meeting her: "We were ushered into the parsonage and Mrs. Liuzzo saw how tired and concerned we were and went out of her way to be nice to us. . . . I will never forget the attention we received and the kindness." Kindness might be a valued quality inside the chapel, but as Liuzzo learned at lunch, it was no protection outside, in Selma's streets. Nonnie Washburne, who grew up in the city, warned her to be careful because she knew from personal experience that "a lot of innocent people in the South had been killed. Women in this area were in as much danger as the men," she claimed. "This was a dangerous place, . . . anywhere police used gas or prods on people is a dangerous place." Liuzzo understood, but whatever dangers might exist, she "had to come because of the brutality in Selma," she said. "I don't see how anyone could keep from coming."[43]

The next day, Sunday, March 21, was sunny but cold—the first day of spring, which many thought a propitious moment for the march to begin. On her way to Brown Chapel that morning, Liuzzo saw Reverend Andrew Young, SCLC's executive secretary, briefing men wearing orange plastic jackets, the marshals who would provide security that day. "Keep the women and children in the middle," he instructed. "If there's a shot, stand up and make the others kneel down. Don't be lagging around, or you're going to get hurt. Don't rely on the troopers, either. If you're beaten on, crouch and put your hands over the back of your head. . . . If you fall, fall right down and look dead. Get to know the people in your unit, so you can tell if somebody's missing or if there's somebody there who shouldn't be there. And listen! If you can't be non-violent, let me know now."[44]

The march was scheduled to begin promptly after a ten o'clock church service, but it took hours to get the thirty-five hundred people organized into columns six abreast with, as Young ordered, the women and children placed safely in the middle of each group. Before leaving, Liuzzo got her first glimpse of Martin Luther King, "bundled in warm woolens and a Ridgeway cap against the 40ish chill." Addressing the crowd in his melodic voice, he said: "You will be the people that will light a new chapter in the history of our nation. Those of us who are Negroes don't have much. We have known the long night of poverty. . . . But thank God we have our bodies, our feet and our souls. Walk together, children, and don't you get weary, and it will lead us to the promised land. And Alabama will be a new Alabama. And America will be a new America." Joining King and other dignitaries at the head of the procession was eighty-two-year-old Cager Lee, Jimmy Lee Jackson's grandfather, who told a reporter that if some good came out of Dr. King's crusade, then "it was worth the boy's dying." Andrew Young placed a group of Catholic nuns near Dr. King and Cager Lee. "Nobody's likely to shoot at us if we have nuns in habits along with us," he told them.[45]

Nobody shot at them as Viola Liuzzo and her colleagues walked down Broad Street, then crossed over the Edmund Pettus Bridge, stopping momentarily where, two weeks before, some had shed blood. "This is the place where State Troopers whipped us," Hosea Williams told Dr. King. "The savage beasts beat us on this spot."[46]

National Guardsmen with bayonets drawn (but sheathed) walked their flanks, while helicopters hovered above and trucks bearing television cameras captured every movement. But their enemies weren't afraid to show themselves. Sheriff Jim Clark was on a street corner, pulling on his lapel to show off his button reading "Never." His posse, armed with their signature billy clubs and cattle prods, followed the marchers along the parade route. Loudspeakers played "Bye, Bye, Blackbird," while bystanders yelled "nigger lover" or shook signs reading "Coonesville, U.S.A." and "Be a Man, Join the Klan." The marchers were not deterred, however. They kept on going.[47]

By sundown the marchers had covered seven miles and stopped at David Hall's farm. Judge Johnson's order allowed only 300 of them to traverse the part of the Jefferson Davis Highway that became a two-lane road, so Liuzzo and most of the others boarded buses and special trains that took them back to Selma. The fortunate 300—280 blacks from four Alabama counties and 20 whites (including one-legged Jim Letherer, who bravely walked on crutches while racists yelled, "Left! Left! Left!")—ate a spaghetti dinner and slept in tents segregated by sex, to fight the rumors of interracial orgies and general debauchery being spread throughout the South. ("Free love among this group is not only condoned, it is encouraged," declared Congressman William Dickinson of Alabama on the floor of the House of Representatives. "Only by the ultimate sex act with one of another color can they demonstrate that they have no prejudice." To which one black marcher replied: "These white folks must think we're supermen to be able to march all day . . . make whoopee all night and . . . then march all day again.") Many had a restless, sex-free night. Ahead lay Lowndes County, whose moss-covered trees and swamps might hide snipers; one report, which the marchers hoped was untrue, claimed that Klansmen planned to set loose deadly snakes at their next campsite.[48]

Viola Liuzzo spent the next two days working at the hospitality desk in Selma and the evenings helping the Jackson family care for their new grandson. One night the baby shrieked for hours, and Willie Lee and daughter Frances thought he was ill and should be seen by a doctor. Liuzzo believed that she knew what was wrong and hurried from the apartment, returning a short time later with several jars of baby food. The baby was only hungry, she said, spooning peas and carrots—his first solid food— into the boy's eager mouth, and, with that, the crying ceased.[49]

One black teenager, who had been beaten on Bloody Sunday, resented Liuzzo's presence, later calling her a "bossy . . . mother hen": "I saw what white people were capable of doing, so I wasn't interested that some white lady came down from Detroit to help me." Mrs. Jackson didn't share this view, and when Liuzzo asked her whether she could take Frances and the baby back with her to Detroit, she quickly agreed. Frances would finish high school while Liuzzo cared for the baby. "We . . . made big plans for it," Willie Lee later noted. It "seemed like things were going to turn out so good and right." Liuzzo was very serious about this; on Wednesday, she telephoned a Detroit clergyman to announce that she intended to adopt the black daughter of the woman with whom she was living.[50]

For Viola Liuzzo, life in Alabama became more interesting on Wednesday, March 24, when Leroy Moton drove her to St. Jude, a medical, religious, and educational complex outside Montgomery that also served as movement headquarters. Here, she was asked to run a first-aid station. Finally she would be able to use the skills she had learned at the Carnegie Institute—and there was no shortage of patients to treat. Most suffered from sunburn or blistered feet or simple exhaustion. At the end of the day, she was given a cot to sleep on but declined; it should go to one of the tired marchers who needed it, she said. By chance, she saw her car parked on the St. Jude grounds, so she slept in it that night.[51]

Liuzzo was up early the next morning, March 25, the day when the demonstrators would gather at the capitol building and Dr. King would speak. A delegation hoped to present Governor Wallace with a petition of grievances, but it was doubtful that he would see them. Before leaving, Liuzzo asked Father Tim Deasy, a priest who worked at St. Jude, if she could go up the church tower to look out on the city. Of course, he said, and together they climbed the stairs. Through the room's narrow windows, she could see before her a river of people, many carrying American flags snapping in the breeze. A strange feeling passed through her, and she turned and ran from the room. When Liuzzo reached the street, she experienced a full-blown panic attack—she was shaking, couldn't breathe, and looked pale. "Father, I have a feeling . . . something is going to happen today," she told Father Deasy and other clergymen who gathered around her. "Someone is going to be killed." Perhaps Governor Wallace, she thought, whose death would then be blamed on the civil rights workers. She went into the church to pray and seemed better when she emerged, ready to join the marchers. She buttoned her coat, capelike, around her neck, took off her shoes, and walked barefoot the four miles from St. Jude to the capitol.

Viola Liuzzo joined a force that by this time numbered between twenty-five thousand and thirty thousand, standing before the state capitol. Atop its dome flew the Alabama and Confederate flags, with the U.S. flag to the side. The demonstrators sang "The Star-Spangled Banner," "The Battle Hymn of the Republic," and "We Shall Overcome." It was on these capitol steps that Jefferson Davis had taken the oath of office as the first (and last) president of the Confederate States of America, and almost one hundred years later that Governor George Wallace proclaimed, "Segregation now, segregation tomorrow, and segregation forever." On this day that exact spot, usually marked by a gold star, was covered with sheets of plywood that Wallace had placed there "to keep that s.o.b. King from desecrating the Cradle of the Confederacy." Reporters covering the event would later note that the governor occasionally peered through his office blinds, watching the demonstrators through a pair of binoculars. Even he, it was said, was in awe of the crowd that was peacefully besieging the building.[52]

At around 3:30, Dr. King climbed atop a flatbed trailer and spoke to those assembled, the largest group ever to gather in the South in support of civil rights. "They told us we would never get here," he said. "And there were those who said we would get here only over their dead bodies, but

Viola Liuzzo on March 25, 1965, participating in the Voting Rights March from Selma to Montgomery. The photograph appeared in the Klan publication *Nightriders*.

all the world together knows that we are here and that we are standing before the forces of power in the state of Alabama, sayin' 'we ain't gonna let nobody turn us around. We are on the move now and no wave of racism can stop us.'

". . . My people, my people, listen! I must admit to you that there are still some difficulties ahead. We are still in for a season of suffering. . . . There are still jail cells waiting for us, dark and difficult moments. But we will go on with faith in the power of nonviolence." The crowd, initially silent, began to respond, especially those who were older and had been with King for a decade since the Montgomery bus boycott in that very city, so they yelled, "Speak! Speak!" and "Yessir! Yessir!"

"Our aim must never be to defeat or humiliate the white man," King continued, "but to win his friendship and understanding. The end we seek is a society at peace with itself. That will be a day not of the white man, not of the black man. That will be the day of man as man."

They were all with him now as he repeatedly called out, "How long?

Not long because no lie can live forever. How long? Not long, because you still reap what you sow. How long? Not long because the arc of the moral universe is long, but it bends toward justice. How long? Not long, 'cause mine eyes have seen the coming of the Lord." And then the crowd joined him, repeating the familiar words: "He is trampling out the vintage where the grapes of wrath are stored. He has loosed the fateful lightning of his terrible swift sword. His truth is marching on. . . . Oh, be swift my soul to answer Him. Be jubilant, my feet. Our God is marching on. Glory, glory hallelujah, glory, glory hallelujah."[53]

When the shouting and applause ended, Hosea Williams, the march's chief organizer, urged people to leave Montgomery quickly but "quietly and with dignity." Night was approaching, and the National Guard and army troops, indeed the entire federal force, would be leaving soon, too. Everyone sang "We Shall Overcome," and then the crowd began to disperse.[54]

Those most afraid that something terrible might happen that day felt wonderful that all went well. President Johnson "breathed a sigh of relief" and conferred with his attorney general, Nicholas deB. Katzenbach, about future events. "What are they going to do when they get through marching?" the president asked during a telephone conversation. "I think King would like to take a little rest," Katzenbach joked. "He's got some sore feet." FBI Inspector Joseph Sullivan, who coordinated the Bureau's effort to protect the marchers, felt that "it had been a very successful venture. . . . There had been visible proof that a peaceful march could be held in any part of the United States. And there was a lot of pride on the part of law enforcement." With King safely on a plane to Atlanta, his lieutenant Andrew Young returned to the Dexter Avenue Church in Montgomery, where he found his colleagues in a joyful mood. "I slipped away to the men's room . . . and locked the door," he later wrote. "Then I just let the tears flow, tears of relief that we had completed the march without any bloodshed, that we had actually pulled it off, this virtual strolling city of five days' duration across the lonely Alabama terrain, a feat we could not possibly have foreseen when we were beginning our campaign. . . . Finally, when there were no more tears, I washed my face, composed myself, and went back out to rejoin my friends."[55]

But for James Orange, one of King's field marshals, there were still problems to worry about. Orange knew that the greatest danger can come after an event has ended. Marchers were eager to go home, so he needed to organize the safest means to transport them from Montgomery to the airport or to the bus and train stations in Selma. With the troops leaving, and possibly with hostile whites roaming around, Orange, at around 5 p.m., called meetings at both Dexter Avenue Church and St. Jude for every-one involved with transportation, from those who drove to those who had only lent their cars to the movement. He warned everyone to go in a cara-van, not alone in a single car. It is likely that Viola Liuzzo received these instructions. Later, Orange couldn't remember seeing her among the fifty to one hundred people attending the meetings; but she did return to St. Jude immediately after the march hoping to find Leroy Moton and her car, so she would have been at the complex when Orange spoke. Further-more, several officials later claimed that when she volunteered to ferry people from one location to another, "we told her, Vi, don't go out there. . . . We've got trucks, we've got busses; there's no reason for you to use your car on that highway." "No, I've got to go," she said. And she did.[56]

Leroy Moton finally arrived at St. Jude around six o'clock with Liuzzo's Oldsmobile, filled with passengers—one wanting to go to the airport and four more headed for Selma. She got behind the wheel and pulled away. The ride to Dannelly Field was uneventful, but as they drove to Selma, they encountered trouble. Orange was right: A single vehicle (and, in Li-uzzo's case, a car with an expired registration sticker on the rear license plate and a banner on the front bumper reading ALL THE WAY WITH LBJ) crowded with three white women in the back seat and a white female driver next to two black men in the front was a target for malicious Alabam-ans. One car filled with white men who apparently thought so began fol-lowing Liuzzo's car closely, and then bumped it several times. "These crazy white people don't have any sense," she said, more irritated than afraid, adding that she would definitely return to Alabama "if Governor Wallace didn't have her killed first." The men eventually grew tired of the prank, changed lanes, and drove off. When she and her passengers stopped for gas, passersby cursed them. Civil rights workers had warned their white allies to avoid integrated cars: "Might attract gunfire," they were told. And if they needed gas, the safest station was located in the black section of Montgomery. Liuzzo seemed unaware or uninterested in such warnings, but Moton, the transportation officer, should have known better.[57]

A few minutes later, another car pulled up very close behind, but in-stead of hitting them, the driver turned on his high beams. "Two can play at that game," Liuzzo said, slowing down to a crawl, until the car went around her and sped off. Then she pursued him and, catching up to the other car, turned on her own bright lights. The driver accelerated, and this time she let him drive away. When they were almost to Selma, another car in front of them decreased its speed while a second came up on the left, boxing them in. Liuzzo hit the brakes so suddenly that the car stopped with a screech; the other vehicles went on. Their final encounter on the road was friendly: A car filled with blacks drove by ("these are our people," she remarked), and she saw that their taillights were broken. Liuzzo honked vigorously and, with the others, yelled at the blacks, urging them to get the lights repaired. Then, they arrived in Selma, and the passengers departed.[58]

Moton still had work to do—another trip to Montgomery to pick up marchers or cars left behind. Liuzzo offered to drive him back. The day's events—the final march to the capitol, King's stirring speech, and the passionate reaction of the crowd—left her too excited to return to Mrs. Jackson's apartment for a quiet evening playing with Frances's baby. Moton said OK, but he was, in fact, worried about Liuzzo's aggressive response to the harassment they had earlier experienced. "Oh, Lord," he thought, "I hope it isn't going to be another of them rides." They decided to eat a quick dinner and meet again at seven o'clock.[59]

Moton's fears were realized not long after they set out for Montgomery. While stopped at a red light, a woman passenger in the car ahead turned around, stared at Liuzzo, and began making faces and sticking her tongue out at her. "Look at her," Liuzzo said—"the people here are sick." Moton stayed quiet, hoping that she would just ignore the woman and "avoid trouble." She did, the light turned green, and both cars moved on.[60]

Around 7:30 p.m., they began crossing the Edmund Pettus Bridge, over which Liuzzo had walked just four days earlier. It was very dark by then and there wasn't much traffic, which worried Moton because this was usually a busy highway. He watched as they passed familiar landmarks —Jet's Drive-In, the Cap Trailer Court, Billups Gas Station, then Craig Air Force Base—while Liuzzo talked about becoming more involved in civil rights work when she returned to Detroit. She planned to leave in the morning and was excited about seeing her family, whom she had telephoned every night that she was away. Moton grew tense: "Everything was so dark and deserted," he later noted. "Mrs. Liuzzo was singing ["We Shall Overcome"] and talking, but I didn't say a word. I almost say to her, we better turn around and go back, but then I say to myself, she probably wouldn't do it anyhow." She decreased their speed to about forty-five miles per hour when they came to the stretch of two-lane road, the approach to Lowndes County and Big Swamp Lake.[61]

It was then, Moton later recalled, that the two noticed a car following them, its headlights on high but too far back to be a nuisance. Probably just another annoyed Alabaman wanting to make a face or stick out a tongue at the interracial couple defying southern tradition. A few minutes later, the car came closer, but then it slowed down, letting them get farther ahead. "That car's still following us," Moton told her. Liuzzo assured him that it was probably one of the staff cars, but Moton, now very worried, disagreed—a staff car would have pulled up behind them and identified itself.[62]

Moton was right. This was no SCLC staff car but a red and white Chevrolet Impala, whose driver and three passengers were members of the Alabama Knights of the Ku Klux Klan. They had spent the day driving around Selma and then Montgomery, armed with revolvers, hoping to do a little missionary work assaulting blacks, or better yet one of those "white niggers" who marched with Martin Luther King. They found them in the blue Oldsmobile when it stopped near them at the red light leading to the Edmund Pettus Bridge. "I'll be damned, look-a-there," said one. "A white lady and a colored man." "Let's get 'em," said the driver, and they took off after the other car, speeding up, then hanging back, waiting for the right moment. Finally, the Impala caught up and swerved into the left lane until it was alongside the other car. The Klansmen rolled down their windows and pulled out their revolvers. "All right, men," the driver cried, "shoot the hell out of them." There was gunfire, and the sound of fourteen bullets breaking glass and hitting metal. The car with the white woman and the black man ran off the road, into a field. "I'm one hell of a shot," said one of the Klansmen. "That bitch and that bastard are dead and in hell."[63]

CHAPTER SEVEN

Night Riders

LEROY MOTON RAN ALONG Highway 80 toward Montgomery as if
his life depended on it. He thought it did. Viola Liuzzo was dead, shot in
the head, but somehow he had managed to escape relatively unscathed
—his shoulder hurt and his face had been cut by flying glass, but he was
alive. He thought the killers were still around, perhaps hiding in nearby
woods or even patrolling the highway looking for him. He tried to stop a
truck, but the driver passed him by. Another stopped, but as he hurried
toward it he fell, and the driver, maybe thinking he was drunk or crazy,
took off. He feared that he was still in Lowndes County, famous for its
adage, "A black man who lived to be 21 was 'a good nigger.'" Moton, the
civil rights worker, was certainly not their idea of a docile "good nigger."
If he was picked up by a Lowndes County cop, he was as good as dead. So
"I just kept runnin' and hoping that someone would come along from the
march," he said later.[1]

A mile down the road, he saw another truck, heading for Selma, but
it was too dark to know whether it was friend or enemy, until he heard
voices calling his name. It was a flatbed truck, its rear filled with young
marchers from Selma, who recognized him. He ran toward them, waving
his arms. The truck stopped, and the driver, Reverend Leon Riley, a young
Disciples of Christ minister from Richmond, California, got out of the
cab. "A woman's been killed!" Moton cried. "She's been shot!" He was

helped into the bed of the truck by the teenage passengers. "Everybody down," screamed Moton, now completely hysterical. "There are men with guns around here! Let's get out of here! A woman has been killed!" "How did it happen?" asked Raymond Magee, another minister. "They . . . shot her through the window, three times I think," Moton said. "They tried to get me, too." Head "bowed," he "huddled" among the others as the truck pulled out for Brown Chapel in Selma.[2]

Reverend Riley and his colleagues were already very much on edge. Earlier that evening, when they were part of a three-truck convoy, state troopers had stopped them. One interrogated Riley while the other examined their truck. They finally ordered Riley to take another road because they were "a nuisance on the highway." When Riley said their truck couldn't travel on a back road, the interrogator said, "We don't give a damn if you don't get back to Selma. It would be just as well if you got shot up." A short time later they were again pulled over, this time for broken taillights, which had worked perfectly before the earlier encounter. Riley was arrested, and while the other two trucks were told to proceed, he and his passengers were taken to a nearby gas station whose owner doubled as justice of the peace. He fined Riley and made their repairs while they nervously waited. After paying almost fifty dollars, they were sent on their way. Now, Riley's new passenger was having a nervous breakdown and claiming that a woman had been killed.[3]

When an automobile passed by, Moton thought the killers had returned and screamed, "There's the car!" His hysteria infected the others, who "pounded the cab and screamed for Riley to stop." Moton jumped to his feet, crying, "I'll stop him," then suddenly fainted. Other cars seemed to follow them, causing the people to yell, "Go fast!" "We expected bullets to fly," Magee said later, but they arrived safely at Brown Chapel around 9:30 p.m. Magee jumped from the truck and ran into the chapel, where he called the local FBI field office. By chance, the agent who answered the phone was veteran inspector Joseph Sullivan. Magee identified himself and said he wanted to report a shooting "on a narrow highway west of Lowndesboro crossroads"; he didn't know whether the victim, a woman, was alive or dead. Sullivan told him to stay at Brown Chapel; two agents would be sent to interview him. Magee also called Montgomery Hospital and asked them to immediately send an ambulance to the scene. While they waited for the FBI, Magee and Riley conferred with civil rights officials, who urged them to hide Moton in the basement of the Dexter Avenue Church to protect him from state troopers or the Selma police, who might harm him.[4]

When the ambulance arrived at Lowndesboro Crossing around 9:45, the attendants found Alabama state troopers already there. About seventy-five minutes earlier, troopers Henry Burgess and Thomas McGehee were giving a motorist a speeding ticket when a truck driver parked his rig nearby and reported that he'd seen a car in a field a couple of miles west of Lowndesboro. It looked like it had run off the road and crashed into a fence. A tall man, perhaps the driver, tried to flag him down, but he drove on until he saw the troopers' flashing red lights. Just an ordinary automobile accident, Burgess thought, so he started to fill out the standard forms as the troopers drove to the scene.

At the Lowndesboro crossroad on U.S. 80, they saw a light blue Oldsmobile, its lights and ignition off, in a field about fifty feet from the edge of the roadway. They tramped through the wet and muddy field, the rain soaking their yellow slickers. This was no simple accident—that was immediately clear. The driver's side window was shattered, leaving a gaping hole through which Burgess shined his flashlight. He saw a white woman slumped against the door, her head covered with blood, which had seeped out the window and run down the side of the car. He also saw blood on the steering wheel and column, the front seat, and the floor mat. It looked like she had been shot in the left side of the head. Carefully, they opened the driver's door, causing the window glass to break further and fall to the ground. First one trooper felt the woman's wrist, searching for a pulse; then the other tried, but she was dead. Moving the flashlight around, they found the woman's purse and, on the right rear floorboard, a .38-caliber bullet.

While Burgess went to alert headquarters, trooper McGehee removed two items from the front seat: a beige plastic handbag and a clipboard whose papers indicated that the woman had been part of the Voting Rights March. The handbag contained cosmetics and personal papers, including the car's registration (which had expired on February 28) and a driver's license. The victim was apparently Viola Gregg Liuzzo of Detroit, Michigan, thirty-nine years old; hair, blonde; eyes, gray; five feet two and a half inches tall; weight, 127 pounds, although she looked much heavier. The car was registered to Anthony J. Liuzzo, presumably the woman's husband. After

Viola Liuzzo's Oldsmobile in a field off Highway 80 after the shooting.
(UPI-Bettmann/Corbis)

The driver's side window and bloodstained door of Viola Liuzzo's car.
(UPI-Bettmann/Corbis)

Burgess returned, the troopers blocked off the area with crime scene tape, and when the Montgomery Hospital ambulance arrived, they told the crew that their services wouldn't be needed.[5]

By 10:00 p.m., the FBI also knew the identity of the victim. Special Agents Robert Frye and Edward Bahlow interviewed the still nervous Leroy Moton at the Selma Police Department, where he had been taken for questioning. Moton reviewed the events of the day and described what little he could remember about the attack. It all happened so fast, and when he was thrown against the dashboard, injuring his shoulder, his glasses also flew off, so he couldn't see a thing. When the bullet hit Mrs. Liuzzo, she "slumped against the driver's side door," bloody and unconscious. The car left the road, and he was helpless until it smashed into a fence and stopped. He turned off the ignition, then thought to start it again to get them back on the road. But the car that had attacked them—a 1955 to 1960 Ford, perhaps—returned, stopped on the roadway, and shined a light at them. Terrified, he pushed himself down as if he were dead, too. After the car left, he just sat there for nearly half an hour before deciding to get help. (In later accounts, Moton claimed that he passed out.)

Back on the road, he saw a small red car, probably foreign, and waved at it. But the driver swerved toward him, as if he wanted to run him down, so he fell back into the gully. He returned to Mrs. Liuzzo's car and again sat there briefly. Then he got out and ran until finally he met Reverend Riley and the marchers, who took him to Selma. He had no idea how many men attacked them, maybe three, but was certain there were no women involved because "they wouldn't be that dirty."[6]

State investigators Rufus Head and Ray Posey failed to elicit additional information, but their manner was insulting and they implied that Moton and Liuzzo had an intimate relationship. Leon Riley and Raymond Magee, the ministers who had rescued Moton on the road, were also at the police station for the interview. "How long did you know this Viola?" Magee recalled Head asking. "You make a practice of goin' round with white women?" When Head read Moton's statement aloud, Magee strongly objected. "The statement is not quite accurate, sir," the Reverend said. "In every instance that you quote Mr. Moton as referring to Mrs. Liuzzo, you have written 'Viola.' Not once in this interview nor before have I heard Mr. Moton refer to Mrs. Liuzzo as 'Viola.'" Leon Riley agreed. The ministers shouldn't take this so seriously, Head replied, but when Magee noted that it was SCLC policy that witnesses should not sign statements without benefit of counsel, he turned ugly. "I order you to quit slowing up these procedures and stand over there in the courtroom," he yelled. Magee did as he was told. Moton was arrested as a material witness to a homicide; he was pushed into a cell as one of the officers said, "Get in there, you bastard." Riley and Magee were told to leave. Later, when Moton complained that his shoulder hurt, his jailers ignored him, and twenty-four hours passed before he received medical attention for a dislocated shoulder.[7]

By eleven o'clock, almost everyone in national authority knew that Viola Liuzzo had been shot in Alabama earlier that evening—the FBI director, the attorney general, even the president—but no one thought to inform the slain woman's husband. It finally occurred to SCLC officials that the call had to be made. Shortly after midnight on March 26, the telephone rang in the Liuzzo home on Detroit's Marlowe Street. Jim and Penny were still awake watching television; Sally, Tony, and Tommy were asleep upstairs in their bedrooms. "I have some very bad news for you," said Reverend Meryl Ruoss, an aide to Hosea Williams. "Your wife has been shot."

"Is it serious?" Jim Liuzzo asked.

"Yes, I'm afraid she's dead." Ruoss heard a thud, the sound of Jim Liuzzo throwing the phone down, and then screams. Ruoss held the line for ten minutes, then hung up.

Tony awakened to hear his sister calling, "[Tony], Tommy, mama is dead, mama is dead." He thought it was a dream. "And then I felt my brother fly across the bed, and get up, and it was like worse than a dream," he later recalled. "It was a nightmare that was real." They ran downstairs into the living room. "My God, Mom's been shot," their father said. "Someone killed Mom," then he began to sob—the first time the boys had ever seen their father cry. As the hours passed, it was bedlam as calls were made and people arrived—relatives, friends, newspaper reporters, photographers, and eventually an army of Teamsters, who, for the next week, cooked and cleaned and, in four-man shifts, guarded the home while the family slept. The always reliable Sarah Evans tried to comfort the children. The phone rang almost continuously; President Jimmy Hoffa of the Teamsters, attending a meeting in Florida, called "about every hour on the hour."[8]

"The dirty rats, the dirty rats," Jim Liuzzo told the reporters, who gathered around him as he sat on the living room couch. "What kind of people are living down there? . . . She thought people's rights were being violated in Selma and she had to do something about it. . . . That was her downfall. I had told her, 'one of these days the humanitarian things you do are going to backfire.'" Penny couldn't stand to hear her mother even mildly criticized, so she leaped to her defense: "Mother felt there was too much talk and not enough action and she wanted to do something." Young Sally, confused by everything, climbed into Jim's lap and asked, "Why couldn't Mommy have just died from being old?"[9]

The victim had been identified and the family notified, but who had killed Viola Liuzzo? There were no leads, no obvious suspects—three men in a Ford was all Moton had told the FBI. It could have been anybody, and they were certainly long gone by now. Solving this crime would be like "looking for a needle in a haystack," J. Edgar Hoover later told President Johnson. But it turned out to be easier than anyone imagined.[10]

The murder of an unidentified white female civil rights worker was first publicly announced in Alabama on the ten o'clock local news. Watching his television, Neil Shanahan winced and said to himself, "Shit." He recalled that Tommy Rowe had told him that morning that he and some other Klansmen were going to Montgomery to observe the Voting Rights March.

Viola Liuzzo's children the morning after their mother's murder. *Left to right:* ten-year-old Tony; six-year-old Sally; eighteen-year-old Penny; and thirteen-year-old Tom. Her other daughter, Mary, is not pictured. (UPI-Bettmann/Corbis)

They might "whip ass" or "skin heads," but Shanahan knew that it was common, when Klansmen got together, for them to do a little "night riding"; he didn't expect serious violence. Rowe had not checked in, but that wasn't unusual. Still, Shanahan was uneasy, afraid that the day might have finally come when Tommy Rowe got himself into a mess that he couldn't talk or fight his way out of.

A half hour later, his worst fears were realized. The phone rang, and Shanahan learned that Rowe had just called the FBI's Birmingham field office, wanting to talk with him immediately. Rowe had long ago given up using code name Karl Cross, given to him when he became an informant in 1960. "Everybody knew who the hell I was," Rowe said later. Shanahan dialed the number; Rowe picked up on the first ring.[11]

"Where are you?" Shanahan asked.

"The phone booth outside the Blue Bird Cafe on Highway II," Rowe said. "Did you hear anything about a woman getting shot in Selma?"

"Yes, it was on the late news."

"I saw it," Rowe told him. "I was in the car with Thomas and the others. I've got to talk to you."

Rowe picked the spot to meet—the parking lot at the West Birmingham Baptist Hospital. Shanahan agreed that it seemed like a good spot; cars were always coming and going during the night; nobody would notice them. Rowe hung up.

Shanahan telephoned his boss, Special Agent in Charge Everett Ingram: "Tommy just called me and he told me he was with Gene Thomas and the guys from Bessemer and they shot a woman somewhere on the highway outside of Selma. I'm going out to see him now."

"OK," Ingram said. "Get back to me when you have some information." He would notify Headquarters in Washington and contact the local authorities to see what they knew.

It was 12:30 a.m. when Neil Shanahan reached the Baptist Hospital parking lot; the darkness and the pelting rain obscured his vision, so it took a moment to find Rowe's black Ford. Pulling alongside, he spoke to Rowe through their open windows. Rowe wanted to talk, but not there— "it wasn't a good place." Shanahan suggested that they go to the FBI field office, but Rowe shook his head. "Take your car and I'll follow you," Shanahan told him, "find some nice, quiet dark place where you can [park] and I'll pick you up." Rowe drove a few blocks, then turned into a dark cul de sac, parked, and climbed into Shanahan's Rambler station wagon. The FBI agent drove aimlessly around the neighborhood until he thought he found a safe place. They began to talk, but suddenly there was a noise nearby and a light flashed on—just a man working in his garage, but Shanahan pulled out anyway and again they drifted for a time. Finally they stopped on a tree-lined street.[12]

The two men had worked closely together during the past seven months, but the Tommy Rowe now sitting next to Shanahan bore little resemblance to the tough, aggressive braggart he knew. Rowe was "very upset," almost in a state of shock. "Are you drunk?" he asked. "No," Rowe said. "We just had a couple of beers during the day."[13]

Had he done any shooting that night? No, Rowe claimed, then took out his .38 Smith and Wesson revolver and gave it to Shanahan. Check it out, Rowe urged. Shanahan smelled the muzzle, then cracked the cylinder and removed the bullets. It didn't appear that the gun had been fired recently, but he suggested that Rowe think about hiring a lawyer. He would have to talk to FBI officials soon, and "decisions about his future would have to be made." Getting a complete statement from Rowe now was probably impossible, Shanahan thought. It was two o'clock on a rainy morning, and he could barely see to take notes. So his first objective was "to settle [Rowe] down . . . where he could become manageable . . . to provide the core information" he needed. He advised Rowe that he had a right to counsel and that any statement he made could be used against him. Rowe nodded, and then slowly, haltingly, he told his story. He had spent the day, he said, with three members of the Bessemer Klavern—Gene Thomas and his friends, a kid named "Wilkinson," and an older bald-headed guy named "Eadon," whom they called "Curly." He couldn't remember their first names. Shanahan knew Thomas, but he didn't recognize the others. Rowe insisted that Shanahan did know Curly and Wilkinson—he had seen them around —and when Shanahan said no, he didn't, Rowe became more agitated.[14]

When he was calm again, Rowe continued. They drove to Montgomery in Thomas's red and white two-door Chevy Impala, arriving at about 10:30 a.m., and watched the marchers for most of the afternoon from a gas station parking lot. "We harassed the marchers, hollered at them, booed them," Rowe recalled, "and got in arguments with some of the colored spectators." Thomas heckled one black man: "Didn't I see you holding hands with a white woman?" "Yes, she's my wife," the man replied. Thomas chased him and "kicked the Negro in the rear," but soldiers arrived in a jeep so they left for Selma, stopping for "two or three beers" at Jack's Tavern.

At 6:20 p.m., they ran through a Highway Patrol "radar trap," and a few minutes later, a police car, its red lights flashing, pulled them over. Thomas got out of the car and asked the officer, "Ole buddy, what you stop me for?" For having a noisy muffler, the officer replied. Thomas protested, showing the officer an honorary police badge from Fairfield County and several ID cards from Bessemer and other Klan-friendly towns, hoping that the man might have Klan connections. But the officer wasn't impressed. Stuffing the ticket in his pocket, Thomas returned to the car and drove to the Silver Moon Cafe, scene of the attack on Reverend James Reeb. While the men drank beer and coffee, Thomas noticed a man sitting alone eating his dinner. "You know who that is?" he asked the others, who said no. "That's the one out on bond for killing that ole preacher. I'm going to talk to him." Thomas was in awe of his fellow Klansman, an impressive figure, six feet tall, 220 pounds, who talked "hard" and proudly of having struck Reverend Reeb in the head with a baseball bat. Finishing their drinks, they got up to leave, running into Thomas's hero, who affectionately "slapped Gene on the shoulder" and said, "God bless you boys. We have done our job, now it's up to you."

After dinner, they tried to get close to Brown Chapel in Selma but a barrier blocked them, so they drove around until they spotted a group of whites and blacks outside a housing project. "Slow up, we'll get their ass," Rowe recalled Wilkinson saying. "Here, baby brother, take this," Thomas said, removing his .38 from the console separating the front bucket seats and handing it to Wilkinson. But Rowe saw an army truck filled with soldiers at the end of the street. "Hold it," he said. Then Thomas saw it and said, "Baby brother, you saved the day. . . . We'll wait. We've got all night." Wilkinson returned the gun to Thomas, who put it on top of the console. Rowe believed that, had the troops not been there, they would have jumped out of the car and "tagged" the blacks—smacking them on the side of the head and frightening them with a show of guns. He didn't expect a shooting.

Heading back to Montgomery, they stopped at a red light. "Look there, baby brother, I'll be damned," Rowe recalled Wilkinson saying as he pointed to the car that pulled up next to them. Despite the darkness and a misty rain, they could see that the driver was a white woman and her passenger a black man. "Wonder where they're going?" somebody asked. Somewhere to have sex, Thomas laughed. Wilkinson said, "Let's take them, maybe we have some brass here." Thomas thought it might be the head man himself, King, or some other important civil rights leader. When the light turned green, Thomas told Rowe and Wilkinson to "get down" as he followed the blue car across the bridge leading to Highway 80. "We're going all the way on this one," Rowe remembered Thomas saying. "We came to get a black and a white together." It was now about eight o'clock.

As they neared Craig Air Force Base, Thomas shifted into the right lane and came abreast of the car. He rolled down his window and picked up his revolver, but Rowe spotted military police ahead and again yelled, "Hold it!" Thomas slowed down, allowing the woman to pull far ahead as the four-lane highway became two narrow roads. If they managed to catch up, Rowe said, they should "whip their ass and let the whole world see them." Wilkinson said, "We know what we're going to do."

Thomas sped up again but quickly slowed down when he reached the radar trap. Passing through safely this time, Thomas increased his speed to 110 miles an hour, and the Oldsmobile soon came into sight. But a station wagon went by in the opposite direction and Thomas said, "They've seen us." Rowe and Wilkinson turned to watch the station wagon disappear and then reappear as the road twisted, then straightened. Soon it was out of sight. Thomas suggested they "sideswipe" the car, forcing it into a ditch. Not a good idea, said Wilkinson, an auto mechanic. The collision would leave paint on Thomas's Impala. Right, Thomas agreed. "Let's go back to Selma and get another one," Rowe said, but it was too late. They were now directly behind the woman. Thomas said, "Get your guns out." Rowe thought they were going to shoot the tires. Eadon pulled out his .22 and began to roll down his front window, as did Wilkinson, who leaned forward to get Thomas's gun. Suddenly, Thomas swerved to the left into the oncoming lane and, as they passed the other car, Eadon fired two shots, which struck the windshield. Then Wilkinson began shooting, shattering the driver's side window. Rowe squeezed in next to Wilkinson and stuck his own .38 out the window, he told Shanahan, but he didn't fire. Thomas sped up, then returned to the right lane, leaving the woman's car far behind. Looking back, Rowe saw the car still behind them, but then it slowly turned off to the side. "You missed!" Rowe told Wilkinson, who looked over his shoulder as the car moved away. "I don't miss!" he gloated. "That bitch and that bastard are dead and in hell."

Farther down the road, the gunmen dumped their shells out the window. Thomas then headed for Bessemer, stopping first at the VFW Club, where he looked for a friend named Bob who he hoped would provide them with an alibi. But Bob was drunk, so they went to Lorene's Cafe, where Thomas found friends who agreed to say that the men had been there most of the evening. Then it was back to Bessemer. On the way, Thomas told Rowe, "You're in the big stuff now. You're number one boy again." When they passed Grand Dragon Bob Creel's home, Thomas wanted to stop and report "a job well done," but the lights were off and nobody wanted to disturb the Dragon while he slept. Thomas said that if they learned that anyone in the car was injured or killed, they should get rid of their guns. He asked Eadon to pick up the revolvers early in the morning and drop them in the blast furnace at the steel mill where he had worked before his recent retirement. And he also warned, "If anyone talks, we'll get their kids." At Thomas's house, Rowe got his car, drove around for a while to make sure he wasn't being followed, and then hurried to contact the FBI.[15]

It was past two o'clock in the morning when Rowe finished talking. Both men were exhausted and sweating from the humidity. Shanahan returned Rowe to his car and told him to go directly home and stay there until he heard from him. The agent drove to the first pay phone he could find and called Ingram at the field office. There had been some developments, Ingram reported. The victim had been identified and her passenger questioned, but beyond that nothing helpful was known. Come in immediately, he told Shanahan.[16]

President Johnson was also up at this late hour, seeking information about the shooting in Alabama. He telephoned FBI Headquarters twice around 1 a.m. and told them they must do everything "to solve this heinous crime." He was assured that everything that could be done was being done. Then the president went to sleep.[17]

There was no sleep for Jim Liuzzo that night. At about the same time Johnson retired, Liuzzo was trying to learn more about what had happened to his wife. His friend Al Koskey offered to help him make some phone calls, which they tape recorded. First they called the Selma Police Department, where an officer said, "This didn't happen in my territory, so I wouldn't have a report. . . . You'll have to talk to somebody in Montgomery." Who? Koskey asked. Colonel Al Lingo, head of the State Police, might be able to help them. Could he give them Lingo's phone number? The officer didn't have it; try the Highway Patrol station in Montgomery, he suggested.[18]

Their call to the state capital was just as fruitless. Lingo wasn't there. "Call back in the morning," one official told them. Koskey said he would talk with anyone, so he was connected to a trooper named Smith. "Have you heard about the slaying?" Koskey asked.

"About the what?" Smith asked.

"About the murder?"

"Yes, sir."

"What can you tell us about it?"

"I couldn't tell you anything," Trooper Smith said. "I don't have a report on it."

"Well, have you heard anything?" Koskey was almost pleading now. "How she died and how she was murdered and who did it?"

"No, I don't know a thing in the world about how it happened. The newspapers and television know more about it than I do." Call the FBI in Selma, Trooper Smith said, and then hung up.

In Selma, they finally reached FBI Inspector Joe Sullivan, who told them what little he knew at that point. The investigation was just beginning, he said; they were "trying to put the pieces together." Mrs. Liuzzo had been driving civil rights workers when she was ambushed.

"She died right away?" Koskey asked.

"As far as we can tell," Sullivan said. There was a witness to the shooting, the inspector added, but he wasn't "capable of furnishing any precise details."

"What was it, a rifle or a pistol?"

"We don't know this yet." An autopsy would be performed to officially determine the cause of death, and ballistics tests would be needed to verify what kind of weapon killed her.

"Where is her body now?"

"It's at the White Chapel Mortuary in Montgomery," Sullivan said, concluding the conversation. "I'm very sorry to have to give you this kind of information, but it's really all we can do right now and we hope to find out more."

"Yes, I realize," Koskey said. "Thank you very kindly, sir."[19]

Sullivan's report only led Jim Liuzzo to crave more information. He was furious at the Alabama authorities, especially Governor Wallace; if only he could have five minutes alone with the governor, he remarked. "You'd think they at least would have the decency to call," he told Koskey, but they didn't, so at around 5:30 a.m., Liuzzo called the White House. He wanted to speak with President Johnson, he told the duty officer who received his call. The president was asleep, he was told; perhaps another person could help him.

"Who?" the angry Liuzzo yelled. "This is very important. . . . My wife died for a cause President Johnson believes in. My children are crying and my wife is lying on a slab in Montgomery, and I can't get any information at all from Alabama. I'll only take a minute of his time." But the duty officer refused to put him through to the president, promising only that Liuzzo's message would be passed along in the morning.[20]

The man who held the key to breaking the case, Gary Thomas Rowe, was brought to the FBI field office at 6:00 a.m. Since Thomas had said that the man named Eadon planned to dispose of the weapons later that morning, identifying the suspects was the top priority. This case was considered "extremely hot," one agent noted; the president had telephoned Headquarters twice that night. Both the Selma and Birmingham offices were to jointly work the case, and agents were told "to keep their mouths shut"; any announcements would come from Washington. To coordinate their efforts, Ingram brought in James L. McGovern, a twenty-four-year veteran of the FBI, who, as a "major case inspector," was already in Birmingham supervising the GREENBOMBS case. Ingram awakened him at 4:30 a.m. and told him to come into the office immediately; there was "an emergency." ("It always happens at four o'clock in the morning," McGovern later said.) It turned out to be one of the most stressful days in McGovern's long career. Asked almost eighteen years later if he remembered March 26, 1965, McGovern said, "I don't think I'll ever forget [it]."[21]

Rowe sat comfortably in an interview room and studied the results of the FBI's "index and file review," which produced three dossiers on the men McGovern and Shanahan thought were a match for those Rowe described: Gene Thomas, Eadon, and the "boy" named Wilkinson. Veteran Klansman Eugene Thomas was the easiest to identify because Shanahan knew him well. The forty-two-year-old Thomas had first been arrested in 1945 for public drunkenness. Two years later he was charged with assault and battery, but the case never went to trial, probably because it was a domestic dispute—Thomas liked to beat his wife. He was again charged with the same crime in 1949, 1950, 1956, and 1963, with an added charge of carrying a concealed weapon. For the past twenty-four years, he had been employed as a machinist at the Fairfield, Alabama, branch of Tennessee Coal and Iron Company. It was in the company's blast furnaces that the guns were to be disposed. Shown a photograph of the tall, lean Bessemer native, Rowe easily identified him as the man who had driven the car the day before.[22]

"Curly" Eadon was William Orville Eaton, who, in 1963, had offered to sacrifice himself by blowing up the Gaston mansion. The file revealed that the forty-one-year-old Eaton, whose bald head earned him the nickname Curly, was also a Bessemer Klansman, with a wife, five children, and a serious heart condition. That illness forced his retirement as a steel port helper from the same plant where Thomas worked. Rowe had no trouble identifying Eaton as the man with the .22.[23]

The boy was Collie Leroy Wilkins, also known as Wilkie or Lee. The twenty-one-year-old Birmingham native was a high school dropout, automobile mechanic, and—like his two buddies—a Bessemer Klansman. Gene Thomas considered him his "protégé" and called him "my boy." He was first arrested at sixteen and pleaded guilty to charges of petty larceny and destroying private property. In 1964, he was arrested three times for possession of an illegal firearm (a sawed-off shotgun) and once for assault with intent to commit murder; currently he was on probation, forbidden to carry any weapon. Rowe said that Wilkins had no gun that day and used Thomas's .38 to shoot at the blue Oldsmobile.[24]

After informing Washington that Liuzzo's alleged killers had been identified, McGovern arranged for the suspects to be put under surveillance until they could be arrested. Then, he, Shanahan, and two other agents asked Rowe to review the previous day's events for a formal statement that he would sign. Rowe repeated the story he had told Shanahan a few hours earlier, emphasizing that while the men talked about beating the marchers, nobody ever mentioned killing them. (McGovern also examined Rowe's revolver, smelling the muzzle and checking for powder residue but found no evidence that the gun had been recently fired.) When Rowe finished his statement, Inspector McGovern informed him of his rights, because legally he was an accomplice and as much a suspect as the three Klansmen. Rowe suddenly became nervous and refused to sign the statement unless he was given immunity from both state and federal prosecution. McGovern said that he could make no promises but would "relay his concerns" to the Justice Department.

When Inspector Joe Sullivan spoke with Rowe, he gave him a preview of what he could expect during the next few months. Rowe "got a charge" from being a "police buff," Sullivan knew, and he quickly disabused him of the notion that he would be treated like a hero. In fact, he should expect to be "derided and abused by his peers," especially when he testified against the Klansmen. Rowe became "very disturbed," Sullivan later noted. "He thought he was being abandoned. He didn't know where his future lay" and hoped the government would help him. Sullivan wasn't reassuring. He was "only beginning to feel the heat, that until he testified, he wouldn't really know what it meant to be scorned and ridiculed and accused of being dishonest and corrupt, and that he could look forward to all of that, too."

Rowe felt better later that afternoon when he was told that Assistant Attorney General John Doar approved immunity for Rowe provided that he had told the truth about the shooting. Doar's action changed the Bureau's response to the murder. Its mission was no longer investigation but corroboration. Already satisfied that Rowe's story was correct, the FBI began to search for the evidence to support it. Anything that suggested that Rowe might have been one of shooters was discounted or ignored.[25]

President Johnson was also up at six o'clock that morning with the Liuzzo case on his mind. Before shaving and showering, he read the morning newspapers and watched—simultaneously—the three television sets he had installed in his bedroom. The TV news carried the story of the Liuzzo killing as well as Jim Liuzzo's inability to reach the president earlier that morning. Johnson immediately called the FBI to get the latest details. There was nothing new to report, the president was told.

Then at 8:10 a.m. J. Edgar Hoover gave Johnson the extraordinary news that the FBI had solved the Liuzzo murder. The president's tape recorder captured the conversation:

HOOVER: One of our men [was] in the car. Fortunately he, of course, had no gun [sic] and did no shooting. But he has identified the two men who had guns and who fired guns. I think there were about ten or twelve shots fired into the car . . .

JOHNSON: Six-shooters or shotgun?

HOOVER: I think they're revolvers.

JOHNSON: Unhuh, unhuh.

HOOVER: And they discussed that . . . if the woman died they were going to throw the guns into the blast furnace where they worked in the steel mills down there. And that's what we're laying for now, to head off these individuals when they come to work this morning and shake 'em down and if we're lucky enough to find the gun on 'em that'll be the big break in the case. But, in any event, whether they find the gun or not, they'll bring 'em in and shake them down—interrogation.

Johnson, whose telephone conversations usually resembled Shakespearian soliloquies, permitted Hoover to dominate the exchange and only expressed relief and gratitude: "Thank you so much, Edgar. As usual, you're right on top of it." Then he asked Hoover what to do about the husband:

JOHNSON: I just heard a little while ago about this fella callin' me, I didn't know anything about it but I think I'll call him. You see no reason why I shouldn't . . . ?

HOOVER: I see no reason why you shouldn't. As the radio said, he was very angry because they wouldn't put him through to you last night. . . . He could have called the FBI. . . . We always have one or two men on duty all the time . . . twenty-four hours a day . . . so that if anything does break they can alert me. And I was alerted.

The men then talked about the Bureau's informant.

HOOVER: We've got the informant in the office and we're talking to him. . . . He's scared to death naturally because he fears for his life . . .

JOHNSON (interrupting): What is an infiltrator—you hire someone and they join the Klan?

HOOVER: Generally, we go to someone who is already in the Klan and persuade him to work for the government. We pay him for it. Sometimes they demand a pretty high price. . . . Now this man that we have now, the informant, he's not a regular agent of the Bureau but he's one of those people we put in, just like we do into the Communist Party. So he keeps us informed and fortunately he happened to be in on this thing last night . . .

JOHNSON: That's wonderful, Edgar. Thank you so much.[26]

Johnson then called the attorney general. Before telling him that the case was nearly solved, Johnson asked what Katzenbach thought he should do about telephoning Liuzzo. All that was known about him was that he worked for the Teamsters Union; Katzenbach recommended caution. "I'd have [White House counsel] Lee White talk to him . . . Mr. President, so you don't get embarrassed by him."

Johnson agreed: "From what he sounded like from radio and television, he's . . . not too restrained and was rather ugly."

Then the president told Katzenbach that the FBI "had an informant in the car . . . they know who they are and they're waiting to pick them up."

"Oh, that's good!" said Katzenbach, astonished.

"The Bessemer Klan did it," Johnson noted, and then wondered what could be done about destroying the Klan once and for all. "Looks like we ought to . . . really move in on the Klan more effectively. They've done a lot of this stuff through the South. . . . Is there anything we can do in the way of legislation?"

Katzenbach had nothing to recommend immediately, but Johnson wanted action: "Outlaw 'em! If we could somehow get a list of all the members and expose it somehow." Then the president had an idea: He would make a statement when the Klansmen were arrested, calling for congressional hearings "to outlaw 'em or increase the penalties on this kind of stuff, make it a federal crime." An announcement from the White House would "be really dramatic, helpful too."[27]

Johnson decided to have Lee White contact Liuzzo, but the president didn't tell his counsel of the FBI's success, not wanting anything to interfere with his planned announcement later in the day. "Tell him the president was up until two o'clock, he's had the FBI workin' around the clock," Johnson instructed. "Everything's being done. . . . We'll let him know as soon as we know something and convey to him my deep sympathies and my deep regrets and so forth. See what kind of person he is . . . whether it might be embarrassing to me to call him. . . . Be sure to take down what he says."

Within minutes White called Liuzzo, and the two spoke of both his personal crisis and the nation's. "Is this going to stop here?" Liuzzo asked.

"You know it's not going to stop," White said.

"All I want to know is where do we go from here?" White had no answer.

Lee White reported to the president that he had found Liuzzo in a "reflective mood," angry at Governor Wallace (who said on the *Today* show that morning that despite the Liuzzo killing, Alabama's highways were still safer than New York's) but supportive of Johnson's efforts on behalf of civil rights. "He . . . wanted to know where do we go from here? . . . Are we going to continue to have to give lives to this cause? Will this ever stop? . . . My judgment, sir, is that if you did call him, he's going to be reasonable and not in any sense uncontrollable or wild." But Johnson still wanted to know more before calling: "Get the FBI to give you right quick a report," he told White.

An impatient Johnson again called Hoover around 9:30. "Before I talk to [Liuzzo] I wanted to . . . have you check . . . if there's any reason why I shouldn't because . . . [he's] a Teamster man."

"Yes, he's a Teamster man," Hoover replied, "one of their so-called 'agents' and he has . . . I wouldn't say a bad character but he's well-known as being one of the Teamsters' strong-armed men." Next, Hoover communicated some false and malicious gossip about the murder victim, which agents had picked up from Alabama's Colonel Al Lingo: "This woman . . . , we found on her body numerous needle points indicating that she may have been taking dope. We can't tell definitely, she's dead." And the reason why the Klansmen went after her was because they saw "this colored man . . . snuggling up pretty close to the white woman . . . it had all the appearances of a necking party."[28]

Johnson was familiar with Hoover's racist views but wanted the case wrapped up quickly. "They're running me crazy over here," he said, referring to reporters seeking news.

"You can make the statement from the White House," Hoover suggested. Johnson, sensitive to Hoover's need for flattery, invited him and Katzenbach to share the glory: "Give me a chance to show what good work the FBI is doin' and how the attorney general is doin' it and we [are] all together . . . workin' this thing and [in] just twenty-four hours you've produced results, and I think [a joint appearance] might make it a little dramatic."

"I think it would be," Hoover agreed, excitedly.

Johnson wanted to make the statement shortly after noon, eleven o'clock Alabama time. "I'll speed the thing up right away," Hoover promised.[29]

Johnson's schedule was a nightmare for FBI Inspector James McGovern. There were a dozen things to do and precious little time in which to do them. Agents were now watching the suspects' homes, but they couldn't arrest them or search their homes and cars without the proper warrants. If the FBI moved too quickly, evidence might be tainted by an illegal search and seizure. Plus, the FBI had to determine what federal law the men had broken. The U.S. attorney in Mobile must quickly produce a formal statement charging them with a specific crime, which the attorney general would approve. The clock was running: "I'm talking back and forth to Headquarters," McGovern later recalled. "I'm interviewing Rowe . . . I'm talking to the U.S. attorney . . . I'm talking to [Inspector Joseph] Sullivan [at the crime scene]. We're attempting to coordinate the surveillance. . . . We're being asked: 'what do we do, they're leaving the house, they're heading for Tuscaloosa. . . . Do we pick them up now?' 'No, you don't' and 11 o'clock is approaching, and the president is going to have a press conference." At 10:55 (11:55 Washington time), McGovern learned that the Justice Department had finally authorized the filing of a complaint charging the Klansmen with conspiracy to violate Section 241, Title 18, of the U.S. Criminal Code—the violation of Viola Liuzzo's civil rights. His agents could now move in and arrest the suspects.[30]

FBI agents in two separate cars had been watching Gene Thomas's house since early that morning, and when he stepped out on the porch to pick up his newspaper, he immediately recognized them. At eleven o'clock, he finally got in his Chevrolet Impala and drove away, ignoring the automobiles that followed him. He made a quick stop at the Grand Dragon's house, where he told Robert Creel about the shooting and asked him to keep his .38 pistol until somebody could pick it up. As Thomas pulled away, Mrs. Creel told her husband she didn't want the gun in her house and telephoned Thomas's wife, who drove down to get it. Mrs. Thomas returned home, leaving her husband's gun in her car's glove compartment. After stopping for gas, Thomas headed for Lorene's Cafe, where he was sipping a Budweiser when Agents Ralph Butler and Lawrence Gettings entered, placed him under arrest, and brought him out in handcuffs. Walking toward Thomas's car, Agents Edward Lahey and John F. Connaughton noticed something on the outside window ledge. "What's this?" Connaughton asked Thomas, pointing to a .22-caliber hollow-point bullet shell lying on the car's window ledge. Both agents saw Thomas's face "turn ashen."[31]

Collie Leroy Wilkins also noticed two cars parked near his house that morning and knew that the men inside them were FBI. When he later drove off, the cars followed him as he aimlessly drove around the Birmingham-Bessemer area, running red lights in the hope of losing them, and then heading south toward Tuscaloosa. That's when the lead car flashed its red light and pulled him over. Special Agent Robert Murphy showed Wilkins his credentials, asked him to get out of his car, and read him his rights. Then he had Wilkins lean against the car so he could search him. Murphy was thorough, patting him down "from his neck to his shoes." "What am I charged with?" Wilkins asked. "Deprivation of civil rights by reason of murder," Murphy said, placing him in handcuffs. Wilkins was so terrified that he defecated in his pants, to Murphy a clear sign that the man was guilty of murder.[32]

William Orville Eaton was probably relieved when he was arrested at his home at 11:16 a.m. Since taking his children to school earlier that morning, he had been followed by the same automobile; it was behind him everywhere he went—at the gas station, tire store, café. Fearing that somebody wanted to kill him, he hurried home, deliberately running a stop sign, expecting that if he was being followed by the police they would pull him over; but the car ran the sign too. When the knock on his front door finally came, it was not some psychopath but rather FBI agents, who took him into custody.[33]

The search of the suspects' homes and cars turned up a variety of weapons, ammunition, and Klan regalia—.22-caliber six-shot revolvers, sawed-off shotguns, a bloodstained bullwhip coiled inside a washing machine, a rusty chain, and a metal-lined rubber hose—all belonging to Gene Thomas. Wilkins's Klan robe and hood were hidden in a suitcase in his bedroom closet. Thomas's wife, Flossie, was annoyed when agents seized her .38 snub-nosed revolver. How would she protect herself now? she asked. "Use your broomstick," one agent replied. But she was kind enough to inform the agents that they could find her husband's .38 in the glove compartment of her car, parked outside. She asked her son Wayne to get it, but Agent Lahey accompanied him to the car and watched as he opened the glove compartment, withdrew the gun, and handed it to him. He removed it from the holster and held it up to the light, but he couldn't see any obvious fingerprints. The FBI never found the .22 that Eaton used that night; they later learned that he had melted it down and buried the remains in his backyard.[34]

With the filing of the complaint at eleven o'clock and the arrest of the suspects a few minutes later, Inspector McGovern had barely but successfully met Johnson's deadline. "I remember very clearly the relief that I felt when I got the radio transmission that all three had been taken into custody without incident," he later recalled. "That was the highlight of the day."[35]

At 12:42 p.m. all national network television programming was interrupted by a special announcement from the president of the United States. Flanked by Hoover and Katzenbach, Johnson told the country that the Liuzzo murder was solved, less than twenty-four hours after the commission of the crime. He thanked the attorney general and singled out for praise Director Hoover ("our honored public servant") and the men of the FBI "who worked all night long starting immediately after the tragic death of

Mrs. Viola Liuzzo," leading to the arrest of Eugene Thomas, William Orville Eaton, Collie Leroy Wilkins, and Gary Thomas Rowe, Jr.—all members of the Ku Klux Klan.

His voice "choked with anger and disgust," Johnson said: "Mrs. Liuzzo went to Alabama to serve the struggle for justice. She was murdered by the enemies of justice who, for decades, have used the rope and the gun, the tar and the feathers, to terrorize their neighbors. They struck by night, as they generally do. For their purposes cannot stand the light of day.

"My father fought them in Texas. I have fought them all my life because I believe them to threaten the peace of every community where they exist. I shall continue to fight them because I know their loyalty is not to the United States but to a hooded society of bigots."

The president then directly addressed the secret order: "If Klansmen hear my voice today, let it be both an appeal—and a warning—to get out of the Klan now and return to a decent society—before it is too late." He had asked the attorney general to create new legislation to bring Klan activities "under effective control of law." He also encouraged Congress to investigate the Klan and other organizations committing violence.[36]

It was an extraordinary moment: Never before had an American president shown such personal interest in the investigation of a crime and then identified the suspects in a special televised event. The announcement dominated the networks' evening news shows that night and was headlined in the nation's newspapers the following morning. Not all Americans were pleased, however. Imperial Wizard Bobby Shelton called the president "a damn liar." "This organization has never used tar and feathers and a rope," he told reporters. "It is he that is using the gun and the rope, his tanks and ammunition against the South." A man from Toledo told Hoover that he didn't look "too happy" on television, "for in your heart you know the kind of Commies, perverts, etc that provoked this march. . . . We are most sad that this white woman was killed! But, what was she doing away from home, five children & a husband, and consorting (?) with niggers for a week like a *2-bit-* . . . . Stick to your guns and don't let LBJ flatter you too much." Other critics would echo these attacks on Liuzzo in the months ahead.[37]

That afternoon, President Johnson telephoned Jim Liuzzo. It was a brief but cordial conversation that television cameras recorded. Liuzzo told the president that he had learned of the arrests and was grateful for his swift action. "Being an Italian and a member of the Teamsters Union, I know what it is to be pushed around and kicked around," he said. Then, his voice choking, Liuzzo added, "Our country needs people like you."

"I was up most of the night," Johnson said, "and I'm glad that we've had some results . . . I'm glad that we were able to move as fastly [sic] and effectively as we could. You know how grieved we are . . . Mrs. Johnson and I . . . know how you must feel and . . . I want you to be brave and [know how] anxious I am to correct it, and to see that your dear wife did not die in vain. And that others will, for years to come, have their lot improved in this country because of the sacrifice she made."

"Thank you, Mr. President," Liuzzo replied. "I don't think she died in vain. It's going to be a battle all out, as far as we're concerned here in Detroit."

"I'm grateful to you, and thank you so much."[38]

In his dramatic announcement, the president said that all the Klansmen were in custody, but that was only partly true; Gary Thomas Rowe, Jr., was not under arrest or in jail. He was very much a free man, traveling over the same ground he had covered the night before. Wearing a homemade disguise—cheap plastic raincoat and what Shanahan called "a go to hell hat" and sunglasses—Rowe showed a carload of agents and Assistant Attorney General John Doar each place the Klansmen had visited on March 25. They drove slowly by the crime scene where agents and state police were still examining Liuzzo's car and the muddy field where it rested. The informant, now the Bureau's most important witness to the killing, pointed out the spot where Thomas told them to empty their pistols. "Now you're gonna go around a little curve and see a bridge," Shanahan remembered Rowe saying; "it was right after that bridge that we threw the shells out the window." Shanahan was skeptical but radioed the office, which sent a group of agents who, just two hundred yards away, found fifteen shell casings—eight from Eaton's .22 and seven from Thomas's .38. "Rowe was right on!" Shanahan later said in amazement.[39]

But Rowe also had to return to his other life inside the Klan. The FBI decided that he should continue the "charade" for as long as possible, so at four o'clock, as they neared the Birmingham Federal Building, he was formally placed under arrest. How should he explain where he had been for the past four hours? he asked the agents. "Just play it cool," he was told. One joked: "Say the FBI picked you up and we rode around . . . trying to swing you over. Tell them we promised you forty thousand dollars and an apple orchard in Wisconsin; LBJ owns a hell of a lot of apple orchards. And you told us to go get screwed." Entering the parking lot, somebody remembered that Rowe should be handcuffed, and it was quickly done. "I'm going to act like I'm a mean tough son-of-a-bitch," Rowe warned the agents.[40]

He did: As Shanahan and the others dragged him into the building, Rowe pushed, shoved, and cursed them. "I thought we had the meanest roughneck Klansman in the world," Shanahan later noted. He was turned over to Deputy U.S. Marshal Bill Funderberk, who put Rowe in a holding cell. When Funderberk returned, he asked to see Neil Shanahan. "Did you search him before you brought him in?" he asked. "Check his pockets?"

"Yes, I did," Shanahan insisted.

Funderberk smiled, nudged Shanahan, and taking his open hand, dropped a bullet and a handcuff key into it. "Oh, thanks a lot," the embarrassed agent said, making a fist to hide the items. (Shanahan later admitted that instead of having the bullet examined, he threw it away.)[41]

At 5:25 p.m., Rowe and the Klansmen were reunited in the courtroom of U.S. Commissioner Louise Charlton, who told them that they were accused of violating Title 18, Section 241 of the U.S. Criminal Code—conspiracy to injure and intimidate Americans exercising their constitutional rights. (They would also soon face state charges of murder in the first degree; Attorney General Richmond Flowers of Alabama had announced that he would seek the death penalty.) Matthew H. Murphy, the Klan's Imperial Klonsel, stepped forward to represent them. Each man entered a plea of not guilty, and bond was set at fifty thousand dollars per suspect, which Klan funds quickly paid.[42]

As the accused were being led away, reporters, photographers, and television crew members moved in for statements and pictures, enraging the Klansmen. "Get those damn lights out of my face!" Wilkins snarled. Eaton crossed his arms in front of his face while Rowe outdid them all: He lunged three times at photographers, and, ducking a cameraman, yelled, "I'm fixin' to bust one of them in the mouth!" "Take it easy," ordered the FBI agent escorting him.[43]

Rowe's violent behavior didn't reassure Klan officials who had long suspected him of being an FBI informer. There would be a meeting that evening at Matt Murphy's office, he was told, and he'd better be there.

When Rowe later entered Murphy's conference room, he found it filled with hostile Klansmen, including Bobby Shelton. Rowe thought, "Oh shit, I'm in a bag of worms."

"Hey baby brother, where the fuck have you been all day?" Rowe later recalled Murphy asking.

"Well, the FBI has had me," Rowe said. "They were trying to get me to tell them what the hell went on."

"What did you tell them?"

"I didn't tell them shit. . . . Get me a lawyer or sue me, or whatever you want to do. I acted really dumb about it."

Shelton didn't believe him. Pounding the desk, he screamed: "God-damned shit! You threw the hell in with them—"

"Hey!" Rowe yelled back. "I never did anything. The goddamned Man got me. What was I supposed to do?"

Murphy asked whether the FBI had threatened him or offered money in exchange for testimony. Rowe said no, and then mentioned the invented story about the $40,000 and an apple orchard. That was the best news the Klansmen had heard in days: "We're going to shoot up the FBI," Murphy said, urging Rowe to "blow up the price to 550 acres of apple trees in Wisconsin plus $186,000 in cash." Tell everybody about the bribe, Shelton told him. They would publicize it widely to embarrass the president: "For once in his life President Johnson has made a terrible mistake." Later, both Shelton and Murphy issued statements attacking the president and accusing him of perverting justice by bribing a Klansman.[44]

They let Rowe leave then, but he wasn't alone. Driving home, he was certain that he was being followed, so he suddenly turned into an alley, and when the other car did too, he slammed on the brakes, jumped out, and pulled a twelve-gauge shotgun from the trunk. Pointing it at the other man, whom he recognized as a Klan investigator, he yelled, "What's your goddamned story?"

The Klansman held his arms up and stuttered, "Hey, Bobby Shelton sent me to be sure the goddamned Bureau didn't pick you up again."

"Get off my ass," Rowe ordered, then returned to his car and drove home, alone.

At 10:50 p.m. that Friday, the body of Viola Liuzzo returned home to Michigan from Alabama, borne by a twin-engine airplane owned by Jimmy

Hoffa, who also offered a five-thousand-dollar reward for information leading to the apprehension and conviction of the killers. Waiting in the cold on the airport tarmac were Jim Liuzzo's co-workers and friends Charles O'Brien and George Kirchner, who had volunteered to receive the coffin. After the plane taxied to a stop, O'Brien and Kirchner, along with the pilot, the copilot, and employees of the Ted C. Sullivan Funeral Home, carefully moved the gray casket to the hearse that stood nearby. A viewing of the body was scheduled for Sunday at the Sullivan Funeral Home, but only for friends and family; a requiem high mass would be held on Tuesday at Detroit's Immaculate Heart of Mary Church, with burial to follow at Holy Sepulcher Cemetery in Smithfield.[45]

Saturday brought the Liuzzo family the news that Governor George Romney of Michigan had declared Monday and Tuesday days of statewide mourning for Viola Liuzzo. Local and national politicians visited the Liuzzo house that day: Mayor Jerome Cavenaugh of Detroit, Senator Philip Hart of Michigan, Congressman John T. Conyers, and Congresswoman Martha Griffiths, who, with "tears in her eyes," had on Friday asked the House of Representatives why Liuzzo's presence on Highway 80 was "a crime punishable by death in Alabama. Is this the law of Alabama?" Governor Romney spent forty-five minutes with the Liuzzos and later told the press that Viola's death "reminded me of the death of Joan of Arc."[46]

Ministers throughout the city—both black and white—spoke of Viola Liuzzo's sacrifice in their Sunday sermons. Reverend Nicholas Hood of the Plymouth Congregational Church likened her murder to Christ's agony at Calvary, reminding his congregation that "in every crucifixion there is a resurrection." His colleague Reverend Fulton Bradley of the Tabernacle Baptist Church proclaimed that "though it is awful that the blood of a noble woman was shed, out of this chaos will emerge an ordered society. Mrs. Liuzzo is another of the great martyrs who lived and died for a cause." Martin Luther King, who had announced that he would attend the Liuzzo funeral, appeared on Sunday's *Meet the Press*, where, as protest against the murders of Jimmy Lee Jackson, Reverend Reeb, and Viola Liuzzo, he proposed the most radical actions of his career. He recommended a national economic boycott of Alabama and the elimination of all federal support for the state, including the removal of federal funds from Alabama's banks. (He later dropped these plans, fearing that they would hurt black as well as white Alabamans.)[47]

The Liuzzos spent most of Sunday at the funeral home. Penny and Tony, looking for the last time at their mother's face, thought her expression seemed "triumphant," as it usually did "whenever Mom won a battle." Later that evening, Vice President Hubert H. Humphrey, long a champion of civil rights, visited the family. He paid special attention to Sally, at one point hugging the child, who cried repeatedly, "I want my mommy."[48]

Telegrams and letters numbering in the thousands arrived at the house. Some came from fellow marchers who remembered "the loving welcome" they had received from Viola when they arrived in Selma. Other people wanted to help. If Jim needed her, a registered practical nurse offered to care for his children. Another woman wired: IF THERE IS ANY-THING I CAN DO—COOK, CLEAN, BABY SIT, PLEASE FEEL FREE TO CALL ME. Many were from blacks, who expressed the same thoughts: YOUR WIFE DIED FOR THE DIGNITY OF COLORED AMERICANS. HER MIND WAS LIKE A CLOUDLESS SKY AND HER CONSCIENCE LIKE A SEA AT REST. . . . SHE DID NOT DIE IN VAIN. From Cleveland, Ohio: WE AS NEGROES SEE IN HER PASSING THE DESTRUCTION OF AN OLD WORLD AND THE BIRTH OF A NEW.[49]

Many letters contained small amounts of money to create a memorial to "the slain martyr." Officials of St. Mary's Dominican College in New Orleans told Jim they would be "privileged and honored to have a daughter of the Anthony Liuzzo family enrolled at St. Mary's," and to make this possible, they promised to give any one of Mrs. Liuzzo's daughters a four-year scholarship worth almost four thousand dollars. From Wyoming came a letter for Sally. Recalling Sally's plaintive question—"Why couldn't Mommy have just died from being old?"—Dan J. Bethell wrote: "That was a terrifying question fate forced you to ask of your daddy. And if he were wiser than Solomon, the answer would still evade him as it does all of us who love you and mourn with you. . . . Perhaps Sally, it will help you to remember this: Now your mother belongs to America. Thank you for sharing her with us." Enclosed was two dollars, part of his children's allowance, which they wanted to share with Sally. "Do not bank it or save it. Just be a little girl and buy something foolish with it."[50]

Viola Liuzzo would have especially enjoyed the NAACP-sponsored memorial service held on Monday night at the People's Community Church. Like Liuzzo herself, it was spirited, inspiring, and defiant. Many of the fifteen hundred to two thousand people who attended had to stand—both inside the sanctuary and outside in the halls and lobby. The choir sang with so much enthusiasm, one observer noted, that when it rendered "Battle Hymn of the Republic" and "We Shall Overcome," "everyone wanted to march . . . and everyone wanted to sing and most did." Two dozen speakers took turns at the lectern—Michigan's lieutenant governor William Milliken; Mary Ellen Riordan, the president of the Detroit Federation of Teachers, who wore a red-and-black suit, saying, "because [black] is the color of grief and . . . red is the color of a martyr's blood"; and representatives of the mayor, the AFL-CIO, and other organizations.

The audience gave a standing ovation to Saginaw native Jim Letherer, the one-legged man on crutches who had completed the fifty-four-mile march from Selma to Montgomery. Wearing his now-famous straw hat with the blue hatband that read "Freedom," Letherer said, "I know Mrs. Liuzzo didn't die in vain, because before she died there were thousands of people sitting on the fence trying to decide when the time was right to join in the civil rights fight—well, she proved the time is right now." Reverend Clarence Theodore Roosevelt Nelson told the crowd that, only a week before, Viola had called him from Selma with the news that she wanted to adopt the black daughter of the woman with whom she was temporarily living. "I'm going to call on the Teamsters," Nelson said, "so that this girl can be found and brought here and raised just as if she was a blood child which is the way Mrs. Liuzzo would have wanted it."[51]

A gentle snow was falling on Tuesday morning as people waited in line to enter the Immaculate Heart of Mary Church to celebrate a requiem mass for Viola Liuzzo. Soon a black hearse appeared, and six Teamsters, led by a black man, carried the gleaming mahogany casket through the doors of the church and down the aisle where it was gently placed before an altar bearing the words "Give me thy heart." The Liuzzo family followed, taking their places in the fourth pew. Jim Liuzzo, his face "contorted with grief," sat alone, a few seats away from his children. Mary looked stunned, "her eyes . . . wide with disbelief." Sally, wearing red patent-leather slippers, clung tightly to Penny, who seemed terrified. Tom and Tony, trying to be brave, held back their tears. The family had invited 100 guests (including Martin Luther King, Jr., who did attend), and after they were seated, others —estimated at about 150—were allowed to join them.[52]

The Reverend Father James J. Sheehan, executive secretary of the Archbishop's Committee on Human Relations, delivered the eulogy in a voice of "controlled fierceness." "Today, America hurts," he said. "None of

Viola Liuzzo's family followed her coffin as it left the Immaculate Heart of Mary Church, March 30, 1965. *Left to right:* Jim Liuzzo, Tom Liuzzo, Penny Liuzzo; *second row:* Barry Johnson, daughter Mary's husband, Mary Liuzzo Johnson (head bowed), and Tony Liuzzo. (UPI-Bettmann/Corbis)

us who has pride in our country is not agonized over the death of Viola Liuzzo. In this the family bears an especially heavy sorrow. We can and do assure them of our sympathy, our prayers, our help in whatever way it may be asked. We wish we could right their wrong."

While praising Viola for her "bravery" on "the highway of hate, the highway of hell," Father Sheehan spoke of the current racial crisis and how poorly white America was responding. "The voice of the white churches on the question of racial justice has been more like a whisper than a trumpet blast. This is . . . the sin of our day. . . . We in the Detroit area have been given a great blessing from God at the expense of the Liuzzo family. He has shown us graphically today the fruit of false prejudice. May we learn this lesson well, so that from Mrs. Liuzzo's death in Christ, there may come new life, not hurt but peace, true peace flowing from truth, justice, love and freedom." The mass ended with the congregation singing "We Shall Overcome."[53]

At the graveside, Jim Liuzzo touched his wife's casket for a moment, then walked away. Penny, still holding Sally's hand, placed it on the casket, then they too, accompanied by Tom and Tony, returned to their car. Reporter Jean Sharley talked with two women who had followed the forty-five-car caravan from the church to Holy Sepulcher Cemetery, Viola Liuzzo's final resting place. "I wanted to see the mother," said Mrs. Donald Kuzawa of Utica. "With 5 children, she should have stayed home." Her friend, Mrs. Carol Nihrany, agreed: "I don't think she did any good. It'll be a hindrance for the children. For a few days they'll feel like martyrs, then they're going to feel offended." Sharley found their comments troubling, and recalling Father Sheehan's eulogy, she concluded that this had not been "a day of peace."[54]

There was also no peace for Gary Thomas Rowe. Since his return home on the night of March 26, he had received numerous threatening telephone calls. "Keep your fuckin' mouth shut or you're a dead man," said one unfamiliar voice, "your fuckin' kids, too." The FBI feared that Klan members now knew that Rowe would testify against their brothers and were therefore planning "immediate action, possibly violence" against him. So on Monday, March 29, agents took him to the Downtowner Motor Inn in East Birmingham, where they guarded him around the clock. Two days later, they moved him to the Guest House Motel, registered as Thomas

Dixon, courtesy of Shanahan's Irish wit: Dixon was the author of the 1913 novel and play *The Clansman*, the inspiration for D. W. Griffith's *Birth of a Nation*. On Friday, Rowe was moved again to the Birmingham Travelodge, but didn't stay long. The next day, April 1, Shanahan and Special Agent John Downey rented a car and, at night, drove Rowe to Pensacola, Florida, some 440 miles south of Birmingham. (Shanahan was not told where he was to take Rowe until the car was gassed up and ready to go.) The Bureau paid all of Rowe's expenses, including three meals a day and a new wardrobe, as well as a sixteen-dollar per diem—the standard government travel allowance. Rowe's ex-wife, Dorothy, received a stipend of sixty-five dollars a week, and she and her children were moved temporarily to a secret location in St. Petersburg, Florida, where the Bureau helped her find employment.[55]

Despite the FBI's efforts to keep Rowe's whereabouts a secret, the Klan learned of his Pensacola holiday. Imperial Klonsel Murphy joked to reporters that Rowe was "living it up in Florida," so the Bureau flew him back to Alabama, housing him at Maxwell Air Force Base. Two days later, "Mr. Dixon" checked in at the Birmingham Holiday Inn. His daily security assured, Rowe now focused on his future. He feared that he would be indicted for murder by the state of Alabama and was uncertain about the federal charges. In exchange for total immunity from prosecution, permanent relocation for his family, and a new life for him, he promised to publicly testify against the Klansmen. His demands were discussed with St. John Barrett, a top aide to Assistant Attorney General John Doar, and he received a quick response from Washington: Assuming that his version of the murder of Mrs. Liuzzo was true, all federal charges would be dropped, and the Department of Justice would "stand by him" should Alabama try to indict him.[56]

The Bureau went further than that. During a meeting with Alabama attorney general Richmond Flowers and his chief assistant Joe Breck Gantt, the FBI told Alabama officials that without immunity from state charges Rowe would not be allowed to testify. Flowers, knowing that there would be no case without Rowe, agreed to the demands, although he cautioned that his decision would not bind future attorneys general. Furthermore, Dorothy Rowe and the children would be permanently relocated, and the government promised to find Rowe a job in one of the three states he had requested—Texas, California, or Hawaii. Rowe was satisfied. Fewer than three weeks after the murder, the federal charges were formally dropped and a grand jury, under Gantt's control, indicted only Thomas, Wilkins, and Eaton.[57]

Tommy Rowe made his first public appearance as a witness for the prosecution on April 21, 1965, when reporters spotted him entering the Lowndes County grand jury room. Dressed in a dark suit and wearing sunglasses, he looked more like a businessman than a former Klansman, except for the holstered revolver on his hip. He told his story convincingly and impressed both state and federal officials. Circuit Solicitor Arthur Gamble, who would prosecute Collie Leroy Wilkins in early May, thought Rowe made "an excellent witness" before the grand jury and was confident that he would hold up well during the ordeal to come. St. John Barrett, who grilled Rowe for five hours about the killing, also came away "highly impressed by the caliber of the informant."[58]

Only one problem—potentially serious—spoiled the confident mood Rowe created. As he left the grand jury room, he saw the next witness enter—a tall, thin black man wearing glasses—Leroy Moton, Liuzzo's passenger on the night of the killing. Rowe thought he looked like a combination "beatnik" and "basketball player," and he asked Shanahan, "Who the hell is that, brother?"

Shanahan looked puzzled: "Don't you know who that is?"

"I've never seen that man before in my life," Rowe said.

Now Shanahan looked worried. "Tom," he whispered, "that's the guy that was in [Mrs. Liuzzo's] car."

"Bullshit," Rowe replied. "That's not the man. . . . Something's wrong here."

Shanahan pushed Rowe into an empty conference room and asked FBI Inspector James McGovern and Justice Department lawyer James Turner to join them. Rowe explained that he had never seen Moton before that moment, that the man sitting next to Liuzzo was Moton's complete opposite in every way—"huge, over two hundred pounds, late 30s or early 40s. He had on a green sport coat with dark checks on it, and a white shirt, tie, [and] a snap brim hat with a feather in the band." The government men didn't know what to make of this discrepancy; the FBI's own investigation indicated that Moton was the passenger that night. At this point, they were willing to live with the fact that Rowe was mistaken, as many witnesses often were. It had been a dark, rainy night, and the black man was visible for only a moment before the chase began. They weren't going to worry about it now.[59]

When Rowe left the room, Shanahan and other agents surrounded him as reporters pursued him down the hall. When photographers tried to take his picture, he cursed them and made "a threatening gesture." Undeterred, *Los Angeles Times* reporter Jack Nelson rushed over to get an interview and saw Rowe "suddenly put his hand on the handle of a revolver" he carried under his coat. "Don't make any sudden moves around him," Shanahan told Nelson. When Nelson tried again to approach Rowe, an FBI agent pushed him against the wall and "blocked the exit with outstretched arms and legs" while Rowe and his keepers successfully made their getaway.[60]

For now, the FBI felt "near jubilation," a journalist later noted, "a feeling that they finally, after years of dire frustration, had the Klan 'by the balls.'" Rowe was elated, too, loving every second as the central figure in a murder case that commanded both presidential and national attention.[61]

CHAPTER EIGHT

This Horrible Brew

THERE WAS A CHILL in the night air on Saturday, May 1, 1965, but it didn't dampen the enthusiasm of the nearly three hundred Klansmen and their families attending a rally in Blandon Springs, Alabama. Besides the usual speeches, members of the crowd were told that they would be honored by the presence of the Klan's latest celebrities—Gene Thomas, Curly Eaton, and, most important, young Lee Wilkins, who was the first to be tried for murdering Viola Liuzzo.

Imperial Klonsel Matthew Hobson Murphy, wearing a "brilliant red robe" and peaked hood, spoke first about the evils of the federal reserve system, foreign aid, and the "Zionist Jew." He was followed by Grand Dragon Robert Creel, whose emerald green robe produced admiring gasps from the audience. "While Murphy's talk was interesting," one reporter later noted, "it was left up to Grand Dragon Creel to comment on what most of those in attendance had apparently come to hear"—a vicious attack on the civil rights movement. They were not disappointed. "My three little children, bless their hearts, will never go to school with a bunch of runny nosed niggers" or the offspring of "race-mixers" like the late Reverend James Reeb, Creel said. "Now, you've been told that old Reeb was beaten to death by Klansmen but that's a damn lie!" Reeb, like all "white niggers," was "rotten with cancer and syphilis, that's what killed him."

Then, as Klansmen moved through the audience collecting donations and distributing membership applications (fifty men joined that night), Creel introduced Thomas, Eaton, and Wilkins. "Do these men look like murderers?" Creel asked the excited crowd. "No!" they screamed back. Matt Murphy invited them to join him at the Hayneville Courthouse on Monday morning to show their support for Wilkins on the opening day of the trial.[1]

Murphy had every reason to feel confident as that day approached. History was on his side: No white man had ever been convicted of killing a Negro or a civil rights worker anywhere in the South. The location of the trial was also propitious: Jurors would hail from "Bloody Lowndes County," so-called because of the brutal treatment blacks had received there since the end of Reconstruction. Although 80 percent of the county's approximately seventeen thousand people were black, every acre of land was owned by a tiny group of white families who dominated the county. Of the almost six thousand blacks who were eligible to vote, none were registered before the advent of the civil rights movement in Alabama, and despite the efforts of activists who began working there early in 1965, not a single black participated in the Voting Rights March that cost Viola Liuzzo her life.[2]

Hayneville was a sleepy little town of four hundred, with a few grocery and merchandise stores, one restaurant, and a town square built around a ten-foot-tall monument dedicated to men from the county who were killed during the Civil War. Reporters from around the world, now invading the town in large numbers, found its citizens resentful of the attention Wilkins and the others were receiving; none of the accused was a local boy, and as far as whites were concerned, "their Negroes" were a happy and contented group. "We grew up with the Negroes and played with them as children," said one woman. "We have never had any trouble getting along. Up until the recent agitation began, there was the best of feeling between us." George Kelly, Hayneville's lone full-time black barber, agreed. "They just haven't started that mixing up [here]," Kelly told *New York Times* reporter Paul Montgomery. "There ain't no discriminating against me."[3]

Most townspeople believed that the accused would be swiftly acquitted, and were angry that Gary Thomas Rowe—the real villain—wasn't being prosecuted. "I wouldn't give a plugged nickel for his life," one citizen told journalist Jack Nelson. "You couldn't pay me enough money to do what he did." These views were shared by the prosecutors: "People here don't like turncoats," County Solicitor Carlton Perdue explained to another reporter, referring to his star witness, Tommy Rowe. Perdue was a "strict segregationist," who once said publicly: "We got ways to keep Nigras in their place if we have to use them. We have the banks, the credit—they can't live without credit. We could force them to their knees if we so choose." Perdue actually envied Matt Murphy and wished that he could defend Wilkins. "Course, you understand, that as a prosecutor ah'm goin' do a good job," Perdue insisted. "But boy would I like to get at that FBI case . . . and rip it apart."[4]

Among those traveling to Hayneville that morning to observe the trial was forty-two-year-old Virginia Foster Durr, a writer and friend of Rosa Parks (Durr and her lawyer husband had helped Parks win her freedom in 1955 after she was jailed for sitting in the white section of Alabama's segregated buses) and a longtime civil rights activist. She drove alone along Highway 80, past meadows that had once been cotton fields but today were "filled with slow-moving fat cattle that drift from one patch of shade to the other," fields "covered with waves . . . of the loveliest and most fragile flower that grows, the wild primrose." Later, she recalled that "a gentle wind rippled the primroses and brought the scent of the honeysuckle and I felt I was in Sleeping Beauty Land, everything was so silent . . . and stretched for miles under the empty sky."[5]

Feeling lonely and scared, Durr left the highway when she saw a store and a gas station. While her car was being checked, she sought directions to a spot she wanted to see. "Where was she shot?" she asked the black attendant. "Just half a mile down the road on the left hand side," he replied, never asking who she was looking for. She had no trouble finding the crime scene—the skid marks were still there, six weeks after the murder, "scarring the dirt where [Viola Liuzzo's] car went off the road with her dead hands on the steering wheel."[6]

Finally arriving in Hayneville, she saw the whitewashed alabaster courthouse, 120 years old, the product of slave labor, the most stately building in town now "surrounded by cars and by State Troopers, great burly men with guns on their hips." Parking proved to be a problem, but she found a spot in front of a "white, green shuttered house . . . with a lovely flowering garden of azaleas." Her first greeting from a Hayneville citizen came next: "You can't park there," an angry woman yelled. "I don't want anyone to park there in front of my house." "This set the tone of the reception the 'outsiders' received in Hayneville that day," she later observed. Returning to her car, she drove off, eventually finding a place to park, and then hurried to the courthouse, fearing that it would be so crowded that she would never find a seat.[7]

But besides the press, few people showed up that day, a handful of curious townspeople, mostly "middle-aged women," so Durr was able to secure a front-row seat at the drama about to begin.[8]

The Klan's Imperial Klonsel, Matthew Hobson Murphy, Jr., caused a stir when he entered the second-floor courtroom and, removing his snap brim straw hat, took his place at the defense counsel's plain oak table. From a bulging briefcase he removed a Bible, reams of documents, crime scene photographs, and two pistols. A "massive man"—six feet three inches tall and weighing more than 220 pounds—with tiny eyes, "firm lips," and a fleshy face, Murphy gave off an air of menace. His right hand had only three fingers, and when he hid his thumb, he could flash a V for victory sign that few who saw it could forget. For Durr, who had known Murphy when they were children, the fifty-one-year-old lawyer epitomized "the last decaying branch of an old aristocratic tree." His mother was a Mississippi Percy whose relatives included U.S. senators and talented novelists, like Murphy's cousin Walker Percy. On his father's side were the De-Bardelebens—one of Birmingham's founding families and owners of the Tennessee Coal and Iron Company, the Bessemer steel mill that had employed Thomas and Eaton. "Here was the descendent and scion of Southern aristocracy," Durr later wrote, "and the unemployed steel workers all combined in this horrible brew of savagery and brutality and indecency."[9]

Imperial Wizard Bobby Shelton was next to arrive, and he worked the room like a good politician—slapping people on the back, chatting, and making a point of "sneering" at one FBI agent who was pointed out to him. He also happily answered questions that journalists put to him. Did he think that Rowe was in any danger, despite being guarded by FBI? "I'd hate to think I had to look over my shoulder everywhere I went," Shelton said. The Klan knew exactly where Rowe was hidden, he boasted: "I don't think he can go anywhere we won't know where he is." Reporters from New York and Los Angeles who knew the Imperial Wizard only by reputation were not impressed by this short, slim, ordinary-looking man. To them, Shelton without his purple robe and tall hat was just "a little bony guy with ears that came up to a red-tipped point." He had come from

Tuscaloosa to see that "these three individuals get a fair trial," he told other members of the press. The Klansmen were "victims of a conspiracy to wipe the KKK off the face of the earth. . . . We want the nation to know the depth that the president of the United States . . . will go to rape the Klan."[10]

Sheriff Jim Clark of Dallas County and Colonel Al Lingo, director of public safety, were also there, subpoenaed to testify for the defense. Both gave Shelton and Murphy warm hellos, and Clark pinned a "NEVER!" button protesting integration on the Imperial Klonsel's left lapel beneath his red Klan insignia. Lingo ignored reporters, but the garrulous Clark chatted and joked, admitting that he had no idea why he had been called. Other Klansmen who knew Rowe well—including Gene Reeves and Robert Thomas—took seats and surveyed the spacious, high-ceilinged courtroom, acting like they owned the place.[11]

Eaton, Thomas, and Wilkins arrived together, looking uncomfortable in dark business suits with folded white handkerchiefs neatly displayed in their coat pockets. "I'm about as ready as I'll ever be," Wilkins told the reporters who gathered around them hoping for a statement. He was just "a shade tree mechanic," Wilkins said, taking work "wherever I can get it." A young Hayneville girl told a journalist that she thought the twenty-one-year-old Klansman "would be dreamy, if he took off a little weight." Other reporters found him less attractive, calling him "fat bellied," "sunken eyed," and "cocky." Gene Thomas was asked whether he was angry at Rowe. No, he said, puffing calmly on a Pall Mall cigarette, just "surprised he made a statement against me. I only met him a couple of times. He didn't bother me." All Eaton would say was that he was retired because of a heart condition and, after telling Wilkins to keep his mouth shut, "stormed off, refusing to talk."[12]

The proceedings officially began at 9:02 a.m. when bailiff Will Lee yelled out, "All rise!" and Judge T. Werth Thagard of the Circuit Court stepped onto the bench. The sixty-three-year-old jurist, "a little bitty wiry fellow—tough as a hickory nut," noted one lawyer, liked to preside with an air of country informality. "I've never tried to hold a tight rein in the courtroom," he once observed. "To be stern is contrary to my nature." Nevertheless, he had assured Solicitor Arthur Gamble that "this trial would be conducted in a decorous, orderly manner and . . . [he] would permit no demonstrations by any parties which might in any way prejudice the jury."

William Orville Eaton (*left*), Eugene Thomas (*center*), and Collie Leroy Wilkins, Jr. (*right*) were arrested for the murder of Viola Liuzzo.

Thagard quickly disposed of previous business before the court and then turned to *State of Alabama v. Collie Leroy Wilkins, Jr.* As the young Klansman rose to his feet to enter his plea of "not guilty," he was interrupted by a sparrow that darted through one of the open windows and flew wildly around the courtroom, provoking laughter until it found a means of escape.[13]

Judge Thagard then asked Murphy for a list of the defense witnesses. The Imperial Klonsel called out dramatically, "Lyndon . . . Baines . . . Johnson, president of the United States of America." Looking around the crowded courtroom for the president, Murphy drawled, "Is he here Mr. Bailiff?" As the courtroom burst into laughter, Murphy muttered, "I don't know how to get him here. It's a matter of law." Murphy also subpoenaed FBI Director J. Edgar Hoover, but he didn't show up, either. Having determined that the president was absent, Murphy then moved for a dismissal of the charges against his clients on the grounds that by announcing their arrest and calling the Klan a "hooded society of bigots," the president had so prejudiced every American against the accused that it was impossible for Wilkins to receive "a fair and impartial trial in any state." Therefore, the trial would be unconstitutional and should be stopped.[14]

"Motion is denied," Thagard replied, and then declared a brief recess before the jury was chosen. At that point, the trial dissolved into a kind of country carnival: Three of Eaton's young children chased one another around the courtroom, while neo-Nazi Edward Fields distributed the current issue of his racist tract *The Thunderbolt*. Nearby stood Ralph Ray Roton, the Klan's publicity director, who looked to Virginia Durr "like a parody of an old Southern colonel, big black hat, string tie, dirty white shirt and dirty white whiskers." He offered "hate literature which went after not only the 'niggers,' but the Jews, the Communists, and Catholics, the U.S. Supreme Court, the President of the United States and the United Nations. Hatred," Durr noted, "seemed to take in everybody."

Featured prominently in that hate literature was Viola Liuzzo. For weeks, the Klan had circulated "wild" rumors about her, hoping to influence potential jurors. Sheriff Jim Clark obtained a confidential file on the Liuzzo family from Detroit police and gave it to the Imperial Wizard. The five-page document described Liuzzo's emotional problems and her spats with employers, the Detroit School Board, and her husband and daughters. Shelton called it Liuzzo's "police record." "There," he said to one reporter, forcing him to take the documents, "that'll show you what kind of woman she was. . . . They portrayed her as being the mother of five lovely children and a community worker. . . . The fact is she was a fat slob with crud that looked like rust all over her body [and] she was braless. You ought to see the one they got on her in Chattanooga. It's rougher'n that."[15]

While Shelton and Murphy waited for the recess to end, they rummaged through Liuzzo's bloodstained pocketbook, which they had received from the prosecutors. People lined up to examine photographs of the Liuzzo children, the victim's lipstick, letters written but not mailed, and the most glorious "trophy" of all—Mrs. Liuzzo's NAACP membership card.

"Let's bring in the jury pool," the judge announced when the trial resumed. Selecting a jury didn't take long. Under Alabama law, a three-man county commission chose potential jurors on the basis of age, race, sex, and status within the community. They excluded men under age twenty-one and over sixty-five, blacks (although they outnumbered white residents four to one), women, and the disabled or others thought unable to serve. The jury finally impaneled consisted primarily of middle-class and middle-aged white men, all Alabama-born save one, who had moved to Lowndes County from Florida. There were two county employees, five farmers, a mechanic, a machinist, an electrician, a bookkeeper, and a night watchman. Unknown to the prosecution was the fact that two jurors had relatives in the Klan, one was a member of the local White Citizens Council, and another was a former member. Virginia Durr thought them an admirable group: "The jurymen, sunburned, angular, lean and white . . . looked like all . . . [the] white men I had seen all my life in all of the little country towns of the South and I liked their looks and felt at once a sense of kinship with them." When a nearby journalist muttered, "Just a bunch of rednecks," she was annoyed. The prosecution was satisfied: "We ended up with the best jury we could have gotten," Arthur Gamble told journalist Murray Kempton. "Of course it wasn't that good."[16]

The jurors were sworn in and given their instructions: "I regret to inform you that it is going to be necessary that you be guests of the county for the duration of this trial," Judge Thagard said. They would spend their nights at special quarters in the Montgomery Courthouse, which at least had the benefit of air-conditioning. They would be carefully watched by bailiffs Hugh Gates and Tom Norris. "When you go to the rest room you will be under the bailiff, and when you go to your meals, you will be under the bailiff. He will see that you are as comfortable as possible and that you have good food to eat, and . . . a good place to stay. . . . You just won't have your usual freedom, and I regret that you have to make that sacrifice, but it is a sacrifice that good citizens have to make occasionally." They would not be inconvenienced for long; he expected the trial to be over within a few days. With a bang of Thagard's gavel, the proceedings ended at 4:50 p.m.[17]

The Klan was well represented on Tuesday, May 5, the first real day of the trial, when Tommy Rowe was expected to testify, and his former colleagues wanted to see Matt Murphy tear him apart. The Imperial Wizard was there, of course, sitting in a comfortable chair in the press gallery. PR man Ralph Ray Roton sat directly behind Shelton as if protecting him from hostile reporters. An aide brought in a large metal file cabinet and placed it next to the Wizard's chair; from it, Shelton and Roton removed newspaper clippings and reels of film. Also in the audience were other Klansmen: Grand Dragon Robert Creel, Grand Titan Robert Thomas, Exalted Cyclops Eugene Reeves, and representatives from Tuscaloosa, Bessemer, and Eastview No. 13, Rowe's old home. Not a single black citizen of Lowndes County was there; not only were they denied admission to the courtroom (unless they were on trial), they couldn't even step on the courthouse lawn.[18]

After the jury came in and the judge was seated, Arthur Gamble rose to deliver a brief opening statement. The circuit solicitor was every bit as physically imposing as Matt Murphy, but thinner and neater, impeccably dressed, with a full head of handsome gray hair. He began by reading the grand jury indictment charging that Collie Leroy Wilkins "unlawfully, and with malice aforethought, killed Viola Gregg Liuzzo by shooting her with a pistol, against the peace and dignity of the state of Alabama." He promised the jurors that the state, through the testimony of its witnesses, would provide them with "positive proof" of Wilkins's guilt. And he reminded the twelve white Alabamans of the oath they had taken to "truly try all issues . . . according to the evidence. According to the evidence, gentlemen," he repeated, "and nothing else." Those two words, "nothing else," referred to all that lay below the surface of the case—that a white woman had come to Alabama to live and work with blacks in a cause every member of the jury hated.[19]

Matt Murphy was uncharacteristically subdued as he addressed the jury. He was there not as an outsider, he said, like Wilkins—a Birmingham boy. No, Matt Murphy hailed from Greensboro and was, therefore, "a nearby neighbor." Lee Wilkins pleaded not guilty, Murphy said, and he was confident that they would find the state's case "riddled with holes."[20]

The prosecution's first four witnesses were all Alabama police officers. Henry Burgess and Thomas McGehee testified about being called to Lowndes County to the site of what they thought was a traffic accident. In a field adjacent to Highway 80, they found an Oldsmobile with a shattered windshield and a woman inside, slumped in the front seat. Burgess "checked the body for life" by taking her pulse, but she was dead. When he found a bullet on the rear floorboard, he knew definitely that a murder had been committed. Burgess and McGehee notified their superiors, and other officers soon arrived—state investigators E. J. Dixon and Willie Painter and County Sheriff Frank Ryals—who secured the automobile and the crime scene. The FBI was also called, and agents were dispatched.[21]

Matt Murphy's cross-examination tried to undermine the officers' investigative abilities by focusing on objects found in Liuzzo's car that Murphy thought suspicious. Showing Officer Burgess State's Exhibit No. 2, a photograph of Liuzzo's body and the interior of the car, he pointed to something in the picture and said: "I see . . . what appears to be a recorder or some electrical device. . . . Now what is that? . . . I refer to this instrument right here, and it appears to be connected by a cord over here with a plug-in device of some sort. What was that?"

"I sure wouldn't know," Burgess replied.[22]

Murphy also questioned Officer McGehee about the "gismo": "Tell me what this device is that appears to be right here with a cord circling right down on the other side. . . . There appears to be a transmitter of some sort, . . . an electrical device. Is it a transmitter?"

McGehee smiled, then replied: "No, sir. That's a button on her coat." Murphy pointed at a similar "device." Another button, McGehee said.[23]

Sheriff Ryals was also asked about the electrical device, but he couldn't identify it either. However, Murphy didn't want the jury to think Liuzzo's "transmitter" was nothing but a button so he continued his questioning. "I refer to this article right here," he said, pointing to the photograph, "this little gismo right down here?"

"I sure don't know what the gismo is," Ryals replied.

"In your judgment is that a button?" Murphy asked.

"There are a million different kinds of buttons. It could be a button."

"But it doesn't look like a button, does it?"

"Not too much."

"Does that look like some sort of transmitter?"

"It looks like it could be, but I sure don't know," Ryals admitted.[24]

Hoping he had convinced the jury that Liuzzo was transmitting secret messages to someone, Murphy next tried to prove that she was on drugs. State's Exhibit No. 1, another photograph of the car's interior, revealed what appeared to be a "tube."

What kind of tube was it and what was in it? Murphy asked each of the witnesses. Investigators Dixon and Painter and Sheriff Ryals said that they never saw a tube. Officer Burgess did but "didn't pay that much attention to it." McGehee recalled seeing it, but under Murphy's questioning he couldn't remember its exact color or what it contained—glue, he thought. Murphy disagreed. He thought the tube contained "some sort of drug."[25]

The Imperial Klonsel took three hours of the court's time for these interrogations, but the judge seemed to enjoy it and was in a good mood as noon approached. "You and the bailiff can now go and get your lunch," he told the jurors; "walk around and have a good time but don't talk about the case and don't let anybody talk to you about the case on the outside." They were instructed to return in an hour to hear the next witness.[26]

Lunching in Hayneville was not the pleasant experience the judge expected. Reporters discovered that the town's only drugstore and Coleman's Restaurant were "closed tight," but the proprietor sold them box lunches through a side window. (He was also the only local source of whiskey, sold in "souvenir-sized bottles," which made him popular with reporters.) Not even Judge Thagard was immune to this treatment: An Associated Press photographer snapped a picture of him eating a piece of fried chicken while sitting on the courthouse lawn. Virginia Durr sat nearby with a group of eastern journalists, and while she ate, she listened to them denounce Alabama. "They looked on this trial as just another of the folkways of a barbaric Southland, for which they felt no affinity and no responsibility," she later noted. "They spoke casually of 'fascism' and Nazism, compared the South to South Africa and seemed to think that . . . the South was the repository of original sin." None of the townspeople wanted to be interviewed, so the reporters peppered her with "a thousand questions," including whether it was true that a man from Lowndes County had murdered fifteen blacks but was never even arrested. Durr had heard the story too and found it difficult to defend her homeland.[27]

When the trial resumed, the prosecution called Leroy Moton, Liuzzo's passenger on the night of her death. Moton sat awkwardly in the witness chair, looking nervous and answering questions so softly that he was almost drowned out by the "twittering of the songbirds in the water oaks outside the courtroom windows." Murphy immediately interrupted Moton's testimony to complain. "Judge," he said, "I can't hear a thing he is saying." Judge Thagard instructed the witness (whom he called "Leroy"; no southern black was ever called "Mister") to "look at that man over in the corner [the court reporter] and talk to him when you answer these questions. Try and make him hear and understand you."[28]

Realizing that Moton was as bad a witness as he feared, Assistant Attorney General Joe Breck Gantt hurriedly took him through the night of March 25, 1965. They had transported a group from Montgomery to Selma, Moton testified, and at about 8 p.m. he and Liuzzo were returning to the capital on Highway 80 when "a car pulled up side of us and shot . . . two or three times." Two holes opened up in the windshield, covering his face with glass fragments and knocking off his glasses. Mrs. Liuzzo slumped toward him, and as they veered off the road into a field, Moton tried to steer but the car ran into a fence and stopped. He turned off the lights and the ignition, and then heard a car, the same car, he thought, and ducked down, pretending that he, too, was dead. He heard the rumble of a truck and the car sped off. He got out of the car and ran toward the highway, but the truck didn't stop. A moment later, a red sports car appeared and when Moton waved, the car accelerated toward him; he jumped into the ditch to avoid being run down. Exhausted and confused, Moton returned to Liuzzo's car, where, he said, he "passed out."[29]

Knowing that the Imperial Klonsel would soon discover the most serious weakness in Moton's testimony, Prosecutor Gantt let Moton reveal it himself: Without his glasses, he couldn't identify the shooters or their car.[30]

Murphy, as *Newsweek*'s correspondent put it, "moved in for the kill." After Murphy had established that Moton was employed by Dr. Martin Luther King's Southern Christian Leadership Conference (earning about one hundred dollars a month) and that he and Liuzzo had transported a racially mixed group from Montgomery to Selma on the night of March 25, the judge interrupted, instructing Murphy to limit his questions to the final "fatal trip." Moton recounted how they were traveling along Highway 80, on the one-lane road, when another car pulled next to them as if it were trying to pass. "What was Mrs. Liuzzo doing?" Murphy asked.[31]

"She was humming 'We Shall Overcome.'"

"She just started singing that, 'We Shall Overcome.' What's the rest of the words that she was singing?" Murphy wondered.

"She was just singing 'We Shall Overcome,'" Moton repeated.

"We shall overcome, we shall overcome, we shall overcome, just over and over again?"

"We shall overcome some day and then come back to that point," Moton said, shifting uncomfortably in the chair.

"What point?"

"We shall overcome."

"What are you trying to overcome?" Murphy yelled, and his audience in the courtroom laughed.[32]

Murphy continued: "Did you smell any whiskey on [Mrs. Liuzzo's] breath?" The prosecution objected and it was sustained before Moton could answer.

Murphy tried again to put Liuzzo and Moton on trial in place of his client: "What did you do to Mrs. Liuzzo while you were there in the car [after the shooting]?"

"I didn't do anything to Mrs. Liuzzo while I was in the car," Moton said.

"Did you reach over and touch her?"

"No, I didn't."

"You didn't lay your hands on her?"

"No, sir."

"What kind of gun did you have with you?"

"I don't carry a gun."

Murphy ignored the answer: "What kind of gun was in the glove compartment?"

"There wasn't no gun in the glove compartment," Moton replied.

"Now who fired the bullet holes in the windshield . . . ? Did you do it?"

"I didn't shoot no gun because I don't have a gun. . . . I didn't do any shooting."

Murphy didn't believe him. "She had her pocketbook with her, didn't she?"

"Yes, she did," Moton said.

"She had a lot of money in that pocketbook, didn't she?"

"I don't know."

"You don't know. I suggest to you that you fired those two shots through the windshield and rifled her purse and got the money."

Moton was beginning to lose patience under this barrage. "I did not fire no shots through the windshield and I did not go through her pocketbook and get no money and I didn't have a gun and I didn't do anything." Then, his voice rising in anger, he said, "You are trying to pin something on me, that's what you're trying to do."

"Oh, I am," Murphy said.

"Yeah."

"Did you have [a] relationship with Mrs. Liuzzo?"

Arthur Gamble objected and the motion was sustained.

Murphy asked Moton how he returned to Selma. Eventually, a truck stopped to pick him up, he explained, civil rights people who were led by, as he remembered (mistakenly), a rabbi from Boston. Murphy thought this was worth discussing. "Who was that rabbi with?" he asked.

"About twenty other people," Moton replied.

"Were they white people or black people?"

"It was an integrated truck."

"Then there were whites and Negroes both in that truck?"

"That's right."

"And a rabbi was driving that truck?"

"That's right."

"You mean a rabbi who teaches a Jewish congregation, is that what you mean?"

"Yes."

"A synagog [*sic*]. You know what a synagog is, don't you?"

"I think so," Moton said.

"A rabbi teaches in a synagog," Murphy explained to the witness and the court. "You have been to a synagog, haven't you?"

"No."

"Was this rabbi dressed up in a rabbi's uniform?"

"No, he wasn't."

"What kind of a uniform did he have on?"

"He just had on plain clothes."

"Who was that rabbi?"

Gamble again objected and was again sustained, but Murphy continued. "Did you have a conversation with a rabbi there?" but before Moton could answer, the judge cut him off, telling Murphy, "I think you have covered it pretty well."

"All right," Murphy said but asked to register an exception. "And with that," the Imperial Klonsel concluded, "I'll cease my examination of that man there."[33]

Time's correspondent thought Murphy's performance despicable and later called it worthy of a circus "tent show." Murray Kempton, reporting for the *New Republic*, also considered it a pitiful spectacle: "Poor Leroy Moton bent under [Murphy's] wild tide of unsupported surmise," he later wrote. "His innocence seemed utterly useless in the face of dementia of conviction so deep." Nonetheless, the journalists failed to appreciate how badly Murphy had hurt the prosecution's case. Under cross-examination, Moton admitted that he didn't see the killers, couldn't identify their car, and didn't know how many shots were fired or the direction from which they came. Furthermore, Murphy created an image of Moton that the jury didn't find appealing: He was a member of King's despised SCLC, a black man who flouted southern convention by riding in cars with white women, and an associate of Jews, who racists believed controlled the civil rights movement with their Communist allies.[34]

The next witness that afternoon was Dr. Paul Shoffeitt, assistant director of the Alabama State Department of Toxicology and Criminal Investigation, who had performed the autopsy on Liuzzo's body. In response to Gamble's questions, Shoffeitt testified that it was after midnight on March 26 when Alabama police delivered the corpse to the White Chapel Funeral Home. First, he took photographs and then removed the victim's blood-soaked clothing—a dress, slip, torso bra, and girdle. No shoes were present, and her feet were "somewhat dirty." The body was washed so that he could better examine it for injuries. Near her left ear he found "a large, ragged hole" as well as "numerous . . . small skin injuries" on the left side of her face and neck, from which he carefully removed "bits of glass and small fragments of lead."

Next, he dissected the head and followed the path the bullet had taken —through the skull in front of the left ear, then moving "inward and slightly upward" until it reached the base of the brain, lodging in the spinal cord, almost severing it. The cause of death was massive brain damage and internal bleeding inflicted by the bullet, which Shoffeitt believed was fired by a .38-caliber handgun. Although the bullet was badly damaged, he felt there were enough grooves and lands present to perform the ballistics tests necessary to identify the gun that fired it. Later that night, police gave him two other bullets, the one found by Officer Burgess when he initially searched the car, and another that investigators discovered inside the right rear door frame—both from .38s and in good enough shape to be tested.[35]

When it was Murphy's turn to cross-examine the witness, he focused on the clothes Liuzzo wore that evening, the condition of her body, and the results of the physical and toxicological studies Dr. Shoffeitt performed. "You say Mrs. Liuzzo had on a dress, a slip and bra and that was all . . . no underpants?" he asked.

"No underpants," he replied.

"Did you find any puncture marks in her arms?"

"No, I did not."

Murphy was incredulous: "No puncture marks in her arms at all where a hypodermic needle might have been used?"

"I did not detect any," Shoffeitt repeated.

"Did you look for it?" Murphy asked.

"Yes."

Perhaps the blood tests might have revealed something incriminating, so Murphy asked what they showed. Just "traces" of two drugs—aspirin and Phenobarbital, which was then commonly prescribed as a sedative. "A type of narcotic?" Murphy wondered (and no doubt hoped).

"It's not a narcotic," Shoffeitt said.

Close enough, according to Murphy: "In the eyes of the law it is a narcotic, isn't it?"

"It does produce sedation," Shoffeitt admitted, "or similar to the action of a narcotic."

"Did you determine whether Mrs. Liuzzo had recently had sexual relations with any individual?"

Gamble objected and it was sustained, but a few minutes later Murphy was permitted to repeat the question.

Dr. Shoffeitt explained that he had taken vaginal smears and examined the area for signs of bruising but found no evidence of intercourse. But wasn't it possible, Murphy asserted, that "some contraceptive device could have been used?" Shoffeitt admitted that it was possible.[36]

"What was the physical condition of her body?" Murphy asked. "I mean was it clean or unclean, and her clothes?"

"It was generally unclean. . . . Her feet were dirty, her hands, beneath her arms. She was not very clean."

"How about odors, did you detect any odors?"

"Nothing other than blood. The body was pretty much saturated with blood and you could certainly detect an odor coming from it."

"Were her clothes dirty or clean?"

"The clothing was not exceptionally clean. They were soiled; you could tell that they had been worn. They were not freshly laundered, and of course they were heavily stained with blood."[37]

None of the prosecutors bothered to point out that Liuzzo spent the last afternoon of her life marching barefoot through the streets of Montgomery and had no opportunity to shower or have her clothes cleaned before she was murdered.

By late afternoon, seven witnesses had been heard, and to one journalist, "the judge and jury [seemed] spent and drowsing in the declining sun and no one [was] quite awake except Robert Shelton, clutching Mrs. Liuzzo's NAACP card." All this changed with the sudden arrival of the state's star witness, Gary Thomas Rowe. Dressed in a neat black suit with white hand-kerchief in the lapel and a thin dark tie, Rowe wore sunglasses and, with his hair cut short and styled, looked very much like the FBI agents who surrounded him. Bill Mobley, covering the trial for the *Birmingham Post-Herald,* dubbed him "the dapper red head." Rowe was always a masterful, if not exactly truthful, storyteller, and for the next fifty-five minutes he held the courtroom spellbound as he publicly described for the first time what had happened on March 25, 1965. As *Time's* correspondent noted, a bit breathlessly, Rowe "told a story that for sheer throat-gripping drama could scarcely be equaled except in fiction."[38]

On the morning of March 25, 1965, Rowe testified, he received ap-proval from his FBI handler to join the other Klansmen, Gene Thomas, Lee Wilkins, and W. O. Eaton, on a trip to Montgomery. It was the day of the big march, and they wanted to see what it was all about. He climbed into the backseat of Thomas's red and white Chevrolet Impala, sitting di-rectly behind Thomas, with Wilkins to his right and Eaton in the front passenger seat. They drove around Montgomery for a while, watching the demonstrators, stopping a few times to have a beer. At around 6 p.m., the Highway Patrol pulled them over and Thomas got a warning for having a faulty muffler. They decided to go to Selma—a dull day, so far.

The judge interrupted Rowe here, Shanahan later recalled. "Son," he said, "move your chair back toward the wall. The Federal Agents have found that you're a sitting target." Looking to his left, Rowe noticed two large open windows, through which a skilled shooter, hidden across the street, could try to kill him. He moved his chair.[39]

Rowe continued: They had dinner at the Silver Moon Cafe, a Klan fa-vorite. There was a celebrity there that night, Thomas noted. Did Rowe and Wilkins know the man sitting over there in the booth? No, they didn't. "Lord, you ought to know him," Thomas told them. He was "one of the men . . . out on bond for the Reeb killing." Thomas went over to talk with him, and when it was time to leave, the man said, "Well, God bless you boys, go do your job, I have already done mine."[40]

At eight o'clock, they got their chance. "Look a-there, baby brother," Rowe recalled Wilkins saying as they sat at a red light near the Edmund Pettus Bridge. "I'll be damn, look-a there." Beside them on their left was

Tommy Rowe, the chief witness for the prosecution in the first murder trial of Collie Leroy Wilkins in May 1965. At right is his favorite FBI handler, Special Agent Neil Shanahan. (UPI-Bettmann/Corbis)

a light blue Oldsmobile with two passengers: "a white lady and a colored man."

The light turned green and the Oldsmobile took off. "Let's get 'em," Thomas said, changing lanes to follow the car. "I wonder where they're going?" Eaton said. "Well," Thomas said, "I imagine they're going out here to park someplace together." But the Oldsmobile stayed on Highway 80. Wilkins wondered how far they were going, maybe all the way to Montgomery. Thomas accelerated to keep up with the woman's car; both vehicles were now going sixty or seventy miles an hour, Rowe thought, maybe more. Thomas opened the compartment next to his seat and removed his .38: "Get your pistol, big brother," he told Rowe. Rowe took out his own .38 and waited. In the rearview mirror he could see lights; there was a car behind them, far back but gaining. He told Thomas, "there's a car coming behind us." Thomas looked and said, "[It's] still a good distance back there, we'll have plenty time to stop them."

Rowe claimed that he urged Thomas to back off. "Gene, the best thing for us to do, they know we are following them, is to go back into Selma, and maybe we will find somebody else to run off."

"No," Thomas said, "we're going to take this car tonight." He thought the woman and "the nigger" would turn off on a side road to look for a secluded spot to park. "We'll just take them when we get a chance."

As Thomas began to pull abreast of the Oldsmobile, Rowe saw that they were approaching Craig Air Force Base. There was a jeep ahead with two MPs standing nearby. He yelled out: "Gene, there're troops over there, God damn, be careful." Then Thomas saw the MPs too, slowed down, and let the Oldsmobile move away. It seemed "to veer to the right," as if trying to drive onto the base. Then it turned back onto the road and raced off.

They caught up with it again. "All right, here we go," Thomas said. "Gene, slow down," Wilkins said, pointing off to the left where two Highway Patrol cars sat in a "radar trap." Thomas took his foot off the gas, hoping that he wouldn't be caught speeding. But the officers were busy with two other cars and ignored both Liuzzo's and Thomas's cars.

For a moment, they thought they had lost the Oldsmobile; then its taillights came into view. Thomas accelerated and again the car was right in front of them. But again it was no good: There was a building off to their right with people—fifty black folks, Rowe thought—congregating around it. Wilkins was annoyed: "Every damn time we go to take them we run across somebody."

"We're not going to give up," Thomas replied.

Rowe disagreed: "Gene, we better get back to Selma . . . we're wasting our time and . . . [we] ought to leave them alone."

Thomas refused, saying, "I done told you baby brother, you're in the big time now, we're going to take that automobile."

They were now on a two-lane road, both cars going more than one hundred miles an hour. "It can't last much longer," Thomas said, "they'll be in Montgomery [soon], we've got to get it." He was going to try again, but two huge trucks barreled past them.

"We ought to go back," Rowe said again, but his protests only seemed to make Thomas angrier.

"We're not going back to Selma. Forget it."

When they came to the area known as Big Swamp Lake, Thomas flicked on his high beams and said, "This is as good a place as any . . ."

But he didn't know how to stop the other car, so he turned to his friends for help. "What you reckon I should do? Bump it from the back, run it off the road or pull up side of it and force it off the road?"

Wilkins opposed running into the Oldsmobile: "Bubba, if you hit that automobile at all, if you touch [it] . . . if you leave any paint or anything on it we've had it."

"How you want to take it?" Thomas asked him.

"If you pull up side of it," Wilkins said, "we'll take it." As Thomas began moving to the left, Wilkins announced, "All right men, get ready." Rowe and Eaton pulled out their guns while Thomas handed his .38 to Wilkins. "You get up side of the automobile," Wilkins said, "it won't take but a minute . . ."

"What're you going to do?" Rowe asked. "Force him off the road?"

"Just a minute," Thomas said, "get ready."

"We are ready," Rowe said, "but how are you going to stop it?"

"Wait and see."

During this long presentation, Rowe was "cool" and "composed," but as he neared the end of his story, Roy Reed from the *New York Times* noticed that he "began to show nervousness. His hands twitched and his voice quavered slightly." Thomas pulled even with the other car, Rowe continued, and Wilkins said, "Give it some gas." Thomas did, and they pulled ahead. Now they were in position: Wilkins rolled down the rear window, and he and Rowe could see the driver. "All right, men," Thomas cried, "shoot the hell out of 'em."[41]

Wilkins stuck his arm out the window and, as the woman turned to look their way, fired two shots. Then he said to Rowe, "Put your gun out here," so Rowe laid his arm on the window sill, pointed his gun at the car, but didn't fire. In the front seat, Eaton shot his .22, which made an odd sound compared with the roar of the .38s. As they pulled farther away from Liuzzo's car, Wilkins twisted around and fired more shots, emptying his revolver.

Looking back, Rowe saw the car "coming just as straight down that road as if anyone in this room was driving it." He told Wilkins, "I believe you missed. The [car] is following us." "Baby brother, I don't miss," Wilkins said, "that so-and-so is dead and in hell." Then Liuzzo's car turned off the highway but so gently that Rowe thought it had taken a side road and said so. "Baby brother, you're just shook up," Thomas said, "there is no side road back there." Wilkins agreed, "I know there is no damn road back there."

The men emptied their pistols out the window, reloaded, and Thomas drove on to Bessemer. They talked of guns and alibis. "What in the world are you shooting there?" Thomas asked Eaton. "It sounds pretty light to me."

"It's my .22," Eaton replied.

".22?" Thomas couldn't believe it: "It's a hell of a time to bring a weapon that light down here."

Eaton assured him that it had done the job: "I'm shooting long rifle hollow points in it. It's a good weapon, and what makes it more better I . . . trim . . . the [bullet] head to make it fit in the cylinder."

Thomas said that he would stop first at the VFW Club on the Bessemer superhighway where his friend Bob could usually be found drinking. Bob would be happy to say that they had all been together that night. But when they arrived at the club at about ten o'clock, they found that Bob was "indisposed." "Drunk or sick?" Thomas asked the bartender. "Drunk" was his answer. Over some beers, they discussed their next move. "Well, let's go to Lorene's," Thomas said, telling Rowe that she was a "real good friend of mine, the organization's, and the sheriff's."

They found Lorene's Cafe deserted, but Lorene was there and while Eaton, Rowe, and Wilkins had a few more beers, Thomas went off to speak with her. He was smiling when he returned: "Well, I have got us an alibi . . . , we can go home and forget about all this."

"How good an alibi?" Rowe asked.

"Real good," Thomas said. "She has alibied for us on several occasions and she has never let us down."

Rowe was still worried—Lorene didn't know him from Adam.

"We took care of you, too," Thomas told him. "We pointed you out to her and she is going to vouch for you."

On the way to Thomas's home, they discussed what to do with their weapons. Once again, Thomas had the answer: If they learned that the woman or "the nigger" was seriously injured, or dead, they were to bring their guns to him for Eaton to pick up; he would throw them in the steel mill's "blast furnace." The shooting had left Thomas excited; he wanted to stop at Bob Creel's house to tell the Grand Dragon "what a good job we did." But when they got there, it was raining heavily and the Creel home was dark: "I believe he's gone to bed," Wilkins said, and "we won't bother him." At Thomas's house, the men ran for their cars, all heading for home except Rowe, who looked for a safe spot to telephone the FBI.[42]

It was 4:30 p.m. when Rowe finished his story and left the courtroom with his federal entourage. "Testifying was hard going," he later wrote. "The atmosphere in the courtroom was icy. I could feel the resentment against me, not for what I was telling but for the way I had acquired the information. If I had been driving down the highway and witnessed this murder, the animosity wouldn't have been as great, but the people of Lowndes County were outraged to discover that a Southerner would infiltrate an organization that supposedly preserved the white race."[43]

The judge thought it a good time to recess for the day. The next day, at 9:00 a.m., Matt Murphy would begin his cross-examination of the FBI "undercover man." Asked to comment on Rowe's testimony as he was leaving the courthouse, Murphy said, "Rowe is a goddamn liar and we'll prove him so tomorrow."[44]

Virginia Durr had difficulty finding a seat on Wednesday: Rowe's appearance and the anticipation of Murphy's response brought out "the largest crowd of spectators so far," filling the courtroom to capacity. Most of the newcomers were citizens of Lowndes County, journalist Roy Reed believed, respectable people who would never join the Klan but shared their views, making a point of greeting the Imperial Wizard and the Grand Dragon before they took their seats. As Murphy approached Rowe to begin his cross-examination, a woman in the courtroom yelled, "All right, son, give it to him with both barrels!"[45]

He needed no encouragement. For almost three hours, Murphy tore into Rowe, calling him "a bastard," a "perjurer," and a "pimp" who was bribed by the FBI to testify against the Klansmen. "Now, Mr. Rowe," Murphy sneered, "you took the oath of allegiance in the United Klans of America, did you not?"

"Such as it was, yes, sir," Rowe replied.

"Such as it was," an angry Murphy yelled. "What do you mean by that?"

"That's my statement," Rowe said.

Murphy's voice boomed out like a backwoods preacher: "Did you hold up your right hand and swear before God the . . . following: 'I most solemnly swear that I will forever keep sacredly secret the signs, words, and grip, and any and all other matters and knowledge . . . regarding which a most rigid secrecy must be maintained . . .'?"

Gamble objected, the judge overruled him, and Murphy continued, "and will never divulge same nor even cause same to be divulged to any person in the whole world, unless I know positively that such person is a member of this Order in good and regular standing, and not even unless it be for the best interest of this Order." Murphy might have stopped then, but he was caught up in the Klan's divine rituals and raced ahead: "I most sacredly vow and most positively swear that I will never yield to bribery, flattery, threats, passion, punishment, persecution, persuasion, nor any other enticements whatever coming from or offered by any person or persons, male or female, for the purpose of obtaining from me a secret or secret information." Murphy was yelling now: "I will die rather than divulge the same, so help me God. Did you swear to such an oath?"

Rowe wasn't at all intimidated: "I could have possibly, yes."

"I will ask you directly, Mr. Rowe, whether you did or did not hold up your hand and signed that oath?"

Rowe smiled: "No, sir, I didn't sign the oath."

Murphy corrected himself: "Did you swear to that oath?"

"I possibly did, yes."

"Did you or didn't you?"

"To the best of my knowledge, yes," Rowe admitted.

"You did do it then didn't you?"

"To the best of my knowledge."

Murphy was triumphant. "All right. . . . After you made those oaths and became a member of . . . a Klavern . . . you . . . divulged the name of each of them, haven't you?"

Rowe said no, but in truth he had, and Murphy knew it. The Imperial Klonsel, "glowering and shaking, whirled around" and walked back to his chair; reporters heard him muttering, "Bastard." Somehow, Murphy failed to realize that his recitation just violated one of the Klan's most solemn rules—maintaining the secrecy of the Klan oath. When reporters, who failed to hear everything he had said, asked him for a copy of the oath, he refused, saying, "I can utter nothing about it."[46]

When the judge declared a fifteen-minute recess, Rowe urged the prosecutors to let him recite the entire Klan oath because it continued with passages he believed "would blast Murphy's argument." Section IV of the oath allowed a Klansman to breach the veil of secrecy and to co-operate with law enforcement officers in cases of "rape, treason against the United States," or "malicious murder." To his disappointment, the prosecutors declined to follow his advice.[47]

Having forced Rowe to admit that he had broken an oath before God, Murphy moved on to other "crimes." Lumbering back and forth before the jury box, Murphy would "suddenly, and without warning, turn and fire questions at Rowe": How much money did the FBI pay him to testify against Wilkins? Gamble objected and was sustained, but Rowe replied, "Absolutely nothing, Mr. Murphy." Was Rowe a member of the NAACP? Objection sustained. Was Rowe "a card carrying member of the Communist Party?" Objection sustained. Was he "a paid informer and a pimp?" Objection sustained. How many guns had he carried on the night of March 25, 1965? "One," Rowe said. "That's all you need, Mr. Murphy." Did Rowe ever receive payments from "Castro or the Communistic Government of Cuba?" That was too much even for the judge: "Mr. Murphy, I think you know that question is improper on cross-examination or otherwise."[48]

If Rowe wasn't on Castro's payroll he was certainly on the FBI's, and Murphy wanted to know sums and dates. Rowe tried to remember as best he could, insisting that patriotism, not profit, had motivated him. (The defense, on redirect, supported Rowe's claim by placing into evidence his financial records from May 1960 to March 1965, revealing that Rowe had received approximately $9,100 from the Bureau for both services and expenses—less than $2,000 per year.)[49]

Murphy also demanded to know why the FBI undercover man did nothing to prevent the shooting of Viola Liuzzo. "I didn't know the shots were going to be fired until they were fired," Rowe said. He thought they were only going to stop the car and beat the passengers.

"You talked about it for a considerable distance," Murphy countered.

"We spoke of stopping the automobile," Rowe replied. "There are various ways of stopping an automobile, I would think."[50]

When a short recess was called, reporters rushed to question Murphy about how the trial was going. The prosecution's star witness, he said, "was a damned liar, ... mixed up with the FBI and other groups ... [like] the Communists and Castro. He is the most treacherous, lying, infected individual I have ever heard ... in my life." Murphy's monologue went on to attack "the United Nations, Alger Hiss and Dr. Martin Luther King,

Jr." Didn't the reporters understand? America was now a prisoner of "World Government."[51]

Finally, Murphy tried to prove that the FBI had bribed Rowe into testifying against Wilkins. With Rowe again on the stand, Murphy questioned him about the meeting they had in his office on the night of March 26, several hours after the Klansmen were arrested. Rowe was still undercover then and tried to explain his whereabouts when Wilkins, Thomas, and Eaton were quickly scooped up by the FBI. He had told Murphy that agents picked him up too and, while he was undergoing a grilling, offered him $40,000 and 55 acres of land to farm in Minnesota if he would cooperate, but he "didn't tell them shit." When Murphy heard that story, an FBI invention, he thought it would prove that the FBI was trying to destroy the Klan. Murphy and Imperial Wizard Bobby Shelton increased the bribe to $186,000 and 550 acres and informed the press.

Now, Murphy returned to that night: "Let me ask you if you didn't tell me . . . that the Federal Bureau of Investigation offered to give you 500 acres in Minnesota, . . . and . . . sufficient money for the rest of your natural life if you would cooperate with them in helping to break the back of the [Klan]?"

Gamble objected but was overruled, which was fine with Rowe, who said: "I would like to answer that. No, sir, Mr. Murphy, you instructed me to put that information out."

At that, Murphy suddenly lost all control. His "pale blue eyes widened in fury, and, in a high-pitched voice, he yelled: 'Are you saying I told you that?'"

"That's correct, Mr. Murphy."

Murphy "flushed and spluttered" and, lurching to the defense table, grabbed his straw hat and "slammed it to the floor." Turning again to Rowe, he stammered, "You, you . . ." Then, realizing his mistake, Murphy said, "I'm sorry, I got mad. I apologize."

Gamble asked for a five-minute break, which the judge approved, saying, "I'll give you time to cool off, Mr. Murphy."[52]

While Murphy smoked a cigarette, he told reporters: "I always say that those who the gods would destroy they first make mad. Well, that boy made me mad." Regardless of how the judge ruled, Murphy swore that he would prove that Rowe was "a traitor and a pimp and an agent of Castro and I don't know what all."[53]

When Murphy finally calmed down, the judge returned to his chair.

"Your honor, I would like to apologize for losing my temper," Murphy said, "and I apologize to the gentlemen of the jury. I did lose my temper and I'm sorry for it, and I repent."[54]

"All right, Mr. Murphy," Thagard said, and then told him to continue his cross-examination. This time, Murphy asked Rowe directly: "How much money have you been offered to come up here and testify in this case?" Gamble objected, and Murphy offered to withdraw the question, but the judge permitted Rowe to answer.

"Absolutely nothing. . . . This I swear to, Mr. Murphy."

Again, Murphy went over the ground that had caused his breakdown: How much money and how many acres did the FBI offer Rowe? But Rowe stuck to his story. "Would you be willing to take a lie detector test with me on that?" Murphy asked. Gamble objected and was sustained. A few minutes later, Rowe left the stand and was hurriedly escorted from the courtroom by his FBI bodyguards. The trial then recessed for lunch.[55]

When the trial resumed, the prosecution completed its case. Alabama State Trooper James D. Hagood testified that he had stopped Thomas's Impala on Highway 80 at 6:20 p.m. on March 25, putting the Klansmen close to the scene where the murder occurred a short time later. FBI Special Agent Archibald L. Riley reported finding seven .38 bullet shells on the south shoulder of the highway, close to the field where Liuzzo's Oldsmobile had come to rest. FBI Special Agents Edward M. Lahey and Lawrence Gettings, part of the team that searched Thomas's home on March 26, testified to seizing a .38-caliber Smith and Wesson revolver, which, with its bullets, was sealed, tagged, and sent to the FBI's ballistics laboratory. Attorney Gamble placed the gun in evidence. Lahey also told the court about discovering a .22-caliber bullet in Thomas's car when he was arrested, which Agent Gettings forwarded to Washington. The bullet bore the mark of W. O. Eaton—its nose was shaved. Neil Shanahan took the stand to relate that Rowe had reported the murder promptly and given him his gun when they met at midnight. To Shanahan's eye (and nose), the .38 had not been fired. Finally, Marion Williams, a twenty-six-year veteran of the FBI's firearms lab, testified that the bullet removed from Liuzzo's brain and the shells found on the highway could only have come from Thomas's gun.[56]

On cross-examination, Murphy tried again to create doubts about each agent's competence, but he scored few points. After Agent Williams laboriously explained how he had tested Thomas's gun and compared the bullets fired with the fragments taken from the crime scene, for example, Murphy demanded to see FBI photographs showing the results of the tests. "I don't have any photographs with me," Williams said.

"Why didn't you bring them down here so we could see them?" Murphy asked.

"You didn't let me finish my answer. I said I do not have them with me at this time."

Believing he had caught Williams in an oversight, Murphy pounced: "They are in Washington?"

"I have them in the next room," Williams said. "They are available."

"You have a magnifying glass in the room also?"

Williams smiled: "Yes, sir."

"You really came prepared didn't you," said a disappointed Murphy.[57]

Murphy also employed what he thought was his most reliable approach: appealing to prejudice. "Shanahan," Murphy mused as he questioned Rowe's favorite agent, "it sounds like an Irish name."

"Yes, sir, it is."

"You are not a Shannie [sic] Irishman though, are you?" (To those, like Murphy, who hated the Irish, a "shanty Irishman" was no better than a derelict.)

"I don't know what that means, Mr. Murphy."

"I don't think you do," Murphy said.[58]

Perhaps the FBI agent was one of the Klan's hated "papists," so Murphy asked: "Are you a Catholic?"

"Yes, sir."

"Well, I'm not."[59]

The next morning the prosecution rested, which surprised Murphy. "I'm sort of off balance," he told the judge and requested fifteen minutes to "get lined up, and I'll really roll." Murphy kept his promise. His defense and his closing argument were so extraordinary that Murphy received prominent attention on the *CBS Evening News with Walter Cronkite* and in most of the nation's newspapers and its major magazines—*Time, Newsweek,* and *Life,* which put Murphy on its front cover. William F. Buckley, Jr., no friend of the civil rights movement, later wrote that Murphy's "final appeal to the jury belongs alongside the sickest literature in the world." Prosecutor Joe Breck Gantt spoke for many when he later said of the events he observed, "You couldn't believe it unless you saw it and heard it."[60]

CHAPTER NINE

A Slight Case of Murder

IT HAD BEEN BOTHERING Clifford McMurphee for most of the trial. The juror, a forty-eight-year-old farmer partial to red hunting jackets and plaid sport shirts, had listened to expert after expert testify about guns, bullets, and shell casings, but neither the prosecutors nor the defense attorney had bothered to ask what, to him, was a critical question. Now, as Murphy prepared to begin his defense, to "really roll," McMurphee rose and addressed Judge Thagard: "Before we start with the witness I would like to ask a question."

"All right," said the judge, a bit startled as jurors almost never asked questions until both sides rested and he explained the law that would guide them to a verdict.

McMurphee wanted to know if any fingerprints had been found on the murder weapon, or on the shell casings found along Highway 80? And was Rowe drunk or sober when Agent Shanahan questioned him the night of the murder?[1]

While the prosecution scrambled to get the ballistics experts back to the courtroom, Murphy used the time to continue attacking Viola Liuzzo. Since her driver's license, used as a form of identification, had been placed into evidence, Murphy demanded that all the documents in her purse receive equal legal standing. Among them were Liuzzo's NAACP membership card; a colleague's SNCC identification card, which, Murphy noted, showed "a black hand shaking a white hand" along with the message "We Shall Overcome"; a Sheraton Motel charge card belonging to Anthony Liuzzo; and a pass allowing Viola Liuzzo to have free meals during her visit to Selma. (Murphy also failed to introduce the card that, in the event of her death, willed Liuzzo's eyes to the Wayne State University Medical School; bringing this card to the jury's attention might have made Liuzzo a more sympathetic figure.) Eventually, Murphy was allowed to introduce into evidence everything in the purse except personal letters and financial records. And to complete the picture of Liuzzo as a dangerous outside agitator, he asked that a "clipboard containing various and sundry papers" be admitted, but the judge overruled this request.[2]

By this time the witnesses had returned, and after questioning and cross-examination, FBI agents Lahey and Williams admitted that they had never tested the pistol, bullets, and shell casings for fingerprints because no one had asked them to. When word of this incredible oversight reached J. Edgar Hoover, he became furious, scrawling on one newspaper's account, "Henceforth I want *all tests* made as a *routine procedure*. This will protect us from charges of not thoroughly and painstakingly conducting our investigations."[3]

Before Murphy began presenting his defense, he called Rowe back for another discussion of apple orchards, farms, and FBI bribes—the subject that had earlier caused him to lose his temper. The Imperial Klonsel slowly approached the judge, shoulders slumped, his face pinched in sadness, his voice, which usually carried all the way to the town square, now low and plaintive. "I stand convicted without trial on what this so-called man up here has said. . . . I'm a lawyer, I'm a member of the bar association . . . a member of an honorable profession, I deeply resent it," Murphy said. If Rowe's testimony that he had coached a potential witness to lie about FBI bribery went unchallenged, he would be in contempt of court, and the bar association's grievance committee should file charges against him. He was "asking and begging to clear this matter up, to clear my good name," and the only way to do it was to submit to a polygraph examination, "a true pentothal test and I will pay for the entire proceedings out of my own pocket."[4]

Gamble interrupted: "Your honor, we object to this. . . . Whatever differences they may have can be settled in their own lawsuit." The judge agreed: "We are not trying you Mr. Murphy," and told him to call his first witness.[5]

Murphy did, but it wasn't the defendant, who never said a word at his own trial. It was the Imperial Wizard, Bobby Shelton, who came forward, took the oath, and was seated. By law, he should not have been permitted to testify because he was in the courtroom throughout the entire proceedings, but the prosecutor didn't protest, and Judge Thagard, sipping Coca-Cola from a bottle, said nothing. The jury members leaned forward, anticipating the start of Murphy's defense of Collie Leroy Wilkins, the shade-tree mechanic facing a charge of first-degree murder. But Murphy only asked Shelton what he had heard Rowe say about the FBI bribe. The prosecution objected and was sustained. "I am an officer of the court," Murphy yelled. "I think the matter should be aired out."

Gamble disagreed: "Your Honor, we say again that this is a personal matter between them. It has nothing to do with the trial of this case." Murphy floundered, searching for a legal way to allow this question to be discussed. It went to credibility, he finally claimed. No, the judge replied, Murphy had not laid the necessary groundwork, "the predicate," to discuss the controversy. Murphy tried again, seeking Shelton's verification that Rowe was "offered a farm [and] 500 acres in Minnesota." Again, the judge cut Murphy off; he was only allowed to have the witness affirm or deny the story. "Yes, he made that statement," Shelton said. Gamble had no questions, so the witness was excused.[6]

The next two witnesses—Klansmen Robert Thomas and Eugene Reeves—were asked only whether Rowe had made the statement Murphy claimed. They said yes and left the stand. Murphy's witnesses were passing one another so quickly that it seemed like they were going through a revolving door. Next was Lorene Frederick, "an arthritic old lady in shower sandals," friend of Gene Thomas and the owner of Lorene's Cafe, where Rowe said the Klansmen had gone looking for an alibi after the murder. Murphy tried to get her to state precisely when she saw Wilkins, early enough to make it impossible for him to have killed Liuzzo and shown up at her place for a beer. Unfortunately, Frederick couldn't say exactly when they arrived: "I didn't time them in and I didn't time them out," she said. Mrs. Mildred Thomas, wife of a Klansman, was asked whether Rowe had told her "he was a card carrying member of the Communist Party," but the words "objection" and "sustained" came so fast that few heard her answer "yes." Then, at 11:28 a.m., to the shock and surprise of just about everyone in the courtroom, Murphy said, "With that, your Honor, the Defendant rests."[7]

Murphy ended so abruptly that reporters couldn't agree on the length of his defense, if this confusing spectacle could be dignified with that title. Fifteen minutes? A half hour? Six witnesses were called; surely it was longer than that. One was positive that it lasted twenty minutes, while correspondents from *Newsweek, Time,* the *New York Daily News,* and the *Los Angeles Times* chose twenty-one minutes when they filed their stories. Murray Kempton and Jimmy Breslin (who thought it a "non-defense") called it at twenty-three, which Murphy himself thought was correct. In any case, they all agreed that it was "one of the shortest defenses in the history of murder trials."[8]

Then it was time for the lawyers' final summations. Everyone waited for Murphy's appearance—his reputation as a great courtroom orator was widely known. William Orville Eaton brought his five children, ranging in age from three to fifteen, and put them in the front row so they wouldn't miss a word. Present, too, were Wilkins's parents, a quiet, well-dressed middle-aged couple seated in the courtroom's fourth row. His mother told reporter Bill Mobley: "I feel my son has always been innocent and I will continue to keep my faith in God. He knows what is right." Wilkins didn't seem to care that they were there.[9]

The county solicitor, Carlton Perdue, began first. Sixty years old and a native of Lowndes County, he was the prosecutor closest to the county's citizens. Quietly, he reviewed the evidence. Gary Thomas Rowe had testified —without contradiction by the defense—that Collie Leroy Wilkins killed Mrs. Liuzzo with a gun belonging to Eugene Thomas. FBI ballistics experts found that the bullet removed from the victim's body, and fragments found in Liuzzo's car, could have been fired only from Thomas's .38 Smith and Wesson. "How much stronger could the evidence be?" Perdue asked the jury. "These men in the car went after that woman like a hound dog after the fox. They pulled up alongside [her car] and then pumped 12 bullets into it." A great deal had been said about oaths at this trial, Perdue continued; well, the gentlemen of the jury also took an oath, "to form your conclusions from the evidence," and now Perdue pointed, "on that stand." "Meet this issue: . . . Thou shall not kill in Lowndes County without just punishment. You have an opportunity today to stand up and say, 'Murders must stop.'"[10]

Matthew Hobson Murphy rose slowly from his chair and approached the jury. He seemed listless and hung over. Almost everyone knew he was "a severe alcoholic," and today he looked it: "greyfaced," Jimmy Breslin thought, his black suit wrinkled, his grayish brown hair askew. Reporters suddenly realized that one rumor was certainly true: The Imperial Klonsel wore a toupee, a bad one. But he suddenly recovered and seemed his old energetic and confident self.[11]

"I'm here to throw you a straight ball. Right down the line. One white man to another white man," Murphy said. He stopped for a moment near a window, his eye caught by something outside: a television crew pointing its camera straight up at him. His audience had grown from perhaps fifty to millions of Americans throughout the country, and he knew it. Suddenly, he began yelling, playing to the camera as well as the courtroom: "What kind of man is this Rowe? What kind of a man is this that comes into a fraternal organization by hook or by crook? What kind of a man is this who took an oath to the You-nighted Klans of America" (it sounded like that to New York reporters, furiously taking notes), "took the oath with his hand raised to his Almighty God? And then sold out like Judas Iscariot. And ah say gentlemen, he betrayed himself, his God, his own oath. He is a liar, perjurer. He'll do anything."[12]

The jury didn't have to wonder what Rowe was capable of—Murphy told them. "He'll accept money from the Communist Party," the Klonsel said.

"He'll accept money from the NAACP.

"He'll accept money from this Martin Luther King organization.

"Yes, he sold his soul for a little gold," Murphy said. Then he quoted Scripture: "What advantage is there for a man to gain the whole world and then lose his soul? Pouring himself out to be a white man. He's worse than a white nigger." Almost lost amid all this bombast was Murphy's only sound legal argument—that Rowe had been in the car with Wilkins and under the law could be considered an accomplice. In Alabama, the accused couldn't be convicted on the basis of the uncorroborated testimony of an accomplice, and the state's witnesses and the FBI agents and their ballistics evidence were not likely to persuade the jury that Rowe's version of events was correct. Prosecutors Perdue and Gantt had also been concerned about this weakness in their case and later admitted that they thought Rowe should have been indicted along with the three Klansmen. But if that had happened, Rowe probably would not have testified, and the prosecution would have had no case at all.[13]

Now Murphy, arms spread, began screaming: "All those nigger people down here. Led by this nigger Martin Luther King. A rabbi. A Jew rabbi. The Jew rabbi puts the nigger in the back of the truck," referring to the rescue of Leroy Moton. "There they are, white woman, nigger man, nigger women, feet to feet. Never! We shall die before we lay down."[14]

Murphy then talked about his archenemies, the men of the FBI— agents Marion Williams (Murphy called him Marvin, implying he was a Jew) and Neil Shanahan. "Marvin, the FBI expert. A great man in the laboratory and the Federal Government of the You-nighted States for 26 years. He lives in Washington." Murphy stopped for a second, then corrected himself: "No, I'm sorry he doesn't. He moved to Virginia . . . where they still fight the battle against integrating and mongrelizing the races," so Williams's children wouldn't have to go to school with "niggers."[15]

"And this other FBI agent, the one who told you that Gary Rowe wasn't drunk when he informed the FBI of the murder. You heard me. I asked him his name. He said 'Shanahan.' . . . I asked him, 'Are you Irish?' and he said, 'Yes.' And I said, 'Are you shanty Irish? Are you a Catholic?' . . . Well, I'm not Catholic. But I know how to deal with these shanty Irish."[16]

Now Murphy turned to Viola Liuzzo: "This white woman who got killed." Murphy stopped, smiled, and said again, "White woman? Hah! Wait a minute." He patted his coat pockets, then looked to the Klansmen seated at the defense table. "Where's that NAACP card?" he yelled. Ralph Ray Roton, keeper of the card, rushed it over to Murphy. Using his three-fingered right hand, Murphy held it out, as if offering it to the jury, but nobody took it. Liuzzo was momentarily forgotten as Murphy had another thought. "Ah never thought I'd see the day . . . when Communists and niggers and white niggers and Jews was flyin' around under the banner of the United Nations, not the American flag we fought for."[17]

Waving his arms and bellowing, he said: "I'm proud to be white and I stand here as a white man and I say we're never going to mongrelize the race with nigger blood and the Martin Luther Kings, the white niggers, the Jews, the Zionists who run that bunch of niggers, the white people are not going to run before them. Jim Clark says 'Never!' I say 'Never' myself." Now he remembered Liuzzo: "You know she was in the car with three black niggers? One white woman and three niggers sittin' back there! Right there. Riding right through your country. And when white people join up to 'em they become white niggers. Black nigger Communists takin' us over." He whirled around and scanned his audience: "Some of 'em even infiltrated this courtroom." Murphy faced the press gallery: "Niggers are against every law God ever wrote. Noah's son was Ham and he committed sin and was banished and his sons were Hammites and God banned them and they went to Africa and the only thing they ever built was grass huts. They live by the tooth and the claw. Black man in a straw hut covered with mud. No white woman can ever marry a descendent of Ham. If you do, you shall be destroyed. That's God's law. I don't care what Lyndon Johnson or anybody else says. You cannot overcome God. Do what the people with God said. White woman, nigger man. You shall be destroyed."[18]

Murphy paused for a moment to catch his breath, taking out a hand-kerchief to wipe his face; a "wet gleaming cowlick" had fallen over his right eye, and he tried to adjust his toupee, which had come unglued in the stifling heat of the courtroom. Reporter Jack Nelson watched as "big beads of sweat rolled down his fleshy face and splattered on the asphalt tile floor of the courtroom." Other reporters noticed that some jurymen "shook their heads" or "cast their eyes down and studied their hands," looking anywhere but into the face of the Imperial Klonsel. Some were edgy, "fidgeting with embarrassment." Two actually glared at Murphy "with cold affront." The judge was sickened, too: *Time's* correspondent noted how, as Murphy raged on, Thagard "slumped deeper and deeper into his brown leather chair as if by doing so, he might disappear altogether."[19]

Murphy stopped, as if searching for a face or a name. It didn't come to him but that didn't matter; everyone recognized that it was Leroy Moton who was his next victim. "You know what that nigger said on the stand?" Murphy gave the room his comic imitation of how Moton spoke, spitting out the words, "'No.' 'Yeah.' 'No.' 'Yeah.' Like a ten year old boy. . . . That black nigger sat up there before this honorable white judge and this white courtroom. He had no respect. He should have been saying 'Yes, sir,' and 'No, sir,' before that honorable white judge." (In fact, that was exactly the way Moton had responded to Murphy's outrageous questions.) In an instant, Murphy transformed himself into an avenger. His face contorted with rage, he shouted: "That's a 20 year old nigger talking, gentlemen. . . . The buck hasn't got the sense, the morals, the decency."

"I'm trying to lay this case on the line," he told the jury, then crouched before them so he could look the jurors in the eye. "You notice [Moton's] ahyes? . . . Oh, Ah did. Ahyes di-lated . . . You see them starin'? Pupils di-lated. You see him talking under the hypnotic spell of narcotics." He seemed to expect the jurors to nod but, when none moved so much as a hair, he said, "Well, Ah did."

He recounted Moton's version of the chase: "I said now look, boy. Look down at your feet. Niggers only understand this kind of talk. How many feets away was that car? So he looked down at his feet and he said about 25 feet away." No such exchange had occurred between Moton and Murphy. Then he ridiculed the idea that Moton just "passed out" for almost a half hour: "What's he doing down there all the time? In that car alone with that woman. . . . We don't know what he did." And Viola Liuzzo had been "singin' 'we will overcome, we will overcome, we will overcome,'" he cried. "What in God's name were they tryin' to overcome? To overcome God himself? And do unto the white people what God said you shall not do because there'll be thorns in your eyes, thorns in your flesh; if you intermarry with a servile race, then you shall be *destroyed.* . . . And Ah tell you as one white man to another that this card carrying member of the Communist Party . . ."

Murphy couldn't finish the sentence. He had spoken for almost sixty-seven minutes and was on the verge of collapse. His suit drenched with sweat, he had the energy only to utter one final sentence: "I urge you as patriotic Americans not to find this young man guilty." The judge cut him off. Murphy stumbled back to the counsel's table and dropped into his chair. His summation was almost three times longer than his defense of Collie Leroy Wilkins. Sitting there in the glow of congratulations from Shelton and other Klansmen, and believing he had done a "good job," Murphy smiled broadly.[20]

During the brief recess that followed, the chief topic of conversation among reporters and townspeople was Murphy's incredible performance. Views split along geographic lines. Jimmy Breslin, a New Yorker, thought that Murphy "gave the saddest performance that we have ever seen a human being give" and couldn't believe that "this buffoon" was allowed to filibuster so hatefully for so long. "Nobody stops him," Breslin later wrote: "The judge does not stop him. The prosecution does not get up and object and try to stop him. Everybody just listens and nobody does anything because the South is not a place where you can just jump up and stop a man from talking like this." Adam Smith, a chicken farmer and county official, disagreed: "The people liked it," he told reporter Jack Nelson. "Mr. Murphy is a damn smart man."[21]

By law and custom, the prosecutors were again allowed to speak, but realizing that the jury was exhausted after Murphy's harangue, they kept their final summations brief and direct. Their strategy was to reassure the jurors that they shared their concerns about race but to shift attention from the South's enemies to the trial's central issue: the murder that had occurred in Lowndes County. "I'm a segregationist," Gantt told the jury, but "I don't want to talk about the Communist Party, or the Teamsters Union, or the NAACP, or segregation or integration, or whites or niggers or marches and demonstrations. I want to talk about a murder—a cold blooded murder of a defenseless woman. She was shot by a yellow bellied coward." He turned and pointed at Wilkins. "I'm saying that this boy—Wilkins—did that murder." If men were permitted to kill just because they went berserk at the sight of a white woman and a black man riding in the same car, then everyone was at risk. Any member of the jury, just driving their family maid or "nigger" cook home after a day's work, could have fallen victim to Wilkins's bullets. "If that's grounds for murder," he warned, "blood will spill in Hayneville streets." If Wilkins was acquitted, "there will be no law [and] justice will be forgotten. Is this what our forefathers fought for in the Civil War, for some yellow bellied murderer to shoot down a defenseless woman?" He closed by quoting Governor George Wallace—"one of the greatest segregationists"—who called Liuzzo's murder "a cowardly act that should not go unpunished."[22]

Last to speak was Arthur Gamble, the circuit solicitor. "Let's keep one thing straight," he began in "a slow commanding voice"; "I want to remain your solicitor." Like them, Gamble did not approve of "this woman's" civil rights work: "It is repugnant to me but, gentlemen, she was here and she had a right to be here on our highways without being killed." Holding himself erect, he urged the jury to think of local pride when they considered their decision. Lowndes County wasn't on trial; the accused and his colleagues lived elsewhere, as did the prosecution's own witnesses. The case was forced on Lowndes County by outsiders. "[Don't] let people like the defendant come into Lowndes County and drag us down from our high moral standards," he said. "This was a cold blooded middle of the night killing that you cannot overlook. . . . Don't put the stamp of approval on chaos, confusion, and anarchy. . . . The bible says, 'thou shall not kill.' It doesn't say who, where, what or when. You've got to face up to it. . . . You must remember your oath and return a guilty verdict to show that murder will be punished in Lowndes County."[23]

At around 3 p.m., the jury received its instructions from Judge Thagard. He had prepared his charge in advance and read it slowly because, he later explained, "I don't trust my ability to express myself in the language of the law well enough to give . . . that charge orally. I might slip and fall, so I took the precaution to prepare the thing in writing." In addition to explaining the concept of reasonable doubt and the law regarding an accomplice's uncorroborated testimony, Thagard told the members of the jury that, according to the indictment, they had a number of choices. They could find Wilkins guilty of murder in the first degree—the willful, deliberate, and premeditated act of murder—in which case it would be up to them to fix the punishment (death by electrocution or life imprisonment). Or they could find him guilty of murder in the second degree—"the unlawful killing of a human being with malice aforethought but without deliberation or premeditation"—punishable by a minimum of ten years plus however long the jury decided the prison sentence should run. Or, finally, first-degree manslaughter—unlawful killing but without malice, carrying a sentence of at least one but not more than ten years in prison.[24]

No jury in the South had ever found an accused person guilty of these or any other capital crime in a racial case, and almost all observers believed that it was unlikely this one would act differently. Traditionally, juries decided quickly, "without even havin' a smoke," as one prosecutor put it. These jurymen were farmers, mechanics, machinists, and bookkeepers, without time to leisurely consider the charges. They were men who needed to return to their work. If the past was any guide, Collie Leroy Wilkins would be home in time for supper.[25]

When the judge finished his charge, he rose and, Coke bottle in hand, directed the jurors to follow senior bailiff Hugh Gates into the room adjacent to the jury box. But they were blocked; the green wooden door wouldn't open. "Door's locked," Gates announced. Deputy Sheriff J. H. Jackson rushed over: "Let me . . . see that thing," he said. He gave the doorknob a hard turn, but nothing happened. "Damned if we ain't all locked out," he laughed. While Gates went downstairs in search of a key, the courtroom relaxed: Jurors reached into their pockets for cigarettes and lit up; reporters rushed to interview the judge; and Wilkins, showing the first sign of animation, left Murphy alone at the defense table to play with Eaton's kids. Soon, Jackson returned, with a smile on his face and a key in hand. If the jurors needed something or wished to report a verdict, they should just knock on the inside door, the judge told them, and the bailiff would come get them. The key worked, and the twelve men slowly filed into the room to begin their deliberations.[26]

An hour later, there was a knock on the door. Some in the courtroom began to collect their belongings, preparing to leave quickly after the jury foreman announced the verdict. Bailiff Gates brought them back to the jury box. All seated themselves except Clifford McMurphee, the jury's foreman. The jury was confused, he said. Were they required to find Wilkins guilty only of first-degree murder, or could they choose a "lesser penalty"? And they wanted a clearer explanation of the guilt of an accomplice. The judge again explained that the jury was free to find the defendant guilty of second-degree murder or manslaughter and was not limited to the most serious offense. The jury seemed satisfied with that answer and left the box. "My god, they're going for a conviction," said a man sitting next to John Frook, *Life*'s correspondent. "But that's impossible," said a local woman sitting behind Frook. "That's never happened before." One of Murphy's aides asked a state trooper, "What does that mean?" "It means that somebody could be in trouble around here," he replied, pointing at Wilkins. Wilkins knew it, too. Jimmy Breslin saw "the . . . sunken eyed cocky Klansman" reach for a cigarette, "but his fat fingers fumbled with trying to pull one out of the pack." "The courtroom was stunned," Breslin later noted. "It seemed to indicate that part of the jury, maybe a good part of it, was for a conviction."[27]

At 6:02 p.m., Judge Thagard called them back and asked whether they were near a verdict. "I don't believe so," McMurphee said. The judge asked the jury members if they wanted supper, but he also said he felt they should deliberate further. If they had not concluded by nine o'clock, they would "get a steak" in Montgomery, spend the night in the air-conditioned courthouse there, and resume in the morning. McMurphee turned to his colleagues, "What is your pleasure, gentlemen?" After a brief discussion, they decided to return to the jury room, armed with a pot of coffee.[28]

The waiting continued. Murray Kempton thought the delay a good sign;

the longer a jury deliberated, the better the chance it would convict. Carlton Perdue disagreed: "You are wrong, boy. I know every man on that jury. There's not five of them that would vote to convict. I did my job and I'm not ashamed of myself. This case was well put together. We didn't even hurt ourselves much with that nigger witness. But convict? I'm just proud of those boys for holding out so long." Townsmen, wearing khaki shirts and suspenders, kept their own counsel. Eaton's kids "whooped and wrestled and cried." Bobby Shelton searched quickly through Liuzzo's letters, as if looking, Murray Kempton thought, for "some revelation at which he could leap into the jury room and cry that he had found the truth and this nonsense could cease." Wilkins sat sullenly, left elbow supporting his chin, right arm draped over the back of his chair. He chain-smoked, idly drew squares on a legal pad, ate peanuts, and frequently bit his fingernails. John Frook of *Life* thought him "a curious specimen—potbellied long before he should be, a bland inexpressive face, slight of forehead and short of neck. . . . Once, walking around the courtroom, he stopped at a . . . lockup in the corner, grabbed the bars and stared at the wall beyond." Wilkins seemed to delight in talking with the Imperial Wizard, who boosted his spirits, causing Wilkins to "take on a kind of swagger as he prowled about."[29]

Another knock at eight o'clock. "What do you say now?" the judge asked. Still no decision, the foreman answered; they weren't even close.

"I think then I will let you go on to Montgomery and get a good night's rest and that might be good for your frayed nerves," Thagard said. "You have had a long hard day, a tiring day, and I think if . . . you get a good meal and a good night's sleep, why maybe everybody might be a little more agreeable." They were to report back at nine o'clock the next morning. "This is worse than the Battle of the Bulge," Murphy remarked as he left the courthouse.[30]

On Friday morning the jurors, after deliberating for forty minutes, returned to their box. They were still confused about the degrees of homicide and the role of the accomplice, and again Thagard explained the law as best he could. They retired but came back at 11:50. McMurphee told the judge that his colleagues were "locked up just as tight as they were the first minute." It was time for lunch, so Thagard told them "to forget this thing entirely and relax." "Oh, damn," said the woman behind John Frook. "I was hoping for a verdict by lunchtime. I wanted to get some television in this afternoon."[31]

During the recess, reporters asked Bobby Shelton whether the Klan would try to harm Rowe. The Imperial Wizard just shrugged, saying, "I wouldn't think we'd have to. A man like that will destroy his own self. Why, we got a . . . FBI informer . . . in an insane asylum in Tuscaloosa. He ratted on his buddies. He didn't last but six or eight months. They threw him out to the wildcats." Joe Breck Gantt and Matt Murphy chatted like a couple of pals, and reporters gathered to listen. Gantt refused to believe that "any American jury would turn loose a cold-blooded killer." "Well, I don't agree with you," Murphy replied, "but I agree with your right to say it." Despite the possibility that his client might still be convicted, the Imperial Klonsel was in a good mood, telling reporters that he was thinking seriously about running for state attorney general. "Well, I guess I'll be out of a job then," Gantt laughed.[32]

Twenty minutes after the jurors resumed their afternoon deliberations, foreman McMurphee wearily reported that the jury was deadlocked: "Your honor, we've discussed this case from every angle, every possible way. . . . We have given a little, up or down, and we are locked just as tight this minute as . . . when the first ballot was taken." Judge Thagard urged them to continue; going through another trial would be "troublesome" and "expensive." "I'm not coercing you; I'm not telling anybody how to vote," Thagard said. "Every man on this jury is the keeper of their own conscience, but . . . we ought to stay here somewhat longer. . . . So, if you will, go back to the jury room and make another effort." Photographers, hoping to snap a picture of the exhausted jurors, rushed around to the south side of the courthouse where they could see through the large open windows of the second-floor jury room. It was hazy with smoke; the men, shirts open, ties askew, walked around or leaned over the table studying documents. A few shook their heads.[33]

When almost three hours had passed without a verdict, the judge asked the bailiffs to bring in the jury. Knowing that this would probably be the last time, the two men vied for the honor and then decided to share it. Tom Norris, wearing what he called his "court shirt," knocked on the jury room door, then put his key in the lock. "You get 'em," he told his partner, Hugh Gates. Gates, his summer suit stained with perspiration, opened the door and yelled inside, "Come awn!" Four jurors appeared and walked to their seats. When no one else came out, he yelled again, "Come awn, boys." That brought out the rest; one limped to his chair,

Matthew Hobson Murphy, the Klan's Imperial Klonsel and Wilkins's defense attorney in his first trial. (UPI-Bettmann/Corbis)

followed by McMurphee, wearing his red hunting jacket and carrying a soft-brimmed hat, obviously ready to go home. Wilkins sat up straighter and tried to read the jurors' faces but showed no emotion.

Were they any closer to a verdict? McMurphee rose slowly, looked out the window for a moment, and stammered: "I don't much think so. We have been hung [at] the same number almost from the outset."

Was the jury "hopelessly deadlocked?"

Yes. Those for conviction were as committed as those for acquittal. The foreman had spoken to every juror and now concluded that "they will remain constant in their beliefs." What was surprising was the way the jury had voted in the twelve ballots taken during the past two days. In their first poll, eight jurors voted for conviction, four for acquittal; but over the course of their deliberations two men had changed sides, so that the final tally was ten to two to convict.

"Well, that sounds just as hopeless as could be," said Thagard.

"I don't know that I have ever seen a jury strive any more diligently or any harder," McMurphee said, almost apologetically.

The judge said he was impressed with their "sincerity," and after asking the others to acknowledge their inability to reach a unanimous verdict —all nodded—he regretfully declared a mistrial. He reminded the jurors to stop by the clerk's office to receive the pay they had earned for their service—thirty-one dollars. "Good-bye and good luck," were his final words.[34]

Klansmen whooped, stomped their feet, and clapped. Wilkins, obviously relieved, "slumped down" in his chair and reached for his cigarettes; his mother rushed over and kissed him on the cheek. She was proud of the way Lee had acted during this ordeal, she told a reporter. "I always told him to look someone straight in the face and to hold his head up high and he's doing just that." Reporters and photographers crowded around the table, flashbulbs popped, and Wilkins yelled, "no comment." As another photographer tried to take his picture, he pointed a finger at him.[35]

Murray Kempton ran into Gene Thomas as he was leaving. "What do you think?" Thomas asked him. Putting a hand on the Klansman's shoulder, the empathetic Kempton, who thought Murphy had been a disaster, said quietly, "Mr. Thomas, you had better go and get yourself a lawyer." John Frook couldn't get away without a final comment from the verbose woman who had befriended him. "Lord sakes," she said, grabbing his elbow, "I'm glad that's over. Y'all can go back North now and let us have some peace and quiet."[36]

Reporters rushed to Joe Breck Gantt for his first reaction to the outcome. Gantt was encouraged. Despite Murphy's efforts to create a racial smoke-screen, the state's message had gotten through: "I think maybe this vote will wake up a few people and show them that there is a slight case of murder involved here." Chances were excellent that Wilkins would be re-tried, and this outcome suggested that the result of another trial could be different from the way such a trial had always gone in Alabama. The state attorney general's office would also continue to pursue its objective—put-ting the Klan "out of business." County Solicitor Perdue said that he was "honestly surprised that we did as well as we did." His colleague Arthur Gamble was also surprised: "No one can blame the jury," he said. "If any-one was at fault it was the prosecution for not convincing the jury of [Wilkins's] guilt."[37]

When reporters reached the courthouse steps, they found the Imperial Klonsel holding a press conference. A very happy man, he played to the crowd—thumping his chest, tipping his hat, and bowing, as if receiving applause. "I'll say to you I did a good job!" he boasted. "I tried the case on my art of cross examination. I only used 23 minutes for the defense be-cause I didn't want to waste the time of that jury . . . but next time a full-scale hearing will be laid on the line. I'll blow that Government case out of the water." When John Frook asked about the close vote, Murphy lost his composure and snarled: "You don't know what the 10 to 2 means. I have no doubt at all that it means 10 to 2 for assault and battery. Maybe not even that." He wasn't far off. Jurors later admitted that from the very beginning there was no support for either a first- or second-degree murder conviction; had they been unanimous, Wilkins would have been found guilty of manslaughter, the least serious charge. "We could not have come that near to any higher charge," said juror Edmund Sallee.[38]

Not everyone thought Murphy's defense and summation "artful." The New York Herald Tribune called both "obscene" and "foul." Life devoted five pages of its May 25 issue to what it called a "Tragicomic Mistrial." Included were an excerpt from Murphy's "violent" summation, several full-page photographs, and to top it off, a cover featuring the Imperial Klonsel hold-ing up two fingers of his right hand in a crooked V for victory sign. News-week's coverage of the trial also reproduced Murphy's "racist diatribe," calling it "disturbing evidence of the enduring difference between some Southerners and most Americans." Conservative columnist William F. Buckley, Jr., weighed in, too: If Murphy's rant were televised to the American people, he argued, it might "persuade the nation to overthrow the jury system."[39]

Even the jurors criticized Murphy. "I think a great many of us were insulted," Sallee told reporters. "He must have thought we were very ignorant to be taken in by that act." Clifford McMurphee agreed, adding: "I don't think he did his case any good with that speech. Personally, he didn't enrich himself with me." The chairman of the New York chapter of the American Bar Association later called Murphy "vicious," "unethical," and guilty of "gross misconduct" and filed a complaint with both the Alabama and national offices of the association, seeking Murphy's expulsion from that body. (Nothing happened: Murphy wasn't a member of the national ABA, and Alabama's branch took no action.)[40]

The two "holdouts" were happy to explain their positions. Both hailed from Fort Deposit, where many Klansmen lived; they denied membership, although they did admit to having belonged to the White Citizens Council. Billy R. Cheatham, a thirty-two-year-old bookkeeper, didn't believe Rowe, "not when he swore before God and broke his [Klan] oath. . . . I'm mad at him for that." Did Cheatham think that Rowe should also have been on trial? "Very, very much so," he said. "We didn't ask for this incident. It came into our county. It should have happened someplace else. I'd be there till hell froze over but I wouldn't change my mind. I stuck by my guns . . . I did my duty." His friend Dan Lee, a mechanic, was more taciturn; he just nodded and said, "Me and him are pretty much on the same side."

Cheatham and Lee were also asked whether they agreed with Murphy's closing argument. "Pretty well," Lee said. "Like I say, he's a lawyer," and Cheatham added, "a sharp one!" When Jimmy Breslin asked Cheatham whether he thought his fellow Alabamans would be angry at him for causing the hung jury, he angrily replied: "No. I got that settled . . . right in that room. I knew that . . . when I said I wasn't going along with them they'd respect me." According to Cheatham, another juror shared their views, and had there been a bit more time, he would have changed sides. All in all, the jury's deliberations proceeded smoothly, affably—feelings not shared by fellow juror Hugh M. Tuberville, who remarked, "This is the worst hell I have ever been through."[41]

Did the ten jurors who voted to convict Collie Leroy Wilkins of manslaughter indicate that the people of Lowndes County were less intolerant than their reputation suggested? Or did Matt Murphy's racist diatribe alienate even the staunchest segregationist who believed that a person shouldn't get away with murder, even if the victim was a civil rights worker? Or was it just a fluke, proof of the lawyer's old adage that you never knew how a jury would vote? The next trials would tell the tale: Wilkins would be retried, probably soon; then the trials of Thomas and Eaton would follow. And there were also the federal charges against the three—violating Viola Liuzzo's civil rights by murder—that trial was likely to occur once the state juries were through with the cases.

Virginia Durr left Hayneville "sick—literally," and more alienated from her fellow southerners than ever. "I cling to the small circle we have," she later wrote friends, "but the great majority of the people frighten me, they are so insane and prejudiced." Driving home alone through "the empty countryside," she experienced "a feeling of terror such as I had never had before." In her rearview mirror, she saw a huge red automobile bearing down on her at what she thought was eighty miles an hour, and she expected it to "deliberately knock [her] off the road." But at the last minute, it pulled around her, and she caught a glimpse of its passengers: "I saw those pale, fanatic, askew faces of [Wilkins, Thomas, and Eaton], Matt Murphy beside them as they roared off up the road. I stopped the car until I could get my breath and my heart could stop beating so hard. I knew killing would strike again. For the white people of Hayneville had condoned the killing, whatever they might say; there was killing in the air."[42]

While the Klansmen celebrated their victory, civil rights workers, energized by Viola Liuzzo's murder and the Wilkins trial, intensified their efforts to register blacks in Lowndes County. Their leader was a twenty-three-year-old veteran activist named Stokely Carmichael.[43]

Born in Trinidad of parents active in the island's rebellion against British rule, Carmichael grew up in New York where he drank deeply from the city's well of radical politics—Marxism, Socialism, the black nationalism of Harlem's street preachers. When he was still in his teens, he joined the civil rights movement; helped organize the SNCC; and participated in sit-ins, Freedom Rides, and demonstrations of all kinds, which landed him in small-town jails and once in Mississippi's notorious Parchman Penitentiary, where he was beaten daily. For Carmichael and many others who felt they were on the front lines of a civil rights war, the nonviolence Martin Luther King, Jr., espoused had little meaning. "I'm not going to let somebody hit up the side of my head for the rest of my life and die," he said in 1961. "You got to fight back!" On March 27, 1965, two days after Viola Liuzzo's murder, Carmichael, with only the clothes on his back and a sleeping bag, set up shop in Lowndes County—in his view, "the epitome of the tight, insulated police state."[44]

Carmichael began traveling the county's back roads—usually at night and often in disguise—meeting with local groups of blacks brave enough to join his movement. It was tough going; no more than sixty blacks were registered to vote by the end of August, but Carmichael, handsome, eloquent, and charismatic, was making his presence felt. And after President Johnson signed the Voting Rights Act into law on August 6, federal registrars came south. Within two months, despite threats of violence and the loss of their jobs, approximately two thousand blacks were on the voting rolls in Lowndes County. With blacks outnumbering whites in the county, their eventual control of the ballot box seemed inevitable.[45]

One southerner who was especially troubled by these "outside agitators" was a fifty-four-year-old Hayneville native named Tom Coleman. The old Lowndes County Courthouse was his second home: His grandfather had been county sheriff early in the twentieth century, and his father, superintendent of the county school system, once had an office there. So did his sister, who currently held that post, as well as the current circuit court clerk, who was married to his cousin. Like his father, Coleman spent time there every day, chatting with bailiffs and court reporters and playing dominoes in the clerk's office. Although lacking a formal education, Coleman eventually became the county's chief engineer whose work crews often included convict labor, which he supervised. One night in August 1959, a black prisoner turned violent, armed himself with broken bottles, and refused to surrender peacefully. He moved toward Coleman, who reacted by firing his shotgun, killing the man. Since this was clearly a case of self-defense, Coleman was never charged. Indeed, local police treated him as a hero, a role he liked. He eventually became an unpaid "special deputy sheriff," formed close friendships with Sheriff Jim Clark and other law enforcement officers, and was proud that his son joined them by becoming a state trooper.

The Wilkins trial, which brought FBI agents and foreign reporters to his beloved home, enraged Coleman. He claimed never to have joined the Klan, but he was active in the local White Citizens Council and, like the Klan, saw himself as a defender of the southern way of life. It wouldn't take much to push Tom Coleman over the edge into madness.[46]

It happened on August 20. That afternoon, Coleman was at the courthouse playing dominoes with his friends as usual, when he learned that Carmichael and his colleagues were about to be released after spending six days in the Hayneville jail for demonstrating. Expecting violence, Coleman got his shotgun and went to the local grocery, where he offered his protection to Virginia Varner, a longtime friend who owned the Cash Store.

As Coleman watched the street outside, four civil rights workers— two white men and two young black women—just freed from their captivity, went together in search of a cold drink on a hot August afternoon. They saw the huge Coca-Cola sign hanging above the front door of the Cash Store and headed for it. As Jonathan Daniels, a twenty-six-year-old Episcopal seminary student and civil rights activist, opened the screen door, followed by Ruby Sales, a college student, they came face to face with Coleman. "Get out, the store is closed," he yelled. "Get off this property or I'll blow your god-damned heads off, you sons of bitches." Shoving Sales aside, Daniels tried to talk with the angry man. He was polite and, with his clerical collar, certainly didn't look like someone who posed a threat. But without further words, Coleman fired his shotgun, blowing a hole in Daniels's chest, killing him instantly. The two other civil rights workers ran, but Richard Morrisroe, a young Roman Catholic priest from Chicago, wasn't fast enough. Coleman fired again, hitting the priest in the back and side, seriously injuring him. After threatening to kill others who approached, Coleman put down his weapon, drove to the sheriff's office, and telephoned Colonel Al Lingo. "I just shot two preachers," he told him. "You better get on down here."[47]

Daniels's and Morrisroe's friends held a rally later that night. "We're going to tear this county down," a saddened and angry Stokely Carmichael said. "Then we're going to build it back brick by brick, until it's a fit place for human beings." Since March, four civil rights workers had been murdered: Jimmy Lee Jackson, Reverend Jim Reeb, Viola Liuzzo, and now Jonathan Daniels. Soon, Carmichael's fury would result in the organization of a separate political party in Lowndes County; its symbol was the black panther, its slogan, "Power for Black People."[48]

To the citizens of Lowndes County, Tom Coleman was a hero—"a hell of a nice guy," people said. County Solicitor Carlton Perdue was probably closer to the mark when he said that Coleman "was like the rest of us. He's strong in his feelings." Tom Coleman and his family were "all good friends" of his, he told reporters who had returned to Lowndes County to cover another murder trial. "If [Daniels and Morrisroe] had been tending to their own business," Perdue continued, "like I was tending to mine, they'd be living and enjoying themselves." These attitudes may explain why the Lowndes County grand jury charged Coleman not with first- or second-degree murder and attempted murder in Morrisroe's case, but with manslaughter and assault and battery. Alabama's attorney general, Richmond Flowers, called the grand jury's action "an abdication of . . . responsibility."[49]

Lowndes County justice proceeded as usual, oblivious to the criticism of outsiders. In fact, the more that the national media attacked southern customs, the more its citizens embraced them. When Flowers asked Judge Thagard, who was trying the Coleman case, for a two-month postponement until Father Morrisroe, his chief eyewitness, had recovered sufficiently to testify, the judge rejected the motion and declared, "The trial of Tom Coleman will begin tomorrow." Flowers refused to participate, so Thagard removed him and asked Carlton Perdue and Arthur Gamble to prosecute.

When the trial began on September 27, the courtroom was packed with Klansmen—including Wilkins, Thomas, and Eaton. Defense witnesses testified that Daniels threatened Coleman with a switchblade knife while Morrisroe pulled a gun, so Coleman was merely protecting himself when he shot them. The jury rejected Ruby Sales's eyewitness testimony, finding these lies more persuasive. In his closing statement, defense attorney Joe Phelps said, "You know Tom Coleman and you know he had to do what he did," while his co-counsel, imitating Matt Murphy, added: "God give us such men! Men with great hearts, strong minds, pure souls—and ready hands!" Coleman had a god-given right "to defend himself."

On Wednesday, September 29, just two days after the trial began, the jury began its deliberations. Awaiting the jury's decision, the "trial watchers" were "busily talking in huddles," not about the verdict—which was never in doubt—but about the next day's football game between the University of Alabama and Ole Miss. After about ninety minutes, the jury found Coleman not guilty of all charges. Thagard thanked the jurors, each of whom, before heading to the clerk's office to receive their stipend, walked over to Coleman and shook his hand. One said, "We gonna be able to make that dove shoot now, ain't we?"[50]

The NAACP called the jury's verdict "a monstrous farce" that encouraged "every Alabama bigot" to declare "open season on Negroes and their white friends." The NAACP was right: Citizens in Fort Deposit were now seen driving cars with bumper stickers that read OPEN SEASON. When one veteran reporter heard the verdict, he thought immediately of Wilkins's next trial, which was soon to begin, and said, "They just tried the Liuzzo case."[51]

CHAPTER TEN

Parable of the Two Goats

ON OCTOBER 18, 1965, less than three weeks after Tom Coleman's acquittal, Collie Leroy Wilkins, puffing on a cigarette and wearing a dark suit, thin tie, and a ten-gallon cowboy hat, returned to the Hayneville Courthouse, this time not as an observer lost in the crowd, but as the defendant, in his second trial for the murder of Viola Liuzzo. To avoid reporters, he ran from the parking area, but the sight of the short, stocky Klansman, coat flapping open to reveal his distended stomach hanging over his belt, was too big to miss; an Associated Press photographer snapped his picture, which ran in the next day's papers.[1]

To outward appearances, little had changed since May. The town was as sleepy as ever, seemingly frozen in amber. A reporter from Detroit found its citizens possessing a "ho-hum attitude" about "its next date with history." The cavernous second-floor courtroom was still stuffy, its windows open despite October's chill. In the great oak tree outside "song birds chirped," an ever present accompaniment to the sounds of people arriving, taking their seats, settling in for another brief entertainment. On the bench, Judge T. Werth Thagard again presided. The state's witnesses were expected to be the same as before: the turncoat Rowe, the skittish Leroy Moton, and others in the supporting cast.[2]

Yet much was different. Most noticeably, Matthew Hobson Murphy, who had been looking forward to a rematch, was gone. "I'm ready to roll and have been gathering new information," he had said in late June. He claimed that because of damaging pretrial publicity created by Lyndon Johnson, his client had been denied a fair trial, resulting in the hung jury. But he recognized that he, too, might have been responsible; his racist appeal had annoyed many jurors, or so he was told. "I figured wrong that last time," Murphy said, "but I won't make the same mistake next time." One man, writing from San Francisco, warned him not to: "I am going to write a letter to the husband of Mrs. Liuzzo offering him $200.00, for him to hire a Negro to shoot . . . you or any member of your family and that of [Wilkins] and see how you feel . . . after you are killed and that of those dirty KKK. If this cannot be done we will pray to God that a misserable [sic] accident may happen to all of you . . . sooner than any man can imagin [sic], and all of you deserve it too." Murphy, afraid for his life, saw no problem in turning to the very agency he had just denounced: He sent the threatening letter to the FBI.[3]

For Murphy, however, there was no second chance. At 3:45 a.m. on August 20, the day Tom Coleman murdered Jonathan Daniels, Murphy's car drifted across the double line on the Tuscaloosa–Birmingham highway, crashing into the rear of an asphalt tanker truck, killing Murphy instantly. The lack of skid marks at the scene suggested that he had fallen asleep at the wheel, although a later investigation revealed that Murphy had been drinking "heavily" at Birmingham's Patio Bar until just before the accident. Grand Dragon Robert Creel had a different explanation: Two hours before Murphy's accident, a white woman driving in the same area was shot and wounded by two unknown assailants. Murphy, armed with a .22 pistol, was trying to determine whether the "nightriders" were "Negroes" when he lost control of his car, the Grand Dragon believed.[4]

Now sitting next to Wilkins at the defense table was his new attorney, forty-eight-year-old Arthur J. Hanes, a former star athlete, former FBI agent (from 1948 to 1951), and former one-term mayor of Birmingham. Tall, handsome, and smartly dressed, he seemed the antithesis of the seedy Matt Murphy, but the two had briefly roomed together while attending college, and Hanes considered Murphy a good friend "who did not have a wicked or evil bone in his body." Hanes was a pallbearer at Murphy's funeral, and one paper noted that he was "near tears throughout the ceremony." He had decided to take the case because he was "incensed over the way President Johnson attacked the Klansmen on national television." "To my knowledge," he told the press, "I have never been within 50 miles of any [Klan] meeting." Perhaps he was being truthful (although Rowe later claimed that Hanes was "a card carrying Klansman"), but in fact he didn't need the robe and hood to espouse the Klan's philosophy or do their bidding.

To Birmingham insiders, Hanes was known as "Bull's boy," the puppet of Bull Connor, who had launched and controlled Hanes's political career. It was during the Hanes administration that Bull Connor's police had attacked young civil rights workers with vicious police dogs and water cannons. Hanes called civil rights demonstrators "the Congolese mob," and Martin Luther King "the witch doctor." He told one audience that he "would never negotiate with the Communists or the rabble rousers of the King type . . . because they haven't got a thing that we want. We have what they want." Hanes may not have had Matt Murphy's flair for the dramatic, but Wilkins was in good hands.[5]

There was also a new prosecutor: the attorney general of Alabama, Richmond Flowers, a tall redhead who was an enemy of the Klan and, as one journalist later noted, "virtually the only force . . . in Alabama which opposed Governor Wallace's segregationist stand, a sort of Alabama Solzhenitsyn." Having been "tossed off" the Coleman case by Judge Thagard, Flowers removed the local solicitors, Perdue and Gamble, and came to Hayneville determined to put Wilkins behind bars. He arrived with armed guards, whom he brought into the courtroom to protect him. Klansmen burned crosses on his lawn almost daily, and death threats were routine. "I wouldn't go down there unless I had my own bodyguard standing immediately behind me and troopers on each side," he later said. "And I wasn't just being fancy. . . . I was scared and I stayed scared a lot of the time. . . . The troopers would tell you, 'You better have protection . . . especially in Hayneville. There's no hate like the hate down there.'" His assistant, Joe Breck Gantt, experienced the same fears: "We lived under the constant threat of being killed," he later recalled.[6]

Flowers harbored no illusion that he could actually win a conviction, despite believing that he had "the strongest criminal case" of his career. So he saw the trial as a historic opportunity to throw light on the inequity of Alabama's jury system. The exclusion of blacks, women, and the disabled so narrowed the group of potential jurors that often the same white men served repeatedly. (One was Tom Coleman, whose name was called when the jury that was to decide his own fate was being selected.) But most serious was the racial prejudice that affected every juror; it made a fair trial almost impossible. Exposing that prejudice and its effect on the judicial system became Flowers's principal goal: He would put the Alabama jury system itself on trial. "We had a kangaroo trial here," he told *Newsweek's* Joseph Cumming, referring to the recent acquittal of Tom Coleman. "We were ridiculed all over the nation. This time, the state of Alabama is going to give them a fight."[7]

The fight began that Monday morning as Flowers and Hanes picked their jury. In the first Wilkins trial, Judge Thagard had conducted the voir dire—the questioning of potential jurors. His questions were traditional: Was any juror related to the victim? The defendant and his lawyer? The prosecutors? Did they have a "fixed opinion" about the case? Were they opposed to the death penalty and would they apply it in a case based on circumstantial evidence? This time, Flowers and Gantt asked questions that were dramatically different from those that potential jurors in Alabama courts were accustomed to hearing—"a gambit," *Newsweek* noted, "virtually unheard of in a small-town Dixie racial case—quizzing each prospective juror about his racial views."[8]

"Do you believe that the white man is superior to the Negro man?" Gantt asked C. E. Bender, an auto mechanic from Fort Deposit and a former member of the Ku Klux Klan. Hanes objected, but the judge permitted the question. "Every white man believes it," Bender replied nonchalantly. So ingrained was such sentiment, as natural as breathing, that during the next three hours, thirteen of fifteen Alabamans responded to Gantt's question, "I believe in white supremacy." Or, as John B. Traylor, Jr., a farmer, put it, "Well, being born here in Lowndes County, and seeing things that I have seen, I would have to say yes." The only two who didn't echo the prevailing sentiment were black men, who were not allowed to serve.[9]

How did the men feel about a white man or woman who "works with the Negroes, lives with Negroes, works with them in civil rights movements, marches, and demonstrations?" Gantt asked. "Do you believe that such a white person is inferior?"

"Yes, sir, I sure do," said Frank N. Lloyd, a car salesman from Fort Deposit who admitted to current membership in the local White Citizens Council. Others were more outspoken about "outside agitators." J. F. Collison, another Lowndes County farmer, said, "If those white people had stayed where they came from, then we wouldn't have had that problem."

Such people "should clean up [their] own backyard first," added O. P. Woodruff, another member of the local White Citizens Council.[10]

Gantt's attempt to elicit potential jurors' views of the Ku Klux Klan also produced troubling but not surprising responses. Did the Klan serve a "useful purpose"? he asked each man. Leon Gilmore, a county employee and former member of the White Citizens Council, thought "it does in some cases. . . . A lot of times things get out of hand and they straighten them out. . . . It shows . . . the right and the wrong way to be." Farmer Traylor agreed with Gilmore because "everybody has some good in them," except blacks and civil rights workers. Others acted as if the Klan hardly existed: "I don't know that much about it," said Hardy M. Owens after the judge asked him to spit out his chewing gum. When asked whether he thought the Klan was a force for good, Wilburn Pettus, a mechanic who admitted to feeling biased toward Klansman Wilkins, replied, "I don't hardly know . . . that much about it." Nevertheless, all but one claimed that they could evaluate the evidence with an open mind and would recommend that Wilkins receive the death penalty if he was found guilty.[11]

Flowers didn't believe them. By the time he and Gantt finished questioning the forty-four prospective jurors on the afternoon of the second day, he was convinced that the state would be unable to receive an impartial hearing. Not only did almost every man believe in white supremacy and think civil rights workers inferior, two-thirds were current or past members of Alabama's White Citizens Council. Faced with the likelihood of another kangaroo court, the attorney general "dropped his bombshell," as *Time* called it. He told the judge that he wanted to challenge eleven of the most outspoken racists for cause. All believed strongly that both blacks and civil rights workers were inferior to whites, and one "shook his head earnestly" when he admitted that he didn't know whether he could send Wilkins to the electric chair just for killing a civil rights worker. "How can the state of Alabama expect a fair and just verdict in this case from men who have already sat in judgment on the victim and pronounced her inferior to themselves?" he asked the judge. "They could not truly render a just verdict on the slaying."[12]

But Judge Thagard rejected the view that prejudice or even stupidity met the legal test for challenging a juror. "The Court is not entitled to administer intelligence tests," Thagard noted in the case of one prospective juror whom he considered "ignorant." Thagard's position was strongly supported by defense attorney Arthur Hanes, who read the appropriate statute defining such grounds—which included having a "fixed opinion" on the defendant's guilt or innocence "which would bias his verdict"; being a felon; or having a relationship with the defendant or the prosecutor and a personal interest in the outcome of the case. Furthermore, Hanes believed that such a mass disqualification would require another time-consuming voir dire and therefore violate Wilkins's constitutional right to a swift trial. Constitutional niceties aside, he also sensed a plot against his client: "This young man . . . has been under terrific pressure . . . [and] in my judgment he has been used as a pawn [for] political gain and I charge [that] the Attorney General for the state of Alabama and the United States are part of it." (Later, Hanes told reporters that Flowers and Attorney General Nicholas Katzenbach had met recently to "cook up" this effort to derail the trial.)[13]

The judge found Hanes's legal argument sound and told Flowers that he would deny every challenge to seating the eleven jurors. The attorney general then surprised everyone by asking for a twenty-four-hour recess so that he could argue his case before Alabama's Supreme Court. Hanes again objected but Thagard replied, "I'm going to give you that opportunity, Mr. Flowers."[14]

The Supreme Court agreed to hear Flowers, and a four-man panel, appointed by Chief Justice Edward Livingston, met at the Montgomery Courthouse on Wednesday morning, October 20. Their ruling came quickly: "If we were to interrupt the trial of the Wilkins case to review . . . the rulings here under consideration," the justices argued, "we would establish a precedent which would in the future operate to impede the progress of all criminal trials while we reviewed . . . various and sundry rulings of the trial courts during the progress of those trials."[15]

A dejected Flowers returned to the Hayneville Courthouse where, less than three hours later, the jury was finally selected. It consisted of six farmers, a construction worker, a car salesman, a county employee, two pulpwood operators, and a timber buyer. Ten of them either had once belonged to the White Citizens Council or were still members. Nearly all had proudly declared their belief in white supremacy and the inferiority of civil rights workers; four were among the group of eleven whom Flowers tried to purge. The defendant, said to be experiencing "terrific pressure," observed these proceedings without a flicker of concern. Roy Reed of the New York Times explained why: "Once again, Mr. Wilkins was surrounded by white people . . . : the white-haired little circuit judge . . . ; 12 neatly dressed jurors; his lawyer . . . a former mayor of Birmingham; red-haired Mr. Flowers and two of his assistants; more than two dozen reporters; Sheriff Frank Ryals and his deputies; six blue-uniformed State Police troopers guarding the doors, and—slouched in cigarette haze, about fifty spectators—all white. . . . [T]he machinery and trappings of justice in Lowndes County [were] in the hands of the white people, where it has always been."

But there were significant differences between the first and second Wilkins trials. This time, Judge Thagard was determined to prevent the "circus like" atmosphere that had prevailed in May. Now, Klansmen were forbidden from swaggering through the courtroom during recesses and stopping off at the prosecutors' table to casually examine the contents of Viola Liuzzo's handbag. The judge also silenced visitors who called out words of encouragement to Wilkins or "laughed and snickered, applauded and even stomped their feet," as they had during the earlier proceedings. Absent was Wilkins's chief cheerleader, Imperial Wizard Bobby Shelton, who that same week was called to testify before the House Committee on Un-American Activities, which, as a result of the Liuzzo murder and President Johnson's call for congressional action, was investigating the Klan.[16]

The lawyers, on both sides, also behaved differently. During the first trial, prosecutors Arthur Gamble and Carlton Perdue sat idly by while Matt Murphy ran roughshod over their witnesses and engaged in racial rants. This time, Attorney General Flowers and his assistant Joe Breck Gantt quickly objected to defense tactics they thought were inappropriate or irrelevant and were often sustained by the judge. For his part, Arthur Hanes, despite his Klan connections, rejected Murphy's emphasis on race, which had contributed to the hung jury, in favor of a more traditional "murder case" strategy. Murphy "was a Klansman . . . he always had been and he tried it that way," recalled Arthur Hanes, Jr., who at age twenty-four assisted his father. "We were just lawyers, we were hired to put on a defense and to put on the best one we could." Hanes also appreciated how advantageous it was to the defense to have a complete transcript of the first trial; they knew the questions the prosecution had asked in May and was now likely to ask again, as well as how the witnesses answered them. "Although I will claim some skill for our side," Hanes later reflected, "it . . . doesn't take a Phi Beta Kappa to figure out that a good defense team will just eat up" the opposition "if they try the second trial" as they did the first. The lawyers Hanes, father and son, had one simple goal: impeach the state's witnesses by looking for inconsistencies in their testimony and uncover those facts that raised reasonable doubt in the jurors' minds.[17]

Hanes's strategy was evident from the first questioning of the Alabama police officials who had been called to the crime scene. Hanes asked the officers about the presence of tire tracks across the road from the meadow where Liuzzo's car had come to rest. Each testified that a small car, perhaps of foreign make, had stopped to view Liuzzo's car, then backed across the road, turned around, and sped away quickly toward Selma. "It got away pretty good," Trooper McGehee noted. The unspoken question was obvious: Did this driver kill Liuzzo?[18]

Murphy's cross-examination of toxicologist Paul Shoffeitt had all been about sex and drugs. Hanes focused instead on the condition of Liuzzo's car. "Based on your examination of that automobile and those holes in that window," Hanes asked, "do you have any judgment as to whether those bullets were fired from . . . a moving automobile, or a parked automobile, or from the ground, or if it was coming head-on from another automobile, or an automobile overtaking it?"

"I don't know where they were fired from, no, sir," Shoffeitt replied.

"You wouldn't have any judgment?"

"No, sir," Shoffeitt repeated.

"It's possible they could have been fired from the ground?" Hanes asked again.

"Yes."

"It could have been fired from an automobile?"

"Yes."

"That's all, doctor. Thank you," Hanes concluded.[19]

Leroy Moton was again a poor witness. Sitting in the witness chair, he was almost "immobile," one reporter noted, "his hands clasped in a prayer grip, his head locked stiffly to the front." As before, he spoke so quietly that Hanes frequently complained that he couldn't hear Moton's answers. The judge agreed: "His voice seems rather weak. . . . We tried before to get him to talk loud and I just don't believe we could get him to do it." Hanes again avoided Murphy's outrageous excesses; he didn't suggest that Moton fired the shots himself or "rifled" Liuzzo's purse and stole her money, but he couldn't entirely resist playing the race card. After Moton described his job as a transportation officer during the march, Hanes sud-

denly asked, "Leroy, was it part of your duties . . . to make love to Mrs. Liuzzo?" Joe Breck Gantt leaped to his feet: "We object, Your Honor. Counsel
knows that is clearly improper."

"Yeah," said Judge Thagard, "I agree with you."

"We're trying a murder case today," Gantt reminded Hanes.

Hanes ignored both men. "Leroy, did you at any time park in an automobile with Mrs. Liuzzo in front of Brown's Chappel [sic]."

This time, Hanes stopped, but the judge said he would allow such
questions if Moton's actions occurred at the time of the killing. So, after
Moton described how Liuzzo's car ended up in the field, Hanes asked,
"Now, when this car stopped, did you touch her?"

"No, I didn't," Moton said.

"Did she touch you?"

"No, sir."

Hanes drew closer to the witness: "At no time you never touched her
[sic]?"

Moton became "rattled," and his voice grew softer: "No, I didn't."

"Or she never touched you?"

"She never touched me or I never touched her," Moton said.[20]

Hanes had better luck questioning Moton about when he had first
met Mrs. Liuzzo. Moton couldn't remember precisely, so Hanes bore in:
"How long had you known Mrs. Liuzzo, two weeks, three weeks, one week,
six days, ten days, do you have any judgment as to how long you have
known her?"

"Well, like I say, I do not remember the exact date on that."[21]

Moton's memory of the shooting was just as bad. "Could you tell what
kind of car it was?" Hanes asked.

"No, I couldn't."

"Did you see any guns?"

"I didn't."

"Did you see any gunfire?"

"No, I didn't."

"Then you don't know whether those bullets came from that car or
not, do you?"

"It's hard to say," Moton replied.[22]

Hanes next asked Moton if he hadn't told both state and federal investigators, and later journalists, that the killers' car was "a 1955 dark Ford

... that fired into your car and went up to the top of the hill and turned around and came back and shined its lights on you and went back to Selma, you told them that, didn't you?"[23]

"I don't recall," Moton said and went on to insist that he hadn't spoken to any member of the press that night or the following day. (Unfortunately, Moton forgot that he *had* told a reporter from the *Detroit Free Press* the following morning about the killing and identified the car as "a red 1959 or 1960 Chevrolet convertible," which was a close match for Thomas's '62 red and white Chevrolet Impala. Had the prosecutors been aware of the *Free Press* story, they might have been able to make Moton a more credible witness.)[24]

Would Rowe be more believable? The attorney general didn't know; he had seen his star witness only once, and the meeting had not been successful. Rowe had been in protective custody on the Maxwell Air Force Base, and access to him was strictly controlled by the FBI. On Tuesday night, October 19, fewer than twelve hours before Rowe was due to testify, Flowers was informed that he could finally see Rowe, but only under conditions dictated by the Bureau. Flowers and Gantt drove first to Montgomery's Holiday Inn East, where they conferred with Inspector James McGovern and Rowe's personal watchdog, Neil Shanahan. "We don't know whether we can let this man testify," McGovern told the prosecutors. This was a shocking way to begin; without Rowe's eyewitness testimony, their case was doomed. The FBI wanted Flowers to grant Rowe immunity from prosecution not just now but in the future as well. They were absolutely "emphatic" about this: "Immunity must be granted . . . before we would be allowed to use [Rowe] as the key prosecution witness," Gantt later recalled. "Absolutely impossible," Flowers replied. He could guarantee Rowe immunity only as long as he was attorney general; his successors would be free to do as they pleased.[25]

The agents weren't happy, so Flowers explained what the law permitted him to do: If Rowe was indicted for murder by a local district attorney, Flowers could replace him and take over the case himself. "If anyone attempts it," he said, "I will do that." As long as he was attorney general, he promised that Rowe would never face prosecution, assuming, of course, that he testified truthfully. This was acceptable to McGovern, so Flowers and Gantt were taken to the Officers' Club at Maxwell Air Force Base for their first and last conference with Gary Thomas Rowe.[26]

As they drove, McGovern explained the ground rules: Only one man at a time could talk with Rowe, and his FBI handlers would remain in the room to advise Rowe which questions he should answer. Only the events of March 25 could be discussed; Rowe's five-year relationship with the FBI was off-limits lest he reveal the secret operations of the Bureau's informant system. When at last Flowers was permitted to see Rowe, he found their exchange "very, very guarded by the FBI." The tale Rowe was allowed to tell was "very vague and sketchy." Neither prosecutor was able to challenge his account. "We really didn't press him," Flowers later recalled; "we couldn't." "Irritated" with the FBI, Flowers left feeling that the prosecution was "hampered badly. . . . Had I been allowed to question . . . Rowe, had I been able to inform myself of the type witness he would have made, I probably wouldn't have used him."[27]

Rowe certainly gave every appearance of still being the state's star witness when he arrived in Hayneville the following morning. Four dark cars driving together in a caravan came to a halt in the courthouse parking lot and deposited their passengers—thirteen men, all dressed alike in plain black business suits. One of them was Rowe, who was immediately surrounded by a dozen FBI agents. They entered the building through a phalanx of state troopers, and Rowe was rushed upstairs to the courtroom, where he was sworn in and seated in the witness chair. His guards remained nearby, stationed at strategic spots, protecting him from harm. Under Joe Breck Gantt's questioning, he once again "kept the packed courtroom spellbound" as he recounted the story of Liuzzo's murder.[28]

"The first thing I knew," Rowe testified, "Wilkins stuck his arm out the window. He had a pistol in his hand almost to elbow length." Rowe stuck his own arm straight out, showing the jury how Wilkins got ready to shoot. Wilkins then told Gene Thomas: "Baby brother, give it some gas and Gene sped up. The woman turned and looked at us, and as she looked Wilkins fired right in the window where the woman was looking."

Speaking without emotion, almost by rote, Rowe said that he thought Wilkins had missed and told him so. "Wilkins slapped me on the right leg and said, 'Baby brother, don't worry about it. That bitch and that bastard are dead and in hell. I don't miss.'" Then the car accelerated, heading toward Montgomery.[29]

Arthur Hanes, on cross-examination, tried to discredit Rowe by first focusing on his personal life. With "acid in his voice," Hanes's questions led Rowe to reveal that he had dropped out of school at age sixteen, worked intermittently, married, and then after the birth of his first child, abandoned his wife and daughter without financial support. His second marriage had fared no better, only now there were four more young children without a father. But there was worse ground to cover as Hanes, drawing on his Klan sources, tried to prove that Rowe was "a trouble-maker" who created riots solely for the purpose of being paid by the FBI to report on them. Case in point: The attack on the Freedom Riders in 1961. Showing Rowe the now-famous photograph of the assault on George Webb, Hanes asked, "This one doing the slugging, is that a picture of Gary Thomas Rowe?"

"No, sir," Rowe replied nonchalantly. "But I see a couple of people in there I recognize."

Hanes pointed at the burly figure crouching over the fallen Webb: "Is this your picture, right here?"

"No, sir."

"Are you telling this Court that this is not your picture here."

"I state that it is not my picture," said Rowe, committing perjury.

"So, Mr. Rowe, this was in 1961, one year after you joined the Klan, [for] God and country, served the FBI, and on your own . . . you were out attacking people, is that right?"

"No, sir," Rowe again insisted, "I protected myself."

"Oh, you left your home . . . and went down to the bus station to protect yourself, right?" There was laughter in the courtroom. "Order in the Court," yelled the bailiff. "Yes," said the judge. "No demonstrations, please."[30]

Hanes asked about Rowe's status within the Bureau: "Now, you are a regular FBI agent, or special agent?"

"No, sir."

"What do they call you . . . ?"

"Undercover investigator," Rowe said.

"Does the FBI address you as Mr. Undercover Agent or do they call you an informer," Hanes snickered.

Rowe's answer took the sting out of Hanes's question: His friends in the Bureau usually called him "Tommy."[31]

Hanes then focused on the day of the killing, drawing his questions from the Klan magazine *Nightriders*. While en route to Montgomery, didn't Rowe and the others pass an accident and almost stop to help until he saw that the injured were black and commented, "That's two niggers that won't make the march." Rowe denied it; Gene Thomas had made the remark, adding, "to hell with them, let's go." At a gas station in the city, didn't Rowe see a shotgun in the office and ask the attendant, "Is that all the guns you all have got?" No, Rowe said. And when the attendant answered, "We don't need any guns," didn't Rowe say, "Just wait till the soldiers leave and we'll see. I left my gun in my car, but I wish I hadn't. I feel half-undressed"? Never said it, Rowe insisted. And when they first saw Liuzzo's car and the interracial couple inside, didn't he say, "Let's stop it . . . let's teach these nigger lovers a lesson"? Rowe finally showed signs of irritation: "Very definitely not, sir," Rowe said "in loud, measured tones."[32]

Hanes tried to force Rowe to lose his composure by asking him directly whether he had tried to prevent the killing of Viola Liuzzo: "Did you tell Wilkins not to shoot?"

"No, sir."

"Did you tell Eaton not to shoot?"

"No, sir."

"Did you make any attempt to move or jostle Wilkins's arm to distort his aim?"

"No, sir."

"Well, you work for the FBI, don't you?" Hanes concluded.

Rowe's reply—"yes, sir"—was drowned out by more laughter in the courtroom.[33]

Believing that he finally had Rowe on the edge of cracking, Hanes asked him to describe at length and in minute detail the route they took from "Big Swamp Creek," where the "alleged escapade" occurred, to the VFW Club, Lorene's Cafe, and finally, Thomas's house. Rowe had no trouble doing it, re-creating the journey street by street, noting sites of particular interest—a gas station on the "old 31 highway," and approximately six miles away, a white motel "that I remember seeing at the intersection, it runs into the freeway."

Hanes interrupted: "I am lost here, Mr. Rowe."

Rowe wasn't: "I will be happy to . . . show it to you, if you're lost."

"I don't want to go see it," Hanes snapped. "We haven't got time to go see it."[34]

Hanes's "grueling" cross-examination lasted more than two hours, but Rowe never broke under the onslaught of questions. Reporters expressed a grudging admiration for the star witness, calling him "intense," "emphatic," and "impermeably cool." Hanes's attempt to undermine Rowe, noted *Newsweek,* left Hanes "ruffled" while "Rowe . . . scarcely batted one of his heavily lidded eyes." But the *Detroit Free Press* had the most colorful comment: "The key state witness, a cocky twice-divorced bartender . . . gives the appearance of swaggering while sitting down."[35]

Arthur Hanes acted unfazed by his failure to destroy Rowe, promising reporters that he would present his case quickly, "within a couple of hours. The jury may have this thing by noon," he said, adding that he was prepared to drop some "bombshells."[36]

But there were no bombshells. The case for the defense was brief— in less than an hour, Hanes presented ten witnesses. Most were Alabama police officers who had interviewed Moton the night of the killing and testified that he believed the shots were fired from an old Ford, not from Thomas's Chevrolet. The most important witnesses were A. F. Nelson and Robert Carroll, two employees of the Bessemer VFW Club who said that Wilkins and the others arrived between 8:45 and 9:15 p.m., which, according to Hanes, made it impossible for the Klansmen to have shot Liuzzo at about 8 p.m. and then travel more than 140 miles from Lowndes County to Bessemer in about an hour.[37]

This was potentially damaging information for the state, so Gantt questioned the witnesses carefully about their memories of that night. Nelson insisted that he had the time right but did admit that he didn't look at his watch when he saw Wilkins drinking a beer at the club. "This is just . . . a guess?" Gantt asked. "Yes, sir," replied Nelson. Carroll did look at the clock above the bar; it was "right after 9:00 o'clock" when he told Nelson that because there were no customers, he was going to lie down on a cot behind the bandstand. Just then, he said, the doorbell rang and he saw Wilkins, Thomas, "and some brothers" enter the bar. He was sure of it. At the first trial, Rowe had testified that Carroll was "drunk" that night and therefore not a suitable alibi witness, but now Carroll denied it: He didn't drink, he testified, a claim supported by his friend Nelson. All that Gantt was able to elicit from Carroll was the fact that he and Thomas were longtime friends and that the Klansmen often visited the Bessemer VFW Club.[38]

At one in the afternoon on Friday, October 22, the attorneys presented their summations to a courtroom packed with visitors—reporters from *Time, Newsweek,* and the *New York Times,* among other news outlets; photographers; and townspeople. "For lack of a better name," Hanes began, "I am going to call this trial the parable of the two goats—the Judas Goat and the scapegoat." The jury was familiar with the story, he said, "You are God-fearing men. You read the bible." Turning to his client, who again sat "stony faced," puffing on a Pall Mall, Hanes shouted, "There is the scapegoat!" The Judas goat was Gary Thomas Rowe, whom Hanes likened to Judas Iscariot, "one of the most loathsome characters in all of history." Rowe broke his Klan oath, betrayed his friends, and demanded money in exchange for information. The jury shouldn't believe anything such a man said because it was a lie, carefully constructed for financial benefit. "[Rowe] fabricates information and then he goes and peddles it," the attorney maintained.[39]

Hanes also raised doubts about Leroy Moton's testimony. "Leroy," as Hanes always called him, claimed the attack occurred around eight o'clock; after bringing Liuzzo's car to a stop, he tried to stop a passing truck, dodged a car that tried to run him down, and then returned to the car where he "passed out" for a half hour. After awakening at around 8:30 p.m., he ran down the road until he met the truckload of civil rights workers who rescued him. How was that possible? Hanes asked. Troopers Burgess and McGehee testified that at 8:30 they found the car and only one dead body. "Where was Leroy?" Hanes laughed. Furthermore, if Moton was running down the road when he said he was, he would have passed the troopers, heading toward the field, but they never saw him. "Where was Leroy?" Hanes asked again. He also strongly implied that Moton had not been in Liuzzo's car at all, pointing to the trajectory of the bullets fired through the driver's side window, one of which embedded itself somewhere "between the top of the car and the door frame over the passenger's side," and another that entered through the windshield. How could the six-foot-four-inch Moton have not been struck? Hanes wondered. For a third time he asked, "Where was Leroy?"[40]

Hanes claimed to offer a more believable explanation for the events that occurred that night: Liuzzo was murdered by civil rights workers hoping to create a martyr for their cause. The real killers were laughing at Lowndes County and poor Lee Wilkins: "Maybe the murderer is from the Watts area of Los Angeles," Hanes said, referring to the recent riot that occurred in the California ghetto. Or perhaps they were hiding somewhere in Georgia, "trying to . . . raise money for their nefarious schemes." This fine jury, Hanes concluded, must acquit the "scapegoat," Collie Leroy Wilkins, because he was an innocent man.[41]

While his bodyguard stood behind him, Richmond Flowers approached the jury with a Bible in his hand. "I'm going to tell you a story too," he said. "It's not going to be a long one"—and he put the Bible on the jury rail—"but it's the truth, and I'll raise my hand and swear it's the truth, the whole truth, and nothing but the truth, so help me God." Rowe had told the truth about how the Klansmen chased Mrs. Liuzzo along Alabama's roads until Wilkins shot her dead, Flowers argued. The jury members may not have approved of the housewife from Detroit, he said, "but she did have a right to be on our highways." He also noted that their own beloved George Wallace, in his recent quest for the presidency, had campaigned in the North, in places where he wasn't welcomed. How would they have felt if he was murdered "simply because [somebody] didn't agree with his being there"?[42]

As for Gary Thomas Rowe, he understood that nobody liked informers, they "strike a little terror into people," but they sometimes serve a useful purpose: "You are thinking that if he had given evidence that a Black Muslim had done this killing he would be a hero. I hope there are informers in [the SCLC], SNCC, the Communist Party and everywhere else that crimes are being done against the peace and dignity of Alabama."[43]

Flowers walked back to his table, put down the Bible, and picked up Gene Thomas's .38-caliber pistol. Showing it to the jury, he reminded them that Rowe said it was the gun that shot Mrs. Liuzzo and FBI ballistics tests proved it. Hanes had argued that some unknown person used that gun, Flowers said, but he never explained how it happened to end up at Eugene Thomas's house. Raising his voice, he cried, "It is absolutely undisputed that this is the gun that killed that woman."[44]

For a moment he was silent, but then, "his voice loud and shaking with emotion," he said: "If you do not convict this man, you might as well lock up the courthouse, open up the jail and throw away the keys!" He returned to the table and put down the pistol. Bending over, he opened his briefcase and removed Black's Law Dictionary. The courtroom grew still as he walked back to the jury box, book in hand. The jurors appeared very relaxed; some smoked cigarettes, others drank soda from bottles. Thumbing the pages of Black's Dictionary until he found what he was looking for, Flowers read the legal definition of a "true verdict": "A verdict that is reached voluntarily . . . and not as a result of an arbitrary rule or order." He was asking them to put aside their prejudices toward blacks and civil rights workers and consider only the facts when reaching a decision. Then he yelled, "If you release this man, you can take 'true verdict' and tear it out of the book and throw it away because it won't mean a thing." Then he ripped out the pages and threw them to the floor in front of the jury box. "The jury snickered a little bit," Art Hanes, Jr., later observed, "but other than that, nobody said anything. . . . It didn't have the dramatic effect he was looking for."[45]

Regaining his composure and speaking more softly, Flowers told the jury: "I want to remind you of one thing. In 15 months, you will have another Attorney General and I will just be history." Some in the audience laughed, one man said, "You *sure* will be out of office," and others whispered loudly, "Amen!" until the judge banged his gavel. Flowers picked up the Bible again and waved it at Wilkins: "But I want to tell you this, gentlemen. The blood of this man's sin, if you do not find him guilty, will stain the very soul of our county for eternity." Then he sat down.[46]

The judge called a brief recess, and when the jury returned he carefully read their instructions. Did the jury wish another break in the proceedings before beginning their deliberations? Thagard asked. "No, sir," said the foreman. At 3:05 p.m., the twelve men filed out.[47]

While the jury discussed the case, other officials were playing football on the courthouse lawn. It was the last round in this brief season between the forces opposing one another in court, which during lengthy recesses moved to the gridiron. On one side were reporters, members of the attorney general's staff, and FBI agents; they called themselves "The Outside Agitators." The other side consisted of Klansmen, Alabama state troopers, Hanes's staff, and segregationists who were proud to be known as "The Local Rednecks." All agreed that touch football was the safest form to play —a serious injury, they feared, might result in litigation.[48]

Those who chose to remain inside the courthouse awaited the jury's decision. Former prosecutor Carlton Perdue "confidently predicted" to anyone who would listen that Wilkins's acquittal was inevitable, but Art Hanes, Jr., was nervous. "Everybody was pacing around the room as you do when you sweat the jury," he later recalled. Then, a man appeared, one of the "locals," who looked at his watch and said to Hanes and his father, "Don't worry, gentlemen, jury will be back by 7:00 on the nose, 'cause the high school kicks off at 7:30." Flowers heard the same rumor, too—and hoped it was wrong.[49]

The timing was a bit off. At 4:52 p.m., just an hour and forty-seven minutes after deliberations began, there came a knock on the jury door. The jurors took their seats. Foreman Lewis McCurdy (formerly of the local White Citizens Council) said they had a verdict, and the piece of paper was handed first to Judge Thagard and then to Clerk Kelly Coleman, Tom Coleman's cousin, who announced the decision: "We the jury in the entitled matter find the defendant, Collie Leroy Wilkins, not guilty." The crowded courtroom "broke into noisy applause," and for the first time that week, Wilkins smiled broadly.[50]

Speaking to the press afterward, Hanes said: "Not only was the verdict of not guilty justifiable, I think the evidence demanded this verdict." Although the verdict didn't surprise Flowers and Gantt, they were, nevertheless, deeply distressed and frustrated. If the killing had occurred just a few miles to the west in Dallas County or to the east in Montgomery County, perhaps "they might have had a chance." But, as Gantt later recalled, "We couldn't have convicted anyone in Lowndes County then. We knew it was futile at the time, but we wanted the nation to know that not everyone in Alabama was like George Wallace."[51]

The Klansmen didn't have long to celebrate Wilkins's victory. He may have won in state court, but also hanging over all their heads was a federal indictment, issued in April by the Hayneville grand jury, accusing them of a federal crime: violating the civil rights of those, like Viola Liuzzo, who participated in the Voting Rights March. The government now moved swiftly to bring the Klansmen to trial on these charges. On November 5, 1965, in the Montgomery courtroom of U.S. District Court Judge Frank M. Johnson, Wilkins, Eaton, and Thomas were arraigned and, with Arthur Hanes beside them, pleaded not guilty and were released on bond. If convicted, they could be sentenced to a maximum prison term of ten years, a five-thousand-dollar fine, or both. Their federal trial was expected to begin within three weeks.[52]

CHAPTER ELEVEN

A Temple of Justice

ARTHUR HANES WAS SURPRISED at how swiftly the Justice Department had acted but relished the chance of having another crack at their star witness, whom one newspaper dubbed "the artful dodger." This time, however, Rowe didn't want to testify, throwing into jeopardy the government's case and perhaps its last opportunity to put Eaton, Thomas, and Wilkins behind bars for the murder of Viola Liuzzo.[1]

Rowe's reluctance to testify was not new. During the first trial in May, he complained about Murphy's brutal treatment and expressed an unwillingness to experience its like again. He was troubled by a letter he received from Joyce Powell, his current girlfriend, who reported that the Klan was "spreading lies about him," claiming he was no "hero," no "patriot," but a "turncoat" out "to save himself." He asked the Bureau to do something to "improve his image," lest it damage his relationship with his family. The FBI asked Inspector Joe Sullivan to "straighten Rowe out," make him appreciate everything they had done for him; without their help, he would be on trial for murder with the other Klansmen. Sullivan thought Rowe was experiencing a temporary "emotional crisis," caused by uncertainty about his future. After all, since April, he had lived out of motel rooms in Birmingham and Pensacola until the end of the first Wilkins trial, when he was transplanted to northern California, where he wasn't very happy. But Sullivan brought him around. By the end of the conversation, which lasted more than an hour, Rowe agreed to testify. But in October, when Wilkins was acquitted, Rowe told the agents: "Don't look for me again; I'm never coming back to Alabama." They didn't take him seriously. Such behavior had become routine for the informant.[2]

On November 23, a week before Rowe was scheduled to testify, the situation became critical. During a meeting with Shanahan and three other agents, Rowe became "highly emotional, distraught [and] tearful." He told the agents that he felt "physically [in]capable of going through with another trial," had no confidence in either state or federal prosecutors, and believed that the Justice Department had "let him down." Anyway, his testimony would be a waste of time since another jury was likely to acquit the Klansmen. Why should he risk his life again? The government could demand that he appear, but if they issued a subpoena, he would resist, even if they used force. And if they managed to get him to the courtroom, he would refuse to answer questions, choosing instead to go to jail.[3]

The next morning Rowe seemed calmer but was still adamant about not testifying unless the Justice Department met certain conditions. First, Attorney General Nicholas Katzenbach must assure him—in writing—that this would be his last appearance in court, regardless of the trial's outcome. Second, once these proceedings ended, Katzenbach must find him a position with either the U.S. Border Patrol or the Immigration and Naturalization Service. Third, if prosecutors asked him whether Leroy Moton was with Liuzzo that night, he would be forced to testify that he wasn't. Fourth, if his family was willing, he wanted all of them—his mother, father, ex-wife, and children—moved to a location near his new post. And fifth, he expected to receive "a substantial sum" after cutting his ties with the FBI; most of the money would go to a college fund for his children. The agents promised to tell Headquarters of Rowe's demands.[4]

J. Edgar Hoover didn't like being threatened, and after reading his agents' message, he scrawled at the bottom of the page: "I think some of his conditions are grossly unreasonable." He sent them on to the attorney general without a recommendation.[5]

A few days later, Katzenbach and Hoover discussed the best way to handle Rowe, who Katzenbach thought needed "to be toned down a bit." Although the attorney general was reluctant to give Rowe the written assurances he wanted, Katzenbach felt that most of his demands could be met, especially a job, perhaps with the INS, and a new place to live. Hoover stated again that he thought Rowe's demands were "unreasonable and that nothing should be put in writing . . . ; that it ought to be made oral because if he does not have that confidence in us, he is not a good witness." He suggested that Justice Department attorneys trying the case meet immediately with Rowe to "size him up to see if he is going to explode on the stand." What worried Hoover most was Rowe's insistence that Moton wasn't in the car. Should he express this doubt, Rowe's credibility would be undermined and jurors might suspect that the FBI was withholding evidence. Other witnesses should establish that the FBI's investigation proved that Moton was Liuzzo's passenger. Katzenbach didn't think it was a major problem but Hoover disagreed; hidden information "could be blown up like a balloon" by the defense.

The two men shared a guarded optimism about the outcome of the case. Hoover felt they had "a better chance of winning it this time," and Katzenbach expressed confidence, shared by Hoover, in the man he picked to prosecute—John M. Doar, the assistant attorney general for civil rights. In the end, however, everything might depend "upon this fellow Rowe," the attorney general said, "and the Bureau's backing of him, as he gets his credibility from his connection with the Bureau." Hoover thought it "important that the case be pressed with vigor because it is a 'symbol' in the minds of the civil rights people."[6]

Rowe met with Doar for six hours on the evening of November 26. Their discussion began well but ended badly. At the outset, Doar said that Rowe's demands "were not considered unreasonable." He recognized that the federal government was obligated to help Rowe and his family in all the areas of Rowe's concern—finding a job, relocation, and reimbursement for "inconveniences" and "loss of income" until he was settled and employed. As for the Moton problem, Doar didn't think it jeopardized the government's case; if asked, Rowe should testify truthfully about the man he believed he saw in Liuzzo's car. But as for any future testimony, the government couldn't give him the written guarantee Rowe wanted. In fact, Doar claimed that it would be worthless because it depended on future events when current officials might not be in office.[7]

But Rowe, "while not antagonistic," refused to give an inch—he wanted all his conditions met. When Doar left at midnight, Rowe continued to talk with Inspector McGovern and Special Agent Shanahan. These were the men Rowe admired most, while Doar was a stranger whom Rowe never trusted and Shanahan (and most of the agents) didn't like because they felt he was arrogant and unsympathetic to the FBI. Shanahan would later recall that before this meeting, Rowe had argued vehemently with Doar about Moton, warning the prosecutor not to use him at trial. Shanahan himself had urged Doar to drop Moton.[8]

In the end, Rowe gave in but not before seeking the advice of two other favorite agents and his ex-wife. Agents Jim Carlisle and Curtis Lynum urged Rowe to testify without a written guarantee, as did Dorothy Rowe. Everything now seemed set, but Rowe still insisted on having a formal letter from Doar regarding any testimony he would give about Moton.[9]

Rowe's insistence that he didn't see Moton in Liuzzo's car puzzled Doar and other Justice Department officials. Nobody could explain it except to argue that witnesses were often confused about what they had seen. But Rowe's insistence on what he had seen went beyond just mistaken identity and toward obsession. Much later, when ABC News investigated the Liuzzo shooting, its reporters thought that it indicated that Liuzzo had been shot by Rowe; if Rowe felt that Moton had seen him do it, he had to discredit Moton by removing him from the car. Another possibility is that Rowe invented this story as a form of extortion. By having a secret that might threaten the government's case, he could ensure that all his demands would be met. In any case, Doar refused to be blackmailed. He acknowledged their differences regarding Moton, and should Rowe be asked about Liuzzo's passenger, Doar instructed him to answer accurately: "The only important rule for any witness is to be truthful," Doar wrote in the formal agreement Rowe demanded. "If you don't remember, say so. Always testify to the facts as you believe them to be." The two "rough draft" letters, one from the attorney general, the other from Doar, gave Rowe everything he wanted: "permanent relocation" for him and his family and assistance "in obtaining suitable employment with either the Federal Government or elsewhere."[10]

To further reassure Rowe, Doar explained that the trial ahead was significantly different from what Rowe had experienced in Lowndes County. This was a federal trial, which would be held in Montgomery in the courtroom of U.S. District Court Judge Frank M. Johnson, a superb jurist, totally unlike the hapless T. Werth Thagard. Arthur Hanes would again try to rattle him, but Judge Johnson wouldn't tolerate the kind of mudslinging the defense had previously engaged in. With luck, even the jury might be better, as it would be drawn from a pool larger than that of Lowndes County. Furthermore, this was not a murder case; the Klansmen were charged with conspiracy to injure American citizens exercising their constitutional rights (which included participating in the Voting Rights March). Therefore, both Moton's and Liuzzo's identities were legally irrelevant. "These defendants set out to harm these people not because of who they were but because they were part of the march from Selma to Montgomery," Doar argued. Rowe's truthful testimony would provide the proof required for conviction. All this was finally good enough for Rowe, who announced that he would willingly testify. That's what everyone now expected, but Rowe still hadn't lost his ability to surprise and confound his FBI handlers.[11]

On the night of November 29, after spending hours testifying at the federal trial, Neil Shanahan was relaxing, watching television in his room at Montgomery's Albert Pick Motel. At around 9 p.m., his telephone rang, the caller a fellow agent guarding Rowe at the Maxwell Air Force Base: "You better come out here," he said. "Tommy is telling us that he's not going to testify tomorrow and everybody is very concerned." Shanahan rushed to his car.

When he arrived at Rowe's quarters, he found him surrounded by frantic FBI agents, everybody talking at once, the sense of panic almost palpable. Rowe appeared to be on the verge of emotional collapse, again claiming that he couldn't go through it all a third time, afraid that "he would break down on the stand." Into this mess stepped John Doar, who asked to interview Rowe one final time before the trial. At first, Rowe refused to see him. Then—with Jim McGovern's help—he agreed to speak with Doar, but the session lasted only five minutes. Shanahan, knowing how volatile Rowe was, capable of swinging from confidence to despair at a moment's notice, told everyone to leave the room, and he and Rowe spent the night together—talking, drinking, playing cards. Finally, near dawn, Rowe's "frame of mind improved," but he still refused to testify.

They slept a few hours, and when they awoke, Shanahan persuaded Rowe to put on his official "going-to-court suit," and the two men walked to the base commissary where they joined Jim McGovern for breakfast. Afterward, Rowe suddenly turned to Shanahan and said, "I'm not going to do it."

"You're going to do it," Shanahan replied, "because we're going to take you in there and everything will be fine."

But Shanahan wasn't sure, so when the car arrived he "grabbed Rowe by the arm" and said, "Let's go, this is it," and pushed him in the car. Shanahan and McGovern stayed with Rowe when they arrived at the courthouse, escorting him to the elevator that took them to the second-floor courtroom. When the bailiff called Rowe's name, Shanahan pushed him into the room, blocked the exit, and watched Rowe walk confidently down the aisle to the witness chair.[12]

Doar was right. This was a different trial, in a different courtroom, with a different prosecutor, presiding judge, and jury. Rowe discovered that John Doar, despite their past squabbles, was a more impressive prosecutor than Perdue, Gamble, Flowers, and Gantt. The tall, curly-haired, forty-three-year-old lawyer was no Washington bureaucrat. In 1960, he had explored rural Mississippi, often disguised, questioning blacks who were being denied the right to vote. In 1961, he had observed firsthand the savage attack on the Freedom Riders when they got off the bus in Montgomery. He had been with James Meredith during the violent insurrection that occurred after the integration of the University of Mississippi in 1962. When NAACP field secretary Medgar Evers was murdered in Jackson, Mississippi, in June 1963, Doar had single-handedly prevented a bloody clash between angry blacks and police and state troopers armed with shotguns, clubs, and tear gas by placing himself between the two groups. He was also part of the Justice Department team sent to Alabama to make sure that the Voting Rights March took place without interference and was therefore especially shaken by the death of Viola Liuzzo. Ironically, this was Doar's first criminal trial, but what he lacked in experience he more than made up for in legal knowledge and personal courage.[13]

Doar was also right about Frank Mims Johnson, Jr., the federal district judge for the Middle District of Alabama. At forty-seven, he was already a southern legend, hated by segregationists and admired by civil rights workers, not because he was their advocate—he was not—but because they knew they would receive a fair hearing in his courtroom. The Klan called him "the most hated man in Alabama." He helped bring an end to racial discrimination in Alabama's schools, courtrooms, and voting booths. For this, his family had been ostracized, his mother's house bombed, and his own life threatened so often that he had to be guarded by federal marshals. Craggy-faced but handsome, he looked like what he was—a descendent of the fiercely independent citizens of Winston County, mountain people who had rejected secession and remained loyal to the Union during the Civil War. The judge's most pronounced feature was his penetrating eyes. "When I see him," Virginia Durr noted, "I always feel he's looking at me down the barrel of a rifle." Tough and strict, he insisted on absolute decorum in his courtroom—there were no smokers or soda pop drinkers in *his* jury box. Young lawyers, aware of Johnson's style, sometimes "fainted dead away with fear" when they faced him. Another lawyer, after trying a case before Judge Johnson, later recalled, "I may have been the only lawyer in history who was threatened with contempt because of the expression on his face."[14]

Would Doar be proved right about this jury? Would it be different from the one that had acquitted Wilkins just five weeks before? Its selection took less than fifteen minutes, with the judge handling the voir dire. In addition to the traditional questions, he asked potential jurors whether they belonged now or in the past to the White Citizens Council or the NAACP. Seven who had such associations were eventually prevented from serving. The final twelve, all white, all male, were, however, more professionally varied than their Hayneville counterparts. One was a school superintendent and nine were businessmen; farmers were in the minority—only two compared with the six who had freed Wilkins. The previous juries had come from Lowndes County, where both racism and hatred for civil rights workers was intense and jurors who voted for conviction might reasonably expect retaliation. This time, the jury pool was drawn from twenty-three counties, whose citizens might be less affected by local thinking and hostility. However, students of southern politics noted that those twenty-three counties were located in a "strongly segregationist section" of southeast Alabama, and all the jurors, except one resident of Montgomery, came from small towns that weren't significantly different from Hayneville, so it was impossible to predict how this group might act.[15]

It was also a different trial because of what Judge Johnson had done the previous March, when King and his allies struggled to win the right to march from Selma to Montgomery. It was Judge Johnson who had made it possible by issuing an order allowing the activists to proceed without interference. Therefore, Viola Liuzzo, and the thousands who participated that day, were under federal protection, and thus her murder was a violation of that court's order and her civil rights. Doar's burden was not to prove Wilkins guilty of murder but to demonstrate that the murder and the

Klansmen's other actions on March 25 were, under Section 241, Title 18, of the U.S. Code, part of a conspiracy to "injure or impede" a federally protected activity.[16]

Past experience showed, however, that it might not be easy to find the Klansmen guilty of such a violation. The statute originated in the Civil Rights Act of 1870, passed by a Congress hoping to protect black freedmen and their white allies from the Ku Klux Klan. Since murder wasn't a federal crime, the Justice Department had once previously used the 1870 Civil Rights Act as a way to prosecute Klansmen and others who killed civil rights workers, but had not been successful.

The last time it had been used was in 1947, and although the government won, the verdict was appealed to the U.S. Supreme Court, which overturned it. Furthermore, in 1965, Section 241 was embroiled in legal controversy. In January 1965, when the killers of civil rights workers Michael Schwerner, James Chaney, and Andrew Goodman were indicted under Section 241, Federal Judge Harold Cox of Mississippi had dismissed those charges because he didn't believe Section 241 applied. A federal judge in Georgia took the same position in the sniper killing of Lieutenant Colonel Lemuel Penn. The government had appealed these decisions to the Supreme Court, but the Court had not yet ruled. So John Doar sought redress in Article III of the Constitution, which established the judiciary. It was here that Judge Johnson's ruling proved critical. Viola Liuzzo's activities that day were protected by Article III of the Constitution because she was "exercising rights covered by Judge Johnson's order protecting the marchers." The Klansmen, the government would argue, violated those rights.[17]

Under Doar's careful questioning, Rowe's testimony on November 30 provided a narrative of the Klansmen's attempts to "injure, oppress, threaten or intimidate" the federally protected marchers. Rowe began by identifying photographs of Wilkins, Thomas, and Eaton at the Klan rally held in Montgomery's Cramton Bowl on March 21 protesting Judge Johnson's order—evidence that the men were authentic Klansmen. He then moved to the events of March 25—the early-morning trip to the capital; the hours spent heckling the marchers; the drive to Selma where they encountered a hitchhiker who seemed, at first, a likely target ("we'll give him a little fun and a surprise," Thomas supposedly said), but when they got closer to him Wilkins said, "No, he's not a marcher, he's too clean to be a marcher."[18]

By nightfall, they were in Selma, looking for victims. At Brown Chapel, they found a huge crowd but couldn't get close, so Thomas circled around until he found "a couple of colored people" walking down the street and slowed the car. "Get ready, baby brother," Rowe recalled him saying, "we're going to take them." But Rowe saw an army truck and troops at the end of the block and warned Thomas off. A few minutes later, while waiting for a stoplight to change, they found what they were looking for. A car approached on their left; inside were a white woman and a black man.[19]

Each word from Thomas or Wilkins was evidence of evil intent: "Looka there, I'll be damned, looka there"; "We're going to get them tonight"; "How do you want me to stop the automobile, you want me to bump it from the back, . . . run it off the road?"; "We're going all the way tonight. . . . This is it, we're going to take them right here."[20]

As if all this were not enough to prove that the Klansmen intended to harm civil rights workers that day, Doar asked: "What was the . . . purpose of this Klan organization you were a member of?"

". . . to maintain white supremacy was the number one order."

"What means were used by the Klan?"

"Any means necessary was the phrase that had been used very often," Rowe said, "whether it be, quote, 'Bullets or ballots.'"

For Hanes, the cross-examination was a rerun of what he had done in Hayneville, but without the sarcasm—Judge Johnson wouldn't permit it. At one point, Hanes made a snide aside, and the Judge snapped, "That is not appropriate. . . . Let's not have any side remarks in the case." When Doar objected to one of Hanes's questions and was sustained, Hanes protested, causing Johnson to rebuke him. "You need not argue the objections or rulings," Johnson said. Hanes's hectoring of Rowe led the judge to interrupt, "Don't argue with him, just question him." So Hanes had to tread more gently, employing a less overtly hostile method to show that Rowe was an unprincipled scoundrel.

Rowe the FBI informant, according to Hanes, was actually an agent provocateur who violated his Klan oath and "agitated and provoked the Klan," as in the attack on the Freedom Riders on Mother's Day 1961. Rowe, lying again, admitted to being at the bus station but claimed he never touched a soul and also denied that his violent action was captured in the photograph Hanes showed him.

At the Klan rally on March 21, didn't he say, "Let's . . . go back to Birmingham, there will be more excitement and action there"? "No, sir, I did not." And, observing the marchers, didn't Rowe say, "Something has got to be done about these people, all you guys do is talk"? "No, sir." "You deny making that statement?" "Yes, sir. I certainly do." Wasn't his car "a rolling arsenal," packed with "submachine guns and shotguns and rifles?" "I hope not," said Rowe, smiling for the first time during the trial. Later, at Jack's Beverages, didn't he "make a pass" at one of the waitresses? "No, sir; I talked with them along with everyone else at the table." And when the so-called attack occurred, did he try to prevent Wilkins or Eaton from shooting or say "Let's quit, let's go back"? "No, sir." Then an explanation of the routes they took on the way home, questions about Rowe's talk with Shanahan and the trip he took with the agents the following morning, and Hanes was done. Rowe never lost his composure or fumbled for an answer.[21]

The trial ended the next day, Wednesday, December 1. John Doar had done an excellent job of presenting the government's case, although his courtroom inexperience showed—the judge admonished him several times for leading his witnesses. Slowly and precisely, and always sticking closely to the facts, he tried to convince the jury that the Klansmen's activities between March 21, when the march began, and March 25, when it reached its triumphant end, were designed to hurt those protected by Judge Johnson's ruling. Among the twenty-seven witnesses he called were Alabama police officers, who had photographs of the defendants at the Klan rally in the Cramton Bowl, and the FBI agents who arrested Thomas and searched his house, obtaining the pistol that ballistics experts testified had fired the bullet that killed Viola Liuzzo. Rowe's account indicated that the Klansmen spent March 25 looking for a victim—the hitchhiker they first thought was a marcher, the black couple walking down the street near the Brown Chapel, and finally the white woman and her black passenger. Hanes, in contrast, seemed out of his element. Unable to appeal to racial prejudice (he didn't dare ask Leroy Moton whether he had made love to Mrs. Liuzzo), he relied on the same few witnesses he had used in Hayneville. Doar's presentation took two and a half days; Hanes's lasted seventy-five minutes.[22]

The lawyers' final summations were dramatically different. Walter Turner, Judge Johnson's law clerk, later called Doar's summation the "most brilliant he ever heard." Without the verbal pyrotechnics of Richmond Flowers, Doar spoke quietly, succinctly, arguing that the Klansmen were guilty as charged, motivated by "animosity and hatred" in their killing of "this poor defenseless woman. . . . They did it because they are people who believe they have the right to take the law in their own hands and do any . . . thing they choose. . . . But they didn't have any right to do this. The rights were all on the other side. The rights . . . were all with the Negroes that were marching from Selma to Montgomery, whether you like it or not. And the rights were there because this court had granted them that right in a court order." He asked the jurors to take their responsibilities seriously, to "put aside . . . your emotions, feelings, anger perhaps" and "decide this case loyal to only one thing, your oath."

Equally effective were the questions put to the jury by Doar's colleague U.S. Attorney Ben Hardeman, who was, like them, an Alabaman: "Are we going to permit . . . in Alabama a return to the medieval system of trial by torture? Are we going to permit a star chamber court, by persons unknown at times and places unknown, who are their own investigators, their own witnesses, their judge, their own jury, and yes, their own executioner? Are we going to have a government of law or of men? We take the flat position that all of these matters should be settled within the halls of a temple of justice such as this one." He reminded the jurors that "this is not a murder trial, although there was a murder in it. . . . And this is not a Klan trial, although there are Klansmen in it." This was a conspiracy trial where the evidence clearly showed that Wilkins, Thomas, and Eaton "were in cahoots" to rob American citizens of "the rights that were ordered and declared by this very court. . . . And I believe that if you consider this evidence fairly and impartially, then I know you will return a verdict of guilty."[23]

Arthur Hanes, in his final comments to the jury, relied on the argument that had worked for him before. Reject the testimony of Gary Thomas Rowe, who was nothing more than a "silver merchant who worked for pay," he insisted. Hanes read from the Bible, Matthew 26:14–15: "Then one of the twelve, Judas Iscariot, went to the chief priests and said, 'What will you give me if I deliver him to you?'" The murder of Viola Liuzzo was "a heinous crime," Hanes admitted, but her killers were "not in this courtroom. I don't know where they are. They are somewhere laughing at the poor, simple fools they made out of the people of Alabama and thinking about their next victim." A conspiracy did exist, he believed, but it had been hatched in Washington: "There are organizations in this country working to divide and destroy us," and his clients were its first victims.[24]

On Thursday, December 2, the jury received its instructions. Judge Johnson's charge was "solemn and dramatic . . . , setting out the law and the jury's responsibility," noted the New York Times. After explaining the legal definition of conspiracy, Johnson spent an hour philosophizing about the "principle of justice" and "the supremacy of the law." Courts were created not to further "any sociological causes or movements" but to be forums in which evidence was analyzed with the strictest impartiality. He expected the jurors to do their duty and produce a just and true verdict.[25]

The jury began its deliberations at 10:40 a.m., broke for lunch two hours later, and at 2:23 informed the bailiff that they wanted to see the judge. Lawyers on both sides hurried to the courtroom. Did they have a verdict? So soon? No, the jury simply wanted a dictionary, but the judge was unable to give them one because none had been introduced as evidence. He offered to define the words they didn't understand. Speaking for his colleagues, Juror James E. Thomas, a Montgomery insurance agent said, "Your honor, the question arises around the word 'conspiracy.'" The judge again gave them the legal definition, which, this time, seemed satisfactory, so they went back to work. At 3:41 they were back with another technical question, and the afternoon dragged on without a verdict. The judge permitted them to call it a day at 5:33 p.m.[26]

But the judge's day wasn't over yet. Suspecting that the jury was having difficulty reaching unanimity and fearing another mistrial, he told his law clerk: "I think we're going to have to give the jury a little dynamite. Get me the Allen charge." Walter Turner brought him the appropriate case, Allen v. United States, decided by the U.S. Supreme Court in 1896. Faced with a deadlocked jury, a judge could order jurors to reexamine their views and listen carefully to their colleagues "with a disposition toward being convinced." If they were in the minority, they should consider how they had come to a decision different from the others. The High Court affirmed Allen, and the action, although rarely used, came to be known as the "dynamite charge," designed to break a logjam and prevent a mistrial.[27]

The jury arrived early at court the next morning and began work around eight o'clock. At 10:09, they asked to see the judge. Looking "haggard and obviously fatigued," the foreman, school superintendent T. H. Kirby, reported: "Your honor, we find that we are unable to reach a verdict and seem to be hopelessly deadlocked."

Johnson's reply, notes a biographer, "was stern, slow and icy. In a deep hill country twang," he told the jury, "You haven't . . . deliberate[d] long enough to be hopelessly deadlocked. . . . This is an important case. This trial has been long and this trial has been expensive." Another trial would be time-consuming and a great cost to both the defendants and the government. "This court is of the opinion that the case cannot again be tried better or more exhaustively than it has been on either side. It is therefore very desirable that you jurors should agree upon a verdict . . . there is no reason to suppose that the case will ever be submitted to twelve more intelligent, more impartial, or more competent to decide it, or that more or clearer evidence will be produced on one side or the other." Then he gave them the *Allen* charge about reconsidering their views and ordered them to continue deliberating.[28]

After the twelve returned to the jury room, Arthur Hanes lodged a strong objection, calling the judge's action "prejudicial" to his clients. It wasn't an unreasonable challenge; critics of the *Allen* charge believed that it would have precisely that effect on a defendant's fate. But as the judge later explained to inquiring reporters, the Supreme Court had upheld it and it was acceptable to give to a jury that had deliberated for many hours without reaching a verdict. Johnson listened to Hanes, then noted his "objection and exception" for the record. The waiting continued. Two additional hours did not produce a verdict, so at 12:23 p.m., the jurors were permitted to go to lunch.[29]

Around two o'clock, the judge was informed that a verdict had been reached. While the jury prepared to return to the courtroom, Johnson cautioned the audience against "uncalled for" demonstrations inside the courtroom or in the hallway outside. When the twelve were seated in the jury box, the foreman was asked whether they had reached a decision. "Yes, sir," he replied, and handed the verdict to the clerk. "Defendants stand, please!" said the judge. Thomas, Eaton, and Wilkins got to their feet along with their lawyer. "Mr. Clerk, you read the verdicts," Judge Johnson directed.

"We the jury find the defendant, Collie Leroy Wilkins, Jr., guilty as charged in the indictment," read Clerk Tim Norris. "We the jury find the defendant, Eugene Thomas, guilty as charged in the indictment. . . . We the jury find the defendant, William Orville Eaton, guilty as charged in the indictment. This the 3rd day of December, 1965, T. H. Kirby, foreman."

"All right, gentlemen," the judge told the jury, "if it is worth anything to you, in my opinion that was the only verdict that you could possibly reach in this case and still reach a fair and honest and just verdict. Of course, I couldn't tell you that beforehand; it wasn't any of my business, because it was your duty and your responsibility to determine the guilt or innocence of these men." The jurors left quickly, but some asked to speak privately to the judge. They were worried that something might happen to them because of the guilty verdict. The judge contacted the FBI, which refused to provide protection but did agree to give each juror the name and phone number of an agent to call if they were threatened. But the day's proceedings weren't over. The judge announced that he would shortly pronounce sentence on the three Klansmen, so the lawyers and clerks waited for that moment.[30]

To one reporter, Arthur Hanes looked "shaken and surprised" after the reading of the verdicts. The attorney and his three "somber" clients "walked aimlessly around the corridor outside the courtroom." No one spoke, but Hanes was very upset and had a lot to say to reporters. He had expected a mistrial, because the jury had spent about eight hours deliberating without reaching a verdict. But the judge's intervention, he thought, "had a great influence" on the jurors; it took them only two and a half hours to convict following Johnson's "dynamite charge." In his view, Wilkins, Thomas, and Eaton had been "railroaded."[31]

Later that afternoon, the Klansmen and their lawyer stood before the judge. Hanes said that he planned to file an appeal. "You certainly have that right," Johnson said, and then asked each man whether he wanted to make a statement. Eaton and Wilkins said they were "innocent," while Thomas mumbled something nobody could hear. Then, in "a soft growl that flowed clearly with a North Alabama twang," Judge Johnson sentenced each man to the maximum penalty prescribed by law—ten years in a federal penitentiary. A ten-thousand-dollar bond would allow them to remain free pending their appeal. Each appeared "stunned" but said nothing. U.S. marshals stepped forward and took the men into custody.[32]

To most observers, the trial had been traditional: The news that a verdict had been reached; the formal passing of the documents to the clerk, who would file it with the court; the repetitious reading of each verdict in the arcane language of the law; the invitation to the guilty parties to speak before sentencing—all were traditional, part of a legal ritual centuries old. But in Alabama in 1965, one word was not traditional—*guilty*. For the first time in American history, a federal jury had found three white men guilty of a crime against a civil rights worker. It was a historic moment.[33]

Reporters rushed to get the prosecutor's reaction. For John Doar, victory came on his birthday, but it was the trial's outcome that gave him the most pleasure. "The court and the jury did its duty," said Doar. "I'm very proud of the system of justice in the country." President Lyndon B. Johnson, recuperating at his Texas ranch from gall bladder surgery, learned of the outcome from an excited attorney general, who telephoned the news. Johnson issued a statement congratulating the prosecutors and the FBI on their excellent work and said that "the whole nation can take heart from the fact that there are those in the South who believe in justice in racial matters and were determined not to stand for acts of violence and terror."

More realistic was Martin Luther King. While pleased by what happened in Montgomery and the outcome of another trial recently concluded in Anniston, where a jury found a white man guilty of second-degree murder for killing a Negro, King believed that it wasn't enough. Since a southern jury was still unable to find a white man guilty of first-degree murder for killing blacks or civil rights workers, legislation was needed to protect them. The two verdicts, he said, "were rays of light and hope which penetrate the darkness which hovers over a long line of unpunished killings," but new laws were a "necessity if justice is to become a day by day reality in the South and routine rather than merely a reality reflected in historic and landmark decisions."[34]

Gary Thomas Rowe had waited anxiously that day for word about the jury's decision. It came late in the afternoon while he was playing cards with the agents who never seemed to leave his side at the Maxwell Air Force Base. The phone rang and, expecting another acquittal—"all that work, worry and money shot to hell"—he was surprised to hear an agent say, "The verdict was guilty, Tom, and Judge Johnson imposed the maximum penalty." He was now free to begin the new life the FBI and the Justice Department promised to create for him as a reward for his services.[35]

He had little doubt that the promises would be kept. Although Rowe might firmly be in the grasp of the FBI, the informant system was mutually reinforcing: Rowe controlled them as well. For the previous eight months, his eyewitness testimony had been the heart of the government's case, so it fulfilled most of his demands. Without a steady source of income, Rowe couldn't pay his living expenses, his debts, or the back alimony he owed to his ex-wife Dorothy. So the Bureau gave him an allowance of $112 a week and paid for his hotel rooms and meals, first in Birmingham and then in Pensacola and Miami. They bought the shirts, ties, and suits he wore for his appearances before the state and federal grand juries. When his creditors began to hound him for about $2,300, the FBI seemed sympathetic to paying these debts (nothing must interfere with the "excellent relationship" between the Bureau and "our informant," one top FBI official told another), but the Justice Department refused to approve it, thus creating a problem that Rowe would later exploit.[36]

The FBI also helped Rowe establish a new identity, moved him far from Alabama, and got him a job in law enforcement. Except when he testified in Alabama, he was known as Thomas Neil Moore and had a Social Security card and other documents to prove it. (He selected "Neil" as a tribute to his most admired handler, Neil Shanahan.) He preferred living in Hawaii (too far away, the Bureau believed) or California (the Bureau's choice), so on May 6, 1965, he and the ever-present Shanahan had flown to San Francisco to look for "suitable living quarters" as well as a job that would both satisfy him and relieve the FBI of Rowe's financial burdens. After driving around for several days, Rowe found that he disliked San Francisco because of the many "mixed couples" he saw, which "infuriated him." So they drove to Los Angeles, but that city didn't appeal to Rowe either. Finally, they returned to San Francisco where agents found him a modest apartment on Second Avenue.[37]

As for a job, Rowe still preferred working for either the INS or the Border Patrol. He told Dorothy that he would soon be a federal agent jumping out of airplanes, although neither agency required such skills. But since he would have to return to Alabama to testify in the second Wilkins trial, he looked for more temporary work. His Bureau connections landed him a position as an "investigator" with the Burns Detective Agency at a salary of one hundred dollars a week. He spent his time doing divorce work—following and taking pictures of men and women engaged in adulterous relationships. Some of his co-workers carried guns, so Rowe wanted one, too, and constantly reminded his handlers that he was now living alone without round-the-clock protection and felt "constantly in danger." He was "fixed in his resolve" to get a gun, but the FBI rejected his request, trying to persuade him that owning a gun might be unwise given his status as a government witness. He accepted that judgment, for now. The San Francisco FBI field office (which assigned two agents to "control Rowe") was able to tell Hoover that the "Informant has been able to establish himself well and has very intelligently and cooperatively followed . . . Bureau instructions and suggestions."[38]

The Bureau's protective custody also extended to Rowe's ex-wife Dorothy and their four children. Fearing that her own knowledge of the Klan threatened her and the children, she accepted the FBI's recommendation that they leave Birmingham for a safer place. Although it meant disrupting the children's lives and giving up her position as a nurse at Birmingham's Carraway Hospital, the idea appealed to her: She wanted "to make a clean break from her own family as well as her in-laws and start life anew," she told the FBI. When she decided where she wanted to live, a team of agents drove them to a hotel in St. Petersburg, Florida, where they stayed until she found a furnished home to rent. These expenses (room and board, first and last months' rent on the house) plus her own past and present debts were all paid by the FBI. Since she also needed a job, the Bureau helped her find one in the medical field. No request was too small to meet: When Dorothy asked for a special nurse's cap that could be obtained only in Birmingham, agents bought one that fit her and mailed it to a special post office box, arranged and paid for by the Bureau; an agent picked it up and personally delivered it to her.[39]

When Dorothy Rowe's life in St. Petersburg proved more expensive than she had anticipated, and with her ex-husband still unable to provide alimony, she again turned to the FBI. Her handlers recommended that Headquarters pay for the babysitter and supplement her income so that she could meet her responsibilities. Hoover agreed to this request and to another seeking reimbursement for her children's dental work. The FBI later estimated that the cost of supporting Gary Thomas Rowe and family during their nine-month period of protective custody came to $11,453.22, almost $4,000 more than it had cost to run Rowe as an informant from 1960 to 1965.[40]

As long as Rowe's testimony was needed, the FBI was willing to put up with Dorothy Rowe's demands and her ex-husband's "peculiarities," which included bouts of melancholia, fits of hysteria, and threats. But with the successful conclusion of the federal trial in December, and the likelihood that Rowe wouldn't testify at the future murder trials of Thomas and Eaton because he was so unpopular in Lowndes County, the FBI began to explore ways to sever its ties with Rowe (and family) but in a way that would guarantee his continued loyalty to the Bureau. Loyalty was a top priority because, as Rowe cleverly told one of his handlers in late December, he possessed "confidential information" about the FBI's war against the Klan—his active participation in a number of violent episodes, and what the agent called Rowe's "knowledge of unusual FBI investigative techniques," specifically the use of illegal wiretaps planted in Klansmen's homes. In short, he was a walking repository of FBI secrets, a time bomb that might go off if he felt he was being badly treated. The FBI's informant system made the agency hostage to information that Rowe believed "might embarrass the Bureau and the Department of Justice" if it ever became public.[41]

To keep Rowe under future control, the FBI chose a two-pronged strategy: forcing the attorney general to find Rowe a satisfactory job and giving their informant a special award. First, after informing the attorney general on December 27 that they planned to end their relationship with Rowe by December 31, Hoover and his top assistants reminded Katzenbach that he had promised (in writing) to find Rowe a permanent job in law enforcement, as well as additional rewards. Katzenbach was furious to learn that he had only a few days to keep this promise and accused the Bureau of "dumping Rowe in his lap without fair warning." He demanded a meeting to discuss these issues.

Hoover sent one of his top assistants, Cartha ("Deke") DeLoach, a "smooth and facile" bureaucratic infighter, to meet with Katzenbach the next morning. DeLoach stood up to the attorney general (nominally his boss as well as Hoover's) on every point. Was the Bureau really going to cut Rowe loose on December 31? Katzenbach asked twice. Definitely, De-Loach replied; the Bureau, unlike the Justice Department, had fulfilled its responsibilities. Had Rowe been relocated and did he like his current job? All the FBI knew was what it had told the attorney general in its memo of December 27—Rowe was now living in San Rafael, California, where he had a temporary job as a warehouse worker at the Oakland Naval Supply Depot. Was the FBI going to obtain another job for Rowe? No, DeLoach insisted, this was up to the Justice Department. Well, if Rowe wanted another job, Katzenbach said, he would try to come up with something, although he was still very upset that the Bureau had put him in this position. DeLoach continued to argue that the Bureau had issued no ultimatum and had not been "impertinent" or "discourteous," as Katzenbach believed. The attorney general's responsibilities in this case were clearly stated in his letter to Rowe, which had been delivered by John Doar before the informant's testimony at the federal trial. All DeLoach promised was to determine whether Rowe was satisfied with his current situation.

DeLoach considered the meeting a victory for the FBI. "The Attorney General was obviously sore," he told his superiors, "that the FBI, who had been pushing the Department time and time again to assume rightful responsibility of the informant, took it upon itself to make the decision that as of [December 31, 1965] we were absolutely through with our responsibilities." Katzenbach was "afraid to accept the responsibility." The FBI, on the other hand, "won [its] point." In short, the Bureau could tell Rowe that as of December 31, it was no longer responsible for protecting and supporting him financially and that responsibility now clearly belonged to the attorney general. In the never-ending bureaucratic war between the FBI and the Justice Department, the Bureau emerged triumphant.[42]

FBI officials in San Francisco spoke with Rowe later that day and learned that his position at the Oakland Naval Supply Depot was far from satisfactory. It was only temporary; Rowe had accepted it to earn enough money to buy Christmas gifts for his family. And Rowe learned that within five days, he could no longer rely on the FBI. However, he assumed that the attorney general would now make good on his promise to find him a permanent job in law enforcement. Katzenbach moved quickly to find something for Rowe and within two days secured him an appointment as a deputy U.S. marshal in San Diego, California, effective January 15, 1966. Rowe received this good news from the FBI on New Year's Eve, along with the notification that his support payments would continue until he assumed his new position. He was overjoyed and accepted the offer; joining the U.S. Marshals Service, with its long history of romance and adventure, was almost as good as being an FBI undercover man.[43]

To guarantee Rowe's silence once their relationship ended and to thank him for his "invaluable service," the FBI also decided to give him a sizable monetary award. Despite the difficulties Rowe had caused them, his achievements couldn't be denied. During his years inside the Klan, he had risked his life, and after Liuzzo was killed he had, "on his own initiative,"

notified the FBI about the shooting and provided the information that led
to the swift arrest of the Klansmen. Without Rowe, they believed, the case
never would have been solved, and his eyewitness testimony was "the real
reason" why Wilkins, Thomas, and Eaton were eventually convicted. But
self-interest also played an important part in their decision: "If Rowe is
terminated without any settlement, it is possible that he would eventually
become critical of the Bureau," the FBI's assistant director Al Rosen wrote
to Deke DeLoach on January 13. "Such a payment would preclude the possibility of any later justifiable criticism . . . and we could obtain a written
release from Rowe that such a payment represents complete satisfaction
of any and all responsibility on the part of the FBI." Rosen also drafted
the receipt Rowe was supposed to sign after receiving the money, telling
DeLoach that the Bureau's "primary concern was to complete negotiations
with [Rowe] and get his signature on the statement." J. Edgar Hoover approved the plan that same morning.[44]

Rowe later called Friday, January 14, 1966, "the greatest day of my
life." Here is how he remembered it: That morning Special Agent Jim
Carlisle called him and said, "I'll pick you up in about 30 minutes. Get
your ass up from the pool and come on out. We got some business to tend
to." After Rowe arrived at the San Francisco Federal Building, he and Carlisle went upstairs to see Special Agent in Charge Curtis Lynum. On Lynum's desk lay "a stack of money," and Rowe thought, "Goddamn, wonder
what they got that from?" Probably "they had made some kind of big bust
or something."

Lynum greeted him warmly, saying: "I want you to know the Bureau's
proud of you. You did one hell of a good job for us. And I think you're going to be surprised who's on this line when he calls."

"Oh, boy, I'm going to get to talk with [my] Mom, huh?"

"No, no, it will be somebody else," Lynum said.

A few minutes later the phone rang, and after Lynum spoke with the
caller, he handed the receiver to Rowe. "Mr. Rowe," a gruff voice said, "are
they treating you all right out there? You know who this is?" Before Rowe
could reply, the speaker said, "It's J. Edgar Hoover."

"Yes, sir," a nervous Rowe replied, feeling "so proud."

"[We've] got a little something there for you. Has anybody mentioned
any money to you yet?"

"No, sir," Rowe said.

"There's $10,000 they are supposed to deliver to you today," Hoover said. "This is on behalf of myself and the F.B.I., for the greatest job we've ever had a man do in your position. You have something, some day, to tell your grandchildren about, that you can be proud of. You're one of the greatest Americans that I've ever had the pleasure to talk to. I wish you well in life, . . . thank you for an outstanding job . . . , you'll always be a credit to this country."

Rowe thanked the director and said, "Mr. Hoover, if there's anything in the world I can ever do for this country, I'll do it."

"I know you will," Hoover said and hung up.

Lynum then brought Rowe to the table and pointed to all the cash that now belonged to him.[45]

FBI records reveal that J. Edgar Hoover did *not* telephone Rowe that day, but the rest of the story was true. Rowe did receive ten thousand dollars, at the direction of Assistant Director Rosen, and it was paid in cash. Agents Lynum and Carlisle were specifically instructed to tell Rowe that "the Director personally wanted him to have this remuneration in appreciation for assistance he has rendered to the FBI." Rowe was "overcome," Lynum later noted, "he became very emotional, wiped tears from his eyes" and said he would miss his friends in the Bureau who had treated him so well for so long. He promised to write the director expressing his thanks and appreciation.[46]

The receipt Rowe signed was three sentences long, reading, in part: "This amount has been accepted by me in full and complete satisfaction rendered voluntarily to representatives of the FBI up to and including January 14, 1966. My acceptance of this amount in fulfillment of the above brings to a close a very pleasant relationship which I have enjoyed with representatives of the FBI." Rowe also expressed his understanding of what was not written—"that if he had other questions or problems in the future they should be taken up specifically with the head U.S. Marshal . . . or with *John Doar,* Assistant Attorney General."[47]

Reporting later to Hoover, Lynum observed: "The mission of paying Rowe . . . has been accomplished, . . . and the receipt signed. The whole operation was carried out smoothly and Rowe was terrifically pleased." The next day, Thomas Neil Moore, unaccompanied by FBI agents for the first time in nine months, flew to San Diego to begin a new job and a new life. But not even Rowe's fertile imagination could have created what was to come: that within two years he would resign in disgrace from the Marshals Service; that within five years he would be broke, unemployed, and nearly homeless; and that within ten years he would again don a Klansman's hood, not on behalf of the FBI, but in a self-declared war against the FBI and the Justice Department.[48]

CHAPTER TWELVE

Taking the Sun Away

THERE WERE NO REWARDS for the Liuzzo family—no financial settlements, no moves to California or Florida, no chance to start life anew. There was only shock and disbelief: first the unbelievable news of Viola's violent death, and then, in the months that followed, the destruction of her character by the Klan and its attorneys.

Three days after the funeral, somebody placed a burned cross on the Liuzzos' lawn. Jim Liuzzo contacted both the police and the FBI, but they never found the guilty party. A week later, he received a special-delivery letter from L. Cecil Rhodes, justice of the peace in Ringgold, Georgia, accusing Viola of loving "Negro scum" better than her own family.

Jim's sister Victoria Aloisio found two disturbing letters in her mail: one written in cursive and signed "a friend," the other printed and without a signature. But both carried the same message: If Viola Liuzzo had just minded her own business and remained at home caring for her children, instead of going south in search of "black meat," she would be alive today.

There were also crank phone calls. Jim's other sister, Helen Liuzzo Farrell, received a call from a man "with a harsh deep voice," asking whether she was related to the woman murdered in Alabama. She hung up on him, but the phone rang frequently the rest of the day and the next morning, when she finally answered it. The same harsh voice repeated the earlier question—was she related to the dead woman in Alabama? "Is this a joke or are you the same jerk who called me yesterday?" she asked. "No, this isn't a joke," the man said. "I'm out to get you unless you tell me." She told him that her phone was tapped, hoping that would end the harassment, but the man became angrier: "Well you don't have to worry about me calling you anymore . . . I'm coming to get you." Farrell called the police and later got an unlisted telephone number. The caller disappeared, but that same day, Jim Liuzzo's cousins, Patrick and Joseph, received similar calls and a trace was put on Patrick's phone; no one was ever apprehended.[1]

At this stage, the burning cross and the annoying phone calls and letters were private annoyances. But soon the attacks on Viola Liuzzo's character became public. With the help of Matthew Hobson Murphy and the Klan's Imperial Wizard, the first Wilkins trial had presented a distorted picture of the dead woman. Their primary source had been a confidential report on the Liuzzo family that Shelton distributed to reporters and promised to disseminate throughout the South. Soon the information began to spread north to Detroit, where ironically, as Jim Liuzzo learned on May 11, some of the charges had originated.[2]

That night, Liuzzo received a call from Walter Rugaber, a *Free Press* reporter, who warned that the paper was about to publish a story about him and his late wife drawn from a report compiled for Sheriff Jim Clark by Marvin G. Lane, former chief of detectives of the Detroit Police Department and now the police commissioner of nearby Warren, Michigan. Liuzzo was furious and called the local FBI field office, telling agents how "upset" he was about "this invasion of his privacy." It was obvious that Lane had some link to the Klan that the FBI should be aware of. He was told that the Bureau had no jurisdiction in this matter, and according to the agent's report, Liuzzo "appeared satisfied with all explanations." A check of the Bureau's own files found no connection between Lane and the Klan. Director Hoover was kept informed of developments, and when Lane was described in one internal memorandum as a past president of the FBI's National Academy Associates and as "widely respected in law enforcement circles," Hoover angrily scrawled on the bottom of the page, "Well, he isn't respected here. Cut him off entirely from the N.A."[3]

Walter Rugaber's front-page article, "Klan gets secret report on life of Mrs. Liuzzo," appeared in the *Detroit Free Press* on May 13, 1965. It described a family in turmoil with "run-away" children, a "disturbed" and "despondent" mother, and a father who earned $860 a week as a Teamsters' "Business Agent." Also listed were the family's creditors and how much was owed to each. When Lane was asked how his six-page report came into the Klan's possession, he admitted to being baffled. On the night of Liuzzo's murder, he explained, he had received a telephone call from Sheriff Clark, asking for information about the dead woman. Although Lane had retired from the Detroit Police Department in 1961, he was able to quickly compile the report, which he sent to Clark on April 2. The envelope was stamped CONFIDENTIAL and was meant only for his fellow law enforcement officer. "If anything got out, the Sheriff was responsible," Lane insisted. The report should *not* have gone to the Klan, but "there's nothing I can do about it. There's nothing in the report other than facts." When Bobby Shelton was asked how he got the report, he denied receiving it from Clark but refused to name his source.[4]

Rugaber's story created an uproar in Detroit, and Jim Liuzzo wondered why he and his late wife were being investigated. Officials in Warren rallied around their beleaguered police commissioner: The president of the Warren City Council maintained that Lane was just "doing his job . . . I'm sure he would respond to a similar request from Highland Park or Dearborn —so why not Selma?" Five city council members and the mayor also supported Lane. But civil rights and labor groups strongly criticized him, with one labor leader calling for Lane's immediate removal from office for "secretly conducting an investigation which was none of his business." Even Congressman Charles Weltner of the House Committee on Un-American Activities, which was about to launch its own investigation of the Klan, promised that the committee would look into the Lane affair.[5]

Sheriff Clark claimed that he had asked for the report because he received a death threat a few hours after Liuzzo's murder from a man who identified himself as a Detroit Teamster. "You've killed the wrong one this time," the caller said. "Now we're going to kill you and your family." Clark gave the report to Lowndes County prosecutors, who probably passed it on to attorney Murphy because of the rules governing legal discovery— although Clark didn't point out that this was tantamount to giving the records directly to the Klan.

On May 18, Detroit chief of detectives Vincent Piersante announced that Inspector Earl C. Miller, head of the Criminal Intelligence Division, had admitted giving the information on Liuzzo to Commissioner Lane "in good faith and on a confidential basis," with no suspicion that it was destined for Alabama. Miller was removed from his post and transferred to the Crime Control Center, although the commissioner defended him and his department's habit of collecting personal information on Detroit citizens. In Liuzzo's case, her funeral would attract many unknown and perhaps dangerous people to the city, so the police action was "a normal precaution" designed to protect everyone, including the Liuzzo family. Commissioner Lane considered the case closed and would not discuss it further.[6]

But the controversy wasn't over yet. Jim Liuzzo did not consider the transfer of one police officer a fit punishment for the pain his family had experienced, so he formally asked the Detroit City Council to investigate the "ill-conceived misdoings" of Miller, Piersante, and others. In a blistering telegram to the council, he requested public hearings and said: "I am confident that the wrong which has been done to [my late wife] by Mr. Miller and others will be avenged." But Lane refused to cooperate and only fueled more public speculation about the Liuzzos by remarking, "I've said all I intend to say about the Liuzzo case. If those people want to drag the survivors back through the public spotlight again, I'm surprised. If they want to embarrass the Liuzzo children, I won't." Liuzzo immediately responded: "My wife never did anything for which she was ashamed. Let the chips fall where they may." But Mayor Jerome Cavenaugh, who just six weeks earlier had paid his respects at the Liuzzo home, was unwilling to help the family now. He supported his police commissioner's actions and refused to intervene. No public hearings were held.[7]

Commissioner Lane's report tarnished Viola Liuzzo's image both nationally and in her own hometown. Before the report, she had been described as "noble" and "courageous." But the week that the first Free Press story appeared, Time magazine called her "a plumpish, perky blonde" who "liked a cause." On Sunday, May 23, the Detroit News continued the trend by publishing a long front-page article titled "The Enigma of Mrs. Liuzzo." Journalist Anthony Ripley tried to create a balanced portrait of Viola, quoting friends and neighbors who called her "a wonderful person," "eminently decent," and "a woman of strength and determination." A fellow student at the Carnegie Institute remembered how she "kept us studying all night and would push us and push us. If it wasn't for her, some of us wouldn't have gotten through school." Her greatest love was her family:

"There's been a lot of remarks that this woman should have been home with her children, not off in Alabama on a freedom march," said one friend. "But nobody talks about the fact that they had help at home. She never left them at home alone uncared for." "She was never a run-arounder," said another. "She wasn't a drinker but she did smoke a lot."[8]

Nonetheless, Liuzzo's unconventional behavior dominated the article and overshadowed her good qualities. Detroit's readers learned for the first time of her one-day marriage at age sixteen to a man more than twice her age; her second marriage at eighteen to a thirty-six-year-old restaurateur that lasted seven years until she divorced him in 1950 to marry Jim Liuzzo; her "metabolic complaint," which led to several hospitalizations; her quixotic struggle with the Detroit School Board and the arrest that followed; her "nervous breakdown" and disappearance that led to her visit to Montreal; and her hasty decision to go to Selma. Even those who considered themselves Liuzzo's friends described her as sometimes "disturbed" and "a little erratic and a little excitable."[9]

But it was the attention that the July issue of *Ladies' Home Journal* gave to Liuzzo that truly revealed why she had become so controversial. Without consciously meaning to do so, Liuzzo challenged popular attitudes about gender and race in the early 1960s.

Intrigued by the Liuzzo story, the magazine asked a major research organization to conduct a national survey of American women to determine whether they thought "that Mrs. Viola Liuzzo . . . had a right to leave her five children to risk her life for a social cause or not." Fifty-five percent of those polled felt the answer was "No," and only 26 percent approved of Liuzzo's decision to go to Alabama.

Finding this result "startling," the *Journal*'s Lyn Tornabene also exchanged views with a specially chosen focus group consisting of eighteen white middle-class suburban housewives. "She was wrong in leaving her home and going down there and meddling," one participant said. "I feel sorry for what happened . . . but I feel she should have stayed home and minded her own business." Did any of them believe that a woman like Liuzzo, a mother with five children, could legitimately "risk her life for a social cause"? Tornabene asked. Suddenly a tension, "almost tangible, gripped the women in the room," she later noted. Then came "an explosion" of voices answering no. Some were very upset: "I don't feel that I have the right to endanger myself and to leave my children motherless," one woman insisted. "The sorrow they would feel at the loss of a mother is greater than any cause. Their sorrow can turn to resentment. . . . If they resent her being killed, she hasn't gained a thing." To Tornabene, the women seemed "constricted by what was appropriate, what they might be criticized for, and what might open them to resentment and anger." She concluded that "the overriding belief of the majority of these women was that civil rights concerns should be left to men." By rejecting this view, Liuzzo left herself open to censure.[10]

That such attitudes dominated American thought becomes even more evident when Liuzzo's experience is compared with that of another victim of Klan violence, Reverend James Reeb.

Like Liuzzo, Reeb decided quickly to go to Selma, despite his wife's concerns; but unlike Liuzzo, who arranged to have Sarah Evans watch her children during her absence, Reeb did not help his wife make extra preparations to care for their four children. Yet only Liuzzo was later attacked for leaving her family to right wrongs that did not directly affect them. No one questioned his emotional stability. Nor did Reeb's activities while in Selma merit special scrutiny. No one questioned, for instance, whether Reeb was having interracial relations. Liuzzo's rejection of traditional gender roles and expectations played a significant role in robbing her of her martyrdom.[11]

So did Liuzzo's attitudes toward race, which differed sharply from those of most Americans in 1965. Especially troubling to many was the "racial mixing" that occurred during the Voting Rights March. Free of prejudice, Viola Liuzzo lived a fully integrated life in Selma: She roomed with a black family in public housing, ate what they served, slept in their beds, and thought nothing of being seen with a black man in an automobile on an Alabama highway. She also openly expressed the desire to adopt a black teenager. Given the dominant racism of the time, Liuzzo's behavior was instinctively questionable to many, and it won her few friends in white America.

Returning to a normal life was all but impossible for the Liuzzo family. At one point, someone even fired a shot through their window, although fortunately it wounded no one. Sarah Evans tried to burn the hate mail before the children could see it, but she didn't fool young Tony: "I knew what was in there. Nobody needed to tell me what was in there." The children may not have read it, but they learned of its contents. "I overheard my father talking about it," Tony later said. "I overheard all the business agents talking about it because the Teamsters Union got flooded with it and our home got flooded with it, and my sisters were talking about it, and our housekeeper was talking about it, and everybody associated with our family was talking about it, but I thank God my father . . . did not let me read it at the time; I don't know what it would have done to me. There was already scars enough."[12]

Somehow, Jim Liuzzo or Sarah Evans missed the copy of the Klan-produced magazine *Nightriders: The Inside Story of the Liuzzo Killing,* which arrived at the house early in 1966. Everyone except Sally saw its cover: an enlarged police photograph of their mother's blood-soaked body slumped in the front seat of her car. Tom read it; "I wasn't supposed to," he said later, "but I did. It said a lot of nasty things about my Momma." Besides including material from Lane's controversial report, *Nightriders* claimed that Viola was "hopped up" on "dope" and that she and Leroy Moton were inseparable in Selma, seen often "holding hands in public or walking around with their arms locked about each others' waists." But in truth, the two hardly saw one another before the night she was killed. One of the magazine's photographs never left Tom's memory: A black man and a white woman were making love, and although their faces were turned away, whoever sent *Nightriders* to the Liuzzos had circled the woman's face and written, "Is this your Momma?"[13]

The agony was unending. Every month Jim Liuzzo made a payment to the mortgage company that owned the title to his wife's car, which remained in the possession of Alabama authorities who wouldn't release it because it was still considered evidence. He also wanted her wedding ring and other personal items returned, but nothing happened. When he wrote to the White House seeking help and compensation for the car, his letter was routinely sent to the FBI, where J. Edgar Hoover appended his own cruel comment: "Liuzzo seems more interested in cash rather than in grief over his wife's death."[14]

Years would pass before any of Viola's personal effects were returned. Jim finally stopped paying on the car and forgot about it until January 1966, when a UPI reporter telephoned him to ask whether he was aware of an ad currently running in the "Business Opportunities" section of the *Birmingham News.* He wasn't, so the reporter read it to him: "NOTICE— Do you need a crowd gatherer? I have 1963 Oldsmobile that Mrs. Viola

Liuzzo was killed in. Bullet holes and everything still intact. Ideal to bring in crowd. $3,500. Write D-46 care *News*." Jim was shocked that "anyone would want to capitalize on this." He called the FBI, which launched a brief investigation and learned that the Birmingham office of the finance company had repossessed the car and sold it to a man who hoped to make "a large profit by resale." The Bureau's files on the man revealed nothing subversive, so it closed the case. Perhaps because of the FBI's interest in the car, the man gave up his original plan, and there is no record indicating that the car was ever used as a "crowd gatherer."[15]

Other problems were more difficult to solve. When Tony returned to school after a two-week absence, bullies beat him up and called him a "nigger lover." Tommy was "ridiculed," and as the rumors about his mother became public, he was forced to answer the awkward questions of his schoolmates. Sally was taunted by her own neighbors, their faces "twisted" with "hate"; they called her the "nigger lover's baby" and threw rocks, which almost hit her. Outraged and worried, Jim put his children in a Catholic school where he thought they would be safer and hired armed guards to protect them at night.[16]

Seventeen-year-old Mary and thirteen-year-old Tommy were the bigots' most serious casualties. After the funeral, Mary and her husband, Barry Johnson, returned to his parents' home in Georgia, but Mary couldn't escape the cold stares of her co-workers or their silence. "The people . . . were afraid to talk to me," she later recalled, "and the other people really didn't care to." It was worse at home. Her marriage, already badly strained, disintegrated at dinner one night when her father-in-law said that her mother "got what she deserved, she shouldn't have been running around with all those niggers." Mary called her stepfather and within days was back at the house on Marlowe Street.[17]

But being home didn't help to relieve the depression Mary began to experience. Her relationship with her stepfather, always difficult, grew worse. Rigid and impatient, unable to relate to his children, Jim Liuzzo couldn't fill the void left by Viola's death, and he soon began to drink heavily. "My dad did the best he could," Mary said later, "but he didn't . . . know what to do." Nor did she. Their mother had been the "nucleus and we revolved around her," Tony Liuzzo later said. "It would be like taking the sun away from the solar system. The family fell apart completely."[18]

For a time, Mary attended night school, hoping to finish her high school degree, but she quit to work as a stock girl at Hudson's Department Store and then moved on to the credit offices at Kresge and Kmart. Although she promised herself after her mother's death "that she would never love anybody enough . . . to cause me that kind of pain," Mary met a young man, and not long after her eighteenth birthday she became pregnant. With no one to turn to, certainly not her father, she had an illegal abortion. An infection set in that went untreated, leading to hospitalization and a serious medical procedure that left her sterile. Only drugs seemed to deaden her pain, and she later admitted to taking most of them at one time or another—LSD, mescaline, speed, "a little bit of cocaine, marijuana, anything."[19]

Returning from a vacation to Mexico in July 1968, she was stopped at the San Antonio airport by U.S. Customs agents, who searched her and found two ounces of marijuana hidden in her underwear. Released on bail pending sentencing, she returned to Detroit and a furious stepfather, who "kicked [her] out of the house." She lived for several months at a "dope house" in Detroit until a judge sentenced her to five months of incarceration at the Federal Reformatory for Women in Alderson, West Virginia. Before leaving for prison in November, she told a reporter that what she regretted most was "knowing how much I've hurt my father. He's been hurt so much. I know I've done wrong. I'll never break the law again." Tom Ethridge, a Mississippi journalist, hearing of Mary's problems, offered a cruel commentary: "At the time the Liuzzo woman was shot, this scribbler (along with many others) suggested that she should have stayed home looking after her children and husband, instead of leaving them to meddle in Alabama. . . . Perhaps her daughter, Mary, would not be mixed up in the narcotics racket if her mother had spent more time with her. Wonder how the other Liuzzo kids are doing these days?"

For Mary, the five months she spent at Alderson seemed like five years; not a single friend or a member of the family ever visited her. She managed to earn her GED during this time, but after her release in 1969 she again "got heavily involved in drugs and alcohol," addictions that would continue for the next ten years.[20]

Her younger brother Tom was also in trouble. Of the five Liuzzo children, Tom had been the closest to his mother, and her murder "devastated" him. He "shut down," retreated into a world of his own, stayed away from school, and then "dropped out as soon as [he] could." In late 1966, when

he was fifteen, he moved to Cincinnati, where he lived with—and off—
a twenty-six-year-old woman named Phyllis Rikos, whom he had known
for a month. While she worked as a waitress, he did occasional odd jobs,
which suited him fine. He developed a drinking problem, which led to an
arrest for breaking and entering. "I didn't steal nothing valuable," he later
explained. "I was just a drunk kid and climbed in a window I shouldn't
have." A juvenile court judge sent him home with a warning not to return
to Ohio, but a month later he was back in Cincinnati. His relationship
with Rikos lasted three more months; after their breakup, he hitchhiked
back to Detroit.

In 1968, he decided to let his hair grow long and go "traveling." Like
millions of young people his age, he was drawn to California, where he
spent the next year "cruising around . . . just trying to find out who I was."
It was "a nice time," he later remembered; "everybody shared on the road,
on the street." He "dropped acid," "flipped out," and battled with police:
"They started beating on me, I beat back. After they beat me half to death
they towed me to the doctor [who] shot me up with Thorazine to bring
me down off the LSD." He spent thirty-three days in jail, reading the Bible
and later claiming that he had a "religious experience." Since he was still
a minor, police didn't press charges, and once again he was put on a plane
for Detroit. His father, fearing that he had become a "drug addict," had
him "taken away in a strait jacket" to St. Clair Hospital, where he remained
until he was clean and sober again.[21]

The other Liuzzo children—Penny, Tony, and Sally—fared a bit better
than their siblings, if only by comparison. Penny, who was living at home
at the time of her mother's death, attended Highland Park Community
College for one semester in the fall of 1965, but her father refused to pay
for her education beyond that, so she worked as a part-time receptionist
at a tile company and for a beautician. In April 1966, she became pregnant
and married Arthur Dupure, a friend of her cousin's whom she had known
less than a year, a young man with few prospects. The marriage lasted
seven years, until Penny became disgusted with her husband's unwillingness to support their two children; that and his habit of "running around
and numerous other things" led to their divorce in 1972.[22]

Tony Liuzzo, watching Tommy, Mary, and Penny drift away, found it
impossible to concentrate on his studies and quit high school in 1972.
Later he said: "Sixteen and lost, I . . . had nobody to turn to, so I turned

to the streets." He worked as a laborer, managed a Mobil gas station, and then joined the army in February 1974. He was discharged a month later because of "tendonitis" and again took any job he could find. On his first day as an ironworker, he slipped on a rainy deck, broke his ankle, and spent the next two months in a cast. When he returned to work at the Bridge Construction Company, he again injured his ankle and underwent two surgeries; he recuperated during the next ten months and lived on workmen's compensation.[23]

Sally's youth insulated her somewhat from her family's difficulties. She considered herself her father's "favorite" and had a closer relationship with him than did the others. "To me, he was wonderful," Sally later said. "He did everything the best he knew how." Sarah Evans took special care of her, too: "She cooked, she gave me baths, she did my hair for school. She did everything a mother did except be a mother." But she also experienced trouble in high school and avoided going: "My dad just said, if you don't want to go, don't go, and I was always absent a lot, . . . and all I used to have to do was wake up and say, 'dad, I'm sick,' and he'd say, 'fine, stay home.'" She quit for a year, but remembering how much her mother valued education, she returned and eventually graduated in 1977. Like her siblings, she struggled to find a good job. For a time she worked at the same gas station brother Tony had once managed, then became a part-time cashier at Sears and eventually joined Michigan Bell, where she sorted and delivered the mail.[24]

For Gary Thomas Rowe, the years from 1966 to 1975 were also hard. The force that held the Liuzzo family's precarious universe together—the "sun," as Tony Liuzzo said—had been Viola; for Rowe, that force, that sun, had been the FBI. Without the Bureau to support and protect him, his world fell apart. And, ironically, it would be Rowe's public breakdown and its consequences that would bring the Liuzzos together again as a family.

Becoming a deputy U.S. marshal was a dream come true for Tommy Rowe, or Thomas Neil Moore, as he was now known. No longer did he have to hide in the shadows or meet his FBI contacts in vacant lots or in cars parked on deserted streets. Now he had the authority to carry a gun on his hip and a gold badge in his pocket—the very figure of authority—admired, respected, feared. But if Gary Thomas Rowe could change his name, he couldn't change his nature. From March 26, 1965, to January 15, 1966, he had been in the FBI's protective custody, which had curbed his drinking, cutting loose, and raising hell. Free of their control, he reverted to his old ways, causing major concerns for his old patron and his current bosses. Although the FBI was rid of him, its top officials in Washington considered him a "troublemaker" who might still embarrass the Bureau. The special agent in charge at the FBI's San Diego field office quickly became aware of Rowe's "emotional instabilities," and his boss feared that if Rowe didn't "learn to control his temper, a serious incident is likely to occur."[25]

One by one the incidents occurred. In March 1966, an "unruly patron" insulted Rowe in his favorite haunt, Betty's Bar in Chula Vista, so he pulled out his snub-nosed .38 revolver and waved it at him until the bartender calmed Rowe down. He drew his gun again in May, this time pointing it at a highway patrolman who had stopped him for erratic driving. The officer thought Rowe "threatening," but when the Highway Patrol officials learned who he was, they simply gave him a warning.[26]

The summer brought more trouble. At Betty's Bar in July, a flirtation with an inebriated woman ("Honey, take me home and love the hell out of me," Rowe said she told him) led to an altercation with an angry husband named John Herbert Haggerty. The two wound up outside, where Rowe again drew his gun and said, "I'll kill you." One police officer called to the scene overheard Rowe and seized his gun. Rowe told the police that Haggerty had pulled a gun on him first, which he denied, calling Rowe "a damned liar."

"Say that one more time and I'm going to knock the hell out of you," Rowe threatened.

"You're a damned liar," Haggerty said again.

Suddenly, Rowe punched Haggerty in the face. The police grappled with Rowe and dragged him away; if there was "one more outbreak of violence," they warned, he would be arrested and jailed.

After an investigation, the district attorney's office concluded that Rowe was guilty of "Exhibiting a Firearm in a Threatening Manner," a violation of the California penal code. John Haggerty never pressed charges, perhaps because of a remark the bartender had made when the fracas began: "Better not mess around with Moore. . . . He could kill [you] and legally get away with it." The only consequences of Rowe's night on the town were some sore knuckles. The authorities informed the U.S. Marshals Service of Rowe's bizarre behavior, preferring to let them worry about their wayward deputy.[27]

Rowe's behavior didn't improve. Just a few weeks after the incident at Betty's Bar, there was another barroom brawl, and this time the San Diego police took Rowe into custody. But after learning who he was, they let him go. His habit of getting drunk, proclaiming to everyone in his company that he was a government agent, and then showing them his badge and gun to prove it, continued through the fall. The local FBI field office was now receiving so many complaints from both the San Diego and Chula Vista police departments that the special agent in charge, incapable of believing that Rowe was actually responsible for all the trouble, began an Impersonation Investigation until he was startled to learn that Rowe *was* causing it all. Wayne Colburn, the U.S. marshal in San Diego and Rowe's boss, told his FBI colleagues that he had recommended that Rowe be "transferred" because he was a "disciplinary problem," news that was passed on to Headquarters. "Rowe apparently has a super-detective complex," San Diego reported to Hoover in November, "and appears incapable of keeping quiet . . . that he works for the . . . U.S. Marshal's office. . . . His true identity has been a closely guarded secret in San Diego and in this office but his behavior, particularly in the past two or three months, can only lead to his exposure." Despite these concerns, or perhaps because of them, the U.S. attorney refused to prosecute and Rowe was not transferred. Protected by the U.S. government from having to pay for his actions, Rowe continued to do as he pleased in the bars of Chula Vista and San Diego.[28]

He was also unpopular with his fellow deputy marshals. There was an air of mystery about him, one that Rowe delighted in and worked to perpetuate. Nobody knew how he came to be a deputy, not even Chief Deputy U.S. Marshal Donald D. Hill, who supervised him. There were only rumors —that he had been "hired" by "someone" in Washington, D.C.; that he had once worked for the Miami Police Department and for the CIA, which still requested his services. (Hill later recalled that Rowe received a two-week leave of absence so he could take part in what he hinted was a clandestine "mission" for the agency, and when he returned, he acted as if he had been injured.) Rowe was "crazy about his background," Hill later said.[29]

Rowe was just as secretive at home with his new wife, Roberta, whom he married in 1967. If her husband seemed a little odd, it was understandable, given what he had told her about his past. A lifelong bachelor, born and reared in Florida, he had worked for the CIA in Africa and most recently had been some kind of "undercover" man in San Francisco. All this explained why he was so "close-mouthed" about his current work. The marriage lasted only two years, with its happiest moment the birth of their daughter, Melinda. (Later, when Roberta learned her ex-husband's real identity and history, she called him "a pathological liar.")[30]

The Marshals Service finally gave up on Tom Moore late in 1967. In October, an argument between Rowe and John Jordan, a janitor at the U.S. Courthouse in San Diego, left Jordan slightly injured. Each accused the other of being responsible for the shouting and shoving that occurred. Nine days after this incident, while driving through Pine Valley with a fellow deputy and two prisoners, Rowe was hailed by a Highway Patrol car, red lights flashing, siren blaring. Officer Billy Sonka had been alerted that the deputies would be in his area on October 19 and was instructed to make sure they received every courtesy. So Sonka was surprised when one of the men—later identified as Deputy Moore—exited the vehicle with a gun pointed at him. Six weeks later, U.S. Marshal Wayne Colburn told Rowe that he must resign from the service or be fired. Rowe later claimed that he refused to go quietly, but Colburn threatened to reveal his identity and location, giving the Klan a chance to kill him. Afraid that Colburn would follow through, Rowe agreed to resign. It's unlikely that Colburn ever made such a threat; Rowe's record certainly justified his dismissal. The news that Rowe was no longer a federal officer came as a relief to the FBI: "There is no longer any need to be concerned with his conduct," Clement McGowan wrote Assistant Director Al Rosen on February 8, 1968. But if the FBI believed it was finally rid of Gary Thomas Rowe, as McGowan's memo suggests, it was sadly mistaken.[31]

CHAPTER THIRTEEN

Digging In

MORE THAN TWO YEARS passed before the Bureau again heard from
Rowe. On December 7, 1970, he visited the San Diego field office, introducing himself to the agents and revealing his past and his current difficulties.
He was broke and unemployed, he said, and was turning again to the
people who had always rescued him—the FBI. He "had the highest praise
for the [Bureau]," the agents later recorded Rowe saying, "and would be
happy to serve in the same capacity he had in the past if he were in a position where he could be of benefit. He felt that he had done a great service for his country."

The tale that followed was typical Rowe—a mixture of truth, fabrica-
tions, and outright lies. Certain things had been "preying on his mind,"
he said, things that he believed the FBI and Mr. Hoover "were not aware
of." John Doar and the Justice Department had treated him badly, breaking
their promises and threatening to have him fired as a deputy U.S. marshal.
He never received the monetary settlement that he had been guaranteed
(the ten thousand dollars, he maintained, was "a personal gift from Mr.
Hoover for a job well done"), and Doar had pressured him several times
to pay the debts he owed his Birmingham creditors. He also blamed Wayne
Colburn for the loss of his job with the Marshals Service. He insisted that
J. Edgar Hoover be personally informed of these charges as well as his
plight. Although it is true that Doar encouraged Rowe to pay his debts,

no threats were made and Rowe conveniently forgot or ignored the fact that the FBI's ten thousand dollars was not a gift but a settlement for services rendered, and the Bureau had his signed receipt to prove it.[1]

In early January 1971, Rowe called the office twice with more details about his troubles. His car and most of his furniture were gone—repossessed—and he was still unemployed. Now he demanded that the FBI get him a job as either a sky marshal or a federal narcotics agent or he would hold a press conference revealing his life as an informant and the shabby way he was being treated. Having communicated with Headquarters, agents now reminded Rowe that his relationship with the Bureau had ended in January 1966 and therefore he should take his complaints to the Justice Department. (Hoover told his own agents that they must not act as a go-between for Rowe.)[2]

No job or settlement was forthcoming, but Rowe remained silent during the next four years. He worked as a private investigator in Los Angeles for a time and then returned to San Diego, where he found work as a security guard in a department store. In April 1975, he turned up at the office of Congressman Lionel Van Deerlin of San Diego. "He was hungry, trying to survive without a job, he was married and his wife was dying of cancer," Rowe told the congressman's assistant, Bill Ackerstein. J. Edgar Hoover, who died in 1972, had personally given him ten thousand dollars (almost half of which he was forced to pay to his creditors at the insistence of Assistant Attorney General John Doar), and FBI agents James McGovern and Neil Shanahan had assured him that an additional thirty thousand dollars was forthcoming from the Justice Department, but it never arrived. Rowe sobbed as he begged Ackerstein to get him a job and especially "the money he felt was promised him."[3]

Again, no job or money materialized, so this time Rowe hired a lawyer who sought the help of President Gerald R. Ford. Rowe's career as an "undercover person was unpleasant and dangerous," attorney Franklin Geerdes wrote the president on July 25, "but he performed in excellent style . . . [and] his service . . . was of great benefit to the Government and black people." Rowe's condition was said to be "dire"; his wife had cancer, his finances were "in bad shape and the family need is great." Presidents Johnson and Nixon had "not cooperated in payment of a proper claim in the amount of approximately $36,400 for service rendered." Geerdes was presently trying to sell a book about Rowe's life and, although nothing had happened, he was encouraging his client to produce another "about his unfavorable experience with the Government." Geerdes hoped that the president would act quickly to help his client.[4]

Geerdes's letter made the rounds of Washington officialdom, with stops at the counsel to the president's office, where it was forwarded to the attorney general, who sent it to the FBI, which stuck to its policy of having nothing to do with Rowe by sending it back to the Justice Department, where it remained unanswered. Rowe continued to bother Congressman Van Deerlin, who finally suggested in September that he contact Senator Frank Church, whose Select Committee on Government Operations (or Church Committee) was investigating the CIA and the FBI in the wake of Vietnam, Watergate, and abuses of power committed in the 1960s and 1970s. Americans were sickened to learn that their government had financed the overthrow of foreign governments in Iran, Guatemala, and Chile and had made attempts to assassinate foreign leaders, especially Cuba's Fidel Castro. They also learned that the FBI had a program called COINTELPRO (a contraction of "counterintelligence program") that sought the destruction of domestic organizations it considered hostile, which included those supporting the antiwar and civil rights movements. A special target of J. Edgar Hoover's wrath was Martin Luther King, Jr., whose extramarital affairs had been tape recorded and sent to the King family with an anonymous note encouraging King to kill himself. As a result of these revelations, only 37 percent of the American people held the FBI in esteem by 1975, down from the 84 percent recorded in 1966. Rowe's own public testimony would further tarnish the FBI's image. This change in public opinion provided Rowe with an opportunity to air his grievances, so he was quick to follow the congressman's advice.[5]

The committee's counsel and staff interviewed Rowe on October 17 and found his testimony so shocking that they leaked it to the press and asked him to appear publicly. On December 1, 1975, the day before he was scheduled to appear, Rowe offered a sample of his charges in an incendiary interview with the *Los Angeles Times*. The FBI, Rowe alleged, had planted electronic listening devices all over Birmingham—in Klansmen's homes, in black churches, and even in a motel room inhabited by Martin Luther King, hoping the bug would produce evidence to destroy the civil rights leader. Rowe recalled an FBI agent telling him that J. Edgar Hoover "hated King with a purple passion."

The Mother's Day attack on the Freedom Riders could have been prevented, Rowe argued, because he had informed the Bureau of the Klan's intentions three weeks before, but the FBI never told the Justice Department of the impending assault. The FBI also knew that the Birmingham Police Department was riddled with Klansmen and that together they had succeeded in shutting down an integrated country club. And there was more: He had given the FBI the names of Klansmen who probably had participated in the 1963 bombing of the Sixteenth Street Baptist Church, yet the crime was still unsolved twelve years later. When the *Times* asked Rowe why he had turned against the Bureau, he said that it was they who had turned against him, breaking promises that included "a lifetime government job." The interview intensified public interest in the story he was about to tell—the personal history of "a double agent" who had worked for two of America's most secret organizations, the FBI and the Ku Klux Klan.[6]

Walking into the immense Russell House Caucus Room on December 2, Rowe discovered a huge audience awaiting him: reporters, photographers, television camera operators, and the curious who wanted to know more about the FBI and the civil rights movement in the 1960s. Some gasped, others laughed, when they saw him: a "chubby" middle-aged man wearing what one reporter called "an extra zinger for the television cameras," an enormous cloth hood with "goggle sized eye holes" to hide his face from potential Klan assassins. The session was "bizarre," noted one writer, but *Newsweek* later called Rowe "a sensational witness." His tale had just the right amount of violence and sex to hold his audience spellbound. Always a superb raconteur, he described how, at the behest of Birmingham police officials Tom Cook and W. W. ("Red") Self, he had arranged the assault on the Freedom Riders in 1961, which the police observed firsthand without intervening. "They couldn't help but see us," Rowe said. "We had baseball bats, we had clubs, we had chains, we had pistols sticking out of our belts. It was just unbelievable. Not one officer in the Birmingham Police Department asked us what was going on." Equally culpable was the FBI, which had also stood by and done nothing except take pictures, although he had informed the Bureau weeks in advance of the plans.[7]

He claimed that his own goal had been to prevent violence. Within the Klan, he was known as "Preacher" because "I would see things that I felt they were fixing to do and I would say, 'come on, it's not worth the hassle. We can do it another time. Don't get involved because we're going

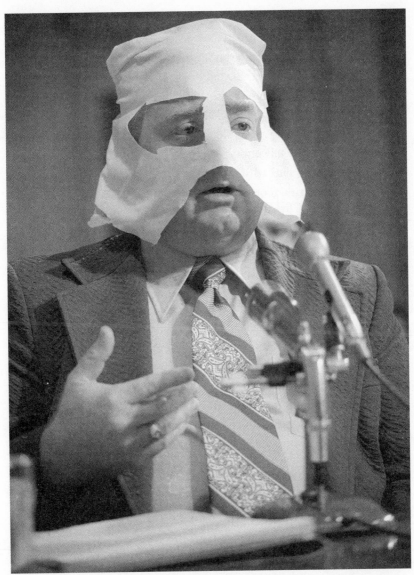

Rowe testifies in December 1975 before the Senate's Church Committee investigating CIA and FBI abuses during the 1960s. (UPI-Bettmann/Corbis)

to blow the damn thing open.'" "Dozens" of violent incidents could have been prevented, but the Bureau always ignored his demands that they protect civil rights activists. He became so angry that he almost quit.[8]

His sexual talents were also put to use in the Bureau's 1964 effort to "disrupt, discredit, or disorganize" the Klan through COINTELPRO. Rowe claimed that his contact agent told him that "the old man [Hoover] has declared war," and that he should "try to sleep with as many wives as I could" because pillow talk always produced "the best information." (Rowe later claimed that he slept with more than a dozen Klan wives.) This evoked laughter in the hearing room and an ambiguous headline in the *San Francisco Chronicle*: "Klan infiltrator tells about FBI's sex drive." But the senators present treated him with respect. In the end, Texas Republican John G. Tower thanked him for his "very significant and helpful testimony."[9]

Rowe's interview and testimony hit Birmingham like an earthquake, shaking up the FBI, Klan families, and the city's police and politicians. After FBI Headquarters learned of Rowe's meeting with the Church Committee staff and received a leaked copy of his deposition, the Birmingham field office was ordered to review Rowe's files and prepare answers to his charges. Its sixteen-page response focused primarily on the incident with the Freedom Riders, admitting that Birmingham authorities had been notified of the impending attack and insisting that the FBI had no legal authority to prevent the violence from occurring, despite the fact that the civil rights workers were involved in interstate commerce, which was subject to federal jurisdiction. After Rowe's testimony, Birmingham sent another teletype report, seventeen pages long, that supported Rowe's claims: Agents did indeed bug all the places Rowe mentioned, including King's motel room. As for Rowe's account of the Mother's Day attack, Associate Director James B. Adams of the FBI noted that he "did not take issue with Rowe's description" of that event.[10]

Rowe's sexual confessions produced fury among some Klan wives. "Mama, did you sleep with [Rowe]?" asked the nineteen-year-old daughter of May Gray, a widow of one Klansman who had remarried outside the Hooded Order. "Now tell me, how would you like your child to ask you something like that?" Gray asked a Birmingham journalist. "How do you think my husband feels? Luckily he stands by me, but some of the old Klansmen . . . are now wondering if their wives might have had something to do with him. . . . I sure never slept with him and [I] talked to another

Klan wife and she says she never slept with him." Gray believed Rowe's comments were a "slur on all of us . . . who didn't sleep with him. . . . I think we all should rise up and fight this thing. . . . It's awful."[11]

In police circles, the word used most to describe Rowe was *liar*. Tom Cook and Red Self, who, with Rowe, had planned the attack on the Freedom Riders, were especially critical of their old friend. Self told the *Birmingham Post-Herald* that "Tommy Rowe will do almost anything to get some attention. There is not a word of truth in what he is saying." Cook, by then a lieutenant with the Birmingham Police Department, "shook his head in exasperation" when he talked with reporters. "The man was an informer, sure. Before the FBI latched onto him, he was my informer. And I learned right away that I had to be careful in using the information he gave me. He's a compulsive liar . . . an oddball. Wants notoriety all the time . . . and would do anything to get it. What I can't understand," he told reporters from the *Birmingham News*, "is how the U.S. Congress would listen to a man who admittedly was in the car—with a gun—when Mrs. Viola Liuzzo was murdered. This is the kind of man they're allowing to attack our whole structure of law enforcement."[12]

Cook also dismissed Rowe's claim that he was essentially nonviolent, pointing out to the press that there was a picture that showed Rowe actually beating one of the Freedom Riders. Once again Langston's photograph of the Klansmen surrounding George Webb was front-page news, this time with an arrow pointed at Rowe's back.[13]

When former police chief Jamie Moore was asked about Rowe's story, he offered an odd comment: "The Birmingham Police didn't openly cooperate with the Klan to do violence to Civil Rights demonstrators." The FBI's former special agent in charge, Tom Jenkins, had no memory of the Klan being given "open season" to wreak havoc before the police moved in. "That's so damn unusual," he said, "if it had come to my attention, I would remember it." Jenkins's poor memory might have been explained by his current position as assistant deputy director of the FBI.[14]

Rowe's testimony also affected local politics. Birmingham city councilman Richard Arrington, a black man, thought Rowe's charges serious enough to warrant a full-scale investigation, not only of the police's alleged role in the attack on the Freedom Riders, but of the city's many unsolved "bombings, beatings and murders." He was challenged by Russell Yarbrough, formerly Bull Connor's executive secretary "before that freedom crap," as he put it, who was now the chairman of the council's Public Safety Committee. He thought Arrington's recommendation was "the silliest thing I ever heard of." Mayor David Vann also opposed a council investigation, fearing that it would only "open old wounds unnecessarily," but he promised to look into the informer's charges. Sergeant Ernest Cantrell and Captain Jack LeGrand would spend the next several years investigating Rowe.

Eventually, after a contentious four-and-a-half-hour hearing on December 9, Arrington's motion calling for a thorough investigation was defeated, pending the mayor's report. Vann blamed Birmingham's past problems on the late Bull Connor, calling them "a blot on the history of this city—but its history, not a current problem." Police Chief James Parsons's own brief investigation found no evidence of collusion between the Klan and the Birmingham police.[15]

In late December, Councilman Arrington, having failed to win additional votes, withdrew his resolution, prompting the *Birmingham Post-Herald* to denounce the city council in an editorial titled "Under the Rug Again." "The circumstances surrounding the Mother's Day, 1961, beating of Freedom Riders at the Trailways Station here may not be exactly as they were outlined by Gary Thomas Rowe," the paper noted, "but his story of an agreement between police and Klansmen . . . is the most plausible explanation yet given to account for the vicious attack. . . . It is unfortunate that the Council could not summon the courage, the curiosity and the compassion to take a look of its own into a matter of utmost gravity."[16]

Although the Church Committee didn't publicly question Rowe about his role in the Liuzzo killing, his old nemesis Arthur Hanes reminded Birmingham's citizens that Rowe had been very much involved in that attack. "It was Gary Thomas Rowe who suggested the trip to Lowndes County to kill some of the Civil Rights Workers," he claimed. "And we have him on record as saying in the courtroom that he had his gun out the window and was shooting along with the rest of them. I found out then that he was the biggest liar in the county," the lawyer added. "I wouldn't believe Rowe on a stack of bibles. He is anybody's dog that will hunt him. I think the real Gary Thomas Rowe is beginning to surface. He turned on his Klan friends and now he's turning on the FBI."[17]

Rowe may have been infamous in Alabama, but in the rest of the country he was a celebrity. Invitations to appear on television talk shows poured in. He always wore his hood but fooled nobody; a San Diego deputy sheriff knew it was Rowe just by the sound of his voice. Publishers urged Rowe to write a firsthand account of his life as an FBI undercover man, so at his lawyer's recommendation he hired a Hollywood agent named Arnold Stiefel to handle all the requests. Eventually Stiefel sold the manuscript to Bantam Books, a prominent paperback house, which—in return for a twenty-five-thousand-dollar advance against future royalties—agreed to publish the ghostwritten memoir as quickly as possible. Its foundation was a manuscript written a decade earlier by Delores Carlisle, the wife of FBI agent Jim Carlisle, who had been Rowe's contact in San Francisco. She eventually severed all connections with Rowe after discovering—to her alarm—that some of the stories he had told her were bogus and because her potential publisher feared lawsuits. Jim Carlisle wrote an angry letter to Rowe's lawyer warning him not to trust Rowe, because Carlisle "did not consider him stable or reliable," especially when drunk.[18]

Six months later, in July 1976, *My Undercover Years with the Ku Klux Klan* appeared in the nation's bookstores. "EXCLUSIVE . . . First time published anywhere . . . an FBI undercover agent tells his violent, terrifying story—how he risked his life to expose the Ku Klux Klan," screamed the book's red cover, which featured a photograph of Rowe wearing his hood and speaking into the Church Committee microphones. *My Undercover Years* was dedicated "To the Klan," an odd choice, since Rowe had assumed a new identity because he believed that they still wanted to kill him. The book was a lively summer read filled with lurid stories of Klan beatings, Rowe's sexual highjinks, and his courage under fire. Chapter 16, "Under Covers with an Undercover Man," recounted Rowe's meeting with a call girl who was more than she seemed: "Not bothering to wait for the privacy of a hotel room, Barbara began to play with me in the car. She blew her breath in my ear, ran her hands through my hair and over my body, and kissed me on the neck. She was really getting to me." But once they arrived at the hotel, Rowe rejected Barbara, having been warned by a Klan wife that it was all a setup: Barbara was to seduce him into admitting his FBI connection, and then Klan hitmen would break into the room and kill him.

To protect himself from lawsuits (or worse), Rowe changed the names of Birmingham cops Tom Cook and Red Self, Klan buddies like Hubert Page, and victims Orman and Pauline Forman. His description of the attack on the Freedom Riders was generally accurate, although he said nothing about beating George Webb, photographer Tommy Langston, or newsman Clancy Lake. Such defects didn't trouble Columbia Pictures, which thought the book would make an exciting television movie and offered Rowe another twenty-five thousand dollars for the screen rights.[19]

With the money earned from his book, Rowe bought a bar in Chula Vista, which he named the Golden Dragon. He quickly became known as a man who enjoyed brawling when drunk, as he demonstrated again on October 17, 1977, when police were called to break up a fight between two "grappling" men. The one wearing a loud Hawaiian shirt was later identified as the bar's owner and seemed to be "the aggressor." Besides refusing to stop fighting when an officer yelled at him to "back off," Rowe was verbally "offensive" and threatened to "knock [the officer's] dick in the dirt." Eventually even Rowe's fourth wife, Elsie, got involved. It took five police officers to finally cuff him and drag him to a squad car, where he continued to yell and even spit in an officer's face, causing the officer to spray Rowe with mace.

After this, Rowe had a reputation as a man who refused to be "pushed around," and customers began to look for other bars where they could drink in peace. A few months later, Rowe sold the bar and he and Elsie moved to Savannah, Georgia, his boyhood home, which he hadn't seen in almost twenty years.[20]

But he found no peace there, either. Almost daily, new investigations into his past were being launched from every quarter. Taking advantage of this situation, Rowe and his California attorney Franklin Geerdes offered to cooperate if the interested parties agreed to pay his round-trip airfare from Savannah to Chula Vista; his daily motel or hotel bills; his meals and "miscellaneous costs"; and payment for his time at a rate of twenty dollars per hour, with a guarantee of at least one hundred dollars a day. Geerdes would receive his usual attorney's fee of sixty-five dollars an hour. Before Rowe agreed to an interview, however, a deposit was required covering his travel and living expenses, the estimated costs of the interview, plus Geerdes's fee. And to top it off, Geerdes also demanded that Rowe receive immunity from prosecution when providing information about his life as an "undercover agent," since his work might have violated "State Penal or civil rights laws." Rowe also expected to receive rewards that were being offered for any crimes he helped solve. Lest anyone consider Rowe's price exorbitant, Geerdes noted that Rowe's usual interview fee was thirty-five dollars per hour, but in certain cases, such as the Sixteenth Street Baptist

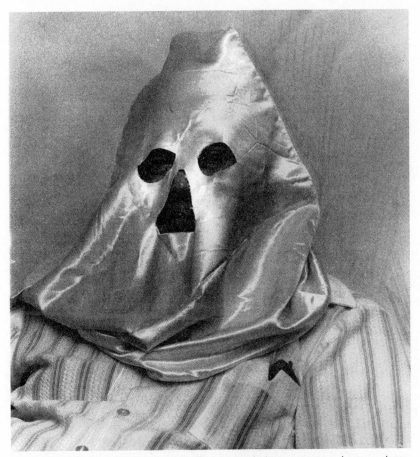

Rowe, hooded to disguise his identity, in a photograph that accompanied a story about him in the *Savannah News Press* on October 8, 1978, three days after he was indicted for the murder of Viola Liuzzo. (Buddy Rich, *Savannah Morning News*)

Church investigation, he was willing to provide a discount because of his desire to help authorities solve that horrific crime.[21]

First to approach Rowe about the church bombing were Birmingham cops Jack LeGrand and Ernest Cantrell and Attorney General Bill Baxley of Alabama. Initially, these twin probes, which began as early as the winter of 1975–1976, were conducted separately and produced conflict. Ever since his student days at the University of Alabama, Bill Baxley had yearned to solve the crime, and now, as attorney general, he was determined to do it. He suspected, correctly, that LeGrand had Klan connections as well as a personal reason to destroy Rowe: LeGrand had loved a Birmingham woman who had dated Rowe and later committed suicide. Therefore, Baxley initially tried to block LeGrand's inquiry, telling Geerdes that LeGrand only wanted "to shoot holes" in Rowe's story and urged him and his client not to cooperate. By 1977, however, the two groups agreed to work together informally, with Baxley pulling rank and dominating the investigation.[22]

Later that fall, Baxley agreed to Geerdes's terms: The attorney received $975, and Rowe was paid a bit more than $1,000 as compensation for his services. Once the checks cleared, LeGrand, Cantrell, and Bob Eddy, Baxley's special assistant, flew to San Diego to meet with Rowe. When they arrived at Geerdes's plush office in Chula Vista, they found Rowe waiting for them in a conference room, sitting at a long table, "hands clasped together," acting as if he didn't have a care in the world. Eddy later recalled that Rowe, although now in his mid-forties, seemed fit—"his reddish hair was close cropped, his face square, the eyes narrow." With his "bullish chest," he still looked like the barroom bouncer he had once been. For the next six hours, they interrogated Rowe about his years in the Klan. If Rowe was truly the FBI's most important informant inside the Eastview Klavern, then he must surely know something important about the church bombing, Eddy told Rowe. In fact, when Baxley and Eddy had interviewed Dynamite Bob Chambliss, the primary suspect and former member of Rowe's Klavern, Chambliss said that Rowe was one of the bombers. Any comment? Eddy asked Rowe. "Bullshit," an angry Rowe replied. "He better have his head checked, he ain't too damn bright. . . . That was a stupid dumb statement. . . . But I would like very much for you to ask me that on the poly[graph]."[23]

They did, and the results, if not definitive, raised serious suspicions about Rowe's participation in the bombing. When Rowe first denied being with the men who had planted the bomb, the machine recorded changes in his physical responses that one polygraphist interpreted as "strong and consistent . . . deception." Rowe then demanded a second test, to be conducted by an expert of his own choosing. Again, the machine noted strong reactions when Rowe answered the questions. But this time, the examiner offered an explanation that differed from the first. "The charts, even though deceptive . . . are not what I would expect to see from a person who is actually responsible for the planting of the bomb," he concluded. "The charts are more consistent with what we see when a person is withholding vital information."[24]

The investigators reacted differently to these reports. Captain LeGrand was convinced "that Rowe drove with Chambliss to the church in the early morning hours of September 15," but probably stayed in the car while Chambliss planted the bomb. The attorney general and his assistants disagreed: "My best evidence was that he knew in advance it was happening," Eddy remarked. "He thought it was going off at 4 a.m., but it went off [later] and killed those kids, and then he can't come forward. How's he going to admit that he knew they were going to put a bomb out and then didn't tell? If he didn't help—if he just had prior knowledge—he's still got a problem. I don't believe the F.B.I. would have given him immunity." In short, they suspected, but could not prove, that Rowe had known about the bombing before it occurred and was possibly even more directly involved. Eddy told the FBI that he believed "Rowe was involved in the actual bombing of the church." But belief wasn't enough without the hard evidence to support it. They had a stronger case against Dynamite Bob Chambliss, which they took to trial in November 1977, winning a conviction that sent the Klansman to prison for the rest of his life.[25]

Eddy also believed that Rowe might have fired the shots that killed Viola Liuzzo. He told one investigator that he and Attorney General Baxley wanted dearly to indict Rowe for murder, but their case was so weak that any good defense attorney would instantly destroy it. They would, however, keep digging.[26]

This interview and another in October also produced some startling new information about Rowe's activities during the 1960s. While being questioned about the multiple bombings, Rowe suddenly changed the subject, revealing that in 1963 he had killed a black man in self-defense during a racial melee. Rowe managed to get away, and when he found a Birmingham cop manning a roadblock, he told him what had happened. According to Rowe, the cop said to forget it and go home. He then informed his contact agent, Byron McFall, who looked into it and eventually told him, "Just sit tight, and don't say anything else about it."[27]

Bob Eddy was puzzled: Why would Rowe admit to a fourteen-year-old murder after getting away with it? Perhaps to get immunity, if somebody uncovered the crime. Charles Hess, Eddy's polygraph operator, had another explanation. "Rowe has a large ego," he told Eddy, and he probably thought that if this latest outrage became public, he would sell more copies of his book and persuade Columbia Pictures to actually produce *My Undercover*

Years in the Klan. Or Rowe "would just keep quiet and hope for the best," Hess added. But Rowe's story troubled Captain LeGrand enough that he added it to his growing list of Rowe's crimes to investigate.[28]

ABC News was also interested in Rowe. During its own investigation into the church bombing, the network's reporters noticed the continual presence of Tommy Rowe: at the Trailways bus station beating Freedom Riders, at or near many of Birmingham's unsolved bombings, in the car with the Klansmen who killed Viola Liuzzo. Intrigued, they shifted the focus of their inquiry to Rowe and Liuzzo. Assigned to lead the investigation was Chuck Lewis, a twenty-four-year-old journalist barely out of college, but what he lacked in experience he more than made up for in energy, intelligence, and zeal. Lewis, assisted by ABC News producer Carol Blakeslee, immersed himself in thousands of pages of trial testimony and FBI records obtained from sources within the Justice Department. He also visited ten states and spent months in Alabama interviewing everyone connected to the story—Klansmen, state troopers, city police, FBI agents, Justice Department officials, prosecutors Richmond Flowers and Joe Breck Gantt, Attorney General Baxley's staff, and many others. Most were willing to talk, except the two most important witnesses to the murder: Eugene Thomas and Collie Leroy Wilkins, who had served their sentences and returned to Alabama. Gone was William Orville Eaton, who had died of a heart attack in 1966.[29]

For weeks, Lewis phoned Thomas's aunt, with whom he was then living, hoping to persuade her that he was an objective journalist without an ax to grind who wanted to hear Gene's story, which he had never told. Lewis also put out feelers through Thomas's former attorney, Arthur Hanes, and a number of the Klansmen he had interviewed. After a long period of silence, there was a possible breakthrough. Late on a Friday night in January 1978, Lewis received a collect call from Thomas. He seemed reluctant to talk but agreed to meet with the reporter in a few days at the Bessemer bar where he worked part-time. With any luck, Lewis would persuade him to talk about the Liuzzo killing not just to him but on camera, for the nation to see and hear.[30]

Lewis had learned from other Klansmen that Thomas had fallen on hard times. In 1966 he had been tried for Liuzzo's murder and acquitted by a jury in Hayneville, just as Wilkins had before him. For his federal conviction, Thomas had entered the maximum-security U.S. penitentiary in

Atlanta on November 27, 1967. He spent the next six years there, working in the industries shop and generally staying out of trouble. During his incarceration, not a single person visited him, not even his two sons or his closest friends. He took no advantage of the prison's educational or vocational services, hoping on release to resume his old job as a machinist at the U.S. Steel plant in Fairfield, Alabama. An attempt to win early release was rejected, despite his generally "good adjustment" to prison life, because, as one official noted, Thomas's past Klan membership would probably lead him again "to resort to other criminal activities." He was released on November 21, 1973, returning to Bessemer and an empty life: His wife had divorced him and U.S. Steel refused to rehire him.[31]

Though Chuck Lewis thought he had an interview with Thomas wrapped up, Thomas called him on Monday afternoon, January 16, with bad news. He had thought about what Lewis had said but decided that he didn't want to talk after all. Fearing that he had lost Thomas for good, Lewis tried to talk him out of it—and succeeded. Thomas again told him to meet him at the Bessemer bar where he worked—before five o'clock when the shift changed. Lewis hurried to his car and drove the twelve miles from Birmingham to Bessemer breaking all speed limits. After losing his way, he finally arrived at his destination with only a few minutes to spare. The place was "a dirty, dilapidated, red-neck bar," whose roof, he feared, might collapse on him. He also worried about the reception that awaited him, dressed as he was in a three-piece suit that prevented him from blending in with the scenery.[32]

Lewis's entrance into the smoky, dimly lit bar was like a scene from an old Western. About a dozen men were drinking or playing pool, and when they saw the young stranger, everything stopped and the room became silent, all eyes turning to Lewis. "Is Gene Thomas around?" Lewis nervously asked the man sitting closest to him. "I'm Gene Thomas," said a tall thin man who approached him with his hand stretched out. Lewis shook it and Thomas took him into the bar's back room, where they had a couple of beers and talked for about an hour and a half.[33]

Both Klansmen had never taken the stand in their own defense and had remained silent for thirteen years, so Lewis became the first reporter to hear Thomas's version of what had occurred that night on Highway 80. It differed significantly from Rowe's account, which the FBI believed unconditionally. According to Thomas, it was Rowe, sitting in the right rear seat of Thomas's car, who first spotted Liuzzo and Moton. He urged Thomas to chase after them and pull out into the oncoming lane alongside the woman's car. Then, using Thomas's .38, Rowe fired the shots that killed Viola Liuzzo.[34]

Chatting over beers was fine with Thomas, but he refused to repeat his story for ABC News on camera. He wanted to put his years in the Klan and the Liuzzo killing behind him and find a permanent job. If he appeared on television, he would revive the entire controversy and would never again find work. Lewis insisted that this would be Thomas's last chance to give his side of the story to the American people; if he remained silent, Rowe's version would inevitably become the accepted history of the murder. Finally relenting, Thomas agreed to an interview but insisted on wearing a hood to disguise his face. And, to Lewis's surprise, Thomas agreed to take a polygraph test. To prevent Thomas from again changing his mind, Lewis set up everything for the next day and promised to pick him up at the bar and drive him to the studio in downtown Birmingham. Lewis left the bar feeling pleased about all he had accomplished.[35]

The following afternoon, as the two men drove to Birmingham's Bell Building, the site of the interview, Thomas again surprised Lewis by declaring that he wouldn't don a hood, like "that coward" Rowe. He wanted to tell the truth directly to the camera and the television audience beyond. Thomas made the most of his opportunity. Surrounded by cameras and sound technicians, with Chuck Lewis and producer Carol Blakeslee leading him through the day's events, Thomas told his version of Viola Liuzzo's murder, with Rowe cast as murderer.[36]

Chuck Lewis thought Thomas was very convincing, but the polygraph test would determine whether or not he was truthful. ABC hired Benjamin Malinowski, a distinguished practitioner, to conduct the examination. First, Thomas was asked to sign a consent form in which he stated that he was voluntarily agreeing to be tested. Then Malinowski reviewed with him the questions he would ask and prepared Thomas for the test, which would measure and record any changes in Thomas's respiration, blood pressure, heartbeat, pulse rate, and galvanic skin response. When the examination was over, Chuck Lewis drove Thomas home. By the time he returned to the studio, Malinowski had completed his report. Thomas's responses to the relevant questions revealed no "deception," so in Malinowski's opinion, Thomas's answers were "truthful."[37]

Having won Thomas's confidence, Lewis now hoped that Collie Leroy Wilkins might be persuaded to go on camera as well. For weeks, he had been trying to get through to Wilkins but managed only to speak on the telephone with his parents and brother. Lewis asked Thomas to help out, but nothing happened and the reporter concluded there was little chance of success. But Lewis was persistent, and on January 29, he again called and this time got through to Wilkins. He knew that Lewis had been calling him, he said, but after leaving prison in 1973, he had been working as a trucker and was away most of the time. But he, too, was ready to talk for the cameras, and even undergo a polygraph. They agreed to meet on February 5.[38]

The Collie Leroy Wilkins whom Lewis met that Sunday was now thirty-four years old, although he looked older; his face was puffy and lined, his hairline was receding, and he wore glasses. He was no longer the dreamy youth the Alabama girls gushed over at his first trial. His story was virtually the same as Thomas's. That's the way it was, Wilkins insisted, although he knew that people would wonder why he and Thomas had waited thirteen years to make things right. Both had told everything to their lawyers, who advised them to remain silent. Taking the stand to accuse Rowe would have resulted in their conviction as accomplices to murder. But events like Watergate and the Church Committee hearings had revealed the FBI's and the government's past crimes, and Wilkins felt that now he and Thomas would be believed.[39]

Later that afternoon, Wilkins signed the consent form and took two polygraph tests, which, like Thomas's, revealed no deception, according to Malinowski. Both Wilkins and Thomas also agreed to testify against Rowe in court, despite the possibility that, if they were found to be lying under oath, they could be prosecuted for perjury and returned to prison.[40]

Using his various sources, Lewis found Rowe in Savannah, and he agreed to be interviewed. Rowe was shocked and visibly upset when Lewis told him what he had learned from the former Klansmen. But he stuck to his original story: It was Wilkins who sat in the right rear seat of Thomas's car and fired the fatal shots. After first resisting a polygraph test, Rowe agreed to be hooked up to the equipment and answered the crucial questions. Victor Kaufman, an eminent polygraphist, later reported that Rowe's responses revealed "strong and consistent deception."[41]

ABC News executives thought Lewis's findings compelling and decided to televise the Liuzzo story in two segments on their show 20/20. The

Washington Post later called the shows "dynamite journalism." It was an apt description. Network television had covered the Liuzzo killing, the two Wilkins trials, and Rowe's testimony before the Church Committee only in brief snippets on their evening news shows. Now, ABC News provided the fullest exposure yet of what it called "the strange career of Gary Thomas Rowe," the FBI informant "who may have instigated the racial violence he was hired to help prevent."

On July 10, 1978, with veteran journalist Sander Vanocur reporting, *20/20* challenged the long-accepted version of Viola Liuzzo's murder. First, it presented Rowe's story—Rowe sitting behind Gene Thomas, Wilkins's arm out the window with a gun, Liuzzo turning her head to look at her killers ("She opened her mouth and . . . she was screaming . . . 'Oh, God.' . . . And the second shot hit her in the face"), driving back to her car to check for survivors, and then Wilkins's boast, "Goddamn little brother, I'm one hell of a shot, I'm just one hell of a shot."

Then Thomas presented his version, in which it was Rowe who had blasted away at Liuzzo and her passenger. He also said that he had long suspected that Rowe was an FBI informant and believed that he and Wilkins had been set up. For his part, Wilkins was typically subdued, but under Vanocur's questioning he stated that he had seen Rowe fire the murder weapon, thus confirming Thomas's account.

Vanocur noted that ABC investigators were "surprised" by the Klansmen's charges and therefore sought the help of expert polygraphists, who had found the two men truthful. Rowe was tested by a separate expert, and his claim that Wilkins had shot Liuzzo was found to be deceptive. "Whom do we believe?" *20/20*'s host Hugh Downs asked Vanocur. "Hard to say," Vanocur replied. "We just don't know. . . . We asked to see both Justice Department and FBI files on the case, and we were refused; and without these files, it is for the moment the word of Rowe against the word of Thomas and the word of Wilkins."[42]

Both *20/20* and its audience were unaware that Rowe had changed his version of the killing. In his initial statements to the FBI following the murder, he had always insisted that the group drove away after the shooting, but now he claimed that Thomas went back and Wilkins actually saw his handiwork. Besides contradicting his earlier statements to the FBI, Rowe's account was inconsistent with the physical evidence: Liuzzo was shot not while looking at her killers but while facing forward, causing the bullet to enter her head below the left ear. Later, Rowe's new account would be part of what his critics called "Rowe's 12 lies."[43]

The second episode of 20/20, broadcast on July 18, provided more details about Rowe's undercover years—his attack on the Freedom Riders and his possible involvement in the Sixteenth Street Baptist Church bombing and other unsolved crimes. Also revealed was Rowe's contention that Moton was not Liuzzo's passenger, to which Moton responded: "Gary Rowe is a liar . . . because I was in the car with Mrs. Viola Liuzzo." Sander Vanocur added that during Rowe's polygraph exam with Victor Kaufman, Kaufman had asked Rowe "if Moton was the black man in the car. Rowe said no. Kaufman's report said Rowe's answer indicated deception."[44]

The most important question, Vanocur insisted, was how the FBI handled its informants. Were there "binding limits" on their conduct, "not just on paper but also in practice?" Were current FBI guidelines adequate to protect American citizens from crimes committed by the Bureau's informants? Former attorney general Nicholas Katzenbach, also interviewed, believed there was little to worry about: "The Bureau had some very stringent regulations . . . and I doubt that they could be improved on," he said. Vanocur wasn't convinced: "What Congress has to find out and what reporters should be trying to find out is if these guidelines are now being implemented. The least that the story of Gary Thomas Rowe suggests is that they probably—and I emphasize probably—were not in the past."[45]

The 20/20 exposé was not the last word on the strange career of Gary Thomas Rowe. The New York Times published a series of front-page news stories on Rowe in the two weeks that followed the broadcast, three of them written by Howell Raines, a Birmingham native and the Times's Atlanta bureau chief. Raines had been conferring with the Alabama investigators, who had become his major sources, leaking documents and passing on other information they had gathered. The portrait of Rowe that Raines painted was of "an agent-provocateur who participated in and helped to plan the incidents that the F.B.I. hired him to monitor." Rowe was now also a major suspect in all of Birmingham's major unsolved bombings, because he had twice flunked polygraph tests when asked about these events. Rowe was said to have admitted to killing Viola Liuzzo "in the presence of two Birmingham policemen." Worse still, Rowe may have been involved in a second murder: He "startled" Birmingham investigators when he suddenly confessed to killing a black man in 1963 and claimed that his FBI contact had instructed him to ignore it. Raines had additional details on this murder: According to two men with Klan connections, Rowe, after describing his involvement in a city race riot, proudly stated, "I shot some niggers." Perhaps the most shocking new revelation was Rowe's claim that Moton wasn't Liuzzo's passenger and that federal prosecutors, led by Assistant Attorney General John Doar, not only ignored his report but "ordered him to keep silent" about it, and lie if necessary.[46]

The stories on *20/20* and in the *Times* created a firestorm of controversy in Washington. "It's unadulterated crap, all of it," said one Justice Department official of Rowe's various crimes. "He didn't shoot Liuzzo. He didn't kill a Black. He didn't bomb the church." Former FBI agent Byron McFall, who was accused of suppressing information about Rowe's black victim, called the murder and its aftermath "an absolute falsehood," invented by Rowe to "gain attention." NBC was at that moment trying to decide whether to air the film about Rowe's undercover life that the network had bought from Columbia Pictures. John Doar refused to comment about Rowe's charges, but his former assistant James Turner denied them. "We told him to tell the truth," said Turner. "If we told him that once, we told him that three million times."[47]

The denials didn't put out the fire. The role of government informants became Washington's primary topic of conversation. The FBI, said to be "alarmed by the allegations about Rowe," nevertheless admitted that during Rowe's time it had six hundred informers reporting on various domestic organizations and groups, and more than ten thousand involved with organized crime. Even FBI agents and Justice Department officials began complaining to the press about the difficulty of handling informants. Yet everyone in law enforcement recognized how important they were in solving crimes, especially those committed by terrorist groups like the Klan. "We desperately needed someone to keep us abreast of what was happening with that bunch of maniacs," said one agent who knew Rowe, "and he was one of the precious few who could do it." Rowe's connection to the death of Viola Liuzzo, the *New York Times* editorialized on July 26, "has forced the nation to take a hard new look at [informers]. How far should they be allowed to go? Who is to make the spot judgments and by what guidelines? . . . And when an informant has nothing on which to inform, is it his job to provoke misconduct?"[48]

There were no easy answers to these questions, but Rowe remained a mystery that many wanted solved. The Senate Judiciary Committee, then drafting new regulations for the FBI, informed Deputy Attorney General Benjamin Civiletti that it was "intensely interested" in knowing the truth about Rowe. In response, the Justice Department asked both the FBI and the Criminal Division to investigate him. After receiving their reports in August, the attorney general decided to create a special task force to answer three questions: Did the FBI act "improperly" in its handling of Rowe? Did the Civil Rights Division attorneys who prosecuted the Klansmen in the federal trial consider Rowe unreliable? And was there any evidence that Rowe had indeed committed the crimes alleged by the media; that is, did he attack the Freedom Riders in 1961? did he kill a black man in 1963? did he participate in the unsolved Birmingham bombings? did he murder Viola Liuzzo?[49]

Rowe's most immediate threat was Colonel Jesse O. Bryan, district attorney for Alabama's Second Judicial Circuit, who was reported to be "shocked" by 20/20's revelations and seemed eager to prosecute Rowe for the Liuzzo murder. "If we can get two people to say Rowe pulled the trigger, I'll take him to trial," Bryan told the press on August 2. Among those called to testify before a hastily called grand jury were Eugene Thomas and Collie Leroy Wilkins, who returned to Hayneville on Monday, September 18. They found that much had changed in the past thirteen years: The town sheriff and his deputy were both black, as were seventeen of the eighteen members of the grand jury, evidence of how the Voting Rights Act had revolutionized southern politics. More blacks were also visible in the crowd that gathered around the courthouse; they had been almost entirely absent in 1965. "I wish I had been picked for this," said one. "Even though this is 13 years old, the truth needs to be known and most of us . . . want to know what it is." But some things remained the same. News reporters in great numbers again invaded the town. "I've lost 10 pounds just opening and closing the courtroom door" for reporters and photographers, said Deputy Willie Ruth Myrick, a sign of the enduring interest of what Bryan called "a murder case that has not been solved."[50]

For more than four hours, the grand jury heard testimony from ten witnesses—former Birmingham police officers, Alabama state troopers, and ex-Klansmen. Lavaughn Coleman, once Rowe's closest friend on the Birmingham police force, recalled meeting with Rowe at Rowe's apartment early on the morning of March 26, just hours after the murder. According to Coleman, Rowe "said that he had smoked a whore or burned a whore . . . in Selma." Supporting Coleman's testimony was Henry Snow, a young acquaintance of Coleman's, who went along on the visit; he, too, heard a very nervous Rowe tell Coleman that "he just screwed up . . . you'll read about it in the papers, baby brother." Snow couldn't remember Rowe's exact phrase but it was something like, "I wasted a white whore or shot a white whore or a nigger loving whore." Wilkins and Thomas repeated what they had said on 20/20: Rowe fired the fatal shots, and a polygraph test proved that they told the truth.[51]

Later that afternoon, the grand jury returned an indictment of first-degree murder, charging that Rowe "unlawfully and with malice afore-thought killed Viola Gregg Liuzzo by shooting her with a pistol" on March 25, 1965. District Attorney Bryan said that he planned to bring Rowe back to Lowndes County to stand trial. Asked by reporters whether he knew where Rowe was, Bryan laughed and said, "If I were him, . . . I'd be in Cuba."[52]

"I'm not going anywhere," Rowe announced from his home in Savannah after learning of the indictment. "I'm not going to let some Ku Kluxers run me out of the country. I feel like a fish in a barrel. If anybody wants me, they get one try, and if they're not careful, they go home in a bag." Despite the characteristic bluster, Rowe was worried. With his name back in the news, he lost his job with a security firm in Savannah, and his wife was afraid he was on his way to the electric chair. "Where were these new witnesses 13 years ago, huh?" he asked Bill Cornwell of the *Birmingham Post-Herald,* who called him for an interview. "Where were they? . . . There's justice and there's the brand of justice in Alabama. I'm going to dig in and fight." To other reporters who asked for his reaction to the news, he said, "The Birmingham Police Department is the granddaddy of the whole thing. They're out to do me in because I embarrassed them."[53]

As Rowe fought to escape Alabama justice, the U.S. Justice Department's task force began its examination of his career. To avoid a conflict of interest, four lawyers were selected who had no connection to the Civil Rights Division. Its chair, Ralph Hornblower III, was a prominent Washington attorney and former Justice Department official. William M. Logan worked for the Tax Division; John R. Fleder, for the Antitrust Division; and Donald L. Burkhalter, for the executive office of the U.S. attorney. Re-

Rowe in February 1979. Living in Georgia at the time of his indictment for murder, he fought his extradition to Alabama. (*Savannah Morning News* file photo)

search was Marydale Drury's responsibility, one that she had already carried out for the Office of Organized Crime and Racketeering.[54]

For two and a half months, the group collected and studied the massive collection of documents Rowe's work had generated in the 1960s. They reviewed eight hundred volumes of FBI records, including Rowe's informant file; field office records from Birmingham, Mobile, Atlanta, and Savannah; the files on the Eastview No. 13 and Bessemer Klaverns; and those covering the Birmingham bombings and the Liuzzo murder. They asked for records from the Civil Rights Division and the Church Committee. They reviewed Rowe's accounts of the murder given to FBI agents, Justice Department officials, grand juries, petit juries, and the Church Committee. Not consulted were Rowe's interviews with Alabama authorities and Chuck Lewis from ABC News. Once their research was completed, they interviewed more than sixty people—FBI officials, informants, and agents (including Rowe's four principal handlers, Barrett Kemp, Byron

McFall, J. Brooke Blake, and Neil Shanahan); Alabama law enforcement officers; Civil Rights Division attorneys and their staff; and those specifically involved in the Liuzzo murder, Collie Leroy Wilkins, Eugene Thomas, and Leroy Moton. And to make sure nothing of importance was missed, they interviewed two of Rowe's former girlfriends.[55]

Task force members flew to Savannah in late February 1979 to interview Tommy Rowe. His local attorney, Alex Zipperer, explained that Rowe intended to answer all their questions "under oath with no restrictions," voluntarily waiving his Fifth Amendment protection against self-incrimination. "I want to do this for the American people," Rowe said. During the next two days, Rowe discussed his years as an FBI informant inside the Klan, covering all the major events, from the attack on Orman and Pauline Forman in 1961 to the murder of Viola Liuzzo four years later. He had done everything the FBI told him to do, he claimed, and always gave them a full report of his activities, most of which the agents didn't want recorded. "I would've done anything they told me to do," he said. "I was a complete asshole about that. . . . My whole life was the FBI. I was a red, white, and blue flag. If they'd told me to go lay down in the damn street, I'd have went and laid down in the street."[56]

He paid a terrible price for his patriotism, he claimed. In the beginning, his wife and parents (who lived with the Rowes) only knew that he had joined the Klan, but not why. His wife wanted him to quit, and his "poppa just didn't believe in that kind of stuff, and he pretty well abused me. You can't believe the bullshit I went through just to live in that house." Eventually, he was forced to choose between his family and his country. He stayed on in the Klan for the FBI, "and it ruined my home, that's all I can say about it."[57]

Yes, he attacked Orman Forman (although he tried to prevent the Klansmen from killing him), the Freedom Riders ("I got my throat cut and damn near died"), and others; but he had no choice, he couldn't stand on the sidelines in the middle of a battle. Then there came a time when the Bureau told him that J. Edgar Hoover had "declared war" on the Klan. "From this day forward," one of his handlers had supposedly said, "screw as many wives as you can; plant as much hate and dissent in the goddamn families as you can; do anything you can to discredit the Klan, period. No holds barred." But there were things he would never do: "I didn't do any bombings. I didn't kill anybody for the Klan and I didn't kill that woman."

After the Liuzzo shooting, "I came straight as my goddamn car would come back to Birmingham . . . and told them, 'Hey, we got a problem.' "[58]

The lawyers were more interested in confronting Rowe with the contradictions they found in his trial testimony and his most recent accounts of the Liuzzo killing. They asked him to again recount the events of March 25, 1965, and he did, but this time he claimed that he saw Wilkins shoot both Mrs. Liuzzo *and* her black passenger. Then, he said, Thomas backed up the car and Wilkins got out to see for himself. When he returned, he gave Rowe a friendly punch on the arms and proclaimed, "Jesus Christ, Big Bro, I'm one hell of a shot. . . . I killed both the fuckers." "Now that's what he told me," Rowe said. "I don't give a damn what anybody in the world says, that's what that man told me."

Attorney John Fleder bore in, quoting Rowe's testimony at trial: "I am very certain that we didn't go back to the Liuzzo automobile." Then he asked, "Now, how do you explain that?"

"I don't know," Rowe said. "I really don't know because in my heart and soul, we did go back."

"You were interviewed by Shanahan, after the shooting that night; you were interviewed by a bunch of agents the next day. . . . You testified three times at trials, and not one time did you ever say that."

Rowe was temporarily at a loss for words. "I'm shocked . . . because in my heart we went back to the car."

Fleder again quoted Rowe's words, then said: "You just couldn't have been any clearer."

"I just don't believe that to be true," Rowe insisted and asked to be hypnotized or given sodium Pentothal.

Fleder continued: "You never testified that you saw that woman shot . . . [or] that you thought the black man had been shot. . . . You never testified once that you thought that either of those people had been killed."

"I can't believe it," Rowe said.

"It's the truth," Fleder emphasized.[59]

Fleder didn't believe Rowe, and at the end of the interview on the next day, he again challenged him. "All right, Tommy, I've just got one more thing to ask you. . . . You testified under oath at the Federal [trial], and at two State [trials]; you wrote a book. . . . You appeared on 20/20; and you talked to us for quite a long time. Let's be honest. There have been a lot of inconsistencies . . . gaping inconsistencies between what you've told us today, and yesterday, and what you said in those trials under oath. What are we supposed to do?"

"Put me under the poly," Rowe begged, "put me under hypnosis, and give me the truth serum."

"Weren't you under the poly on 20/20?" attorney Don Burkhalter asked him.

"I passed that goddamned poly," Rowe said, and then went off on a tirade, claiming that the ABC News polygraphist told him "there's . . . no problem here. You're as innocent as a baby." Then he had asked Rowe for an autographed copy of his book. His wife had witnessed that moment, and she was willing "to take a poly." Later, somebody falsified the results. The task force members gave up, thanked Rowe and his attorney, and ended the interview. For once, Rowe was in a position from which he couldn't extricate himself. He had always out-talked his adversaries, and if that failed he used his fists. This time, his words didn't convince his opponents and physical force wasn't an option. The lawyers left Savannah convinced that Rowe had lied to them, not only about the Liuzzo murder but about other aspects of his career as well.[60]

The task force report, completed in July 1979, was very critical of the FBI's informant system. Although top FBI officials insisted that informants were warned to avoid violence, field agents admitted that such warnings were unrealistic because, in order to obtain information and protect themselves, they had to convince their fellow Klansmen that they, too, were willing to "skin heads" or do anything necessary to stop the civil rights movement. The report also noted that although the FBI had guidelines about controlling agents, none dealt specifically with the issue of how much, if any, "minor or unlawful conduct" was permissible. Contact agents were on their own.[61]

Were Rowe's contact agents guilty of suppressing information that he committed violence? "Yes," the report stated. It happened at least four times between 1960 and 1964, most dramatically in the attack on the Freedom Riders. Evidence, including the photograph that had appeared in the *Birmingham Post-Herald*, indicated that "of the hundreds of people at the station that day, . . . Rowe was one of a handful most intensely involved in the violence," and his handler failed to inform his superiors. This important event early in Rowe's career established the way that agents responded to Rowe's future activities: "Reports that Rowe was deeply involved in Klan violence apparently never triggered investigations into precisely what he was doing. . . . As long as he was providing good intelligence, the Birmingham field office appeared willing to overlook Rowe's own involvement." Other informants, like John Nigger Hall, whose recruitment the attorneys noted with concern, were receiving similar treatment.[62]

Was Rowe involved in the bombing of the Sixteenth Street Baptist Church or the other bombings in 1963? The attorneys found no evidence that Rowe had participated in the church bombing or the other events, with the possible exception of the Center Street shrapnel bombing, where they thought Rowe knew more than he told his handler. (During the course of their research, they discovered Hoover's refusal to prosecute Robert Chambliss, Tommy Blanton, Herman Cash, and Troy Ingram in 1964, and noted their opposition to his decision.) For some reason, the task force did not examine the bombing of the Gaston Motel—a serious oversight.[63]

Did Rowe murder Viola Liuzzo? In perhaps its most unsatisfactory conclusion, the task force was unwilling to identify a killer. Although the report devoted almost half of its three hundred pages to the shooting, the attorneys found none of the suspects credible: Rowe's various accounts were filled with "jarring discrepancies," and the testimony of Wilkins and Thomas couldn't be trusted given their desire for revenge and their failure to offer their own version of events until 1978, thirteen years after the shooting. Complicating the task force's examination of the event was its desire to do nothing to prevent Rowe, now under indictment for murder, from receiving a fair trial.[64]

The task force offered no recommendations. Since the FBI was in the process of tightening its informer guidelines and none of Rowe's handlers (except Shanahan) were still with the Bureau, nobody was selected for censure. They sent fifteen copies of their report to Attorney General Griffin Bell, but the Justice Department decided not to publish it. The hefty volume probably would have gone unnoticed, filed away and ultimately destroyed, except for the action of one person, a member of the task force perhaps, or a Justice Department official who, after seven months passed, leaked the report to Howell Raines of the *New York Times*.[65]

"Federal report says Hoover barred trial for Klansmen in '63 bombing" was the page-one headline in the *Times* on February 18, 1980. Although Raines focused on Hoover and BAPBOMB (noting that more evidence against Chambliss and the others existed in 1964 than Bill Baxley presented in

1977), Rowe and the FBI's informer system also received attention. Rowe's assertion that the FBI knew and covered up his attacks on blacks was supported by the task force's findings, Raines argued. And while they may have cleared him of involvement in the church bombing, nothing was said about Rowe's polygraph tests, which indicated that he had withheld "vital information" that might have implicated him in the crime.[66]

Rowe's success as an informant, Raines explained, led the FBI to recruit people of even more questionable character, like Nigger Hall. FBI documents obtained by the task force indicated that Hall was so dangerous he was added to the Secret Service's list of people considered a threat to the president. Hall, Raines revealed, received dynamite from Chambliss, volunteered to murder Reverend Fred Shuttlesworth, and was a chief suspect in the church bombing. Hall was also allowed to continue assaulting blacks while he was on the FBI's payroll. Robert Murphy, Hall's contact agent, was quoted as saying that he never bothered to warn Hall to avoid "knocking a nigger on the head" because "it was not in the man's constitutional makeup to not engage in violence." Murphy claimed that he did report Hall's activities except "how much blood ran out of the wound."[67]

Raines's report about rogue informants must have worried Rowe as he waited for a resolution of his own case, which dragged on for a year after his indictment. Rowe's lawyers argued that he had received immunity from prosecution in 1965 and that Alabama was violating his constitutional rights by indicting him for murder. "The state of Alabama and the federal government gave him their solemn promise," Rowe's Alabama attorney, J. Paul Lowery, insisted. "Now Mr. Rowe is a man without a country and he has no remedy. There's no way for this man to defend himself." Furthermore, all the evidence—the Klansmen's guns, bullets, casings, ballistics tests, and the like—no longer existed; it had been destroyed years ago, robbing Rowe of the chance to use such evidence to defend himself. Rowe stated his position more bluntly: "From day one I've said this has been a conspiracy to get revenge against me by the Birmingham police, Alabama officials and the Ku Klux Klan." District Attorney Bryan argued that Rowe had never received official immunity, only a promise, and that new evidence provided by eyewitnesses (especially Wilkins and Thomas, who were now willing to tell their stories) required that the prosecution go forward.[68]

Finally, in October 1980, twenty-seven months after 20/20 first aired its stories about Rowe, U.S. District Court judge Robert Varner, after a formal hearing, issued a permanent injunction freeing Rowe from Alabama's threats. In a thirteen-page opinion, the judge accused Alabama of "bad faith" and "harassment"; a prosecution would violate Rowe's constitutional rights and harm law enforcement. "If the word of a prosecutor is worth anything," Varner wrote, "if the right of an informant to protection—if this invaluable source of information is to be left open to law enforcement, Rowe and those who follow in his footsteps, must know they'll be protected and Rowe must be protected now." The FBI could not have presented a better case for its informant system. Rowe received more good news a month later when the Justice Department released a brief summary of the Rowe task force report, which noted that no "credible evidence" existed proving that Rowe had killed Viola Liuzzo. District Attorney Bryan appealed Varner's ruling to the U.S. Court of Appeals for the Eleventh Circuit, but on May 19, 1982, the court affirmed Varner's decision prohibiting Alabama from prosecuting Rowe.[69]

"I'm tickled to death," Rowe remarked when learning of the court's ruling. "I'm proud and I'm happy that justice has finally been done. I didn't do it. I honest-to-God didn't do it." As for the future, he planned to remain in Savannah; he thanked "all the people of Georgia who stood behind me, who had faith in me. Georgia sure's been good to me." But his troubles weren't over yet. Although Judge Varner may have ended the possibility of a murder conviction and even enhanced Rowe's reputation as a public servant, another threat to his "character and credibility" lay ahead.[70]

CHAPTER FOURTEEN

Pain and Anguish

THE TRANSFORMATION OF Gary Thomas Rowe from undercover agent and star witness into FBI critic hiding behind a hood surprised the Liuzzo family. In 1965, they admired Rowe, the man who risked his life identifying the killers and then testifying against them in three trials. Tony Liuzzo later recalled: "I was so happy and so relieved that the FBI had solved the case so fast, and to me, Gary Thomas Rowe was a hero above all heroes, that he would risk his life and stand up and talk against the Klan like he did."[1]

Now, another Gary Thomas Rowe appeared: a man who would not or could not stop Klan violence against civil rights activists like Viola Liuzzo. Tom Liuzzo had always thought that "something stank" about his mother's death but was preoccupied with trying to put the past behind him after leaving the drug rehabilitation program at St. Clair Hospital early in 1969. He joined a "Christian Street Group," went to work for a construction company, married in 1971, and a few years later became a father. The marriage lasted only four years before Tom's wife "split with a friend of mine three days before Christmas," in 1975. That same month, Rowe appeared before the Church Committee, and Tom, now twenty-four, became obsessed with the man in the hood. "Call it a hunch," he later said. "I felt there was a lot more to be told."[2]

In his spare time, he began to read everything he could about his mother's murder. Tony Liuzzo later remembered the moment, early in 1976, when his brother showed him the crumpled article on Rowe he had been carrying around. The article said that Rowe "had forewarned his control agents . . . that he was going to Montgomery that day and it also said that he forewarned them on many occasions about the violence he was going to do." Tom, yearning to try to somehow right the wrong of his mother's murder, said, "We can sue them." It made sense to Tony: "Never once did we hear that Gary Thomas Rowe was in constant contact with his control handlers and that he called them on a daily . . . basis and he was involved in major violence. No, never once did we hear that."[3]

The Liuzzo brothers now began their own investigation. They lived at the city's two largest libraries, reading reel after reel of microfilmed newspaper articles and stories about the case. They filed Freedom of Information Act requests with the FBI seeking documents about their mother's death but were told they must wait in line with all the others—journalists, historians, ordinary people—requesting information.

The more they dug, the more confused they became. For instance, their mother had been an unusually aggressive driver (once, angry at her husband, she rammed his car), so they didn't believe that she would have just run from her pursuers. The woman they knew would have turned around and attacked the Klansmen—unless she was blocked by another car, the Ford that Moton first mentioned as being the car that chased them. And why did Rowe insist that he didn't see Moton sitting in the car? If Moton was, in fact, the passenger, how did a six-foot four-inch man avoid being shot? Why did the FBI, supposedly the most sophisticated law enforcement agency in the world, fail to test Rowe's and Thomas's guns for fingerprints? Did the agency have something to hide?

Ultimately, Tom and Tony concluded that their mother's death was no accident. Birmingham police and Alabama state troopers sympathetic to the Klan, if not Klansmen themselves, had sought to avenge the disruptions caused by the civil rights movement, and the FBI covered up the crime because it had been committed by their own informant. Tom also believed that his mother had been killed because she was the link between the civil rights and labor movements, which threatened J. Edgar Hoover's version of America. "Our Government had its hands on the gun that shot my mother," Tony later said. In the climate of post-Watergate America, when the country learned of the Bureau's past abuses and that conspiracies were a political reality, it is perhaps not surprising that the Liuzzo brothers concluded that their mother had been the FBI's special target.[4]

Tony urged Tom to find a lawyer. He spoke with one who thought the family had a strong case against the FBI, but nothing happened, so he called the Atlanta office of the NAACP. Its longtime southeast regional director, Ruby Hurley, who had marched in Selma, was answering the phone that day. "Mr. Liuzzo," she told him, "there hasn't a day gone by that I haven't prayed for Viola Liuzzo and her family." She put him in touch with famed civil rights attorney Charles Morgan, Jr., who suggested he contact a lawyer closer to home—Michigan's Dean Robb. Although one FBI agent would later call Robb an "ambulance chaser looking to make a buck," such was clearly not the case. A graduate of the University of Illinois and the Wayne State University Law School, Robb was an eminent personal-injury attorney who had fought for the rights of handicapped children, Native Americans, and victims of spousal abuse. He was also a passionate supporter of civil rights. In 1950, fresh out of law school, he had joined the "first known integrated law firm in the United States," Detroit's Crocker, Goodman, and Eden. Robb agreed to take their case. On October 12, 1977, he filed, on behalf of the Liuzzo family, a claim against the U.S. government, charging "personal injury and the wrongful death" of Viola Liuzzo, for which they sought $2 million for compensation. Robb was also able to persuade the American Civil Liberties Union to work with him.[5]

When two months passed without a response from the government, Robb called a press conference at the ACLU's Detroit office, announcing the government's inaction and informing the FBI that if nothing was done, he would file a lawsuit against it. Jim Liuzzo told reporters that, despite their seeking monetary compensation, the family's main interest was achieving "personal justice and human dignity."

The press conference, which Jim attended in a wheelchair, was his last public appearance. His wife's murder and the disintegration of his family had led him deeper into alcoholism and a final criminal act. Two years earlier, on April 15, 1975, an undercover police officer, working with the Wayne County Organized Crime Task Force, arrested Jim Liuzzo and two accomplices, charging them with arson. He and the others had allegedly conspired to set fire to a small grocery store in return for part of the insurance settlement. Two weeks later, he suffered a massive stroke that left him paralyzed. When his case came to trial, he pleaded guilty, and the judge sentenced him to five years' probation because of his failing health. Not long after Robb's press conference, Jim moved into a nursing home but encouraged his sons to keep on fighting until they learned the truth about their mother's murder.[6]

When more than two years passed without receiving the FBI's records, which the Liuzzos believed might solve the mystery of their mother's death, they turned to Senator Donald Riegle of Michigan in the fall of 1978 for help. He arranged for them to meet with William H. Webster, newly appointed FBI director, the fourth man to hold the post since Hoover's death in 1972. As Tony later remembered it, Webster seemed surprised that he was going to have to waste his time answering the questions of a scruffy Detroit construction worker: "He just looked at us and looked at Riegle like, *What the shit is this?*" Tony demanded to know why it was taking so long to receive the records they had requested. Webster asked what purpose such a release would serve because the documents alleged that his mother was on drugs and had been sexually intimate with black men. Why was the Bureau "trying to smear" his mother's reputation? Tony shot back. Webster denied the accusation and disarmed everyone by announcing that he would immediately release the documents they wanted.[7]

The fifteen hundred pages of heavily censored documents only intensified Tony's anger. He found Hoover at his worst: memos of conversations with President Johnson and Attorney General Katzenbach, for instance, describing puncture marks and necking parties; Hoover's comment that Jim Liuzzo was "more interested in cash rather than in grief over his wife's death" when Jim tried to have her car returned to him. From these records, Tony became certain that Hoover had orchestrated a smear campaign against his mother in order to prevent her from becoming a heroine of the civil rights movement and to divert attention from the FBI's catastrophic decision to let Rowe go to Montgomery.[8]

Tony's interpretation of this evidence later became an accepted part of the Liuzzo story. FBI TRIED TO 'SMEAR' MRS. LIUZZO, proclaimed a headline in the *Detroit News*. But this view may not be entirely correct. The FBI's swift arrest of the killers was considered a triumph, winning Hoover praise from President Johnson, powerful members of Congress, and even Martin Luther King. It's doubtful that Hoover would have done anything to soil that achievement. To be sure, Hoover despised King and the civil rights movement, but the records don't reveal a conscious effort to destroy

Viola Liuzzo's reputation. For example, when the Lane report was sent to Sheriff Jim Clark and details from it later ended up in Klan publications like *Nightriders,* Hoover was furious. "[Lane] isn't respected here. Cut him off entirely," Hoover noted and told aides to remove Lane's name from a list of national police officers often invited to FBI social functions. Other documents from Confidential Informants were even more critical of Jim Liuzzo, but they remained hidden in FBI files. The effort to defame Viola Liuzzo originated with Alabama authorities and was organized by Klan officials, not by the FBI. Ironically, by publicly releasing the FBI records to support their case, the Liuzzo children inadvertently provided information critical of their parents.[9]

Tom Liuzzo was the last family member to see the FBI documents. In the fall of 1978, he was in Lowndes County, living not far from where his mother had died. When Alabama indicted Rowe that September, Tom changed his name to Thomas Gregg Lee and, with his second wife, Janet, and seven-year-old son Jacob, moved there to observe the coming trial. They rented a ramshackle house without heat or indoor plumbing, but he felt good being so close to his mother's spirit. When Tom first drove along that stretch of Highway 80 where the attack occurred, he began to cry and had to pull over to the side of the road. "It was the most moving experience of my life," he later said. "I thought to myself, this is where she laid her life down for what she believed in. I wondered if I could have done the same." Once people knew who he was they welcomed him to Lowndes County.[10]

Then something went wrong: Perhaps it was disappointment that Rowe was never prosecuted, or anger toward Dean Robb because the lawsuit seemed to be going nowhere, but Tom now saw enemies where before he had seen friends. He said that he was receiving death threats from "small-minded, white trash racists," who slammed the door in his face when he asked for work and even denied him the fuel he needed to heat his house during a cold winter. "I think they hated just the fact that I came down here and they couldn't kill me," he said. "They hated the fact that I didn't give them anything to talk about. . . . I've never been uncouth or not a gentleman towards people and they've hated that."[11]

Black friends thought Tom was responsible for his difficulties. They lent him money, found him a place to live, and gave him a van to drive. "We've done everything in the world possible for Tom," said Lowndes

County's first black deputy sheriff, Julius Bennett. "We got him jobs and he wouldn't hold them. . . . We really felt obligated to Tom because of his mother. We think she's a hero." In December, Tom learned that his father had suffered another stroke and died, but he was too poor to attend the funeral. Not long afterward, someone "blasted" their home with buckshot. Local police suspected that Tom, distraught over his father's death, might have attacked his own home. Some neighbors were certain he had done it "to attract attention."[12]

When the government continued to ignore the Liuzzo family's administrative claim, Dean Robb finally filed a formal lawsuit against the FBI on July 5, 1979, this time in Michigan's federal court. The lawsuit charged that "(1) FBI informant Gary Thomas Rowe wrongfully murdered Viola Liuzzo; or (2) that Gary Thomas Rowe wrongfully failed to prevent the murder of Viola Liuzzo; (3) that the FBI wrongfully recruited, trained and supervised Rowe; (4) that the FBI wrongfully authorized Rowe to participate in illegal activities; (5) that the FBI wrongfully failed to prevent Viola Liuzzo's murder; each of which directly or indirectly caused Mrs. Liuzzo's death; and (6) that the FBI wrongfully abused and mishandled Viola Liuzzo's body after her death, and that as a proximate cause of such actions, plaintiffs suffered severe injuries, including emotional distress and mental anguish." If successful, the Liuzzo children would receive $1 million in damages for the death of their mother and another $1 million for the "mental anguish" the family had experienced.[13]

An ACLU spokesman called the suit pioneering "because it would contend that the Bureau was responsible for the actions of its informants." The Bureau "faced a choice in the Liuzzo case," said Howard Simon, executive director of the ACLU's Detroit chapter, "protecting the lives of American citizens or guarding the cover of their informants. They made the second choice," the wrong choice, and would now have to pay for it. "What I want most from this case," said Penny Liuzzo, "is that if someday I stand up for my beliefs, I want to know that I'm not going to have to worry about being killed." Dean Robb noted that the Liuzzos were the underdogs in this venture. "We have no illusions that this is not a difficult case," he told reporters. "The family lives with this every day. If we can do something to put this to rest properly, we should."[14]

Robb hoped that this new action would force the government to treat the Liuzzo family's claim more seriously, and the strategy worked. On

August 31, 1979, the Department of Justice replied that the federal courts had no jurisdiction in such cases because Rowe was never a government employee. Furthermore, "to say that the U.S. caused Ku Klux Klan violence is an unsupportable argument," Justice Department attorney Mark Kurzman told the court. "The FBI was engaged in a massive battle against the Ku Klux Klan to stem the violence in the South. Mr. Rowe was one of the FBI's most important informers on Klan activities." Howard Simon thought it significant that Kurzman was responding instead of the U.S. attorney in Detroit. This signified that the Justice Department was now treating the matter very seriously indeed and would use its most skillful attorneys against them. U.S. District Court judge Charles W. Joiner told each party to submit written arguments on the motion within two weeks.[15]

The contesting lawyers met for the first time on September 16. Mark Kurzman urged the judge to dismiss the case because the law, according to the Supreme Court, held that the government couldn't be sued for negligence when a federal policy was being carried out, and that Rowe was never a government employee so the government wasn't required to protect Mrs. Liuzzo. Besides, the FBI's program of infiltrating the Klan was so extensive that there was "bound to be a certain amount of slippage."

That remark infuriated ACLU attorney Jack Novik: "I can't believe that the government would try to brush Mrs. Liuzzo's death aside in such a manner," he told the court. He argued that, although the government was protected from lawsuits because of an overall policy, courts had ruled that it was responsible for what its agents did as they implemented policy on a daily basis. The FBI knew that Rowe, a "violent and brutal person," enjoyed working for the Klan and was therefore responsible for protecting citizens from any crimes he committed on its behalf. He also showed the court an FBI voucher indicating that Rowe was paid for his services during the period when Mrs. Liuzzo was killed. Was this not evidence that Rowe was a government employee? The judge said that he would study their briefs and then issue an opinion. The Liuzzos were encouraged by a remark Judge Joiner made during the arguments: "I don't understand how the government can put such violent people out on the street and not expect to have to pay somewhere down the line."[16]

While the Liuzzo attorneys awaited the judge's decision, they suddenly faced a new problem—combating the cinematic version of Gary Thomas Rowe and the FBI. NBC and Columbia Pictures had spent $1 million turning Rowe's memoir into a film for television and finished the project—then titled *Freedom Riders*—in the summer of 1978. But Rowe's indictment that September forced a postponement. "The movie has been completed and nobody at this point knows when it is going to be aired," said an NBC executive at that time. "It could be in the fall or it could be later; we don't know." They finally decided to go ahead a year later, despite the fact that none of the legal issues were resolved. The film, now called *Undercover with the KKK*, was scheduled for airing on Tuesday night, October 23, 1979. The *Detroit Free Press* obtained a copy and invited the Liuzzo family for an advance preview showing.[17]

When Tony and Sally Liuzzo, accompanied by their lawyers, arrived at the *Free Press* screening room, they found there another casualty of the civil rights clashes in Alabama, Walter Bergman. Bergman, now sixty-six and confined to a wheelchair, was one of the original Freedom Riders, and the injury he sustained that day on the bus had led to a stroke from which he never recovered. He, and his colleague James Peck, also severely beaten, were both suing the government, thanks to Rowe's testimony that the FBI knew in advance that the assault was coming and failed to stop it. He was eager to see how Hollywood portrayed that event.

The first person seen on screen as the film began had nothing to do with the actual story. Robert Stack, the former star of the popular television series *The Untouchables*, delivered a disclaimer that would presumably prevent future lawsuits: "The film you are about to see is a fictionalized version of certain incidents which occurred during the six years Gary Thomas Rowe was employed as an FBI informant." He acknowledged that Rowe had recently been indicted for Viola Liuzzo's murder and that his role "is still unclear."[18]

"Fictionalized" is an accurate description of the film. The "Tom Rowe" portrayed by former football star "Dandy" Don Meredith was a mild-mannered, likable "good old boy" who infiltrated the Klan for the FBI. He was rarely seen committing violence, and when his contact agent urged him to sleep with Klan wives to obtain information, this Rowe remarked, "That's immoral." Viola Liuzzo, described as a woman who was "very big in the labor movement," was played by an uncredited actress who had no lines and was seen only briefly during the chase sequence, which occurred in daylight on deserted backcountry roads. The murder itself consumed less than five minutes of air time. After the shooting, everybody left the car to check on Liuzzo and her black passenger. "It's a total wipeout," said one of the Klansmen when they found two dead bodies—Liuzzo and her black passenger. With no eyewitness to the crime, the FBI selected a young black man willing to testify that he was in the car and survived the attack. Rowe objected to these illegalities, but government attorneys argued that now it was "a case we can win."

The three Klansmen, named Barker, Mitchell, and Eakin, were acquitted, leaving Rowe a ruined but heroic man whose wife left him because his FBI work interfered with their marriage. At the film's end, as Rowe was ready to depart for his new life in Oregon, FBI special agent Raleigh Porter asked him how he "got sucked into this, a no-win proposition all the way." Rowe, in the moment closest to reality, replied that he was the son of an illiterate redneck sharecropper who grew up with little self-respect. "You came along and I jumped at the chance to do something, be somebody. And it didn't work out the way I wanted it to. Hell," Rowe said, "now, I don't have any respect for you either." As the final credits rolled, Robert Stack repeated the disclaimer and informed viewers that the Klansmen were eventually found guilty of violating Liuzzo's civil rights.[19]

The film was bad history, but for the Liuzzos it packed an emotional punch. As the Klansmen pursued her mother, Sally "put her hands over her face and cried." She asked a reporter, "Does she look like my mother?"

"Yes. She does. To me at least," said the reporter.

"Is there a lot of blood?"

"No, there's not a lot of blood."

Tony tried to comfort her, but she continued to cry throughout the rest of the movie. When it was over and the lights came on, she had no comment for reporters. Neither did Tony, but he was obviously angry. Walter Bergman asked whether they could repeat the Freedom Riders sequence, and after watching it again, he said that "the incident on the screen bore little resemblance to what happened to him." And he thought that on film Rowe was even more sympathetic than he was in his own book.[20]

On Tuesday morning, Dean Robb held a press conference to "alert Americans to a gross, malicious distortion of the role played by Gary Thomas Rowe. . . . Rowe was a 'violence groupie.' He was not a reporter of criminal acts; he was a perpetrator of criminal acts." Robb called NBC's decision to air the film that night "one of the most astonishingly irresponsible acts ever committed by a major network. . . . Rowe's version of his days in the KKK . . . portrays both Rowe and the FBI as heroes, when, in truth and fact, the FBI's and Rowe's conduct was . . . disgraceful." The *Free Press*, in a follow-up story, contacted NBC, asking to speak to those who had produced the film, but they were told that the two executives no longer worked for the network. Howard Simon of the ACLU also met with the manager of NBC's affiliate in Detroit, persuading him to view the movie before running it. Despite these protests, the movie was shown that night in Detroit and throughout the nation. Reaction from those close to the events continued to be critical. District Attorney Jobie Bryan, who hoped to prosecute Rowe for murder, called the film "real boring. . . . It certainly won't win any Academy Awards." And in Birmingham, a small group of Klansmen picketed Channel 13 for an hour while the film ran. On Wednesday, a Klan spokesman claimed that *Undercover with the KKK* was "a biased attempt by the network to distort" the Klan's contribution to American life.[21]

Life for the Liuzzo lawyers was a series of continuing crises. On November 28, another occurred, this time the result of a Supreme Court decision. *United States v. William A. Kubrick* overturned a lower court award to a veteran who had sued the government for malpractice, on the grounds that Kubrick had failed to file his suit within the two-year statute of limitations required by the Federal Tort Claims Act. Kubrick had known he was injured and who had caused the injury but didn't file his claim in a timely fashion. This decision seemed to give the government new ammunition to use against the Liuzzos. It could now charge that the family members had known enough about Rowe's role in their mother's death in 1965 to file no later than March 25, 1967. Therefore, they were a decade too late to sue the government. Judge Joiner asked the attorneys to consider the relevance of *Kubrick,* and they argued again early in February 1980.

The government believed that *Kubrick* was exactly on point and urged the judge to dismiss the case. The Liuzzo attorneys rejected this motion, arguing that in 1965 the family had no reason to suspect that Rowe and the FBI were anything but heroes; the case had been solved within twenty-four hours by brave FBI agents on the strength of Rowe's information. It wasn't until December 1975, when Rowe appeared publicly before the Church Committee, that they first learned of his violent past and the Bureau's knowledge of it. Therefore, the original claim filed in October 1977 was within the tort law's statute of limitations.

The Liuzzo family wasn't used to receiving good news, so the judge's decision on February 28, 1980, delighted them. In a thirty-three-page opinion, Joiner rejected the government's claim, arguing that in 1965 the Liuzzos were not aware of who might have really killed their mother; those responsible appeared to be the three Klansmen who had been arrested, tried, and later convicted. The FBI would have been the unlikeliest suspect given President Johnson's televised praise of the Bureau and the government's eventually successful prosecution of Wilkins, Eaton, and Thomas. But when Rowe went public a decade later, their suspicions were reasonable; therefore, the statute of limitations had begun on December 2, 1975. The government's motion to dismiss was denied.[22]

Howard Simon called a press conference to publicize their victory and told reporters that the Liuzzo children were "ecstatic." He hugged Tony and Tom, who was now back in Detroit, once again seeking to learn the truth about his mother's murder. "Rowe was a pawn of the FBI," Tom said, with tears in his eyes. "He was used all along. . . . Their finger was on the trigger right along with his." In pursuing the lawsuit, the family members were carrying on their mother's work: "I feel like I'm defending her honor. She's gone and the dream she believed in with Martin Luther King is gone now too."[23]

But Tom's happiness over the legal success didn't last long. As the months passed, his emotional problems intensified. He argued with his brother about the case and thought Tony was trying to reach a financial settlement with the government rather than move all the way to a trial. Although destitute, Tom fought this move, believing that a trial was the only way to finally learn who had killed his mother. Arguments grew into physical altercations, and Tom's paranoia grew. In May 1980, Tom showed up at Tony's home brandishing a shotgun. Tony called the police, who took Tom to Detroit General Hospital for psychiatric observation. A short time later, Tony and his aunt had Tom forcibly committed to Northfield State Hospital. Mary Liuzzo later denied that the family had discussed a settlement. She thought that the emotional cost of searching for his mother's killer had caused Tom to become "paranoid and frightened of everybody and everything right down to believing that the family itself was part of the conspiracy."[24]

Tom spent almost three weeks in the hospital before being released in late June. Although he felt better, he remained obsessed with his mother's murder. When he learned that a public hearing was scheduled in mid-July to determine whether Gary Thomas Rowe should be extradited to Alabama, Tom again moved his family to Alabama to observe the proceedings. Earlier, his sister Mary had called Rowe's indictment "a tremendous victory for the family," but Tom was doubtful. He now believed that Rowe was a scapegoat and the FBI was "probably more to blame than Rowe." "They'll make a sacrificial offering out of him to save face," he said, expecting the trial to be a "Gary Thomas Rowe witch hunt . . . one man, . . . fixing to go to trial . . . for murder, and everybody else [is] going to skate." At the Atlanta capitol building, he ran into Rowe and his attorney, J. Paul Lowery, and spent half an hour with them having coffee and discussing the case. Lowery later put Tom on the stand, but his testimony seemed so "crazy" that the judge halted the hearing, interviewed Tom in chambers, and then prevented Lowery from using him as a witness. Although disappointed that no trial ever occurred to resolve his new doubts, Tom and his family remained in Alabama, but he refused to tell his brothers and sisters where he lived or what he was doing.[25]

Dean Robb found Tom's disappearing act annoying (he needed Tom for a deposition), but there were other, more important problems to solve as he began to prepare the case. First, he was buried in paper: The legal discovery process required the government to give Robb and his associates Rowe's records as well as those pertaining to the incidents in which he had been involved. Box after box arrived at Robb's office—fifteen thousand documents, approximately thirty thousand pages in all—five years of informant reports and the quarterly reports the contact agents had prepared documenting Rowe's activities to persuade Headquarters to keep him on the payroll. The investigations of the attack on the Freedom Riders, the bombing of the Sixteenth Street Baptist Church, and the Liuzzo murder were voluminous. There were also transcripts of two state trials and one federal civil rights trial to review; alone, these amounted to thousands of pages. Everything needed to be organized, catalogued, and examined. There were legal issues to analyze, affidavits to prepare, and witnesses to depose. Robb needed an army of legal assistants just to help him get through the documentary record ("it would take ten years to know this case," Robb noted), and this immense workload led to a break with the ACLU.[26]

By the fall of 1980, it was clear to Robb that his relationship with the ACLU lawyers had become strained to the breaking point. The lawsuit essentially belonged to the ACLU and was a prisoner of the time, energy, and money it could afford to devote to this one case, however important it was. The distance that separated Robb's base in Michigan from that of the other lawyers in New York also proved difficult. The result was "divided leadership" and a "lack of cohesion" that Robb feared would affect the case. So in October, he and the ACLU agreed to part company, and with the Liuzzo family's approval, Robb received help from three excellent lawyers: Grant Gruel, former president of the Grand Rapids Bar Association and president-elect of the International Academy of Trial Lawyers; Jeff Long, a former prosecutor who had practiced law in Ann Arbor for a decade; and Joseph Cotchett of San Mateo, California, a member of the American Board of Trial Advocates and author of several important legal texts, including *Federal Courtroom Evidence*. Students at the University of Michigan Law School volunteered their services. Robb and the others would also work in association with Trial Lawyers for Public Justice, a Washington-based group of attorneys seeking "to curb lawlessness in government and in the private sector."[27]

Robb believed that the surest way to win the case was to prove that Rowe had killed Viola Liuzzo. That meant learning all that he could about Rowe, his years in the Klan, and what really happened the night of March 25, 1965. So, after thoroughly studying the records, he went to Alabama three times in 1982 and 1983, accompanied by his private investigator, Warren Hanson, and Tony Liuzzo, the family's representative now that Tom was no longer able to participate. Among their first stops was that point on Highway 80 where Viola Liuzzo died. With a police report as their guide, Hanson and Liuzzo took photographs and made measurements, while Robb got a feel for the scene, recording his impressions with a tape recorder. The place was not at all what he imagined, he observed. The scattered houses, the "rolling farmlands, . . . clumps of trees, and hedgerow fences" reminded him of rural Illinois where he grew up. "It's a strange feeling being here with Tony, where his mother was killed," he said. "He is so obsessed with this that the sadness doesn't come through. He's . . . like a young doctor trying to figure out where everything is and what went wrong."

He then pretended he was delivering his opening statement to the court. "Judge, this isn't a very difficult case. The master and servant law goes back into antiquity when the master . . . was liable for the misdeeds of his servant . . . In this case, Judge, the master's name is FBI, . . . the employee is Gary Thomas Rowe. . . . Anybody who would open their eyes . . . could have known from at least 1961 . . . that he was a mad dog, . . . an agent provocateur . . . he was creating violence . . . and getting paid for it by the American government. His employers were sitting there in their offices, meeting him in motels and saying, 'Good job, Gary, go get them baby.' "[28]

Rowe needed no encouragement, claimed former Klansmen Bill Holt, Robert Creel, and Eugene Thomas when they met with Robb, Liuzzo, and Hanson. For most of his life, Tony Liuzzo had dreamed of killing Gene Thomas, the man who had chased down his mother and provided the weapon that killed her. Now Thomas was an ally, eager to testify against Rowe. It was a difficult adjustment to make, Tony later admitted: "It was a real mixed emotion looking at him. He apologized, said he was very, very sorry, that nothing could ever correct what was done. He was a changed man, believing in the Lord. I accepted it for a man to come face to face to apologize. I can accept that." Thomas proclaimed that he was no longer "as mean as the Devil himself" but was now a born-again Christian who belonged to an integrated church in Bessemer, Alabama. "After I gave my testimony over at the Assembly of God Church," Thomas recalled, "two black ladies came over and one of them hugged me and said, 'I love you.' And I said, 'I love you, too. I see your soul. I don't see no color.' . . . A day before I got saved, I didn't care about what happened. But today I have to look at it in a different light. I see everything in a different light these days."[29]

Thomas and the others told their visitors what they wanted to hear. Rowe always seemed to be "looking for trouble," former Grand Dragon Creel recalled. Thomas remembered the Bessemer carnival, where Rowe "hit a nigger with a chain, and he went sprawlin'. . . . He hit him a good hit. I heard it." Robb read off a list of Rowe's alleged activities—beating blacks at a baseball game, attacking demonstrators at a variety store— when Holt interrupted him. "Rowe wasn't in that," he said. "He would take something that happened and say he done it; . . . I couldn't understand him. . . . Either he was trying to make himself look big for the FBI, or he was doing it to falsify himself." All said they thought Rowe was an FBI informant, and if the Bureau didn't know that he "agitated after violence," then the Bureau was the "stupidest organization . . . in our government."

"They had to know," Holt said. "There's no doubt in my mind. . . . They were very successful in using people like Rowe."[30]

If they knew Rowe was an informant, why did they allow him to remain in the Klan? Robb asked. If they kicked him out, Creel explained, he would "go out and do stuff on his own, and we'd get blamed for it." With Rowe inside the Klan, they would know "what he's trying to pull off. If he's out there by himself, you don't know what the hell he's doing."[31]

Later that night, Thomas met alone with Robb, Hanson, and Liuzzo to discuss the murder. Grand Titan Robert Thomas had asked them to go to Montgomery, Gene Thomas said, to observe the marchers, who turned out to be a "crummy looking bunch of people. Been laying out on the road, walking around them cornfields . . . you can imagine what they looked like when they come tumbling down the street." He repeated his claim that Rowe had first seen Liuzzo and Moton (a "skinny nigger," not the fat man Rowe said he saw) and urged Thomas to follow them. Thomas believed that Rowe was a "braggert" and "bullshit artist" and would never actually shoot. But he did. Given a choice, Thomas said, he would have shot the black man, while he thought Rowe didn't care whether his victim was black or white, "just so he hit somebody." Then they sped away, never turning back as Rowe claimed. "Do you think if Rowe had not been with you, you would have made that chase?" Robb asked. "No," Thomas said, "I definitely would not have."[32]

Did he try to stop Rowe? Robb asked. No, Thomas admitted, he was unarmed—Rowe had his gun. When they had parked the car in Montgomery that morning, Rowe asked Thomas if he could borrow his gun because he had dropped his own while cleaning it the night before. Rowe felt "naked without a gun," Thomas recalled Rowe saying; he wouldn't even go to the bathroom without it. Rowe returned his gun at the end of the night, slipping it back into Thomas's holster. The next day, when the FBI seized it, it was still in the holster, and if they had tested it for fingerprints, Thomas believed, they would have found Rowe's on it.[33]

Robb also went over the question of who sat where in the car. Denying Rowe's story that he had been behind Thomas the entire day, Thomas said, "Lee always sat behind me. . . . It was that way all the time." Toward the end of the conversation, Thomas repeated his charge that the FBI had arranged the whole thing, along with Robert Thomas, who he now believed was also an FBI informant. He knew the FBI had followed them to Montgomery that day, "watching . . . just like a hawk. They watched it every minute it was down there. They knew where we was, what we was doing."[34]

The next day, Thomas took them to meet with Lee Wilkins and their discussion continued. Robb had Wilkins run over the story, too, checking for inconsistencies or contradictions. His account was generally the same. What was motivating them to help now? Robb asked. The FBI said it was revenge. Thomas admitted that he did have "a certain amount of revenge in my head for [Rowe]—I'd like to stomp a mud puddle in him and then stomp him dry . . . to be perfectly honest about it." After all, it was Rowe's fault that they got into trouble; he should have gone to prison, too. Then he remembered that he was a born-again Christian and told Robb that he was no longer the man he had been—supporting the Klan, drinking, smoking, cursing "as much as the people I hung out with." The years had not changed Wilkins very much; he was still a segregationist, he said, and would be until "the day I die. . . . There ain't no use in changing now." Perhaps time had "mellowed" him a bit, but it wasn't likely he'd be attending an integrated church with Gene. Despite their Klan history and Wilkins's current prejudices, they were the only eyewitnesses to claim that Rowe had fired the fatal shot, so Robb decided to use them at trial.[35]

Robb's meeting with a local prosecutor who had observed the Hayneville trials was more helpful. John Andrews gave Robb access to the district attorney's files, as well as documents from the investigation conducted by Birmingham policemen LeGrand and Cantrell. Andrews noted that the first prosecutor, Arthur Gamble, never had a chance to meet with Rowe, who was sequestered by FBI agents before his testimony in court. "I've got a witness I can't even talk to," Andrews recalled Gamble saying. "He always bitched about that." Even better was a copy of an interview with Rowe's friend and Birmingham cop Lavaughn Coleman. Coleman had testified before the grand jury in 1978 that he and Henry Snow had visited a nervous Rowe the day after the killing, and Rowe said "that he killed a woman in Selma [sic] and that they'd be reading about it." Later, Coleman and Snow put some boxes in Rowe's car and, opening the trunk, saw "carbines and guns." The two men immediately became potential witnesses in Robb's case.[36]

There was an even stranger document Robb had never seen before: a police report describing an event that had occurred on January 15, 1965. A policeman found Rowe lying unconscious on a Birmingham street, his current girlfriend nearby trying to revive him. When Officer Lester Robinson tried to pick him up and place him in the car, Rowe suddenly awoke and tried to attack him. Robinson thought Rowe was "demented" but was more troubled to learn that inside the trunk of Rowe's car were three rifles. The girlfriend just wanted to take Rowe home, and since he had broken no laws, Robinson let them go, but the policeman seized the guns. Six weeks later Rowe came to the police station to pick up his property. "Oh, man," Tony Liuzzo remarked. "That's the beginning of March." "Right in the beginning of March," Robb agreed, "they give him all those guns back."[37]

One question had "always bugged" John Andrews, and he asked it now: "What in the hell good did it do" to have an informant in the Klan unless you used that informant to *curtail* Klan activities rather than merely report on them? "I mean," Andrews continued, "are you keeping a tab, the Klan's killed 15 this month and . . . we know all about this because we've got a super informant in there telling us about the damn thing." What good, if any, informer Rowe may have done would also be examined at the trial.[38]

The government's preparation was also thorough, but its treatment of the Liuzzo family was harsh and at times abusive in the examinations of them during pretrial depositions. Since the Liuzzo children's lawsuit sought financial compensation for injuries caused by their mother's death, Justice Department attorneys Ann Robertson and Alan Mishael wanted to know just how they had been damaged. "You've asked for several million dollars," Robertson told Tony Liuzzo on November 30, 1982. "What are the reasons you want the money? What is it supposed to do?"

"To reconcile for our loss," Tony said.

"And what loss is that?" Robertson asked.

"For the loss of my mother, for the loss of her caring and nurturing and love, her knowledge and teaching, for the lost and vacant feeling that's in my life. . . . For the nightmares that I've lived, for the torment that my family has been put through . . . the fear of living with armed guards in our house for two years, from crosses being burned in our backyard, from being called a nigger lover over and over again. . . . To watch my father turn into an alcoholic and destroy himself. . . . To watch my brother go wild."[39]

Robertson was unmoved, and when Robb tried to stop her from continuing, she said to him, "We had a lot of questioning about what they would have done and what they would have been had their mother been alive; I think I have a right to make an inquiry." Then she offered a deal: If the Liuzzos dropped their claim, "then I'll cease and desist this inquiry immediately." Robb wouldn't accept such a deal.[40]

Tom Liuzzo agreed to be questioned but again refused to say where he lived and what he was doing. Attorney Robertson wanted to know whether the family's alleged differences regarding a settlement led to his breakdown. It was "nobody's business what went on," he replied.

"Unfortunately Mr. Liuzzo or Mr. Lee, I'm going to have to ask you to tell me," Robertson said. "Since you subjected yourself to the lawsuit . . . there is a certain amount of inquiry that has to be made. What were the circumstances surrounding your being involuntarily committed?"

Dean Robb objected again: "Is this conceivably relevant to the issues? . . . Isn't there any shame involved here?" he asked Robertson. "This is a matter of public record. You probably already have it in your file. Why drag him through it?"

"It don't bother me," Tom said before Robertson could respond.

"It bothers me!" his sisters Mary and Sally said as one.[41]

Robertson resumed her questioning, asking Tom how he had arrived at the $2 million figure. It was a symbol, Tom said, a "token . . . for wrongs done, . . . for damages inflicted and incurred."

"Compensation for what?" Robertson asked.

"Just the pain and anguish."

"Pain and anguish, anything else?" Robertson impatiently asked.

"Yeah, there's a lot else," Tom shot back.

"Tell me. . . . Give me some specifics."

"Specifically, her care as a mama, . . . She could have come back from Alabama and died any number of ways, but the fact is she didn't. She was murdered and that changed everything in my life from that point on."

"Or at least you think so," Robertson noted.[42]

Alan Mishael asked Mary Liuzzo Silverberg to explain specifically how she had allegedly suffered after her mother's death. Had her mother been alive, Mary believed, she would have received help when she became pregnant, would not have had the abortion and the complications that followed, and would now be able to have children. She also felt that her mother's death affected her ability to form lasting relationships. Finally, it had been devastating to watch her family disintegrate. Mary had always wanted to become a physician, which her mother had encouraged. "I believe I would have gotten back on the right track if she had been around," Mary said. "There just wasn't anybody."[43]

Both Penny Liuzzo Herrington and Sally Liuzzo Lauwers believed that if their mother had lived, they, too, would have gone to college and become "professional people." "She was the driving force," Penny said, always making sure they did their homework and attended school. Penny at least had many memories, but Sally, the youngest, had only a few. "How did your mother's death affect you?" Mishael asked her. "Well," Sally replied, her voice choking, "I never got to know what it was like to have a mother. That's about it. I never had a mother."[44]

The government also scrutinized the life of Viola Liuzzo, hoping to find in her psychological history evidence to prove that she had been responsible for her own death. Her psychiatrist, Dr. Abraham Elson, was subpoenaed and required to bring Liuzzo's files to the deposition. When Elson protested that this would violate professional ethics, as well as doctor-patient confidentiality, Justice Department attorney Alan Mishael snapped, "We're not here to listen to you . . . ventilate your views."

"I would like to just ask one simple question, if you would indulge me, sir," Elson said: What were the legal consequences if he declined to answer questions about his dead patient?

"And my simple answer is: I'm not going to give you legal advice," Mishael replied. "We'll move back to the original question: Did you . . . ever meet Viola Liuzzo?"[45]

Elson uncomfortably revealed Liuzzo's bouts of depression, family conflicts, and suicide attempt, which Mishael thought proved his theory: Viola Liuzzo had a "death wish" and deliberately went to Selma to be killed. Elson rejected this scenario. "She did not court danger," he told the attorney. She had "a zest for life and living and being the Queen of her family and having them admire her."

Mishael tried other routes to reach his goal. If Liuzzo didn't have a "death wish," was she, perhaps, "reckless or careless"? "Impulsive" was as far as the doctor would go, adding, "wanton recklessness wasn't her style."

Mishael tried again: If, as the doctor testified, Liuzzo craved affection and recognition, would she take a risk, if it created such feelings in her fellow civil rights workers? "If she felt a deep devotion to a cause [like] the Civil Rights Movement," Elson conceded, "I think it's possible." That was enough for Mishael.[46]

Attorney Jeff Long, representing the Liuzzos, sought clarification. "You're familiar with Abraham Lincoln, is that correct?" he asked Elson. The doctor was. And the doctor knew that President Lincoln had been assassinated at Ford's Theatre? Yes. Alan Mishael objected, calling the questioning "just . . . ridiculous." Long continued: Did Elson feel that "Lincoln was suicidal when he put himself in the position where someone could assassinate him at Ford's Theatre"? No, said the doctor.

Long was finished, but Mishael had one final question for the witness: "Were you the treating psychiatrist for Abraham Lincoln?"

"No, sir," Elson said.

"That's all," Mishael said, bringing the deposition to a close.[47]

Both sides were now ready for trial, which was scheduled to start on March 21, 1983, eighteen years to the day after the start of the Voting Rights March, which had ended four days later with the death of Viola Liuzzo.

CHAPTER FIFTEEN

A Search for the Truth

THE MANY TRIALS RELATED to Viola Liuzzo's death—five in all—
tracked, in reverse, her journey into history. First were the two trials of
Wilkins in Hayneville, then the federal trial in Montgomery; Hayneville
again when Thomas was acquitted; now Ann Arbor, Michigan, at the federal building, home of the FBI. An observer of the earlier trials would
have found *Liuzzo v. United States of America* stranger than the others.
The Klansmen once tried for murdering Viola Liuzzo and convicted for
violating her civil rights were now the Liuzzo family's allies against the
FBI, which presumably had solved the crime and apprehended the criminals. Gary Thomas Rowe, the FBI's top Klan informant and star witness
in the 1960s, was now, eighteen years later, the Bureau's bitter enemy.

This final trial was also ignored by the nation's media, which had lost
interest in the Liuzzos' quest for justice. The major networks and most
of the nation's top newspapers didn't cover it. The *New York Times* showed
an interest, but its daily accounts were relegated to the paper's back pages,
small articles lost between stories about labor negotiations and Jane Fonda's
health spa. It had become a local story reported only by Michigan's daily
papers.[1]

This time, it was also a trial without a jury. Because the family was
suing the government in a wrongful death lawsuit under the Federal Tort
Claims Act, a jury trial was barred; federal judge Charles Joiner alone would

consider the arguments and decide in favor of the plaintiffs or the defendants. Although the sixty-seven-year-old jurist had been appointed to the bench by President Richard Nixon in 1972 and was considered a conservative, his three earlier rulings encouraged Robb that they might win the suit. Joiner had dismissed the contention that the government could not be sued for negligence; he had rejected its motion that the statute of limitations for filing a suit had run out; and he also had granted Robb's request that the plaintiffs be allowed access to the Rowe task force report, over the objections of Ann Robertson. It therefore appeared that Judge Joiner would adjudicate the case with an open mind.[2]

In his opening statement, Dean Robb argued that the FBI knew Gary Thomas Rowe was "a violent, unstable man" in 1960 when it hired him to penetrate the Klan and that his career—from the attack on the Freedom Riders to the murder of Viola Liuzzo—indicated that he had become a rogue elephant, totally out of control. Given Rowe's violent temperament, FBI handler Neil Shanahan should not have allowed Rowe to accompany Wilkins, Thomas, and Eaton on their trip to Montgomery, a city on the verge of racial explosion. Or, having permitted him to go, Shanahan should have taken extraordinary measures to have Thomas's car watched by local police or the FBI. Therefore, the FBI was "careless and negligent" and contributed to Liuzzo's death.[3]

Ann Robertson painted a different Gary Thomas Rowe for the court: the informant whose primary job was not to protect Americans who put themselves at risk but to collect information that only he could obtain. "The informant business is a strange business," she said. "Sunday school teachers don't become informants. Informants are people who can get into the underbelly of society and report on it. Rowe had to appear tough to survive." She would prove that Rowe tried to stop the Klansmen from pursuing Liuzzo and, when that failed, just pretended to shoot while Wilkins fired the fatal shots. Furthermore, on the morning of March 25, 1965, when the Klansmen set out for Montgomery, there was no way for Shanahan to know that a murder might occur, and therefore the government should not be held responsible for failing to prevent it. Wilkins's and Thomas's charges were clearly tainted by their Klan connections; their revived memories were the product of hatred and the desire for revenge. The FBI had acted efficiently throughout the case, and were it not for Gary Thomas Rowe's information, the killers would have escaped justice entirely.[4]

The trial that followed conformed to these two strategies. To prove that Rowe killed Liuzzo, Robb first asked Eugene Thomas and Collie Leroy Wilkins to testify. Thomas agreed to appear in person, but Wilkins claimed to be too busy, so his testimony was videotaped. Within minutes of taking the stand, Thomas committed perjury. Asked whether the Klan had ever used violence to prevent integration, he said, "I haven't seen any, but I've heard—this would be hearsay—and I couldn't say." What about the violence against blacks at the Bessemer carnival in 1962? asked Robb's associate, Joseph Cotchett. All Thomas knew was what he had heard: There had been a "knock down drag out fight," but he wasn't there at the time. Attorney Robertson objected to hearsay testimony, and the judge told Cotchett to move on. (Cotchett couldn't bring up Thomas's statement to Robb that he had seen Rowe "hit a nigger," as that would have undermined the credibility of his own witness.) But Thomas did state that he saw Rowe beating a black man during the assault on the Freedom Riders and that, generally, Rowe was "capable of violence, I'll guarantee you on that."[5]

Rowe's violent nature showed itself best on March 25, 1965. Thomas claimed that Rowe urged him to follow the "cream of the crop"—the white woman with a black man. Rowe said he was going to shoot them, and Thomas heard the back window roll down and felt the wind on his neck. He saw Rowe using Thomas's own .38 to shoot and heard Eaton's .22, and when Liuzzo's car drifted off the highway Rowe said, "I got them . . . that was damn good shooting." Wilkins, sitting in his traditional spot behind Thomas, had no gun and said nothing during the chase and the shooting. Then they went on to Lorene's Cafe to set up their alibi and returned home.[6]

During Joseph Cotchett's questioning, Thomas tried to prove his veracity by stating that a Lowndes County jury had found him not guilty of Liuzzo's murder in 1966. He had passed three polygraph tests then and was more than willing to take a fourth if Judge Joiner ordered it. Was there any doubt in his mind where Rowe sat or who fired the shot? Cotchett asked in conclusion. "No, sir," Thomas said, "not in my mind."[7]

Collie Leroy Wilkins supported Thomas's version of events during his videotaped deposition. He testified that from his position in the left rear seat, he saw Rowe shoot Liuzzo "four or five times" with a .38 Smith and Wesson revolver. Wilkins's testimony "marked the first time in court that Rowe was identified positively as the triggerman," noted the Detroit News.[8]

On cross-examination, Ann Robertson tried to impeach Robb's witnesses by showing that their earlier statements about the murder contradicted what they were now saying. In his first statement to the FBI, Thomas claimed no knowledge of Liuzzo's shooting, but now he did. He also said that Rowe sat behind him, but now he claimed Wilkins did. How did he explain these differences? Robertson asked. Thomas didn't recall making those statements in 1965, but today, as a born-again Christian, he said, he was obligated to be truthful.

Wilkins had the same problem, Robertson showed. In 1965, after his acquittal, he told a Canadian journalist that he thought Moton had killed Liuzzo, but now he told a different story. Wilkins admitted that maybe he had said that, but he couldn't recall. Had Robertson examined Wilkins's interview with the Rowe task force, she would have found other inconsistencies: Wilkins said they never tried to establish an alibi, but Thomas now testified that they did. Thomas claimed that Rowe said, "That was damn good shooting"; Wilkins told the task force that Rowe never made that statement.⁹

Robertson also showed the judge that Thomas and Wilkins were not the mild-mannered "good ole boys" they appeared to be in their testimony. Wasn't it true, she asked Thomas, that when the FBI searched his house they found a bullwhip, an illegal sawed-off shotgun, a two-and-a-half-foot rusty chain, and a fifteen-inch metal hose? "Yes, ma'm," Thomas said, "that was there." And as far as Wilkins was concerned, she had him describe the time when he was eighteen that he shot a man in the stomach at the Bessemer Moose Lodge. It was clear that both men were capable of violence, including murder.¹⁰

Robertson also found it incredible that the men had waited so long to accuse Rowe of the murder. Thomas blamed his attorneys, saying that Matt Murphy and Arthur Hanes had advised him not to take the witness stand during Wilkins's trial or his own and, after he was convicted in federal court, to remain silent until he served his sentence. What if he had received a life sentence; would he have gone to his death in prison never telling that Rowe was the real killer? asked Robertson. The judge accused her of arguing with the witness, so Thomas never answered. When Wilkins was asked why it took him thirteen years before first telling his story on 20/20, he replied, "Well, . . . nobody had ever asked me." But that wasn't true, Robertson countered. Didn't he remember that before being sentenced in federal court, Judge Johnson had asked him whether he wished to make a statement and Wilkins had declined? "The bucket had done poured out," Wilkins told Robertson. "There wasn't nothing I could say to do any good." Robertson didn't believe him. "What did you do in that federal penitentiary for five years, 11 months and 18 days?" "Kept my mouth shut and minded my own business," he replied. "That's the onliest way to get by in one of them places."[11]

To prove that Wilkins's racism could drive him to the most violent act, Robertson questioned him about his attitudes toward blacks and the civil rights movement. "What would you call a black person?" she asked Wilkins.

"They're niggers. They always have been."

"You didn't believe that white people and black people should go to school together, did you?"

"No, ma'am."

"And you wouldn't go to the same bathroom."

"No, ma'am."

"Tell us a little about your philosophy concerning the mixing of races . . . in 1965."

"I don't believe that it is right for the races to mix. They've always been separated."

Everything was quiet in the South until the outside agitators arrived, Wilkins claimed. "We didn't have any trouble until they come down here and started all this rabble-rousing."

So then Viola Liuzzo "got what she deserved?" Robertson asked.

"I think so," Wilkins said.[12]

Still hoping to prove that Rowe killed Liuzzo, Robb called three more witnesses to support his case. Highway Patrolman James Hagood, who had testified at the other trials, recounted again how he stopped Thomas's automobile and cited him for having a noisy muffler. He still thought that the youngest man in the car, Wilkins, sat on the left side behind the driver, but, as he acknowledged on cross-examination, he wasn't sure. Lavaughn Coleman and Henry Snow had more positive evidence—their claim that Rowe told them he killed Liuzzo. Both men repeated the testimony they gave to the Lowndes County grand jury that had indicted Rowe in 1978. Coleman also said that he had another meeting with Rowe where he repeated his story, this time adding that the men he was with had wanted to kill a police officer, and to prevent it Rowe had to shoot a "whore."

Robertson undermined Coleman's testimony by asking about specific dates and times, to which he often replied, "Ma'am, I don't even remember the year, let alone the day." Indeed, over the years, Coleman gave vague and contradictory testimony about these meetings: To Birmingham investigators in 1975 and 1976 and to the grand jury in 1978, he mentioned meeting Rowe only once, at a motel. Asked during the 1976 interview what Rowe said, Coleman replied: "I don't remember exactly what he said. . . . I really don't." But in 1983, he remembered perfectly. Now he suddenly claimed that there was a second meeting at Rowe's apartment early on the morning of March 26, 1965. Although Snow testified that he was with Coleman and Rowe at that time, it's unlikely this meeting occurred. At six o'clock that morning, FBI agents were interviewing Rowe, and he spent most of the day with them until he appeared at his arraignment late in the afternoon. Why would Snow and Coleman lie? Coleman was said to be "the Klan's biggest supporter" on the Birmingham police force (Rowe claimed he was an actual card-carrying member), and Snow admitted that he once applied for Klan membership, and although he wasn't invited to join he generally shared their views. Their attempt to damage Rowe may have been influenced by these associations.[13]

To counter Robb's contention that Rowe killed Liuzzo, Robertson relied on the testimony of the Justice Department officials who were in charge of the case in 1965. James P. Turner, a trial attorney with the Civil Rights Division, said that he interviewed Rowe extensively in the days after the shooting, and once his investigation was completed, he concluded that Rowe "had not violated any federal law." John Doar, who prosecuted the Klansmen in the civil rights trial, told the court that he had made the original decision to grant Rowe immunity only after he, too, was convinced that the informant "had not committed a crime." St. John Barrett, another Civil Rights Division trial attorney, testified that he interrogated Rowe for five hours on April 1, 1965, and felt that Rowe was not just innocent but actually had tried to prevent the shooting by telling Thomas, "Let's go back to Selma and get another one" and "if we're going to do anything at all, we ought to whip their ass and let the whole world see them." Unfortunately, for Thomas a flogging was insufficient; he wanted "to go all the way."[14]

If Robb was unable to persuade the judge that Rowe killed Liuzzo, as was now becoming apparent, he had a "fall-back position." He and his team would amass enough evidence to show that Rowe was emotionally unstable, a "violence junkie" who should never have been allowed to go to Montgomery that day without special FBI surveillance. The sight of happy demonstrators, blacks and whites together, marching and singing, would, as happened, provoke the Klansmen into committing some heinous act. The FBI should have anticipated this, and its failure to do so would prove negligence.[15]

One witness who could reveal Rowe's emotional state two months before the shooting was former Birmingham police officer Lester Robinson, whom Robb first learned about during his trip south. Through a videotaped deposition, Robinson took the court back to January 15, 1965, when he was a twenty-three-year-old patrolman assigned to the canine unit. While patrolling in Avondale that night, he saw a man lying on the ground, a woman nervously walking around him. He pulled over. The man was obviously no derelict; he was "heavy set, neatly dressed." He later said his name was Thomas Rowe. He appeared almost comatose; when Robinson shook him or asked questions, he didn't respond. The woman told Robinson that he had been "acting strange all night." Should he call an ambulance? Robinson asked. No, the woman said. If the officer could just get him into their nearby car, she would drive him home and put him to bed. Robinson was six feet two inches tall and weighed more than two hundred pounds, so he didn't hesitate to lift up Rowe. As he tried to put him in the car, however, Rowe awoke and "came up fighting." Robinson backed away, and for a few minutes, there was a "standoff."

Robinson was armed and this seemed to make Rowe madder. If he pulled the gun, Rowe said, "he was going to make [Robinson] eat it." A crowd was beginning to surround them, and one man asked the officer if he could help. Just open my car door and let the dog out, Robinson told him. He did and a large German shepherd bounded out and "heeled" to Robinson's right side. "If you sic that dog on me, I'll kill him," Rowe supposedly said. "You ain't going to kill my dog," Robinson told him, and despite Rowe's bluster, he began to calm down. Sergeant Guy arrived at the scene and the two policemen and the woman discussed what to do. They could arrest Rowe for disorderly conduct, but he seemed "more sick" than a threat to anyone. The "girl volunteered to take him on home," Robinson testified, "but . . . she was a little bit scared of him" and was worried about Rowe's weapons. What weapons? Robinson asked, and she took them to the back of the car, opened the trunk, and pointed to three M-1 carbines.

Robinson was familiar with carbines; he had carried one during the 1963 riots that followed the bombings. Rowe said that the weapons belonged to him and "there was nothing wrong with them." But the officers took the weapons anyway, telling Rowe that he could pick them up when he was feeling better, and allowed Rowe and his friend to leave.[16]

"Did you form an opinion as to his mental stability . . . [when] you had this encounter with him?" Robb asked Robinson. "Anybody that comes up fighting me . . . was nuts," he replied. Robinson had used the word "demented" in his report, Robb said, so he asked him to explain what he meant. "To me, demented means that a person is . . . crazy, not within control of his faculties. . . . I felt he was extremely unstable."[17]

Ann Robertson, on cross-examination, tried to blame Robinson for the confrontation that occurred. Rowe was simply lying in the street, unconscious: "Was he breaking any law?" she asked. "No, ma'm," Robinson replied. Then, when the officer moved Rowe, he awoke "in the arms of a stranger," surprised and probably frightened, so there was nothing especially unusual about that, wouldn't he agree? Robinson didn't: "Surprise could be a word. Violent could be another one." But the officers didn't arrest Rowe; he broke no laws, was sent home, and later picked up his guns? Correct, Robinson said. Attorney Robertson couldn't resist one final parting shot. Since Robinson was in Birmingham's canine corps, had he ever been in Kelly Ingram Park, where black demonstrators had been attacked by vicious police dogs in 1963? No, he'd never been there, Robinson said, a bit annoyed. In 1963, he was a motorcycle patrolman and didn't have anything to do with dogs at that time.[18]

The man who could best describe Rowe's penchant for violence was Rowe himself, so Robb asked him to testify in person. Rowe declined. All his public appearances had left him "battered and beat up," but he did agree to a videotaped deposition, which took more than twenty hours to record over three days. Robb showed it to the court after Robinson testified. Rowe was now fifty-two, his red hair flecked with gray. He was a bit more portly and less energetic, but he had lost none of his talent for colorful storytelling. Robb was hoping to hear about the happy hell-raiser. Instead, the Tommy Rowe who testified resembled his cinematic counterpart: the mild-mannered family man who joined the Klan as an undercover man at the behest of "God," in this case the FBI. He described how he ingratiated himself with his colleagues, having beers with them after meetings to just "bullshit around," until he entered the inner circle where the missionary work was planned.[19]

In every incident during his five-year career, he tried to prevent violence, and when he was forced to participate, he did so reluctantly and only in self-defense. Yes, he put that pillowcase over old man Forman's head, but only because Bill Holt had said, "Let's kill him here." He knew he could "save that man's life" if he could just get him away from the others and into his car. But then Mrs. Forman appeared, blasting away with her pistol, and it was every man for himself. Yes, he reported the plans to attack the Freedom Riders to the FBI, warning Agent Kemp that "there was going to be beatings, bombings, murders." But his contact agent assured him this would never happen: the U.S. marshals and the Eighty-second Airborne would come to the rescue. When they didn't, Rowe was enraged: "You let me down," he recalled telling Kemp. "I almost died. . . . There were people killed all over the damn place. I can't believe you let all those people get hurt." He quit, vowing never again to work "for the goddamn Bureau." But Kemp explained that the FBI was just an investigative agency, not a police force, and they desperately needed his help. So he stayed on, because he "believed in the Bureau . . . believed in justice . . . believed in the American citizen," while Kemp resigned to pursue his personal ambitions.[20]

Robb asked him about the beatings at the Krystal Kitchen. He had defended himself against violent Negroes, he said. The Bessemer carnival? "In my mind I said, 'I can avert this.' I tried to stop that from happening." The Gaston Motel bombing? "I didn't bomb any motel." The Center Street shrapnel bombing? "I didn't set that bomb." The Sixteenth Street Baptist Church bombing? "I was never involved in any bombings," and he solved that case by telling the FBI he saw Chambliss and Blanton hanging around the church two nights before the bombing. He always kept the FBI fully informed of everything he learned and everything he did and "was never reprimanded for wrongdoing." In the days before the Voting Rights March, he alerted the Bureau to the Klan's plan to drop grenades on the marchers, along with the arms transfer in Selma, but nobody seemed to take his warnings seriously.[21]

On the morning of March 25, 1965, Robert Thomas told him he "would be doing something for the Klan [he] would always remember for the rest of his life." Neil Shanahan told him to go; if Shanahan had said don't go, "Jesus Christ would have had a hard time getting me to go there." When they saw the white woman and her black passenger, he never dreamed there would be a shooting, a flogging perhaps, but nothing more serious. "It all happened so fast": Wilkins picking up Thomas's gun and shooting over and over again. The woman turned toward them, he claimed: "I don't care what the whole damn world says, I saw it." The black man was hit, too; he saw him slump down. He wanted to stop it, order them at gunpoint to pull over; "that's the truth, . . . but my whole system told me, if you do, you're going to die right here tonight."[22]

After Thomas turned back and Wilkins left the car to check his victims, they headed for Bessemer, stopping first at a filling station where the other Klansmen bought Cokes and cigarettes and used the bathroom. He stayed in the car, sat there, "perplexed as hell . . . emotionally upset . . . my damn heart was bursting. I just seen a man kill a woman. . . . My better reasoning told me, try to get to town. I knew I was going to tell Neil the very second I could get to him."[23]

Robb hammered away at the contradictions between Rowe's earlier statements and his current testimony, but Rowe wouldn't give an inch: "I'm telling you what transpired then." Nor would he admit that he was mistaken about the black passenger: "I've told the government at that moment and I'm telling the world today, I did not see Leroy Moton in that automobile. I saw a middle-aged, mature man, well dressed."[24]

What about 20/20's polygraph, which showed that on these questions, Rowe wasn't being truthful? Robb asked. Rowe insisted that he had actually passed all the tests: His charts were "as smooth as glass." Anything to the contrary might be explained by something he learned shortly afterward —he was a diabetic with high blood pressure, and that accounted for faulty readings. Would he take another test now? Robb asked. He would be "very happy" to be tested again. "Take Gene Thomas, take Collie Leroy Wilkins and myself, run us through the polygraph, same examiner, have an unbiased party . . . a priest, a rabbi, preacher, somebody that we feel we can respect. Put us in a known institution, a hospital someplace, videotape the whole thing, put us under truth serum and let the whole world know. I'd do that in a heartbeat."[25]

Rowe's testimony was so favorable to the government that Ann Robertson didn't try impeaching him. Instead, she added to the self-portrait that Rowe had painted. She had Rowe describe how Thomas drove around Brown Chapel on March 25, looking for an integrated couple to attack.

When he found one, Rowe quickly pointed to a National Guard jeep nearby, which caused Thomas to pull away, saving the couple from a beating. "During your informant years with the Klan, did you frequently do things like that?" Robertson asked. "Yes, ma'am, every opportunity I could," Rowe replied. Robertson listed other times that Rowe prevented violence: informing the Bureau that the armed Klansmen were going to Tuscaloosa, and the incident at the Tutweiler Hotel when he saved Agent Blake's life. And wasn't it also true that after the shooting on March 25, Rowe immediately contacted Agent Shanahan, met with him for hours describing every detail of what had occurred, voluntarily turned over his gun, and later took the agents on a tour of the route the Klansmen drove the night before?

"That's correct," Rowe said.

"And you told the truth concerning who shot Mrs. Liuzzo?"

"Yes, ma'am, with all my heart, I did."[26]

If Rowe seemed less a murderer now (although Robb still believed he had killed Liuzzo), his testimony helped the second part of the Liuzzos' case—the FBI's failure to adequately alert authorities on March 25 that a group of dangerous Klansmen were going to Montgomery. Just how dangerous was brought out in Rowe's testimony about his three Klan colleagues. William Orville Eaton, he said, was "a pretty sick man," suffering from a heart condition the doctors thought terminal. Believing he only had a short time to live, his greatest desire, Rowe said, "was to kill a nigger before he died." Eugene Thomas was a "hard core redneck Klansman" whom Rowe saw beating Negroes at the Bessemer carnival. Lee Wilkins was "a strong, powerful young man . . . kind of dense, a little slow but very dedicated to the Klan." Putting these men together in an automobile heading to the Voting Rights March was like throwing "a torch in an open pail of gasoline," Robb believed. Yet Neil Shanahan, in composing his telegram that morning, had failed to alert the appropriate federal, state, and city officials that the Klansmen were "armed and dangerous."[27]

Shanahan also made a mistake four days earlier that added weight to Robb's case. On the night of March 21, Rowe told him that during his trip to Montgomery with Robert Thomas, they stopped in Selma where a cache of arms and landmines was transferred from one Klan group to another. Shanahan, who had spent the day running around Birmingham defusing bombs in the GREENBOMBS case, was exhausted and preoccupied and let several days pass before informing Washington and the Mobile field office.

For that oversight, he had received a "letter of censure" from J. Edgar Hoover.

To support his position, Robb asked Highway Patrolman James Hagood what would have happened if he had known that the car he stopped for a noisy muffler contained four dangerous Klansmen. He would have checked the men for guns, he testified, and if he learned they had no permits, they would have been arrested. If the permits were valid, he still would have contacted his supervisor before letting them depart. William R. Jones, head of Alabama's Investigative Division in 1965, told the court that he would have acted in a similar fashion. News that "Klukers" with guns were in his area was always a matter of great concern, and he would have ordered his men to locate and determine whether the Klansmen were armed and their permits were in order. On cross-examination, Ann Robertson partly undermined Robb's contention by having both former police officers acknowledge that, if the gun permits had been good, they would have sent the Klansmen on their way. Had they done otherwise, Robertson noted, Hagood and Jones would have violated the Klansmen's civil rights and be lawbreakers themselves. Nevertheless, Robb was hopeful that when the judge saw all the events in concert—the Klan's discussion on March 19 of a new strategy of using one or two men to lob grenades at demonstrators, the arms transfer on March 21, and word of the Klansmen's impending visit to observe the marchers—he would surely consider both of Shanahan's failures as solid evidence of FBI negligence.[28]

Neil Shanahan became Robb's chief target. Two months earlier, he had been deposed for four days, his testimony filling four long volumes. He felt the case against the FBI was groundless and that the Liuzzo lawyers, interested only in money, had persuaded the grieving family to bring suit. On the second day of testimony, Shanahan lost his temper and lashed out at Robb and his colleague Eleanor Langer. "I'm really getting upset," he said, "and . . . I'm tired of getting jerked around. . . . I object to the tone and tenor of the questions, and the innuendo." He had tried to make them understand how difficult it was being an informant. Rowe had infiltrated a dangerous group of terrorists to collect information for the FBI but was told never to start or participate in violent activities. Collecting information came first. Rowe was not expected to be "a peacemaker in the Ku Klux Klan." But to protect his cover and, more important, to become part of the inner circle where a small group of Klansmen hatched their plots, he might have to commit the very violence he had been ordered to avoid. "Many, many times I told him I did not want him participating in violent or illegal activities," Shanahan said, "knowing full well that the time would come when maybe he would be in a situation where he couldn't control it. . . . Life is a contradiction, and a trade-off. It's a very, very difficult problem and I'm not sure there is any resolution to it."[29]

On March 25, 1983, the eighteenth anniversary of Viola Liuzzo's murder, Shanahan was called to the stand to defend himself against the charge that he had mishandled his informant. Regarding the censure, he admitted to making a mistake but argued that there were extenuating circumstances. When he received the report of the arms transfer, he was involved in the GREENBOMBS case, and then, a few days later, the shooting occurred and he was responsible for making sure that Rowe provided a full account and that it could be verified. It was a matter of priorities, he claimed. His so-called failure to alert the authorities that the visiting Klansmen were armed and dangerous was also misunderstood. Those words were usually used by agents in cases where indicted fugitives were on the run or a crime had been committed and the suspect was about to be arrested. Neither was true in the case of Rowe and his colleagues.[30]

Those two incidents were symptomatic of a greater problem, Robb and his colleagues argued in response to Shanahan's testimony. Just how well did Shanahan know Tommy Rowe? The attorneys noted that Birmingham was only Shanahan's second assignment as a young FBI agent and he had received no formal training on the handling of racial informants like Rowe. Shanahan had reviewed Rowe's file before taking him on in 1964 but admitted to knowing little about his past activities. Yes, he knew that Rowe had been involved in the assaults on Orman Forman and the Freedom Riders but had never asked for details. He knew that Rowe had been near the Center Street bombings but accepted his story of just being in the neighborhood when the bombs went off. Was it not significant that Headquarters ordered Rowe to resign as head of the Klavern's Action Squad in 1964? Joseph Cotchett asked. Didn't this mean that J. Edgar Hoover himself feared that Rowe might have crossed the line and become a creator of the violence he was supposed to just observe? Shanahan rejected this interpretation of Hoover's order. The Bureau didn't want Rowe to be in a policymaking position where he was responsible for developing violent plans; instead, he should be a "passive member . . . of an Action

Squad who could be right [close] to the action, and not participate in it, and report on everybody else who did." But Shanahan did admit that being passive in an Action Squad would be "a rather difficult position to be in."[31]

Wasn't Shanahan also concerned about reports from other informants that Rowe beat blacks at a baseball game, or was thought to be demented by a Birmingham police officer, or just a few days before the Liuzzo killing was seen fighting with a man—they pulled guns on each other—whose wife Rowe was not-so-secretly courting? Weren't these signs that Rowe was emotionally unstable? Again, Shanahan disagreed with that conclusion. All those events occurred during Rowe's spare time and had nothing to do with his work for the Bureau. In fact, Shanahan didn't want to know about Rowe's personal life—his marital or financial problems, his habit of getting into fights. None of it was significant, he argued, because Rowe was never arrested for committing a crime. It seemed more serious to Robb: Who really dominated the informant-agent relationship, Rowe or Shanahan? If Rowe was allowed to do what he wanted, then of course, there was no need to worry about his visit to Montgomery, no need to warn others that the Klansmen were coming. If this wasn't negligence, Robb didn't know what was.

Ann Robertson must have thought Robb's argument threatening because she called upon two of the FBI's most experienced agents to destroy it: Joseph Sullivan and James L. McGovern, who together had supervised the investigation of the Liuzzo murder. McGovern had recommended that Shanahan be censured, but now he called it "a dark day in my life" and didn't consider Shanahan's dereliction "a major event." Indeed, it was less important than Shanahan's "superb" handling of Rowe from their midnight talk to Rowe's testimony in the successful federal trial. Nor did he see any need for Shanahan to add "armed and dangerous" to the March 25 communiqué. McGovern had reviewed "thousands of communications on Klan matters, internal security matters, [and] domestic intelligence matters" during his twenty-five years with the FBI and couldn't remember "an instance in which that cautionary statement appeared." But he, too, admitted that he didn't know Rowe very well, except for the time he spent with him before the federal trial. In an earlier deposition, hadn't McGovern said, "I defy anyone to control [Gary Thomas Rowe]?" Cotchett asked. What he really meant, McGovern said, was total, absolute control, around the clock; that would have been impossible. Had anyone suggested to him that he should elaborate on that original answer? Cotchett asked. Yes, McGovern admitted, the government's attorneys.[32]

Joseph Sullivan, famed within the Bureau for solving the case of three civil rights workers murdered by the Klan in Mississippi in 1964, also felt Shanahan had acted appropriately. In fact, he thought it would have been a "serious mistake" to add "armed and dangerous" to the teletype; Klansmen observing civil rights demonstrations was a common occurrence during those years.

Since Sullivan was responsible for coordinating the massive effort to protect the marchers in 1965, didn't he feel "sad" that an FBI informant was in the "murder car"? Robb asked. Sullivan did regret that a woman had died, but he had no reservations about Rowe's presence. There was no way that he could have predicted what happened, he claimed.

Robb disagreed: The Bureau had gone to great lengths to monitor the activities of Klansmen and other dangerous racists. At the Klancade on March 21, agents recorded license plate numbers and took photographs of participants. When FBI agents in South Carolina learned that Grand Dragon Robert Scoggins was coming to Alabama, they immediately notified the authorities, using the words "armed and dangerous." When hate monger Jesse B. Stoner, who once proclaimed "I think we ought to kill all Jews," showed up, agents kept him under surveillance. (Robb might well have added the Bureau's presence after the Sixteenth Street Baptist Church bombing, when agents followed the suspects' every move.) Shouldn't Shanahan, knowing how dangerous Thomas and Wilkins were, have done more than send a vague announcement? Wasn't it a massive failure for the FBI to have permitted Thomas's car to slip through their net?[33]

"It would have been very difficult to have prevented the chain of events that actually transpired," Sullivan continued to insist.

For the first time during the trial, Robb lost his temper: "Sir, would it have been difficult . . . when you knew before they even got out of their garage that they were coming, for the Federal Bureau of Investigation . . . to have not kept that car under surveillance . . . ? Forget about stopping them, just let the [FBI] be there . . . so they wouldn't go tearing down the road at 100 miles per hour shooting up the Liuzzo car, would that have been difficult?"

Sullivan paused, searching for a correct response. Finally he said,

"You're talking about a set of facts I didn't have any control over. . . . So, I don't think I should answer your question."

But Robb wouldn't let Sullivan escape so easily: "It would have been a piece of cake . . . to prevent the Thomas car and its occupants [from going] through that whole area, all day; go to Selma, drive around; stop at a bar; go around by the church where all the people were celebrating; go back down the main streets of Selma. . . . For them to be able to do that, do you think that is using reasonable care?"

Sullivan fell back on the explanation that the Bureau often used when it failed to take action: There was no law that would allow them to stop the Klansmen. "Until they committed some overt lawless act, we were in no position to interfere with the freedom of these people."

"Surveillance, letting them know you're watching them, tracing them like you did [at the Klancade], taking pictures . . . letting them know you're there, you could do that."

It was being done in Montgomery, Sullivan insisted, along the marchers' route.

"But you're not dealing with the issue of Thomas's car," Robb said, his voice rising. "You didn't find it. Correct?"

"Correct."

"And it slipped through?"

Ann Robertson objected but the judge let Robb continue.

"Slipped through what?" Sullivan asked.

"Slipped through all the security people—"

"Slipped through to what?" Sullivan repeated. "Mrs. Liuzzo wasn't a civil rights principal. She wasn't in the parade scene, in the march area . . . I didn't know she was there."[34]

But he could have known that Thomas, Eaton, Rowe, and Wilkins were there if Shanahan had provided a fuller, more detailed alert or called for surveillance. Among all the government forces amassed that day, U.S. marshals, National Guardsmen, army personnel, and seventy FBI agents, the Bureau could have spared one car to follow Thomas. If Shanahan had not been so exhausted by the GREENBOMBS crisis or so accustomed to hearing the Klan's angry rhetoric and mostly empty threats, Viola Liuzzo's life might have been saved.[35]

Two days after Robb's confrontation with Joseph Sullivan, a new and unexpected crisis developed. It came in the person of a tiny woman named Flossie Louise Creel, Eugene Thomas's ex-wife. She had watched with interest Thomas's interviews with the *Birmingham Post-Herald* and Lori Denard of television station WBCR before his leaving for Ann Arbor. Thomas praised the Lord and asserted that Rowe was the real killer. "I think Rowe ought to pay for what he's done," he said. "I want my name cleared. When President Johnson got up on television, he told the whole world we was guilty. I want to prove to the whole world—that's the reason I went on 20/20 television; that's the reason I've gone through all these trials, to tell the truth about this thing. I'm a Christian and I don't want people to think I'm lying."[36]

Flossie Louise Creel was delighted that her ex-husband had become a born-again Christian but was troubled by his continuing attacks on Rowe. She looked back on their twenty-seven-year marriage with little pleasure. There were the "terrible times" when Thomas drank heavily and enjoyed beating her. She had him arrested three times for assault and battery but later dropped the charges. After an especially severe beating in 1956, she fled with their two sons and filed for divorce. But she returned to their small house in Bessemer a few months later and withdrew the suit. In 1957, over her opposition, Thomas joined the Klan and soon rose to the second highest position in the state organization, quite an achievement for the thirty-five-year-old high school dropout. "I begged him to get out of it," she said later. "I tried to get him to stop because I knew sooner or later that he would get in trouble but he wouldn't listen to me." So for the next ten years she was a good Klansman's wife, attending a few pleasant social functions, but she warned Thomas never to tell her what he was doing. "They would come in and get the bullwhip and leave," she said. "I never asked him anything."[37]

Trouble finally came in March 1965, but she stuck with him despite the "shame" and "embarrassment" she felt and the late-night phone calls that threatened her children. Three years after Thomas entered prison, she filed for divorce, got a job, and later remarried. When Thomas returned to Bessemer in late 1975, she met with him occasionally at his aunt's home —neutral ground—where they discussed ways to help their eldest son, who had been convicted of rape and faced a twenty-year jail sentence. Now Thomas was back in the news, on television, and about to testify again in another trial. She was shocked: "My goodness, I got to do something about this," she later said. "I can't stand it any longer. I thought he would straighten up. I decided I was going to tell this now, whether it does any good or not." She phoned Margy Searcy, Dean Robb's local associate, who had recently interviewed her, but she wasn't there. She tried Channel Six's Lori Denard, too, but Denard didn't return her call. Finally, on March 25, 1983, she contacted the FBI's Birmingham field office, which sent two agents to interview her. Attorneys Robertson and Mishael were told, and a few days later, she was flown to Michigan to testify in court as a government witness.[38]

The press called her "a surprise witness" when she took the stand on Wednesday, March 30, eight days after Thomas described how Rowe had murdered Viola Liuzzo. Ann Robertson identified her for the court and then went right to the heart of the matter: "Directing your attention to March and April 1965, did something happen between you and your husband?"

"Yes, ma'am," Creel said. She had just entered her home after taking her youngest son to school when Thomas yelled to her to come to the bedroom. She found him lying on the bed, "propped up on his elbow, smoking a cigarette." There were tears streaming down his face, a shocking sight because she had never seen him cry in the thirty years she had known him. He asked her to sit down on the bed. "I want to talk to you," he said. "This is a terrible thing we've done."

"What do you mean?" she recalled saying. "Did you do it?"

"No, I didn't do it," Thomas said. "Collie Wilkins did it and did it with my gun, but I told him to do it, and I'm as guilty as he is."

"That is the words that he said," Creel told the court.

Anticipating Robb's first question on cross-examination, Robertson asked why it took her so long to tell this story. "Lots of reasons," she said. First, she knew that a wife couldn't testify against her husband, so that explained her silence during the early trials. After his 1965 civil rights conviction, she needed to create a new life for herself and her sons. "I tried to hide," she said. "I was scared of him—threatened and beaten so many times. . . . The reason I come forth here at last now, . . . I have got a divorce and remarried, I don't have to live with him anymore, don't have to depend on him." She, too, was a born-again Christian and couldn't stand his lies: "I don't believe in using a lie to win a case, . . . and in my heart I know he's lying. . . . I can't stand the embarrassment, I don't want that on my children and decided that I'm going to tell this now whether it does any good or not."[39]

Did she ever hear Thomas say that he wanted "to get even with Mr. Gary Thomas Rowe?" Robertson asked.

Yes. She recalled a conversation with her ex-husband in 1978 when Rowe was facing extradition to Alabama. Thomas said, "You know, all the time while I was in prison, I had made up in my mind that I would get even with Rowe myself. But, the courts can handle it and do a better job." That was proof to her that Thomas still had "vengeance in his heart, and he's determined to get even."[40]

Robb moved quickly to counteract this serious blow. Didn't she still feel "a lot of anger" against Gene Thomas? he asked. "He beat you, mistreated you, and put the Klan before you . . . and your children." Yes, she once had those feelings, she said, "hard feelings," but that was in the past and she now forgave him. "I'm a born-again Christian . . . I don't have any [anger]."

Robb increased the pressure. When Thomas lied on 20/20, did she call ABC? "No, I didn't." When Rowe was indicted for first-degree murder in 1978, did she contact the Alabama authorities? "No, I didn't." And, wasn't it also true that he and his associate Margy Searcy had just interviewed her and she said nothing about Thomas's confession? "No, I didn't." The reason for this sudden recall of a conversation eighteen years old was her "anger," Robb insisted, "your pent up anger for all the mistreatment and the jealousy and the beatings . . . [anger] is coming out right now, isn't it?"

"No, sir," Flossie Louise Creel said softly. Robb had no further questions, so the witness was excused.[41]

Despite this setback, Robb was still confident as the trial ended, and he and his colleagues prepared the plaintiff's final summation. It would consist of three parts, he told Judge Joiner on the morning of April 1, 1983. He would focus on "the real Tommy Rowe, what he was asked to do, and what he did do," as well as describe what the FBI claimed was "the proper role of an informant," and show how Rowe had violated it. His colleagues Joseph Cotchett and Grant Gruel would deal with the legal questions under the Federal Tort Claims Act—the FBI's liability, the theory of "concerted action," and causation. Robb began by stating that they were not "trying the FBI" or testing whether it is "legal or proper to have informants."

Theirs was "a simple negligence case": whether the government, "in taking control of and handling Gary Thomas Rowe was reasonable, under all the circumstances." The judge himself had posed the fundamental issue: "Somewhere along the line, it's wrong for the government to hire someone that it knows is going to cause all kinds of damages without paying for it later."[42]

The FBI's own records, its history of Rowe's years as an informant, lead to one inescapable finding, Robb told the judge: "that Tommy Rowe was an unstable, violent, pugilistic racist, an unguided missile, a violence junkie," a person by character and temperament unsuited to be an informant. Indeed, he didn't become a traditional informant, the kind defined by the FBI, the observer and reporter, who avoids violence. He became instead an "undercover agent," always at the center of Klan violence, uncontrolled by the FBI. He then recounted that history—the attacks on Orman Forman, the Freedom Riders, the black diners at the Krystal Kitchen, and all the rest—culminating in the murder of Viola Liuzzo.

Robb also noted how often Rowe had changed his account of that event. At first, Rowe barely mentioned Liuzzo's black passenger to Shanahan and his other interviewers; then he never stopped talking about him, the heavy-set, middle-aged man in a green checked coat and a Russian hat, whom he saw die with his own eyes. At first, during the state and federal trials, Rowe said they proceeded straight on to Montgomery after the shooting. Then to the Church Committee, the Rowe task force, to this court in deposition, he said they returned to the scene of the crime so Wilkins could make sure the victims were dead. Such contradictions, Robb claimed, were evidence of guilt, a "preponderance of evidence," proving that Rowe killed Viola Liuzzo.

"The government's agents could control his activities," Robb said in conclusion, "but they could not suppress his genius for mayhem. . . . It became only a matter of time before the partnership between the Klan and Gary Thomas Rowe, acting under the sponsorship of the Bureau, brought tragedy into the lives of innocent people. Not only the Liuzzo family, but an entire nation looks now to the government for an acknowledgment of that error. . . . But the government, still, is unwilling to admit it. Your Honor, we ask that you speak for the government on this matter."[43]

Joseph Cotchett and Grant Gruel followed, arguing that the government was negligent in its handling and control of Rowe, whose actions, "in concert" with Eaton, Thomas, and Wilkins, led to the death of Viola Liuzzo. Then, Ann Robertson addressed the court. "The evidence is abundantly clear," she said, "that the plaintiffs have failed, totally, to convince this court or anyone else that Gary Thomas Rowe pulled the trigger that killed Viola Liuzzo." Under the plaintiff's theory, the court was expected to believe that Collie Leroy Wilkins, a symbol of Klan "lunacy," who, in 1964, fired his sawed-off shotgun at black demonstrators trying to integrate bathrooms, sat in Gene Thomas's car "doing nothing" as the attack occurred. And then he waited thirteen years before telling the world that another man had actually committed the crime for which he went to prison. "The evidence is abundantly clear," Robertson said, "that Collie Leroy Wilkins is a murderer and . . . a liar."[44]

The court was also expected to believe Thomas when he stated that Rowe sat in the right rear seat and shot Viola Liuzzo, when not twenty-four hours after the murder he told the FBI that Wilkins sat there, she said. Thomas, a "forty-year-old man who runs around with nineteen-year-old kids . . . under cover of night . . . and beat[s] his wife," came before this court and "perjured himself." He lied, and not just once, according to the testimony of his ex-wife, to whom he confessed his guilt and that of Wilkins. Thomas's testimony was "totally unpersuasive, totally incredible."

Gary Thomas Rowe was the real injured party. The FBI's top informant "avoided participation wherever possible" and neither encouraged nor joined the others, who "ran around together; got into mischief; got bull-whips out" and, acting "in concert," committed violence on March 25, 1965. Although Robertson didn't say it, she implied that Rowe was the real hero that day. Admittedly, some of Rowe's testimony was inconsistent, "muddled." But that was understandable given the passage of time and the traumas Rowe experienced—"his cover was burned . . . he's completely jerked up out of his environment and . . . put entirely in a new life." Still, he did his job, informing on men who otherwise would never have been punished for any crime. The government had acted reasonably and with care. The plaintiffs, she concluded, had failed "in their burden of proof on any of these counts."[45]

Judge Joiner thanked them and expressed gratitude for their hard work. He hoped to render a decision on federal liability "as rapidly as I can."[46]

Now the waiting began. Robb felt so optimistic about the outcome that he drafted a two-page victory statement to distribute to the press.

Tony Liuzzo and his attorney Dean Robb leave a Michigan courtroom April 1, 1983, after the conclusion of *Liuzzo v. United States of America*. (UPI-Bettmann/Corbis)

When thirty days passed without a decision, the Liuzzos grew nervous but remained hopeful: "We beat the pants off them," Tony thought, expecting good news. Another week went by, and then another. Finally, on Thursday, May 26, Robb was notified that the judge had reached a decision and should bring his clients to court the next morning to receive it. That morning, Tony put on his "good luck charms," his father's worn cardigan sweater and a silver and turquoise ring that belonged to Dean Robb, and drove to Ann Arbor.[47]

At 9:00 a.m., in a conference room of the federal building, Judge Joiner's clerk gave copies of the sixteen-page decision first to the attorneys, then to Tony and Sally Liuzzo. Tony could see the stricken look on Robb's face and broke into tears. The judge ruled against them in the strongest way possible, rejecting every facet of their case. Rowe was not a "violent, dangerous man," but a model public servant—"perhaps the best informer" in the South. Joiner accepted the government's interpretation of events: Rowe did not murder Liuzzo, nor did he aid or encourage others to do so: "Collie Leroy Wilkins shot her and . . . he was encouraged . . . by Eugene Thomas." Neither the government nor FBI agents conspired with Wilkins and Thomas to kill Liuzzo. "Rowe was dispatched to obtain information. The fact that, in the process of getting information and protecting his cover, he did not act to prevent an assault certainly cannot impose liability on the Government. Rowe's failure to act was less important than his prompt reporting of the murder," which led to the arrest and eventual conviction of the Klansmen.

The most striking part of Joiner's decision, thought the *New York Times*, was Rowe's transformation from villain back to hero: Rowe had been long attacked by civil rights leaders and congressional investigators for his alleged role in the Liuzzo murder, but Judge Joiner's decision "rehabilitated the name and reputation of Gary Thomas Rowe."[48]

"We're engaged in a search for the truth in this case," Judge Joiner had noted during the proceedings. Did he or any of the other lawyers find it? Only in part: An impartial analysis of the evidence finds that Wilkins, not Rowe, killed Liuzzo. Lost in the thousands of FBI documents produced by the discovery process and missed by both Robb's and Robertson's staff members is a report by Philip Mabry, "a spy-courier" who worked for the National States Rights Party but also moved comfortably back and forth between the party, the Klan, Alabama's top cop Al Lingo, and even the

FBI, which interviewed him in 1967. Mabry recalled that sometime in March 1965, while visiting Grand Dragon Robert Creel, he met Collie Leroy Wilkins, "who was boasting that he would get away with what he had done and that he thought that they had killed the Negro also, as well as the white woman . . . whom they shot." Wilkins noted that Alabama state troopers stopped them that night, but they weren't detained long. "It was fortunate," Mabry recalled Wilkins saying, "that he and his companions had not been stopped by federal authorities." While not absolutely conclusive, Mabry's recollections add weight to the evidence that it was Wilkins who killed Liuzzo.[49]

Yet Rowe may have contributed to, and the FBI been complicit in, the killing in subtler ways. Rowe's status as an FBI informant covered him, and his closest friends in the Klan, with a cloak of immunity. In the Freedom Riders case, the government prosecuted those who bombed the bus in Anniston and ignored Rowe's friends who beat the activists in Birmingham. Tommy Langston's famous picture showed the FBI a few of those directly involved in the attack on George Webb; besides Rowe, they included Gene Reeves and Bill Holt. But the Bureau never bothered them because it might have revealed Rowe's participation and their advance knowledge. Similarly, Hoover blocked prosecution of the Sixteenth Street Baptist Church bombers in part to protect Rowe and his newest informant, John Nigger Hall. Klansmen who suspected Rowe of being an informant may have realized that Rowe's FBI connections protected from federal and state prosecution anyone who associated with him. To be sure, it took little to incite either Thomas or Wilkins to commit violence, but they might have thought that Rowe's presence provided extra insurance, adding to their recklessness—particularly on that March night in 1965.

Furthermore, on that night, Gene Thomas, who had long detested Rowe and suspected him of being an informer, may have seen an opportunity to seek vengeance against him. In 1962, Rowe had tried to alert police to the impending attack at the Bessemer carnival, which almost robbed Thomas of being the first Klansman that night to strike a blow against blacks. Then, Rowe tried to block the bombing of A. G. Gaston's mansion in 1963 when Thomas wanted a more violent assault and procured the explosives to achieve it. At the Tutweiler Hotel in 1964, Rowe had intervened to stop Thomas from shooting Agent Blake, and Thomas's plot to bomb the Flame Club ultimately failed because Rowe planted pills and liquor on the premises, which closed the club. When the two men found themselves together in Montgomery in 1965, Thomas may have seen that embroiling Rowe in a murder would ensure his loyalty to the Klan, embarrass the Bureau, and be sweet revenge for the times when Rowe had tried to thwart him or successfully done so. Indeed, when Rowe urged the Klansmen not to attack the Liuzzo car and go back to Selma, Thomas told him, "We're going all the way on this one." And after the shots were fired, Thomas said: "You're in the big stuff now. You're number one boy again."

Robb called an impromptu news conference later that day. On the verge of tears, he said that he was "shocked" by the judge's decision, which he called "gutless," and pointed out that the government "could not have written a better decision for itself." He also noted that just down the hall from the courtroom were the offices of the U.S. attorney and the FBI, implying that the former was an extension of the latter: "They are all drawing the same pensions and they all have the same buddies." If a jury had been allowed to hear the case, Robb thought the outcome would have been completely different, and he urged Congress to pass legislation permitting jury trials in lawsuits against the federal government. Tony, his eyes still red from crying, said: "This is not just a defeat for our family but for the American people. My mother was a heroine, a martyr. She gave her life for her country. . . . The fight isn't over!"[50]

But the judge had the final word. On June 2, he informed the Liuzzos that they would have to pay the government's court costs, which, according to the Justice Department, amounted to eighty thousand dollars. "I think this is ridiculous," Tony told reporters. "They would never have spent the money if they hadn't killed my mother. Now they're billing an American family that was trying to find out about their mother's death. The estate has no money . . . and I would go to jail first. No," he added, "I wouldn't pay even if we had the money." The government's latest move sparked editorial opposition from Michigan newspapers and the ACLU, which called the Justice Department's action "vindictive" and recommended that it be overturned. Perhaps stung by this criticism, Judge Joiner later reduced the fee to thirty-six hundred dollars. The case was now over.[51]

In April 1985, two years after the final disposition of the Liuzzo case, Gary Thomas Rowe returned to Alabama for one last battle with Bobby Shelton and the United Klans of America. Despite the FBI's efforts to disrupt the Klan, it continued to survive in the 1970s and 1980s. But now it had a new and aggressive enemy: the Southern Poverty Law Center, which kept an eye on hate groups, represented victims of their violence, and used class-action lawsuits against various state Klans and similar organizations. Rowe was asked to participate in the case of *Beulah Mae Donald v. United Klans of America* and reluctantly agreed to do so.[52]

The case grew out of a shocking event in 1981: Two Alabama Klansmen, members of Shelton's group, kidnapped and murdered a nineteen-year-old black man named Michael Donald and hung his dead body from a tree on a quiet suburban street in Mobile. But much had changed since the time when Klansmen could murder blacks with impunity. Donald's killers were captured, tried, and convicted. Morris Dees, the founder and leader of the Southern Poverty Law Center, saw the case as an opportunity to shut down Shelton's organization for good. Using a novel legal theory, Dees treated the United Klans of America as a corporation, which, in a civil case, could be held responsible for the actions of its employees. Part of his strategy depended on proving that violence was an officially sanctioned Klan policy, and he needed a former Klansman to so testify. He turned to Gary Thomas Rowe.[53]

At first, Rowe refused to help. "That part of my life is behind me," he told Dees in their initial telephone conversation. But knowing of Rowe's thirst for fame, Dees emphasized how important he would be to their case. "Man, if you believe what you believed in 1965 when you helped the FBI, then it's even more important now to stop these Klansmen," Dees told him. "You're the only one who can do it, Tommy. You'll be the star of the show." Seduced by Dees's flattery, Rowe agreed to give a deposition describing the violent history of Shelton's Klan.

Rowe in person looked to Dees like "the stereotypical Southern Sheriff; central casting couldn't have picked a better bully." Next to a fistfight, Rowe loved being in the limelight, and he was ready to put on a good show. From the moment the deposition began "it was clear he'd come to perform," Dees later wrote, "a loud, bragging, know-it-all thug who had been made a hero for what would have sent most men to prison." Dees needed Rowe to put Robert Shelton at the center of Klan violence, and that's exactly what he did, even if it meant adding invented facts to his now-familiar story.[54]

As Rowe told it, Shelton was at his side during every major event of his career. In 1961, when Rowe and the Birmingham cops met at Ivan's Drive-In Restaurant to plot the attack on the Freedom Riders, Shelton was there, too. On Mother's Day, Shelton "was totally in charge," directing the action inside the Trailways bus station. Rowe also recalled "vividly" a Klavern meeting before the Voting Rights March when Shelton told Grand Dragon Creel: "Dammit, the white people [need] to go in there and clean that shit up. . . . Just do what you have got to do." Then, as if it were a two-part plan, Creel later called Rowe: "Hey, I'm going to tell you something. I have laid awake and prayed and cried and prayed over this thing for two or three days. . . . Listen to me good, I've saved your ass a couple of times. Half of the people in the Klan think you're [a] fucking FBI agent, but in my heart, I know better. But . . . I will kill you today . . . I will kill your children . . . if you mess me up, . . . because this is going to be the . . . day . . . you will remember until the day you die." Rowe went on to describe Liuzzo's killing in awful detail, now adding that he saw "blood running down the side of the lady's face." In short, Rowe's mission to Montgomery on March 25, which ended with Liuzzo's murder, was specifically ordered by Bobby Shelton.[55]

"Rowe's testimony was perfect," noted Bill Stanton, Dees's investigator. Dees himself couldn't have been happier. While listening to Rowe's monologue, he wrote the Klan's initials, UKA, on his legal pad and drew "a hangman's noose around them." The jury found Rowe's words equally compelling when Dees's other investigator, Joe Roy, read them aloud at trial. (Dees didn't want Rowe to personally appear and be subject to Klan attorney John Mays's cross-examination.) "Rowe had enough skeletons in his closet to make him suspect," Dees believed, so he asked the questions and Roy answered them. Because Mays refused to attend Rowe's deposition (he didn't wish to be anywhere near that "judas goat"), he could not now impeach Rowe's testimony so it became evidence, not open to challenge.[56]

"No amount of money can ever truly compensate Mrs. Donald for her son's death," Dees said in his closing argument. "But if you return a large verdict—a very large verdict—you will be telling Mrs. Donald and this nation that her son's life was as valuable and precious as anyone's. No matter what you decide, Michael Donald will take his place in history along with others whose lives were lost in the struggle for human rights. And when the final roll is called in heaven—when they call Dr. Martin Luther King, and Medgar Evers, and Viola Liuzzo—they will also call Michael

Donald. I hope the verdict you reach will also go down in history on the side of justice." Four and a half hours later, the jury presented its verdict: Dees and his client won, and Mrs. Donald was awarded $7 million in damages. The United Klans of America had no assets except its headquarters —an imposing building in Tuscaloosa. Mrs. Beulah Donald became its new owner, but not for long. She sold the building for about sixty thousand dollars, half of what it was said to be worth, and purchased a home—her first—in downtown Mobile.[57]

Dees's victory rested in part on Rowe's false testimony. While there is no doubt that Robert Shelton was a hate merchant who advocated violence as the Klan's policy, it took Rowe's lies to defeat him in the courtroom. The incident symbolized Rowe's career as an informant: the use of questionable, even illegal, means to achieve a beneficial end.

Dealing with the Devil

THE LIUZZOS BORE THE costs of weaknesses in the informant system. In the years following their legal defeat, the family scattered. Tom remained in Alabama, hiding somewhere unknown to his siblings. Mary, Penny, and Sally moved to the West Coast. Only Tony Liuzzo stayed in Detroit, hoping to put the experience behind him and rebuild his life with his wife and children. He took some comfort from the news in late 1983 and early 1984 that Walter Bergman and James Peck had won their cases against the FBI. In the Bergman case, Judge Richard Enslen, like Joiner a Michigan judge, held that because the FBI had advance warning of the attack against the Freedom Riders, the Bureau was guilty of "dereliction of duty and negligence" for not preventing Bergman's injuries that day. Bergman had asked for $1 million in compensation but received only $35,000. In his case, Peck received $25,000, not the $500,000 he had asked for. Despite these victories, or perhaps because of them, the Liuzzos' defeat remained disappointing and painful. "I lost a lot, I gave a lot," Tony Liuzzo told a reporter in 1985. "It took its toll on my personal life." So for a time he concentrated on home and his work as a long-haul truck driver. But he couldn't escape the past; his sons came to him with questions about their grandmother, a figure now in their schoolbooks.[1]

In 1992, he injured his back and it never healed correctly, ending his career as a truck driver. Out of work and on disability, he briefly devoted himself to civil rights. He established the Viola Gregg Liuzzo Institute for Human Rights and taught classes on the civil rights movement at a local junior college. But his interest waned; nothing seemed to last except the emotional pain that only liquor could numb. He was rarely sober, and his marriage began to fall apart until one day in 1996 when he found himself alone at home, praying to God for help; he thought his prayers were answered, because he stopped drinking.

His life changed again when he bought a secondhand shortwave radio and listened to the voices in the night: people attacking the "New World Order," the United Nations, and, above all, the omnipotent federal government. It all made sense to Tony Liuzzo, so in 1998 he joined a branch of the Michigan Militia called the Wolverines, one group among many that were being closely watched by Morris Dees's Southern Poverty Law Center. Tony rose quickly to second in command, and when its leader, Mark Koernke, was jailed for assaulting a police officer, Tony inherited his popular radio show "The Intelligence Report." His broadcast emanated from a makeshift studio he built adjoining his new home—a trailer deep in the Michigan woods. He armed himself with a .45 pistol and learned how to use it, as did his wife. When a friend asked him what he was doing, he laughed and replied: "I'm doing what I've always done—fighting tyrannical government. There's nothing new about this. I'm doing my mother's work."[2]

When terrorists attacked New York and Washington, D.C., on September 11, 2001, Tony activated the Wolverines. Although nobody came after him, he grew increasingly nervous; he heard military helicopters in the night sky, patrolling, he thought, and getting too close to home. Not long after Congress passed the USA Patriot Act, authorizing the FBI to more actively pursue what the government considered threats to national security, Tony and his wife disappeared into the militia underground. Liuzzo family members feared they would never see him again.[3]

But their fears were unfounded: Tony later surfaced, and it was because his mother had again become the subject of national interest. In 2000, the filmmaker Paola di Florio, attracted to the story of Viola Liuzzo, decided to make a documentary about her life and death and how both affected the lives of her children. It took four years to amass the 1960s film footage, interview the principals, write the script, and edit and score the film. Stockard Channing, co-star of the popular television series West Wing, agreed

Viola Liuzzo's daughters at the Sundance Film Festival, January 2004, which premiered *Home of the Brave*, directed by Paola di Florio. *Left to right:* Penny Liuzzo Herrington, director di Florio, Mary Liuzzo Lilleboe, and Sally Liuzzo. (Jeff Vespa, Wire Image)

to do the voiceover narration for the film, titled *Home of the Brave*. It debuted at the Sundance Film Festival in January 2004, with Liuzzo's daughters Mary, Penny, and Sally in attendance, and later was shown at film festivals across the country. Reviews were favorable, with critics calling it "fascinating" and "a powerful film worthy of a truly extraordinary American."[4]

Its greatest effect was on Liuzzo's sons and daughters. "Not only has my mother been made whole again, I've been made whole again," said Mary, now living in Oregon with her husband, Dan Lilleboe. She told one interviewer that her brother Tony was said to be "overjoyed that the film managed to have the impact that he had fought for since her mother's death." When the film was screened at the International Cleveland Film Festival in March, Tony was there. Mary had not seen him in six years. Afterward, the two answered questions from the audience, which included a young black man who told them that their mother "had not died in vain, as he felt himself to be living proof of [her] victories." In October, Janet

Liuzzo-Lee informed Detroit's *Metro Times* that her ex-husband Tom was "doing fine" but did not wish to see *Home of the Brave*. "Basically he is happy living in the present," Liuzzo-Lee said, "and just wants to be left alone."[5]

Gary Thomas Rowe, aka Thomas Neil Moore, spent his last years in Savannah, Georgia, "hiding—in the open," as one journalist put it, until he died of a heart attack on May 28, 1998, at age sixty-four. (He survived both Gene Thomas and Lee Wilkins, who died earlier in the decade.) He was bankrupt and sixty thousand dollars in debt. None of his neighbors on Old Louisville Road knew of his past, although he did tell most of his closest friends. He was a "cop buff" to the end; it was both his greatest pleasure and his final occupation as a private detective and security guard for Savannah's United Detective Agency. It wasn't much like the old days— he examined auto accidents for insurance companies and ran background checks on people seeking employment. He also dabbled a bit in local politics, working to elect Republican congressman Jack Kingston, although after his death, Kingston's spokesperson announced that the congressman "didn't know him."[6]

His funeral on June 2 was sparsely attended; among the mourners were a few FBI agents, some friends, and his children (one of whom he had told, "I love you, but I don't have time for you in my life") from various marriages. If there were any Klansmen there, they didn't announce themselves. "He was a very likable individual," said his employer Pete Liakakis, a city alderman. "Tom was mostly a loner the last couple of years, but he was a really good guy."[7]

A loner perhaps, but not entirely alone. As usual, there was a woman in his life, whom he regaled with tales of his days with the FBI and CIA (he embellished his résumé to the very end). Linda Seigler considered him a patriot. "I can honestly say that he loved his country and he possibly gave up everything for it," she told a reporter after his death. Tony Liuzzo, asked to comment, strongly disagreed: "He was a violence junkie . . . a pit bull. He didn't do it for God and country, he did it for the excitement."[8]

Rowe was buried in Savannah under a headstone simply inscribed:[9]

Thomas Neil Moore
1934–1998

What does Rowe's experience tell us about the effectiveness of the FBI's informant system? As terrorism has increased throughout the world, there have been many calls for more "human intelligence" to combat it, including the aggressive recruitment of informants. It is difficult to generalize from Rowe's experience. At the height of the FBI's war against the Klan in the late 1960s, the Bureau claimed to have two thousand informants inside the Hooded Order—about 20 percent of the organization's membership. Without access to FBI records, it's impossible to document with certainty just how effective informants were overall in disrupting the Klan. It is unlikely that such records will become available to historians in the near future, if at all, because the Bureau fiercely guards informant identities and activities.

Rowe's career was also different from that of other Klan informants. Traditionally, as J. Edgar Hoover told President Johnson soon after Liuzzo's death, the FBI created informants from existing Klansmen. Rowe, however, as Hoover noted, was "one of those people we put in, just like we do in the Communist Party." The distinction is important because Rowe, an outsider, was suspect from his first day in the Klan and therefore had a greater need to prove himself, which meant participating in violent missionary work.

There were successes: When the Bureau acted on Rowe's information, it was able to prevent violence, and in the case of Reverend Fred Shuttlesworth, murder. But these are the exceptions. More often, the FBI ignored the information Rowe brought forward. It ignored Rowe's advance warning of the attack on the Freedom Riders, claiming that jurisdictional problems blocked it from intervening. Yet the Freedom Riders, traveling across state lines, were surely covered by federal statutes governing interstate commerce. By failing to alert the attorney general, who probably would have sent U.S. marshals to Birmingham, the Bureau needlessly let innocent people suffer. In its aftermath, the federal injunction against Klan interference, which for a time inhibited Klan action, suggests that a strong federal response in 1961 might have prevented later violence. Rowe, at the least, probably knew that a bomb was planted at the Sixteenth Street Baptist Church, and his failure to report it before it exploded makes him an accessory to that awful crime. Just as bad was Hoover's decision to protect his informants instead of prosecuting the bombers, illustrating how the informant system sometimes interfered with or prevented law enforcement.

FBI agents considered Rowe's swift reporting of the Liuzzo murder vindication of the informant system, and perhaps they are correct. If Rowe had simply gone home that night, it is likely that the Klansmen would never have been brought to justice. On the other hand, if Rowe's presence in the car contributed to the murder of Viola Liuzzo, then the system is partly responsible for the tragedy. Did Rowe flunk the ultimate test when he failed to prevent Liuzzo's murder? Here was a man who boasted of his physical strength and courage, yet at the critical moment when both were being tested, he put self-preservation ahead of acting like the heroic under-cover man he believed himself to be.

Rowe's achievements as informant were therefore limited and often ambiguous, reflecting the informant system itself. Sometimes, even he wondered whether infiltrating the Klan was necessary; by his calculation, there were about a dozen violent Klansmen in Eastview Klavern No. 13, and everybody knew who they were. Put them under close surveillance, and violence would disappear, he believed. The others in the Klavern were content to listen to racist screeds, watch *The Birth of a Nation*, and enjoy the companionship of like-minded folks.

Other weapons in the FBI's arsenal were ultimately more effective than Rowe and the informant system in weakening the Klan. The FBI's meddling through COINTELPRO drove Klansmen crazy: They received threatening letters purportedly from the Mafia that were actually written by the Bureau; the Bureau financed the establishment of rival Klaverns; revelations of Klan corruption were widely publicized by media picked by the FBI; Klansmen were followed, harassed, and publicly embarrassed. Even Bobby Shelton admitted that "the FBI's counterintelligence program hit us in membership and weakened us for about ten years." Unfortunately, Hoover used the same tactics against Martin Luther King, Jr., and later the antiwar movement, which tarnished the FBI for a generation.[10]

The problematic nature of the FBI's informant system didn't end with Rowe leaving the Klan in 1965. His name was back in the news in 2003, but even Rowe might not have approved of the company he was in: Gregory "The Grim Reaper" Scarpa and Joseph "The Animal" Barboza, among others. Each was guilty of a host of crimes, including murder, robbery, loan-sharking, gambling, and racketeering, committed while they worked as FBI informants within organized crime. Gary Thomas Rowe was among those whom the *San Diego Union-Tribune* called "FBI Informants Who Caused Mayhem on the Side."

In a March 2003 story, the *Union-Tribune* and other newspapers were now reporting on the Bureau's misuse of informants in the war against organized crime. The most shocking scandal occurred in Boston where, from the 1960s to the 1980s, the FBI used informants in the Irish Winter Hill Gang against their rivals in the Patriarca family. With Washington's knowledge, FBI agents were allowed to ignore what their charges were doing, which included homicide on a grand scale. Eventually, the Winter Hill Gang, protected by the FBI, emerged victorious until 1995, when state prosecutors brought them to trial and revealed the FBI's misdeeds. One congressional committee later called the Bureau's Organized Crime Informant Program "one of the greatest failures in the history of law enforcement."[11]

What at first seemed like a local story was soon found to be more serious: an epidemic of FBI-sanctioned lawlessness from coast to coast. In response to media criticism, nine former FBI agents, who had worked in twenty-five field offices across the country during long careers, expressed public support for the FBI's informant system, yet at the same time they revealed its inherent dangers. For those who knew of Rowe's career, their comments were familiar. Informants, "mavericks willing to deal with the devil to bring down [the] Mafia," were the FBI's "eyes and ears" inside criminal groups, providing information agents could obtain in no other way. "The bureau has to encourage these guys to be themselves and do what they do," said a former New York FBI supervisor. Policies issued by Washington were often ignored in the field. Did agents know that their informants were withholding information about their activities? "Absolutely," said a former director of the FBI's organized crime unit. It was "a don't ask, don't tell situation." Sometimes agents refused to listen to informant plans that might involve violent crimes. "I didn't want to be involved," said one agent who had worked in Texas and New Jersey. "It just opened a Pandora's box." Their overwhelming conclusion was that the weaknesses of the informant system were less the fault of individuals, informants like Rowe and their handlers, than they were endemic to the system.[12]

That system's problems continued in the years after 9/11. On November 15, 2004, a bearded middle-aged man screamed "Allah" and then set himself afire in front of the White House. He was rushed to the Washington Hospital Center with burns covering 30 percent of his body. The following day, the *Washington Post* reported that the victim, Mohamed Alanssi, a fifty-two-year-old Yemeni, claimed to be an FBI informant who was assisting the Bureau in its war against terrorism. While the Bureau refused to comment on the tragedy, the *Post* revealed a now familiar story to observers of the FBI's informant system. In November 2001, Alanssi had volunteered his services to the FBI and, despite a checkered past, became a Confidential Informant. He supplied the Bureau with "reliable information" and played a key role in a January 2003 sting operation leading to the arrest of a Yemeni cleric accused of financing al-Qaeda. Whether Alanssi would be well enough to testify at the cleric's trial scheduled to begin in January 2005 was unclear as of this writing.

In return for his services, the FBI paid Alanssi $100,000 (which Alanssi considered nothing more than a "tip"), but in May 2003 he was charged with felony bank fraud, which the Bureau "tried to keep quiet." He also "bilked" thousands of dollars from friends after telling them "teary stories" about personal problems. Although the FBI set him up in business with a $50,000 down payment and paid the rent on a comfortable apartment in Falls Church, Virginia, Alanssi told the *Post* that the Bureau had failed to fulfill its promises of more cash and permanent residency in the United States. Before his self-immolation, he said that he was "very scared and nervous" and regretted his relationship with the FBI. "It is my big mistake that I have cooperated with the FBI," he said. "The FBI have already destroyed my life and my family's life and made us in a very dangerous position." Still, he was proud of the job he had done "for all American people. I like them very much. When I do anything to protect them from bad people, I feel happy."

"Alanssi's dramatic act put the murky, secretive world of informants under a rare spotlight," the *Post* concluded. "It is a world become doubly important since the 2001 terrorist attacks, as U.S. intelligence and law enforcement agencies strive to infiltrate . . . terrorist networks to prevent attacks. Alanssi's highly publicized suicide attempt may make that task more difficult, some experts say." Rowe's career, for one, suggests that that concern is unfounded. There will always be people willing to trade their ordinary lives for a chance to enter the "murky, secretive world" of the informant.[13]

NOTES

Unless otherwise noted, all FBI records are housed at FBI Headquarters, Washington, D.C. All depositions taken for and testimony during the trial *Anthony Liuzzo, Jr., et al., v. United States of America et al.* are available in the Dean A. Robb Papers in Mr. Robb's possession (cited as Robb Papers) and appear in the form Dep–Liuzzo or Testimony–Liuzzo.

ABBREVIATIONS

ASAC	assistant special agent in charge
BN	*Birmingham News*
BPH	*Birmingham Post-Herald*
Dep	deposition
DFP	*Detroit Free Press*
DN	*Detroit News*
LAT	*Los Angeles Times*
NYHT	*New York Herald Tribune*
NYT	*New York Times*
SA	special agent
SAC	special agent in charge
WP	*Washington Post*

CHAPTER 1. UNDERCOVER MAN

1. Gary Thomas Rowe, Jr., *My Undercover Years with the Ku Klux Klan* (New York: Bantam Books, 1976), 3, 5.
2. U.S. Department of Justice, *The FBI, the Department of Justice and Gary Thomas Rowe, Jr.: Task Force Report on Gary Thomas Rowe, Jr.*

(Washington, D.C.: 1979), 33–34, 35, 36, 38–39. Hereafter cited as Rowe Task Force Report.

3. Ibid., 5–13.

4. Ibid., 30–33; Identification Record, Gary Thomas Rowe, FBI file No. 44-1236-84; Barrett G. Kemp Trial Testimony, *James Peck v. United States of America,* January 28, 1982, 1099–1100, Robb Papers, hereafter cited as Kemp Testimony–Peck; author's interview with Neil Shanahan, May 2004, Warminster, Penn., hereafter cited as Shanahan Interview.

5. Rowe Task Force Report, 31–32.

6. Ibid.; Shanahan Dep–Liuzzo, Vol. 2, 95.

7. Rowe Task Force Report, Appendix III, 16–17.

8. Ibid., 16–18.

9. Ibid., 39–40.

10. Gary Thomas Rowe, Jr., interview with Gary Thomas Rowe, Jr., 5–10, Task Force, Office of Professional Responsibility, Department of Justice, Washington, D.C., February 20, 1978, hereafter cited as Rowe Interview–Rowe Task Force; Rowe Dep–Liuzzo, 178.

11. Rowe Interview–Rowe Task Force, 14–15.

12. Ibid.

13. On Bill Holt, see Diane McWhorter, *Carry Me Home: Birmingham, Alabama, the Climactic Battle of the Civil Rights Revolution* (New York: Simon and Schuster, 2001), 208, 434; "APPLICATION FOR CITIZENSHIP IN THE INVISIBLE EMPIRE OF THE KU KLUX KLAN," May 21, 1960, Robb Papers.

14. "APPLICATION FOR CITIZENSHIP."

15. Rowe Dep–Liuzzo, Vol. 1, 1, 2; Rowe Task Force Report, 15–17; Rowe, *My Undercover Years,* 8–9.

16. SAC, Birmingham to Director, September 5, 1962, 2; Rowe Task Force Report, 39–41; Kemp Dep–Liuzzo, 42; deposition of Barrett G. Kemp for *James Peck v. United States of America,* January 23, 1981, 55, Robb Papers, hereafter cited as Kemp Dep–Peck; Shanahan Dep–Liuzzo, 173–174.

17. Kemp Dep–Peck, 30; Rowe Task Force Report, 50–51.

18. Kemp Dep–Peck, 30–32; Rowe Task Force Report, 50–51, 39–40.

19. Gary Thomas Rowe Informant Report, June 30, 1960, 2, FBI file No. 170-9-?, hereafter cited as Informant Report.

20. Rowe, *My Undercover Years,* 11.

21. Rowe testimony in *The State of Alabama v. Collie Leroy Wilkins, Jr.,* in the Circuit Court of Lowndes County, Alabama, May term, 232–233. Hereafter cited as First Wilkins Trial.

22. Rowe, *My Undercover Years,* 12.

23. Wyn Craig Wade, *The Fiery Cross: The Ku Klux Klan in America* (New York: Touchstone, 1988), 31–111. The quotations are on pages 62 and 79, respectively; see also David Chalmers, *Hooded Americanism: The History of the Ku Klux Klan* (Durham, N.C.: Duke University Press, 1987), 8–21, and *Backfire: How the Ku Klux Klan Helped the Civil Rights Movement* (Lanham, Md.: Rowman and Littlefield, 2003).

24. Wade, *The Fiery Cross*, 119–275; Chalmers, *Hooded Americanism*, 28–303.

25. Wade, *The Fiery Cross*, 276–306; Chalmers, *Hooded Americanism*, 343–374. For a brief discussion of the White Citizens Council, see Robert Weisbrot, *Freedom Bound: A History of the Civil Rights Movement* (New York: Penguin, 1991), 12, 39, 131; McWhorter, *Carry Me Home*, 98–106 (quotation on p. 98). The best study of the White Citizens Council is Neil R. McMillen, *The White Citizens Council: A History of Organized Resistance to the Second Reconstruction, 1954–1964* (Urbana: University of Illinois Press, 1971).

26. Physical characteristics of Eastview Klansmen can be found in "Members of Eastview Klavern, United Klans of America, Inc.," no FBI file number. For a description of a typical Klansman of the 1960s, see Sullivan Testimony–Liuzzo, Vol. 6, March 28, 1983, 165–166. For more on the composition of the Klan, see Chalmers, *Backfire*, 145–162.

27. Rowe Task Force Report, 29.

28. Informant Report, August 25, 1960, 3, FBI file No. 170-9-38.

29. Informant Report, November 10, 1960, 3, FBI file No. 170-9-69; Informant Report, July 14, 1960, 2, FBI file No. 170-9-16.

30. Informant Report, July 7, 1960, 2, FBI file No. 170-9-13.

31. Informant Report, August 27, 1960, 3, FBI file No. 170-9-40; Informant Report, July 14, 1960, 2, FBI file No. 170-9-16.

32. Informant Report, July 24, 1960, 2, FBI file No. 170-9-18; Informant Report, August 4, 1960, 2, FBI file No. 170-9-27.

33. Informant Report, September 22, 1960, 3, FBI file No. 170-9-49.

34. Informant Report, September 29, 1960, 2, FBI file No. 170-9-54.

35. Informant Report, August 9, 1960, 2, FBI file No. 170-9-28; Informant Report, August 12, 1960, 2–3, FBI file No. 170-9-32; Informant Report, August 7, 1960, 2, FBI file No. 170-9-22; Informant Report, August 9, 1960, 2, FBI file No. 170-9-28; Informant Report, August 30, 1960, 2, FBI file No. 170-9-39; RE: The Alabama Knights, September 16, 1960, 1, FBI file No. 157-227-10.

36. Informant Report, August 3, 1960, 2–3, FBI file No. 170-9-26.

37. Rowe Dep–Liuzzo, Vol. 1, 52–57; Rowe Interview–Rowe Task Force, 67–71.

38. Informant Report, August 25, 1960, 3, FBI file No. 170-9-38; Informant Report, September 1, 1960, 3, FBI file No. 170-9-39.

39. Rowe Dep–Liuzzo, Vol. 1, 43.

40. Ibid.

41. SAC, Birmingham to Director, July 25, 1960, 3–4, FBI file No. 170-9-17; Director to SAC, Birmingham, August 8, 1960, FBI file No. 170-9-23; Rowe Task Force Report, 34.

42. Informant Report, August 18, 1960, 2, FBI file No. 170-9-35.

43. Ibid.

44. Ibid., 4; Rowe Task Force Report, 34; Director to SAC, Birmingham, November 16, 1960, FBI file No. 170-9-67.

45. Informant Report, September 1, 1960, 2, FBI file No. 170-9-43; SAC, Birmingham to Director, 10/70/60, and memorandum enclosed, 1–2, FBI file No. 170-9-50.

CHAPTER 2. ONE HELL OF A GOOD JOB

1. Deposition of Gary Thomas Rowe, Jr., for *Walter Bergman and Frances Bergman v. Clarence M. Kelly* and for *James Peck v. United States of America*, 114, Robb Papers, hereafter cited as Rowe Dep–Bergman/Peck; Rowe Dep–Liuzzo, Vol. 1, 74–75; Shanahan Dep–Liuzzo, Vol. 2, 187; memorandum, April 8, 1961, attached to SAC, Birmingham to Director, 4/8/61, 2–3, FBI file No. 157-71-5; SA Byron McFall to SAC, Birmingham, October 22, 1963, FBI file No. 170-9-SF-203. Diane McWhorter argues that the black child was a mulatto (a "fudge ripple baby"), the offspring of a white woman and black soldier, but the documents indicate otherwise. See Diane McWhorter, *Carry Me Home: Birmingham, Alabama, the Climactic Battle of the Civil Rights Revolution* (New York: Simon and Schuster, 2001), 192.
2. McFall to SAC, October 22, 1963; memorandum, April 8, 1961, 2.
3. Rowe Dep–Bergman/Peck, 114–115; Informant Report, April 4, 1961, 2, FBI file No. 170-9-SF-39; SA Byron E. McFall to SAC, Birmingham, April 11, 1961, 2, FBI file No. 157-71-7; Rowe Dep–Liuzzo, 73.
4. Memorandum, April 8, 1961, 2–3.
5. McFall to SAC, October 22, 1963.
6. Rowe Dep–Bergman/Peck, 117; Rowe Interview–Rowe Task Force, 229–230; Rowe Task Force Report, 42–43.
7. Rowe Dep–Bergman/Peck, 118, 120–121; memorandum, April 8, 1961, 3; Rowe Task Force Report, 43; Rowe Interview–Rowe Task Force, 230–231.
8. Memorandum, RE: Racial Situation, Birmingham Div, April 8, 1961, 1, with McFall to SAC, October 22, 1963.
9. Teletype, April 7, 1961, 1–2, FBI file No. 157-71-1; memorandum, RE: Racial Situation, April 7, 1961, no file number, 1–2, FBI records; memorandum, April 8, 1961.
10. Kemp Dep–Peck, January 23, 1981, 3, 50; deposition of Barrett G. Kemp for *Walter Bergman and Frances Bergman v. Clarence M. Kelley, et al.*, U.S. District Court for the Western District of Michigan, No. G-77-6 CA, October 3, 1980, 37, hereafter cited as Kemp Dep–Bergman; Kemp Dep–Liuzzo, 67.
11. Deposition of Gary Thomas Rowe, Jr., October 17, 1975, before the U.S. Senate Select Committee to Study Governmental Operations with Respect to Intelligence Activities, chaired by Frank Church, 94th Congress, 1st session, December 2, 1975, 117, Robb Papers, hereafter cited as Rowe Dep–Church Committee.
12. SAC, Birmingham to Director, April 11, 1961, FBI file No. 157-71-7; Rowe Task Force Report, 44; SAC, Birmingham to Director, June 9, 1961, 2, FBI file No. 137-698-74.
13. Rowe Task Force Report, 48; deposition of Gary Thomas Rowe, Jr., by Bill Baxley, December 1, 1975, 39, Robb Papers, hereafter cited as Rowe Dep–Baxley.
14. Harvard Sitkoff, *The Struggle for Black Equality* (New York: Hill and Wang, 1993), 88–91, quotation 89; Juan Williams, *Eyes on the Prize: America's Civil Rights Years, 1954–1965* (New York: Penguin Books, 1987), 145–148.

15. Deposition of Gary Thomas Rowe, Jr., for *Walter Bergman and Frances Bergman v. United States of America*, U.S. District Court for the Western District of Michigan, No. G-77-6 CA, November 25, 1980, 22–23, hereafter cited as Rowe Dep–Bergman; Rowe Task Force, Vol. 2, 94–95.

16. Kemp Dep–Liuzzo, 42–43; Rowe Dep–Bergman, 33; SAC, Birmingham to Director, April 19, 1961, FBI file No. 170-9-93; SAC, Birmingham to Director, April 24, 1961, FBI file No. 170-9-94; SAC, Birmingham to Director, April 26, 1961, FBI file No. 137-698-97; Informant Report, April 24, 1961, 1–4, FBI file No. 170-9-SF-42.

17. Informant Report, May 4, 1961, 3, FBI file No. 170-9-SF-43; Informant Report, May 10, 1961, 3, FBI file No. 170-9-SF-44; teletype, SAC, Birmingham to Director, May 12, 1961, FBI file No. 170-9-SF-47.

18. Informant Report, May 10, 1961.

19. Ibid.

20. Deposition of Eugene Thomas for *Anthony Liuzzo, Jr., et al., v. United States of America*, 10–11, hereafter cited as Eugene Thomas Dep–Liuzzo.

21. Rowe Task Force Report, 54–55; quoted in deposition of Thomas J. Jenkins for *Walter Bergman and Frances Bergman v. Clarence M. Kelly* and for *James Peck v. United States of America*, June 22, 1979, 115, 144, Robb Papers, hereafter cited as Jenkins Dep–Bergman/Peck.

22. Hoover statement in A. Rosen to Mr. Parsons, May 18, 1961, FBI file No. 157-373-16; Kemp Dep–Bergman, 42–43, 51.

23. Rowe Task Force Report, Appendix III, 40; K. N. Raby to SAC, May 13, 1961, FBI file No. 157-48-29; Jenkins Dep–Bergman/Peck, 144; teletype, SAC, Birmingham to Director, May 14, 1961, 3, FBI file No. 149-1684-2; Jenkins Dep–Bergman/Peck, 144, 145; Freedom Riders records, May 23, 1961, 130, FBI Headquarters, Washington, D.C., hereafter cited Freedom Riders.

24. Mary Spicer Webb interview, May 25, 1961, 1, Freedom Riders.

25. John P. Patterson interview, May 17, 1961, 1–2, Freedom Riders; Charles Arthur Person interview, May 17, 1961, 1, Freedom Riders; Isaac Reynolds interview, May 18, 1961, 21, Freedom Riders; Herman Harris interview, May 18, 1961, 1, Freedom Riders.

26. Taylor Branch, *Parting the Waters: America in the King Years, 1954–1963* (New York: Simon and Schuster, 1988), 417–418; Patterson interview.

27. Person interview, 23; Patterson interview, 2; Branch, *Parting the Waters*, 419.

28. Person interview, 23, 28–29; James Douglas Peck interview, May 18, 1961, 1, 45, Freedom Riders; *BN*, May 15, 1961; Dr. Walter Gerald Benjamin interview, May 18, 1961, 35, Freedom Riders; Mary Spicer Webb interview, 2; Branch, *Parting the Waters*, 419; Ivor Moore interview, May 18, 1961, 16, Freedom Riders; Reynolds interview, 20; Harris interview, 8.

29. Peck interview, 45; interview with Frances Worner Bergman, May 17, 1961, 41, Freedom Riders; *DN*, February 19, 1980, 1; Person interview, 29; Harris interview, 7; Patterson interview, 3.

30. Peck interview, 45; C. D. DeLoach to Al Rosen, May 4, 1961, FBI records, Washington, D.C.; Branch, *Parting the Waters*, 420.

31. Deposition of Howard K. Smith for *Walter and Frances Bergman v. United States of America, et al.*, 10–11, Robb Papers, hereafter cited Smith Dep–Bergman; ASAC Carl F. Freeman to SAC, Birmingham, December 3, 1975, 15, FBI file No. 170-9-550; interview with Thomas Lankford, May 19, 1961, 1, Freedom Riders.

32. Smith Dep–Bergman, 2.

33. Lankford interview, 1; interview with James Gordon Atkins, May 23, 1961, 1–2, Freedom Riders; on Stoner, see Wyn Craig Wade, *The Fiery Cross: The Ku Klux Klan in America* (New York: Touchstone, 1988), 282–283; Smith Dep–Bergman, 1; Rowe Dep–Bergman, 63–64, 186.

34. Rowe Dep–Bergman, 61–62; quoted in *NYT,* July 17, 1978; Smith Dep–Bergman, 3.

35. Gary Thomas Rowe, Jr., *My Undercover Years with the Ku Klux Klan* (New York: Bantam Books, 1976), 42.

36. Interview with Marshall Long, May 19, 1961, 1, Freedom Riders; Peck interview, 45.

37. SA B. G. Kemp to SAC, May 15, 1961, 1, FBI file No. 149-16-20; Peck interview; Person interview; Milton E. Hall interview, May 19, 1961, 1, Freedom Riders; Moore interview, 11, 12; statement of Jesse Oliver Faggard, May 16, 1961, 6, Cantrell deposition exhibits, Robb Papers.

38. Rowe Interview–Rowe Task Force, 105; interview with John Hampton Thompson, May 26, 1961, 1, Freedom Riders; Earle Incident Report, May 14, 1961, Birmingham Police Department records, Cantrell file, Robb Papers; Smith Dep–Bergman, 12–13.

39. Person interview, 23–24.

40. Peck interview, 45–46; Smith Dep–Bergman, 15, 45; interview with Paul Sutter, May 19, 1961, Freedom Riders; Frances Bergman interview, 41–42; Walter Bergman interview, 41–42; *BN,* May 15, 1961; Reynolds interview, 20; Branch, *Parting the Waters*, 423–424.

41. Frances Bergman interview, 41; Rowe Interview–Rowe Task Force, 105–106; Rowe Dep–Liuzzo, 117; Smith Dep–Bergman, 27.

42. Moore interview, 12; *BN,* May 15, 1961; Mary Spicer Webb interview, 3; interview with George Edward Webb, May 25, 1961, 1–3; Webb statement, June 2, 1961, 1–4, Birmingham Police Department records, Cantrell file; Hall interview, 2; Moore interview, 1–3; interview with John W. Bloomer, May 19, 1961, 2, Freedom Riders; Hall interview, 2; interview with Ossie Hines, May 18, 1961, 2, Freedom Riders; interview with Bud Gordon, May 19, 1961, 1, Freedom Riders; *BN,* May 15, 1961.

43. Interview with Jerry D. McLoy, May 20, 1961, 2, Freedom Riders.

44. Interview with Thomas Earl Langston, May 21, 1961, 1–2, Freedom Riders; SA Barrett G. Kemp to SAC, May 15, 1961, 1, FBI file No. 149-16-20; Hall interview, 2; Bloomer interview, 2; Gordon interview, May 19, 1.

45. Interview with Julian A. "Bud" Gordon, May 16, 1961, 1–2, Freedom Riders; interview with Bud Gordon, May 21, 1961, 1–2, Freedom Riders; statement of J. A. Gordon, June 26, 1961, 1–2, Birmingham Police Department records,

Cantrell file; interview with Thomas Lankford, May 20, 1961, 2, Freedom Riders; Bloomer interview, 1–2; interview with Thomas Dygard, May 19, 1961, 2, Freedom Riders; SA Barrett G. Kemp to SAC, Birmingham, May 17, 1961, 3.

46. Clancy Lake, *BN*, May 15, 1961, 1; interview with Clancy Lake, May 18, 1961, 1, Freedom Riders.

47. Lake, *BN*, May 15, 1961; SA Barrett G. Kemp to SAC, Birmingham, May 17, 1961, 3.

48. Lake, *BN*, May 15, 1961; A. Rosen to Mr. Parsons, May 15, 1961, FBI file No. 149-16-841.

49. McWhorter, *Carry Me Home*, 208.

50. SA Barrett G. Kemp to SAC, May 15, 1961, 1, FBI file No. 170-9-SF-48.

51. McWhorter, *Carry Me Home*, 211; Rowe, *My Undercover Years*, 46.

52. Rowe, *My Undercover Years*, 46.

53. Rowe, *My Undercover Years*, 46; for FBI records describing Rowe's activities, see SA Barrett G. Kemp to SAC, May 15, 1961, 1, FBI file No. 170-9-SF-48SA; Barrett G. Kemp to SAC, Birmingham, May 17, 1961, 3.

54. Kemp Dep–Bergman, 51; Kemp Dep–Liuzzo, 51–52.

55. Lake, *BN*, May 15, 1961; SA Barrett G. Kemp to SAC, Birmingham, May 17, 1961, 5, FBI file No. 170-9-SF50; *BPH*, May 15, 1961.

56. Rowe Dep–Bergman, 186; Kemp to SAC, May 17, 1961, 5.

57. Kemp Testimony–Peck, 1188; Kemp Dep–Bergman, 38–39.

58. Rowe Dep–Liuzzo, 123; Rowe Interview–Rowe Task Force, 107.

59. Rowe Task Force Report, 250.

60. SA Barrett G. Kemp to SAC, Birmingham, May 17, 1960, 2–3, FBI file No. 149-16-62.

61. Ibid.

62. Rowe Task Force Report, 48.

63. Teletype, SAC, Birmingham to Director, May 14, 1961; teletype, SAC, Birmingham to Director, May 21, 1961. File numbers unreadable.

64. SAC, Birmingham to Director, June 12, 1961; SAC, Birmingham to Director, September 12, 1961.

65. SAC, Birmingham to Director, May 18, 1961, FBI file No. 137-6295-6; SAC, Birmingham to Director, May 18, 1961, FBI file No. 170-9-100.

66. Birmingham Police Department interview with Jesse Oliver Faggard, May 16, 1961, 3, 9, 12; statement of Jesse Oliver Faggard, Birmingham Police Department, May 24, 1961; Birmingham Police Department interview with Jesse Thomas Faggard, May 17, 1961; Birmingham Police Department interview with John Hampton Thompson, June 7, 1971; on Dove and Acker, see "Notes," Cantrell file.

67. Branch, *Parting the Waters*, 426.

68. A. Rosen to Mr. Parsons, May 15, 1961, FBI file No. 149-68-4; SA Barrett G. Kemp to SAC, Birmingham, May 29, 1961, 1, FBI file No. 170-9-SF-52; Branch, *Parting the Waters*, 423–429.

69. SA Barrett G. Kemp to SAC, Birmingham, May 17, 1961, 1.

70. Sitkoff, *The Struggle for Black Equality*, 105–106.

71. Ibid., 108.
72. Ibid., 108–110.
73. SA Barrett G. Kemp to File, May 17, 1961, 1, FBI file No. 170-9-99; SA Barrett G. Kemp to SAC, Birmingham, May 18, 1961, 2, FBI file No. 170-9-SF-4; Kemp Dep–Bergman, 51; Kemp Testimony–Peck, 1195.
74. Kemp Dep–Bergman, 62–64, 68; Kemp Dep–Peck, 84–90; Kemp Testimony–Peck, 1196–1197; Kemp Dep–Liuzzo, 58–59.
75. Kemp Dep–Liuzzo, 58–60.

CHAPTER 3. SERIOUS BUSINESS

1. Rowe Interview–Rowe Task Force, 57–58; C. B. Stanberry testimony, *James Peck v. United States of America*, January 27, 1983, 990, hereafter cited as Stanberry Testimony–Peck; Rowe Dep–Bergman, 201–202.
2. Rowe Interview–Rowe Task Force, 57–58; Gary Thomas Rowe, Jr., *My Under-cover Years with the Ku Klux Klan* (New York: Bantam Books, 1976), 52; Kemp Dep–Liuzzo, 59.
3. Rowe Dep–Liuzzo, Vol. 3, 13–14; Byron T. McFall Testimony, *James Peck v. United States of America*, January 21, 1983, 473, 474, 479, 482, Robb Papers, hereafter cited as McFall Testimony–Peck; Rowe Dep–Bergman, 202.
4. Informant Report, June 1, 1961, 2, FBI file No. 170-9-SF-55; SA Barrett G. Kemp to SAC, June 8, 1961, FBI file No. 170-9-SF-56.
5. SA Ernest H. White, Jr., to SAC, June 13, 1961, 2, FBI file No. 170-9-SF-57.
6. Informant Report, June 15, 1961, 3, FBI file No. 170-9-SF-59; SAC, Birmingham to Director, October 13, 1961, 2, FBI file No. 137-6275-8.
7. Informant Report, June 21, 1961, 2–3, FBI file No. 170-9-SF-63; Informant Report, June 22, 1961, FBI file No. 170-9-SF-64; Informant Report, July 16, 1961, 3, FBI file No. 170-9-SF-67.
8. Informant Report, June 23, 1961, 3, FBI file No. 170-9-SF-65.
9. Informant Report, June 29, 1961, 3–5, FBI file No. 170-9-SF-66; Informant Report, July 16, 1961, 3; Wyn Craig Wade, *The Fiery Cross: The Ku Klux Klan in America* (New York: Touchstone, 1988), 312–313.
10. Informant Report, August 10, 1961, 4, FBI file No. 170-9-SF-75; Informant Report, October 12, 1961, 2–3, FBI file No. 170-9-SF-82.
11. Informant Report, September 14, 1961, 2–3, FBI file No. 170-9-SF-179; Informant Report, October 19, 1961, 4, FBI file No. 170-9-SF-83.
12. Informant Report, October 24, 1961, 2, FBI file No. 170-9-SF-85.
13. Informant Report, October 28, 1961, 2, FBI file No. 170-9-SF-86.
14. Ibid.
15. Ibid., 2.
16. Informant Report, November 9, 1961, 2, FBI file No. 170-9-SF-88.
17. Informant Report, November 19, 1961, 2, 4, FBI file No. 170-9-SF-89.
18. SAC, Birmingham to Director, April 11, 1962, 1–3, FBI file No. 137-6245-11; C. L. McGowan to Mr. Rosen, April 12, 1962, FBI file No. 137-6295-10.
19. Informant Report, December 7, 1961, 2–4, FBI file No. 170-9-SF-91.
20. SAC, Birmingham to Director, February 13, 1962, 4, FBI file No. 170-9-145.

21. Informant Report, December 4, 1961, 2–4, FBI file No. 170-9-SF-90; FBI index, n.d., 2–3, FBI file No. 105-722-800; FBI interview with Emory Anthony, October 25, 1963, FBI records; FBI interview with Delores Anthony, October 25, 1963, FBI records; SAC, Birmingham to Director, February 13, 1962, 4–5; Rowe Interview–Rowe Task Force, Vol. 2, 273–277; Rowe Dep–Liuzzo, 132–133.

22. SAC, Birmingham to Director, February 13, 1962, 4–5, FBI file No. 137-6295-9; see also Liuzzo documents, Vol. 1–3, 15, Robb Papers.

23. SA Byron E. McFall to SAC, Birmingham, January 17, 1962, no file number; SAC, Birmingham to Director, June 14, 1962, 1–8, FBI file No. 137-6295-12; see also McWhorter, *Carry Me Home*, 259.

24. SAC, Birmingham to Director, June 14, 1962, 5; SA Byron E. McFall to SAC, April 12, 1962, FBI file No. 170-9-164; Rowe Dep–Liuzzo, 137–142; Rowe Interview–Rowe Task Force, 78–80.

25. Taylor Branch, *Parting the Waters: America in the King Years, 1954–1963* (New York: Simon and Schuster, 1988), 187–188; Shuttlesworth is quoted in Diane McWhorter, *Carry Me Home: Birmingham, Alabama, the Climactic Battle of the Civil Rights Revolution* (New York: Simon and Schuster, 2001), 187.

26. Rowe Task Force Report, 68–70; see also Racial Situation–Birmingham Division, July 23, 1962, 1–2, FBI records.

27. SAC, Birmingham to Director, July 20, 1962, 1–4, FBI file No. 100-3080-1505; FBI report, July 20, 1962, 1–2, FBI file No. 170-9-SF-123; see also Racial Situation–Birmingham Division, 1–2; Rowe Task Force Report, 68–70; on Holt's remark, see Conversation with Thomas-Creel-Holt, n.d., 8, Thomas-Creel-Holt file, Robb Papers.

28. SAC, Birmingham to Director, July 20, 1962, 4.

29. SAC, Birmingham to Director, July 23, 1962, 2, FBI file No. 100-3070-1497.

30. SAC, Cleveland to Director, et al., July 21, 1962, FBI file No. 100-3080-1496; SAC, Birmingham to Director, July 25, 1962, FBI file No. 100-3080-1498; see also Andrew M. Manis, *A Fire You Can't Put Out: The Civil Rights Life of Birmingham's Reverend Fred Shuttlesworth* (Tuscaloosa: The University of Alabama Press, 1999), 318–319.

31. SAC, Birmingham to Director, July 23, 1962, 2, FBI file No. 100-3070-1497; SA Byron McFall to SAC, Birmingham, September 19, 1962, 2, FBI file No. 170-9-198; Rowe Task Force Report, 68–72; McWhorter, *Carry Me Home*, 276.

32. Rowe, *My Undercover Years*, 110; SAC, Birmingham to Director, June 14, 1962, 8, FBI file No. 170-9-171.

33. SAC, Birmingham to Director, FBI, September 5, 1962, 1, FBI file No. 170-9-193.

34. Ibid., 2–3.

35. Director, FBI, to SAC, Birmingham, September 13, 1962, 1, FBI file No. 170-9-197.

36. SAC, Birmingham to Director, June 14, 1962, 2, FBI file No. 137-6295-12;

SAC, Birmingham to Director, February 14, 1963, 3–4, 6, FBI file No. 170-9-226; SAC, Birmingham to Director, June 12, 1963, FBI file No. 137-6295-8.

37. SAC, Birmingham to Director, June 12, 1963, 2–3; Informant Report, April 23, 1963, 2, FBI file No. 170-9-SF-164.

38. Informant Report, April 11, 1963, 3, FBI file No. 170-9-SF-16; Informant Report, April 23, 1963, 2; Informant Report, April 30, 1963, 1, FBI file No. 170-9-SF-163; SAC, Birmingham to Director, June 12, 1963, 5; on Walker, see Gerald Posner, *Case Closed: Lee Harvey Oswald and the Assassination of John F. Kennedy* (New York: Anchor Books, 1994), 98, 112–115.

39. McWhorter, *Carry Me Home*, 483–485; Robert Chambliss's niece notes that the group was called the "Cahaba boys." See Elizabeth H. Cobbs and Petric J. Smith, *Long Time Coming: An Insider's Story of the Birmingham Church Bombing That Rocked the World* (Birmingham: Crane Hill Publishers, 1994), 57.

40. Branch, *Parting the Waters*, 536–537, 548–549, 628–630; Stephan B. Oates, *Let the Trumpet Sound: The Life of Martin Luther King, Jr.* (New York: Plume, 1982), 189–201.

41. Harvard Sitkoff, *The Struggle for Black Equality* (New York: Hill and Wang, 1993), 120.

42. Oates, *Let the Trumpet Sound*, 211.

43. Ibid., 232–235.

44. Ibid., 240–241.

45. Informant Report, April 23, 1963, 3, FBI file No. 170-9-SF-164. For other Klavern activities at this time, see Informant Report, April 18, 1963, 1–3, FBI file No. 170-9-SF-160; Informant Report, April 30, 1963, 1–3, FBI file No. 170-9-SF-163; Informant Report, April 30, 1963, 1–3, FBI file No. 170-9-SF-165.

46. SAC, Birmingham to Director, June 12, 1963, 6, FBI file No. 170-9-246.

47. Branch, *Parting the Waters*, 793–794; McWhorter, *Carry Me Home*, 427.

48. McWhorter, *Carry Me Home*, 430–434; Glenn T. Askew, *But for Birmingham: The Local and National Movements in the Civil Rights Struggles* (Chapel Hill: University of North Carolina Press, 1997), 300–303.

49. SA Byron McFall to SAC, Birmingham, May 12, 1963, 1–2, FBI file No. 170-9-SF-16.

50. SAC, Birmingham to Director, June 12, 1963, 2, FBI file No. 137-6295-8.

51. Diane McWhorter's account of Rowe's involvement in the motel bombing is in *Carry Me Home*, 434–437. For Hall's remarks, see SA Byron E. McFall to SAC, October 18, 1963, 2, FBI file No. 170-9-SF-19.

52. Blake Dep–Liuzzo, 35.

53. McFall to SAC, October 18, 1963, 1–2; SAC, Birmingham to Director, FBI, June 12, 1963, 6, 7, FBI file No. 170-9-246; on Rowe and Holt, see Cantrell exhibits, 32; SA Byron E. McFall to SAC, Birmingham, May 19, 1963, FBI file No. 170-9-242.

54. SAC, Birmingham to Director, FBI, et al., June 7, 1963, 1–2, FBI file No. 170-9-243.

55. SAC, Birmingham to Director, FBI, June 9, 1963, FBI file No. 170-9-SF-16;

Rowe Dep–Baxley, 17; Rowe Dep–Liuzzo, 148; McWhorter, *Carry Me Home,* 456; Rowe, *My Undercover Years*, 81.

56. SAC, Birmingham to Director, June 12, 1963, 3, FBI file No. 137-6295-8; *BN*, June 9, 1963, in Cantrell Dep and Docs, Robb Papers; on Cash's possible involvement in the Gaston Motel bombing, see SA Stanberry to SAC, September 6, 1963, FBI file No. 157-241-1125, and SAC, Birmingham to Director, May 8, 1964, FBI file No. 157-881-306; McWhorter, *Carry Me Home*, 456.

57. Rowe Dep–Baxley, 18; McWhorter, *Carry Me Home*, 457.

58. Rowe Dep–Baxley, 17–19; McWhorter, *Carry Me Home*, 457.

59. SAC, Birmingham to Director, June 8, 1963, 1–2, FBI file No. 170-9-244; Rowe Dep–Baxley, 19; *BN*, June 9, 1963, Cantrell Dep and Docs.

60. Rowe Dep–Baxley, 21–22, 34; Gary Thomas Rowe, Jr., November 25, 1975, 4, Robb Papers; Rowe interview, 1977, 20, Cantrell exhibits, Robb Papers; *BN*, June 9, 1963; Gary Thomas Rowe, Jr., FBI file No. 44-1232-388; SA Pierce A. Pratt to SAC, Birmingham, April 2, 1965, FBI file No. 44-1232-156; Task Force Report, 73.

61. President Kennedy is quoted in Sitkoff, *The Struggle for Black Equality,* 146; for Rowe's comment, see McWhorter, *Carry Me Home*, 461.

62. David J. Garrow, *Bearing the Cross: Martin Luther King, Jr. and the Southern Christian Leadership Conference* (New York: William Morrow and Co., 1986), 269; Stewart Burns, *To the Mountaintop: Martin Luther King Jr.'s Sacred Mission to Save America, 1955–1968* (New York: HarperCollins, 2003), 208; for the assassination of Medgar Evers, see Adam Nossiter, *Of Long Memory: Mississippi and the Murder of Medgar Evers* (New York: De Capo Press, 2002); Maryanne Vollers, *The Ghosts of Mississippi: The Murder of Medgar Evers, the Trials of Byron De La Beckwith, and the Haunting of the New South* (Boston: Little, Brown, 1995).

CHAPTER 4. BOMBING MATTERS

1. Informant Report, December 23, 1964, 2, FBI file No. 170-9-SF-306; SA Byron E. McFall to SAC, Birmingham, October 9, 1963, 3, FBI file No. 170-9-SF-194.

2. Informant Report, July 19, 1963, 2, FBI file No. 170-9-SF-181; SA Joseph P. Ayers to SAC, Atlanta, December 11, 1963, FBI file No. 157-582-334; author's interview with confidential source who spoke about the Blantons.

3. Rowe Dep–Peck, 228; FBI interview with Robert Chambliss, October 1, 1963, Birmingham 157-390, 604–614, FBI records; Diane McWhorter, *Carry Me Home: Birmingham, Alabama, the Climactic Battle of the Civil Rights Revolution* (New York: Simon and Schuster, 2001), 72–75, 98–99, 114–118; Elizabeth H. Cobbs and Petric J. Smith, *Long Time Coming: An Insider's Story of the Birmingham Church Bombing That Rocked the World* (Birmingham: Crane Hill Publishers, 1994), 38–85.

4. Informant Report, December 23, 1964, 3–4, FBI file No. 170-9-SF-306.

5. RE: Unknown Subjects, FBI, August 27, 1963, 1–6, FBI records; Informant Report, August 20, 1963, 3, FBI file No. 170-9-SF-186.

6. SAC, Birmingham to Director, FBI, May 8, 1964, 1–2, FBI file No. 157-331-83.

7. Tidwell was officially admitted to Eastview Klavern No. 13 on August 22; see Informant Report, August 22, 1964, 2; interview of Gary Thomas Rowe by Captain Jack LeGrand and Officer Ernest Cantrell, September 12, 1977, 7, 10–11, 33–34, Robb Papers, hereafter cited as Rowe Interview–LeGrand; Rowe mentioned the bombing briefly in an interview with Alabama Attorney General Bill Baxley on December 1, 1975 (see Rowe Dep–Baxley, 12–13), and he discussed it with the Rowe Task Force (see Rowe Interview–Rowe Task Force, Vol. 2, 69).

8. For Rowe's reports on his activities on August 8 and August 15, 1963, see Informant Report, August 8, 1963, 1, FBI file No. 170-9-SF-187, and Informant Report, August 15, 1963, 1, FBI file No. 170-9-SF-188.

9. McWhorter, *Carry Me Home*, 494–496.

10. Rowe Interview–LeGrand, 6; McWhorter, *Carry Me Home*, 498–501.

11. SAC, Birmingham to Director, FBI, October 15, 1963, 1–10, FBI file No. 137-62905-19; "Bombing Matters," October 4, 1963, 3, FBI file No. 157-352-1401; Informant Report, May 7, 1964, 3–4, FBI file No. 170-9-SF-255.

12. Rowe Interview–Rowe Task Force, Vol. 1, 100–105.

13. Ibid., 110–118; see also Bob Eddy to George Beck, October 11, 1977, Cantrell Dep and Docs, Robb Papers, and Memorandum by Investigator M. R. Roye III, Alabama Bureau of Investigation, Cantrell file; McFall is quoted in Rowe Task Force Report, 100.

14. Rowe Interview–LeGrand, 10; Dan T. Carter, *The Politics of Rage: George Wallace, the Origins of the New Conservatism, and the Transformation of American Politics* (New York: Simon and Schuster, 1995), 173; McWhorter, *Carry Me Home*, 503–504.

15. Rowe Interview–LeGrand, 11–12.

16. Rowe Interview–LeGrand, 11; Rowe Interview–Rowe Task Force, Vol. 3, 2–3, 6.

17. Rowe Interview–LeGrand, 12–14; Rowe Interview–Rowe Task Force, Vol. 3, 7–8; McWhorter, *Carry Me Home*, 504; Gary Thomas Rowe, Jr., *My Undercover Years with the Ku Klux Klan* (New York: Bantam Books, 1976), 94–95.

18. Rowe Interview–LeGrand, 39–40; SAC, Birmingham to Director, October 15, 1963, FBI file No. 137-62905-19; "Bombing Matters," October 4, 1963, FBI file No. 157-352-1401; Informant Report, May 7, 1964, FBI file No. 170-9-SF-255.

19. First quotation is from *Newsweek*, September 30, 1963; SAC, Birmingham to Director, et al., September 15, 1963, FBI file No. 157-352-1; Frank Sikora, *Until Justice Rolls Down: The Birmingham Church Bombing Case* (Tuscaloosa: University of Alabama Press, 1991), 9–19; Cross's remarks are on 14–15.

20. SA John Culpepper to SA John C. Newsom, September 15, 1963, 1–2, FBI file No. 157-352-44; SA Roy Osborn to SAC, September 15, 1963, FBI file No. 157-352-47; A. Rosen to Mr. Belmont, September 16, 1963, 2–3, FBI file No. 157-1025-28, Subject: Birmingham, Alabama, Sixteenth Street Church

Bombing/September 15, 1963, Part I, FBI records; SAC, Birmingham to Director, September 16, 1963, FBI file No. 157-205-45; *NYT*, September 16, 1963; *Newsweek*, September 30, 1963; *NYHT*, September 17, 1963; Sikora, *Until Justice Rolls Down*, 14.

21. A. Rosen to Mr. Belmont, September 16, 1963, 1–2; *Washington Star*, September 17, 1963; C. D. DeLoach to Mr. Mohr, September 17, 1963, FBI file No. 157-1025-57.

22. A. Rosen to Mr. Belmont, September 16, 1963, 1–2; A. Rosen to Mr. Belmont, September 17, 1963, FBI file No. 137-1025-62, for Hoover's remark, see 3.

23. W. S. Hyde to Mr. Mohr, September 16, 1963, FBI file No. 157-1025-64; A. Rosen to Mr. Belmont, September 15, 1963, 1–3; *Newsweek*, September 30, 1963.

24. The quotation is from the *NYHT*, September 17, 1963; *Washington Star*, September 17, 1963.

25. SAC, Atlanta, to Director, September 16, 1963, FBI file No. 157-1025-41; SAC, Savannah to Director, and SAC, Birmingham, September 17, 1963, FBI file No. 157-1025-31; SAC, New Orleans to Director, September 17, 1963, FBI file No. 157-1025-30; SAC, Knoxville to Director, September 17, 1963, FBI file No. 157-1025-36; SAC, Jacksonville to Director and SAC, Birmingham, FBI file No. 157-1025-37; SAC, Tampa to Director, September 17, 1963, FBI file No. 157-1025-38. Quotations are from Atlanta and Tampa FBI field offices. Klansman quotation is in SAC, Atlanta to Director, September 18, 1963, 1, FBI file No. 157-1025-78.

26. A. Rosen to Mr. Belmont, April 10, 1964, FBI file No. 157-1025-938; C. A. Evans to Mr. Belmont, September 16, 1963, FBI file No. 157-1025-67.

27. C. D. DeLoach to Mr. Mohr, September 20, 1963, FBI file No. 157-1025-144; "Redacted Name" to Mr. J. Edgar Hoover, September 15, 1963, FBI file No. 157-1025-160.

28. *NYHT*, September 21, 1963, FBI file No. 157-1025-310. On Green, see SAC, Birmingham to Director, September 27, 1963, 6, FBI file No. 157-1025-259.

29. Garry [*sic*] Thomas Rowe, Jr., November 25, 1975, 4, Robb Papers. This is a fragment of an interview with Rowe done by an unidentified person.

30. SA Byron E. McFall to SAC, September 15, 1963, 1, FBI file No. 170-9-SF-204.

31. McFall to SAC, September 15, 1963, 1–2; SAC, Birmingham to Director, October 15, 1963, 6, FBI file No. 170-9-270.

32. McFall to SAC, September 15, 1963, 2–3; SAC, Birmingham to Director, October 15, 1963, 7A.

33. SAC, Birmingham to Director, October 15, 1963, 6, 7.

34. Rowe Dep–Baxley, 6–7; McWhorter, *Carry Me Home*, 535–536.

35. Informant Report, October 19, 1963, 2, FBI file No. 170-9-SF-193.

36. SA Byron E. McFall to SAC, September 25, 1963, 1–2, FBI file No. 157-407-18; E. H. Cantrell, "Memo," March 17, 1976, Cantrell Dep and Docs; SA Harry T. Posey to SAC, Birmingham, September 25, 1963, 1, FBI file No. 157-407-5.

37. Posey to SAC, Birmingham, September 25, 1963, 3; McFall to SAC, September 25, 1963; Rowe Task Force Report, 90–91.
38. SA J. Brooke Blake to SAC, May 6, 1964, 1, FBI file No. 170-9-SF-253; Rowe Task Force Report, 92–93; McWhorter, *Carry Me Home*, 543; for Rowe's later confused account of the Center Street shrapnel bombing, see Rowe Interview–LeGrand, 24–27.
39. McFall is quoted in Rowe Task Force Report, 94.
40. SA Byron E. McFall to SAC, Birmingham, March 26, 1963, FBI file No. 170-9-SF-159; telephone interview with Mrs. Helen Odle, June 16, 1976, Cantrell file. Emphasis is in the original document.
41. Informant Report, January 19, 1964, 3, FBI file No. 170-9-SF-225.
42. FBI interview with Robert Chambliss, September 26, 1963, Birmingham field office file No. 157-407, FBI records; SAC, Birmingham to Director, September 25, 1963, 4, FBI file No. 157-352-733; interview with Robert Chambliss, October 29, 1963, 1–2, Birmingham field office file No. 157-352.
43. Interview with Robert Chambliss, October 29, 1963, 1–2.
44. FBI interview with Thomas Edward Blanton, October 1, 1963, F-G, Birmingham field office file No. 157-352; SAC, Birmingham to Director, October 8, 1963, 5, FBI file No. 157-416-169.
45. Thomas Edward Blanton, October 4, 1963, 12–13, no file number.
46. SAC, Birmingham to Director, October 26, 1963, 2–6, FBI file No. 157-352-1066; FBI interview with Mrs. Troy Ingram, October 3, 1963, 1–2, Birmingham field office file No. 157-352-1714.
47. "Bobby Frank Cherry," FBI report, n.d.
48. For Hall and Cagle, see John Wesley Hall, September 25, 1963, 2–3, and Charles Cagle, September 25, 1963, 3–4, both in Birmingham field office file No. 157-352; SAC, Birmingham to Director, October 1, 1963, 2, FBI file No. 157-1025-297.
49. On the FBI's difficulties, see SAC, Birmingham, to Director, October 26, 1963, 1–3, FBI file No. 157-352-2528; SAC, Birmingham to Director, September 25, 1963, 3, FBI file No. 157-352-733; on the arrest, see A. Rosen to Mr. Belmont, September 30, 1963, 1–4, FBI file No. 157-1025-275; on Lingo and the arrest, see SAC, Birmingham to Director, October 1, 1963, 2, FBI file No. 157-1025-297; A. Rosen to Mr. Belmont, March 27, 1964, 2, FBI file No. 157-1025-904; Carter, *The Politics of Rage*, 189–193; McWhorter, *Carry Me Home*, 501–502, 547–550, 552–553.
50. SAC, Birmingham to Director, June 19, 1964, FBI file No. 157-331-108; for Hoover's view, see "Memorandum for the Attorney General," September 30, 1963, 1, FBI file No. 157-10253, Sixteenth Street Baptist Church Bombing records, Vol. 2; *BPH*, June 23, 1964; Carter, *The Politics of Rage*, 187–191.
51. John Wesley Hall statement, September 25, 1963, 43, FBI report; John Wesley Hall statement, September 25, 1963, EE-FF, FBI records.
52. John Wesley Hall statement, October 4, 1963, 91–92, FBI report; SAC, Birmingham to Director, October 5, 1963, 3, FBI file No. 157-352-1381; SAC, Birmingham to Director, October 16, 1963, 3, 4, FBI file No. 157-352-1924;

John Wesley Hall statement, November 2, 1963, John Wesley Hall File, Robb Papers.

53. Gary Thomas Rowe, Jr., Task Force to Michael E. Shaheen, Jr., December 4, 1979, 5–6, Office of Professional Responsibility, Department of Justice Records, Washington, D.C.; see *NYT*, February 18, 1980; for testimony by Hall's contact agent, Robert Murphy, see Murphy Testimony–Liuzzo, Vol. 4, 5–27; on Hall and his wife, see Rowe Dep–Baxley, 31, and Rowe Interview–Rowe Task Force, Vol. 1, 17.

54. Byron E. McFall to SAC, November 30, 1964, FBI file No. 170-9-275; SAC, Birmingham to Director, January 9, 1964, 2, FBI file No. 137-6295-21; Director to SAC, Birmingham, January 17, 1964, FBI file No. 170-9-283; for Rowe's February 1962 payments, see SA Byron E. McFall to SAC, Birmingham, March 9, 1962, FBI file No. 170-9-153.

55. SAC, Birmingham to Director, FBI, January 9, 1964, 3; Byron E. McFall to SAC, October 17, 1963, 1, FBI file No. 170-9-SF-202; Byron E. McFall to SAC, October 29, 1963, 4–6, FBI file No. 170-9-SF-208.

56. Informant Report, May 7, 1964, 4, FBI file No. 170-9-SF-255; Rowe Dep–Baxley, 2–5; Rowe Interview–LeGrand, 41–43.

57. FBI report, n.d., Y-Z, FBI records; Rowe Interview–LeGrand, 43; Rowe Interview–Rowe Task Force, Vol. 2, 21–23, 33–35, 42–49; McWhorter, *Carry Me Home*, 524.

58. On McCord's absence, see Rowe Interview–LeGrand, 41–42; on the Bureau's view of Rowe, see Blake Dep–Liuzzo, 12; Rowe Interview–Rowe Task Force, Vol. 2, 21.

59. McWhorter, *Carry Me Home*, 511–514.

60. Director, FBI to SAC, Birmingham, April 24, 1964, 3, FBI file No. 157-352-SF2-143; SAC, Birmingham to Director, FBI, May 13, 1965, 4, FBI file No. 157-1025-1411; Director, FBI to SAC, Birmingham, May 19, 1965, FBI file No. 157-352-5741; *NYT*, February 18, 1980.

61. Eleven microphones and seven phone taps were employed. See SAC, Birmingham to Director, November 21, 1963, 1–4, FBI file No. 157-352-SF2-53; A. Rosen to Mr. Belmont, December 2, 1963, FBI file No. 157-1025-1556; Director, FBI to Mr. Fred M. Vinson, Jr., December 7, 1966, 1–4, FBI file No. 157-1025-1558; Fred M. Vinson to Director, December 19, 1966, FBI file No. 157-1025-155-?; Director, FBI to Mr. Fred M. Vinson, Jr., January 6, 1967, FBI file No. 157-1025-1559; Memorandum, FBI General Investigative Division, December 20, 1966, no file number.

62. For Baxley's prosecution see Sikora, *Until Justice Rolls Down*, 39–168; McWhorter, *Carry Me Home*, 573–575; for coverage of the Blanton trial, see *NYT*, April 13, 16, 24–27, 29, May 1, 3–5, June 1, July 11, 17, 29 (Diane McWhorter), all 2001; and Cherry trials, see relevant issues of the *New York Times*.

CHAPTER 5. CAT AND MOUSE

1. Author's interview with confidential source; Rowe Dep–Liuzzo, Vol. 2, 56; Blake Dep–Liuzzo, 4–5, 8–9, 46.

2. Blake Dep–Liuzzo, 5–6, 9, 45; Rowe Interview–Rowe Task Force, Vol. 2, 28.

3. Informant Report, January 24, 1964, 2, 4, FBI file No. 170-9-SF-222; Informant Report, February 7, 1964, 3–4, FBI file No. 170-9-SF-223; Informant Report, February 17, 1964, 2, FBI file No. 170-9-SF-231; Informant Report, February 19, 1964, 2, FBI file No. 170-9-SF-228.

4. Informant Report, February 7, 1964, 4; Blake Dep–Liuzzo, 26; Rowe Interview–Rowe Task Force, 77.

5. Informant Report, February 9, 1964, 2–3, FBI file No. 170-9-224; Informant Report, February 10, 1964, 2, FBI file No. 170-9-SF-233; Rowe Interview–Rowe Task Force, 78; Blake Dep–Liuzzo, 26.

6. Rowe Interview–Rowe Task Force, 78–81.

7. For Rowe's contemporaneous account, see Informant Report, February 10, 1964, 2, FBI file No. 170-9-SF-233; for Justice Department investigator John Fleder's remark, see Rowe Interview–Rowe Task Force, 81; Blake Dep–Liuzzo, 25–26, Blake quotation is on 25. Rowe's account in his memoir is grossly exaggerated. See Gary Thomas Rowe, Jr., *My Undercover Years with the Ku Klux Klan* (New York: Bantam Books, 1976), 102–106.

8. SA J. Brooke Blake to SAC, Birmingham, January 21, 1964, 3, FBI file No. 170-9-284; Informant Report, January 27, 1964, 2–4, FBI file No. 170-9-SF-222; Diane McWhorter, *Carry Me Home: Birmingham, Alabama, the Climactic Battle of the Civil Rights Revolution* (New York: Simon and Schuster, 2001), 477–478.

9. Informant Report, February 3, 1964, 3, FBI file No. 170-9-SF-226; Informant Report, February 24, 1964, 2; Informant Report, March 26, 1964, FBI file No. 170-9-SF-243; SAC, Birmingham to Director, FBI, March 30, 1964, 2, FBI file No. 157-352-SF(2)-88; Rowe Dep–Baxley, 8–9.

10. Informant Report, April 15, 1964, 2–3.

11. Informant Report, April 14, 1964, April 15, 1964, 2, FBI file No. 170-9-SF-246.

12. Ibid., 2–4.

13. Ibid., 3.

14. SA, Birmingham to Director, August 14, 1965, 3–4, FBI file No. 137-6295-28; telegram, FBI Birmingham to FBI Washington, D.C., April 18, 1964, no file number. On Thomas, see Informant Report, April 8, 1964, 2, FBI file No. 170-9-SF-247; Informant Report, April 19, 1964, 2, FBI file No. 170-9-SF-250.

15. Informant Report, April 19, 1964, 2.

16. Informant Report, April 24, 1964, 3, FBI file No. 170-9-SF-26.

17. On Rowe's removal as head of the Action Squad, see Airtel, Director to SAC, Birmingham, April 13, 1964, FBI file No. 170-9-295; SAC, Birmingham to Director, April 14, 1964, 1–3, FBI file No. 170-9-296; Director to SAC, Birmingham, May 4, 1964, FBI file No. 170-7-299A; teletype, Birmingham to Bureau, April 18, 1964, FBI file No. 170-9-298; for Rowe's fight at the ballpark, see Rowe Interview–Rowe Task Force, Vol. 2, 262–264; Rowe Task Force Report, 115–116.

18. Informant Report, July 6, 1964, 2, FBI file No. 170-9-SF-264; Dan T. Carter, *The Politics of Rage: George Wallace, the Origins of the New Conservatism, and the Transformation of American Politics* (New York: Simon and Schuster, 1995), 216–217.

19. Informant Report, July 6, 1964, 3. For Thomas's belief that Rowe was an informant, see Thomas Interview–Rowe Task Force, 54, 72, 83; Rowe Task Force Report, 191–192; Eugene Thomas Affidavit, n.d., 1, Eugene Thomas File, Robb Papers; Eugene Thomas Interview, "Birmingham Bombings," March 24, 1976, 9, 11, 18, 19, Robb Papers.

20. SAC, Birmingham to Director, July 18, 1964, FBI file No. 157-331-111; Birmingham to FBI, July 16, 1964, 170–? (number unreadable); Rowe, *My Undercover Years*, 125.

21. FBI Birmingham to FBI Washington, D.C., July 21, 1964, 1–3, FBI file No. 157-1025-105; SAC, Birmingham to Director, August 14, 1965, 8–9, FBI file No. 170-9-319; Rowe Interview–Rowe Task Force, Vol. 2, 43–45; Rowe, *My Undercover Years*, 127–129; Informant Report, August 17, 1964, 3–4, FBI file No. 170-9-SF-272; Blake's comment can be found in Blake Dep–Liuzzo, 29. Rowe's account of the "showdown" in his memoir is wildly exaggerated, but I have quoted some dialogue where it conforms to contemporary FBI documents.

22. SAC, Birmingham to Director, December 17, 1964, 1–2, FBI file No. 137-6295-29; Shanahan Dep–Liuzzo, Vol. 1, January 18, 1983, 72, 73, 79; SA Neil P. Shanahan to SAC, Birmingham, January 5, 1965, FBI file No. 170-9-344.

23. Blake Dep–Liuzzo, 4; Shanahan Dep–Liuzzo, 59–64.

24. Informant Report, September 26, 1964, 3, FBI file No. 170-9-SF-280; Informant Report, September 29, 1964, 3, FBI file No. 170-9-SF-280; SAC, Birmingham to Director, September 29, 1964, 2, FBI file No. 157-2045-7.

25. Birmingham to Director, September 29, 1964, 1–2, FBI file No. 157-842-5; RE: Planned Bombing of Negro Night Club, September 29, 1964, 1, FBI file No. 170-9-SF-277; teletype, Birmingham to Director, September 29, 1964, 1, FBI file No. 157-842-5; A. Rosen to Mr. Belmont, September 30, 1964, 1–2, FBI file No. 157-2045-6.

26. Teletype, Birmingham to Director, October 1, 1964, 1–2, FBI file No. 157-2045-8; SAC, Birmingham to Director, October 2, 1964, 1–2, FBI file No. 170-9-SF-281A; SAC, Birmingham to Director, October 2, 1964, 1, FBI file No. 157-881-341; Informant Report, October 5, 1964, 2, FBI file No. 170-9-SF-284.

27. Informant Report, October 15, 1964, 2, FBI file No. 170-9-SF-293.

28. Informant Report, October 23, 1964, 2–3, FBI file No. 170-9-SF-285; SAC, Birmingham to Director, December 17, 1964, 6, FBI file No. 137-6295-29.

29. Fred Powledge, *Free at Last?: The Civil Rights Movement and the People Who Made It* (Boston: Little, Brown, 1991), 612–614.

30. Harvard Sitkoff, *The Struggle for Black Equality* (New York: Hill and Wang, 1993), 174; Carter, *The Politics of Rage*, 241–246.

31. SA Neil P. Shanahan to SAC, February 19, 1965, 1–2, FBI file No. 170-5-SF-310.

32. FBI memorandum, November 28, 1964, 157–85, FBI records.

33. George B. Leonard, "Midnight Plane to Alabama," in *Reporting Civil Rights Part Two: American Journalism, 1963–1973* (New York: The Library of America, 2003), 329.

34. Carter, *The Politics of Rage*, 250–251.

35. President Johnson is quoted in Sitkoff, *The Struggle for Black Equality*, 180; aide Eric F. Goldman is quoted in Doris Kearns Goodwin, *Lyndon Johnson and the American Dream* (New York: St. Martin's, 1991 edition), 229.

36. Sitkoff, *The Struggle for Black Equality*, 180–181.

37. "Informant Information," April 1, 1965, 1, FBI file No. 44-28601-207.

38. SAC, Birmingham to Director, SAC Selma, March 20, 1965, 1–2, FBI file No. 157-920-8; see also "Informant Information," 5–6; Rowe, *My Undercover Years*, 160.

39. "Informant Information," 7; the dates and times of Rowe's communications with Shanahan are on 1–8.

40. "Informant Information," 7–8; FBI Birmingham to Director, Mobile and Selma, March 21, 1965, 1–2, FBI file No. 157-920-11; "EUGENE THOMAS, ET AL.," November 23, 1965, 1–2, FBI file No. 44-28601-581; Rowe, *My Undercover Years*, 162. The FBI later tried to identify the man in the hotel room but found no obvious suspects. See "EUGENE THOMAS, ET AL.," 3–5.

41. "EUGENE THOMAS, ET AL.," 1–2.

42. Shanahan Dep–Liuzzo, Vol. 2, 38–40; McGovern Dep–Liuzzo, 7–8.

43. Shanahan Dep–Liuzzo, Vol. 2, 230–231; see also Birmingham to Bureau, and Mobile (Selma), March 25, 1965, FBI file No. 44-2844-355; Birmingham to Bureau and Mobile (Selma), FBI file No. 157-920-53.

CHAPTER 6. SEASON OF SUFFERING

1. Clark Dep–Liuzzo, 26–27; for King's fears, see Marshall Frady, *Martin Luther King, Jr.* (New York: Viking, 2002), 164.

2. Tape, March 25, 1965, Lyndon Baines Johnson Library, Austin, Texas, hereafter cited as LBJ Library.

3. Viola Liuzzo to Dr. Mohsen, n.d., FBI report, 56.

4. Mary Stanton, *From Selma to Sorrow: The Life and Death of Viola Liuzzo* (Athens: University of Georgia Press, 1998), 83.

5. Author's interview with Gordon Green, February 27, 1990, hereafter cited as Green Interview; author's interview with Rose Mary Sprout, March 9, 1990, hereafter cited as Sprout Interview.

6. Geraldine Brown, "Notes," FBI report, April 1, 1965 (hereafter cited as Notes–FBI Report); Stanton, *From Selma to Sorrow*, 84.

7. Notes–FBI Report; Stanton, *From Selma to Sorrow*, 84.

8. Green Interview; Notes–FBI Report; Stanton, *From Selma to Sorrow*; interview with Mary Liuzzo Silverberg, March 8, 1990, hereafter cited as Silverberg Interview.

9. Richard R. Lingeman, *Don't You Know There's a War On?* (New York: G. P. Putnam and Sons, 1970), 399–402; Stanton, *From Selma to Sorrow*, 88–89.

10. Sproat Interview; Silverberg Interview.

11. Green Interview.

12. Silverberg Interview; Stanton, *From Selma to Sorrow,* 90; Herrington Dep–Liuzzo, 20.

13. Silverberg Interview; Stanton, *From Selma to Sorrow,* 90.

14. Jack Mendelsohn, *The Martyrs: 16 Who Gave Their Lives for Racial Justice* (New York: Harper and Row, 1966), 177–178.

15. Admission Record attachment, Wayne County General Hospital and Infirmary, January 15, 1963, 1–2, Government's Exhibit No. 1, March 8, 1983, *Anthony Liuzzo, Jr., et al. v. United States of America,* hereafter cited as Admission Note.

16. Silverberg Interview; Tony Liuzzo is quoted in Stanton, *From Selma to Sorrow,* 104.

17. Silverberg Interview; Sproat Interview; Herrington Dep–Liuzzo, 10, 11, 22–23; Lauwers Dep–Liuzzo, 9.

18. Stanton, *From Selma to Sorrow,* 100; author's interview with confidential source, March 7, 1990; Silverberg Interview.

19. Silverberg Interview, 1, 4.

20. Ibid.; author's interview with confidential source; Stanton, *From Selma to Sorrow,* 100.

21. Silverberg Interview; Lee Dep–Liuzzo, 78.

22. Lee Dep–Liuzzo, 77–78, 81–82.

23. Stanton, *From Selma to Sorrow,* 65–66.

24. FBI interview with Sidney Kopernick, M.D., April 1, 1965; Stanton, *From Selma to Sorrow,* 66.

25. Admission Note, 1.

26. Ibid., 2.

27. Elson Dep–Liuzzo, 35–36, 61; see also Herrington Dep–Liuzzo, 8–12.

28. Elson Dep–Liuzzo, 35, 61; see also Herrington Dep–Liuzzo, 8–12.

29. Elson Dep–Liuzzo, 36.

30. Viola Liuzzo to "Dearest mom and dad," March 19, 1965, FBI report, 3–5; Elson Dep–Liuzzo, 45–51; Notes–FBI Report, 7–8.

31. "Unknown Subjects," March 27, 1965, 1–2, FBI records.

32. Ibid., 2; interview with Eugene Plowden, April 1, 1965, FBI records; Mendelsohn, *The Martyrs,* 180.

33. "Unknown Subjects," 1–2; Stanton, *From Selma to Sorrow,* 60–62.

34. Lee Dep–Liuzzo, 65–66; Green Interview; Stanton, *From Selma to Sorrow,* 103–104; Mendelsohn, *The Martyrs,* 180.

35. Johnny Green, "Did the FBI Kill Viola Liuzzo?" *Playboy,* October 1980, 102; Lee Dep–Liuzzo, 78.

36. Report of SA Mahlon F. Collier, April 1, 1965, 9, FBI records; Detroit Memorial Hospital Discharge Summary, October 5, 1964, 1–2; Herrington Dep–Liuzzo, 24; Elson Dep–Liuzzo, 65–67.

37. Elson Dep–Liuzzo, 81; Mendelsohn, *The Martyrs,* 182; Stanton, *From Selma to Sorrow,* 137.

38. Herrington Dep–Liuzzo, 30; on Liuzzo's comment to Penny, see Michael Beschloss, *Reaching for Glory: Lyndon Johnson's Secret White House Tapes, 1964–1965* (New York: Simon and Schuster, 2001), 244; the Liuzzos are quoted in Mendelsohn, *The Martyrs*, 182, and Beatrice Siegel, *Murder on the Highway* (New York: Four Winds Press, 1993), 55; see also *NYT*, March 27, 1965.

39. Interview with Samuel Leroy Edmonson, April 2, 1965, FBI report; interview with Lewis Julius Miller, April 2, 1965, FBI report.

40. Mendelsohn, *The Martyrs*, 182–183; FBI interview with Mrs. Willie Lee Jackson, March 29, 1965, FBI records.

41. On Moton and Liuzzo, see "Moton, Leroy Jerome," March 29, 1965, 1, 4, Personal file No. 22, Robb Papers; see also "Conversation with Leroy Moton," Justice Department Records, n.d., 2, 3–4, Robb Papers.

42. FBI interview with Mrs. Willie Lee Jackson; Hanson-Jackson interview, n.d., 11, Robb Papers; Stanton, *From Selma to Sorrow*, 155.

43. Stanton, *From Selma to Sorrow*, 156; FBI interview with Mrs. Nonnie Lea Washburne, March 20, 1965, FBI records.

44. Renata Adler, "Letter From Selma," in *Reporting Civil Rights Part Two: American Journalism, 1963–1973* (New York: The Library of America, 2003), 368–369.

45. Andrew Young, *An Easy Burden: The Civil Rights Movement and the Transformation of America* (New York: HarperCollins, 1996), 363; King is quoted in Stanton, *From Selma to Sorrow*, 156–157.

46. Paul Good, ". . . It Was Worth the Boy's Dying," in *Reporting Civil Rights*, 354.

47. Adler, "Letter From Selma," 370–371; Stanton, *From Selma to Sorrow*, 157; memo by SA M. L. Alexander, November 24, 1965, Birmingham field office file No. 44-1236-751 2A; report by M. L. Alexander, November 24, 1965, Birmingham field office file No. 44-1236-751.

48. Adler, "Letter From Selma," 371–374; Stanton, *From Selma to Sorrow*, 144.

49. Hanson-Jackson interview, 4, 11, Robb Papers.

50. Stanton, *From Selma to Sorrow*, 36, 155; Doc Green, "The Big Point Still Is Murder," *DN*, March 30, 1965.

51. Stanton, *From Selma to Sorrow*, 164.

52. Adler, "Letter From Selma," 391; Stanton, *From Selma to Sorrow*, 169.

53. Quoted in Stewart Burns, *To the Mountaintop: Martin Luther King Jr.'s Sacred Mission to Save America, 1955–1968* (New York: HarperCollins, 2003), 281; Adler, "Letter From Selma," 393; Frady, *Martin Luther King, Jr.*, 163–164; Harris Wofford, *Of Kennedys and Kings: Making Sense of the Sixties* (New York: Farrar, Straus and Giroux, 1980), 199–200; Stephan B. Oates, *Let the Trumpet Sound: The Life of Martin Luther King, Jr.* (New York: Plume, 1982), 363–364.

54. Adler, "Letter From Selma," 394.

55. Tape, March 25, 1965, LBJ Library; Beschloss, *Reaching for Glory*, 242; Sullivan Dep–Liuzzo, 153; Young, *An Easy Burden*, 367–368.

56. Orange Dep–Liuzzo, 9–10, 13–14, 20–21, 27–31, 38; Siegel, *Murder on the Highway*, 75.

57. Stanton, *From Selma to Sorrow*, 176; George B. Leonard, "Midnight Plane to Alabama," in *Reporting Civil Rights*, 334–335.

58. SAC, Mobile (Selma) to Director FBI, April 12, 1965, "Section VI: Interviews with Passengers in Car of Viola Liuzzo on Montgomery to Selma Trip," March 25, 1965, 87–95, FBI file No. 44-28061-29.

59. Moton is quoted in David Truskoff, *The Second Civil War* (New York: Sidney T. Black Publishing, 2001), 91–92.

60. "Conversation with Leroy Moton," 12.

61. Moton, Leroy, Interview, 6, FBI records.

62. Ibid.

63. Thomas is quoted in Rowe Testimony, in *The State of Alabama v. Collie Leroy Wilkins, Jr.*, in the Circuit Court of Lowndes County, Alabama, October Term, 183, hereafter cited as Second Wilkins Trial; Gary Thomas Rowe, Jr., FBI statement, March 29, 1965, 7–8, FBI file No. 44-28601-35.

CHAPTER 7. NIGHT RIDERS

1. David Truskoff, *The Second Civil War* (New York: Sidney T. Black Publishing, 2001), 92–93.

2. Moton is quoted in *DN*, March 27, 1965; memo, RE: telephone call of Roy J. McGee [*sic*], March 25, 1965; FBI interview with Ray J. Magee, March 26, 1965, both in report by Joseph R. Connors, 38–39; enclosure with "Director, FBI, to The Attorney General," March 26, 1965, FBI file No. 44-28601-288, hereafter cited as Connors Report.

3. FBI interview with Leon Millard Riley, March 26, 1965, in report by Joseph R. Connors, 40–42.

4. *DN*, March 27, 1965; see also Raymond J. Magee, "The Hard, Hard Road to Freedom," unpublished essay, n.d., 1, 4–5, 9–10, Robb Papers.

5. Connors Report, 126.

6. FBI interview with Leroy Jerome Moton, March 26, 1965, 44–46, in report by Joseph R. Connors.

7. Magee, "The Hard, Hard Road to Freedom," 14–16. See also SAC, Mobile to Director, March 28, 1965, 2, FBI file No. 44-28631-2; A. Rosen to Mr. Belmont, March 26, 1965, FBI file No. 44-28631-?; author's interview with Reverend Raymond Magee, November 26, 2004.

8. Tony Liuzzo Dep–Liuzzo, 5.

9. *DN*, March 27, 1965.

10. Michael Beschloss, *Reaching for Glory: Lyndon Johnson's Secret White House Tapes, 1964–1965* (New York: Simon and Schuster, 2001), 246.

11. Rowe Interview–Rowe Task Force, Vol. 2, 31.

12. Shanahan Interview; Shanahan Dep–Liuzzo, Vol. 4, 38–42.

13. Shanahan Dep–Liuzzo, 38–42.

14. Shanahan Dep–Liuzzo, 218–228; see also Rowe Testimony in *United States of America v. William Orville Eaton, Collie Leroy Wilkins, Jr., and Eugene Thomas*, Criminal Case No. 11, 736-N, U.S. District Court for the Middle District, Alabama, 390–563, hereafter cited as Federal Trial.

15. Rowe Testimony–Federal Trial, 390–420.
16. Memo by Neil P. Shanahan, March 29, 1965, B-D, FBI file No. 170-9-377; Gary Thomas Rowe statement, March 29, 1965, 5–14, FBI records.
17. Tape, March 25–26, 1965, LBJ Library.
18. "Telephone Calls From Liuzzo Residence," 1, Robb Papers.
19. Ibid., 2–7.
20. Quoted in *DFP*, March 27, 1965. For Liuzzo's remark about Wallace, see Johnny Green, "Did the FBI Kill Viola Liuzzo?" *Playboy*, October 1980.
21. SAC, Birmingham to File, March 27, 1965, 2, FBI file No. 44-1236-116; A. Rosen to Mr. Belmont, March 26, 1965, FBI file No. 44-28601-156; A. H. Belmont to the Director, March 26, 1965, FBI file No. 44-28601-33; McGovern Dep–Liuzzo, 10–11, 36.
22. McGovern Dep–Liuzzo, 27.
23. Connors Report, 167–168.
24. Ibid., 195; Wilkins Rap Sheet, FBI file No. 44-28601-158.
25. McGovern Dep–Liuzzo, 26, 39, 41; for Sullivan's talk with Rowe, see Sullivan Testimony–Liuzzo, Vol. 6, 172–173.
26. Tape, March 26, 1965, LBJ Library; A. Rosen to Mr. Belmont, March 26, 1965, FBI file No. 44-28601.
27. Tape, March 26, 1965, LBJ Library.
28. For Wallace's comments, see Dan T. Carter, *The Politics of Rage: George Wallace, the Origins of the New Conservatism, and the Transformation of American Politics* (New York: Simon and Schuster, 1995), 258; tape, March 26, 1965, LBJ Library.
29. Tape, March 26, 1965, LBJ Library.
30. McGovern Dep–Liuzzo, 32.
31. Lahey Testimony–Federal Trial, 653–659, 709–710, 713–714; Bud Gordon, *Nightriders: The Inside Story of the Liuzzo Killing* (Birmingham, Ala.: Bralgo Publications, 1966), 41–42, Robb Papers; *Nightriders* was a Klan-commissioned magazine based on interviews with Thomas, Wilkins, and Eaton. It should be used cautiously. See also FBI Report, 46–47.
32. Murphy Testimony–Liuzzo, 31–34; Wilkins Dep–Liuzzo, 5–7.
33. Gordon, *Nightriders*, 43–44.
34. Lahey Testimony–Liuzzo, 182; FBI Report, 14–15; Lahey Testimony–Federal Trial, 667–687; Shanahan Interview.
35. McGovern Dep–Liuzzo, 32.
36. Johnson is quoted in *DN*, March 27, 1965, FBI file No. 44-643-Nic 35-1840; *The Evening Star*, Washington, D.C., March 26, 1965, FBI file No. 44-643-Nic 38-1831; Rowe Task Force Report, 153–154; Richard Gid Powers, *Secrecy and Power: The Life of J. Edgar Hoover* (New York: The Free Press, 1987), 410.
37. Shelton is quoted in *DFP*, March 27, 1965; "A Citizen of the United States to Edgar Hoover, March 29, 1965," enclosure Office of the Director, March 31, 1965, FBI file No. 44-28601-6; redacted to Honorable Sir, 26 March '65, enclosure with Office of the Director, March 31, 1965, FBI file No. 44-28601-52, emphasis in original.

38. Tape, March 26, 1965, LBJ Library.

39. Connors Report, 151; Shanahan Dep–Liuzzo, Vol. 4, 45–47; Shanahan Interview.

40. Shanahan Dep–Liuzzo, Vol. 2, 155.

41. Ibid.

42. Ibid., 151.

43. A. Rosen to Mr. Belmont, April 5, 1965, FBI file No. 44-28601-162.

44. Rowe Interview–Rowe Task Force, 236–242.

45. For other services in Liuzzo's honor, see *DN*, March 26, 29, 30, 1965; *DFP*, March 31, April 4, 1965; *DN*, April 4, 1965; Mary Stanton, *From Selma to Sorrow: The Life and Death of Viola Liuzzo* (Athens: University of Georgia Press, 1998), 87; on O'Brien see *DFP*, April 5, 1965.

46. *DN*, March 28, 1965; *DFP*, March 28, 1965; *DN*, March 29, 1965; on Griffiths and extortion charge, see Detroit to Director and Selma, March 26, 1965, 2, FBI file No. 44-28601-118.

47. *DN*, March 29, 1965; *DFP*, March 28, 1965; *DFP*, March 29, 1965; and Memorandum, Selma, March 26, 1965, 2, FBI file No. 44-28601-118; on King, see Stanton, *From Selma to Sorrow*, 176.

48. Penny and Tony Liuzzo are quoted in Jack Mendelsohn, *The Martyrs: 16 Who Gave Their Lives for Racial Justice* (New York: Harper and Row, 1966), 177; *DN*, March 29, 1965; *DFP*, March 28, 1965; *DFP*, March 29, 1965.

49. Mrs. Shirley Scoggins and Mrs. Resa Gilbert to Anthony Liuzzo, March 26, 1965; Beulah Saffold to Anthony Liuzzo and family, March 28, 1965; N. Burkett to Anthony Liuzzo, n.d.; A. S. Wright to Anthony Liuzzo, March 28, 1965; A. H. Jarmon to Bereaved Family of Mrs. Anthony Liuzzo, March 28, 1965, all in "Wires of Condolence" file, Robb Papers; see also *DFP*, March 28, 1965.

50. Sister Mary Louise to Mr. Anthony Liuzzo, March 30, 1965, Liuzzo Viola File No. 26, Robb Papers; Bethell letter is quoted in *DN*, March 30, 1965.

51. Letherer, Sayers, and Nelson are quoted in Doc Green, "The Big Point Still Is Murder," *DN*, March 30, 1965, and Lawrence J. Green, "Rector Asks Ala. Bishop to Resign," *DN*, March 30, 1965; see also Stanton, *From Selma to Sorrow*, 176–177.

52. Stanton, *From Selma to Sorrow*, 70; *DFP*, March 28, 1965.

53. "Viola Liuzzo's Funeral Homily," Robb Papers; *DFP*, March 28, 1965.

54. Quoted in *DFP*, March 31, 1965.

55. Birmingham to Director, April 1, 1965, FBI file No. 170-9-389; Birmingham to Director, April 2, 1965, FBI file No. 170-9-393.

56. SAC, Birmingham to Director, April 3, 1965, FBI file No. 170-9-387.

57. Birmingham to Director, March 29, 1965, 1–3, FBI file No. 170-9-384; Birmingham to Director, March 31, 1965, 2, FBI file No. 170-9-387; Inspector J. L. McGovern to SAC, Birmingham, April 1, 1965, 1, FBI file No. 170-9390.

58. *DN*, April 21, 1965, 7; Director to SACs Mobile, Birmingham, 1–2, April 16, 1965, FBI file No. 44-2086-263; interview of Gary Thomas Rowe by St. John Barrett, April 1, 1965, 1, exhibit with Shanahan Dep–Liuzzo, January 21,

1983; *WP*, April 20, 1965, in FBI file No. 44-20860-265; *NYT*, April 22, 1965, in FBI file No. 44-2086-259.

59. San Francisco to Director, November 12, 1965, 2, FBI file No. 44-28601-559; Rowe Dep–Church Committee, 43–47; author's interview with confidential source.

60. *LAT*, May 23, 1965.

61. Author's interviews with confidential sources; FBI Mobile to Director, April 21, 1965, 3, FBI file No. 44-20861-265; Birmingham to Director, March 31, 1965, 1, FBI file No. 170-9-387; Mobile to Director, April 20, 1965, 1, FBI file No. 44-28601-2480.

CHAPTER 8. THIS HORRIBLE BREW

1. Mobile to Director, May 2, 1965, FBI file No. 44-28601-258; A. Rosen to Mr. Belmont, May 3, 1965, 2, FBI file No. 44-28601-293; FBI memorandum, May 4, 1965, FBI file No. 44-1236-403; *Choctaw Advocate*, Butler, Ala., May 6, 1965.

2. Tim Unsworth, "Murder in Black and White," *U.S. Catholic*, February 1998, unpaginated.

3. Quoted in Charles Eagles, *Outside Agitator: Jon Daniels and the Civil Rights Movement in Alabama* (Chapel Hill: University of North Carolina Press, 1993), 116.

4. *LAT*, April 22, 1965; Breslin in *NYHT*, May 14, 1965; Eagles, *Outside Agitator*, 200; *NYT*, May 4, 1965; Mobile to Director, May 1, 1965, FBI file No. 44-28601-272.

5. Eliza Heard, "Economics and a Murder Trial," *New South*, October 1965, 2. The author is actually Virginia Durr using a pseudonym. I'm grateful to Diane McWhorter for bringing this article to my attention.

6. Ibid., 3.

7. Ibid.

8. Ibid.; *BN*, May 4, 1965.

9. Patricia Sullivan, ed., *Freedom Writer: Virginia Foster Durr, Letters from the Civil Rights Years* (New York: Routledge, 2003), 329, 330; see also *NYT*, May 7, 1965.

10. C. B. Stanberry to SAC, Birmingham, May 12, 1965, 3, file number unreadable; *NYT*, May 4, 1965; *NYHT*, May 9, 1965; *LAT*, May 4, 1965; *BN*, May 3, 1965.

11. *LAT*, May 5, 1965.

12. Ibid.

13. "Conference Art Hanes, Jr.," January 10, 1983, 2, Robb Papers; FBI Mobile to FBI Washington, D.C., April 30, 1965, 2, FBI file No. 44-28601-272.

14. Mobile to Director, May 3, 1965, 2, FBI file No. 44-28601-289; *NYT*, May 4, 1965.

15. *LAT*, May 9, 1965; Heard, "Economics and a Murder Trial," 5.

16. First Wilkins Trial, 3–15; *LAT*, May 4, 1965; *Time*, May 14, 1965, 27; Heard, "Economics and a Murder Trial," 3; Murray Kempton, "Klan Trial a Turning Point," *New York World Telegram*, May 8, 1965.

17. Mobile to Director, May 3, 1965, FBI file No. 44-28601-289; *BN*, May 3, 1965; *BPH*, May 4, 1965; First Wilkins Trial, 16.

18. C. B. Stanberry to SAC, Birmingham, May 12, 1965, 1, 2, 5, FBI records; Jimmy Breslin, "Aftermath in Alabama Murder Trial," *NYHT*, May 9, 1965.

19. First Wilkins Trial, 18–19.

20. Ibid., 19.

21. Ibid., 20–29, 30–31, "Report of SA Robert Frye," May 25, 1965, 11, FBI records, hereafter cited as Frye Report.

22. First Wilkins Trial, 38.

23. Ibid., 50–51.

24. Ibid., 61.

25. Ibid., 37, 51, 62, 95.

26. Ibid., 103.

27. Ibid., 3–4.

28. *Newsweek*, May 17, 1965; First Wilkins Trial, 107.

29. First Wilkins Trial, 106.

30. Ibid., 107–110.

31. Ibid., 110–121.

32. Ibid., 129; Murray Kempton, "Trial of the Klansman," *The New Republic*, May 22, 1965.

33. First Wilkins Trial, 135, 143–149; Frye Report, 11–12; *Newsweek*, May 17, 1965.

34. *Time*, May 17, 1965; Kempton, "Trial."

35. First Wilkins Trial, 150–157; Frye Report, 12.

36. First Wilkins Trial, 175, 177.

37. Ibid., 174–176.

38. Kempton, "Trial"; *BPH*, May 5, 1965; *Time*, May 14, 1965.

39. Gary Thomas Rowe, Jr., *My Undercover Years with the Ku Klux Klan* (New York: Bantam Books, 1976), 195; Shanahan Interview.

40. First Wilkins Trial, 186–187.

41. *NYT*, May 5, 1965.

42. First Wilkins Trial, 183–219; Frye Report, 12–14; *Time*, May 14, 1965, 28; *Newsweek*, May 17, 1965, 40–41.

43. Rowe, *My Undercover Years*, 195.

44. Quoted in Robert M. Mikell, *Selma* (Charlotte, N.C.: Citadel Press, 1966), 149.

45. *NYT*, May 6, 1965, 28; *NYT*, May 7, 1965.

46. First Wilkins Trial, 231–233; *LAT*, May 6, 1965; *Time*, May 14, 1965, 28.

47. Rowe, *My Undercover Years*, 196–197.

48. First Wilkins Trial, 240, 277, 278, 286, 288, 290; *Time*, May 14, 1965, 28; *WP*, May 7, 1965.

49. First Wilkins Trial, 228, 234–236, 242–247, 279–285.

50. First Wilkins Trial, 267–268; *LAT*, May 6, 1965.

51. *LAT*, May 7, 1965.

52. First Wilkins Trial, 289; *Washington Daily News*, May 6, 1965; *LAT*, May 7, 1965; *Newsweek*, May 17, 1965.

53. *NYT*, May 6, 1965.
54. First Wilkins Trial, 289–290.
55. Ibid., 289–294.
56. Ibid., 295–297, 299–306, 307–318, 323–327, 328–332, 342–364, 390–391.
57. Ibid., 383.
58. Ibid., 341.
59. Ibid.; for Murphy's cross-examination of others, see First Wilkins Trial, 298, 306–307, 318–323, 327, 332–342.
60. First Wilkins Trial, 399; William H. Buckley, Jr., "Liuzzo Trial Dealt Blow to Local Law," *DFP*, May 13, 1965; *LAT*, May 14, 1965.

CHAPTER 9. A SLIGHT CASE OF MURDER

1. First Wilkins Trial, 399; Jimmy Breslin, "Klan Trial Goes to Jury," *NYHT*, May 7, 1965.
2. First Wilkins Trial, 401–406.
3. Ibid., 407–412; Hoover's words appear in the *WP*'s story of May 7, 1965, FBI file No. 44-28601-893. The emphasis is Hoover's.
4. First Wilkins Trial, 416–417.
5. Ibid., 417.
6. Ibid., 422–423.
7. Ibid., 423–430; *LAT*, May 7, 1965.
8. *Washington Daily News*, May 7, 1965, FBI file No. 44-28601-A; *Time*, May 14, 1965; *Newsweek*, May 17, 1965; *New York Daily News*, May 7, 1965; *LAT*, May 7, 1965; Murray Kempton, "Trial of the Klansman," *The New Republic*, May 22, 1965; Breslin, "Klan Trial." The quotation is from the *New York Daily News*.
9. *BN*, May 6, 1965.
10. Summations are not recorded by the court reporter, so the historian must rely on contemporary newspapers. Perdue is quoted in *BN*, May 6, 1965; *New York Daily News*, May 7, 1965; *Evening Star*, May 7, 1965; *LAT*, May 7, 1965; *WP*, May 7, 1965; *New York World Telegram*, May 8, 1965. Copies can also be found in FBI file No. 44-28601-A.
11. Jimmy Breslin, "Aftermath in Alabama Murder Trial," *NYHT*, May 9, 1965; on Murphy's drinking, see Diane McWhorter, *Carry Me Home: Birmingham, Alabama, the Climactic Battle of the Civil Rights Revolution* (New York: Simon and Schuster, 2001), 550.
12. Quoted in *Newsweek*, May 17, 1965, 41; quoted in *Life*, May 21, 1965; quoted in Breslin, "Aftermath."
13. *New York Daily News*, May 6 and 7, 1965; *NYT*, May 7, 1965; quoted in Breslin, "Aftermath."
14. Breslin, "Aftermath."
15. Ibid.; *LAT*, May 7, 1965.
16. Breslin, "Aftermath."
17. Ibid.; quoted in *Life*, May 21, 1965.
18. Breslin, "Aftermath"; quoted in *Life*, May 21, 1965; quoted in *Newsweek*, May 17, 1965.

19. Kempton, "Trial"; *Time*, May 14, 1965.
20. Breslin, "Aftermath"; quoted in *NYT*, May 7, 1965; quoted in *Newsweek*, May 17, 1965; *Time*, May 14, 1965; *LAT*, May 7, 1965.
21. Breslin, "Aftermath"; *LAT*, May 7, 1965.
22. Gantt is quoted in *NYT*, May 7, 1965; *Time*, May 14, 1965; *Newsweek*, May 17, 1965.
23. Quoted in Charles Eagles, *Outside Agitator: Jon Daniels and the Civil Rights Movement in Alabama* (Chapel Hill: University of North Carolina Press, 1993), 16; *BN*, May 6, 1965; *NYT*, May 7 and 14, 1965; *LAT*, May 7, 1965; *Time*, May 14, 1965.
24. First Wilkins Trial, 433, 451.
25. *NYHT*, May 8, 1965; *Newsweek*, May 17, 1965.
26. First Wilkins Trial, 443; *NYHT*, May 7, 1965.
27. *Life*, May 21, 1965; Breslin, "Aftermath."
28. First Wilkins Trial, 444–445; *Evening Star*, May 7, 1965.
29. *New York World Telegram*, May 8, 1965; *Life*, May 21, 1965.
30. First Wilkins Trial, 444–445; *BN*, May 6, 1965.
31. *NYT*, May 8, 1965; quoted in *Life*, 38.
32. *NYT*, May 8, 1965; *St. Petersburg Times*, May 8, 1965.
33. *Life*, May 21, 1965.
34. First Wilkins Trial, 453–455; Mobile to Director, May 7, 1965, 1, FBI file No. 44-28601-328; *BN*, May 8, 1965; Kempton, "Trial," 13.
35. *BN*, May 8, 1965.
36. Kempton, "Trial," 10; quoted in *Life*, 38.
37. Quoted in *BPH*, May 8, 1965, and *St. Petersburg Times*, May 8, 1965.
38. Murray Kempton, "Klan Trial a Turning Point," *New York World Telegram*, May 8, 1965; *Life*, 38; *Time*, May 14, 1965; *LAT*, May 8, 1965; Mobile to Director, May 7, 1965, 2.
39. *NYHT*, May 8, 1965; *Life*, 32–37 and cover; Buckley in *BN*, May 14, 1965.
40. *LAT*, May 7, 1965.
41. The jurors are quoted in *BN*, May 8, 1965; *St. Petersburg Times*, May 8, 1965; *New York Journal American*, May 9, 1965; *LAT*, May 8, 1965.
42. Patricia Sullivan, ed., *Freedom Writer: Virginia Foster Durr, Letters from the Civil Rights Years* (New York: Routledge, 2003), 328; Eliza Heard, "Economics and a Murder Trial," *New South*, October 1965, 6.
43. *LAT*, May 26, 1965; *BPH*, May 17, 1965; *BN*, May 20, 1965.
44. Eagles, *Outside Agitator*, 127; Milton Viorst, *Fire in the Streets: America in the 1960s* (New York: Touchstone, 1979), 347–361. Carmichael is quoted in Viorst, 353.
45. Viorst, *Fire in the Streets*, 363, 367.
46. Eagles, *Outside Agitator*, 185–194.
47. *LAT*, May 26, 1965; *BPH*, May 17, 1965; *BN*, May 20, 1965; Eagles, *Outside Agitator*, 179–180, 194; Jack Mendelsohn, *The Martyrs: 16 Who Gave Their Lives for Racial Justice* (New York: Harper and Row, 1966), 209–210. Coleman is quoted on 210.

48. Viorst, *Fire in the Streets*, 367–368.

49. Eagles, *Outside Agitator*, 196, 203; quotation in Eagles, 203; Mendelsohn, *The Martyrs*, 210–211.

50. Eagles, *Outside Agitator*, 240–241; *DN*, October 1, 1965.

51. Quoted in Eagles, *Outside Agitator*, 245; for account of the trial, see 213–249; *DN*, October 1, 1965.

CHAPTER 10. PARABLE OF THE TWO GOATS

1. *DN*, September 30, 1965; *WP*, October 19, 1965; both in FBI file No. 44-28601-A.

2. *DN*, September 30, 1965.

3. *BN*, May 20, 1965; *BPH*, May 23, 1965; redacted to Atty. Matt Murphy, May 19, 1965, "Matthew Hobson Murphy," FBI file No. 9-43808-2, hereafter cited as Murphy FBI File; RE: Matt H. Murphy–VICTIM, June 10, 1965, Murphy FBI File; *BPH*, June 23, 1965; redacted to Atty. Matt Murphy, May 19, 1965, Murphy FBI File; RE: Matt H. Murphy–VICTIM, June 10, 1965, 1–2, Murphy FBI File; report of SA redacted, Matt H. Murphy–VICTIM, July 14, 1965, Murphy FBI File; *BN*, August 8, 1965; *The Tampa Times*, August 20, 1965, all in Murphy FBI File.

4. C. L. McGowan to Mr. Rosen, August 20, 1965, FBI file No. 44-28601-436; *Mississippi Clarion-Ledger*, August 22, 1965; RE: Matt H. Murphy–VICTIM, June 10, 1965, Murphy FBI File; Report of SA Redacted, Matt H. Murphy-VICTIM, Murphy FBI File; *Mississippi Clarion-Ledger*, August 21, 1965; *BN*, August 20, 1965; *The Tampa Times*, August 20, 1965.

5. *BPH*, August 28, 1965; *DN*, October 21, 1965; Diane McWhorter, *Carry Me Home: Birmingham, Alabama, the Climactic Battle of the Civil Rights Revolution* (New York: Simon and Schuster, 2001), 187–188, 192, 252, 312, 433, 443–444. Hanes's quotation on King is on 444.

6. *LAT*, October 14, 1965; John Hayman, *Bitter Harvest: Richmond Flowers and the Civil Rights Revolution* (Montgomery, Ala.: Black Belt Press, 1996), 226–227; *BN*, September 27, 1965.

7. Quoted in *Newsweek*, November 1, 1965; *NYT*, October 18 and 19, 1965; Hayman, *Bitter Harvest*, 228.

8. Second Wilkins Trial, 13–14; *Newsweek*, November 1, 1965.

9. Second Wilkins Trial, 38 (Bender), 190 (Traylor).

10. Second Wilkins Trial, 121–122 (Lloyd), 76 (Collison), 201 (Woodruff).

11. Second Wilkins Trial, 83 (Gilmore), 188 (Traylor), 158 (Owens), 164–165 (Pettus).

12. Second Wilkins Trial, 105–107, 262–263; *Time*, October 29, 1965; *NYT*, October 20, 1965; Edward W. Knappman, ed., *American Trials of the 20th Century* (Detroit, Mich.: Visible Ink Press, 1995), 310–311.

13. Second Wilkins Trial, 261–262, 265–268; *NYT*, October 20, 1965.

14. Second Wilkins Trial, 263–265, 268; teletype, Mobile to Director and Birmingham, October 19, 1965, 1–2, FBI file No. 44-28601-532; see also Mobile to Director, October 19, 1965, 1–2, FBI file No. 44-28601-534.

15. Quoted in *NYT,* October 21, 1965; *BPH,* October 21, 1965; see also *Flowers v. Thagard,* 278 Ala. 537, 179 So. 2d. 286, 1985.

16. Second Wilkins Trial, 638; *Time,* October 29, 1965; *LAT,* October 21, 1965; *NYT,* October 21, 1965; *BPH,* October 21, 1965. For the investigation of the Klan by the House Committee on Un-American Activities, see Wyn Craig Wade, *The Fiery Cross: The Ku Klux Klan in America* (New York: Touchstone, 1988), 354–361, and Walter Goodman, *The Committee: The Extraordinary Career of the House Committee on Un-American Activities* (New York: Farrar, Straus and Giroux, 1968), 488–495.

17. *LAT,* October 21, 1965; "Conference Art Hanes, Jr.," January 10, 1983, 3, Robb Papers.

18. Second Wilkins Trial, 328–329; for the others' testimony about the tracks, see 306–307 (Burgess), 341–342 (Ryals), 356–357 (Painter), 377–378 (Dickson).

19. Second Wilkins Trial, 460.

20. *DN,* October 21, 1965; Second Wilkins Trial, 405–406, 417; see also 419–420; *BN,* October 21, 1965.

21. Second Wilkins Trial, 404.

22. Ibid., 415.

23. Ibid., 426.

24. Ibid., 427; see also *DFP,* March 27, 1965.

25. "Oral deposition of Hon. Richmond Flowers, 19–22, in *Gary Thomas Rowe v. Hon. Fob James, et al.,* U.S. District Court, Middle District of Alabama, Northern Division, Civil Action No. 80-0255-N, hereafter cited as Flowers Dep–James; "Deposition of Joe Breck Gantt," October 26, 1978, 3, in RE: Extradition of Gary Thomas Rowe, Bill of Particulars, State of Georgia, Executive Department, State of Alabama Rowe Prosecutive File, Robb Papers.

26. Flowers Dep–James, 22.

27. Ibid., 15, 23, 28.

28. *BN,* October 22, 1965.

29. Second Wilkins Trial, 505; quoted in *NYT,* October 22, 1965.

30. Second Wilkins Trial, 510, 516.

31. Ibid., 499–504, 516, 589; *DN,* October 22, 1965.

32. Second Wilkins Trial, 541–542, 549–552, 570–571; *LAT,* October 22, 1965.

33. Second Wilkins Trial, 577.

34. Ibid., 584–585.

35. *LAT,* October 22, 1965; *NYT,* October 22, 1965; *Newsweek,* November 4, 1965; *DFP,* October 22, 1965.

36. *New York Journal American,* October 22, 1965.

37. Second Wilkins Trial, 763–779, 791–799.

38. Ibid., 794, 798–799.

39. Quoted in *LAT,* October 23, 1965; *Jackson Daily,* October 23, 1965; *NYT,* October 22, 1965; *Time,* October 29, 1965.

40. Second Wilkins Trial, 722–723; "Conference Art Hanes, Jr.," 8, Robb Papers.

41. *Time,* October 29, 1965; *Newsweek,* November 1, 1965; *NYT,* October 22, 1965.

42. Second Wilkins Trial, 808; Gary Thomas Rowe, Jr., *My Undercover Years with the Ku Klux Klan* (New York: Bantam Books, 1976), 205.

43. Second Wilkins Trial, 808; *Mississippi Clarion-Ledger*, October 23, 1965.

44. Quoted in *NYT*, October 23, 1965.

45. Quoted in *Mississippi Clarion-Ledger*, October 23, 1965; *NYT*, October 22, 1965; *Newsweek*, November 1, 1965; "Conference Art Hanes, Jr.," 4, Robb Papers. For Black's definition of "true verdict," see Bryan A. Garner, ed., *Black's Law Dictionary* (St. Paul, Minn.: West Group Publishers, 2001), 747.

46. *NYT*, October 22, 1965.

47. Second Wilkins Trial, 808–820.

48. "Conference Art Hanes, Jr.," 1–2, Robb Papers.

49. *LAT*, October 23, 1965; "Conference Art Hanes, Jr.," 2, Robb Papers; *NYT*, October 27, 1965.

50. *LAT*, October 23, 1965; *Time*, October 29, 1965; *Newsweek*, November 1, 1965; *NYT*, October 22, 1965; *Mississippi Clarion-Ledger*, October 23, 1965.

51. Hanes film footage in the documentary *Home of the Brave*, directed by Paola di Floria, released in 2004; for King's reaction to the verdict, see *NYT*, October 24, 1965.

52. Federal Trial, 7–10; *DN*, November 7, 1965; *NYT*, November 6, 1965; *BPH*, November 6, 1965; *NYT*, April 8, 1965.

CHAPTER 11. A TEMPLE OF JUSTICE

1. "Conference Art Hanes, Jr.," January 10, 1983, 9, Robb Papers; *DN*, November 7, 1965.

2. Shanahan Dep–Liuzzo, 169; Gary Thomas Rowe, Jr., *My Undercover Years with the Ku Klux Klan* (New York: Bantam Books, 1976), 206; see also teletype, San Francisco to Director and Birmingham, May 25, 1965, FBI file No. 44-28601-304; SAC, San Francisco to Director, November 9, 1965, 1–3, FBI file No. 44-28601-557.

3. San Francisco to Director, November 23, 1965, 1–2, FBI file No. 44-28601-583. See also SAC, San Francisco to Director, November 9, 1965, FBI file No. 44-28601-557; San Francisco to Director, November 12, 1965, FBI file No. 44-28601-559; SAC, San Francisco to Director, November 15, 1965.

4. San Francisco to Director, November 23, 1965, 3–4, FBI file No. 44-28601-583.

5. Ibid., 5.

6. Memorandum for Mr. Tolson, et al., November 24, 1965, 1–2, FBI file No. 44-28601-635, and Memorandum for Messrs. Tolson, Belmont, Rosen, DeLoach, November 24, 1965, 3, enclosure; see also A. Rosen to Mr. Belmont, November 24, 1965, 1–2, FBI file No. 44-28601-599.

7. Inspector J. L. McGovern to Director, November 28, 1965, no file number, 1–2.

8. Shanahan Interview.

9. McGovern to Director, November 28, 1965, 3; Jim McGovern to Al Rosen, December 8, 1965, no file number, 1–2.

10. Nicholas de B. Katzenbach to Mr. Gary Thomas Rowe, November 27, 1965, FBI file No. 44-28601-628; Assistant Attorney General John Doar to Mr. Gary Thomas Rowe, November 27, 1965, 2, FBI file No. 44-28601-628.

11. McGovern to Director, 4–6; see also C. L. McGowan to Mr. Rosen, November 28, 1965, 1–2, FBI file No. 44-28601-602; Rowe, *My Undercover Years*, 208.

12. Shanahan Dep–Liuzzo, 170–171; McGovern to Rosen, December 8, 1965, 2.

13. For a brief sketch of Doar, see Taylor Branch, *Parting the Waters: America in the King Years, 1954–1963* (New York: Simon and Schuster, 1988), 331–335, 826–827; for Johnson admonishing Doar, see Federal Trial, 401, 413, 422.

14. On Johnson, see Jack Bass, *Taming the Storm: The Life and Times of Judge Frank M. Johnson, Jr., and the South's Fight over Civil Rights* (New York: Doubleday, 1993); Tinsley E. Yarbrough, *Judge Frank Johnson and Human Rights in Alabama* (Tuscaloosa: University of Alabama Press, 1981); Robert F. Kennedy, Jr., *Judge Frank M. Johnson, Jr.: A Biography* (New York: Norton, 1978); Hollinger F. Barnard, ed., *Outside the Magic Circle: The Autobiography of Virginia Foster Durr* (Tuscaloosa: University of Alabama Press, 1985), 27; the quotations are from "Judge Frank M. Johnson, Jr., 1918–1999," The Third Watch, http://www.uscourts.gov/ttb/aug99ttb/johnson.html; Barnard, *Outside the Magic Circle*, 303, and Kennedy, *Judge Frank M. Johnson, Jr.*, 127.

15. *DN*, November 30, 1965; *DFP*, November 30, 1965; *BN*, November 30, 1965; all in FBI file No. 44-643NC-80; see also *NYT*, December 4 and 5, 1965.

16. Yarbrough, *Judge Frank Johnson*, 112–124.

17. For Hanes's and Doar's legal arguments, see Federal Trial, 20–37; on the 1870 Civil Rights Act, see Wyn Craig Wade, *The Fiery Cross: The Ku Klux Klan in America* (New York: Touchstone, 1988), 90; on the "Mississippi Burning" case, see Seth Cagin and Philip Dray, *We Are Not Afraid* (New York: Doubleday, 1989); quotation is from Bass, *Taming the Storm*, 257. See also Yarbrough, *Judge Frank Johnson*, 130–131.

18. Federal Trial, 409–417, 709.

19. Ibid., 417–425.

20. Ibid., 426–439.

21. Ibid., 444–549; for Johnson's remarks, see 526, 527, 447, 532, respectively.

22. *BN*, November 30, 1965; *BPH*, November 30, 1965; *NYT*, November 30, 1965; *NYT*, December 1, 1965; for Johnson admonishing Doar, see Federal Trial, 401, 413, 422.

23. Federal Trial, 911–918 (Doar), 942 (Hardeman); also quoted in Yarbrough, *Judge Frank Johnson*, 133–134; see also *NYT*, December 2, 1965; *BN*, December 2, 1965.

24. Quoted in *BPH*, December 2, 1965; *NYT*, December 2, 1965.

25. Federal Trial, 75–102; Yarbrough, *Judge Frank Johnson*, 134; Bass, *Taming the Storm*, 257; *NYT*, December 3, 1965.

26. Federal Trial, 106–108, 109–112.

27. Kennedy, *Judge Frank M. Johnson*, 23; Bass, *Taming the Storm*, 257; Yarbrough, *Judge Frank Johnson*, 134.

28. Kennedy, *Judge Frank M. Johnson*, 23; Federal Trial, 114–117; *NYT*, December 4, 1965; Yarbrough, *Judge Frank Johnson*, 134–135; Bass, *Taming the Storm*, 257–258.

29. Federal Trial, 117–118; Kennedy, *Judge Frank M. Johnson*; *NYT*, December 4, 1965.

30. Federal Trial, 120–121; *BN*, December 4, 1965; A. Rosen to Mr. Belmont, December 3, 1965, FBI file number unreadable.

31. *Mississippi Clarion-Ledger*, December 3, 1965; "Conference Art Hanes, Jr.," January 10, 1983, 9–10, Robb Papers; *BPH*, December 4, 1965.

32. Federal Trial, 53–58; *BPH*, December 12, 1965.

33. Federal Trial, 120–121; Knappman, *American Trials*, 309.

34. For Doar's and President Johnson's reactions, see *NYT*, December 4, 1965; *BPH*, December 4, 1965; *DN*, December 4, 1965; for King, see *DN*, December 4, 1965. For other reactions, see *DFP*, December 6, 1965; *DN*, December 7, 1965; *BPH*, December 4, 1965; and Fred Graham, "The Law," in *NYT*, December 5, 1965. Hoover and Johnson also exchanged congratulatory telegrams: See Mr. DeLoach to Mr. Belmont, December 4, 1965, file number unreadable; Lyndon B. Johnson to Hon. J. Edgar Hoover, December 4, 1965, file number unreadable; J. Edgar Hoover to The President, December 4, 1965, all in FBI records.

35. Rowe, *My Undercover Years*, 212.

36. C. L. McGowan to Mr. Rosen, April 6, 1965, FBI file No. 44-28601-197; ? to Director and Birmingham, n.d., FBI file No. 44-28601-211; SAC, Miami to Director, April 9, 1965, FBI file No. 44-28601-177; Birmingham to Director, May 14, 1965, 2, FBI file No. 137-6295-33; A. H. Belmont to Mr. Tolson, April 1, 1965, 1–2, FBI file No. 44-28601-126; A. Rosen to Mr. Belmont, May 21, 1965, 1–2, FBI file No. 44-28601-382; see also Director to SAC, Birmingham, May 26, 1965, FBI file No. 44-28601-369; SAC, Birmingham to Director, May 31, 1965, FBI file No. 44-28601-370. On the Justice Department's refusal to pay Rowe's debts, see teletype from Director, June 1, 1965, 1–2, FBI file No. 44-28601-375; Director to SAC, Birmingham, June 24, 1965, 1–2, FBI file No. 44-28601-403; Director to Mr. John Doar, July 12, 1965, 1–2, FBI file No. 44-28601-414; Director to SAC, Birmingham, July 9, 1965, FBI file No. 44-1236-527.

37. FBI San Francisco to FBI Birmingham, May 21, 1965, FBI file No. 44-28601-451; Inspector James L. McGovern to SAC, Birmingham, May 6, 1965, 2, FBI file No. 44-1236-376; Inspector James L. McGovern to SAC, May 13, 1965, FBI file No. 170-9-430; SAC, Birmingham to Director, May 14, 1965, file number unreadable; SAC, San Francisco to Director, June 4, 1965, FBI file No. 44-28601-383; San Francisco to Director, November 1, 1965, FBI file No. 44-28601-542; Director to SAC, San Francisco, November 12, 1965, FBI file No. 44-28601-542; A. Rosen to Mr. Belmont, November 8, 1965, FBI file No. 44-28601-556.

38. Director to SAC, San Francisco, May 21, 1965, FBI file No. 44-28601-488; San Francisco to Director and Birmingham, May 21, 1965, file number un-

readable; SAC, San Francisco to Director, June 5, 1965, file number unreadable; A. Rosen to Mr. Belmont, June 8, 1965, 1–2, FBI file No. 44-28601-389; General Investigation Division Memo, n.d., FBI file No. 44-28601-391; Urgent Radiogram, San Francisco to Director, June 11, 1965, FBI file No. 44-28601-397; Director to SAC, San Francisco, June 12, 1965, FBI file No. 44-28601-397; San Francisco to Director, June 14, 1965, FBI file No. 44-28601-399; Director to SAC, San Francisco, June 17, 1965, FBI file No. 44-28601-399.

39. A. Rosen to Mr. Belmont, April 6, 1965, FBI file No. 44-28601-197; redacted to Director and Birmingham, April 6, 1965, FBI file No. 44-28601; ? to Director and Birmingham, April 10, 1965, 1–2, FBI file No. 44-28601-176; Director to Birmingham, April 16, 1965, no file number; Director to SACs, Birmingham, and redacted, April 21, 1965; SAC (redacted) to Director, n.d., 1965, FBI file No. 44-28601-282; Director to SAC (redacted), April 21, 1965, FBI file No. 44-28601-303; redacted to Director, April 28, 1965, no file number; redacted to Director, May 17, 1965, no file number.

40. SAC, Miami, to Director, April 9, 1965, FBI file No. 44-28601-177; C. L. McGowan to Mr. Rosen, April 6, 1965, FBI file No. 44-28601-197; redacted to Director and Birmingham, April 6, 1965, FBI file No. 44-28601-211; A. H. Belmont to Mr. Tolson, April 1, 1965, 1–2, FBI file No. 44-28601-126; A. Rosen to Mr. Belmont, May 21, 1965, 1–2, FBI file No. 44-28601-382; see also Director to SAC, Birmingham, May 26, 1965, FBI file No. 44-28601-369; SAC, Birmingham to Director, May 31, 1965, FBI file No. 44-28601-370; on the costs of supporting the Rowe family, see A. Rosen to Mr. Belmont, December 28, 1965, FBI file No. 137-6295-46; A. Rosen to Mr. DeLoach, February 16, 1966, FBI file No. 137-6295-?; A. Rosen to Mr. Belmont, December 28, 1965, FBI file No. 137-6295-46.

41. SAC, San Francisco to Director, November 15, 1965, 1, FBI file No. 44-28601-578; A. Rosen to Mr. Belmont, November 18, 1965, 3–4, FBI file No. 44-28601-579; SAC, San Francisco to Director, December 27, 1965, FBI file No. 44-28601-657.

42. A. Rosen to Mr. Belmont, December 21, 1965, 1–3, FBI file No. 44-28601-675; Director to the Attorney General, December 27, 1965, FBI file No. 44-28601-676; A. Rosen to Mr. Belmont, December 27, 1965, file number unreadable; for the DeLoach-Katzenbach meeting, see C. D. DeLoach to Mr. Tolson, December 28, 1965, 1–5, FBI file No. 44-28601-677.

43. Director FBI to SACs, Birmingham, Mobile, San Francisco, December 29, 1965, FBI file No. 44-28601-65?; the Attorney General to the Director, December 30, 1965, 1–2, FBI file No. 144-2-470; Director to the Attorney General, January 3, 1966, FBI file No. 137-6295-42?; Director to Mr. James J. P. McShane, January 3, 1966, FBI file No. 44-28601-702; A. Rosen to Mr. DeLoach, January 6, 1966, FBI file No. 44-28601-653.

44. A. Rosen to Mr. DeLoach, January 13, 1965, 2–3, FBI file No. 44-28601-703. See bottom of p. 4 for Hoover's approval.

45. Rowe Interview–Rowe Task Force, 179–183.

46. A. Rosen to Mr. DeLoach, January 14, 1966, 1–2, FBI file No. 44-28601-695; SAC, San Francisco, January 14, 1966, 1–2, FBI file No. 44-28601-696; Curtis O. Lynum to Mr. J. Edgar Hoover, January 17, 1966, 1, FBI file No. 44-28601-704; for Rowe's letter to Hoover, see Gary Thomas Rowe to Mr. J. Edgar Hoover, January 14, 1966, 1–2, FBI file No. 44-28601-705.

47. Statement of Gary Thomas Rowe, January 14, 1966, no file number; Doar is italicized in the original, SAC San Francisco to Director, January 14, 1966, 2.

48. A. Rosen to Mr. DeLoach, January 14, 1966, 2.

CHAPTER 12. TAKING THE SUN AWAY

1. For the Rhodes letter, see SAC, Detroit to Director, April 13, 1965, FBI file No. 9-43611-2; Detroit to Director and Atlanta, April 11, 1965, 1–2, FBI file No. 9-43611-4; SAC, Atlanta, to Director, April 20, 1965, FBI file No. 9-43611-7; SAC, Detroit to Director, April 13, 1965, FBI file No. 9-43611-2; FBI report on Lee Cecil Rhodes, April 20, 1965, 3, FBI file No. 9-43611-6; for the crank phone calls, see SAC, Philadelphia to Director, April 23, 1965, 3–5, FBI file No. 44-28601-9; Detroit to Director, April 3, 1965, FBI file No. 44-1236-192; SAC, Buffalo to SAC, Detroit, April 8, 1965, 1–2, FBI file No. 44-643-39.

2. Untitled paper enclosure in Detroit to Director, May 12, 1965, FBI file No. 44-28601-354; DN, May 23, 1965; a copy of the Lane report was also deposited in the Mississippi Sovereignty Commission records—see Liuzzo, Viola, SCR ID No. 3-14A-3-21-1-1-1, Commission Records, Mississippi Department of Archives and History, Jackson, Mississippi. The Mississippi Sovereignty Commission records are also available online at http://www.mdah .state.ms.us./arlib/contents/er.

3. Detroit to Director, May 12, 1965, 1–2, FBI file No. 4-643-43; Hoover's comment is on 5; ASAC Thomas J. Nally to SAC, Detroit, May 13, 1965, FBI file No. 4-643-48.

4. DFP, May 13, 1965; see also RE: Eugene Thomas, et al., May 12, 1965, FBI file No. 44-645-44; Detroit to Director, May 12, 1965, 1–5, FBI file No. 44-643-55.

5. SAC, Detroit to Director, May 13, 1965, 1–2, FBI file No. 44-643-49; DN, May 12, 1965; DFP, May 13, 1965.

6. DN, May 13, 1965; DFP, May 13, 1965; DN, May 18, 1965; BN, May 18, 1965.

7. DN, May 21, 1965.

8. Anthony Ripley, "The Enigma of Mrs. Liuzzo," DN, May 23, 1965.

9. Ibid.

10. Quoted in Mary Stanton, From Selma to Sorrow: The Life and Death of Viola Liuzzo (Athens: University of Georgia Press, 1998), 170–172; for the poll, see Ladies' Home Journal 82 (July 1965), 42–44; see also Lyn Tornabene, "Murder in Alabama: American Wives Think Viola Liuzzo Should Have Stayed Home," reprinted in Molly Lad-Taylor and Lauri Umansky, eds., "Bad" Mothers: The Politics of Blame in Twentieth Century America (New York: New York University Press, 1998), 273–279.

11. My discussion of the Liuzzo-Reeb comparison is influenced by Professor

Jonathan L. Entin's article "Viola Liuzzo and the Gendered Politics of Martyr-dom," *Harvard Women's Law Journal*, Vol. 23, Spring 2000, 262–263. I am grateful to Professor Entin for sending me a copy of his important essay.

12. Tony Liuzzo Dep–Liuzzo, 17–19.

13. *Nightriders: The Inside Story of the Liuzzo Killing* (Birmingham, Ala.: Bralgo Publications, 1966), 23; for Mary's reaction to *Nightriders*, see Silverberg Dep–Liuzzo; for Tom's reaction, see Lee Dep–Liuzzo, 60–61.

14. A. Rosen to Mr. Belmont, June 28, 1965, 1–2, FBI file No. 44-28601-407.

15. Ibid.; RE: Eugene Thomas, et al., January 17, 1966, 1–2, FBI file No. 44-28601-687; SAC, Birmingham to Director, January 19, 1966, 1–2, with enclosure of advertisement from the January 15, 1966, edition of *BN*, FBI file No. 44-28601-684. Liuzzo is quoted in unnamed newspaper article also enclosed.

16. Silverberg Dep–Liuzzo, 39; Tony Liuzzo Dep–Liuzzo, 16, 22; Stanton, *From Selma to Sorrow*, 180–182; Beatrice Siegal, *Murder on the Highway: The Viola Liuzzo Story* (New York: Four Winds Press, 1993), 106–107.

17. Silverberg Dep–Liuzzo, 28.

18. Ibid., 49, 50; Stanton, *From Selma to Sorrow*, 180.

19. Silverberg Dep–Liuzzo, 35–36.

20. Ibid., 29–36, 49, 54; Tom Ethridge, "Mississippi Notebook," *Mississippi Clarion-Ledger*, November 26, 1968.

21. Lee Dep–Liuzzo, 50–59, 62–63.

22. Herrington Dep–Liuzzo, 16–19.

23. Tony Liuzzo Dep–Liuzzo, 25–34; "Plaintiff's Individual Answers to Defen-dant's First Set of Interrogatories," 3, *Anthony Liuzzo, Jr., et al. v. United States of America*, Robb Papers.

24. Lauwers Dep–Liuzzo, 5, 6, 9–11, 13.

25. C. L. McGowan to Mr. Rosen, January 3, 1967, FBI file No. 137-6295-?; A. Rosen to Mr. DeLoach, November 6, 1967, FBI file No. 137-6295-64.

26. San Diego to Director, December 12, 1975, 5, FBI file No. 137-6295-?.

27. Officer's Report, Police Department, Chula Vista, California, July 14, 1966, 1–3; Investigator's Follow-Up Report, Chula Vista Police Department, August 22, 1966, both enclosures in Director to the Deputy Attorney General, Au-gust 29, 1966, FBI file No. 44-28601-735.

28. C. L. McGowan to Mr. Rosen, January 3, 1967, FBI file No. 44-28601-786; SAC, San Diego to Director, November 3, 1966, 1, FBI file No. 137-6295-60.

29. Interview with Donald D. Hill, January 23, 1979, Pizitz, Hill and Snow File, Robb Papers.

30. Interview with Mrs. Roberta Faye Beldin, April 23, 1979, Robb Papers.

31. On Rowe's fight with the janitor, see interview with John D. Jordan, October 24, 1967, 3–4, in FBI report on Gary Thomas Rowe, October 13, 1967, FBI file No. 137-6295-61; enclosure with Thomas Neil Moore, October 25, 1967, 1–12, FBI file No. 137-6295-63; for Rowe and the Highway Patrol, see Director to the Deputy Attorney General, November 6, 1967, 1; on Rowe's resignation, see SAC, San Diego to Director, December 11, 1967, FBI file

No. 137-6295-66; A. Rosen to Mr. DeLoach, December 19, 1967, FBI file No. 137-6295-67; Director to the Deputy Attorney General, December 20, 1967, FBI file No. 137-6295-66; SAC, San Diego to Director, January 22, 1968, FBI file No. 137-6295-68; Rowe's version is in SAC, San Diego to Director, December 8, 1970, 3, FBI file No. 137-6295-70; C. L. McGowan to Mr. Rosen, February 8, 1968, FBI file No. 137-6295-?.

CHAPTER 13. DIGGING IN

1. San Diego to Director, December 8, 1970, 1–3, FBI file No. 137-6295-71; on Doar, see Memorandum to the Attorney General, February 9, 1966, 1–3, FBI file No. 137-6295-52; C. D. DeLoach to Mr. Tolson, February 10, 1966, 1–4, FBI file No. 137-6295-52; C. D. DeLoach to Mr. Tolson, February 14, 1966, 1–5, FBI file No. 137-6295-53; Rowe Dep–Church Committee, 54, 56, 61.

2. SAC, San Diego to Director, January 6, 1971, FBI file No. 137-6295-71; SAC, San Diego to Director, December 8, 1970, 4, FBI file No. 137-6295-72; Director to SAC, San Diego, January 11, 1971, FBI file No. 137-6295-71; J. G. Deegan to Mr. W. R. Wannall, August 18, 1975, FBI file No. 137-6295-74.

3. Author's interview with confidential source.

4. Franklin Geerdes to Hon. Gerald T [sic] Ford, July 25, 1975, 1–2, FBI file No. 137-6295-74.

5. Inspector C. F. Brown to Mr. H. N. Bassett, April 15, 1975, FBI file No. 137-6295-73; Philip W. Buchen to Mr. Franklin Geerdes, July 29, 1975, FBI file No. 137-6295-74; Barry N. Roth, Memorandum for Office of the Attorney General, July 29, 1975, FBI file No. 137-6295-74; W. R. Wannall to J. G. Deegan, August 18, 1975, FBI file No. 137-6295-74; Director to Assistant Attorney General, August 20, 1975, FBI file No. 137-6295-74.

6. *LAT,* December 1, 1975; *BN,* December 3, 1975; Rowe Dep–Church Committee, 2–68.

7. *BN,* December 3, 1975; *San Francisco Chronicle,* December 3, 1975; *BN,* December 3, 1975; *Newsweek,* December 15, 1975; *BPH,* July 25, 1978; testimony of Gary Thomas Rowe before the U.S. Senate Select Committee to Study Governmental Operations with Respect to Intelligence Activities, chaired by Frank Church, 94th Congress, 1st session, December 2, 1975, 118, Robb Papers; hereafter cited as Rowe Testimony–Church Committee.

8. Rowe Testimony–Church Committee, 118, 125, 127, 129.

9. *San Francisco Chronicle,* December 3, 1975; Rowe Testimony–Church Committee, 118, 131; on Rowe's sex life, see Rowe Task Force Report, 9.

10. Supervisor A. Lewis Barnett to SAC, Birmingham, November 12, 1975, FBI file No. 170-9-546; SAC, Birmingham to Director, December 4, 1975, 1–16, FBI file No. 137-6295-76; Birmingham to Director, December 2, 1975, FBI file No. 137-6295-75; on bugging, see 1–4.

11. *BPH,* June 10, 1976; SA Mildred H. Gipson to SAC, Birmingham, May 19, 1976.

12. *BPH,* December 3, 1975; *BN,* December 3, 1975; *BN,* December 4, 1975.

13. *BPH,* December 3, 1975.

14. Ibid.
15. *BN*, December 4, 1975; *BPH*, December 4, 1975; *BN*, December 6, 1975; *BPH*, December 9, 1975; *BN*, December 9, 1975; *BN*, December 10, 1975; see also SAC, Birmingham to Director, December 11, 1975, FBI file No. 137-6295-78.
16. *BPH*, December 19, 1975.
17. Quoted in *BN*, December 4, 1975; *San Francisco Chronicle*, December 5, 1975.
18. *BPH*, July 13, 1978; SAC, San Diego to Director, December 4, 1975, FBI file No. 137-6295-? (no number), Director to the Attorney General, December 12, 1975, no file number, 2; Franklin L. Geerdes to Delores Zinn Carlisle, February 11, 1975, no file number, 1–2; Delores Zinn Carlisle to Franklin L. Geerdes, February 15, 1975, no file number, 2; enclosures, San Diego to Director, February 24, 1975, 1–2, FBI file No. 137-6295-88; Inspector C. F. Brown to Mr. H. N. Bassett, April 15, 1975, FBI file No. 137-6295-73; on the sale of Rowe's book, see *Newsweek*, July 24, 1978.
19. Gary Thomas Rowe, Jr., *My Undercover Years with the Ku Klux Klan* (New York: Bantam Books, 1976), dedication, n.p.; for Rowe and Barbara, see 111; on the Freedom Riders incident, see 38–50; on the book and movie rights, see *Newsweek*, July 24, 1978.
20. Chula Vista Police Department Crime Report, October 18, 1976, 1–5.
21. Franklin Geerdes to Deputy Attorney General George Beck, Captain Jack LeGrand, July 6, 1977, 1–4, Cantrell file, Robb Papers.
22. Ibid., 2.
23. George Beck to Honorable Franklin Geerdes, August 2, 1977, Cantrell Dep and Docs, Robb Papers; Frank Sikora, *Until Justice Rolls Down: The Birmingham Church Bombing Case* (Tuscaloosa: University of Alabama Press, 1991), 65; Cantrell-Rowe Tape, September 12, 1977, 44, Cantrell Dep Exhibits, Robb Papers.
24. Quoted in *NYT*, July 9, 1977.
25. Quoted in ibid.; Eddy's view is in Birmingham to Director, March 10, 1977, 1, FBI file No. 157-1025-1770; see also Sikora, *Until Justice Rolls Down*, 53; for a brief description of the Chambliss trial, see 123–155.
26. *NYT*, July 9, 1978; author's interview with Chuck Lewis, hereafter cited as Lewis Interview.
27. Bob Eddy to George Beck, October 11, 1977, 1, Cantrell Deposition Docs; *Time*, July 2, 1975.
28. Ibid., 2.
29. Shanahan Interview; *BPH*, March 11, 1966.
30. Lewis Interview.
31. On Thomas's prison experience, see Parole Progress Report, January 26, 1971; Offense Report, December 31, 1971; Quarterly Work Reports for March and December, 1973; Evaluation of Release Readiness, March 15, 1973, 1, all in "Eugene Thomas Prison File," Federal Bureau of Prisons, U.S. Department of Justice.
32. Lewis Interview.

33. Ibid.
34. Ibid.; Thomas quotes from *20/20* broadcast, July 10, 1978.
35. Lewis Interview.
36. *20/20* broadcast, July 10, 1978.
37. *20/20* broadcast, July 18, 1978; details on the polygraph examination came from a description of a similar test Malinowski conducted on Jack Ruby: see *House Select Committee on Assassinations, Hearings Vol. VII* (Washington, D.C.: 1979), 197–222.
38. Lewis Interview.
39. Ibid.; *20/20* broadcast, July 10, 1978; for a photograph of Wilkins taken in September 1978, see *BN*, September 19, 1978.
40. *20/20* broadcast, July 10, 1978.
41. Ibid.
42. *20/20* broadcast, July 10, 1978; see also Charles Lewis, "J. Edgar's Man in the Klan," *Inquiry*, November 24, 1980, 7–8.
43. Johnny Green, "Did the FBI Kill Viola Liuzzo," *Playboy*, October 1980, 108.
44. *20/20* broadcast, July 18, 1978.
45. Ibid.
46. *NYT*, July 9, 11, 12, 13, 14, and 19, 1978; see also *BPH*, July 11, 1978.
47. *Time*, July 24, 1978; *NYT*, July 10, 1978; *NYT*, July 19, 1978; for Liuzzo's comment, see *NYT*, July 12, 1978.
48. *Time*, July 24, 1978; *NYT*, July 23, 1978; *NYT*, July 26, 1978.
49. *Time*, July 24, 1978; Rowe Task Force Report, 1–3.
50. *BN*, August 2, 1978; *BN*, August 5, 1978; *BN*, August 10, 1978; *BN*, September 19, 1978.
51. Ibid.; *BN* listed the identities of the witnesses who later testified in the wrongful death lawsuit. See also *BN*, September 18, 1978; Coleman Testimony–Liuzzo, 15; Snow Testimony–Liuzzo, 8–9; *Gary Thomas Rowe v. Hon. Fob James, et al.*, Civil Action No. 80-255-N, 33–34, Robb Papers; the indictment is quoted in *BN*, October 5, 1978.
52. *BPH*, September 19, 1978.
53. *BPH*, September 20, 1978; *NYT*, September 20, 1978; *BPH*, September 22, 1978; *NYT*, October 8, 1978; *Gary Thomas Rowe v Hon. Fob James, et al.*, July 17, 1980, 116–119.
54. Rowe Task Force Report, 3.
55. Rowe Task Force Report, Appendix I, 1–7, 161–162.
56. Rowe Interview–Rowe Task Force, Vol. 1, 1, 53; Vol. 3, 116–117.
57. Rowe Interview–Rowe Task Force, Vol. 1, 25–26.
58. Ibid., 39, 49–50, 53–54.
59. Ibid., 191–192, 202–204.
60. Rowe Interview–Rowe Task Force, Vol. 2, 309–317.
61. Ralph Hornblower III to Michael E. Shaheen, Jr., 8, Rowe Task Force records, Office of Professional Responsibility, Justice Department; see also Rowe Task Force Report, Appendix III, 12–50.
62. Ibid., 9; see also Rowe Task Force Report, 48–64, 135–149. The latter section

NOTES TO PAGES 313–320   411

dealing with Hall is heavily redacted so the best source of this information is *NYT,* February 18, 1980.

63. Hornblower to Shaheen, Rowe Task Force records, 3–4; see also Rowe Task Force Report, 78–96.

64. Hornblower to Shaheen, Rowe Task Force records, 6–7; see Rowe Task Force Report, 149–237.

65. Hornblower to Shaheen, Rowe Task Force records, 9; see also John R. Fleder, Jr., to Michael E. Shaheen, Jr., July 27, 1969, Rowe Task Force records, Office of Professional Responsibility, Justice Department; Gary Thomas Rowe, Jr., Task Force to Michael E. Shaheen, Jr., 1–5, Rowe Task Force records.

66. *NYT,* February 18, 1980.

67. Ibid.

68. Lowery is quoted in *BN,* December 14, 1979; *BPH,* December 12, 1979.

69. For Varner's decision, see *Rowe v. Griffin,* 497 F. Supp. 610 (M.D. Ala. 1980); *NYT,* October 7, 1980. For the Court of Appeals' decision, see *Rowe v. Griffin,* 676 F. 2d. 524 (11th Cir. 1982).

70. Rowe is quoted in *BPH,* May 19, 1982, and *DN,* May 19, 1982.

CHAPTER 14. PAIN AND ANGUISH

1. Tony Liuzzo Dep–Liuzzo, 6; Silverberg Dep–Liuzzo, 9, 12–13, 14, 15–16.

2. Lee Dep–Liuzzo, 12–17, 85–86.

3. Tony Liuzzo Dep–Liuzzo, 7–8.

4. Silverberg Dep–Liuzzo, 9; Johnny Green, "Did the FBI Kill Viola Liuzzo?" unpaginated reprint of article from *Playboy,* October 1980, Robb Papers; Ken Fireman, "Babe I'm Going to Alabama," *DFP,* March 28, 1982; Tony Liuzzo Dep–Liuzzo, 9.

5. Lee Dep–Liuzzo, 10–24, 28–32, 44–45; *"Liuzzo v. United States:* A Case History," n.d., 3, Robb Papers; Howard Simon to Jack Novik, January 2, 1980, 1–2, Robb Papers; *DN,* December 29, 1977; Green, "Did the FBI Kill Viola Liuzzo?"; *DFP,* March 3, 1983.

6. Lauwers Dep–Liuzzo, 9, 12–13; Tony Liuzzo Dep–Liuzzo, 19–20, 24; Lee Dep–Liuzzo, 29–30; *DN,* April 16, 1975; *DN,* December 12, 1978; Fireman, "Babe I'm Going to Alabama."

7. Green, "Did the FBI Kill Viola Liuzzo?" emphasis in original; Fireman, "Babe, I'm Going to Alabama"; Howard L. Simon to Mr. William Webster, February 24, 1978, Robb Papers; Allen H. McCreight to Howard L. Simon, March 13, 1978, Robb Papers; William H. Webster to Howard L. Simon, n.d., Robb Papers.

8. Green, "Did the FBI Kill Viola Liuzzo?"; Fireman, "Babe, I'm Going to Alabama."

9. *DN,* October 28, 1978; for a Confidential Informant's report on Jim Liuzzo, see EUGENE THOMAS, ET AL., April 1, 1965, FBI file No. 44-28601-83; Hoover's comment on Lane is handwritten on Detroit to Director, May 12, 1965, FBI file No. 44-28601-354; on the FBI-Klan conspiracy, see Mary Stanton, *From Selma to Sorrow: The Life and Death of Viola Liuzzo* (Athens: University of

Georgia Press, 1998), 190; the fullest statement of this view is presented in the documentary *Home of the Brave*, directed by Paola di Floria and released in 2004.

10. *Selma Times Journal*, November 2, 1978; *Tuscaloosa News*, December 30, 1979.

11. Lee is quoted in *Tuscaloosa News*, December 20, 1979.

12. *Tuscaloosa News*, December 20, 1979; Lee Dep–Liuzzo, 44, 47; *BN*, October 11, 1979.

13. Dean A. Robb to Office of the Director, Federal Bureau of Investigation, January 24, 1978, Robb Papers; Dean A. Robb to Office of the Director, Federal Bureau of Investigation, January 25, 1978, Robb Papers; Litigation Plan: *Liuzzo v. United States*, 1, Litigation Plan File, Robb Papers; *Anthony Liuzzo, Jr., et al. v. United States of America and its agency, the Federal Bureau of Investigation*, "Complaint," July 5, 1979; see also *Anthony Liuzzo, et al., v. United States of America, et al.*, "Amended Complaint," Civil Action No. 972564, February 27, 1981.

14. Simon is quoted in *NYT*, July 5, 1979; *DFP*, July 6, 1979; *BN*, July 6, 1979.

15. Howard L. Simon to Mary, Penny, Tommy, Tony, and Sally, December 11, 1979, 1, Robb Papers; *DN*, September 17, 1980; *WP*, September 17, 1980.

16. The attorneys and the judge are quoted in *DN*, September 17, 1979.

17. *BPH*, July 13, 1978; *DFP*, October 23, 1979.

18. *Undercover with the KKK*, NBC–Columbia Pictures (1979); on the Bergman lawsuit, see *Walter Bergman and Frances Bergman v. United States of America, et al.*, U.S. District Court for the Western District of Michigan, No. G-77-6 C.A., November 18, 1982, and *Civil Liberties* (published by the ACLU), November 1978, 74.

19. *Undercover with the KKK*.

20. *DFP*, October 23, 1979.

21. Liuzzo Attorneys' Statement, October 23, 1979, 2, Robb Papers; Howard L. Simon and Ira Glasser to Fred Silverman, October 23, 1979, 1–2, Robb Papers; *DFP*, October 23, 1979; *BPH*, October 24, 1979.

22. For Joiner's decision, see *Liuzzo v. United States*, 485 F. Supp. 1274 (1980); *NYT*, March 1, 1980.

23. The Liuzzos are quoted in *DFP*, March 1, 1980; see also Howard L. Simon to Margaret Standish, October 15, 1980, 3, Robb Papers.

24. Lee Dep–Liuzzo, 32–47; Silverberg Dep–Liuzzo, 51–52.

25. *Selma Times Journal*, November 2, 1978; *BN*, October 4, 1978; Jack Novik to Howard Simon, September 19, 1980, Lake Headley File, Robb Papers; for Tom Lee's testimony, see *Gary Thomas Rowe v. Hon. Fob James, et al.*, C.A. No. 80-255-N, 39–48, Robb Papers; Lee Dep–Liuzzo, 41–44.

26. Dean to Penny, Mary, Tommy, Tony, and Sally, October 30, 1980, Liuzzo—Pertinent Correspondence with ACLU File No. 26, Robb Papers; Agenda for Tuesday Meeting—Liuzzo, n.d., 6, Lake Headley File No. 2, Robb Papers.

27. Dean to Penny, Mary, Tommy, Tony, and Sally, October 30, 1980; draft letter to Jack Novik, November 3, 1980, Liuzzo—Pertinent Correspondence; TLP to Liuzzo file, October 30, 1980, Liuzzo—Pertinent Correspondence;

Sharonn M. Bruley to All Attorneys of Record, March 21, 1983, 5, New Media File—Liuzzo, Robb Papers; "Fellow Students," n.d., Lake Headley File No. 2, Robb Papers.

28. Transcription 8/82 Tape, 1, Robb Papers.
29. Thomas is quoted in *BPH*, December 18, 1980; *DN*, March 22, 1982.
30. Conversation with Thomas/Creel/Holt, n.d., 1, 11, 17, Robb Papers.
31. Ibid., 5, 11, 12.
32. Interview with Eugene Thomas, November 15, 1982, 1–2, 4–5, 9–15, Robb Papers.
33. Ibid., 5, 21, 26–28.
34. Ibid., 18–23, 24–25.
35. Lee Wilkins and Eugene Thomas RE March 25th, January 9, 1983, Part II, 11–12, 14, 16, Robb Papers.
36. Liuzzo Trial Preparation, July 27, 1982, 3, 6, 13, Robb Papers.
37. Ibid., 8.
38. Ibid., 17.
39. Tony Liuzzo Dep–Liuzzo, 10–17.
40. Robertson is quoted in ibid., 32.
41. Lee Dep–Liuzzo, 33–38.
42. Ibid., 61–63.
43. Silverberg Dep–Liuzzo, 47–52.
44. Herrington Dep–Liuzzo, 26–31; Lauwers Dep–Liuzzo, 10–12.
45. Elson Dep–Liuzzo, 14–15.
46. Ibid., 64–85.
47. Ibid., 94–96.

CHAPTER 15. A SEARCH FOR THE TRUTH

1. *NYT*, March 31, 1983, 15:1.
2. *DFP*, March 1, 1980; *DN*, March 20, 1983; *Ypsilanti Press*, March 22, 1983.
3. *Anthony Liuzzo, Jr., et al., v. United States of America*, March 21, 1983, Vol. 1, 4–48.
4. Ibid., 48–70; *DN*, March 22, 1983.
5. Thomas Testimony–Liuzzo, Vol. 1, 120–126, 136–137, 143–144. Thomas also lied to the Rowe Task Force about his role in the Bessemer carnival assault. See interview with Eugene Thomas, Gary Thomas Rowe Task Force, February 9, 1979, 75–76, hereafter cited as Thomas Interview–Rowe Task Force.
6. Thomas Testimony–Liuzzo, 166–178; *DN*, March 22, 1983; *Ann Arbor News*, March 22, 1983; *DFP*, March 22, 1983.
7. Thomas Testimony–Liuzzo, 192–202.
8. Wilkins Dep–Liuzzo, 9, 10, 18–19; *DN*, March 23, 1983; *DFP*, March 22, 1983; *NYT*, March 23, 1983.
9. Thomas Testimony–Liuzzo, 37–49; Wilkins Dep–Liuzzo, 38–45; interview with Collie Leroy Wilkins, Rowe Task Force Report, February 9, 1979, 91–92, 93, hereafter cited as Wilkins Interview–Rowe Task Force.
10. Thomas Testimony–Liuzzo, Vol. 2, 19–20. During an argument, Thomas

also shot his father but not fatally; see Thomas Interview–Rowe Task Force, 106–107; Wilkins Dep–Liuzzo, 33.

11. Thomas Testimony–Liuzzo, 54–55; Wilkins Dep–Liuzzo, 23–24, 36–37.

12. Wilkins Dep–Liuzzo, 30–31, 45–47.

13. James D. Hagood Dep–Liuzzo, 10–12; Lavaughn Coleman Dep–Liuzzo, 11–45; on Rowe statement, see Rowe Dep–Liuzzo, Vol. 3, 81; Henry L. Snow Dep–Liuzzo, 5–27; Sgt. Lavaughn Coleman, December 12, 1975, 1, Lavaughn Coleman File, Robb Papers. In this interview Coleman also said that Rowe never rode with him in his police car.

14. James P. Turner Testimony–Liuzzo, 64–94; John Doar Testimony–Liuzzo, 98–101; St. John Barrett Testimony–Liuzzo, 104–111.

15. RE: Liuzzo v. USA—Memorandum to File by Dean Robb, February 20, 1983, 2–3, Robb Papers.

16. Robinson Dep–Liuzzo, 4–11, 15.

17. Ibid., 16–17.

18. Ibid., 18–22.

19. Rowe Dep–Liuzzo, Vol. 3, 158–159; Vol. 1, 24, 50, 67.

20. Ibid., Vol. 3, 72, 78, 79, 80–82, 94, 99, 100–101, 124–127.

21. Ibid., 14–17, 130–136, 139–140, 140, 146, 150, 161, 181–182; Vol. 2, 15–16, 18–19, 24–28, 101.

22. Ibid., Vol. 2, 32, 34–35, 55, 57.

23. Ibid., 60–61; Vol. 3, 140.

24. Ibid., Vol. 2, 64–69.

25. Ibid., 70–74.

26. Ibid., Vol. 3, 97–98, 100–101, 104–111, 143.

27. Ibid., 99, 103–104, 123–124. Robb's comment is in RE: Liuzzo v. USA, 6.

28. Hagood Dep–Liuzzo, 13–19; Jones Dep–Liuzzo, February 17, 1983, 12–20.

29. Shanahan Interview; Shanahan Dep–Liuzzo, Vol. 1, 140–141; Shanahan Dep–Liuzzo, Vol. 2, 14.

30. Shanahan Testimony–Liuzzo, Vol. 5, 57–60, 132–143; for more on Shanahan and GREENBOMBS, see Shanahan Dep–Liuzzo, Vol. 1, 86–87; Vol. 2, 38–42; Vol. 4, 44.

31. Shanahan Testimony–Liuzzo, Vol. 5, 61–104.

32. McGovern Testimony–Liuzzo, Vol. 8, 17–34; for McGovern's earlier comment on Rowe, see McGovern Dep–Liuzzo, 55; Michigan Daily, March 26, 1983; DN, March 26, 1983.

33. For Scoggins, see Wyn Craig Wade, The Fiery Cross: The Ku Klux Klan in America (New York: Touchstone, 1988), 314, 358, 361; on Stoner, see Diane McWhorter, Carry Me Home: Birmingham, Alabama, the Climactic Battle of the Civil Rights Revolution (New York: Simon and Schuster, 2001), 130, 132–134, 240–241.

34. Sullivan Testimony–Liuzzo, Vol. 6, 138–238.

35. Ibid.

36. Eugene Thomas Dep–Liuzzo, 92–94.

37. Creel Testimony–Liuzzo, Vol. 7, 138–139, 164.

38. Ibid., 148–151; for Gene Thomas's various statements to the press, see *WP*, September 21, 1978, and *BN*, February 2, 1979.

39. Creel Testimony–Liuzzo, 142–144, 150, 163.

40. Ibid., 144–145.

41. Ibid., 151–168.

42. Closing argument by Mr. Robb, *Liuzzo v. United States of America*, April 1, 1983, Vol. 9, 5–8.

43. Ibid., 8–27, 100–101.

44. For Cotchett and Gruel's arguments, see ibid., 27–63; for Robertson's closing argument, see ibid., 68–70.

45. Ibid., 72–98; see also *NYT*, April 4, 1983.

46. Robertson closing argument, *Liuzzo v. United States of America*, 102.

47. *DN*, May 28, 1983; *DFP*, May 28, 1983.

48. *DN*, May 28, 1983; Joiner is quoted in *NYT*, May 28, 1983. For Joiner's decision, see *Liuzzo v. U.S.*, 565 F. Supp. 640 (D.C. Mich. 1983).

49. FBI interview with Philip Thomas Mabry, October 27, 1967, 20–21, Birmingham field office file No. 174-6; Birmingham field office file No. 157-32; for a brief reference to Mabry, see McWhorter, *Carry Me Home*, 473.

50. Quoted in *DN*, May 28, 1983.

51. *Grand Rapids Press*, August 3, 1983; *Ann Arbor News*, August 5, 1983; *DFP*, August 5, 1983.

52. On the Southern Poverty Law Center, see Bill Stanton, *Klanwatch: Bringing the Ku Klux Klan to Justice* (New York: Mentor-Penguin Books, 1992), 1–199; for Dees's own account, see Morris Dees with Steve Fiffer, *A Season for Justice: The Life and Times of Civil Rights Lawyer Morris Dees* (New York: Charles Scribner's Sons, 1991), 1–209.

53. Stanton, *Klanwatch*, 200–228; Dees, *A Season for Justice*, 218–220.

54. Dees, *A Season for Justice*, 262–265; Stanton, *Klanwatch*, 231–237.

55. Deposition of Gary Thomas Rowe for *Beulah Mae Donald, et al. v. United Klans of America, Inc., Knights of the Ku Klux Klan, et al.*, Civil Action No. 84-0725-C-S, U.S. District Court for the Southern District of Alabama, April 27, 1985, 18–21, 30–37, 47; see also Stanton, *Klanwatch*, 237.

56. Stanton, *Klanwatch*, 232, 254; Dees, *A Season for Justice*, 262, 264, 322.

57. Dees, *A Season for Justice*, 328–331; Stanton, *Klanwatch*, 259–262.

EPILOGUE. DEALING WITH THE DEVIL

1. Liuzzo is quoted in *DFP*, March 3, 1985. For a brief discussion of the Bergman-Peck lawsuits, see Fred Powledge, *Free at Last?: The Civil Rights Movement and the People Who Made It* (Boston: Little, Brown, 1991), 271–275 (Judge Enslen's comment is on p. 275). See also Diane McWhorter, *Carry Me Home: Birmingham, Alabama, and the Climactic Battle of the Civil Rights Revolution* (New York: Simon and Schuster, 2001), 572.

2. *DFP*, May 31, 2001.

3. Ibid., and the documentary film *Home of the Brave* (2004).

4. In the interest of open disclosure, the writer was interviewed for *Home of*

the Brave in March 2000. For information on the production of *Home of the Brave*, see the Emerging Pictures Website, www.emergingpictures.com/home_of_the_brave.htm; Terry Lawson, "Sundance is sweeter the second time around," ContraCostaTimes.com, http://www.thestate.com/mld/cctimes/entertainment/movies/7715850.htm (accessed November 28, 2004); *Christian Science Monitor*, October 29, 2004, http://www.csmonitor.com/2004/1029/p14s02-almo.html (accessed November 28, 2004); Scott Foundas, "Home of the Brave," *Variety*, February 2, 2004, http://www.variety.com/ac2005_review/VE1117922944?nav=reviews&categoryid=1798&cs=1 (accessed November 28, 2004).

5. Mary Liuzzo Lilleboe is quoted in David Person, "Reclaiming Viola Liuzzo," *The Huntsville Times*, October 15, 2004, 2–3, http://www.al.com/opinion/huntsvilletimes/dperson-ssf?/base/opinion/10978318083132 (accessed November 28, 2004); Joanne Laurier, "Interview with Mary Liuzzo Lilleboe," June 7, 2004, World Socialist Website, http://www.wsws.org/articles/2004/jun2004/mary-j07.shtml; Batya Weinbaum, "Women's Eye View of the Twenty-eighth International Cleveland Film Festival," Goldamag.com, 1, http://goldamagazine.com/printedversion.asp?article_id=41 (accessed November 28, 2004); Janet Lee, Letters to the Editor, Metro Times Detroit, http://www.metrotimes.com/editorial/story.asp?id=6833 (accessed November 28, 2004).

6. *Savannah Morning News*, October 7, 1998.

7. Ibid.; author's interview with Brandi Singley, March 17, 1999.

8. The quotations are from the *Savannah Morning News*, October 7, 1998; author's interview with Linda Seigler.

9. I'm grateful to Luciana Spracher of Savannah's Bricks and Bones Historical Research for sending me a photograph of Rowe's gravesite marker.

10. For a discussion of COINTELPRO, see David Cunningham, *There's Something Happening Here: The New Left, the Klan, and FBI Counterintelligence* (Berkeley: University of California Press, 2004), 67–78, 109–167, 188–190; Wyn Craig Wade, *The Fiery Cross: The Ku Klux Klan in America* (New York: Touchstone, 1988), 361–363.

11. *Boston Globe*, January 9, 2001, and November 21, 2004; for the Boston story, see Dick Lehr and Gerard O'Neil, *Black Mass: The Irish Mob, the FBI and a Devil's Deal* (New York: Public Affairs, 2000); Jeff Dunn, "Mob Informant Scandal Involved Highest Levels of FBI, Documents Show," Associated Press, July 27, 2002, online at http://www.ratical.org/ratville/JFK/JohnJudge/linkscopy/MobFBI.html (accessed September 17, 2004).

12. Jeff Dunn, "Do the Crime, Do the Time," *Capitol Hill Blue*, March 2, 2003.

13. For information on the Alanssi incident, see Caryle Murphy and Del Quentin Wilber, "Terror Informant Ignites Himself Near White House," *WP*, November 16, 2004, and Caryle Murphy, "Informant's Fire Brings Shadowy Tale," *WP*, November 21, 2004.

INDEX

ABC News, 120, 254, 300–309, 311, 345, 354
Acker, Herschel, 47
Alabama Christian Movement for Human Rights (ACMHR), 63, 65
Alabama National Guard, 49, 54, 77, 125, 142, 146; federalization of, 89, 121
Alanssi, Mohamed, 370–371
Allen, Ben, 76–77
Allen v. United States, 262, 263
Allred, J. D., 94, 95
American Bar Association, 227
American Civil Liberties Union, 318, 321, 322, 324, 327–328, 360
American National Bank of Birmingham, 108, 109, 110, 111
Andrews, John, 331, 332
Anthony, Emory and Delores, 59, 60
anti-Catholicism: Cahaba Boys and, 79–80, 96; Klan and, 12–13, 14, 190, 210, 213, 216
anti-Communism, 198; FBI informants and, 3, 30, 368; Klan and, 14, 28, 36, 55, 56, 66, 90, 190, 207
anti-Semitism, 14, 56, 70, 184, 190, 198, 216

Argyris, George, 128–129, 130
Arrington, Richard, 293–294
Article III (U.S. Constitution), 258

Barboza, Joseph ("The Animal"), 369
Barnett, Ross, 74, 111
Barrett, St. John, 181, 341
Baxley, Bill, 104, 298, 299, 300, 313
Beckwith, Byron de la, 78
Belcher, Raymond, 16, 109, 110, 116
Bell, Griffin, 313
Bergman, Frances, 33–34, 36, 37
Bergman, Walter, 33–34, 36, 37, 323, 324, 364
Bessemer carnival, 61–62, 112, 329, 338, 344, 346, 359
Bessemer Klavern, 6, 28, 29, 47, 55–59, 62; bombings and, 86, 87; Liuzzo murder and, 158, 159, 164–165, 168, 191; Selma march and, 122, 124; weapons arsenal of, 119
Bethell, Dan J., 177
Beulah Mae Donald v. United Klans of America, 361–363
Birmingham City Council, 67, 294–295
Birmingham FBI. *See* Federal Bureau of Investigation; informant system

Birmingham Klan. *See* Eastview Klavern No. 13; Ku Klux Klan

Birmingham News, 42, 77, 279, 293

Birmingham police: Center Street bombing and, 94–95; complicity in anti-black violence, 16, 27–28, 29, 34, 35, 38, 40–42, 46–48, 53, 59–60, 63, 64, 69, 82, 84–85, 88, 110, 290, 295, 341; FBI vague warning to, 30–31; planned bank attack and, 109; race riot violence and, 83, 84; report of Rowe's weapons arsenal by, 331–332, 342–343; Rowe as hanger-on with, 2–3, 5; Rowe's charges against, 290, 293, 295; Rowe's murder indictment and, 307–308, 314, 341

Birmingham Post-Herald, 38–39, 42, 200, 293, 295, 308, 312, 352

Birth of a Nation, The (film), 67, 80, 113, 181, 369

Black Muslims, 61, 86, 90, 99

Blake, J. Brooke, 100, 101, 105–109, 115, 309; resignation of, 114; Rowe's rescue of, 107–108, 111, 112, 346, 359

Blakeslee, Carol, 300, 302

Blanton, Thomas ("Pop"), 79, 102

Blanton, Thomas, Jr. ("Tommy"), 313; bombing conviction of, 91, 104; extremism of, 79, 93, 97; Sixteenth Street Church bombing and, 96–97, 99–104, 344

Bloody Sunday (1965), 119–120, 138

bombings, 60–61, 79–104, 109, 294, 314; on Center Street, 94–95, 96, 100, 348; difficulties in solving, 89; dynamite availability and, 89; dynamite possession arrests and, 98; FBI dynamite discoveries and, 123–124; as FBI GREENBOMBS case, 124, 164, 346, 348, 351; of Gaston Motel, 70–73, 76–78, 96, 99; of Gaston's country house, 85–87; interstate commerce restraints and, 88; Klan dynamite arsenal and, 118–119; polygraph tests and, 96–97; race riots following, 71, 81, 83, 84; Rowe's suspected involvement in, 61, 305, 307, 313, 344; of Shores's house, 81–84,

85; University of Alabama anti-integration plot and, 74–77. *See also* Sixteenth Street Baptist Church bombing

Booker, Simeon, 34, 37

Boyd, Malcolm, 138

Boynton, Amelia, 118

Bradley, Fulton, 176

Bragg, Robert, 16

Breslin, Jimmy, 214, 215, 218, 221, 227

Brown v. Board of Education of Topeka (1954), 13, 27

Bryan, Jesse O. ("Jobie"), 307, 308, 314, 315, 325

Buckley, William F., Jr., 210, 227

Burgess, Henry, 152, 154, 192–193, 198, 247

Burkhalter, Donald L., 308, 312

bus desegregation, 18, 26–49

Butterworth, Wally, 55, 56–57, 58

Cagle, Charles ("Arnie"), 23, 24, 44, 45; bomb plots and, 74–75, 77, 82, 84; as Sixteenth Street Church bombing suspect, 92–93, 95, 98, 100, 103, 104

Cahaba Boys, 68, 79–80, 86, 93, 95–96, 108

Cantrell, Ernest, 294, 297–298, 331

Carlisle, Delores, 295

Carlisle, Jim, 253, 270, 271, 295

Carmichael, Stokely, 228–229, 230

Carroll, Robert, 246

Cash, Herman, 74–77, 99, 101, 313

Catholicism. *See* anti-Catholicism

Cavenaugh, Jerome, 176, 276

CBS News, 35, 210

Center Street South shrapnel bombing, 94–95, 96, 100, 348

Chambliss, Bob ("Dynamite Bob"), 40, 72, 84, 86, 96, 313, 344; arrest and acquittal of, 98, 313; bomb expertise of, 93, 97; church bombing and, 91, 100–104, 298, 299; conviction of, 91, 104, 299; extremism of, 80, 82, 314; Tidwell and, 108, 109, 110

Chaney, James, 258

Channing, Stockard, 365–366

Cheatham, Billy R., 227
Cherry, Bobby Frank, 23, 24, 61, 97, 100, 102; bombing skill of, 93; conviction of, 91, 104
Church, Frank, 289
Church Committee, 289–292, 296, 303, 309, 316, 325, 355
Civiletti, Benjamin, 307
Civil Rights Act of 1870, 258
Civil Rights Act of 1960, 30, 88
Civil Rights Act of 1964, 111, 117
civil rights movement: Birmingham police and, 27–28; countrywide emotional support for, 120; Doar and, 256; effect of Liuzzo's death on, ix–x, 177–178, 321, 365; FBI and, 3, 52–53, 289, 290, 312; federal protection for, 48–49, 63, 74, 77, 101, 121, 258, 261; Freedom Riders and, 26–49; Hoover's view of, 30, 253, 319; intensification of, 228–231; Johnson (Lyndon) and, 111, 118, 120–121, 229; Kennedy (John) and, 78; King's revised tactics and, 68–69; Klan's reemergence and, 13–14, 16, 184–185; nonviolence and, 68, 81; racists' view of, 78, 197–198, 212, 229, 236; Sixteenth Street Church bombing and, 90–91; workers' murders and, 230, 256, 258, 265, 350. See also desegregation; Liuzzo murder; Selma–Montgomery march; voting rights
Clansman, The (Dixon), 181
Clark, Jim, 71, 118, 119–120, 142, 229; Detroit report on Liuzzo and, 274, 275, 319; Liuzzo murder trial and, 188, 190, 216
Clark, Ramsay, 125
class-action suits, 361
COINTELPRO, 289, 292, 369
Colburn, Wayne, 286, 287
Coleman, Lavaughn, 307–308, 331, 340–341
Coleman, Tom, 229–232, 234–236, 250
Collins, Addie Mae, 87–88
Collins, Sarah, 87–88

Columbia Pictures, 296, 299–300, 306, 322–323
Communism. See anti-Communism
Communism on the Map (film), 57
Congress of Racial Equality, 26, 28–29, 33, 43, 49, 63
Connor, Theolphilus Eugene ("Bull"), 27, 28–29, 34, 48, 80, 294, 295; Hanes's political career and, 235; King's civil rights tactics and, 69, 70; Shuttlesworth plot and, 63
Conyers, John T., 176
Cook, Tom, 27–28, 29, 31, 34, 35, 41, 42–43, 63, 64, 290, 295; "liar" charges against Rowe of, 293
Cooper, Rodney, 59, 60
Cotchett, Joseph, 328, 338, 348, 349, 350, 354, 355–356
Cox, Harold, 258
Crawford, Jack, 15, 122
Creel, Flossie Louise (formerly Flossie Thomas), 170, 171, 352–354
Creel, Robert, 28, 55–57, 118, 184, 185; charges against Rowe of, 113, 114, 329, 330; Gaston house bombing and, 86, 87; Liuzzo murder and, 161, 170, 191, 204–205, 359; on Murphy's death, 234; Selma march and, 121–122, 362

Daniels, Jonathan, 230, 231, 234
Dees, Morris, 262, 361, 362, 365
de la Beckwith, Byron, 78
DeLoach, Cartha ("Deke"), 90, 268, 269, 270
Denard, Lori, 352, 353
desegregation: of buses, 18, 26–49; of public schools, 13, 21, 55, 79, 83; of universities, 73–74, 256
Detroit Board of Education, 136, 190, 278
Detroit Free Press, 246, 274–275, 276, 323, 325
Detroit News, 276, 319, 338
Detroit Police Department, 274, 275–276
Detroit race riot (1943), 129–130
Dexter Avenue Church, 146, 147, 152
Dickinson, William, 142–143
di Florio, Paola, 365

Dixie Speedway, 55, 57, 58

Dixon, E. J., 192, 193

Dixon, Thomas, 180–181

Doar, John, 49, 166, 173, 181, 271, 287, 288, 341; civil rights background of, 256; Liuzzo case prosecution by, 253–261, 265, 306

Doles, Curtis, 115, 116

Donald, Beulah, 361, 362–363

Donald, Michael, 361, 362–363

Dove, Melvin, 47

Downey, John, 100, 107, 181

Drury, Marydale, 308

Durr, Virginia Foster, 186–187, 190, 191, 194, 205, 228, 257

"Dynamite Hill," 68, 80, 81, 82

Eadon, "Curly." See Eaton, William Orville

Earle, L. B., 24, 29, 37

Eastview Klavern No. 13, 10, 13–15, 192; defectors from, 79–80; distrust of Rowe in, 7, 17, 28, 65, 73, 75, 111–114, 329–330; Exalted Cyclops post and, 108–111; FBI and, 47, 53; financial problems of, 66–67; Freedom Rider attacks and, 28, 29, 38–48; inaction of, 17–19, 57–59, 66–68; meetings of, 14–15, 20, 67; "missionary" violence and, 22–26, 58–59, 61–62, 73–78, 115–117; rally fiasco and, 57; Rowe's rise in, 20–21; Rowe's trial by, 113–114; rumors of informer in, 77, 111; Selma march and, 118–119, 121–124; Shuttlesworth assassination plot and, 63–78; violent members of, 369; warnings against "snitching" by, 53; weapons of, 16, 18, 29, 48, 118–119. See also bombings

Eaton, William Orville ("Curly"), 159–162, 164, 187, 231; charges against, 174; death of, 300; fanaticism of, 86–87, 346; FBI arrest of, 171, 172; FBI dossier on, 164–165; federal indictment of, 250; federal trial of, 251–264, 270, 326; Klan celebrity of, 184, 185; Liuzzo murder and, 200, 201–205, 209, 221, 222, 228, 258, 337, 351, 356; prison sentence of, 264; state indictment of, 182; Wilkins trial and, 188, 190, 214

Eddy, Bob, 298, 299

Edmonson, Sam, 138–139

Edmund Pettus Bridge, 119–120, 142, 149, 200

Edwards, Eldon, 13

Elson, Abraham, 135–138, 334–335

Ethridge, Tom, 281

Evans, Courtney, 90

Evans, Sarah, 129, 130, 134, 138, 156, 278, 279

Evers, Medgar, 78, 256, 362

Faggard, Jesse Oliver (son), 46–47

Faggard, Jesse Thomas (father), 47

Farley, Michael Lee, 88

Farmer, James, 26, 27

Farrell, Helen Liuzzo, 273–274

Faulkner, Ernie, 63, 64, 86

Federal Bureau of Investigation: Alabama civil rights violence and, 52–53 (see also bombings; Freedom Riders; Liuzzo murder; Sixteenth Street Baptist Church bombing); "armed and dangerous" warning and, 346, 348, 349, 350; Catholic agents and, 79–80, 96, 210, 216; Civil Rights Act (1960) powers of, 30, 88; COINTELPRO and, 289, 292, 369–370; illegal wiretaps and, 103, 268, 289, 292; and informants (see informant system); jurisdictional role claimed by, 30, 88, 292, 351, 368; Justice Department relations with, 88–89, 103, 269, 307, 312–313; Liuzzo's reputation and, 273, 319–320; media charges against, 306; negligence charges against, 323, 324, 346–348, 355–356, 364; non-sharing of information by, 88–89, 103; and post–September 11 terrorism, x, 365, 370–371; public concerns about, 289, 317–318, 369; Selma march and, 121, 124, 125, 146, 344, 346–351, 355; Senate investigations of, 289–292, 306–307; Shuttlesworth assassination plot and, 64–65; tarnished image of, 289, 369. *See also* Hoover, J. Edgar

Federal Tort Claims Act, 325, 336, 354

Feminine Mystique, The (Friedan), 135

Fields, Edward, 35–37, 43, 45, 86, 190

Fiery Cross, The (Klan newspaper), 55, 58

Flame Club, 115–117, 359–360

Fleder, John R., 308, 311

Flowers, Richmond, 174, 181, 231, 235–239, 242, 256, 300; as Klan enemy, 235–236; prosecution summation of, 248–249, 260; Wilkins acquittal and, 250

Ford, Gerald R., 288

Forman, Orman and Pauline, 22, 23–24, 61, 74, 295, 310, 344, 348, 355

Forrest, Nathan Bedford, 12

Fountain Heights. *See* Dynamite Hill

Frederick, Lorene, 204, 213

Freedom of Information Act, 317, 319

Freedom Riders, 26–49, 69, 70, 71, 74; FBI and, 26–31, 34, 35, 44–49, 52, 53, 91, 290, 312, 323, 324, 359, 364; federal protection of, 49, 73; interstate travel and, 26–27, 36, 368; Justice Department and, 26, 29, 48, 49, 256, 368; photo of Klan violence and, 26, 38, 42–43, 46–47, 53, 244, 293, 295, 312, 359; Rowe as FBI hero and, 46–47, 66; Rowe's accounts of, 42, 91, 290, 292, 294, 295–296, 344, 362; Rowe's violence and, 36–46, 244, 259, 295–296, 300, 305, 307, 310, 312, 338, 348, 355, 359

Friedan, Betty, 135

Frook, John, 221, 222, 225–226

Funderberk, Bill, 174

Gamble, Arthur, 182, 188, 191, 192, 196, 197, 207–209, 212, 213, 219–220, 226, 231, 235, 239, 256, 331

Gantt, Joe Breck, 181, 194–195, 210, 215, 219, 223, 226, 300; second Liuzzo trial and, 235–243, 246, 250, 256

Gaston, A. G., 86, 87, 112, 164, 359; bombing of country house of, 86, 87, 112, 164, 359

Gaston Motel, 68–69; bombing of, 70–73, 75–78, 86, 96, 97, 99, 313, 344

Gates, Hugh, 191, 220, 221, 223

Geerdes, Franklin, 288–289, 296–298

gender roles, x, 135, 277–278

Gettings, Lawrence, 170, 209

Goodman, Andrew, 258

Graves, Ray, 40, 41

Green, Gordon, 128, 130, 137

Green, Willie, 90–91

GREENBOMBS case, 124, 164, 346, 348, 351

Gregg, Eva Wilson, 128, 130, 136, 137

Gregg, Heber, 126–129, 130, 137

Griffith, D. W., 67, 181

Griffiths, Martha, 176

Grimes, Clarence, 6

Gruel, Grant, 328, 354, 355–356

Hagood, James D., 209, 340, 347

Hall, John ("Nigger"), 63, 64, 72, 80–81, 113, 119; arrest of, 98–99; bombings and, 82–83, 84, 92–93, 95, 98–103, 314; as FBI informant, 99–100, 313, 314

Hanes, Arthur J., 63, 294, 300; federal Liuzzo trial defense and, 250, 251, 254, 259–264; racism of, 235; state Liuzzo trial defense and, 234–250, 339

Hanes, Arthur J., Jr., 239–240, 249

Hanson, Cecil, 110, 115, 116

Hanson, Warren, 328, 329, 330

Hardeman, Ben, 261

Harris, Herman, 32, 33, 37

Hart, Philip, 176

Henson, Fred, 16, 21–25, 53, 58

Hess, Charles, 299, 300

Hill, Donald D., 285

Hoffa, James R., 133, 156, 175–176

Holt, Bill, 7, 9–10, 20, 53, 58, 100, 106, 107; bombings and, 71–72, 73, 84, 86, 92–95, 101, 102; doubts about Rowe of, 10, 17, 72, 73; formal charge against Rowe of, 112, 113–114, 329–330; Forman "mission" and, 23–25, 344; Freedom Riders attack and, 29, 38, 40–45, 47, 359; Shuttlesworth assassination plot and, 63, 64, 92

Home of the Brave (film), 366, 367

Hood, James, 73
Hood, Nicholas, 176
Hoover, J. Edgar, 61, 73, 319, 347; Birmingham bombings and, 31, 87–90, 98, 103, 104, 313, 368; control of investigations by, 88–89, 91, 103; field office misinformation to, 46; Freedom Riders attack and, 29–30; hostility toward King, 30, 289, 319, 369; informant system and, x, 2, 4, 91, 104, 111, 368; Liuzzo murder and, 166–167, 168–169, 171, 172, 189, 212, 253, 274, 279, 317, 319–320; Rowe and, x, 19, 20, 66, 252–253, 267, 268, 270–271, 285, 287, 288, 292, 310, 348–349, 359
Hornblower, Ralph, III, 308
House Committee on Un-American Activities, 239, 275
Humphrey, Hubert H., 177
Hurley, Ruby, 318

Immaculate Heart of Mary Church, 176, 178–180
informant system, ix–xi, 3–4; assessment of, 347–348, 368–371; career criminals and, 4, 99; ends vs. means and, 363; handler rapport and, 106–107; Hoover's confidence in, 91; ideal candidate for, 3, 4; Justice Department defense of, 305, 322, 337; Justice Department task force critique of, 312–313; Liuzzo family suit and, 321, 347–348; as mutually reinforcing, 265–266, 268; organized crime and, 306, 369–370; protection of, x, 19–21, 26, 30–31, 44–46, 64, 103–104, 312–315, 359; recruitment for, 4, 314; revelations of, 290, 295–296, 305–306, 313–314; violence as inherent in, x, 9, 21, 26, 38–47, 52, 60–61, 103, 305, 312–314, 322, 348–349, 369–371; warnings against violence in, 25. See also Rowe, Gary Thomas, Jr.
Ingram, Everett, 158, 162, 164
Ingram, Troy, 72, 80–81, 86, 93, 97, 100, 101, 313

interracial sex, 14–15, 58–59, 110, 111, 115–117
Interstate Commerce Commission, 26, 49
interstate travel: FBI powers and, 30, 88, 292, 368; federal injunction protecting, 49, 52, 63; Freedom Riders' test of, 26–27, 36, 368; Klan interference with, 30

Jackson, Frances, 139, 141, 143, 148
Jackson, Jimmy Lee, 119, 138, 142, 176, 230
Jackson, Willie Lee, 139, 141, 143, 148
Jenkins, Thomas, 30–31, 45, 46, 50, 51, 293
Jews. See anti-Semitism
John Birch Society, 67
Johnson, Barry, 138, 179, 280
Johnson, Frank M., 142; fairness of, 256–257, 259, 260, 265; Liuzzo federal trial and, 250, 254, 262–265, 339; Voting Rights March protection by, 121, 257, 258
Johnson, Lyndon B., 125–126, 146; anti-Klan campaign of, ix, 168, 172, 188, 189–190, 239; civil rights bills and, 111, 118, 120–121, 229; Liuzzo case involvement of, ix, 162, 163, 164, 166–169, 170, 171–173, 175, 189, 234, 265, 319, 326, 352
Joiner, Charles W., 322, 325–326, 336–337, 355, 356; Liuzzo suit decision of, 358–359, 360
Jones, Doug, 104
Jones, John, 22, 25
Jones, William, 76, 347
Justice Department: basis of prosecuting civil rights deaths, 258; civil rights protections and, 49, 52, 74, 87, 125, 256; FBI conflict with, 88–89, 103, 269; Freedom Rider attacks and, 26, 29, 48, 49, 256, 368; Liuzzo family suit against, 322, 332–335, 337–360; Liuzzo murder and, 166–170, 173, 181, 251–265, 300, 304, 341; Rowe investigation task force of, 26, 29, 46, 77, 95, 104, 307–315, 337, 339;

Rowe's demands and, 252–255, 265, 266, 268–269, 272, 287–289; Sixteenth Street Church bombing and, 89–91, 104

Katzenbach, Nicholas deB., 146, 167–168, 169, 171, 238, 252–253, 268–269, 305, 319
Kaufman, Victor, 303, 304
Keith, Ross, 73–76, 81–84, 92, 95, 100, 102, 110
Kelley, Clarence M., 6
Kemp, Barrett G. ("Barry"), 2–9, 18–21, 30, 309; efforts to curb Rowe's violence, 25, 42; protection of Rowe, 19–21, 26, 45–46, 49; resignation of, 50; Rowe's reports to, 14, 15, 25, 42, 344
Kempton, Murray, 191, 197, 214, 221–222, 225
Kennedy, John F., 48, 49, 67–68, 69, 89; civil rights bill and, 78, 90; Klansmen's hatred of, 14, 15, 56
Kennedy, Robert F., 29, 48, 49, 56, 89, 90, 96
King, A. D., 70–71, 81, 124
King, Martin Luther, Jr., 27–28, 63, 78, 87, 207, 216, 229, 362; changed tactics of, 69; FBI wiretaps and, 292; federal protection of, 49; Gaston Motel bombing and, 68, 70–74; Hoover's hostility toward, 30, 289, 319, 369; Liuzzo murder and, 176, 178, 265, 319; Nobel Peace Prize and, 118; Voting Rights March and, 118, 121, 125, 141–142, 144–146, 257
Kingston, Jack, 367
Kirby, T. H., 262, 263
Klan. See Ku Klux Klan
Klan Bureau of Investigation, 1, 15
Klanvocation (1964), 106–107
Klaverns (Klan divisions), 1–2, 6, 11
Koskey, Al, 162–163
Krystal Kitchen attack, 59–60, 74, 344, 355
Ku Klux Klan, 10–21; appeal of, 13–14; application form of, 7; attempt to broaden range of, 51, 55–56; Birmingham Klaverns of, 6 (see also Bessemer Klavern; Eastview Klavern No. 13); characteristics of, 3, 13–14; congressional investigation of, 239, 275; convention (1964) of, 106–107, 112; defeats for, 77–78; extremist splinter groups and, 35, 179–180; FBI informants in (see informant system; Rowe, Gary Thomas, Jr.); fear of enemies within, 16–17, 53–54; federal conspiracy charges against, 255, 258, 261, 262; federal injunction against, 49, 52–53, 74, 368; Freedom Rider violence and, 26–47, 289, 290, 359; hate literature of, 190; hate targets of, 12–15, 28, 56, 58–59, 66; history of, 12–14; Imperial Wizard of (see Shelton, Bobby); initiation fee and monthly dues of, 6, 7, 55, 66; initiation ritual of, 10–12; Johnson (Lyndon) warning to, ix, 168, 172, 188, 189–190; Liuzzo defamation campaign of, 169, 172, 190, 195–196, 198, 211–212, 216, 273–286, 320; and Liuzzo murder (see Liuzzo murder; Liuzzo trials); militarization of, 54–57; Montgomery headquarters of, 6; oath of, 205–207, 215, 227; police support for, 27–28; problems of, 56–58; rallies of, 55–57, 58, 70, 184–185; Rowe testimony against, 165–166, 243–246, 251, 258–259, 361–363; Selma march and, 121–124, 258, 346–351; Sixteenth Street Church bombing arrests and, 98–99; successful suit against, 361–363; "Ten Questions" of, 11; titles of officers of, 11, 14, 108–111; violent "missionary work" of, 9, 13–14, 19, 22–26, 361; weapons and, 16, 18, 29, 48, 55, 77. See also bombings
Kurzman, Mark, 322

Ladies' Home Journal, 278
Lahey, Edward M., 170, 171, 209, 212
Lake, Clancy, 40–42, 45, 46, 49, 296
Lane, Marvin G., 274–276, 279, 319

Langston, Tommy, 38–39, 42, 45, 47, 53, 293, 295, 359

Lankford, Tom, 39–40

Lee, Cager, 142

Lee, Thomas Gregg (aka Tom Liuzzo), 320

LeGrand, Jack, 294, 297–300, 331

Leonard, George B., 120

Letherer, Jim, 142, 178

Lewis, Chuck, 300–304, 309

Lewis, John, 48

Life (magazine), 210, 221, 226

Lingo, Al, 98, 119, 162, 169, 188, 230, 358

Liuzzo, Anthony, Jr. ("Tony," son), 131, 136, 137, 155, 156, 177, 178–180, 323, 324; case against government of, 316–319, 326, 328–331, 358; case's verdict and, 360; defense of damages sought by, 332; hate campaign against family and, 278–279, 280, 319; personal life of, 282–283, 364–366, 367

Liuzzo, Anthony James ("Jim," husband), 130–138, 152, 155–156, 162–163, 177, 178, 212; death of, 321; FBI documents on, 320; hate campaign against family and, 273–280, 319; Johnson (Lyndon) and, 163, 166–169, 172–173; personal disintegration of, 280–283, 318–319; suit against government and, 318–319, 358

Liuzzo, Mary (daughter), 130, 131–132, 133, 136, 137, 138; case against government and, 326, 333–334; documentary film and, 366; hate campaign against family and, 280–281; mother's murder and, 178–180; personal life of, 138, 280, 281, 333–334, 364

Liuzzo, Penny (daughter), 130, 132, 135, 136, 137, 138; case against government and, 321, 334; documentary film and, 366; mother's murder and, 155, 156, 177, 178–180; personal life of, 282, 334, 364

Liuzzo, Sally (daughter), 131, 155; case

against government and, 333, 358; documentary film and, 366; hate campaign against family and, 280; mother's murder and, 156, 177, 178–180; personal life of, 283, 334, 364; Rowe TV film and, 323, 324

Liuzzo, Thomas ("Tom," son), 131, 136, 137, 155; case against government of, 319, 326, 327, 333; hate campaign against family and, 279, 280, 319; investigation of mother's murder by, 316–317; mother's murder and, 156, 178–180; personal life of, 281–282, 316, 364, 367; personal problems of, 320–321, 326–327, 333

Liuzzo, Viola, 125–149; background and early life of, 126–129, 277; as civil rights hero, 177, 321; as controversial figure, x–xi, 169, 172, 180, 277–278; death of (*see* Liuzzo murder); death premonition of, 125, 144; decision to go to Selma, 138, 334–335; documentary film on, 365–366; emotional problems of, 134–137, 190, 277; FBI records and, 124, 319; historical importance of, x, 11–12; identification with suffering of, 120, 126; interracial friendship of, 129, 130, 278; malicious campaign against, 169, 172, 190, 195–196, 198, 211–212, 216, 273–279, 319, 320; motherhood vs. activism and, 277–278; personal traits of, 128–131, 133, 134, 136, 137, 317, 334–335; return home of body of, 175–176; risk-taking by, 147–149; self-fulfillment search of, 130–135; Selma experiences of, 139–144; services for, 176–180; southern roots of, 126, 128, 137; tributes to, 176–180; warnings to, 141

Liuzzo-Lee, Janet (Tom's ex-wife), 366–367

Liuzzo murder, ix, 86, 124, 149, 150, 151–183, 185–210, 362; ABC News investigation of, 300–306; accounts of, 149, 150, 157–162, 165, 182, 203–204, 243–248, 258–260, 270, 293, 294, 301–304, 310–313, 329–331,

338, 345, 362, 368–369; alibis and, 161, 204, 213, 246, 338, 339; arrest of suspects and, ix, 171–172, autopsy report and, 198–199; as civil rights violation, 228, 250, 257, 258; crime scene of, 152–154, 173, 186, 192, 209, 240, 328; evidence and, 170, 171, 198, 209, 211, 213, 304; evidence destruction and, 164, 314; family's problems following, 273–283, 364–367; FBI and, 124, 151–174, 180–183, 192, 212, 270, 301, 304, 319, 346–353, 359–360, 368–369; five trials for, 336 (see also Liuzzo trials); grand jury indictments and, 182, 192; Justice Department task force report and, 313; national impact of, ix, 155, 171–172, 176–177; public announcement of, 156–157; Robb's investigation of, 328–329; Rowe as alleged perpetrator of, 245, 254, 299–313, 315, 328, 329–331, 338; Rowe's arrest for, 173–174; Rowe's FBI protection and, 180–184; Rowe's immunity and, 166, 181–182, 242, 341; Rowe's inconsistent accounts of, 304, 311–312, 345, 355, 356; Rowe's indictment for, 307–308, 313, 320, 323, 327, 340; Rowe's suspect identification and, 164–166; Rowe's TV film version of, 323–324; "Rowe's 12 lies" charge and, 304; state charges and, 174; state defense version of, 247–248; Thomas's confession to ex-wife about, 353–354; Thomas's version of, 301–302, 304, 313, 329–331, 338; weapon fingerprints and, 211, 317, 330; weapons and, 161–162, 164, 170, 171, 203, 204, 214, 248, 330, 338, 345, 353; Wilkins as perpetrator of, 358, 359; Wilkins's version of, 303, 313, 338

Liuzzo trials
—first, of Wilkins, 184, 185–210, 211–230, 274, 304, 336; final summations in, 214, 216–220; jury deadlocked in, 223, 225, 226, 227–228; mistrial declared in, 225; reactions to, 225–230; second trial contrasted with, 236, 239–240
—second, of Wilkins, 233–250, 304, 336; final summations in, 246–249; jury deliberations in, 249–250; Wilkins acquitted by jury, 250, 257
—third (federal), of Eaton, Thomas, and Wilkins, 174, 250, 251–265, 336, 341; civil rights basis of, 228, 255, 257–258; contrasted with state trials, 254–258; jury deliberations in, 262–263; Rowe's reluctance to testify at, 251–256; Rowe's testimony in, 258–259, 260, 311; summations in, 260–261; Wilkins, Thomas, and Eaton convicted in, 263–265
—fourth, of Thomas, 300, 336, 338
—wrongful death suit against U.S. government, 318–335, 336–360; charges of, 321, 355; court costs, 360; damages sought in, 318, 321, 332–333; final summations in, 354–356; government's case in, 322, 338–341; judge's ruling in, 358, 360; Liuzzo family's situation after, 364–367; Rowe and, 316, 321, 337–346

Livingston, Edward, 238
Lloyd, Frank N., 236
Logan, William M., 308
Long, Jeff, 328, 335
Long, Marshall, 32, 36
Lorene's Cafe, 161, 170, 204, 213, 245, 338
Los Angeles Times, 183, 214, 289
Lowery, J. Paul, 314, 327
Lynum, Curtis, 254, 270, 271

Mabry, Philip, 358–359
McCord, Mary Louise, 100, 101, 102
McCurdy, Lewis, 250
McFall, Byron, 2, 52, 309; Klan plots and, 64, 71, 73–77, 92–95, 101, 106; protection of Rowe by, 60, 65–66, 73, 95, 99, 299, 306; rapport with Rowe of, 52; resignation of, 105; Rowe's

McFall, Byron (*continued*)
  reports to, 54, 59–60, 61, 62, 74,
    81–84, 85, 87, 92, 94, 95, 101
McGehee, Thomas, 152, 192, 193, 240,
    243, 247
McGovern, James L., 164–165, 169–171,
    242; Liuzzo suit testimony of, 349–
    350; Rowe's trust in, 253, 255, 288
McGowan, Clement L., Jr., 39, 64, 286
McMurphee, Clifford, 211, 221–223, 225,
    227
McNair, Denise, 87
McWhorter, Diane, 72
McWhorter, Loyal, 1–2, 3, 5, 6, 7
Mafia. *See* organized crime
Magee, Raymond, 151–152, 155
Malinowski, Benjamin, 302, 303
Malone, Vivian, 73
Marshall, Burke, 89
Mays, John, 362
Meredith, Don ("Dandy"), 323
Meredith, James, 256
Metcalf, Helen, 75, 94, 95, 101, 102
Michigan Militia, 365
Miller, Earl C., 275–276
Miller, Louis ("Tadpole"), 138–139
Milliken, William, 178
Mishael, Alan, 332–335, 353
Mobley, Bill, 200, 214
Moore, E. James, 42, 106, 293
Moore, Ivor, 33, 37
Moore, Jamie, 30–31
Moore, Thomas Neil (Rowe's new iden-
    tity), 266, 271, 283–284, 367
Morgan, Charles, Jr., 318
Morris, Monti, 31, 38
Morrisroe, Richard, 230, 231
Moton, Leroy, 139, 143, 147–149, 216,
    279, 310, 339; federal trial and, 254;
    Liuzzo murder and, 150–152, 154–
    155, 156; Liuzzo murder testimony
    of, 154, 194–195, 246, 317; Rowe's
    testimony and, 182–183, 252–254,
    305, 306, 317, 345, 355; state trials
    and, 194–197, 217–218, 233, 240–
    242, 247; Thomas's account and,
    301–302, 330
Murphy, Matthew Hobson, Jr., 112, 113–

114, 174–175, 181, 184, 231; critics of,
    226–227; death of, 234; family back-
    ground of, 187; hate speech of, 184,
    207–212, 216–220, 226–227, 228,
    234, 239, 274; Klan secret oath reve-
    lation by, 205–207; Liuzzo murder
    defense case of, 185–199, 205–223,
    228, 233–234, 239, 275, 339; physi-
    cal appearance of, 187, 215
Murphy, Robert, 170, 314
My Undercover Years with the Ku Klux Klan
    (Rowe), 295; TV film version of,
    299–300, 306, 322–323

NAACP, 14–15, 78, 207, 232, 257, 318;
    Liuzzo membership in, 138, 190,
    200, 211, 216; Liuzzo memorial
    service of, 177–178
National Guard. *See* Alabama National
    Guard
National States Rights Party, 35, 67, 86,
    91, 358
NBC television, 126, 306, 322–325
Nelson, A. F., 246
Nelson, Clarence Theodore Roosevelt, 178
Nelson, Jack, 183, 185, 217
New Republic (magazine), 197
Newsweek (magazine), 195, 210, 214, 226–
    227, 236, 246, 290
New York Herald Tribune, 226
New York Times, 86, 118, 185, 203, 238–
    239, 246, 290, 336, 358; series on
    FBI of, 305–306, 313–314
Nightriders (Klan magazine), 244, 279,
    319
Norris, Tom, 191, 223, 263
Novik, Jack, 322

Orange, James, 146–147
organized crime, 306, 318, 369–370
Oswald, Lee Harvey, 68
Owens, Hardy M., 237

Page, Hubert, 15, 18, 20, 21, 53, 57, 74, 79,
    295; and Freedom Rider attacks, 27,
    28, 34, 35, 39, 47, 48; and Gaston
    Motel bombing, 71; and Klan rally,
    55, 56, 57–58; Rowe's slit throat story

and, 41–42; and Shuttlesworth assassination plot, 63, 64, 65; and Sixteenth Street Church bombing, 94, 101, 102

Painter, Willie, 192, 193

Patriot Act (2001), 365

"Patriot's Rally Against Tyranny" (1964), 111–112

Patterson, John, 49, 54, 64

Patterson, Pat, 31–33, 34

Peck, James, 33–37, 45, 323, 364

Peek, Albert, 17

Penn, Lemuel, 258

Percy, Walker, 187

Perdue, Carlton, 186, 214, 215, 222, 226, 231, 235, 239, 249, 256

Person, Charles, 32, 33, 36, 45

Pettus, Wilburn, 237

Phelps, Joe, 231

Pickle, George, 72, 80

Piersante, Vincent, 275–276

Porter, Raleigh, 324

Powell, Joyce, 251

Pritchett, Laurie, 68, 69

Raines, Howell, 305–306, 313–314

Reconstruction, 12

Reeb, James: family obligations of, 278; murder of, 120, 138, 159, 160, 176, 184, 200, 230

Reed, Roy, 203, 205, 238–239

Reeves, Gene, 16, 22, 25, 29, 36, 38, 59; bomb plots and, 74–76, 84, 98, 102; as Exalted Cyclops, 111; first Liuzzo murder trial and, 188, 191, 213; photo of Freedom Riders beating and, 359

Reynolds, Isaac, 33

Rhodes, L. Cecil, 273

Riegle, Donald, 319

Rikos, Phyllis, 282

Riley, Archibald L., 209

Riley, Leon, 150–152, 155

Riordan, Mary Ellen, 178

Ripley, Anthony, 276

Robb, Dean, 320, 321–335, 337, 340–342, 345–358, 358; background of, 318; case against FBI of, 346–349, 350–351; judge's decision and, 360; on Rowe's true nature, 324–325, 341–342

Robertson, Ann, 332–333, 337–350, 353, 355–356, 358

Robertson, Carole, 87

Robinson, Lester, 342

Romney, George, 176

Rosen, Al, 89, 90, 270, 271, 286

Roton, Ralph Ray, 190, 191, 216

Rowe, Dorothy (second wife), 3, 4, 41, 65, 66, 254, 266; FBI relocation of, 181, 252, 267

Rowe, Elsie (fourth wife), 296, 305

Rowe, Gary Thomas, Jr. ("Tommy"), ix–xi; ABC News investigation of, 300–306; achievements for FBI of, 269–270; agent-provocateur charges against, 259, 305, 306, 329, 337, 342; assessment of career of, 368–369; background of, 2–3; barroom brawls and, 284–285, 296; bombings and, 81–87, 94–95, 313 (see also Sixteenth Street Baptist Church bombing); as center of national attention, 183, 294–295; Church Committee testimony of, 289–292, 295, 316, 325; credibility of, 91–92, 100–102, 253; death of, 367; emotional instability of, 252, 255, 267, 271, 284, 295, 342–343, 349, 355; employment problems of, 114, 266, 283–286, 287–288; exaggerations and lies of, 72–73, 77–78, 286, 287–288, 290, 292, 293, 299, 329, 330; FBI code name of, 9, 157; FBI doubts about, 18–20, 65–66; FBI final payment and sign-off of, 269–271, 287, 288; FBI handlers of (see Blake, J. Brooke; Kemp, Barrett; McFall, Byron; Shanahan, Neil); FBI payments to, 42, 46, 99, 181, 207, 266, 269–270; FBI protection of, 26, 44–47, 53, 60, 62, 63, 180–182, 242–243, 265–267, 284, 305, 312–314, 329–330; FBI ratings of, 19, 21, 99, 115, 117; FBI recruitment of, 2–6, 368; FBI relations with, 14, 15, 21, 25, 42, 49, 51–62, 72–73, 74,

Rowe, Gary Thomas, Jr. (*continued*) 99–100, 251–255, 268–270; as FBI's enemy, x, 272, 289–292, 336; financial problems of, 288; grievances of, 287–288; hooded identity cover of, 290, 291, 294, 295; Hoover's alleged phone call to, 270–271; Justice Department investigation of, 307–314; Justice Department problems with, 253–256; Klan activities of, 10–12, 14, 15, 20–21, 23–29, 34–35, 41–42, 49, 54, 58–77, 80–81, 91, 105–124; Klan activity testimony of, 165–166, 243–246, 251, 258–259, 361–363; Klan colleagues' testimony against, 329–330, 338–339; Klan distrust of, 7, 17, 28, 65, 72–73, 75, 111–114, 174–175, 359, 368; Klan oath and, 206–207, 215, 227, 259; as Klan prospect, 1–2, 3, 6–11; Klan threats to, 180–187, 200; Klan violence deposition of, 360–363; Klan weapons arsenal and, 118–119; last years of, 367; Liuzzo family reactions to, 316–317; and Liuzzo murder (*see* Liuzzo murder); Liuzzo wrongful death suit against, 321–358; love of guns, 2, 16, 266–267, 284, 332, 342–343; love of limelight, 183, 299, 361; marital troubles of, 65–66, 114; marriages of, 2, 19–20, 244, 285–286, 296; memoirs of, 105, 295–296; new identity of, 254, 266, 271, 283–284; *New York Times* investigative report on, 305–306; perjury of, 244, 259; personal traits of, x, 3, 106, 115, 246, 255, 284, 361; physical appearance of, 7, 298, 343, 361; as police buff, 1–3, 4, 5, 106, 165, 367; polygraph tests of, 102–103, 298, 299, 303, 304, 305, 312, 314, 345; press characterizations of, 245–246; reinstatement as hero, 357, 358–359; relocation demands of, 252, 254, 266, 269; relocation of, 251–252, 266, 269, 283–296; sexual tales of, 292–293, 295, 310; storytelling skill of, 200, 243, 290, 343–344; TV film on, 296, 299–300, 322–323, 325; "undercover agent" self-image of, xi, 9, 244; violence ameliorated by, 105–111, 290, 292, 310, 344, 346, 359; violence proneness of, x, 21, 23, 26, 38–46, 52, 53, 59–62, 73, 84–85, 95, 102, 244, 259, 284–286, 293, 295, 310, 312, 317, 324, 329–330, 337, 338, 342–343, 348–349, 355, 359, 369; warnings against violence to, 25, 348; womanizing of, 3, 52, 65, 66, 112

Rowe, Roberta (third wife), 285–286
Rugaber, Walter, 274–275
Ruoss, Meryl, 155–156
Russell, Richard B., 90
Rutherford, Leroy ("Monk"), 15, 54, 122, 123
Ryals, Frank, 192, 193, 239

Sales, Ruby, 230, 231
Sallee, Edmund, 226, 227
Samet, Norman T., 134–135
San Diego Union-Tribune, 369–370
Scarpa, Gregory ("The Grim Reaper"), 369
school desegregation, 13, 21, 55, 79, 83; of universities, 73–74, 256
Schwerner, Michael, 258
Scoggins, Robert, 350
Searcy, Margy, 353, 354
Seigenthaler, John, 48, 49
Seigler, Linda, 367
Self, W. W. ("Red"), 27–28, 38, 40, 42, 49, 290, 293, 295
Selma–Montgomery march, ix, 117–126, 138–150, 185, 205; Bloody Sunday halt to, 119–120, 138; description of, 141–147; FBI negligence charges and, 346–348, 355; federal protection for, 121, 125, 142, 254, 257, 258, 260, 261; King's speech and, 144–146; "Klancade" against, 121–123, 350; Klan's Imperial Wizard and, 121, 122, 362; peaceful last leg of, 121–124; Rowe's reported actions during, 159, 344–346; tributes to Liuzzo and, 178. *See also* Liuzzo murder

Senate Judiciary Committee, 306–307
Senate Select Committee on Government
Operations. *See* Church Committee
September 11 attack (2001), 365, 370–371
Shanahan, Neil: censure of, 347, 348, 349;
defense of informant program by,
347–348; Justice Department task
force and, 309, 313; Liuzzo murder
and, 124, 156–162, 164, 165, 173,
174, 181–183, 211, 311, 337, 344, 346,
348–350; Liuzzo murder federal
trial and, 252, 254, 255–256; Liuzzo
murder state trial and, 200, 209,
210, 216; as Liuzzo wrongful death
trial target, 346–349; photo of
Rowe's violence and, 44–45; as
Rowe's handler, 115–119, 122–124,
181, 200, 242, 253–254, 266, 288,
344, 349
Sharley, Jean, 180
Sheehan, James J., 178, 180
Shelton, Bobby, 6, 14–15, 17, 67, 72, 78,
81, 86, 172; business boycott and, 70;
Chambliss's bombing skills and, 93;
congressional Klan investigation
and, 219; FBI counterintelligence
and, 369; federal injunction and, 74;
Freedom Riders attack and, 27, 28,
35, 41, 362; on informants, 65; Klan
rally and, 55–57; Klan revamping
by, 53–55, 58, 66; Klanvocation and,
106; Liuzzo family confidential report and, 274, 275; Liuzzo first murder trial and, 187–188, 191, 200, 205,
213, 218, 222, 223; political strategy
and, 116, 117; Rowe's deposition
against, 360–363; Rowe's questioned
loyalty and, 28, 63, 75, 112, 175, 208,
223; Selma march and, 121, 122, 362;
Sixteenth Street Church bombing
arrests and, 98, 102
Shoffeitt, Paul, 198–199
Shores, Arthur, 80–85, 97, 110, 123
Shuttlesworth, Fred L., 37, 47, 80, 83;
assassination plot against, 63–64,
73, 91, 92, 99, 314, 368
Silver Moon Cafe, 120, 159–160, 200
Simon, Howard, 321, 325, 326

Sims, Larry Joe, 88
sit-ins, 16, 28, 69
Sixteenth Street Baptist Church bombing,
87–104, 106; convictions for, 91,
104, 299; *New York Times* series on,
313, 314; polygraph tests and, 96–
99; Rowe and, 91–93, 95–97, 100–
103, 105, 290, 296–300, 305, 313,
314, 344, 368; twin 1970s probes of,
297–298
Smith, Adam, 218–219
Smith, Al, 12
Smith, Howard K., 35, 37, 38
Snow, Henry, 308, 331, 340, 341
Sonka, Billy, 286
Southern Christian Leadership Confer-
ence (SCLC), 63, 118, 139, 141, 155,
195, 197
Southern Poverty Law Center, 361–363,
365
Spicer, Mary, 31, 32, 33, 37, 38
Stack, Robert, 323, 324
Stanberry, Charles B. ("C.B."), 2, 51–52
Stanton, Mary, 133
Stiefel, Arnold, 295
Stoner, Jesse B., 35, 350
Student Nonviolent Coordinating Com-
mittee (SNCC), 111–112, 118, 211–
212, 228
Sullivan, Joseph, 146, 151, 163, 165, 169,
251–252, 349, 350–351
Sundance Film Festival, 366
Supreme Court, U.S., 13, 18, 23, 258, 262,
263, 322, 325

Teamsters union, 130, 133, 156, 167, 169,
173, 175–176, 178, 275, 279
television, 78, 118, 126; images of civil
rights violence on, 69, 120; Liuzzo
murder coverage by, 156, 166, 168,
171–172, 215, 303–304. *See also* ABC
News
terrorism, x, 306, 365, 370–371. *See also*
bombings; Ku Klux Klan
Thagard, T. Werth, 188–194, 199, 205,
206, 208–213, 217, 220, 231, 233,
235, 236, 254; jury deadlock and, 221,
222, 223, 225; Murphy's summation

Thagard, T. Werth (*continued*)
and, 217, 218; second trial and, 236–241, 249, 250
Thomas, Eugene ("Gene"), 62, 87, 107, 110, 112, 114–117, 182, 187, 188, 225, 231; ABC News investigation and, 300–302, 352; arsenal of, 119, 171, 339, 352; born-again Christian claims of, 329, 331, 339, 352; death of, 367; ex-wife's testimony against, 352–354, 356; FBI arrest of, 170, 172, 174; FBI dossier on, 164; federal conviction of, 263–264, 270; federal indictment of, 250; federal trial of, 251–265, 326; Justice Department task force investigation and, 310; Klan prominence of, 184, 185, 352; Liuzzo family suit and, 330–331, 337–339, 350, 351, 353–354, 356, 359; Liuzzo murder accounts and, 124, 158, 159–162, 164, 200, 201–205, 209–210, 213, 214, 228, 242, 243, 245, 246, 248, 258, 259, 300–302, 304, 330–331, 338, 339, 344, 356; perjury of, 338; polygraph test of, 302, 304, 308, 338; Rowe testimony about, 307, 308, 345–346; Rowe vendetta of, 329–331, 352–354, 359–360; state indictment of, 182; state trial jury's acquittal of, 300, 336, 338; violent history of, 164, 352, 356, 359–360
Thomas, Flossie (Gene's wife), 170, 171, 352–354
Thomas, James E., 262
Thomas, Mildred (Robert's wife), 93, 108, 213
Thomas, Robert, 14, 20, 22–23, 57, 69, 86, 101, 188, 191, 213; as Grand Titan, 109; Klan plots and, 72, 74, 77, 81; Klansmen critics of, 108; pullback in Klan activities by, 53, 108; Rowe and, 110–111, 112, 116, 117; Selma march and, 118, 121–123, 330, 344, 346; on Sixteenth Street Church bombing, 93–94, 102; Tidwell's proposed violence and, 109, 110

Thompson, Earl ("Shorty"), 10–11, 15, 16, 20, 29, 48, 58–60; Cahaba Boys and, 80, 81; pullback of Klan activities by, 53, 58; as Sixteenth Street Church bombing suspect, 94, 95, 102
Thompson, John Hampton, 47
Thunderbolt, The (racist tract), 190
Tidwell, Ira, 108
Tidwell, Ronnie, 82, 108–110, 111, 115
Time (magazine), 197, 200, 210, 214, 217, 237, 246, 276
Tornabene, Lyn, 277–278
Tower, John G., 292
Traylor, John B., Jr., 236, 237
Tuberville, Hugh M., 227
Turner, James, 306, 341
Turner, Walter, 262, 269
20/20 (TV program), 303–308, 311, 312, 314, 339, 345, 352, 354

Undercover with the KKK (TV film), 323–325
United Americans for a Conservative Government, 67, 85–86
United Klans of America. *See* Ku Klux Klan
United States v. William A. Kubrick, 325
University of Alabama, 73–78, 346
University of Mississippi, 74, 256
USA Patriot Act (2001), 365
U.S. marshals, 49, 54; Rowe's post with, 269, 272, 283, 285–286, 287

Van Deerlin, Lionel, 288, 289
Vann, David, 294
Vanocur, Sander, 304, 305
Varner, Robert, 314–315
Varner, Virginia, 230
Vines, Jimmy, 94, 95
Volunteers for Alabama, 67–68
voting rights, ix, 117, 118, 120–124, 185, 228, 229
Voting Rights Act of 1965, ix, 229, 307
Voting Rights March. *See* Selma–Montgomery march

Walker, Edwin A., 67–68
Walker, Harry, 51, 84, 109–110

Wallace, George C., 67, 83, 86, 90, 111–112, 147, 248, 250; as Klan convention speaker, 106; Liuzzo murder and, 163, 168, 219; "Segregation forever" speech, 144; Selma march and, 121, 144; Sixteenth Street Church bombing and, 98; university integration and, 74, 77, 78

Ware, Virgil, 88

Washburne, Nonnie, 141

Washington Post, 118, 303, 370–371

Weaver, Macon L., 90, 91

Webb, George, 31, 37–40, 42, 45, 47, 295; photo of beating of, 244, 293, 359

Webster, William H., 319

Weltner, Charles, 275

Wesley, Cynthia, 87

Wheeler, Glenn, 14, 15

White, H. A. ("Sister"), 82, 83, 84, 92–93, 95, 100

White, Lee, 167, 168

White Citizens Council, 13, 67, 118, 191, 227, 230, 236, 237, 238, 250; jury membership and, 257

white supremacy, 11, 12, 13, 236–238, 259; Alabama organizations, 35, 68–69

Wilkins, Collie Leroy ("Wilkie" or "Lee"), 159, 160, 161, 231, 258, 310, 331; ABC News investigation and, 300, 302–303; charges against, 174, 214; death of, 367; FBI arrest of, 170, 172; FBI dossier on, 165; federal indictment of, 250; federal trial of, 251–264; guilty verdict and, 263–264, 270, 326; Klan celebrity of, 184, 185; Liuzzo family suit and, 331, 337–340, 350, 351, 356, 359; as Liuzzo's murderer, 200–205, 243, 304, 311, 345, 353, 356, 358, 359; physical appearance of, 222, 303; polygraph test of, 303, 304, 308; prison sentence of, 264–265, 339–340; Rowe as alleged murderer and, 307, 308, 331, 339; Rowe's testimony and, 258, 259, 303, 311, 345, 346; state indictment of, 182, 192; state trial of (first), 185, 186–210, 211–228, 304; state trial of (second), 233–250, 304; state trial jury's acquittal of, 250, 252, 257

Williams, Hosea, 142, 146

Williams, Marion, 209–210, 212, 216

Winter Hill Gang (Boston), 370

wiretaps, 103, 268, 289, 292

Wolverines (militia group), 365

Woodruff, O. P., 237

Yarbrough, Russell, 293–294

Young, Andrew, 141, 142, 146

Zipperer, Alex, 310

ABOUT THE AUTHOR

GARY MAY was born in California and received his Ph.D. from UCLA. His previous books include *China Scapegoat: The Diplomatic Ordeal of John Carter Vincent*, winner of the Society of American Historians' Allan Nevins Prize, and *Un-American Activities: The Trials of William Remington*, selected for inclusion in the Gryphon Library of Notable Trials. He is Professor of History and Director of the Master of Arts in Liberal Studies Program at the University of Delaware.